Learn Microsoft Power BI

Third Edition

A comprehensive, beginner-friendly guide to real-world business intelligence

Greg Deckler

Learn Microsoft Power BI
Third Edition

Portfolio Director: Sunith Shetty
Relationship Lead: Apeksha Shetty
Project Manager: Shashank Desai
Content Engineer: Tiksha Abhimanyu Lad
Technical Editor: Seemanjay Ameriya
Copy Editor: Safis Editing
Indexer: Manju Arasan
Proofreader: Tiksha Abhimanyu Lad
Production Designer: Pranit Padwal
Growth Lead: Bhavesh Amin

First published: September 2019
Second edition: February 2022
Third edition: August 2025

Production reference: 1040825

Published by Packt Publishing Ltd.
Grosvenor House
11 St Paul's Square
Birmingham
B3 1RB, UK.

ISBN 978-1-83664-741-6

www.packtpub.com

I would like to dedicate this book to my son Rocket who graduated from high school on June 7th, 2025

– Greg Deckler

Editorial Reviews

The third edition of Learn Power BI provides an updated step-by-step guide to utilizing primary features in data transformation, semantic modeling and analysis, interactive data visualization, and content distribution. Additionally, valuable project planning and data governance considerations are reviewed, including user and capacity-based licensing, row-level security roles, and alternative models for deploying Power BI for an organization.

– Brett Powell, author of Mastering Microsoft Power BI and Microsoft Power BI Cookbook

There's something powerful about a tool that doesn't just visualize data, but transforms how an organization *thinks*. Power BI is one of those tools. And this book? It's not just a technical guide. It's a structured blueprint for elevating decision-making at every level of a business, from the frontline analyst to the C-suite strategist.

When I started Onyx Data, my mission was clear: to help people unlock the value of their data. But too often, I'd see brilliant individuals overwhelmed by dashboards that confused more than clarified, or semantic models that hid insights behind complexity. That's why this book resonates so deeply. It doesn't just teach Power BI, it teaches *business intelligence* the right way, by starting with the why, and guiding you through the how with clarity and intent.

Across the book, Greg shows you what makes great BI work:

- A commitment to **business-first thinking** (Chapter 1)
- A disciplined approach to **project planning and stakeholder alignment** (Chapter 2)
- A mastery of **building reliable semantic models** that scale across departments (Chapters 4–5)

This book doesn't shortcut the fundamentals. It walks you through transforming raw data into decision-ready assets, all while keeping the end-user experience front and center. From shaping data in Power Query to publishing secure reports to Microsoft Fabric, Greg strikes the right balance between precision and practicality.

What I also appreciate is how it speaks to the real-world scenarios we face every day, tailoring reports for execs, defining row-level security, optimizing licensing decisions, and ultimately, creating tools that people actually use.

If you're here to learn Power BI to get ahead in your role, modernize your organization, or build solutions that stand the test of scale, you're in the right place. My advice? Don't just follow the clicks, understand the *thinking*. Because when data professionals combine tooling with strategic intent, the results aren't just visual, they're transformative.

Let this book be your guide. And then go build something remarkable.

– *Leon Gordon, Microsoft MVP, Forbes Tech Council, Gartner Ambassador, LinkedIn Top Voice, and CEO of Onyx Data*

Reading Greg's books is always an entertaining experience. He often provides deep, sometimes unconventional, and thought-provoking insights and methods for working with Power BI. Hence, I was excited to read the third edition of his extremely popular book, Learn Microsoft Power BI. This book doesn't disappoint in that regard. Learn Microsoft Power BI takes you on a thoughtfully sequenced journey – from grasping general business intelligence principles to deploying enterprise-grade solutions using Microsoft Power BI. The opening chapters demystify high-level BI strategy and project planning before diving into hands-on work with Power BI Desktop. By the time you reach the report-building and sharing chapters, you've already mastered the under-the-hood mechanics, ensuring that dashboards aren't just pretty but also performant and reliable.

– *Nikola Ilic, founder of Data Mozart, Microsoft Data Platform MVP*

The book is written well, and the copy and tech editing are handled well. I was particularly impressed to see that Art Tennick was a tech reviewer. I regularly mention Art's books. The book is targeted at beginners and starts by describing why on Earth you might be using these tools in the first place. The book has a good discussion on how to use the various transformations in Power Query and achieve good visualizations in reports. Finally, I liked the discussion on career paths and so on at the end of the book. I've not seen that mentioned in other books, yet it's certainly useful for beginners. Overall, I really enjoyed this book. It's exactly the right length and provides a good coverage of the topic. Great work, Greg!

– *Dr. Greg Low, Founder and Principal Mentor at SQL Down Under, long-term Microsoft MVP and RD*

Contributors

About the author

Greg Deckler is a seven-time Microsoft MVP for Data Platform and an active member of the Columbus Ohio IT community, having founded the Columbus Azure ML and Power BI User Group (CAMLPUG) and presented at many conferences and events throughout the country. An active blogger and community member interested in helping new users of Power BI, Greg actively participates in the Power BI community, having authored over 200 Power BI Quick Measures Gallery submissions and over 7,500 authored solutions to community questions. Greg is also vice president at a global consulting firm.

My sincere thanks to the entire Power BI community for your support through the years. In addition, I want to thank the entire team at Packt for giving me the opportunity to write books.

About the reviewers

Art Tennick is the author of 20 computer books and over 2,000 magazine, blog, and LinkedIn articles. He wrote one of the first books on DAX way back in 2009. He is an independent freelance consultant on Power BI, Analysis Services, Fabric, Python, R, and SQL Server. This is the fourth book for Packt for which he has been a technical reviewer. You can find him on LinkedIn.

Thank you, Rita and Emma, as always.

Peter ter Braake started working in IT after graduating in Physics from the University of Utrecht in 1993. After a few years, data became his primary focus. In 2002, Peter became a Microsoft Certified Trainer and has since divided his time between teaching and consultancy. This has led to extensive experience across a wide range of companies and industries.

Join our community on Discord

Join our community's Discord space for discussions with the authors and other readers: https://discord.gg/hvqvgyGH

Table of Contents

Chapter 10: Understanding Dashboards, Apps, Metrics, and Security 275

Chapter 11: Refreshing Content   305

Part 4: The Future   333

Chapter 12: Deploying, Governing, and Adopting Power BI   335

Preface

To succeed in today's fast-paced business world, organizations need **Business Intelligence** (**BI**) capabilities more than ever in order to make smarter decisions that allow them to be more efficient, effective, and profitable. This book is an entry-level guide specifically designed to get you up and running quickly with Power BI, including data import and transformation, data modeling, visualization, and analytical techniques, without any prior knowledge of BI or Power BI.

You will find this book useful if you want to become knowledgeable about the extensive Power BI ecosystem. You'll start by understanding basic BI concepts and how BI projects are conducted. In short order, you will have Power BI Desktop installed and understand its major components. As you progress, step-by-step instructions are provided for using the Power Query Editor to ingest, cleanse, and transform your data, creating simple and complex DAX calculations, and visualizing your data in ways that truly bring your data to life. Additionally, you'll gain hands-on experience in creating visually stunning reports that speak to business decision-makers and understand how to share and collaborate with others. Finally, you will understand how Power BI is deployed, governed, and adopted within organizations, the job and career opportunities available to BI professionals, and how to continue your learning.

By the end of this book, you'll be ready to create effective reports and dashboards using the latest features of Power BI.

Who this book is for

If you are new to BI or you are a business analyst or other technical or non-technical user who is new to Power BI, then this book is for you. No prior experience in BI or Power BI is required in order to proceed.

What this book covers

Chapter 1, Understanding Business Intelligence and Power BI, provides an introduction to key concepts of business intelligence, an overview of the Power BI ecosystem, and licensing options for Power BI, and introduces Power BI Desktop and the Power BI service.

Chapter 2, Planning Projects with Power BI, explains how BI projects are planned and executed, including identifying stakeholders, goals, requirements, required resources, and data sources, and introduces the example scenario used throughout the rest of the book.

Chapter 3, Up and Running with Power BI Desktop, provides instructions for downloading and installing Power BI Desktop and an overview of the major components of the Desktop including Report, Data and Model views, the menu tabs, the filters, and the Visualizations and Fields panes. It also introduces the creation of tables and visualizations.

Chapter 4, Connecting to and Transforming Data, introduces the Power Query Editor for importing and transforming data, including transposing data, creating custom columns, adding index columns, splitting columns, referencing queries, appending and merging queries, additional transformation functions, and importing data.

Chapter 5, Creating Semantic Models and Calculations, demonstrates how to create a data model by using the model view to create relationships between tables, and how to create and troubleshoot data analysis calculations.

Chapter 6, Unlocking Insights, introduces analysis concepts such as groups and hierarchies, row-level security, report navigation using drill through and buttons, question and answer, bookmarks, and advanced analysis techniques such as analysis, summarization, filtering, gauges, key performance indicators, What if parameters, conditional formatting, quick measures, report page tooltips, and advanced visuals such as the Key Influencers visual.

Chapter 7, Creating the Final Report, provides step-by-step instructions for creating a professional, multi-page report that provides data insights to business decision-makers.

Chapter 8, Publishing and Sharing, demonstrates how to publish the final report to the Power BI service and share the report with a larger audience.

Chapter 9, Using Reports in the Power BI Service, focuses on using reports in the Power BI service including all of the various report functions such as editing reports, embedding, exporting, bookmarks, lineage view, comments, subscriptions, and Microsoft Teams integration.

Chapter 10, Understanding Dashboards, Apps, Metrics, and Security, provides information on creating and working with dashboards, including pinning and managing tiles, the creation and distribution of apps, the creation of scorecards and goals, and an overview of permissions and security.

Chapter 11, Refreshing Content, demonstrates how to install, configure, and manage a data gateway, and how to schedule automatic refreshes for datasets within the Power BI service.

Chapter 12, Deploying, Governing, and Adopting Power BI, introduces different deployment usage models for Power BI within organizations, the concept of governance of Power BI systems including all of the various Power BI Service tenant settings, and how to drive the adoption of Power BI within an organization.

Chapter 13, Working with Microsoft Fabric and Copilot, introduces you to the powerful capabilities of Microsoft Fabric and Copilot within the context of scaling a Power BI solution for enterprise use, including the full process of building and managing Fabric items such as dataflows, warehouses, and semantic models. It also introduces Microsoft Copilot, showcasing how generative AI can assist with data preparation, report creation, SQL generation, and troubleshooting across Fabric workloads.

Chapter 14, Putting Your Knowledge to Use, describes the overall opportunities available in BI, the various types of BI jobs, roles, and responsibilities, the differences between consulting and internal employees, job search strategies, interviewing and compensation negotiation tips, and finally, information on blogs and other websites to continue your journey of learning Power BI.

To get the most out of this book

No prior experience in BI or Power BI is necessary. A keen interest in data and data analytics is helpful as well as prior experience with other BI tools. Running the Power BI Desktop and Data Gateway both require using a computer with Windows as the operating system.

Chapter 10, Understanding Dashboards, Apps, Metrics, and Security, includes material that requires a **Fabric trial capacity** or **Premium Per User (PPU)** licensing.

Chapter 13, Working with Microsoft Fabric and Copilot includes material that requires a **Fabric trial capacity.**

If you are using the digital version of this book, we advise you to type the code yourself or access the code from the book's GitHub repository (a link is available in the next section). Doing so will help you avoid any potential errors related to the copying and pasting of code.

Join the Power BI Community at https://community.powerbi.com!

Download the example code files

The code bundle for the book is hosted on GitHub at https://github.com/PacktPublishing/Learn-Microsoft-Power-BI_3E. We also have other code bundles from our rich catalog of books and videos available at https://github.com/PacktPublishing. Check them out!

Download the color images

We also provide a PDF file that has color images of the screenshots/diagrams used in this book. You can download it here: https://packt.link/gbp/9781836647416.

Conventions used

There are a number of text conventions used throughout this book.

Code in text: Indicates code words in the text, database table names, folder names, filenames, file extensions, pathnames, dummy URLs, user input, and X/Twitter handles. Here is an example: "The first parameter is the Hours table, on line 4, and a filter, on line 5."

A block of code is set as follows:

```
Column 3 =
    VAR __Employee = [EmployeeID]
    VAR __Table =
        FILTER(
            ALL('Hours'),
            [Category] = "Billable" && [EmployeeID] = __Employee
        )
    VAR __Result = SUMX( __Table, [Hours] )
RETURN
    __Result
```

Bold: Indicates a new term, an important word, or words that you see on screen. For instance, words in menus or dialog boxes appear in **bold**. Here is an example: "**Power Platform** includes Power BI datasets and dataflows, as well as the Dataverse."

> Warnings or important notes appear like this.

> Tips and tricks appear like this.

Get in touch

Feedback from our readers is always welcome.

General feedback: If you have questions about any aspect of this book or have any general feedback, please email us at customercare@packt.com and mention the book's title in the subject of your message.

Errata: Although we have taken every care to ensure the accuracy of our content, mistakes do happen. If you have found a mistake in this book, we would be grateful if you reported this to us. Please visit http://www.packt.com/submit-errata, click **Submit Errata**, and fill in the form.

Piracy: If you come across any illegal copies of our works in any form on the internet, we would be grateful if you would provide us with the location address or website name. Please contact us at copyright@packt.com with a link to the material.

If you are interested in becoming an author: If there is a topic that you have expertise in and you are interested in either writing or contributing to a book, please visit http://authors.packt.com/.

Share your thoughts

Once you've read *Learn Microsoft Power BI, Third Edition*, we'd love to hear your thoughts! Scan the QR code below to go straight to the Amazon review page for this book and share your feedback.

https://packt.link/r/1836647417

Your review is important to us and the tech community and will help us make sure we're delivering excellent quality content.

Your Book Comes with Exclusive Perks - Here's How to Unlock Them

Unlock this book's exclusive benefits now

UNLOCK NOW

Scan this QR code or go to packtpub.com/unlock, then search this book by name. Ensure it's the correct edition.

Note: Keep your purchase invoice ready before you start.

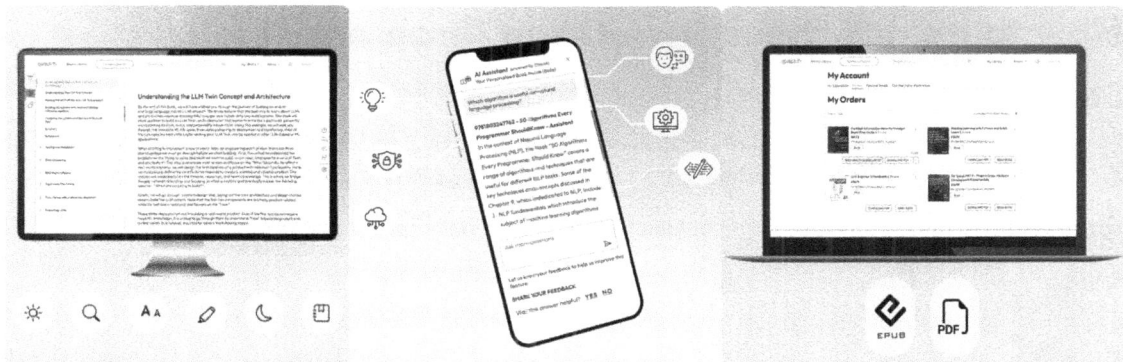

Enhanced reading experience with our Next-gen Reader:

☁ **Multi-device progress sync:** Learn from any device with seamless progress sync.

📑 **Highlighting and notetaking:** Turn your reading into lasting knowledge.

🔖 **Bookmarking:** Revisit your most important learnings anytime.

🔅 **Dark mode:** Focus with minimal eye strain by switching to dark or sepia mode.

Learn smarter using our AI assistant (Beta):

✦ **Summarize it:** Summarize key sections or an entire chapter.

✦ **AI code explainers:** In the next-gen Packt Reader, click the **Explain** button above each code block for AI-powered code explanations.

> **Note:** The AI assistant is part of next-gen Packt Reader and is still in beta.

Learn anytime, anywhere:

📖 Access your content offline with DRM-free PDF and ePub versions—compatible with your favorite e-readers.

Unlock Your Book's Exclusive Benefits

Your copy of this book comes with the following exclusive benefits:

☁ Next-gen Packt Reader

✦ AI assistant (beta)

📄 DRM-free PDF/ePub downloads

Use the following guide to unlock them if you haven't already. The process takes just a few minutes and needs to be done only once.

How to unlock these benefits in three easy steps

Step 1

Keep your purchase invoice for this book ready, as you'll need it in *Step 3*. If you received a physical invoice, scan it on your phone and have it ready as either a PDF, JPG, or PNG.

For more help on finding your invoice, visit https://www.packtpub.com/unlock-benefits/help.

> **Note:** Did you buy this book directly from Packt? You don't need an invoice. After completing Step 2, you can jump straight to your exclusive content.

Step 2

Scan this QR code or go to `packtpub.com/unlock`.

On the page that opens (which will look similar to Figure X.1 if you're on desktop), search for this book by name. Make sure you select the correct edition.

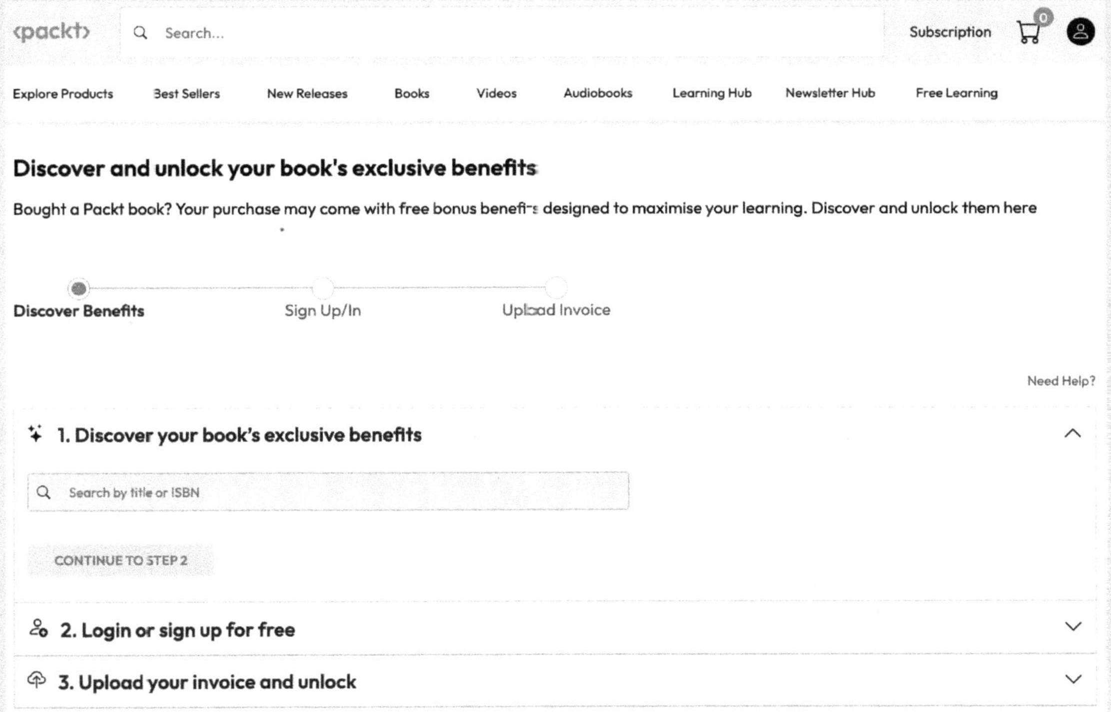

<packt>   Search...   Subscription   🛒   👤

Explore Products   Best Sellers   New Releases   Books   Videos   Audiobooks   Learning Hub   Newsletter Hub   Free Learning

Discover and unlock your book's exclusive benefits

Bought a Packt book? Your purchase may come with free bonus benefits designed to maximise your learning. Discover and unlock them here

Discover Benefits   Sign Up/In   Upload Invoice

Need Help?

✦ 1. Discover your book's exclusive benefits   ⌃

   Search by title or ISBN

   CONTINUE TO STEP 2

⅗ 2. Login or sign up for free   ⌄

⊕ 3. Upload your invoice and unlock   ⌄

Figure 0.1: Packt unlock landing page on desktop

Step 3

Sign in to your Packt account or create a new one for free. Once you're logged in, upload your invoice. It can be in PDF, PNG, or JPG format and must be no larger than 10 MB. Follow the rest of the instructions on the screen to complete the process.

Need help?

If you get stuck and need help, visit https://www.packtpub.com/unlock-benefits/help for a detailed FAQ on how to find your invoices and more. The following QR code will take you to the help page directly:

Note: If you are still facing issues, reach out to customercare@packt.com.

Part 1

The Basics

The objective of this part is to introduce you to the key concepts of business intelligence and Power BI, understand how Power BI projects are conducted, and introduce you to the example scenario used throughout the rest of this book.

This part of the book includes the following chapters:

- *Chapter 1, Understanding Business Intelligence and Power BI*
- *Chapter 2, Planning Projects with Power BI*

1

Understanding Business Intelligence and Power BI

Power BI is part of a powerful ecosystem of **business intelligence** tools and technologies from Microsoft. But what exactly is business intelligence, anyway? Simply stated, business intelligence is all about leveraging data to make better decisions. This can take many forms and is not necessarily restricted to just business. We use data in our personal lives to make better decisions as well. For example, if we are remodeling a bathroom, we get multiple quotes from different firms. The prices and details in these quotes are pieces of data that allow us to make an informed decision regarding which company to choose. We may also research these firms online. This is more data that ultimately supports our decision.

This book explores **Microsoft Power BI** as well as **Microsoft Fabric**, covering everything from foundational concepts to semantic modeling, visualization techniques, and more. You are given step-by-step instructions for connecting to various data sources, transforming and shaping data using Power Query, building effective semantic models, and creating interactive reports and dashboards. In addition, topics such as **DAX** (short for **Data Analysis Expressions**), AI-powered analytics, and performance optimization strategies are covered. With practical examples and real-world scenarios, this book seeks to teach you the skills needed to leverage Power BI for data-driven decision-making and business intelligence solutions.

In this chapter, we explore the fundamental concepts of business intelligence, as well as why business intelligence is important to organizations. In addition, we take a high-level tour of the **Power BI ecosystem**, including Microsoft Fabric, as well as covering licensing and core tools—**Power BI Desktop** and the **Power BI service**.

The following topics are covered in this chapter:

- Exploring key concepts of business intelligence
- Discovering the Power BI ecosystem
- Choosing the right license
- Introducing Power BI Desktop and the Power BI service

Exploring key concepts of business intelligence

In the context of organizations, business intelligence is about making better decisions for your business. Unlike the example in the introduction, organizations are not generally concerned with bathrooms but rather with what can make their business more efficient, effective, and profitable. The businesses that provided those quotes on bathroom remodeling need to answer questions such as the following:

- How can the business attract new customers?
- How can the business retain more customers?
- Who are the competitors and how do they compare?
- What is driving profitability?
- Where can expenses be reduced?

There are endless questions that businesses need to answer every day, and these businesses need data coupled with business intelligence tools and techniques to answer such questions and make effective operational and strategic decisions.

While business intelligence is a vast subject in and of itself, the key concepts of business intelligence can be broken down into five areas:

- Domain
- Data
- Model
- Analysis
- Visualization

Now, let's look at these areas in greater detail.

Domain

A **domain** is simply the context where business intelligence is applied. Most businesses are composed of relatively standard business functions or departments, such as the following:

- Sales
- Marketing
- Manufacturing/production
- Supply chain/operations
- Research and development
- Human resources
- Accounting/finance

The domain helps in narrowing down the focus regarding which questions can be answered and what decisions need to be made. For example, within the context of *sales*, a business might want to know which sales personnel are performing better or worse, or which customers are the most profitable.

Business intelligence can provide such insights as well as helping to determine which activities enable certain sales professionals to outperform others, or why certain customers are more profitable than others. This information can then be used to train and mentor sales personnel who are performing less effectively or to focus sales efforts.

Within the context of *marketing*, a business can use business intelligence to determine which types of marketing campaigns, such as email, radio, print, TV, and the web, are most effective in attracting new customers. This then informs the business where they should spend their marketing budget.

Within the context of *manufacturing*, a business can use business intelligence to determine the **mean time between failure (MTBF)** for machines that are used in the production of goods. This information can be used by the business to determine whether preventative maintenance would be beneficial and how often such preventative maintenance should occur.

Clearly, there are endless examples of where business intelligence can make an organization more efficient, effective, and profitable. Deciding on a domain in which to employ business intelligence techniques is a key step in enabling business intelligence undertakings within organizations since the domain dictates which key questions can be answered, the possible benefits, as well as what data is required in order to answer those questions.

Data

Once a domain has been decided upon, the next step is identifying and acquiring the **data** that's pertinent to that domain. This means identifying the sources of relevant data. These sources may be internal or external to an organization and may be structured, unstructured, or semi-structured in nature.

Internal and external data

Internal data is data that is generated within an organization by its business processes and operations. These business processes can generate large volumes of data that is specific to that organization's operations. This data can take the form of net revenues, sales to customers, new customer acquisitions, employee turnover, units produced, cost of raw materials, and time series or transactional information.

This historical and current data is valuable to organizations if they wish to identify patterns and trends, as well as for forecasting and future planning. Importantly, all the relevant data to a domain and question is almost never housed within a single data source; organizations inevitably have multiple sources of relevant data.

In addition to internal data, business intelligence is often more effective when internal data is combined with **external data**. Crucially, external data is data that is generated outside the boundaries of an organization's operations. External data includes things such as overall global economic trends, census information, customer demographics, household salaries, and the cost of raw materials. All this data exists irrespective of any single organization.

Each domain and question will have internal and external data that is relevant and irrelevant to answering the question at hand. However, do not be fooled into believing that simply because you have chosen manufacturing/production as the domain, other domains, such as sales and marketing, do not have relevant sources of data.

If you are trying to forecast the required production levels, sales data in terms of pipelines can be very relevant. Similarly, external data that points toward overall economic growth may also be extremely relevant, while data such as the cost of raw materials may very well be irrelevant.

Structured, unstructured, and semi-structured data

Structured data is data that conforms to a rather formal specification of tables with rows and columns. Think of a spreadsheet where you might have columns for the transaction ID, customer, units purchased, and price per unit. Each row represents a sales transaction. Structured data sources are the easiest sources for business intelligence tools to consume and analyze. The most common structured data sources are relational databases such as Microsoft SQL Server, Microsoft Access, Azure SQL Database, Oracle, MySQL, IBM Db2, Teradata, PostgreSQL, Informix, and Sybase. In addition, this category also includes such things as Azure Table storage and relational database standards such as **Open Database Connectivity (ODBC)** and **Object Linking and Embedding Database (OLE DB)**, which are supported standards for accessing a wide variety of relational databases as well as other data storage systems.

Unstructured data is effectively the opposite of structured data. Unstructured data cannot be organized into simple tables with rows and columns. Such data includes things such as video, audio, and images. Text documents, social media posts, and online reviews are also examples of largely unstructured data. Unstructured data sources are the most difficult types of sources for business intelligence tools to consume and analyze. This type of data is either stored as **Binary Large Objects (BLOBs)**, online files or posts, or files in a filesystem, such as the **New Technology File System (NTFS)** or the **Hadoop Distributed File System (HDFS)**.

Semi-structured data has a structure but does not conform to the formal definition of structured data, that is, tables with rows and columns. Examples of semi-structured data include tab and delimited text files, **eXtensible Markup Language (XML)**, other markup languages such as **HTML** and **XSL**, **JavaScript Object Notation (JSON)**, and **Electronic Data Interchange (EDI)**. Semi-structured data sources have a self-defining structure that makes them easier to consume and analyze than unstructured data sources but require more work than true, structured data sources.

Semi-structured data also includes so-called **NoSQL** databases, which are specifically designed to store both structured and unstructured data. They include data stores such as:

- **Document databases:** Document databases generally store data in JSON, **Binary JSON (BSON)**, or XML and include Microsoft Azure Cosmos DB, MongoDB, Cloudant (IBM), Couchbase, and MarkLogic.
- **Graph databases:** Graph databases represent and store data using graph concepts such as nodes, edges, and properties. Examples include Neo4j and HyperGraphDB.
- **Key-value stores:** Key-value stores, also known as dictionaries or hash tables, treat data as records that can each have a different number and type of fields. Basho Technologies' Riak, Redis, Aerospike, Amazon Web Services' DynamoDB, Couchbase, DataStax's Cassandra, and MapR Technologies are examples of key-value stores.
- **Wide-column stores:** Wide-column stores organize data into column families versus rows like traditional relational databases. Examples include Cassandra and HBase.

Finally, semi-structured data also includes data access protocols, such as **Open Data Protocol (OData)** and other **Representational State Transfer (REST) application programming interfaces (APIs)**. These protocols provide interfaces to data sources such as Microsoft SharePoint, Microsoft Exchange, Microsoft Active Directory, and Microsoft Dynamics; social media systems such as X/Twitter and Facebook; as well as other online systems such as Mailchimp, Salesforce, Smartsheet, Twilio, Google Analytics, and GitHub. These data protocols abstract how the data is stored, whether that is a relational database, NoSQL database, or simply a bunch of files.

Most business intelligence tools, such as Power BI, are optimized for handling structured and semi-structured data. Structured data sources integrate natively with how business intelligence tools are designed. In addition, business intelligence tools are designed to ingest semi-structured data sources and transform them into structured data. Unstructured data is more difficult but not impossible to analyze with business intelligence tools. In fact, Power BI has some features that are designed to ease the ingestion and analysis of unstructured data sources. However, analyzing such unstructured data has its limitations.

Model

A **model**, also known as a semantic model or data model, refers to the way in which one or more data sources are organized to support analysis and visualization. Models are built by transforming and cleansing data, which helps define the types of data within those sources, as well as to categorize the data according to specific data types. Building a model generally involves three elements:

- Transforming and cleansing
- Defining and categorizing
- Organizing

Transforming and cleansing

When building a semantic model (also known as a data model), it is often (read: always) necessary to clean and transform the source data. Data is never clean— it must always be massaged for bad data to be removed or resolved. For example, when dealing with customer data from a **Customer Relationship Management (CRM)** system, it is not uncommon to have the same customer entered with multiple spellings. The format of data in spreadsheets may make data entry easy for humans but can be unsuitable for business intelligence purposes. In addition, data may have errors, missing data, inconsistent formatting, or even something as seemingly simple as trailing spaces. These types of situations can cause problems when performing business intelligence analysis. Luckily, business intelligence tools such as Power BI provide mechanisms for cleansing and reshaping the data to support analysis. This might involve replacing or removing errors in the data, pivoting, unpivoting, or transposing rows and columns, removing trailing spaces, or other types of transformation operations.

Transforming and cleansing technologies are often referred to as **Extract, Transform, Load (ETL)** tools and include products such as Microsoft's **SQL Server Integration Services (SSIS)**, Azure Data Factory, Alteryx, Informatica, Dell Boomi, Salesforce's MuleSoft, Skyvia, IBM's InfoSphere Information Server, Oracle Data Integrator, Talend, Pentaho Data Integration, SAS's Data Integration Studio, Sybase ETL, and QlikView Expressor.

Defining and categorizing

Semantic models also formally define the types of data within each table. These data types include text, decimal number, whole number, percentage, date, time, date and time, duration, true/false, and binary. The definition of these data types is important as it defines what kind of analysis can be performed on the data. For example, it does not make sense to create a sum or average of text data types; instead, you would use aggregations such as count, first, or last.

Finally, semantic models also define the data category of data types. While a data type such as a postal code might be numeric or text, it is important for the model to define that the numeric data type represents a postal code. This further defines the type of analysis that can be performed on this data, such as plotting the data on a map. Similarly, it might be important for the semantic model to define that a text data type represents a web or image **Uniform Resource Locator** (URL). Typical data categories include such things as address, city, state, province, continent, country, region, place, county, longitude, latitude, postal code, web URL, image URL, and barcode.

Organizing

Semantic models can be extremely simple, such as a single table with columns and rows. However, business intelligence almost always involves multiple tables of data, often coming from multiple sources. Thus, the model becomes more complex as the various sources and tables of data must be combined into a cohesive whole. This is done by defining how each of the disparate sources of data relate to one another.

As an example, let's say you have one data source that represents a customer's name, contact information, and perhaps the size of the business by revenue and/or the number of employees. This information might come from an organization's CRM system. The second source of data might be order information, which includes the customer's name, units purchased, and the price that was paid. This second source of data comes from the organization's **Enterprise Resource Planning** (ERP) system. These two sources of data can be related to one another based on the unique name or ID of the customer.

Some sources of data have prebuilt models. In other words, there are defined relationships between data entities or tables within the data source. This includes traditional data warehouse technologies for structured data as well as analogous systems for performing analytics over unstructured data. Data warehouses are traditionally built upon **Online Analytical Processing** (OLAP) technology and include systems such as Microsoft's Analysis Services, Snowflake, Oracle's Essbase, AtScale cubes, SAP HANA and Business Warehouse servers, and Azure Synapse. With respect to unstructured data analysis, technologies such as Apache Spark, Databricks, and Azure Data Lake Storage are used.

> Note that OLAP refers to a method of storing data that optimizes read operations for reporting purposes. This is in contrast to **Online Transaction Processing** (OLTP) systems, which store data in a manner that is optimized for write operations.

Analysis

Once a domain has been selected and data sources have been combined into a model, the next step is to perform an analysis of the data. This is a key process within business intelligence as this is when you attempt to answer questions that are relevant to the business using internal and external data.

For example, simply having data about sales is not immediately useful to a business. To predict future sales revenue, it is important that such data is aggregated and analyzed. This analysis can determine the average sales for a product, the frequency of purchases, and which customers purchase more frequently than others. Such information allows better decision-making by an organization.

Data analysis can take many forms, such as grouping data, creating simple aggregations such as sums, counts, and averages, as well as creating more complex calculations, identifying trends, correlations, and forecasting. Many times, organizations have, or wish to have, **Key Performance Indicators (KPIs)**, which are tracked by the business to help determine the organization's health or performance. KPIs might include such things as employee retention rate, net promoter score, new customer acquisitions per month, gross margin, and **Earnings Before Interest, Tax, Depreciation, and Amortization (EBITDA)**. Such KPIs generally require that the data is aggregated, has calculations performed on it, or both. These aggregations and calculations are called metrics or measures and are used to identify trends or patterns that can inform business decision-making. In some cases, advanced analysis tools such as programming languages, machine learning and artificial intelligence, data mining, streaming analytics, and unstructured analytics are necessary to gain the proper insights.

There are numerous programming languages that have either been specifically designed from the ground up for data analytics or have developed robust data analytics packages or extensions. Two of the most popular languages in this space include R and Python. Other popular languages include SQL, **Multidimensional Expressions (MDX)**, Julia, SAS, MATLAB, Scala, and F#.

There is also a wide variety of machine learning and data mining tools and platforms for performing predictive analytics around data classification, regression, anomaly detection, clustering, and decision-making. Such systems include TensorFlow, Microsoft's Azure Machine Learning, DataRobot, Alteryx Analytics Hub, H2O.ai, KNIME, Splunk, RapidMiner, and Prevedere.

Streaming analytics becomes important when dealing with **Internet of Things (IoT)** data. Streaming analytics processes data in real time or near real time. In these situations, tools such as Striim, StreamAnalytix, TIBCO Event Processing, Apache Storm, Azure Stream Analytics, Oracle Stream Analytics, and Microsoft Fabric's Real-Time Intelligence workload are used.

When dealing with unstructured data, tools such as Pig and Hive are popular, as well as tools such as Apache Spark and Azure AI for vision, speech, and sentiment analysis.

Of course, any discussion around data analytics tools would be incomplete without including Microsoft Excel. Spreadsheets have long been the go-to analytics tool for business users, and the most popular spreadsheet today is Microsoft Excel. However, other spreadsheet programs, such as Google Sheets, Smartsheet, Apple Numbers, Zoho Sheet, and LibreOffice Calc, also exist.

Visualization

The final key concept in business intelligence is visualization or the actual presentation of the analysis being performed. Humans are visually oriented and thus it is advantageous to view the results of the analysis in the form of charts, reports, and dashboards. Charts may take the form of tables, matrices, pie charts, bar graphs, and other visual displays that help provide context and meaning to the analysis, and multiple charts are combined to make **reports** and **dashboards**. In the same way that a picture is worth a thousand words, visualizations allow thousands, millions, or even trillions of individual data points to be presented in a concise manner that is easily consumed and understandable. Visualization allows the analyst or report author to let the data tell a story. This story answers the questions that are originally posed by the business and thus delivers the insights that allow organizations to make better decisions.

Individual charts or visualizations typically display aggregations, KPIs, and/or other calculations of underlying data that have been summarized by some form of grouping. These charts are designed to present a specific facet or metric of the data within a specific context. For example, one chart may display the number of web sessions by the day of the week, while another chart may display the number of page views by browser.

Business intelligence tools allow multiple individual tables and charts to be combined on a single page or report. Modern business intelligence tools such as Power BI support interactivity between individual visualizations to further aid the discovery and analysis process. This interactivity allows the report consumer to click on portions of individual visualizations, such as bar charts, maps, and tables, in order to drill down, highlight, or filter the information presented or determine the influence of a particular portion of a chart on the rest of the visualizations in a report. This goes beyond typical legacy visualization tools such as **SQL Server Reporting Services (SSRS)** or SAP Crystal Reports, which only provide minimal user interactivity when it comes to choosing from predefined filters. For example, given the two charts we referenced previously, the report consumer can click on a particular day of the week in the first report to display the page visit breakdown per browser for the chosen day of the week in the second chart:

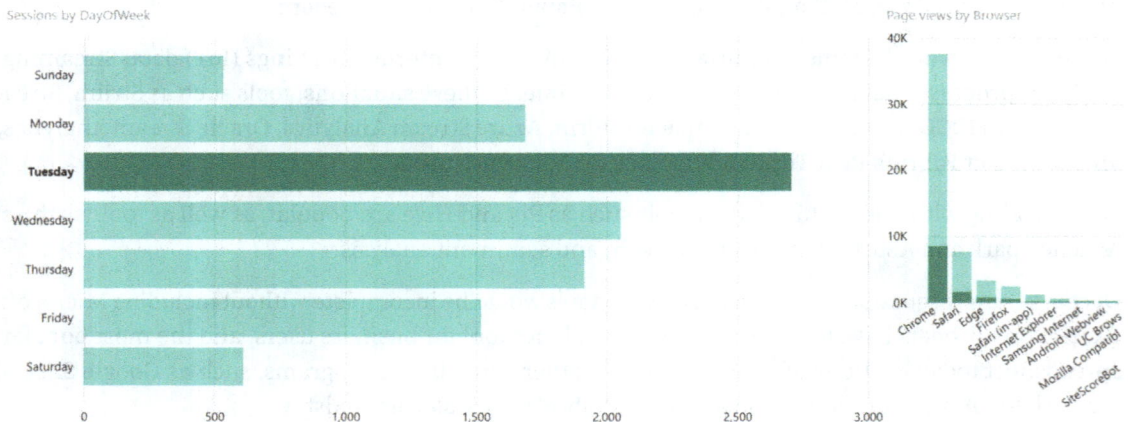

Figure 1.1 – Two bar charts: (L) sessions by DayOfWeek; (R) Page views by browser

Finally, dashboards provide easy-to-understand visualizations of KPIs that are important to an organization. For example, the CEO of a corporation may wish to see only certain information from sales, marketing, operations, and human resources. Each of these departments may have its own detailed reports, but the CEO only wishes to track one or two of the individual visualizations within each of those reports. Dashboards enable this functionality.

Visualization software includes venerable tools such as SSRS and Crystal Reports, as well as software such as Birst, Domo, MicroStrategy, Qlik Sense, Tableau CRM, SAS Visual Analytics, Sisense, Tableau, ThoughtSpot, and TIBCO Spotfire.

Now that we have examined the key concepts and overarching themes of business intelligence, it is time to delve a layer deeper and discover the technologies that enable business intelligence within the Power BI ecosystem.

Discovering the Power BI ecosystem

While Power BI is often classified as a visualization tool, the reality is that Power BI is not a single tool but rather part of a collection of interrelated tools and services that form a complete business intelligence ecosystem. This ecosystem spans the entire business intelligence spectrum: domain, data, model, analysis, and visualization. In addition, this ecosystem includes components that are specific not only to Power BI itself but also to other Microsoft technologies that encompass and interoperate with Power BI, as well as third-party integrations. This interoperation with other Microsoft tools and technologies, as well as third parties, makes Power BI a formidable business intelligence platform, whose value far exceeds that of more siloed business intelligence tools in the market.

While the Power BI ecosystem is vast and complex, this ecosystem can be broken down into the following categories:

- Core and Power BI-specific
- Core and non-Power BI-specific
- Non-core and Power BI-specific
- Natively integrated Microsoft technologies
- Extended ecosystem

Core and Power BI-specific

Core and Power BI-specific technologies are systems that are specific to Power BI and fundamental to its use. Core and Power BI-specific technologies include the following:

- **Power BI Desktop** is a free Windows-based application that is installed on a local desktop or laptop computer. It is the primary tool used to ingest, cleanse, and transform various sources of data, combine the data into models, and then analyze and visualize the data through the creation of calculations, visualizations, and reports. Once reports have been created in Power BI Desktop, these reports are often published to the Power BI service for sharing and collaboration.

- The **Power BI service** is a cloud-based **Software as a Service (SaaS)** online platform. The Power BI service can be used for light report creation and editing, dashboard creation, and sharing, collaborating on, and viewing reports. Some data sources can be connected directly from the Power BI service, but the ability to model and analyze that data is limited.

Core and non-Power BI-specific

Core and non-Power BI-specific technologies are technologies that are a core part of Power BI but are also used in other software and systems. These include the following:

- **Power Query** is the Microsoft technology that provides data connectivity and transformation. This technology allows business users to access hundreds of different sources and transform the data as required. Data sources supported by Power Query include many different file types, databases, Microsoft Azure services, and third-party services. Power Query also provides a **Software Development Kit (SDK)** that allows for the creation of custom connectors so that third parties can create their own data connectors that seamlessly interoperate with Power Query. Power Query is used within Power BI Desktop, Microsoft Excel, Microsoft SQL Server Data Tools for Visual Studio, and Microsoft Dataverse (formerly Common Data Service).

- **DAX** is a language that consists of a collection of functions, operators, and constants that can be used to write formulas or expressions that return calculated values. Similar to Excel functions or MDX, DAX helps you create new information from data that's already in your model.

- A **data gateway** is software that is installed to facilitate access from the Power BI service to on-premises data sources. A data gateway allows the Power BI service to refresh data from one or more data sources housed within on-premises systems. The data gateway comes in two modes – Personal and Enterprise. Personal mode can only be used with Power BI, while Enterprise mode can be used with Power BI as well as Power Automate, Microsoft Power Apps, Azure Analysis Services, and other Azure Logic Apps.

- **Analysis Services tabular modeling** is an evolution of Microsoft's multidimensional cubes. This technology is available outside of Power BI within Analysis Services but is also fundamental to Power BI. Models that are built within Power BI are actually built using SSAS Tabular, and Power BI Desktop runs a full instance of SSAS Tabular under the hood, so to speak. Thus, when building models in Power BI Desktop, you are actually building an Analysis Services tabular model.

- **Microsoft AppSource**, or simply AppSource, is a marketplace for finding apps, add-ons, and extensions to Microsoft software, including Microsoft 365, Azure, Dynamics 365, Cortana, and Power BI. Within Power BI, AppSource hosts custom visuals that can be downloaded and added to Power BI reports that have been authored within the desktop. These visuals are supported within the Power BI service as well.

Non-core and Power BI-specific

Non-core and Power BI-specific technologies are technologies that are specific to Power BI but not necessarily required to use Power BI. These include the following:

- **Power BI Report Server (PBIRS)** is an on-premises technology that is a superset of SSRS. Similar in function to the Power BI service, PBIRS allows Power BI reports authored in Power BI Desktop and Excel to be published and viewed while remaining fully on-premises. Because PBIRS is a superset of SSRS, it can also host paginated reports (.rdl).

- **Power BI Embedded** is a system of REST APIs that can be used to display visualizations (charts), reports, and dashboards within custom applications that serve customers that are external to an organization. Power BI Embedded is often used by **Independent Software Vendors** (ISVs) and developers.

- **Power BI mobile applications** are native Android, iOS, and Windows applications that are downloadable from the respective platform stores: Google Play, the Apple App Store, and the Microsoft Store. Power BI mobile apps are touch-optimized for viewing and interacting with Power BI reports that are published to the Power BI service.

Natively integrated Microsoft technologies

Natively integrated Microsoft technologies include the following:

- **Microsoft 365** is Microsoft's ubiquitous line of subscription services, which includes traditional Office applications, plus other productivity services that are enabled via the cloud (the internet). Central to Microsoft 365 is the concept of a tenant, an organization's very own slice of Microsoft 365. Power BI integrates natively with Microsoft 365 so that when a user subscribes to Power BI, the email address is checked for existing Microsoft 365 tenants, and if one exists, the Power BI user will be added to that tenant. If an Microsoft 365 tenant does not exist, Power BI will provision a new Microsoft 365 tenant, sometimes called a shadow tenant, and the Power BI user will be added to that tenant.

- **Excel** incorporates many underlying Power BI technologies as native add-ons. These include Analyze in Excel and Power Pivot, which provides access to Power Query, and the same underlying semantic model used by Power BI (Analysis Services tabular models). Excel is also a first-class citizen within the Power BI service and is called Workbooks within the Power BI service.

- **Power Platform** is an encompassing ecosystem that includes Power BI as well as Power Automate, Power Apps, and Power Virtual Agents:

  - **Power Automate** is a workflow technology that has a native connector for Power BI that supports both triggers and actions. Triggers are based on the Power BI service's data alerts, and actions support both streaming and non-streaming datasets in the service. In addition, there is a Power Automate visualization available in AppSource.

  - **Power Apps** is a form-based technology from Microsoft that provides a native connector to Power BI, as well as a default visualization. In addition, Power BI tiles can be embedded into Power Apps applications. Finally, Power Apps uses Power Query technology as part of its data integration feature.

  - **Power Virtual Agents** enables the creation and use of intelligent agents or *bots* that can perform tasks or have intelligent, contextual conversations with humans. Power Virtual Agents chatbots can be integrated into Power BI workspaces.

- The **Microsoft Visio** desktop application has a custom visual for Power BI that was built by Microsoft. This visual allows you to link data within Power BI to a Visio diagram where the data is displayed using values or colors within the Visio drawing.
- **SharePoint** provides the ability to embed Power BI reports within SharePoint via a native Power BI report web part.
- **Dynamics 365** provides the ability to embed Power BI visuals natively within Dynamics 365 reports and dashboards. In addition, Power BI has native connectors for Dynamics. Finally, there are several apps available for Dynamics in the Power BI service.
- **Dataverse** (formerly Common Data Service) is actually central to Power Automate, Power Apps, Power Virtual Agents, Dynamics 365, and Power BI. Dataverse allows an organization to store and manage data from numerous business applications within a set of standard and custom entities. Entities allow an organization to create a business-focused definition of their data and use this data within apps. Power BI has a native connector for Dataverse.
- **Azure Machine Learning** technologies are becoming pervasive within Power BI. This includes the ability to create columns from examples within Power Query, as well as custom visualizations, such as the key influencers visual. In addition, dataflows in Power BI Premium capacities can leverage **Automated Machine Learning (AutoML)** and Azure AI services.
- One of the native outputs from **Azure Stream Analytics** is Power BI. This allows you to stream data that is running through Azure Stream Analytics and display it on Power BI's dashboard tiles.
- **Report Builder** is a venerable Microsoft tool for the creation of paginated reports (.rdl). These reports can be published to the Power BI service or PBIRS on-premises.

The extended Power BI ecosystem

One of the biggest changes in the Power BI ecosystem, as of May 2023, is that Power BI is now part of a larger ecosystem called **Microsoft Fabric**. Microsoft Fabric is a unified platform for enterprise data and analytics. This platform includes data ingestion, transformation, and processing as well as semantic modeling, experimentation, real-time event routing, alerting and workflows, and report building. Within this larger ecosystem, Power BI primarily serves as the report-building component. We will explore Microsoft Fabric in greater detail later in this book.

Microsoft has also created numerous APIs and SDKs that enable the creation of custom visuals, data source connectors, and automation via PowerShell and other coding languages. As a result, there is a large extended ecosystem of third-party custom visuals, connectors, apps, and add-on products for Power BI. In addition, Power BI integrates with other non-Microsoft programming languages, such as Python, R, and **Scalable Vector Graphics (SVG)**.

The Power BI community is a large ecosystem of users focused on the education and use of Power BI within local communities. To find a Power BI user group in your area, go to https://www.pbiusergroup.com.

In addition to local user groups, there is a general community website that provides forums and galleries where Power BI users can get questions answered about using Power BI. To access this community website, go to https://community.powerbi.com.

As you can see, Power BI is part of a large ecosystem of tools and technologies that enables business intelligence as well as supporting the business processes that benefit from informed decisions. However, to get the most out of these tools and technologies, it is important to understand how Power BI is licensed.

Choosing the right license

Power BI provides numerous licensing options that provide flexibility and affordability for individuals and organizations of any size. These various licensing options come in two primary categories:

- Shared capacity
- Dedicated capacity

Shared capacity

Think of **shared capacity** like an apartment building. While each tenant within the apartment building has their own personal living quarters, certain infrastructures, such as a common entryway, electrical wiring, and plumbing, are shared. Shared capacity licensing options for Power BI work similarly. While each tenant within the shared capacity of the Power BI service has their own personal area for publishing datasets, reports, and dashboards, the memory and processing capacity of the entire Power BI service is shared among all of the tenants using the Power BI service within an Azure data center. And, just as a tenant in an apartment building playing loud music can affect that tenant's neighbors, so too can tenants impact other tenants within the same shared capacity by using resources within the Power BI service.

There are two options for using shared capacity within Power BI:

- Free
- Pro

Free

Power BI Desktop is free to download, install, and use. In addition to simply sharing Power BI files (.pbix), which are the files that are created by the Power BI Desktop program, Microsoft provides a free method of using the Power BI service so that you can publish and view reports. However, the Free license does not allow sharing reports with others. There is one exception to this inability to share and that is a feature called **Publish to web** Publish to web creates a web browser link or URL to a report that's published in the Power BI service. While this URL is long and cryptic and these reports are not indexed by search engines, anyone with the link can browse the report anonymously. This means that there is no real security other than simple obfuscation.

It is important to note some of the limitations of this option:

- Publish to web is the only sharing mechanism available with a Free license of Power BI. All other sharing, collaboration, and export features are not available with the free Power BI service. This includes app workspaces for collaboration, sharing of reports and dashboards, as well as exporting to Microsoft PowerPoint/**Comma Separated Values (CSV)** and embedding within Microsoft SharePoint.

- The Free licensing of Power BI also comes with certain restrictions on the automatic refreshing of data. Only online sources of data can be refreshed automatically. While both online and internet-based data sources can be refreshed, these data sources can only be refreshed 8 times per day, and the minimum time between refreshes is 30 minutes.
- Finally, the Free Power BI license restricts the total size of any single semantic model that's published to the Power BI service to 1 GB and the total size of all semantic models that are published to the service for each user to 10 GB.

Pro

The classic way to license Power BI that provides more secure sharing and collaboration is called **Power BI Pro**. Pro is a subscription license for authoring, sharing, and consuming shared reports within the Power BI service and is suitable for individuals as well as small and medium businesses with fewer than approximately 500 active users. Each user who authors, shares, or consumes a shared report must purchase Power BI Pro for a commercial list price of $14 per user per month.

Pro licensing in Power BI enables all sharing, collaboration, and additional features that are not available with a Free license. However, Pro has the same restrictions in terms of dataset size and total capacity as Power BI Free licenses. This means that the total size of any single semantic model that's published to the Power BI service is restricted to 1 GB and the total size of all semantic models that are published to the service for each user cannot exceed 10 GB. In addition, the data refresh frequency limitations are the same as Free licenses.

Dedicated capacity

While shared capacity is analogous to an apartment building, think of dedicated capacity as individual houses. With dedicated capacity licensing options, each tenant has dedicated memory and processing power that only that tenant can utilize, thereby protecting each tenant from *noisy neighbors*.

There are four options for using dedicated capacity within Power BI:

- Microsoft Fabric
- **Premium Per User (PPU)**
- Embedded
- PBIRS

Microsoft Fabric

Microsoft Fabric is a capacity-based subscription license with capacity sizes that scale from small businesses to mid-sized organizations as well as enterprises. Fabric capacities include additional features for Power BI as well as additional workloads such as **Data Warehouse, Data Engineering, Data Science, Data Factory, Real-Time Intelligence**, and **Data Activator**.

The additional features that Fabric capacities provide include such things as increased model size limits, increased refresh rate limits, advanced dataflow features, deployment pipelines, XMLA (XML for Analysis) endpoint connectivity, and advanced **artificial intelligence** (AI).

Fabric SKUs range in size from F2 to F2048 in increments that double the number of the previous SKU. Thus, the next size up from an F2 SKU is an F4 SKU and then an F8 SKU, etc. The SKU number represents the total number of **capacity units (CUs)** available to the capacity. CUs are simply a measure of computing power so each level of F SKU has twice as much computing power as the previous SKU.

Pricing for Fabric varies across geographic regions and also varies depending on whether you reserve an instance of Fabric or adopt a pay-as-you-go strategy. Fabric reservations are typically approximately 40% less expensive than pay-as-you-go instances. However, pay-as-you-go instances allow you to turn off (suspend) the capacity when not in use and therefore not be charged for compute.

It is important to note that building and sharing reports in Fabric capacities requires additional licensing in the form of Power BI Pro or Power BI PPU licenses.

Fabric SKUs that are F64+ include additional features, namely, the ability of users with a Free license to view shared reports as well as Copilot in Fabric. Copilot is Microsoft's generative AI product. Finally, F64+ reserved SKUs also include a license for PBIRS.

Premium Per User

Power BI PPU licensing fills the gap for small and medium-sized customers that require the Enterprise Power BI features included in Microsoft Fabric capacities but do not require the additional Fabric workloads. PPU works exactly like Pro licensing in that each individual user accessing a PPU workspace must have a PPU license. Workspaces designated as PPU include almost all of the advanced Enterprise features of Microsoft Fabric capacities, such as increased model size limits, increased refresh rate limits, advanced dataflow features, deployment pipelines, XMLA endpoint connectivity, and advanced AI. A small number of features, such as Multi-Geo support, Report Server licensing, and Microsoft Copilot, are not included. PPU licenses cost $24 per user per month.

Embedded

Power BI Embedded is a capacity-based subscription license. This means that increments of capacity in the form of virtual CPU cores and memory are purchased on an hourly basis. These increments of capacity are called **node types** and range in size from an A1 with a single virtual core and 3 GB of RAM for approximately $750 per month to an A6 with 32 virtual cores and 100 GB of RAM for approximately $24,000 per month. Power BI Embedded *A* SKUs are purchased via the Azure portal. In addition to this capacity licensing, report authors also need to license Power BI Pro for the standard license cost of $14 per user per month.

Power BI Embedded is intended for use by developers and ISVs that use APIs to embed Power BI visuals, reports, and dashboards within their custom web applications. These applications can then be accessed by external customers.

Power BI's embedding technology can be used to create applications that are accessed by internal users; however, this requires different SKUs, the Power BI Premium *EM* SKUs.

Finally, it is worth noting that A1 and A2 nodes run on non-dedicated capacity, while A3 to A6 nodes run on dedicated capacity. This is important, as dedicated capacity can prevent noisy neighbor scenarios that may impact overall performance.

Power BI Report Server

PBIRS is intended for customers who wish to keep their data completely on-premises. PBIRS is a superset of SSRS and, therefore, can be licensed by purchasing a license of SQL Server Enterprise Edition with **Software Assurance (SA)** or by purchasing any Microsoft Fabric F64+ reserved capacity instance. The details of SQL licensing are beyond the scope of this book, but typical costs will range in price from $4,000 to $7,000 per core. In addition, report authors also need to license Power BI Pro for the standard license cost of $14 per user per month.

> It should be noted that there is a free developer edition of PBIRS that can be used in non-production environments.

Importantly, PBIRS does not provide the same level of functionality as the Power BI service. For example, PBIRS does not allow reports to be created or edited like in the Power BI service. In addition, features such as workspace apps, dashboards, Q&A, quick insights, and native R and Python visuals are not supported within PBIRS. However, PBIRS can access and refresh online and on-premises data sources without requiring a gateway.

Next, let's get acquainted with the predominant components of Power BI.

Introducing Power BI Desktop and the Power BI service

After learning about the entire breadth and depth of the Power BI ecosystem and licensing, you may be wondering how on earth a single book can possibly cover everything there is to know about Power BI. The short answer is that it is not possible. Entire books exist dedicated to just a single topic, including Power Query, DAX, and Power BI Embedded. Even books that claim to be complete references to Power BI inevitably leave out some components of the entire Power BI ecosystem. Thus, this book is intended for those who wish to learn about the basic, core components of the Power BI ecosystem, namely, the following:

- Power BI Desktop, including Power Query and DAX
- The Power BI service, including the data gateway

Learning about these core technologies and, while doing so, learning how to build and share reports with meaningful business intelligence insights means that by the end of this book, you will have learned about all of the core components and become a participant within the Power BI ecosystem.

Power BI Desktop

As mentioned previously, Power BI Desktop, or simply Desktop, is a free Windows-based application that can be installed on a local desktop or laptop computer. Desktop is the primary tool used by analysts to ingest, shape, analyze, and visualize data. More specifically, Power BI Desktop is useful for the following tasks:

- **Getting data:** The first step in working with Power BI Desktop is to connect to data sources. There are currently over 100 connectors that can be used to connect to different data sources, including many general-purpose connectors, such as the web connector, OData Feed, and the JSON connector, which enable connections to hundreds, if not thousands, of different sources of data.

- **Creating a semantic model:** Connecting to a data source creates a query within a tool called the Power Query editor. The Power Query editor utilizes Power Query technology and provides a graphical interface that allows the user to create a series of steps that are recorded and then replayed every time data is loaded or refreshed from the source. This means your data always ends up in your desired form.

  Queries load data into structured data tables within Power BI Desktop. Once these tables of data have been loaded, a semantic model can be constructed by relating these tables to one another.

- **Analyzing data:** The data used within the model does not have to come solely from data sources. Power BI uses a programming language called DAX, which allows users to create calculations in the form of calculated columns, measures, and even entire tables. This allows analysts to create simple measures, such as gross margins and percentage of totals, as well as more complex measures, such as year-over-year revenue.

- **Creating and publishing reports:** Once a semantic model has been built and analyzed, visuals can be created on report pages by dragging and dropping fields onto the report canvas. Visuals are graphical representations of the data within the model. There are 37 default visuals within Power BI Desktop, but hundreds more can be imported from Microsoft AppSource and used within Power BI Desktop. Multiple visuals can be combined on one or more pages to create a report. These visuals and pages can interact with one another as users click within the report. Once the reports have been finalized, the reports can be published to the Power BI service. These reports can then be shared with other users.

The Power BI service

The Power BI service is a hosted web application that runs on Microsoft's cloud platform, Azure. The service is free to use, with restrictions around the sharing of reports, as covered previously.

> The service can be accessed at https://app.powerbi.com, but do not go there just yet! We will cover the service in greater detail later in this book.

The service is useful for the following tasks:

- **Viewing and editing reports:** Reports that are published to the service can be viewed within a web browser. This provides the same interactive experience as Desktop. In addition, reports can be marked as favorites, subscribed to for email delivery, and downloaded as PDFs or PowerPoint files. Existing reports can be edited, and new reports can be created from the published datasets.

- **Creating dashboards:** The Power BI service allows visuals from one or more reports to be combined into dashboards. Dashboards highlight the most important information and metrics. Dashboards can be marked as favorites, subscribed to for email delivery, and have alerts created that notify the user when thresholds have been exceeded.

- **Sharing and collaborating with others:** Reports and dashboards can be shared with others. This allows a report author's published work to be easily distributed to a wider audience. Other users can set their own personal report bookmarks, as well as engaging in discussions about data. Multiple individuals can even collaborate within workspaces to create reports and dashboards. The security settings allow authors and collaborators to control who sees which dashboards, reports, and data.

- **Accessing and creating apps:** Microsoft and third parties have created built-in apps within the service that provide bundles of data, reports, and dashboards. These apps can be subscribed to from within the service and added to your personal Power BI workspace. Authors can even bundle their own data, reports, and dashboards into an app and distribute it to other users in their organization.

- **Refreshing data:** The service allows users to schedule automatic refreshes of online and on-premises data. This means that once a refresh has been configured for a published report, the data is always current, with no further work required by the author. The service provides its own refresh gateway for online data. On-premises data requires an on-premises data gateway to be installed on a local network.

Now, let's wrap up with a quick summary of what we've learned in this chapter.

Summary

In this chapter, we were introduced to business intelligence and its key concepts. Then, we took a broad look at the Power BI ecosystem. Finally, we explored some more specific capabilities of Power BI Desktop and the Power BI service. Because Power BI is all about business intelligence, it is difficult, if not impossible, to understand Power BI without first understanding the broader context of making informed business decisions. Understanding the full scope of business intelligence and the Power BI ecosystem helps you understand the context in which the Power BI technologies covered in this book are applied.

In the next chapter, we will dig deeper into the methodology and process for Power BI projects within corporations and set up the example business intelligence project used throughout the rest of the book.

Questions

As an activity, try to answer the following questions on your own:

- What is business intelligence?
- What does business intelligence do for an organization?
- What are the five key concepts of business intelligence?
- What are the five different categories of data?
- Which word best describes everything that comprises and integrates with Power BI?

- What are the two primary licensing mechanisms for Power BI?
- Which tools are covered in this book?
- What can you do with Power BI?
- Which six additional workloads does Microsoft Fabric add in addition to Power BI?

Further reading

To learn more about the topics that were covered in this chapter, please take a look at the following references:

- Business intelligence: https://en.wikipedia.org/wiki/Business_intelligence
- Power BI pricing: https://powerbi.microsoft.com/en-us/pricing/
- *What is Microsoft Fabric?*: https://learn.microsoft.com/en-us/fabric/get-started/microsoft-fabric-overview
- *What is Power BI Report Server?*: https://docs.microsoft.com/en-us/power-bi/report-server/get-started
- Power BI Embedded: https://azure.microsoft.com/en-us/services/power-bi-embedded/

Join our community on Discord

Join our community's Discord space for discussions with the authors and other readers: https://discord.gg/hvqvgyGH

2

Planning Projects with Power BI

Power BI projects are essentially the same as business intelligence projects involving alternative tools such as Tableau, Qlik, MicroStrategy, **SQL Server Reporting Services (SSRS)**, or even Crystal Reports. In fact, all business intelligence projects follow (or should follow) a similar process, with only minor variations depending on the specific technology being implemented.

In this chapter, we explain the general process for business intelligence projects with specific callouts for planning considerations specific to Power BI. In addition, we introduce the specific business scenario that is used throughout this book.

The following topics will be covered in this chapter:

- Planning business intelligence projects
- Example scenario: utilization reporting

Planning business intelligence projects

As explained in the previous chapter, in the *Power BI Desktop* section, Power BI business intelligence projects involve getting data from data sources, creating a data/semantic model, and then creating and publishing reports and dashboards that are consumed by the business and used to answer specific questions or support the analysis of the efficiency, effectiveness, and profitability of the business. However, successfully delivering the desired insights and analysis to the business requires careful planning and should include the following activities:

- Identifying stakeholders, goals, and requirements
- Procuring the required resources
- Defining the data sources
- Designing a model
- Planning reports and dashboards

We'll look at each of these activities in detail in the following sections.

Identifying stakeholders, goals, and requirements

Business intelligence projects are most often driven by the business as opposed to IT. This means that one of the business domains, such as sales, marketing, manufacturing/production, supply chain/ operations, research and development, human resources, or accounting/finance, is attempting to answer specific questions about the business or better understand how to make the business more efficient, effective, and profitable. Therefore, it is imperative that any business intelligence project starts with identifying the specific **goals** or objectives of all interested parties or **stakeholders** that are championing the business intelligence project, as well as any specific **requirements** in terms of data security, the granularity of the data, the amount of historical data, and the availability of data.

Stakeholders

Simply stated, stakeholders are individuals or groups with an interest in the outcome of a business intelligence project. Stakeholders are vitally important to the success of any business intelligence project, as they define the goals and requirements of the business intelligence project and, ultimately, determine whether the business intelligence project meets or fails to meet the desired outcomes.

It is not uncommon to have multiple stakeholders for a given business intelligence project, and even stakeholders that span multiple business domains. For example, sales and marketing often share similar interests and need answers to similar questions. Start by identifying the business domains as stakeholders for the business intelligence project and then identify the specific individuals within those business domains that can provide the goals and requirements for the project.

In most corporate environments, it is often advantageous to identify a single individual as a special kind of stakeholder, a **project sponsor**. Project sponsors help secure the funding and/or prioritization of resources for the business intelligence project.

Goals

Goals or objectives are the purpose of the business intelligence project or the questions the business is trying to answer. As you can imagine, these goals can be quite varied. Sales may be attempting to analyze overall sales and compare those sales with their plan. Marketing may wish to understand and compare the effectiveness of different marketing campaigns or the effectiveness of different customer trigger events on a corporate website. Production may wish to plan raw material levels more efficiently in order to avoid running out of stock.

The goal or goals of the business intelligence project should be clearly stated and written down in one or two easily understood sentences (minimal business or technical jargon). The goal or goals should be ever-present in the minds of those implementing the business intelligence project in order to guide the project toward success and avoid increasing the scope of the project unnecessarily or, even worse, failing to fulfill the intended goals.

Goals help determine what data will be required in order to fulfill the purpose of the business intelligence project. For example, in the case of the sales goal stated previously, this helps identify that all corporate sales transactions, as well as online and reseller sales transactions, are required as well as the yearly sales budget.

For the marketing scenario, this means that marketing campaign dates, click-through rates, and website data are required. Finally, for the production scenario, the goal statement clearly indicates that both production and inventory data will be necessary.

Requirements

Requirements help define the size and scope of a business intelligence project. As with goals, requirements can come in all shapes and sizes. However, there are particular requirements that should be collected by all business intelligence projects. These requirements include the following:

- *Who will be accessing the reports and dashboards?*

  This can be defined in terms of individuals or groups/roles such as sales managers, salespeople, marketing, and production managers. Defining who will be accessing the reports and dashboards helps determine the required security as well as how reports and dashboards are distributed or shared.

- *Approximately how many individuals will need to access the reports and dashboards?*

  If groups or roles are used to define who will be accessing a report, it is important to understand how many individuals will be accessing the reports, as this helps identify the licensing mechanism, licensing costs, and the overall scale required in terms of system resources. For example, if hundreds of individuals require the ability to view the reports and dashboards, this might mean that Fabric licensing is preferred over Power BI Pro licensing or that a Fabric F64 capacity needs to be upgraded to an F128 capacity.

- *How frequently will users be checking the reports and dashboards?*

  As with the previous bullet, the frequency with which users will access the report can help determine the scale required in terms of system resources.

- *Should some individuals or groups only see a subset of the data, reports, and dashboards?*

  This requirement dictates whether specific security features of Power BI, called **Row-Level Security** (**RLS**) or **Object-Level Security** (**OLS**), are required to secure certain data from some individuals or groups. RLS secures individual rows within tables in the data model while OLS is used to secure columns within tables or even entire tables in the data model. The scenario for this book includes the implementation of RLS.

- *Are there any regulatory concerns regarding the data, such as PCI, DSS (short for Payment Card Industry Data Security Standard), HIPAA (Health Insurance Portability and Accountability Act), or GDPR (General Data Protection Regulation)?*

  Understanding the sensitivity of the data being accessed is advisable in order to avoid any regulatory pitfalls. In general, dealing with sensitive or regulated data will add time and complexity to the business intelligence project.

- *What is the lowest level of data granularity required, such as individual transactions/orders/records/ lines or aggregated hourly, daily, weekly, monthly, or yearly?*

  It is important to understand the required data granularity, as the more granular the data, the larger the data model. Data granularity in this context refers to the detail required of the main data or facts being analyzed. For example, consider sales information that consists of a sales order, which may contain multiple individual sales lines for specific products. Is it important that the detailed sales lines are preserved and accessible in the data model or is simply the sales amount of the entire sales order required? If the specific products sold in the sales order are necessary, can this data be aggregated by day, week, or month?

- *How will the data be analyzed, such as by date, customer, department, account, country, region, territory, city, or ZIP code?*

  This requirement identifies the facets or dimensions across which the fact tables will be analyzed. This also helps to identify the granularity of data required. In the example from the previous bullet, where product sales can be aggregated daily, if the requirement is to analyze that data by ZIP code, then the granularity of the fact data is increased from simply *by product by day* to *by product by ZIP code by day*.

- *How much historical data is required – days, weeks, months, or years?*

  More historical data increases the overall size of the data model. There are limitations to the size of Power BI data models using **Import** mode and thus extremely large models may require the use of a Power BI technology called **DirectQuery**, or the latest Microsoft Fabric technology, **Direct Lake**. Import models ingest data from the source systems into the Power BI data model and must be periodically refreshed. DirectQuery models produce report visualizations by querying the source data system directly in real time when the visualizations are displayed. It is not important that you fully understand these technologies now. The scenario for this book focuses on building an Import mode data model; additional information about both Import and DirectQuery storage modes is included within this chapter under the heading *Designing a data model*.

- *How current must the data be, such as real-time, near-real-time, daily, weekly, or monthly?*

  This requirement helps determine the deployment model for the Power BI data model. Real-time or near-real-time data requirements mean that Power BI technologies such as DirectQuery or Microsoft Fabric Real-Time Intelligence are required, while non-real-time data means that Import data models can be considered.

- *What are the core **Key Performance Indicators (KPIs)** or business metrics required and what are their definitions?*

  Identifying the KPIs or metrics used by the business and the definition of those KPIs assists in determining the required data as well as the potential required calculations. Some KPIs may be straightforward, such as defining total sales as the number of units sold multiplied by the unit price. Other KPIs, such as **Mean Time Between Failure (MTBF)**, are more complex.

Many KPIs have near-universal definitions, such as gross margin percentage being defined as follows:

$$\frac{(price - cost)}{price}$$

However, some businesses have their own more obscure or unique KPIs or may have slight variations to common KPIs.

- *What calendar is used by the business?*

  Nearly all Power BI data models include some kind of calendar or date table or the requirement to analyze data based on dates. It is vitally important to understand the calendar used by the business. Many businesses use a calendar based on the standard Gregorian calendar year. However, many businesses also use a **fiscal calendar** that does not conform to a standard calendar year. Businesses may define their fiscal year to run from July to June, instead of from January to December. Businesses may also use fiscal calendars that define their own months and quarters/periods in order to ensure that each quarter or period contains the same number of days.

Procuring the required resources

Power BI projects require a number of different skill sets and areas of expertise. These skill sets can be broken down into the following roles that must be fulfilled in order to successfully execute a Power BI project:

- Domain expert
- Data modeler
- Report author
- Administrator

In smaller organizations, all of these roles may be fulfilled by the same individual, while in larger organizations or for more complex projects, each role is fulfilled by one or more different individuals. In addition, these roles can be filled either by technical IT resources or business resources. In the past, all of these roles (except potentially domain expert) would traditionally be filled by IT technical resources. However, Power BI lends itself to self-service business intelligence that allows business resources to fulfill these roles. It is not uncommon to have technical IT resources fulfill the data modeler and administrator roles while business users fulfill the report author role.

Domain experts

Domain experts come in two forms: **business users** with domain expertise over the subject area of the business intelligence project and **technical domain experts** with expertise over source systems.

Business domain experts have extensive business expertise regarding such subjects as sales, marketing, manufacturing, supply chain, research and development, human resources, accounting and finance, and so on. Business domain experts understand the KPIs and other metrics important to the business. Stakeholders most often serve as business domain experts.

Technical domain experts are experts in sophisticated source systems such as SAP, Dynamics 365, Oracle, and so on. These experts understand the structure of the source system as well as what tables and fields map to the desired data. This can become quite complex with **enterprise resource planning** (**ERP**) systems, **customer relationship management** (**CRM**) systems, and other advanced business systems. Understanding the technical details regarding how such systems are installed and configured ensures that the right data is collected from these systems.

Data modelers

As previously explained, Power BI projects require connecting to source data systems via queries that load data into structured data tables. These structured data tables and their relationships are called **models** and it is the job of the data modeler to build these models. Data modelers are responsible for creating the queries that connect to the source data systems. In addition, data modelers transform or shape the data as necessary and define the relationships between the tables within the model. Data modelers are also responsible for defining the data types within the model (setting columns within data tables to be text or numbers), setting default summarizations such as sum, average, first, and last, and specifying data categories such as country, ZIP code, latitude, longitude, and web URL. Finally, data modelers often create any necessary calculations such as **Year-To-Date** (**YTD**) sales or gross margin percentage.

Queries and models are key components of Power BI solutions. Well-designed queries and models are critical to the success of Power BI projects, as improperly designed queries and models will lead to a poor user experience, complex calculations, and unnecessary consumption of system resources.

Key skills for data modelers include a robust knowledge of Power Query (and the associated M coding language), the DAX programming language, and data modeling best practices. In addition, knowledge of source data technologies such as SQL, OData, JSON, and XML is often helpful.

Report authors

Report authors are responsible for data analysis and the creation of visuals that comprise reports and dashboards. Generally, report authors serve as business analysts, gathering reporting requirements and understanding the KPIs and metrics desired by the business as well as how the business wishes to analyze and visualize the data to answer important business questions.

Since the reports and dashboards created by report authors are the most visible product of a Power BI project to the business, it is important that report authors have solid skills in visualization and design best practices. Visualization choices, color choices, font choices, symmetry, and the layout of reports are key aspects of building a good user experience.

In addition to visualization and design skills, report authors should be familiar with the use of as many features and capabilities of Power BI reports as possible, including the use of visual interactions, drillthrough, drilldown, bookmarks, buttons, conditional formatting, and mobile layouts.

Administrators

Administrators have a special role within a Power BI tenant, the **Fabric administrator** role. Users assigned to this role can access the full capabilities of the **admin portal** within the Power BI service. The admin portal allows administrators to monitor the usage of the Power BI service, as well as to enforce organizational governance policies through the **tenant settings**. For example, administrators can use the tenant settings to enable or disable certain functionality, such as the use of public embedded codes for reports, the use of R and Python visuals, the exporting of reports, and the creation of workspaces. Administrators are also responsible for setting up enterprise data gateways that facilitate data refresh for models, as well as creating and assigning permissions for data connections used by these data gateways. Finally, administrators can restrict the use of custom visuals and configure capacity settings used by Microsoft Fabric capacities.

Administrators are generally not heavily involved in Power BI projects, but their assistance may be required depending on the particular needs of individual projects. For example, certain types of projects may require enabling or disabling certain Power BI service tenant settings or the creation of data source connections on enterprise data gateways.

Administrators should have in-depth knowledge of the Power BI service with respect to available tenant settings and security. In addition, administrators should be knowledgeable regarding the creation and configuration of enterprise data gateways. Finally, administrators should understand organizational policies and governance guidelines related to data access and security.

Defining the data sources

Once the base requirements are gathered and resources procured, the next step is to determine the required data sources that will comprise the model. Data modelers and report authors will need to collaborate with both IT and the business to discover the required source data repositories. These source data repositories may be transactional systems such as ERP systems, CRM systems, data warehouses, or even individual files maintained by the business, such as Excel spreadsheets.

An important aspect of this step is ensuring that the required data sources are configured in such a way as to support access and/or data refresh within Power BI. The Power BI reports generated will eventually be published to the cloud in the Power BI service or to an on-premises instance of Power BI Report Server. The service or server must be able to access these data sources. Thus, for example, an Excel file stored locally on someone's laptop or desktop is not an optimal configuration and should be moved to a shared network file storage location or similar technology. For transactional systems and data warehouses, it is likely that IT will need to provide login and access credentials for the source systems and want to understand the potential impact with regard to system processing load on source systems.

Designing a data model

With the base requirements gathered, resources procured, and data access granted, it may be tempting to dive right in and start creating models and reports. While Power BI lends itself to an iterative, agile style of development, it is always better to spend some time on upfront design work. A good design approach can help identify potential issues and gaps, confirm feasibility, and set realistic expectations regarding what can and cannot be accomplished.

A semantic or data model design includes the following steps:

- Identifying **facts** and **dimensions**
- Creating a **bus matrix**
- Determining a **model storage mode**

Identifying facts and dimensions

For Power BI, it is best to think in terms of facts and dimensions. Fact tables, or facts, are the tables that contain numeric information about particular business processes such as sales, marketing, production, and inventory. Each row in a fact table represents a particular *event* associated with that business process, such as a change in inventory or a sale to a customer. Columns in the fact table include such things as the amount of inventory change, the number of units sold, and the unit sale price.

Dimension tables, or dimensions, contain information about people, places, or things involved in the business process. As opposed to storing event information, dimensions store detailed information about people, places, and things. For example, a store dimension table would contain a row for every store in the organization and would include columns such as latitude, longitude, address, country, the date the store opened, and other detailed information that describes each store. Similarly, a product dimension table would include a row for every product sold and might include such columns as color, size, and category.

In a simple scenario of a corporate sales team wishing to compare sales to their planned budget, the fact tables involved would be a *sales table* and a *budget table*. Dimensions would include tables for *date*, *customer*, *product*, and *territory*.

Creating a bus matrix

A **bus matrix** is a data warehouse planning tool created by Ralph Kimball. It is useful for visualizing the relationships between facts and dimensions. In the simple scenario cited previously of a sales team wanting to compare sales to a planned budget, the bus matrix would look like the following:

			Dimensions			
Facts	**Grain**	**KPIs/Measures**	**Date**	**Product**	**Customer**	**Territory**
Sales	Sales Order Line	# of Units, Unit Sale Price, Total Sale Price	X	X	X	X
Budget	Monthly	Budget Amount	X			X

Figure 2.1 – Example bus matrix

As shown in *Figure 2.1*, the fact tables representing the business processes are on the left, and columns describing the grain and important KPIs/measures are included as additional information. The dimension tables describing the people, places, and things associated with the facts are on the right. The Xs indicate which dimensions are associated with the different facts.

The bus matrix provides an organized overview of the most important elements comprising the data model and is simple to understand and easily referenced. From the bus matrix, we can quickly understand the granularity of the fact tables, the KPIs and measures most important to those fact tables, and which dimensions are related to which fact tables. For example, it is clear from the bus matrix that the budget fact table has a monthly grain and is broken down by sales territory but not by product.

Determining a model mode

Deciding on the model mode is an important design decision that should be addressed early in the planning process. Power BI supports the following model storage modes:

- Import
- DirectQuery
- Live
- Composite
- Direct Lake (Microsoft Fabric)

Power BI's default model mode is Import. This means that all of the data from source data systems is ingested into a local model to the Power BI Desktop file. Import mode allows the full functionality of all Power Query and DAX functions and supports the extension of the model with DAX calculated columns as well as fast performance for DAX measures. Because of the columnar compression technology used with Import mode models, it is possible to import millions or, depending on the circumstances, even tens of millions of rows while still maintaining acceptable performance for complex calculations. In addition, Import mode models allow you to combine multiple different data sources into a single model. However, there are certain disadvantages to Import mode data models:

- One disadvantage is the limit to model sizes. Users using a Pro license can publish models to the service that are up to 1 GB in size, while **Premium Per User (PPU)** and Fabric licensing allows initial model sizes up to 10 GB in size to be published to the service.
- Another consideration for Import mode data models is that the data will need to be refreshed from the source systems. Pro users can schedule up to 8 refreshes per day in the service, while **Premium Per User (PPU)** and Fabric users can schedule up to 48 refreshes per day.

DirectQuery mode models do not ingest any data into the local model. This avoids the model size limitations and refresh requirements associated with Import mode models. However, this approach means that when reports are displayed, network traffic and source system processing load are generated as information is retrieved from the source data systems. In addition, there are additional restrictions and limitations with DirectQuery mode models, including the following:

- DirectQuery mode only allows a single source system to be accessed as part of the data model. While multiple tables within a single source system can be used in the model, you cannot use tables from different source systems (see the discussion on composite models).
- DAX calculated columns are not supported for DirectQuery mode models.
- Certain DAX functions are not supported or optimized for role-level security or DirectQuery performance.
- Many Power Query M functions cannot be used with DirectQuery to transform or shape data.

Live connection models generally have the same strengths and weaknesses as DirectQuery. In fact, while not exactly the same, one can consider Live connections as specialized DirectQuery connections for use with Power BI semantic models and Analysis Services with additional limitations. The main difference is that with a Live connection, the Power BI file no longer contains any kind of semantic model definition but rather simply a "pointer" to a semantic model. With the more recent development of being able to use DirectQuery for Power BI semantic models and Analysis Services, there are fewer reasons to use Live connections.

Composite models allow you to mix DirectQuery and Import sources, or even multiple DirectQuery sources. While more complex, when configured correctly, composite models can combine the ability to retrieve near-real-time data from DirectQuery sources with the high query performance of Import models. When using composite models, the storage mode for each table can be specified within the model. Thus, composite models still retain the same limitations as DirectQuery but now on a per-table basis.

Direct Lake is a data model mode only available with Microsoft Fabric and has very niche applications, mainly for larger data models that are difficult to manage as Import mode models. When creating a lakehouse in Microsoft Fabric, a corresponding semantic model in Direct Lake mode is automatically created. Limitations include the inability to create calculated columns, calculated tables, or MDX user hierarchies.

Planning reports and dashboards

As mentioned previously, Power BI lends itself to an agile, iterative development process where feedback from stakeholders is collected on a regular basis and used to inform and adjust the development process. This is especially true when authoring reports and dashboards. That said, it is still useful to include some upfront design work for reports. This often takes the form of one or more whiteboarding sessions with key stakeholders where different layouts for reports are discussed and mock-ups or wireframes of report pages are created. The goal of these design sessions is to understand the KPIs and metrics the business wants to be displayed on reports, understand whether there will be multiple report pages, and discuss potential interactivity between visual elements and features in the report, such as the use of slicers, drillthrough, and drilldown.

That covers all five elements of planning your Power BI project. Next, we will put this planning knowledge to use in defining an example use case that we'll be using throughout the rest of the book.

Example scenario: utilization reporting

The following chapters of this book primarily focus on a single, real-world scenario. This section introduces the scenario and implements the planning process introduced in this chapter for the example scenario.

The organization at the heart of this scenario is a regional professional services firm with offices located in Charlotte, Nashville, and Cleveland providing professional services related to technology, accounting, and management consulting. This firm recently conducted a yearly employee survey that highlighted a strong employee demand for increased flexibility regarding **Personal Time Off** (PTO). As a result, human resources have decided to implement unlimited PTO.

While time off still needs to be approved, employees no longer have a set amount of days of PTO per year. This is an enormous benefit to employees but, in order to stay profitable, it is now imperative that the organization is able to closely track and report on utilization so that managers can make informed business decisions around requests for time off.

In this scenario, you will take on the persona of Pam, a finance controller who works at the firm and has access to all of the division budgets as well as the daily time reports from employees. As such, it has fallen to Pam (you) to implement better utilization reporting and distribute that information throughout the firm.

Identifying stakeholders, goals, and requirements

Since the subject of the business intelligence project revolves around the utilization of consultants, the business domain falls into the delivery organization as opposed to sales or marketing. As part of the project planning process, Pam has identified the following stakeholders:

- Partners and executive management
- Branch managers (Charlotte, Nashville, and Cleveland)
- Division managers (technology, accounting, and management)

Pam has identified Mike, her boss and **Chief Financial Officer (CFO)**, as the project sponsor. In conversations with Mike and the other stakeholders, Pam formulated the following project goal statement:

Report and analyze % utilization by employee, branch, and division across any date range, including the ability to identify trends and forecasts. The ability to also compare revenue against budgets is desirable but not an absolute requirement at this time.

Finally, Pam collected the following requirements from Mike and the other stakeholders:

Question	Business Requirement
Who will be accessing the reports and dashboards?	Partners, executive management, branch managers, and division managers.
Approximately how many individuals will need to access the reports and dashboards?	10–12.
How frequently will users be checking the reports and dashboards?	Daily.
Should some individuals or groups only see a subset of the data, reports, and dashboards?	Yes, branch and division managers should only see the branches and divisions they are responsible for.
Are there any regulatory concerns regarding the data, such as PCI, HIPAA, or GDPR?	No.
What is the lowest level of data granularity required, such as individual transactions/ orders/records/lines or aggregated hourly, daily, weekly, monthly, or yearly?	Daily for hours and % utilization. Budget data is by month.

How will the data be analyzed, such as by date, customer, department, account, country, region, territory, city, ..., or ZIP code?	Date, division, branch, employee, and project.
How much historical data is required – days, weeks, months, or years?	1 year.
How current must the data be, such as real-time, near-real-time, daily, weekly, or monthly?	Weekly.
What are the core KPIs or business metrics required and what are their definitions?	% utilization. Utilization for sub-contractors and hourly employees is always 100%. For salaried employees, % utilization is defined as the sum of billable hours divided by the sum of potential billable hours. Each day is categorized as either a working day or a non-working day (holidays and weekends). A working day is assumed to have the potential for 8 billable hours.
What calendar is used by the business?	Standard calendar year.

Table 2.1 – Questions and answers regarding business intelligence

With this information gathered, Pam must next acquire the necessary resources to fulfill the company's needs.

Procuring the required resources

As this is a relatively small business intelligence project and the firm only has approximately 450 active employees across all employee types, it has fallen to Pam to be both the data modeler and report author for the percent utilization project. Pam will work with Paul in the IT division, who is the Power BI administrator for the firm.

Defining the data sources

Pam knows that all of the firm's employees and reported hours are contained within the firm's Dynamics 365 Business Central tenant. In addition, Pam maintains an Excel spreadsheet on a network file share that holds budget information for all branches and divisions by month.

Designing a model

Pam has identified the following facts for the data model:

- **Hours:** Contains reported hours for every employee by day
- **Budget:** Contains a forecasted budget by month for each division and branch

Pam has also identified the following dimensions for her model:

- Date
- Branch
- Division
- Employee
- Project

The following bus matrix was created to represent the design of the data model:

			Dimensions				
Facts	Grain	KPIs/Measures	Date	Branch	Division	Employee	Project
Hours	Daily	Billable hours, % Utilization	X	X	X	X	X
Budget	Monthly	Budget Amount	X	X	X		

Figure 2.2 – Bus matrix for the example scenario

After reviewing the requirements, Pam has decided to use an Import data model. This decision was based upon the requirement that the report data be kept up to date on a weekly basis. Employees report hours at the end of every week. With approximately 450 employees and a daily grain on the **Hours** fact table, Pam estimates that a year's worth of data will only be about 160,000 rows of data. In addition, Dynamics 365 Business Central does not support DirectQuery or Live connections, which then also rules out a composite model. Since Pam is developing the report locally, she will not be using Microsoft Fabric and thus Direct Lake is also not an option. Finally, Pam needs to combine two different sources of data – the **Hours** information coming from Dynamics 365 Business Central, and the **Budget** information stored in an Excel spreadsheet. All of these reasons make Import mode a good choice.

Planning reports and dashboards

Pam holds design sessions with each of the stakeholder groups. All groups agree that report pages should be kept concise and clean with no more than four or five visuals on a page. The stakeholder groups also agree that there should be simple filtering of the reports by date range, branch, division, and employee type. Mike suggests that the reports also include the ability for users to dynamically set the target utilization as different branches and divisions have slightly different utilization targets.

Partners and executive management desire an executive summary page that includes the % utilization for the entire calendar year as well as a visual that displays the % utilization trend by month. Finally, partners and executive management also desire that the % utilization be displayed across branches and divisions.

Division managers want similar information but displayed somewhat differently. Division managers are also interested in the % utilization for the year and % utilization broken down by branch. However, division managers also want visuals that display the total hours and % utilization by project code as well as employee type.

Finally, division managers desire the ability to quickly see the total hours broken down by categories such as billable time, PTO, project non-billable time, bench time, and sales support.

Branch managers want extremely similar information to division managers, with the main difference being that branch managers want to see hours and % utilization by employee rather than by project code.

Finally, all stakeholders feel that it is important to be able to drill down into additional detail pages that display hours and utilization per employee and per project code in order to analyze and determine the cause of utilization issues.

Pam envisions a report with multiple pages, all resembling the following:

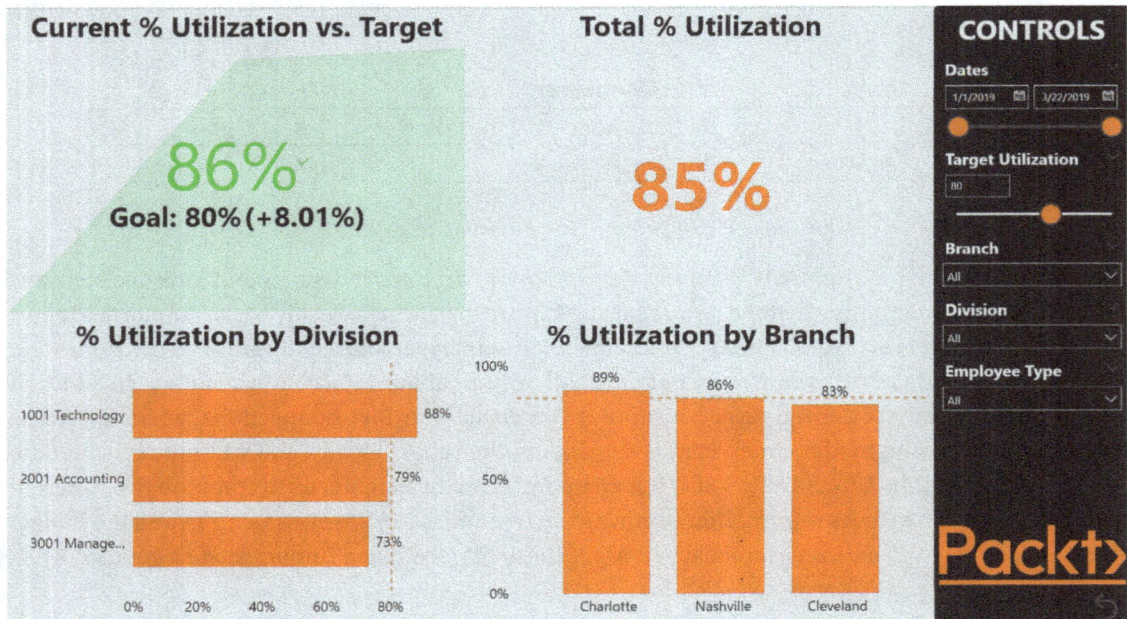

Figure 2.3 – Bus matrix for the example scenario

This book demonstrates exactly how to create this report along with additional information for sharing and collaborating within the Power BI service and how to operationalize the report via automatic refreshes and Microsoft Fabric.

Summary

In this chapter, we introduced the planning process for Power BI business intelligence projects. Upfront requirements such as gathering, planning, and design are critical steps in ensuring the success of any business intelligence project, and projects involving Power BI are no exception. We then introduced the specific scenario that will be used throughout the rest of this book. As finance controller, you (Pam) have been tasked with creating a data model and report that will assist a regional consulting firm in visualizing and analyzing the % utilization of employees across divisions, branches, and projects.

In the next chapter, we will install Power BI Desktop, explore its interface, and familiarize ourselves with some of its functionality.

Questions

As an activity, try to answer the following questions on your own:

- What are the five elements of planning a business intelligence project?
- What three things must a business intelligence project identify?
- A project stakeholder that helps procure funding and prioritize resources is called what?
- What are the four roles required for Power BI projects?
- What is the difference between facts and dimensions?
- What visual tool is used to design and organize a data model?
- What are the five semantic model modes that Power BI supports?

Further reading

To learn more about the topics that were covered in this chapter, please take a look at the following references:

- **Implementing different calendars in reporting**: https://www.sqlshack.com/implementing-different-calendars-in-reporting/
- **The matrix**: https://www.kimballgroup.com/1999/12/the-matrix/
- **The matrix: revisited**: https://www.kimballgroup.com/2005/12/the-matrix-revisited/
- **Semantic model modes in the Power BI service**: https://learn.microsoft.com/en-us/power-bi/connect-data/service-dataset-modes-understand
- **Manage workspaces**: https://learn.microsoft.com/en-us/fabric/admin/portal-workspaces

Unlock this book's exclusive benefits now

Scan this QR code or go to packtpub.com/unlock, then search for this book by name.

Note: Keep your purchase invoice ready before you start.

Part 2

The Desktop

In this part, you will install Power BI Desktop, get acquainted with the major components of the desktop's interface, import and transform data, create a working semantic model, create DAX calculations, explore many of the desktop's various features and functionality, and finally, create a professional report.

This part of the book includes the following chapters:

- *Chapter 3, Up and Running with Power BI Desktop*
- *Chapter 4, Connecting to and Transforming Data*
- *Chapter 5, Creating Semantic Models and Calculations*
- *Chapter 6, Unlocking Insights*
- *Chapter 7, Creating the Final Report*

3

Up and Running with Power BI Desktop

The first step to being able to do almost anything in Power BI is to get Power BI Desktop up and running and have some data loaded to use in creating visualizations. This chapter will get you up and running quickly with Power BI by showing you how to download and install Power BI Desktop, familiarizing you with the Power BI Desktop interface, and then showing you how to work with some simple data and visualizations.

By the end of this chapter, you will have Power BI Desktop installed, be familiar with the different areas and basic features of Power BI Desktop, know how to generate data using **Data Analysis Expressions** (**DAX**) and use that data to construct basic visuals such as tables, cards, and slicers, and understand how these visuals can interact with one another.

The following topics will be covered in this chapter:

- Downloading and running Power BI Desktop
- Touring the desktop
- Generating data
- Creating visualizations

Technical requirements

The following are some requirements to successfully complete the instructions in this chapter:

- You will need a connection to the internet.
- You will need Windows 8 or later or Windows Server 2012 R2 or later.
- .NET 4.6.2 or later.
- Internet Explorer 10 or later.
- At least 2 GB of memory (RAM).
- 1440x900 or larger display resolution.

Downloading and running Power BI Desktop

There are actually three different versions of the Power BI Desktop application. Each version has its own methods for downloading and installing. The three versions of Power BI Desktop are as follows:

- Power BI Desktop (the trusted Microsoft Store app)
- Power BI Desktop (EXE)
- Power BI Desktop (Report Server edition)

Downloading Power BI Desktop

Downloading and installing Power BI Desktop varies slightly based on the version being downloaded. Let's look at each of the three available options.

Power BI Desktop (the trusted Microsoft Store app)

Power BI Desktop (the trusted Microsoft Store app) is the preferred Power BI Desktop application to install and use. Microsoft recommends this version of Power BI Desktop as it is specifically built for use on 64-bit Windows 10/Windows 11 and keeps itself updated automatically. This version of the Power BI desktop has the additional requirement of Windows 10 version 17134.0 or higher.

This version of the desktop works like other Windows apps, as in, it is automatically updated when there is a new version, which is every month! There are three methods for installing the app version of the desktop.

To download Power BI using the first method, follow these steps:

1. In a web browser, enter `http://aka.ms/pbidesktop` into the browser bar and press the *Enter* key.
2. The Microsoft Store app will open automatically to the Power BI Desktop app. You may be prompted to **Open** the Microsoft Store app.
3. Click **Get** and this will start the download and installation process. Note that this used to say **Install** instead of **Get**, so the interface may change over time.
4. Once the download and installation process are complete, the **Install** button will turn into an **Open** button.
5. Click the **Open** button.

To download Power BI using the second method, follow these steps:

1. Press the *Windows* key on your keyboard, type `Microsoft Store`, and then press the *Enter* key.
2. The Microsoft Store app will launch.
3. Click the **Search** icon in the upper-middle of the page, type *Power BI Desktop*, and then select the app from the drop-down menu.
4. The Power BI Desktop app page will load.
5. Click **Get** and this will start the download and installation process.
6. Once downloading and installation are complete, the **Install** button will become an **Open** button.
7. Click the **Open** button.

To download Power BI using the third method, follow these steps:

1. In a web browser, enter `https://powerbi.microsoft.com/desktop/` into the browser bar and press the *Enter* key.
2. Click **Download now**.
3. The Microsoft Store app will open automatically to the Power BI Desktop app. You may be prompted to **Open** the Microsoft Store app.
4. Click **Get**, which will begin the download and installation process.
5. Once downloading and installation are complete, the **Install** button will turn into an **Open** button.
6. Click the **Open** button.

Power BI should now be up and running!

Power BI Desktop (EXE)

For a variety of reasons, it may not be possible to install the trusted Microsoft Store app version of Power BI Desktop.

Use the following procedure to install the EXE version of Power BI Desktop:

1. In a web browser, enter `https://powerbi.microsoft.com/desktop/` in the browser bar and press the *Enter* key.
2. Click **Advanced download options**.
3. A new browser tab will open.
4. Select your language and then click **Download**.
5. Choose **PBIDesktopSetup.exe** or **PBIDesktopSetup_x64.exe** and then click **Download**. Note that the **_x64** version is for 64-bit operating systems and that the other file is for 32-bit operating systems. You will most likely want to install the same type of application as your Microsoft Office installation. If you are not sure, choose the **_x64** version. You can always uninstall and reinstall the other version if you make the wrong choice.
6. Once the download is complete, run the `EXE installer` file.
7. Once the installation launches, follow the prompts.

Power BI should now be up and running!

Power BI Desktop (Report Server edition)

The **Report Server (RS)** edition of Power BI Desktop is optimized to work with **Power BI Report Server (PBIRS)**. If you plan on using PBIRS, this is the version of Power BI Desktop that you want since this version provides an option for publishing to PBIRS. Note that the RS version is only updated four times a year, versus every month.

Follow these steps in order to download and install the Report Server edition:

1. In a web browser, enter `https://powerbi.microsoft.com/report-server/` in the browser bar and press the *Enter* key.
2. Click **Advanced download options**.
3. A new browser tab will open.
4. Select your language and click **Download**.
5. Choose **PBIDesktopSetupRS.exe** or **PBIDesktopSetupRS_x64.exe** and then click **Next**.
6. Once the download is complete, run `EXE installer`.
7. Once the installation launches, follow the prompts.

Power BI Desktop (Report Server edition) should now be up and running!

Running Power BI Desktop

When running Power BI Desktop for the first time, you will be greeted with a series of splash screens. For now, simply click **No thanks** or the **X** in the upper-right corner to close these splash screens. These splash screens provide some useful information but are not necessary in terms of the operation or configuration of the desktop.

With Power BI up and running, let's take a brief tour of the desktop.

Touring the desktop

If you are familiar with Microsoft Office programs, many of the user interface elements of Power BI Desktop will look familiar. The following screenshot depicts the nine major interface elements of Power BI Desktop:

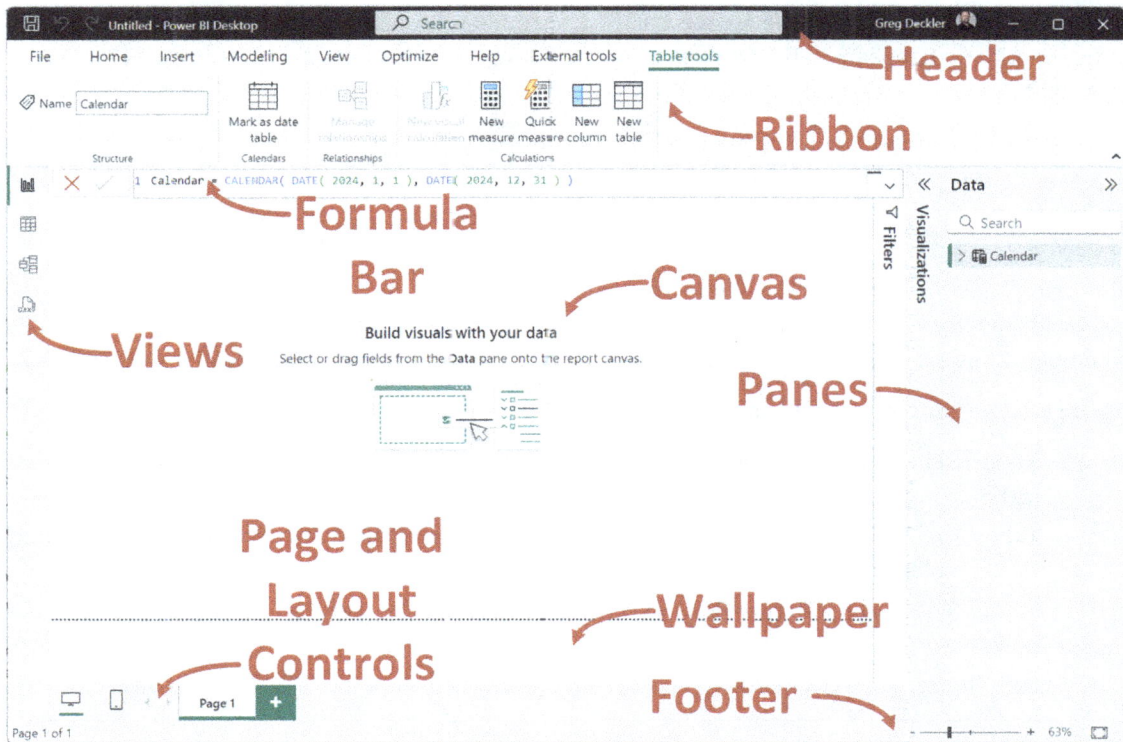

Figure 3.1 – Power BI Desktop interface elements

Let's delve deeper into each of these areas.

Header

In the preceding screenshot (*Figure 3.1*), the **Header** is the small strip at the top of Power BI Desktop. This area is standard for Windows applications, including the **Minimize, Restore down/Maximize,** and **Close** icons in the upper-right corner.

In the far-left corner are icons for **Save, Undo the last action,** and **Redo the last action you undid.** To the right of these icons is the name of the currently opened file, or **Untitled** if the file has not been saved; next to that is the name of the application. For Power BI Desktop, this will be **Power BI Desktop.** For Power BI Desktop Report Server, this will include the release month and year of the version of the Power BI Desktop.

In the middle of the header is a **search** bar. The search bar can be used to easily find and use any functionality that appears in the **Ribbon**. Simply clicking in the search bar will bring up a list of suggested actions.

Finally, the header includes a **Sign in** link. This link allows you to sign in to your Microsoft 365 account. If you are already signed in, this link is replaced with your name and profile image.

Views

Referring back to *Figure 3.1*, the **Views** area currently provides four different options. These views primarily modify what is displayed within the **Canvas** area, but also contextually determine what tabs and operations are available in the ribbon, as well as modifying which **Panes** are displayed.

There are four different views available:

- **Report:** The **Report view** allows for the authoring of reports through the creation of visualizations on one or more pages.
- **Table:** The **Table view** provides an interface for exploring the data contained within the individual tables of a semantic model.
- **Model:** The **Model view** provides an overall look at all of the tables in the semantic model and how those tables relate to one another.
- **DAX Query:** The **DAX query view** provides the ability to view and run **DAX** queries.

Panes

Referring back to *Figure 3.1*, **Panes** are contextual within the Power BI application. Only one pane, the **Data** pane, is omnipresent. This pane displays a list of tables, columns, and measures present within the semantic model.

Other panes include the following:

- **Filters:** The **Filters** pane is available within the **Report** view and displays a list of filters currently active on reports, pages, and visualizations.
- **Visualizations:** The **Visualizations** pane is also available when in the **Report** view and provides access to the various visualization types available within the report. Tabs exist for configuring and formatting visualizations and adding analytics to visualizations, as well as for configuring filters and drill-through capabilities for reports, pages, and visualizations.
- **Bookmarks**, **Selection**, **Performance Analyzer**, and **Sync Slicers:** These panes are only available while in **Report** view and provide additional capabilities that we will explore later.
- **Properties:** The **Properties** pane is only present in the **Model** view. This pane provides the ability to associate metadata (data about data) for various fields or columns within the tables of the semantic model. This includes the ability to specify synonyms and descriptions as well as data types, data categories, and default aggregations or summarizations.
- **Quick measure:** Certain Preview features enable the display of a **Quick measure** pane when creating a quick measure.

Canvas

Referencing *Figure 3.1*, the **Canvas** is the main work area within the desktop. This area is contextual depending upon the view. When in the **Report** view, this area is the place where visualizations are created in order to build reports. When in the **Table** view, this area displays the underlying data for a selected table within the semantic model. When in the **Model** view, this area displays all of the tables within the semantic model and their relationships to one another. Finally, when in the **DAX query** view, this is the area where you author DAX queries and display results.

Wallpaper

As shown in *Figure 3.1*, the **Wallpaper** area is only available in the **Report** view. There is little functionality other than the ability to set a background color or image for a report.

Page and Layout Controls

Referring back to *Figure 3.1*, the **Page and Layout Controls** area is contextual based upon the current view. While in the **Report** view, the **Page and Layout Controls** area provides the ability to create new pages, rename pages, and reorder pages within a report. In addition, the left two icons switch between **Desktop** and **Mobile** report layouts. There is no **Page and Layout Controls** area in the **Table** view. In the **Model** view, this area provides the ability to create new layouts, rename layouts, and reorder layouts for the semantic model. In the **DAX Query** view, this area provides the ability to create new queries, rename queries, and reorder queries.

Footer

Referencing *Figure 3.1*, the **Footer** area is contextual based upon the current view. In the **Report** view, the footer provides basic information regarding how many pages are in the report and which page is currently selected by the user. In addition, zoom controls are included on the right-hand side. Finally, if connected live to an Analysis Services cube or using DirectQuery, the footer displays connection information.

In the **Table** view, the footer provides basic statistics of a selected table and/or column, including the number of rows in the table and the number of distinct values in a column. In the **Model** view, the footer provides various viewing controls, such as the ability to zoom in and out, reset the view, and fit the model to the current display area. Finally, in the **DAX Query** view, the footer provides information on the number of queries as well as basic zoom controls.

Ribbon

As shown in *Figure 3.1*, below the header is the **Ribbon**. Users who are familiar with modern versions of Microsoft Office will recognize the function of this area, although the controls displayed will be somewhat different.

The ribbon consists of three permanent tabs and a number of contextual tabs. The permanent tabs are as follows:

- **File:** The **File** tab actually displays a fly-out menu when clicked that allows overall file operations, such as opening and saving Power BI Desktop files. Power BI Desktop files have the .pbix file extension. Other operations include importing data, exporting, and publishing.
- **Home:** The **Home** tab provides a variety of the most common operations, such as copying and pasting, getting data, inserting visuals, creating calculations, and other common actions.
- **Help:** The **Help** tab includes useful links for getting help with Power BI, including links to the Power BI Community site, documentation, guided learning, and training videos.

Contextual tabs appear in the ribbon depending upon the view selected, what items are selected in the interface, and whether or not additional tools are installed. These tabs include the following:

- **Insert:** The **Insert** tab only appears in the **Report** view and has options for adding pages, visuals, and visual elements such as textboxes, images, and buttons.
- **Modeling:** The **Modeling** tab only appears in the **Report** view and provides operations common to the semantic modeling process, including creating calculations, new tables, and new parameters, as well as operations related to security, questions, and answers.
- **View:** The **View** tab only appears in the **Report** view and has actions related to themes, page views, and mobile page layout, as well as options related to laying out visual elements on a page, such as gridlines and snap to grid. Finally, the **View** tab includes options for showing or hiding panes, such as the **Filters** pane, **Bookmarks** pane, and **Performance Analyzer** pane.
- **Optimize:** The **Optimize** tab provides access to optimization settings such as query reduction, the ability to pause visuals, etc.
- **Format:** The **Format** tab is all about formatting how visuals interact with one another or are displayed in relation to one another. This tab appears while in the **Report** view when a visual is selected on the canvas.
- **Data/Drill:** The **Data/Drill** tab provides operations focused on Power BI's ability to drill into data and see the raw data that makes up a visualization. This tab only appears in the **Report** view when a visual is selected on the canvas.
- **Table tools:** The **Table tools** tab provides options for adjusting the properties of tables as well as creating new tables, measures, and columns. This tab is displayed in the **Report** and **Table** views when a table is selected in the **Data** pane.
- **Column tools:** The **Column tools** tab provides options for adjusting the properties of columns in the semantic model. This tab is displayed in the **Report** and **Table** views when a column is selected in the **Data** pane.
- **Measure tools:** The **Measure tools** tab provides options for adjusting the properties of DAX measures. This tab is displayed in the **Report** and **Table** views when a measure is selected in the **Data** pane.
- **External tools:** This tab is displayed in the **Report, Data,** and **Model** views when external tools, such as **DAX Studio** or **Tabular Editor**, are installed.

The Formula Bar

Referring back to *Figure 3.1*, the **Formula Bar** is a contextual element. This means that the **Formula Bar** only appears when creating or editing calculated columns, measures, and calculated tables.

The formula bar allows the user to **DAX** code in order to create columns, measures, and tables in the semantic model. DAX is a formula language comprised of functions, operators, and values and is used in Analysis Services (Tabular), Power BI Desktop, and Power Pivot in Excel.

This completes our tour of Power BI Desktop. Let's now delve a bit deeper into DAX, in order to generate some data that we can use to create visuals.

Introducing DAX

The syntax of DAX is not dissimilar to Excel's function language. In fact, there are a large number of functions that are named and work nearly identically to Excel's formula language. However, do not be fooled by these similarities. DAX is an extremely powerful programming language that works very differently from Excel's formula language.

While Excel's formula language is optimized for dealing with cells in a spreadsheet, DAX is optimized to deal with tables of data consisting of columns and rows. Hence, unlike Excel, it is not possible to reference an individual cell within a table. Instead, you use DAX to identify a table and a column and then filter down to a single row or rows.

As mentioned previously, DAX allows for the creation of the following:

- **Calculated columns** are columns that are added to an existing table within the semantic model. These columns are defined by the DAX formula entered for the column. This formula is used to create a calculated value for each row in the table.
- **Measures** are DAX formulas that are not tied to any particular table except as referenced within the DAX formula itself. These calculations are dynamic and can change values based upon the context within which the formula is calculated.
- **Calculated tables** are entire tables within the semantic model whose columns, rows, and values are defined by a DAX formula.

There are several hundred DAX functions that can be used in formulas, and these functions can be infinitely nested to create extremely complex calculations. However, all DAX formulas have the same format: `Name = Formula`

The portion to the left of the equals sign becomes the name of the object created. The portion to the right of the equals sign is the actual formula calculation consisting of DAX functions and operators.

DAX function names are always followed by beginning and ending parentheses, such as **FILTER( )**. As you type, Power BI provides contextual help, such as available function names, as well as input parameters for DAX functions. Use the *Tab* key to accept a suggestion and have Power BI autocomplete the remainder of the suggestion.

You will learn more about DAX in later chapters, but for now, let's use some simple DAX to generate some data that we can then use to create visualizations.

Generating data

Power BI Desktop is all about connecting to data, modeling that data, and then visualizing that data. Therefore, it makes sense that you cannot really do much within Power BI without data. So, in order to get started, we are going to create some data to familiarize you with basic operations within the desktop.

Creating a calculated table

First, we will create a calculated table as follows:

1. If not already there, switch to **Report** view.
2. Click on the **Modeling** tab.
3. Choose **New table** from the **Calculations** section of the ribbon. The formula bar will appear with the words Table =, and the cursor will become active within the formula bar.
4. Type the following formula into the formula bar, replacing the existing text in its entirety:

```
Calendar = CALENDAR( DATE( 2017 ,1 ,1 ), DATE( 2019 ,12 ,31 ) )
```

> 💡 **Quick tip:** Enhance your coding experience with the **AI Code Explainer** and **Quick Copy** features. Open this book in the next-gen Packt Reader. Click the **Copy** button
>
> **(1)** to quickly copy code into your coding environment, or click the **Explain** button
>
> **(2)** to get the AI assistant to explain a block of code to you.
>
> ```
>                                                            Copy        Explain
> function calculate(a, b) {
>   return {sum: a + b};                                      1            2
> };
> ```
>
> 🔒 **The next-gen Packt Reader** is included for free with the purchase of this book. Scan the QR code OR visit packtpub.com/unlock, then use the search bar to find this book by name. Double-check the edition shown to make sure you get the right one.
>
>

5. Press the **Enter** key on the keyboard to create a table called **Calendar** in your semantic model.

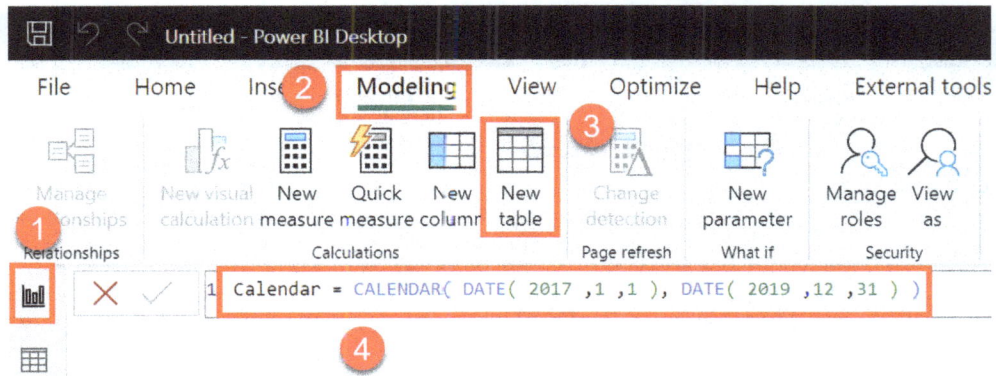

Figure 3.2 – New table creation using the DAX Formula bar

Congratulations! You have just written your first DAX formula!

> **Note**
>
> The preceding and subsequent formulas in this book are created and tested for the English language version of Windows and Power BI Desktop. Different language settings for Windows or Power BI may impact these formulas slightly. To make the formulas as compatible as possible, spaces have been added before commas preceded by numbers to account for cultures that use commas for decimal points. This may look a bit odd, but this is the most compatible approach with various cultures.

This formula creates a table named **Calendar** that has a single column called **Date**. This table and column will appear in the **Data pane**. The CALENDAR function is a DAX function that takes as input a start date and an end date. We used another DAX function, DATE, to specify the start and end dates of our calendar. The DATE function takes a numeric year, month, and day value and returns a date/time data type representative of the numeric inputs provided.

Switch to the **Table** view to observe the table created:

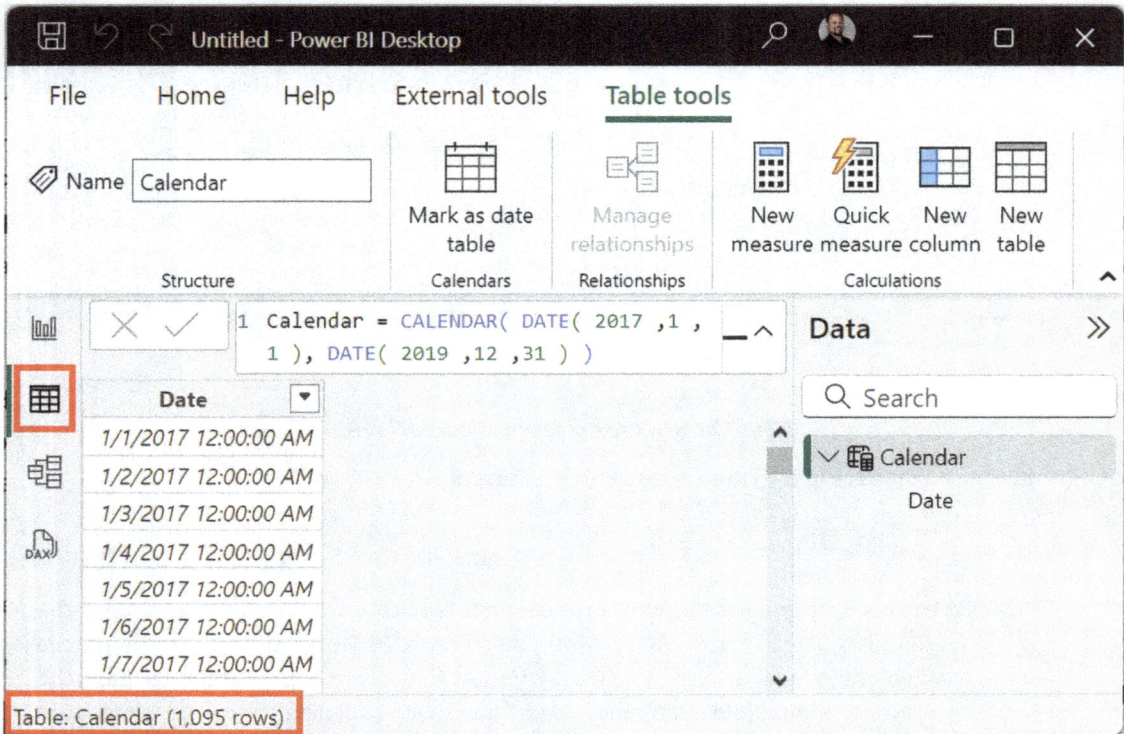

Figure 3.3 – Initial Calendar table with a Date column

Note, in the footer at the bottom, that this table consists of **1,095** rows of data. In fact, this table contains a row for every date inclusive of, and between, *January 1, 2017*, and *December 31, 2019*. If you do not see this information in the footer, make sure to select the **Calendar** table in the **Data pane**.

Creating calculated columns

While we are in the **Table view**, let's add some additional data to our simple, single-table semantic model:

1. Make sure that the **Calendar** table is selected in the **Data pane,** and then click the **Table tools** tab in the ribbon.

2. Click on **New Column** in the ribbon, and a new column named **Column** will appear in your table.

3. Type this new formula into the formula bar, completely replacing all existing text, and press the *Enter* key to create the column:

```
Month = FORMAT( [Date],"MMMM" )
```

Here, we use the **FORMAT** function to create a friendly month name, such as **January** instead of **1**. Within this formula, we refer to our **Date** column created previously using the column name prefixed and suffixed with square brackets ([ ]).

When referring to columns or measures within DAX formulas, these column and measure names must always be surrounded by square brackets. You should now have a new column called **Month** in your table with values such as **January**, **February**, and **March** for every row in the table.

4. Repeat the preceding procedure to create six new columns using the following DAX formulas:

    - `Year = YEAR( [Date] )`
    - `MonthNum = MONTH( [Date] )`
    - `WeekNum = WEEKNUM( [Date] )`
    - `Weekday = FORMAT( [Date],"dddd" )`
    - `WeekdayNum = WEEKDAY( [Date],2 )`
    - `IsWorkDay = IF( [WeekdayNum] < 6 ,1, 0 )`

5. You should now have a total of eight columns in your **Calendar** table:

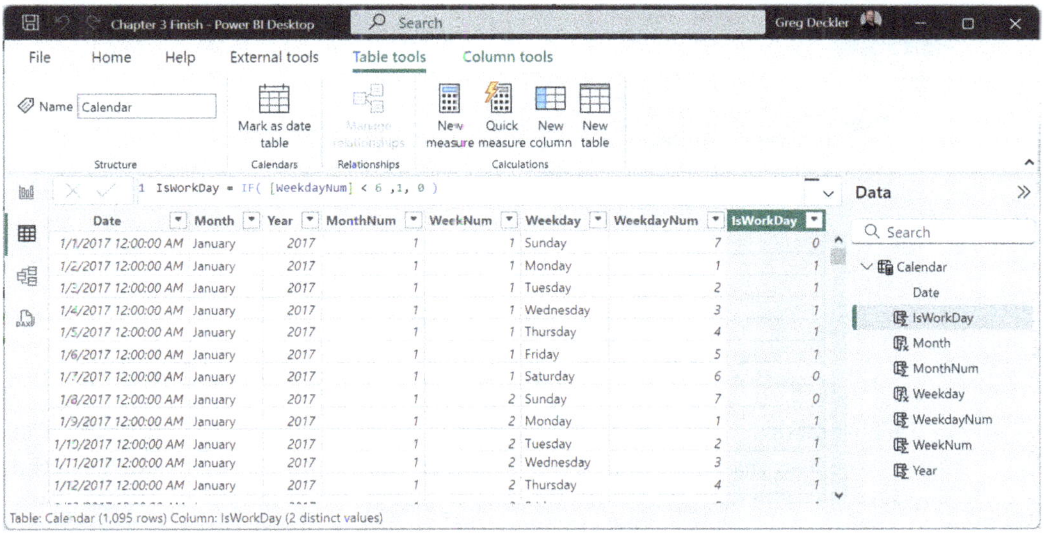

Figure 3.4 – Calendar table with eight columns

The columns include our original **Date** column, our text **Month** column, and the six columns shown in the preceding screenshot. The first five columns—**Year, MonthNum, WeekNum, Weekday**, and **WeekdayNum**—all refer to the original **Date** column and use simple DAX functions that return the year, numeric month, week number of the year, weekday name, and lastly, weekday as a numeric value between 1 for Monday and 7 for Sunday. The last column, **IsWorkDay**, uses the IF DAX function.

The IF function works identically to Excel's IF function. The first input parameter is a true/false expression, the second parameter is the result returned if that expression evaluates to true, and the last parameter is the result if that expression evaluates to false. In this case, we are returning 1 for Monday–Friday, and 0 for Saturday and Sunday.

Formatting columns

Now that we have a single-table semantic model and some columns, let's take a closer look at what we can do with this data:

1. Start by clicking on the **Date** column and then choose the **Column tools** tab of the ribbon.

2. Change **Data type** by clicking on the drop-down arrow and select **Date**. **Format** automatically changes to *Wednesday, March 14, 2001 (Long Date)*, and all of the values for the **Date** column in the rows of your table are automatically updated to match this format. Note that this could be slightly different depending on your language settings:

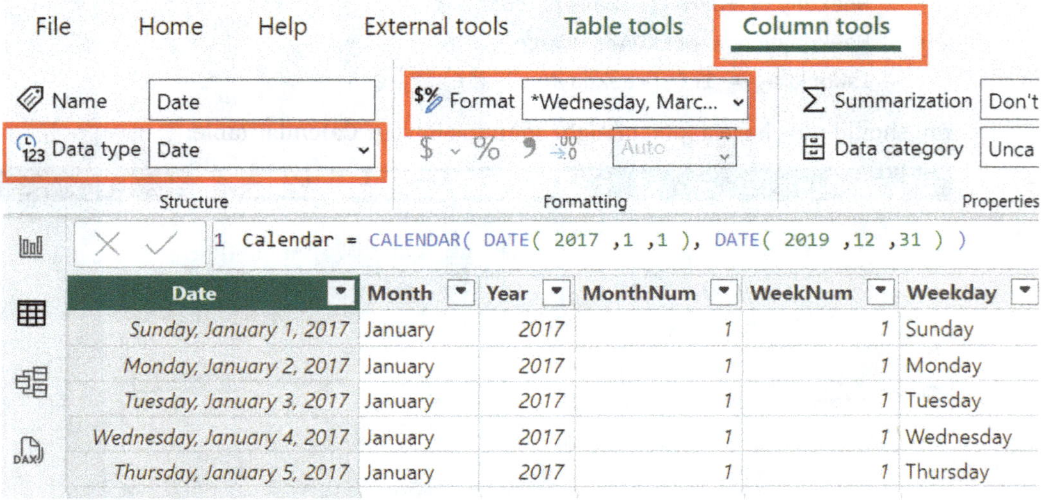

File	Home	Help	External tools	Table tools	Column tools

| | Name | Date | | $% Format | *Wednesday, Marc... ⌄ | | Σ Summarization | Don't |
| ₁₂₃ Data type | Date | ⌄ | $ ⌄ % 9 .00→.0 | Auto ⌄ | | Data category | Unca |

| Structure | Formatting | Properties |

```
1 Calendar = CALENDAR( DATE( 2017 ,1 ,1 ), DATE( 2019 ,12 ,31 ) )
```

Date	Month	Year	MonthNum	WeekNum	Weekday
Sunday, January 1, 2017	January	*2017*	*1*	*1*	Sunday
Monday, January 2, 2017	January	*2017*	*1*	*1*	Monday
Tuesday, January 3, 2017	January	*2017*	*1*	*1*	Tuesday
Wednesday, January 4, 2017	January	*2017*	*1*	*1*	Wednesday
Thursday, January 5, 2017	January	*2017*	*1*	*1*	Thursday

Figure 3.5 – Data Type and Format options in the ribbon of the Column tools tab

3. In the **Format** dropdown, under **Date format,** select the first listed format, *3/14/2001 (Short Date)*. Note how many different date formats are available! The **Date** column in the rows in your table is again updated to match this new format.

4. Click on the **Month** column and note that **Data type** and **Format** both read **Text**. Also, note that the lettering in the table for the **Month** column is non-italicized and left-justified. This is a visual cue that indicates that this column is text.

5. Click on the **Year** column and note that **Data type** and **Format** both read as **Whole Number**. Observe that the lettering in the table is italicized and right-justified. Again, this is a visual cue that indicates that this column is a number. Click the dropdown for **Data type** and choose **Text**. While a year is certainly a number, it does not make any sense to sum, average, or otherwise aggregate a year, so we will specify the column as **Text**.

6. Click on the **MonthNum** column. In the **Properties** section of the **Column tools** tab, note that **Summarization** is set to **Sum**. Again, it is unlikely that summing a column of month numbers is going to aid us in our analysis, so set the **Summarization** field to **Don't summarize** instead. Repeat this process for the **WeekNum** and **WeekdayNum** columns.

Congratulations! You have just built your very first semantic model! Sure, it is an extremely simple semantic model at the moment, but there are big things in store for this **Calendar** table in the next chapter, when we will add more data tables and relationships.

Before we move on, save your work by choosing **File** and then **Save** in the ribbon. Save your work with the filename LearnPowerBI. The file extension is .pbix. After saving, notice that the **Header** changes from **Untitled** to **LearnPowerBI**.

Now that we have some data, we can start creating some visualizations of our semantic model.

Creating visualizations

Human beings are visual creatures. In the same way that *a picture is worth a thousand words*, so too can visualizations of data convey information and insights in a manner that is just not possible otherwise Since Power BI Desktop is designed to be a data visualization and analysis tool, let's explore the basics of creating, formatting, editing, and adding analytics to visuals.

Creating your first visualization

Follow these steps to create your first visualization:

1. Begin by clicking on the **Report** view in the **Views** area.

2. In the **Data** pane, if your **Calendar** table is not already expanded so that you can see the column names in the table, simply click the > icon to the left of the table name to expand the table and show the columns.

3.   Start by clicking on the **IsWorkDay** column and drag and drop this column onto the canvas. Power BI will create a visual based on the **IsWorkDay** column. This visual may be a table visual, card visual, or some other visual. Switch the visual to a clustered column chart visual by clicking the fourth icon from the left in the top row of the **Visualizations** pane. In addition, ensure that the **IsWorkDay** column is in the Y-axis field and switch the aggregation for the **IsWorkDay** column to **Sum** using the down arrow icon. See *Figure 3.6*:

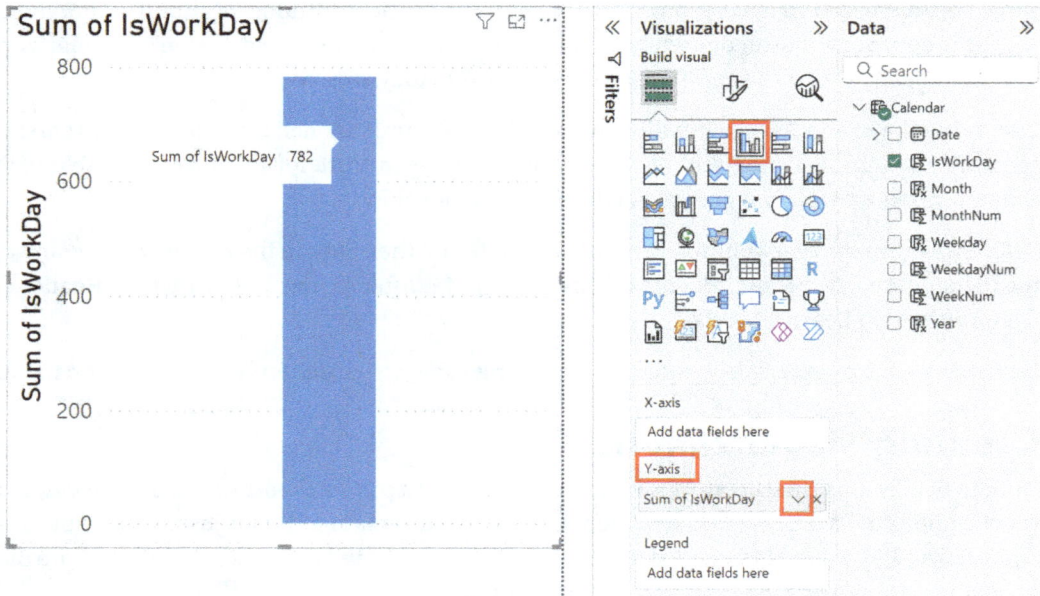

Figure 3.6 – Your first visualization – a simple column chart

Obviously, this is not the world's greatest visualization, but it is a start!

If you hover your mouse over the column, you will see the text **Sum of IsWorkDay 782** displayed. This pop-up is called a **Tooltip,** and this indicates that there are **782** combined working days (Monday-Friday) in the years 2017, 2018, and 2019. Sure, this is a little high because we are not accounting for holidays, but we will get to that later. Note that in the **Visualizations** pane, **Sum of IsWorkDay** has been added to the **Y-axis** field, and the text **Sum of IsWorkDay** appears in the upper-left corner of our visual as a title for the visual and also appears as a label on the *y* axis.

4.   Drag the **Month** column from the **Data pane** into this same visualization. Now, our visualization has 12 columns of varying heights, and, in the **Visualizations** pane, the **Month** column has been added to the **X-axis** field. Also, the visual title now displays **Sum of IsWorkDay by Month**, and **Month** appears as an *x*-axis label. However, if you are being observant, you will notice that the months are in a seemingly strange order. In fact, the months are currently being sorted by the value of **IsWorkDay**. Let's change that.

5. Click the ellipsis (**...**) in the upper-right or lower-right corners of the visual and then choose **Sort axis** followed by **Month**. Click on the ellipsis again, and this time choose **Sort axis** and then **Sort ascending**. Hmm, it's still not quite right. Our visual is sorted by **Month** now, but our month names are still in the wrong order from what we would expect. This is because the **Month** column is **Text**, and therefore the names of the months are being sorted alphabetically instead of what you would expect—in the order they occur within a year. Not to worry.

6. In the **Data pane**, click on the **Month** column. The **Column tools** tab of the ribbon becomes active. In the ribbon, in the **Sort** section, click **Sort by column** and then **MonthNum**:

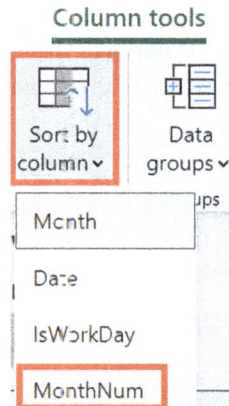

Figure 3.7 – Sort by column

There we go. All fixed! Now, our visual's *x* axis lists the month names in the correct order! Your visual should now look similar to the following. The specific values in your *y* axis may vary:

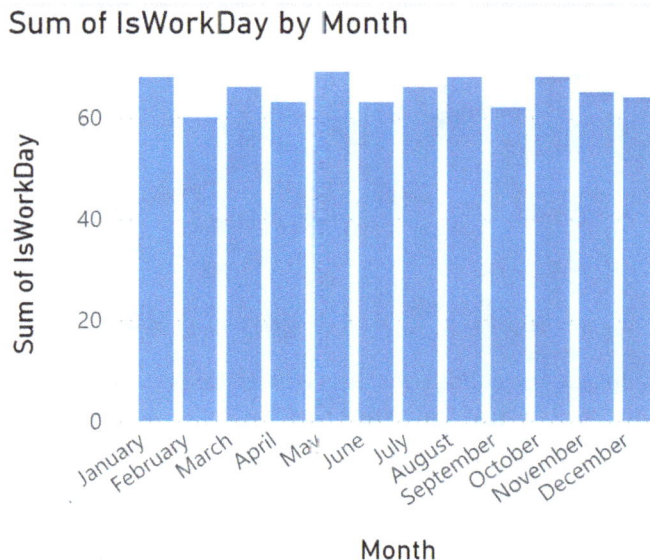

Figure 3.8 – Correctly sorted column chart by MonthNum

Note that with this visual selected on the canvas, in the **Visualizations** pane, the fourth icon to the right in the top row is highlighted. This indicates what type of visual is currently displayed. Visualizations can be changed instantly by simply selecting a different visualization icon.

Formatting your visualization

Now that we have a visualization, let's do some simple formatting, starting with moving and resizing our visual:

1. Click the mouse cursor anywhere inside the visual and drag the visual down to the lower-left corner of the canvas.

2. Observe the sizing handles on the edges of the visual. Hover the mouse over the upper-right sizing handle and notice that the mouse cursor changes from the standard pointer to two arrows.

3. Click this sizing handle and drag it up and to the right. The goal is to resize the visual to consume exactly one-quarter of the screen. Drag your handle until you observe two dotted red lines, one horizontal and one vertical, and then unclick. The dotted red lines are called **Smart Guides**, and, in this case, they indicate when the canvas has been bisected. You should now have a resized visual that takes up exactly one-quarter of the canvas.

Next, let's tackle that small text size in our visualization. Power BI Desktop defaults to a rather small font size. Let's make this visual easier to read:

1. Ensure that your first visualization is selected in the canvas. You know that the visualization is selected if the visual is outlined and the sizing handles are displayed. Look at the **Visualizations** pane. Just under the palette of visualization icons, there are three icons: one that looks like cells in an Excel spreadsheet, a paint brush and a chart, and a magnifying glass. These are known as the **Build**, **Format**, and **Analytics** tabs, as shown here:

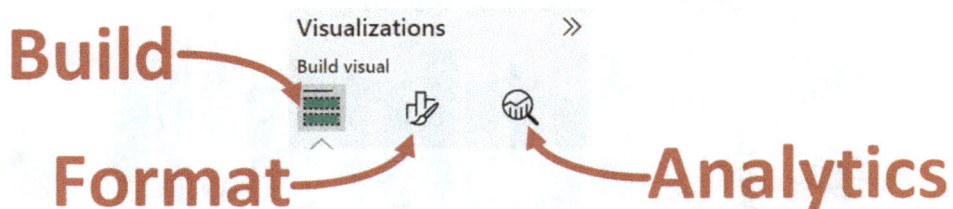

Figure 3.9 – Visualizations pane – Tabs for Build, Format, and Analytics

2. As shown in *Figure 3.9*, the subtitle for the **Visualizations** pane is **Build visual** and the **Build** icon is filled with the color teal, indicating that this is the currently selected sub pane within the **Visualizations** pane.

3. Select the **Format visual** icon and note that the middle icon is filled with the color teal, and the subtitle changes to **Format visual**. Within this tab are a number of expandable sections. Within the **Visualizations** pane, there are tabs called **Visual** and **General**. Common visual settings such as position, size, title, effects, header icons, tooltips, and alternative text have sections under the **General** tab, while settings specific to the visual itself are listed under the **Visual** tab.

4. While on the **Visual** tab, expand the **X-axis** card, expand the **Values** sub-card, and change the **Font size** to 11. Scroll down and expand the **Y-axis** card, the **Values** sub-card, and again set the **Font size** to 11.

5. Switch to the **General** tab, expand the **Title** card, and set the **Font size** to 16. Near the bottom of the card, select the middle **Alignment** icon to center the title within the visualization. Note the changes happening to our visual as you perform these operations. The text size for our x and y axis values increases, as well as the size of the text of our title.

6. At the top of the **Title** card, modify **Text** to read **Number of Working Days by Month**.

7. Switch back to the **Visual** tab and expand the **Data labels** card. Notice that everything is grayed out and cannot be modified.

8. Activate this section by using the toggle icon to the right of the **Data labels** text. Numeric values appear above the columns in our visualization. Expand the **Value** sub-card and increase the **Font size** to 11. Expand the **Options** sub-card and change **Position** to **Inside end**. Finally, toggle on **Background** using the toggle for the **Background** card.

9. Expand the **Background** card and change the **Color** field to the default top orange color and set **Transparency** to 25%.

Your visual should now look like the following:

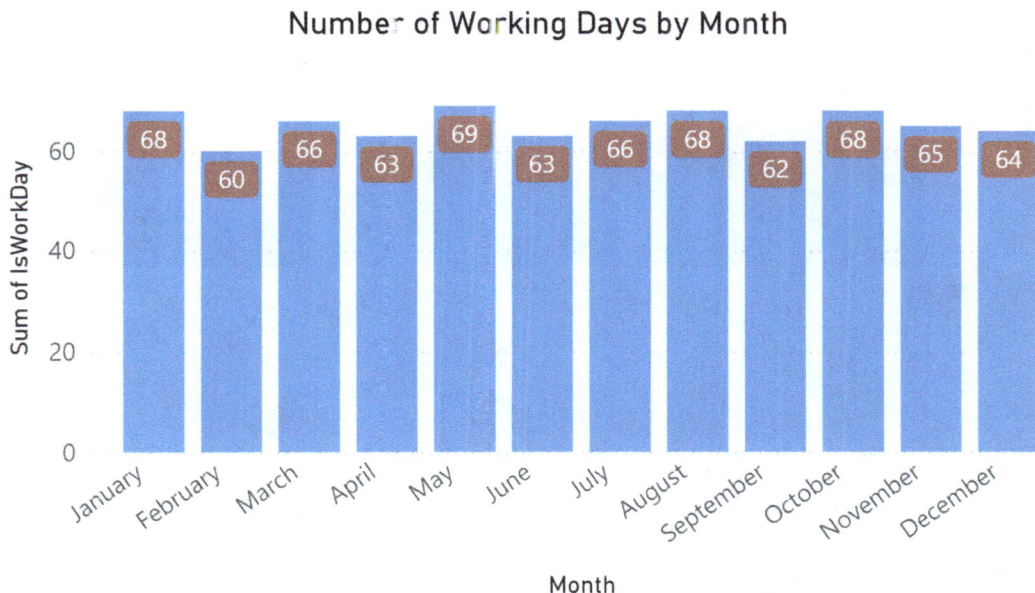

Number of Working Days by Month

Figure 3.10 – Improved column chart visualization

Now that our visual is formatted, let's add some simple analytics.

Adding analytics to your visualization

We can add analytics to our visualization using the **Analytics** tab in the **Visualizations** pane:

1. Ensure that your first visualization is selected in the canvas.
2. Click on the **Analytics** tab. Here again, we see several expandable sections.
3. Expand the **Average Line** section and then click + **Add line**. Note the dotted line that appears on your visual.
4. Change the text **Average Line 1** to **Average Working Days**.
5. Expand the **Line** card, change **Color** to black, and change **Position** to **Behind**.
6. Toggle on **Data label** and expand the card. Change **Color** to black, change **Style** to **Both**, and finally, change **Horizontal Position** to **Right**.

Your visual should now look like the following screenshot:

Number of Working Days by Month

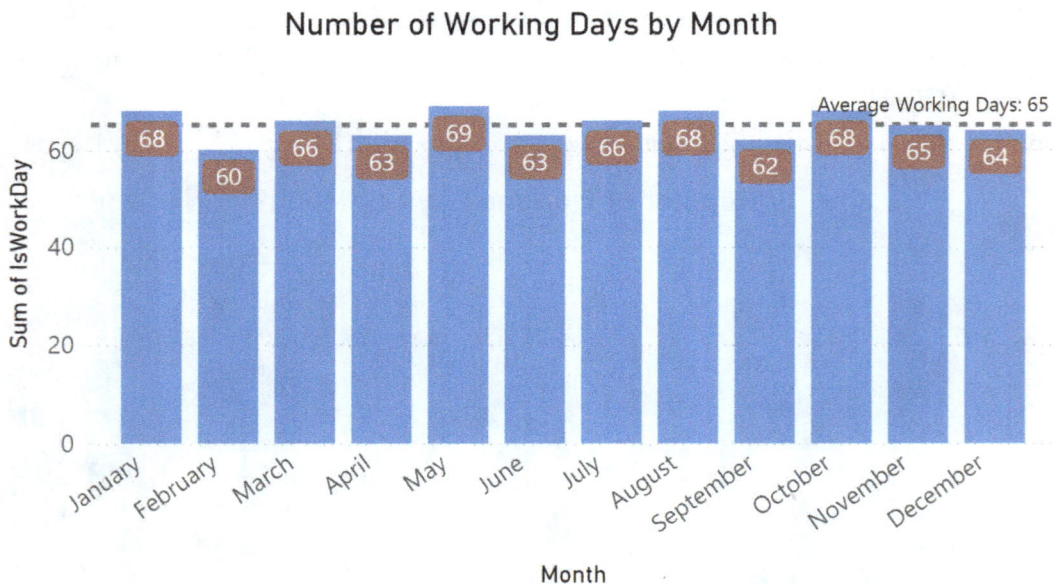

Figure 3.11 – Analytics added to Number of Working Days by Month visual

Your first visualization is now finished. Let's move on to adding some additional visuals to the page.

Creating and using a slicer

Your first visualization is starting to look a little better! And now you also know that there is an average of 65 working days per month for all of the years 2017, 2018, and 2019 combined. But, let's be honest, it's a little weird having the number of working days summed for each month spanning three different years. What you really would like to see is the number of working days per month for each year.

One method to accomplish this is to use the **Small multiples** feature. To see how small multiples work, do the following:

1. Ensure that your first visual is selected and change to the **Build** tab in the **Visualizations** pane.

2. Drag the **Year** column from the **Data** pane into the **Small multiples** field in the **Visualizations** pane. Your visualization is now divided into four quadrants with each year displayed individually, as shown in the following screenshot:

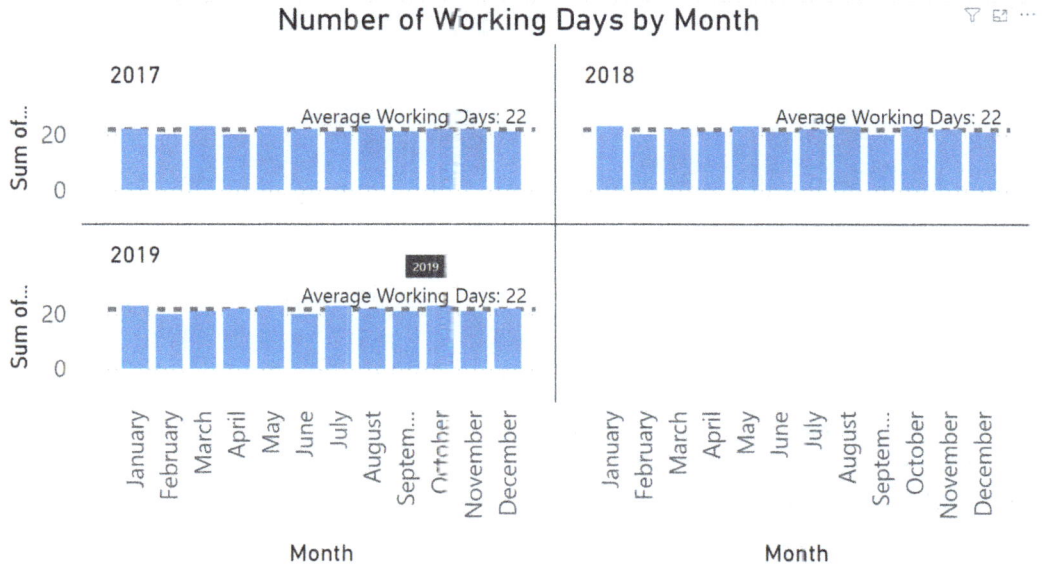

Figure 3.12 – Small multiples

However, instead of using **Small multiples**, we are going to use a **slicer**. Slicers are a type of visual in Power BI that are useful for providing user-selected values that filter the data in the semantic model that is presented within a report. Now, let's see how they work:

1. First, with your first visual selected, click on the **X** to the right of the **Year** column in the **Small multiples** field to remove the **Year** column from the visual. Your visual now displays a single column chart, as before.

2. Click on any empty portion of the canvas—on any place except your visual. This deselects the visual.

3. Find the visualization icon in the **Build** tab of the **Visualizations** pane, which has a small funnel, as highlighted here:

Figure 3.13 – Slicer visualization

4. Hover your mouse over this icon and you will see **Slicer** displayed in a pop-up. Select this visual with your mouse and observe that a new, blank slicer visual is created that consumes the upper-left quadrant of the canvas. Power BI attempts to intelligently position and size new visuals based on existing visuals on the canvas.

5. Drag and drop the **Year** column from your **Data pane** into this new visual. You should now have a list of years for **2017**, **2018**, and **2019** displayed in a vertical column with small boxes beside them. The word **Year** appears as the title of your visual.

6. Click on each year in the slicer in turn. Notice that your columns change heights. In addition, the *y* axis and data labels change, as well as your average analytics line. What is going on? When you click on a year in a slicer, the slicer filters the column chart visual so that it is filtered to only rows in the semantic model for the selected year. Hence, your column chart goes from displaying all three years to just a single year. If you want to see two years, start by selecting a year. Then, hold down the *Ctrl* key and select another year. Now, both years are selected in the slicer, and your column chart also displays data for both of those years.

7. As with all visuals, slicers can also be formatted. Let's try formatting it. First, ensure that your new slicer is selected on the canvas, and then click on the **Format** tab of the **Visualizations** pane.

8. On the **Visual** tab, expand **Slicer settings** and then expand the **Selection** sub-card.

9. Toggle **Show "Select all" option** and notice that a new item is added to your slicer at the top that reads **Show "Select all" option**. Selecting this option in the slicer selects all of the slicer options.

10. Toggle on **Single select**. Notice that the other options go away, and your slicer selection controls change from boxes to radio buttons (circles). This slicer mode enforces single selection only within the slicer, such that holding down the *Ctrl* key no longer works for selecting multiple items within the slicer.

Let's now do a final few edits to the format of our slicer:

1. Under the **Slicer header** card, expand the **Text** sub-card, and change the **Font size** to **16**.
2. Under thew **Values** card, expand the **Values** sub-card, and change **Text size** to **16**.
3. In the **Slicer settings** card, expand the **Options** sub-card, and change **Style** to **Tile**.
4. Move and resize your slicer by using the middle-bottom sizing handle to shrink the visual until all three boxes appear in a single row. Your slicer should look like this:

Figure 3.14 – Horizontal slicer

We now have two visuals on the page, but let's create some more!

Creating more visualizations

Create some additional visualizations by following these instructions:

1. Click a blank area on the canvas to ensure that no visuals are selected.
2. Drag the **Date** column from the **Data** pane onto a blank area of the canvas.
3. Notice in the **Visualizations** pane that the **Date** column is displayed in the **Columns** field with a hierarchy of **Year**, **Quarter**, **Month**, and **Day**. Four corresponding columns appear in the visual.

> Default settings in Power BI create an automatic hierarchy in the semantic model for every column of the **Date** type. We cover hierarchies in more detail later in this book.

4. For now, switch the hierarchy to just the **Date** column by selecting the chevron to the left of the X and to the right of the **Date** column in the **Columns** field. Note that a checkbox appears to the left of **Date Hierarchy**. In this dropdown, choose **Date** instead, as shown in the following screenshot:

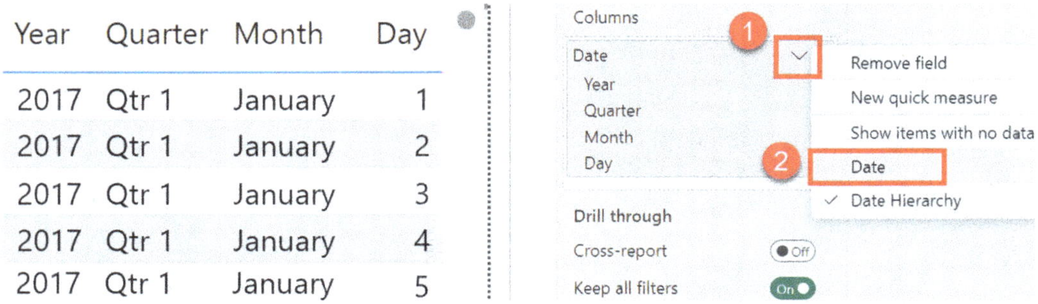

Figure 3.15 – Changing from Date Hierarchy to Date column

5. With the visual selected, switch the visual type to **Slicer** by simply clicking the **Slicer** icon in the **Visualizations** pane.

6. In the **Format** tab of the **Visualizations** pane, expand the **Slicer settings** card, expand the **Options** sub-card, and set **Style** to **Between** if it is not already set to Between.

7. Move this slicer to the upper-right corner of the page.

8. Resize this slicer by first using the middle-left sizing handle to expand this slicer so that it consumes half of the page horizontally. Use the bottom-middle sizing handle to shrink the visual vertically until a red dotted line appears. This indicates that it is the same height as our first slicer.

Let's create two additional visuals:

1. For the first visual, drag the **Weekday** column in the **Data** pane onto a blank area of the canvas. Note that a single-column table of the distinct values for the days of the week appears.

2. Drag the **Date** column from the **Data pane** into this new visual. Four columns are automatically created for **Year, Quarter, Month,** and **Day**. As before, change this from **Date Hierarchy** to just **Date**.

3. Change this visual to **Clustered bar chart**. That is the third visual over from the left in the top row.

4. In the **Build visual** tab within the **Visualizations** pane, drag and drop **Date** from the **Legend** field to the **X-axis** field. Note that the text changes to **Count of Date**.

5. Drag and resize this visual to consume the lower-right quadrant of the canvas.

6. Notice that the weekdays are not in order. Use the ellipsis (**...**) in the visual to change **Sort axis** to **Weekday** and **Sort ascending**.

7. Click on the **Weekday** column in the **Data pane** and then, from the **Column tools** tab, choose the **Sort by** column and then **WeekdayNum**. This new visual now displays **Monday** at the top and **Sunday** at the bottom.

8. Finally, format this visual to display **Data labels**.

9. Click on a blank area of the canvas and select the **Card** visual. By default, this is the visual in the fourth row from the top and farthest to the right, as shown in *Figure 3.16*.

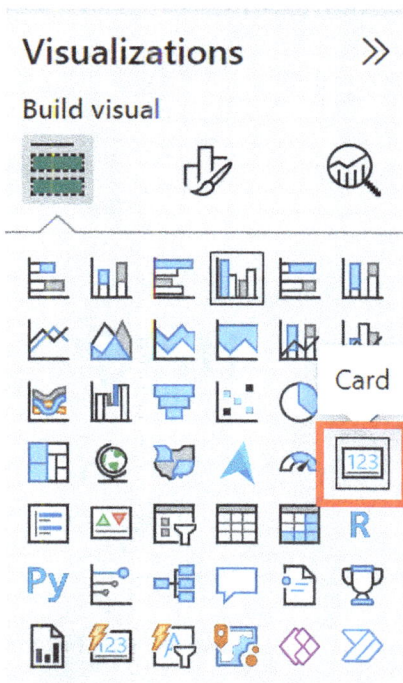

Figure 3.16 – Card visual in Visualizations pane

10. Drag **Date** from the **Data** pane into this visual.

11. In the **Build visual** tab of the **Visualizations** pane, use the drop-down arrow next to **Earliest Date** and change this to **Count**.

12. Lastly, reposition the **Card** visual to be in the center of the blank area of the canvas and resize the visual to be just big enough to fully display the **Count of Date** text.

Feel free to explore the **Format** and **Analytics** options for these new visuals. You will note that some visuals, such as slicers and card visuals, do not have any analytics available. When you are done, save your work by selecting **File** and then **Save** from the ribbon. Your canvas should look something like the following screenshot:

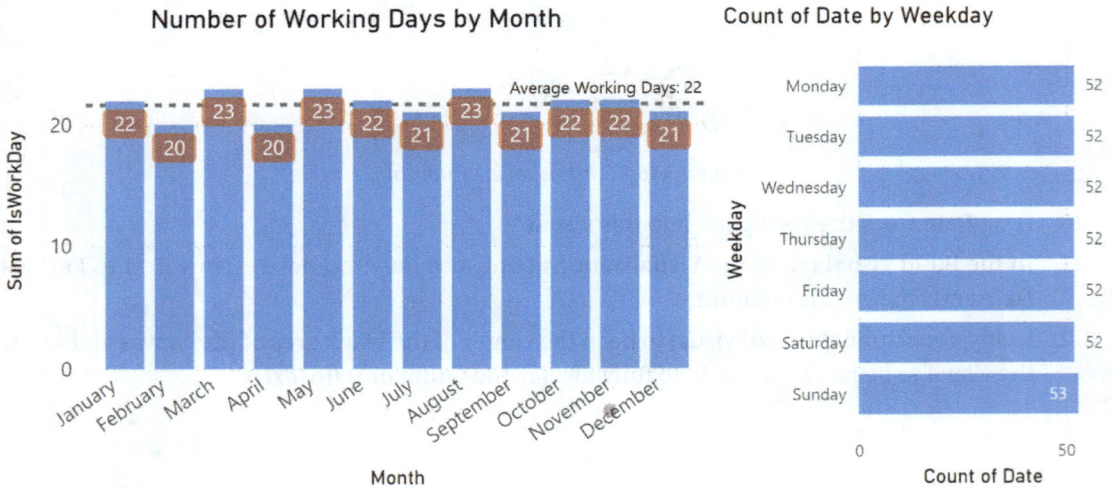

Figure 3.17 – Page of visuals

Now that we have multiple visuals on a page, let's explore how these visuals interact with one another.

Editing visual interactions

As you have already seen, visuals on a page interact and modify the display of other visuals on a page. We can explore how these visuals interact with one another as well as how we can control visual interactions by doing the following:

1. Start by making sure that **2019** is selected in the slicer in the upper-left corner of the page.

2. Click on **July** in the column chart in the lower left-hand corner of the page. The **July** column becomes highlighted in the visual. Also, notice that the card visual changes to display **31** and that the bar chart bars shrink to highlight just the number of weekdays in the month of July 2019. This behavior is called **Highlight**.

3. Click on **July** again in the column chart to return the charts to their original state.

4. Click on **Monday** in the bar chart. Again, **Monday** becomes highlighted, our card visual changes to **52**, and our column chart changes to show the number of Mondays in each month of the year.

5. By default, this highlighting mechanism is not additive. For example, with **Monday** chosen in the bar graph, hover your mouse over the highlighted portion of **July** in the column chart. Observe that additional information is displayed in the tooltip. In addition to **Month** and the **Sum of IsWorkDay**, **Highlighted** appears and reads **5**. However, try clicking on the highlighted portion of the column chart. You might expect that our filters would now be **Monday** and these five days in **July**. Instead, the charts simply switch to only have **July** selected. However, we can make these filters additive.

6. With **Monday** selected in the bar chart, hover your mouse over **July** again, but this time, hold down the *Ctrl* key and then click the July column. Note that the **Card** visual changes to read **5**. By using the *Ctrl* key, we can make values selected within visuals additive with one another.

But what if you do not want your visuals to highlight or filter one another? Well, you can control that as well. If you have been paying attention, you may have noticed that the date slicer in the upper-right corner has not been changing when selecting elements of the other visuals. If you have been paying really close attention, you might also have noticed that, when you select a visual, the ribbon changes to display two additional tabs, **Format** and **Data / Drill**. Let's explore the **Format** tab with respect to editing the interactions between visuals:

1. Select the slicer in the upper-left corner.

2. Click on the **Format** tab in the ribbon and then click on **Edit interactions**, which is the button on the far left-hand side. Notice that the **Edit interactions** button becomes shaded and small icons appear at the top or bottom of all of our other visuals:

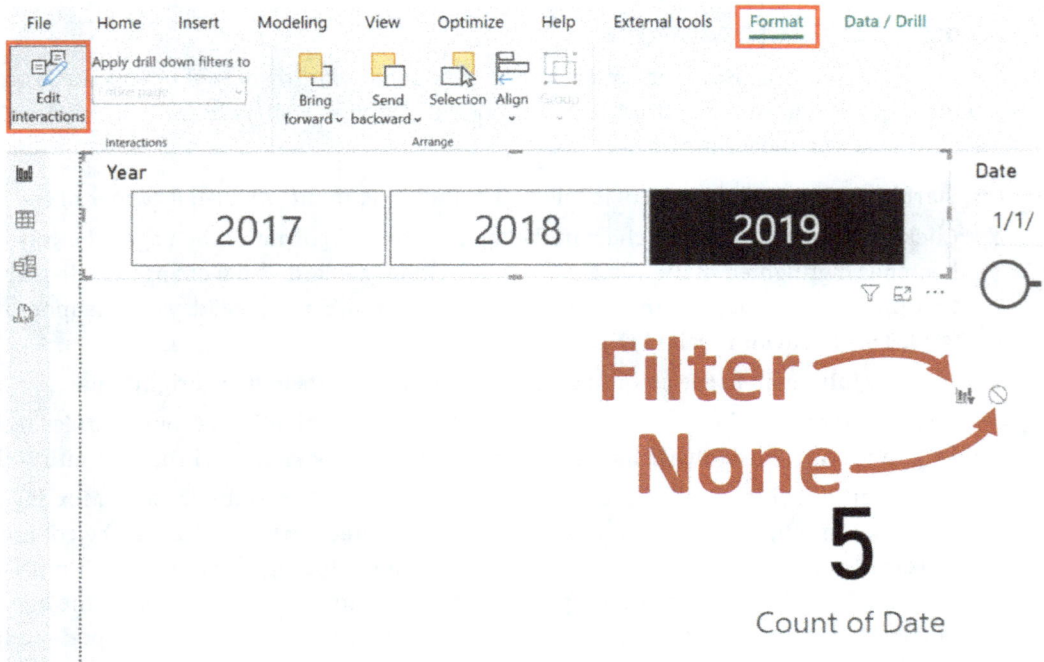

Figure 3.18 – Edit interactions

One icon looks like a column chart with a small funnel, and the other is a circle with a line through it. If you hover over these icons, you will see that the chart icon is called **Filter** and the circle icon is called **None**. The icon that is shaded in gray is the currently active interaction mode.

3. Hover your mouse over the date slicer visual and then click on the **Filter** icon. The **Filter** icon becomes active and the **None** icon becomes inactive.

4. With the slicer visual in the upper-left corner still selected, hover over the **Card** visual and select the **None** icon.

5. Select the column chart visual in the lower-left corner and hover your mouse pointer over the bar chart. Notice that a third icon appears that is simply shaded in the column chart. This is the **Highlight** icon, which explains the behavior of this chart when we click on months within our column chart:

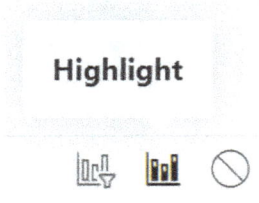

Figure 3.19 – Highlight interaction icon

6. With the column chart still selected, hover over the **Card** visualization and choose the **None** filter icon.

7. Repeat this same procedure for the bar chart visual in the lower-right corner so that the bar chart does not filter the **Card** visual. In addition, change the column chart to **Filter** instead of **Highlight**.

8. Click on the **Card** visual and notice that all of the **Filter, Highlight,** and **None** icons disappear. This is because card visuals cannot filter other visuals.

9. Click on the **Format** tab of the ribbon and deselect **Edit interactions** by clicking on the button.

Let's see what happens now as we click elements within our visualization:

1. First, unselect any selections for the bar and column charts.

2. Click on **2017** in the horizontal slicer visual in the upper-right corner and notice that the date slicer changes to a range that only includes dates in **2017**.

3. Click back onto **2019** and the date slicer changes to only include dates in **2019**. Notice that this entire time, the **Card** visual has continued to display **1095**. This is because the slicer is no longer filtering the **Card** visual.

4. Move the date range in the date slicer. Notice that our horizontal slicer changes to only include **2019**. Also, notice that the **Card** visual changes numbers. This is because the date slicer is filtering the **Card** visual.

5. Click on a weekday in the bar chart visual. Notice that the column chart visual no longer does highlighting but is filtered instead. Click on a month in the column chart visual to observe the different behavior between **Filter** and **Highlight**.

6. Use the eraser icon to clear the selections of the **Date** slicer to reset the **Year** slicer.

Figure 3.20 – Clear selections icon (eraser)

🔍 **Quick tip:** Need to see a high-resolution version of this image? Open this book in the next-gen Packt Reader or view it in the PDF/ePub copy.

🔒 **The next-gen Packt Reader** is included for free with the purchase of this book. Scan the QR code OR go to packtpub.com/unlock, then use the search bar to find this book by name. Double-check the edition shown to make sure you get the right one.

Once again, save your work using **File** and then **Save** from the ribbon.

Summary

In this chapter, we downloaded and installed Power BI Desktop. We then took a quick tour of the desktop application's major user interface components, generated some working data to create a simple semantic model, and created some basic visualizations of that semantic model. We also learned how to format and add analytics to these visuals, as well as how to control the way in which visuals interact with one another on a page.

In the next chapter, we explore Power BI Desktop's data ingest capabilities and add more data to our semantic model.

Questions

As an activity, try to answer the following questions on your own:

*   What are the three different versions of Power BI Desktop?
*   What are the nine major areas of the Power BI Desktop user interface?
*   What are the four different views available in Power BI Desktop?
*   What is DAX?
*   What is DAX used for?

- What are the nine different panes that can be displayed in Power BI Desktop?
- What are the three tabs available in the **Visualizations** pane?
- What three types of interactions can there be between visuals?

Further reading

To learn more about the topics that were covered in this chapter, please take a look at the following references:

- **Get Power BI Desktop:** `https://docs.microsoft.com/en-us/power-bi/fundamentals/desktop-get-the-desktop`
- **Getting started with Power BI Desktop**: `https://docs.microsoft.com/en-us/power-bi/desktop-getting-started`
- **Learn DAX basics in Power BI Desktop**: `https://docs.microsoft.com/en-us/power-bi/desktop-quickstart-learn-dax-basics`
- **Add visualizations to a Power BI report (part 1)**: `https://learn.microsoft.com/en-us/power-bi/visuals/power-bi-report-add-visualizations-i`
- **Add visualizations to a Power BI report (part 2)**: `https://docs.microsoft.com/en-us/power-bi/visuals/power-bi-report-add-visualizations-ii`

Join our community on Discord

Join our community's Discord space for discussions with the authors and other readers: `https://discord.gg/hvqvgyGH`

4

Connecting to and Transforming Data

So far, we have learned about the basics of the Power BI interface. However, to truly unlock the power of Power BI, we need to expand our semantic model. To do that, in this chapter, we will learn about the **Power Query Editor** and how to relate multiple tables of data to one another to create a more complex semantic model. Every good visual report starts with a good semantic model, so we must learn how to properly ingest, transform, and load our data into Power BI.

The following topics are covered in this chapter:

- Getting data
- Transforming data
- Merging, copying, and appending queries
- Verifying and loading data

Technical requirements

You will need the following to follow the instructions in this chapter:

- An internet connection.
- Microsoft Power BI Desktop.
- Download Chapter 4 Start.pbix and the Budget and Forecast.xlsx, People and Tasks.xlsx, and Hours.xlsx files from GitHub at https://github.com/PacktPublishing/Learn-Microsoft-Power-BI_3E.

Getting data

Power BI is all about working with and visualizing data. Thus, we must incorporate some additional data into our model. In *Chapter 2, Planning Projects with Power BI*, we covered the data and data sources that Pam required. To emulate this data, we will use Excel files, so ensure that you have the Excel files from this chapter's *Technical requirements* section downloaded. If you are continuing from the last chapter, ensure that your LearnPowerBI.pbix file is open in **Power BI Desktop**. Otherwise, download and open Chapter 4 Start.pbix and save the file as LearnPowerBI.pbix.

In this section, you will create your first query and then add some additional data to your semantic model.

Creating your first query

To determine whether or not **Personal Time Off** (PTO) should be approved, it is important to understand where the company is concerning budgets and forecasts. Whether or not the company, department, and/or location is on target in terms of its budget can be an important consideration when approving or denying time off.

Unlike the calendar table from *Chapter 3, Up and Running with Power BI Desktop*, where we used DAX to create a calculated table, this time, we will import data into our semantic model using a **query**. A query is simply a series of recorded steps for connecting to and transforming data.

To create a query, follow these steps:

1. In **Power BI Desktop**, choose **Get Data** from the **Home** tab of the ribbon. Note the default list of potential data sources and select **More...** at the bottom of the list:

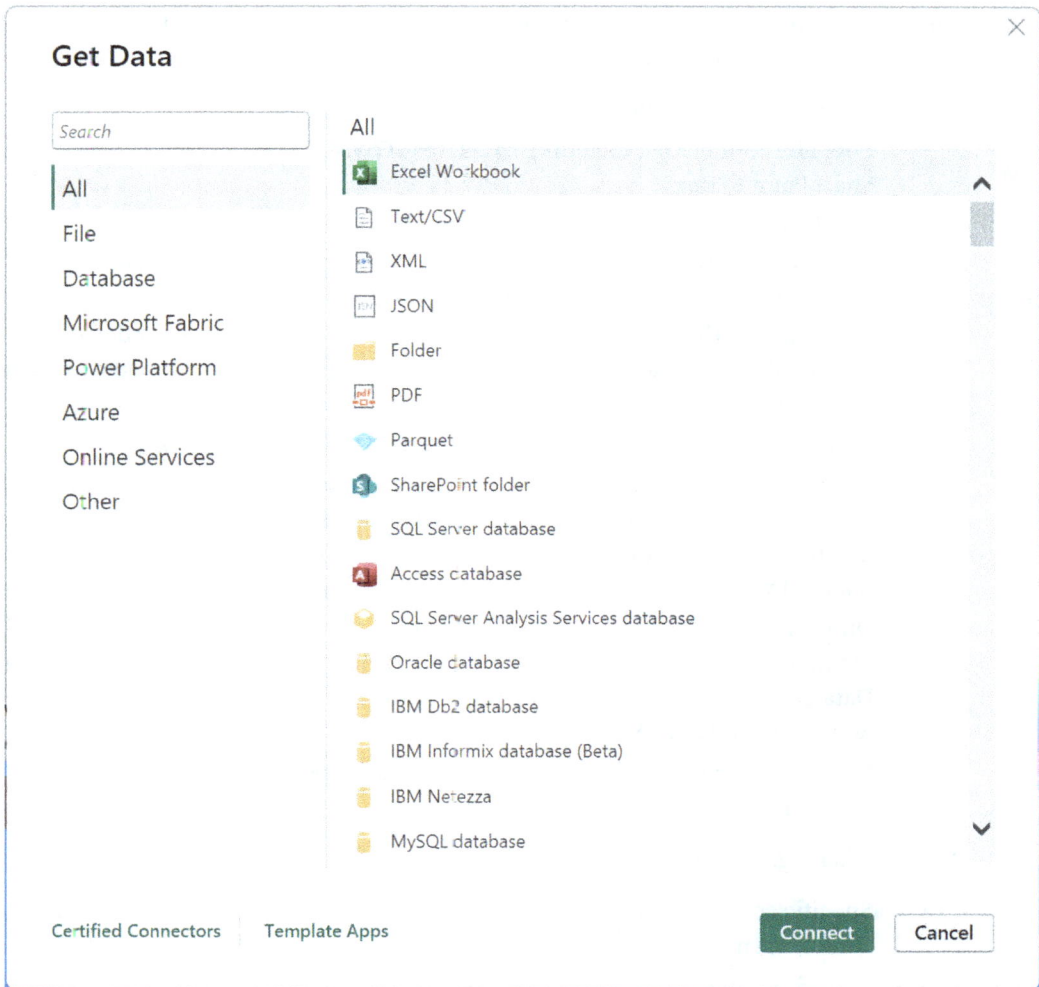

Figure 4.1 – The Get Data section

There are approximately 200 default **connectors** available for ingesting data. These connectors are broken down into several categories:

- **All:** This lists all of the available connectors.
- **File: File** connectors, including Excel, text/CSV, XML, JSON, folder, PDF, Parquet, and SharePoint folders.
- **Database:** The **Database** section lists sources such as SQL Server, Access, Oracle, IBM DB2, IBM Informix, IBM Netezza, MySQL, PostgreSQL, Sybase, Teradata, SAP, Impala, Google BigQuery, Vertica, Snowflake, Essbase, and AtScale.
- **Microsoft Fabric:** Includes traditional Power BI assets such as semantic models, Datamarts, and Dataflows, as well as Fabric assets such as Warehouses, Lakehouses, and KQL Databases.
- **Power Platform: Power Platform** includes Dataflows and Dataverse.
- **Azure: Azure** lists many different services, such as Azure SQL Database, Azure Synapse Analytics, Azure Analysis Services, Azure Blob Storage, Azure Table Storage, Azure Cosmos DB, Azure Data Lake Storage, Azure HDInsights (HDFS), Azure HDInsights Spark, Azure Data Explorer (Kusto), Azure Databricks, and Azure Cost Management.
- **Online Services:** There is a substantial collection of online services, including Microsoft technologies such as SharePoint Online, Exchange Online, Dynamics 365, Common Data Service, DevOps, and GitHub, as well as third parties such as Salesforce, Google, Adobe, QuickBooks, Smartsheet, Twilio, Zendesk, and many others.
- **Other:** Other connectors include Web, OData, Spark, Hadoop (HDFS), ODBC, R, Python, and OLE DB.

You can also regard connectors as specific and generic:

- **Specific connectors** connect to proprietary technologies, including IBM DB2, MySQL, Teradata, and many more.
- **Generic connectors** are included under the **Other** category and support connecting to any technology that supports industry standards, such as ODBC, OData, web (HTML), and OLE DB. Because there are hundreds, if not thousands, of data sources that are not specifically listed that support these standards, there is an almost unlimited number of data sources that can be connected to within Power BI.

At the bottom of *Figure 4.1*, there are two links. The first is a link that reads **Certified Connectors.** One of the reasons Power BI has so many data source connectors available is Microsoft has created the ability for customers and third parties to extend the data sources supported by Power BI through custom connectors.

By default, Power BI only allows connectors that have been certified through Microsoft's certification process to be used in Power BI. This can be changed by going to **File** | **Options and settings** | **Options**, selecting **Security**, and then adjusting **Data Extensions**. Custom connectors are placed in the Power BI Desktop installation folder, under the [Documents]\Microsoft Power BI Desktop\Custom Connectors folder. This folder was created after installing and running Power BI.

The second link is for **Template Apps**. **Template Apps** are prepackaged dashboards and reports that can be connected to live data sources. Clicking the **Template Apps** link opens a web browser window or tab connected to the **Power BI Apps marketplace**.

2. Click on the **All** category and select the first item in the list; that is, **Excel Workbook**.

3. Browse to your **Budgets and Forecast.xlsx** file and click **Open**. The dialog that's displayed is known as the **Navigator**:

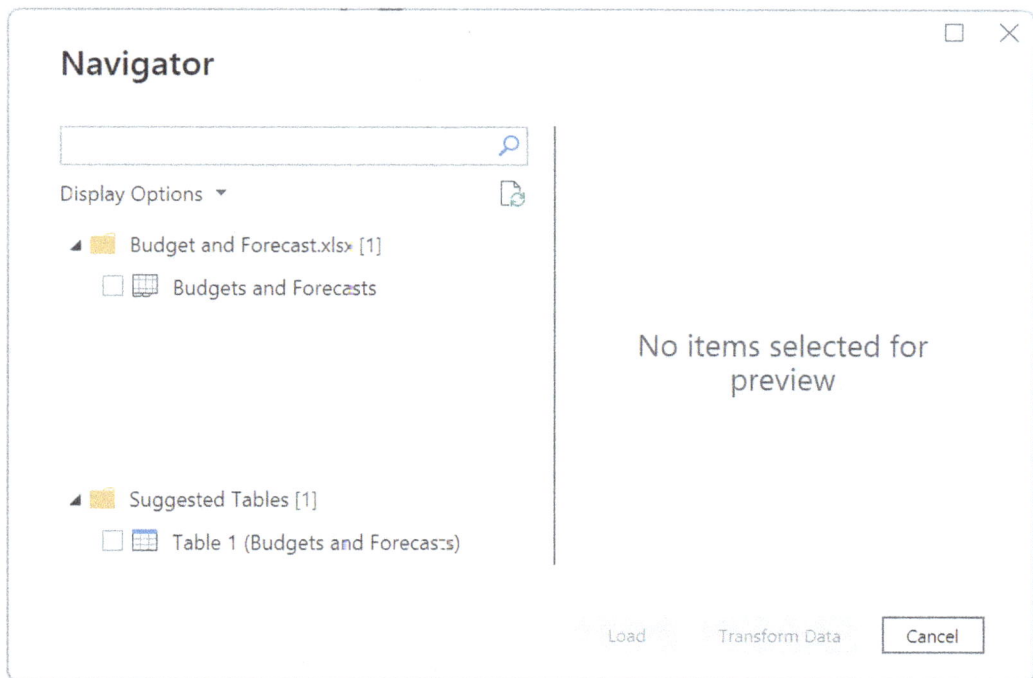

Figure 4 2 – The Navigator dialog

For Excel files, the **Navigator** dialog lists all the pages and tables within the Excel file. The suggested tables are the areas in Excel that are specifically marked as tables.

4. Click the checkbox next to **Budgets and Forecasts** and observe that a preview of the data is loaded in the right-hand pane:

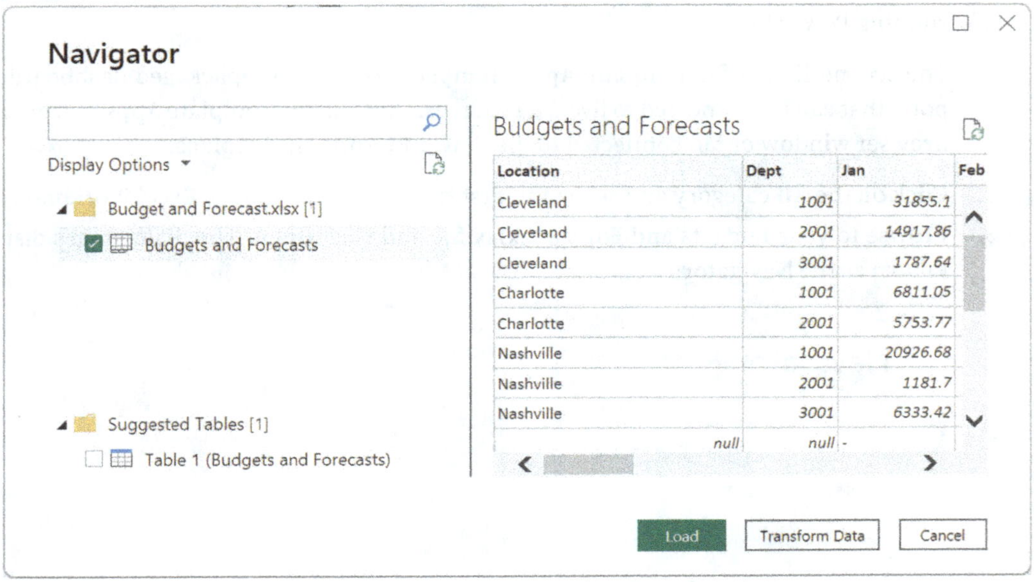

Figure 4.3 – Navigator dialog with a preview of the data

Note that three buttons are available at the bottom of the page: **Load, Transform Data,** and **Cancel.**

5.   Click the **Load** button. Once the loading dialog completes, click on the **Data** view and then the **Budgets and Forecasts** table to see this data loaded into the semantic model:

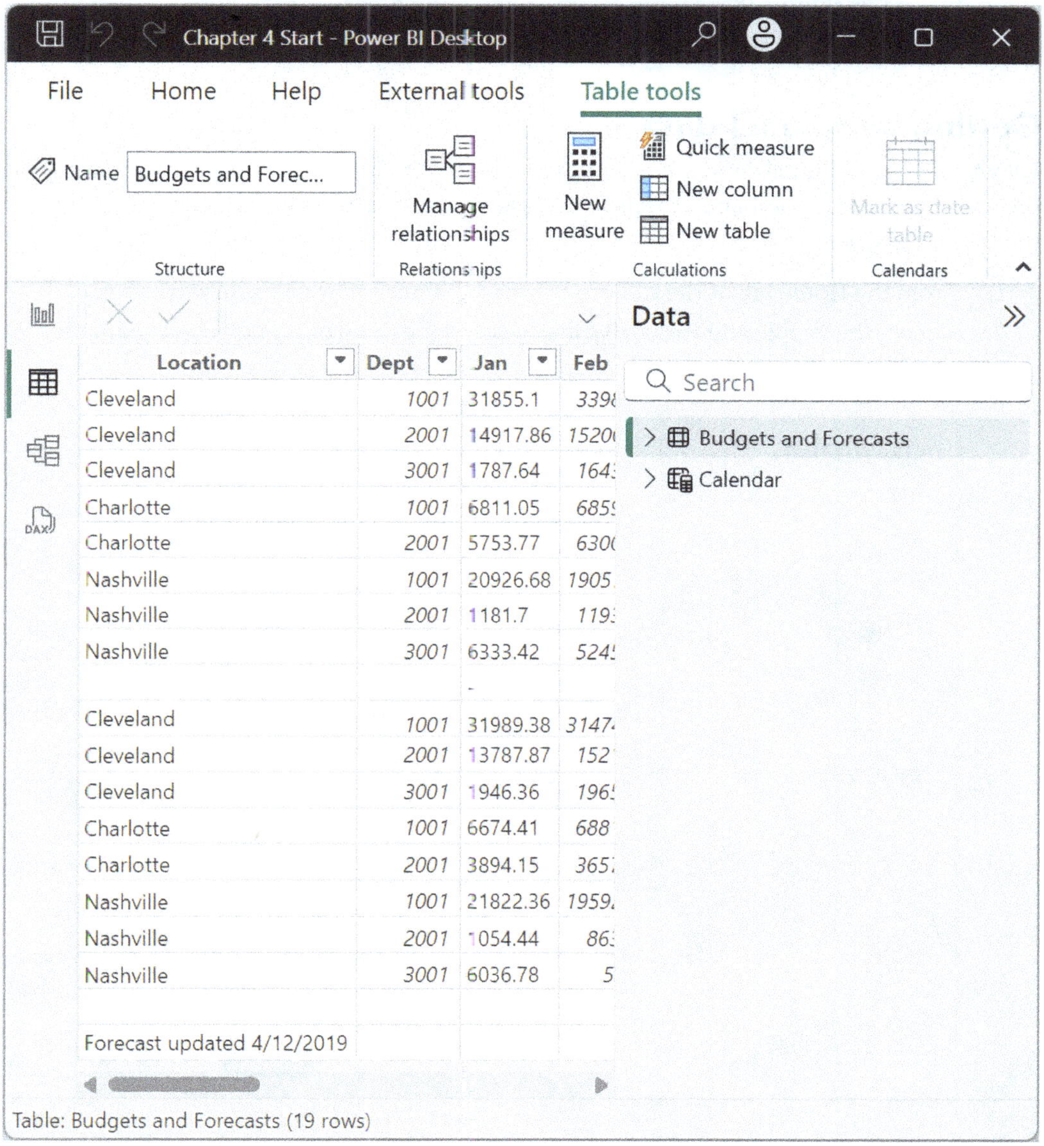

Figure 4.4 – Budgets and Forecasts table

The data that's displayed represents the budget and forecast information for our fictional professional services firm. Behind the scenes, Power BI created a query and attempted to make intelligent decisions about the data, including identifying column names and data types.

Congratulations! You have created your first Power BI query!

Getting additional data

Let's get some additional data. Since we are tracking PTO for people, we need to get some data about the employees at the company, as well as the tasks that they are performing. To get this data, perform the following steps:

1. From the **Home** tab of the ribbon, choose **Get Data** and then **Excel workbook**.
2. Choose the **People and Tasks.xlsx** file and click the **Open** button. The **Navigator** dialog displays the following:

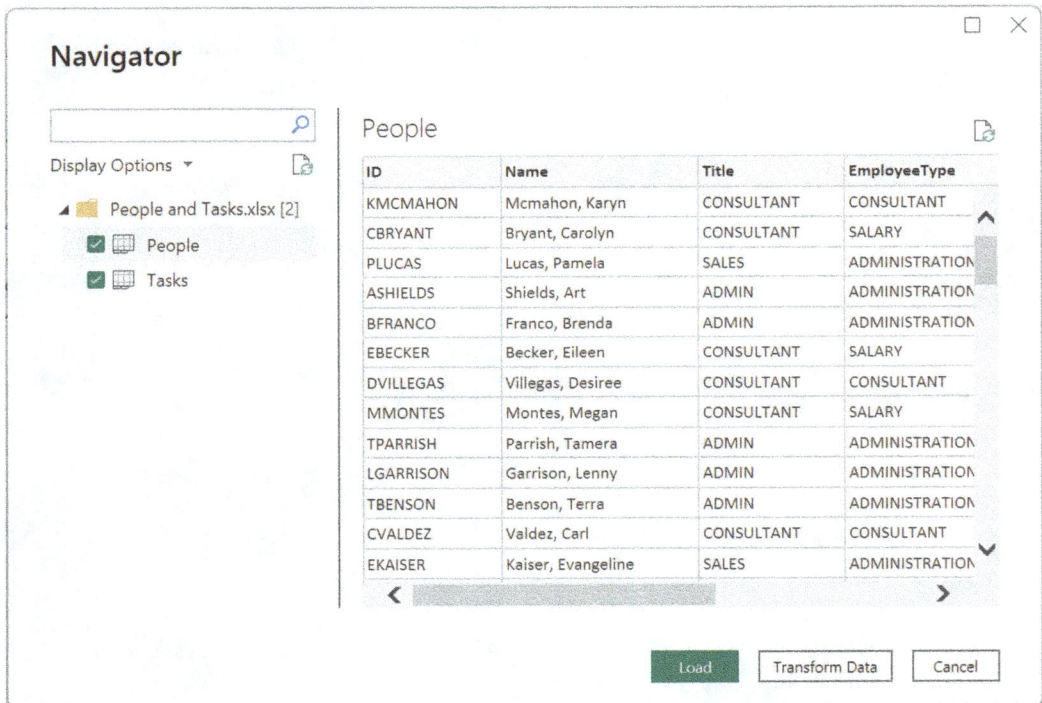

ID	Name	Title	EmployeeType
KMCMAHON	Mcmahon, Karyn	CONSULTANT	CONSULTANT
CBRYANT	Bryant, Carolyn	CONSULTANT	SALARY
PLUCAS	Lucas, Pamela	SALES	ADMINISTRATION
ASHIELDS	Shields, Art	ADMIN	ADMINISTRATION
BFRANCO	Franco, Brenda	ADMIN	ADMINISTRATION
EBECKER	Becker, Eileen	CONSULTANT	SALARY
DVILLEGAS	Villegas, Desiree	CONSULTANT	CONSULTANT
MMONTES	Montes, Megan	CONSULTANT	SALARY
TPARRISH	Parrish, Tamera	ADMIN	ADMINISTRATION
LGARRISON	Garrison, Lenny	ADMIN	ADMINISTRATION
TBENSON	Benson, Terra	ADMIN	ADMINISTRATION
CVALDEZ	Valdez, Carl	CONSULTANT	CONSULTANT
EKAISER	Kaiser, Evangeline	SALES	ADMINISTRATION

Figure 4.5 – Creating queries for People and Tasks

3. As shown in the preceding screenshot, check both the **People** and **Tasks** pages and click the **Load** button.

    While exploring this data back in the **Data** view of **Power BI Desktop**, we can see that we now have two additional tables: **People** and **Tasks**.

    The **People** table contains information about the employees of the company. By looking at the **People** table, we can see that we have information such as **ID**, **Name**, **Title**, **EmployeeType**, **TermDate**, **HireDate**, and **Location**.

    The **Tasks** table contains information about the projects or tasks that employees work on and whether or not those tasks are billable. In the **Tasks** table, we can see that **TaskID** and **Category** are in the first row, but we can also see that these are not our column names. Not to worry; we will fix that later when we transform this data.

The final data that we need is the actual hours that employees are working. To do this, perform the following steps:

1. Click on the **Home** tab of the ribbon, choose **Get Data**, and then **Excel workbook**.
2. This time, choose the **Hours.xlsx** file and click the **Open** button.
3. In the **Navigator** dialog, this time, just choose **January** and click **Load**.

Now that we have loaded all of our data, we can move on to transforming the data as necessary. As you become more familiar with Power BI, you will likely choose the **Transform Data** button instead of the **Load** button while you are importing data.

Transforming data

While Power BI did a good job of automatically identifying and categorizing our data, the data is not entirely in the format required for analysis. Therefore, we need to modify how the data gets loaded into the model. In other words, we need to **transform** the data. Transforming can take many forms such as unpivoting columns of data, removing header rows, changing the data types of columns, and correcting errors in the data. Many additional data transformations are also possible. In order to transform data, we will cover using a powerful sub-application known as **Power Query Editor**.

Touring Power Query Editor

Similar to how we provided a tour of Power BI Desktop in *Chapter 3, Up and Running with Power BI Desktop*, this section provides a tour of Power Query Editor. **Power Query Editor** can be launched from the **Home** tab by choosing **Transform data** in the **Queries** section of the Ribbon.

Once launched, the following screen is displayed:

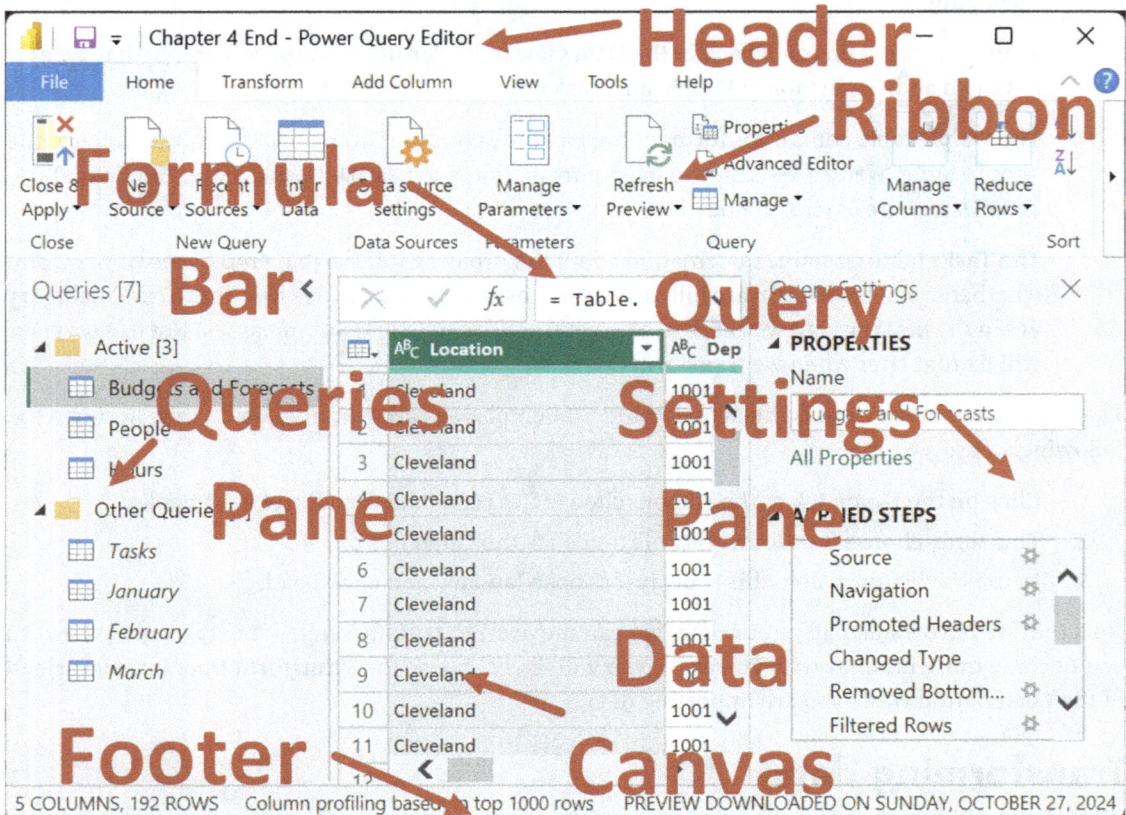

Figure 4.6 – Power Query Editor

As you might expect, the **Power Query Editor** interface shares similar elements with Power BI Desktop. The **Power Query Editor** user interface is comprised of seven main areas. Refer to the preceding screenshot while reading about these seven areas in the subsequent sections.

Header

Nearly identical to Power BI Desktop, the **Header** is the small strip at the top of the **Power Query Editor** window. This area is standard for Windows applications. Left-clicking the application icon in the left-hand corner provides the standard sizing and common exit commands, such as **Minimize**, **Maximize**, and **Close**.

Next to this icon is the **Quick Access Toolbar**. This toolbar can be displayed above or below the ribbon, and commands within the ribbon can be added to this toolbar by right-clicking an icon in the ribbon and selecting **Add to Quick Access Toolbar**. By default, only the **Save** icon is displayed.

To the right of the **Quick Access Toolbar** is the name of the currently opened file and next to that is the name of the application, **Power Query Editor**. Standard minimize, maximize, and close icons appear on the far right.

Ribbon

Below the **Header** is the Ribbon. Users who are familiar with modern versions of Microsoft Office will recognize the function of this area although the controls that are displayed will be somewhat different. The ribbon consists of six tabs:

- **File:** The **File** tab displays a fly-out menu when clicked that allows Power BI Desktop files to be saved, as well as **Power Query Editor** to be closed, and changes made within **Power Query Editor** to be applied.

- **Home:** The **Home** tab provides a variety of the most common operations, such as connecting to sources and managing parameters and common transformation functions, such as removing rows and columns, splitting columns, and replacing values.

- **Transform:** The **Transform** tab provides data manipulation functions that let you transpose rows and columns, pivot and unpivot columns, move columns, add R and Python scripts, and many scientific, statistics-related, trigonometry, date, and time calculations.

- **Add Column:** The **Add Column** tab provides operations that focus on adding calculated, conditional, and index columns. In addition, many of the functions that are available from the **Transform** tab are also available in this ribbon.

- **View:** The **View** tab includes controls for controlling the layout of the Power Query interface, such as whether or not the **Query Settings** pane is displayed, and whether the **Formula bar** area is displayed.

- **Tools:** The **Tools** tab includes access to diagnostic tools that can be helpful in optimizing the performance of queries.

- **Help:** The **Help** tab includes useful links for getting help with Power BI, including links to the Power BI Community site, documentation, guided learning, training videos, and much more.

Formula Bar

The **Formula Bar** allows the user to view, enter, and modify the Power Query (**M**) code. The Power Query formula language, commonly called M, is a functional programming language comprised of functions, operators, and values. M is the underlying data connection and transformation technology for Microsoft Power Automate, PowerApps, Power BI Desktop, and Power Query in Excel.

M is the language behind queries in Power BI. As you build a query in **Power Query Editor**, behind the scenes, this builds an M script that executes to connect to, transform, and import your data. In reality, each of the applied steps in a query is a line of Power Query M language code. You do not need to worry about that just yet, but we will explore this in the *Merging, copying, and appending queries* section.

Queries Pane

The **Queries Pane** displays a list of the various queries associated with the current Power BI file. As queries are created, those queries are displayed here. This area also allows you to group queries, as well as display any errors that are generated by data rows within queries.

Data Canvas

Data Canvas is the area within **Power Query Editor** where a preview of the data that's been loaded into the model is displayed. This area is contextual, displaying the data table for the currently selected step of a query. This area is similar to the **Data** view within Power BI Desktop and is the main work area for viewing and transforming data within queries.

Query Settings

The **Query Settings** pane provides access to properties of the query, such as the name of the query. By default, the name of the query becomes the name of the table within the semantic model.

More importantly, the **Query Settings** pane includes a list of **Applied Steps** for a query. A query is just a series of applied steps, or transformations, of the data. As you transform the data that's been imported by a query, a step is created for each transformation. Thus, executing a query to refresh data from a data source is just a matter of re-executing these steps, or using transformation operations.

Footer

The Footer area is contextual and is based on what is selected within **Power Query Editor**. Helpful information, such as the number of rows and columns in a table and when the last preview of the data was loaded, is displayed here.

Transforming budget and forecast data

Now that we have connected to our data, we need to perform some transformation steps to clean up the data and prepare it for our semantic model. To do this, follow these steps:

1. In the **Power Query Editor** window, select **Budgets and Forecasts** from the **Queries** pane on the left.

    Looking at the data, we can see that we have a blank row in the middle and several extraneous rows at the end. Looking at the column headers, we can see that Power BI has identified that our first row contains column names and has already categorized our columns as text (**ABC**), whole numbers (**123**), and decimal (**1.2**).

	$^{ABC}_C$ Location		1^2_3 Dept		$^{ABC}_{123}$ Jan		1.2 Feb	
1	Cleveland		1001		31855.1		33985.1	
2	Cleveland		2001		14917.86		15200.85	

    Figure 4.7 – Column headers and data type icons

    The table contains columns for **Location**, **Dept**, and then a column for each month. As we scroll horizontally to the end, we can see a column called **Type**.

2. In the **Query Settings** pane, under **APPLIED STEPS**, we can see that some steps have already been applied to our query. These steps were automatically created by Power BI.

    A query is just a collection of applied steps. If we click on these steps, we can see how our query changes our data table at each step.

3. Clicking on the **Navigation** step, we can see that our column headers are labeled **Column1, Column2,** and so on.

4. When we click on the **Promoted Headers** step, we can see that the first row has been promoted to column headers, but that all of our columns are labeled **ABC123.**

5. Clicking on the **Changed Type** step, we can see that this is where our columns are categorized according to their data types.

Now that we understand how applied steps transform the data, let's apply some of our transformation steps!

Cleaning up extraneous bottom rows

Let's clean up those extraneous rows at the end. To do that, ensure that the last step, **Changed Type,** is selected in the **Query Settings** pane and then follow these steps:

1. From the Ribbon, select the **Home** tab.

2. Select the **Remove Rows** button in the **Reduce Rows** section.

3. Select **Remove Bottom Rows:**

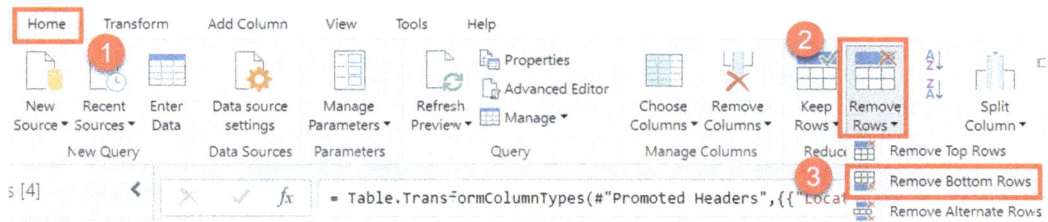

Figure 4.8 – Removing rows

4. In the following dialog, type *2* and then click the **OK** button:

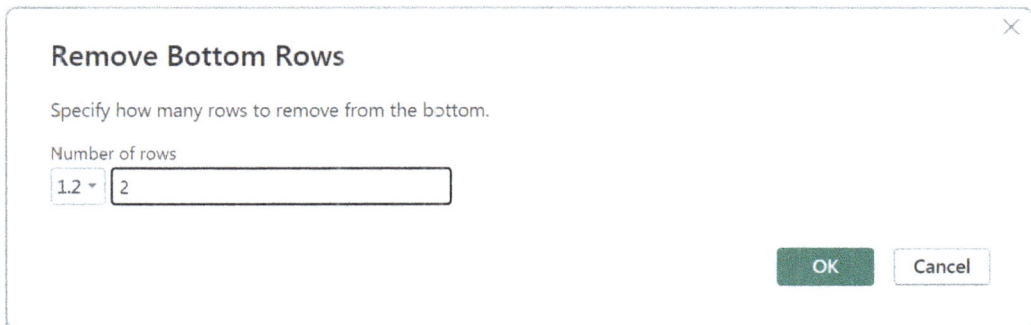

Figure 4.9 – Remove Bottom Rows dialog

Observe that the last two rows have been removed from the Data Canvas and that an additional step, **Removed Bottom Rows,** has been added to the bottom of our query steps in the **APPLIED STEPS** area of the **Query Settings** pane.

Filtering rows

Now, let's clean up that mostly blank row in the middle, row 9. To do this, follow these steps:

1. In the **Location** column header, click the drop-down arrow and notice that there are several options, including sorting, text filters, and a search bar. The **Text Filters** area presents several useful text filtering options, including filters such as **Equals**, **Does Not Equal**, **Begins With**, **Does Not Begin With**, **Ends With**, **Does Not End With**, **Contains**, and **Does Not Contain**. Also, note that all of the distinct values that appear in the column are listed, including **(null)**, **Charlotte**, **Cleveland**, and **Nashville**. As datasets become larger, you may see a **List may be incomplete** warning message. This occurs because Power Query Editor samples the first 1,000 rows of data.

    If you see this message, you can click on the **Load more** link to have Power Query Editor analyze all the rows of data:

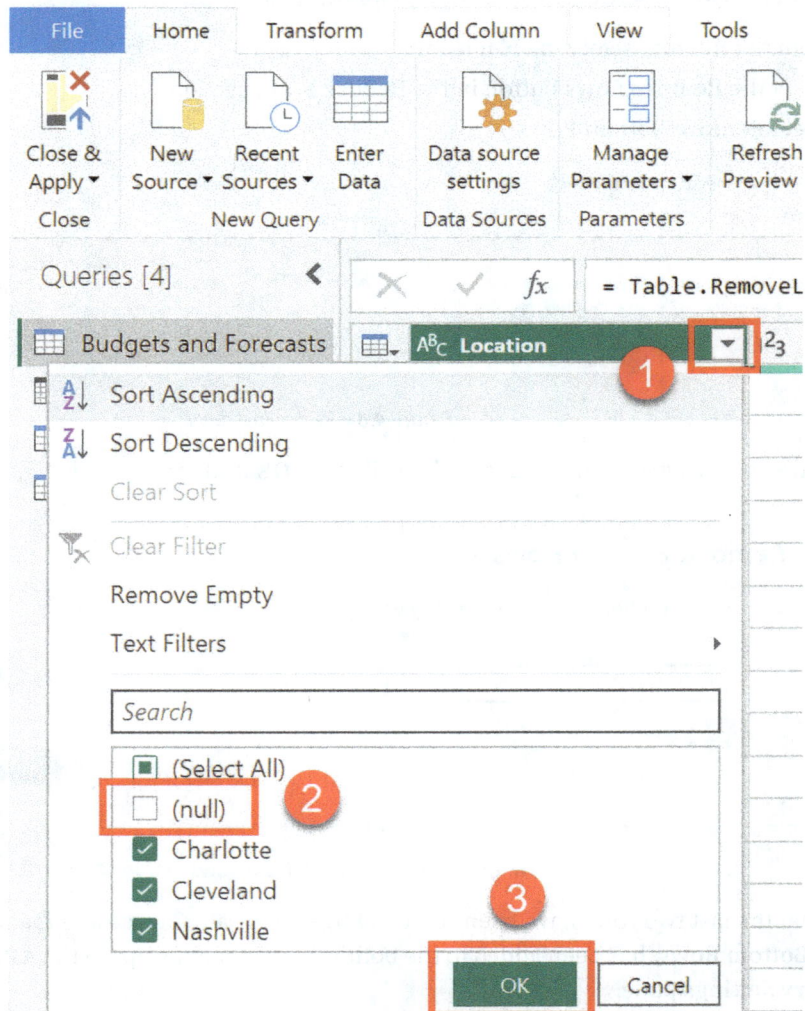

Figure 4.10 – Filtering rows

2. As shown in the preceding screenshot, uncheck the box next to **(null)**.

3. Then click on the **OK** button.

Notice that the row of null values in the data table has been removed and that a new step has been added to the query called **Filtered Rows** in the **APPLIED STEPS** area of the **Query Settings** pane. Also, notice that a small funnel icon appears in the **Location** column's header button, indicating that there is a filter on this column.

Unpivoting data

Let's put this data into a better format for analysis. Since the numeric data that we need to analyze appears in multiple columns (the month columns), this can make analysis difficult. The data is much easier to analyze if we transform this data so that all of the numeric data is in a single column. We can do this by unpivoting our month columns. To unpivot our month columns, perform the following steps:

1. Start by selecting the column header for **Jan**.

2. Scroll horizontally to the right until you see the last column, **Type**.

3. Hold down the *Shift* key and then select the column header labeled **Dec**.

4. Now, all of the columns between and including **Jan** through **Dec** are highlighted, indicating that they are selected.

5. Click on the **Transform** tab.

6. Choose **Unpivot Columns** from the **Any Column** section of the Ribbon:

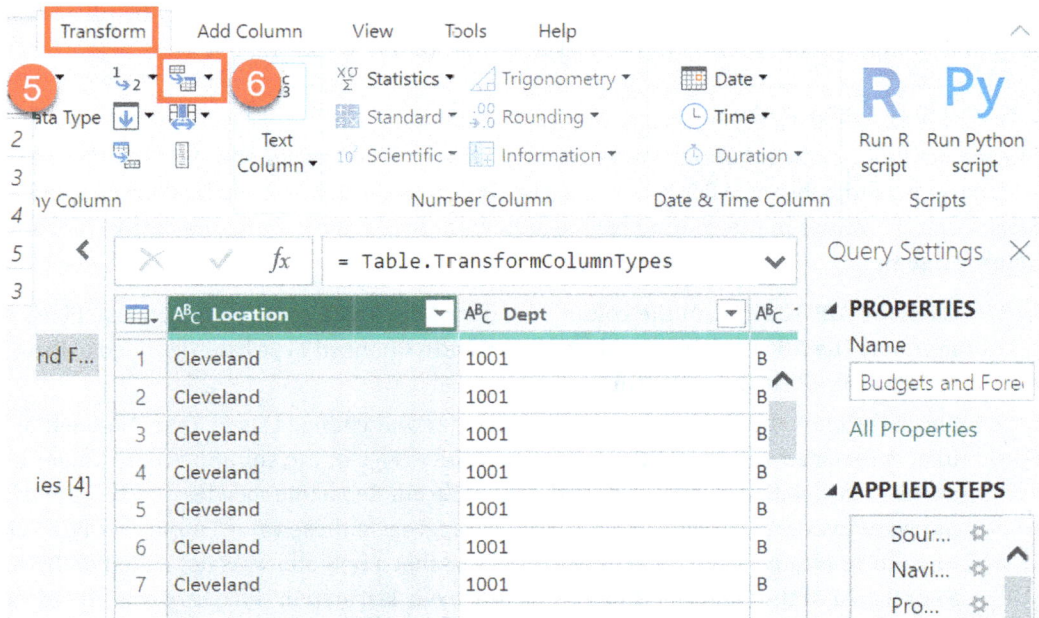

Figure 4.11 – Unpivoting columns

As shown in the preceding screenshot, our month columns are now transformed into two columns called **Attribute** and **Value**. Our former column names, **Jan, Feb, Mar, Apr, May**, and so on, now appear as row values under the **Attribute** column, and our numeric values appear in the column called **Value**. A new **Unpivoted Columns** step appears in our **APPLIED STEPS** area.

7. Double-click the **Attribute** column header and rename this column Month. A **Renamed Columns** step now appears in the **APPLIED STEPS** area of the **Query Settings** pane.

Unpivoting data is a common operation with Excel-based data as spreadsheets are generally designed for easy data entry. However, having multiple columns for the same data element is almost always a bad idea for data analysis in Power BI.

Using Fill

Now, we want to fix our **Type** data. Notice that the **Type** column contains spotty information. The first 12 rows contain the word **Budget**, and then there is a gap until row **97**, where the next 12 rows contain the word **Forecast**, and then another gap. We want all of these rows to contain either **Budget** or **Forecast**. To fix the data, we can use the **Fill** functionality by performing the following steps:

1. Select the **Type** column, then right-click in the **Type** column header and choose **Fill**, and then **Down**.
2. Notice that our **Type** column now contains a value for each row and that a **Filled Down** step appears in the **APPLIED STEPS** area of the **Query Settings** pane.

The **Fill** operation takes the latest value found in the column and replaces any blank or null values with that value until a new value is found. Then, this operation repeats.

Changing data types

In the data table, notice that our **Value** column is categorized as general data. As shown in *Figure 4.11*, we can tell this by the **ABC123** icon that appears in the **Value** column header. The **ABC123** label means that the values in the column can be either text or numeric. To fix the data type, perform the following steps:

1. Click the **ABC123** icon in the column header of the **Value** column and choose **Fixed decimal number**. The ABC123 icon is replaced by a $ and a **Changed Type1** step is added to the **APPLIED STEPS** area of the **Query Settings** pane.
2. Similarly, click the **123** icon in the **Dept** header and change this to **Text**. Notice that the **123** icon is replaced with an **ABC** icon and that the values in the column are no longer italicized and are left-justified versus right-justified. While our department codes may be numeric, we do not want to ever sum, average, or otherwise aggregate these values numerically, so changing them to be treated as text makes sense. Notice that a new step was not added to the **APPLIED STEPS** area of the **Query Settings** pane. Since our last step in the query was already a step to change the data type of a column, this new operation for the **Dept** column was simply added as part of the current **Changed Type 1** step.

Changing data types also affects the sort order, so sometimes, leaving the data type as numeric and using a default summarization of don't summarize can also be effective.

Transforming People, Tasks, and January data

Now, let's move on to ensuring that our other tables are ready for analysis. In the following sections, we perform similar operations on the **People**, **Tasks, and**, and **January** queries as we did in the *Transforming budget and forecast data* section.

Transforming the People query

To transform the **People** query, perform the following steps:

1. In **Power Query Editor**, click on the **People** query in the **Queries** pane. Notice that four steps have already been created in this query: **Source**, **Navigation**, **Promoted Headers**, and **Changed Type**. Power BI has automatically added several query steps to make the first row of data the column names as well as to identify the data types of the columns. The first four columns – that is, **ID**, **Name**, **Title**, and **EmployeeType** – have all been identified as text (**ABC**). The next two columns, **TermDate** and **HireDate**, have a calendar icon. These are date columns. The final column, **Location**, is a text column (**ABC**).

2. Ensure that all of these columns have the correct data type. If not, change their data type by either clicking on the data type icon in the column header or choosing the **Transform** tab of the Ribbon and using the **Data Type** dropdown in the **Any Column** section. When you are finished, your data types should be the same as the ones shown in the following screenshot:

ABC ID	ABC Name	ABC Title	ABC EmployeeType	📅 TermDate	📅 HireDate	ABC Location
KMCMAHON	Mcmahon, Karyn	CONSULTANT	CONSULTANT	1/1/1900	1/1/1900	Charlotte
CBRYANT	Bryant, Carolyn	CONSULTANT	SALARY	5/15/2015	1/1/1900	Charlotte
PLUCAS	Lucas, Pamela	SALES	ADMINISTRATION	1/1/1900	1/1/1900	Charlotte
ASHIELDS	Shields, Art	ADMIN	ADMINISTRATION	1/1/1900	1/1/1900	Charlotte

Figure 4.12 – Column data types for the People query

These are all the transformations required for the **People** query. Now, let's move on to the **Tasks** query.

Transforming the Tasks query

To transform the **Tasks** query, perform the following steps:

1. In **Power Query Editor**, click on the **Tasks** query in the **Queries** pane. Notice that there are only three **APPLIED STEPS** in this query: **Source**, **Navigation**, and **Changed Type**. There are two columns named **Column1** and **Column2**. Also, note that the first row contains the **TaskID** and **Category** values. We want the values in this first row to be the names of our columns.

2. Click the **Navigation** step in the **APPLIED STEPS** area of the **Query Settings** pane.

3. Click the **Transform** tab and choose **Use First Row as Headers,** the second icon from the left. An **Insert Step** message will be displayed, asking you to confirm that you wish to insert a step into the query:

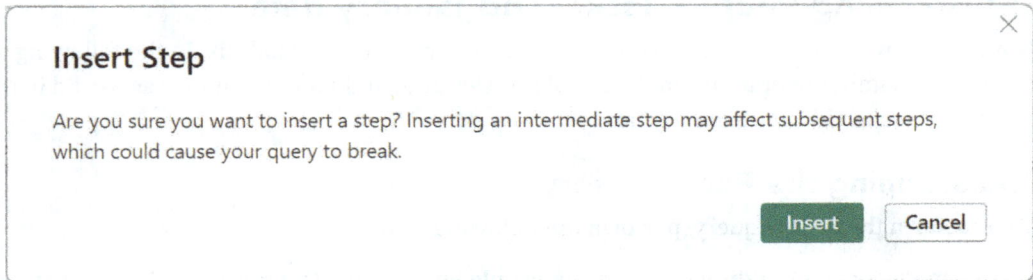

Insert Step

Are you sure you want to insert a step? Inserting an intermediate step may affect subsequent steps, which could cause your query to break.

Insert   Cancel

Figure 4.13 – Insert Step dialog

4. Click the **Insert** button. Notice that a **Promoted Headers** step has been inserted between the **Navigation** step and the **Changed Type** step. Our column headers are now **TaskID** and **Category.**

5. Click on the **Changed Type** step and notice that an error is displayed. This is because the **Changed Type** step was referring to the columns as **Column1** and **Column2,** but now, these columns are called something different.

6. Remove the **Changed Type** step by clicking on the X icon to the left of the step name.

7. Now, change the data types of both columns to **Text** by either clicking on the data type icon in the column header (**ABC123**) or choosing the **Transform** tab of the Ribbon and using the **Data Type** dropdown in the **Any Column** section.

The transformations for the **Tasks** query are now complete. The next query to transform is the January query.

Transforming the January query

Moving on to the **January** query, perform the following transformation steps:

1. In **Power Query Editor,** click on the **January** query in the **Queries** pane. Note that four **APPLIED STEPS** options exist: **Source, Navigation, Promoted Headers,** and **Changed Type.**

    The **EmployeeID, TaskID, JobID, Division, TimesheetBatchID, TimesheetID,** and **PayType** columns are all **Text** columns (**ABC**).

    The **Date, PeriodStartDate,** and **PeriodEndDate** columns are all **Date** columns (calendar icon).

    The **Hours, HourlyCost, HourlyRate, TotalHoursBilled,** and **TotalHours** columns are all decimal number (**1.2**) columns.

2. Make sure that the **Changed Type** step is selected and then change **HourlyCost** and **Hourly-Rate** to **Fixed decimal number** by either clicking on the data type icon in the column header (**1.2**) or choosing the **Transform** tab of the Ribbon and using the **Data Type** dropdown in the **Any Column** section. A **Change Column Type** prompt will be displayed each time. Choose the **Replace current** button each time, as shown in the following screenshot:

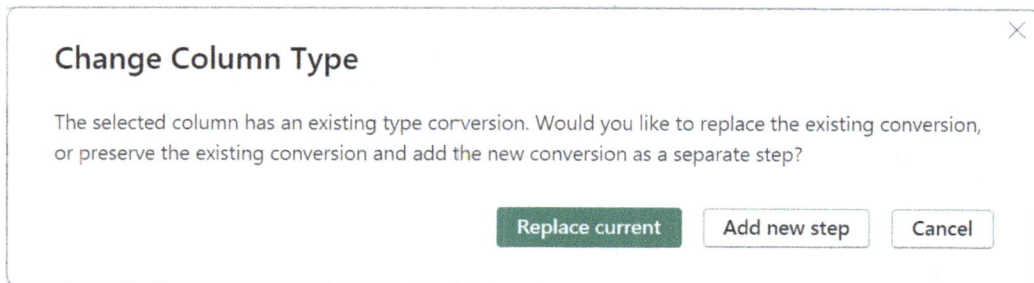

Change Column Type ✕

The selected column has an existing type conversion. Would you like to replace the existing conversion, or preserve the existing conversion and add the new conversion as a separate step?

[Replace current] [Add new step] [Cancel]

Figure 4.14 – Change Column Type dialog

This finishes the basic transformation work we must perform on our queries. However, we have not finished transforming our data yet. We will now move on to more complex data transformations.

Merging, copying, and appending queries

Now that we have cleaned up our data, we still require some additional data and transformations to occur to prepare our data for analysis. Specifically, we need to add our additional month data around hours billed to customers, as well as some additional transformations.

In the following sections, we perform more advanced transformations of our data, including merging queries, expanding tables, and appending queries.

Merging queries

Note that in the **January** query, there is a column called **TaskID**. The values in this column match the values in the **TaskID** column from our **Tasks** query. This **Tasks** query has additional information about each of these tasks regarding whether or not the task is **Billable**, or some other category, such as **PTO**, **Int Admin**, **Sales Support**, and **Training**. We want this information included in our **January** table. To accomplish this, we can merge the two queries by performing the following steps:

1. In **Power Query Editor**, start by selecting the **January** query in the **Queries** pane.

2. Select the **Home** tab from the ribbon and then, in the **Combine** section of the ribbon, choose **Merge Queries**.

The **Merge** dialog is displayed, as shown in the following screenshot:

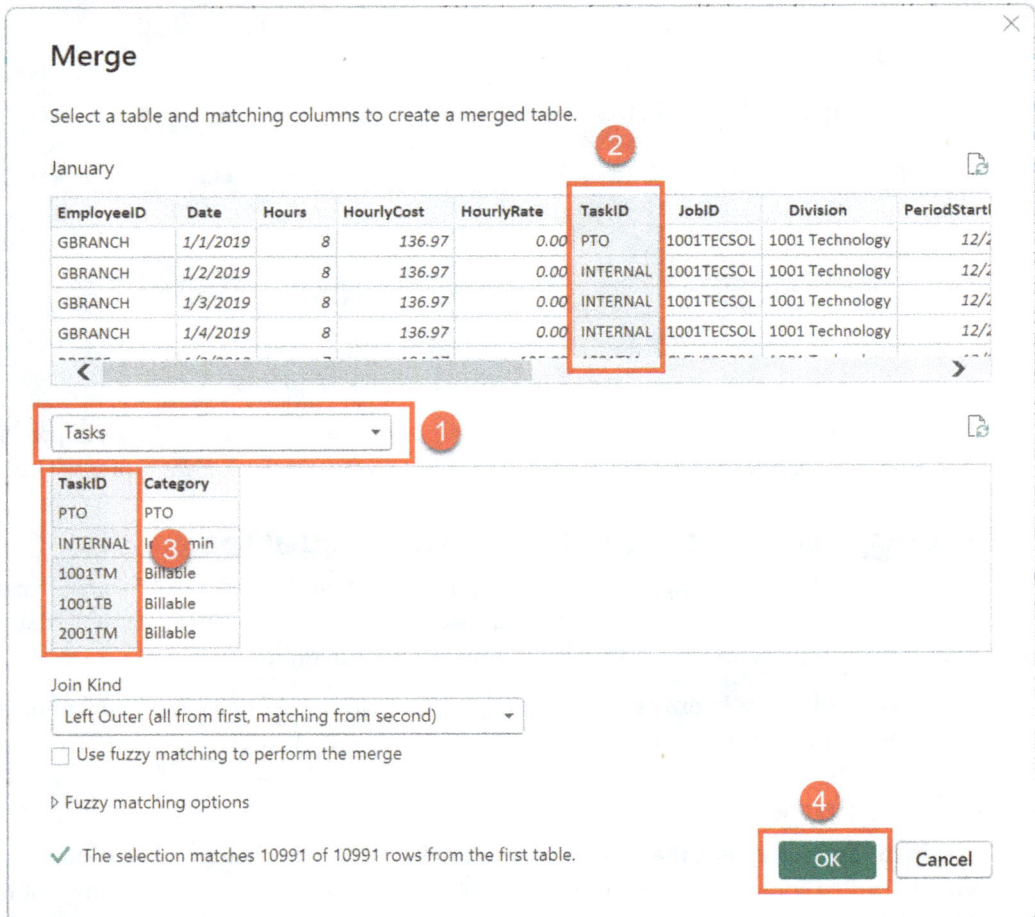

Figure 4.15 – Merge dialog

3. The **January** query is listed at the top of the dialog, along with a preview of the columns and rows returned by that query. In the drop-down box just below this table, use the drop-down arrow and choose the **Tasks** query, as shown in the preceding screenshot. Again, a preview of the columns and rows returned by the **Tasks** query will be displayed. This is the query that we will be merging with our **January** query.

4. As shown in the preceding screenshot, select the **TaskID** column of the **January** table.

5. Select the **TaskID** column of the **Tasks** table and note that the **OK** button becomes active.

Be aware that, at the bottom of the **Merge** dialog, information is displayed indicating **The selection matches 10991 out of 10991 rows from the first table.**

The **Join Kind** dialog displays **Left Outer (all from first, matching from second)**. Other types of joins are listed in the dropdown, including the following:

- **Left Outer (all rows from first table, matching from second)**
- **Right Outer (all rows from second table, matching from first)**
- **Full Outer (all rows from both)**
- **Inner (only matching rows)**
- **Left Anti (rows only in first)**
- **Right Anti (rows only in second)**

Leave this as **Left Outer (all from first, matching from second)**.

Below **Join Kind**, there is a checkbox for **Use fuzzy matching to perform the merge** and an area for **Fuzzy matching options**.

A **fuzzy merge** allows similar but not identical items to be matched during a merge. Options include a **Similarity threshold**, which is optional. The **Similarity threshold** is a number between **0.00** and **1.00**. A value of **0.00** causes all values to match, while a value of **1.00** causes only exact values to match. The default is a value of **0.80**.

Additional options include the ability to **Ignore case**, as well as the ability to **Match by combining text parts**. For example, by ignoring case, mIcrOSoft could match Microsoft, and by combining text parts, Micro and soft could be combined to match Microsoft.

When performing fuzzy merges, it is possible to have multiple values match. You can use the optional **Maximum number of matches** setting to control how many matching rows are returned for each input row. This is a number that can range from 1 to 2,147,483,647 (the default).

Finally, there is an option to use a **Transformation table**. This allows you to specify a table of values with **From** and **To** columns that can be used during the merge process. For example, the merge table might contain a value in the **From** column for USA that maps to a **To** column of United States.

6. Leave the **Use fuzzy matching to perform the merge** checkbox unchecked and click the **OK** button to exit the **Merge** dialog and perform the merge.

Now that you have learned how to merge queries, we will move on to expanding tables.

Expanding tables

Back in **Power Query Editor**, note that an additional step has been added to this query called **Merged Queries**, as shown in the following screenshot. In addition, an additional column has been added called **Tasks**. This column's row values say **Table** in colored text. We wish to expand this table. To do this, perform the following steps:

1. Click the diverging arrows icon to the far right of the column header for the **Tasks** column. This icon can be used to expand the columns that contain table information.
2. Uncheck the checkbox next to **TaskID**.

3. Uncheck the checkbox for **Use original column name as prefix**, as shown in the following screenshot; otherwise, instead of the column being called **Category**, the column will be called **Tasks.Category**:

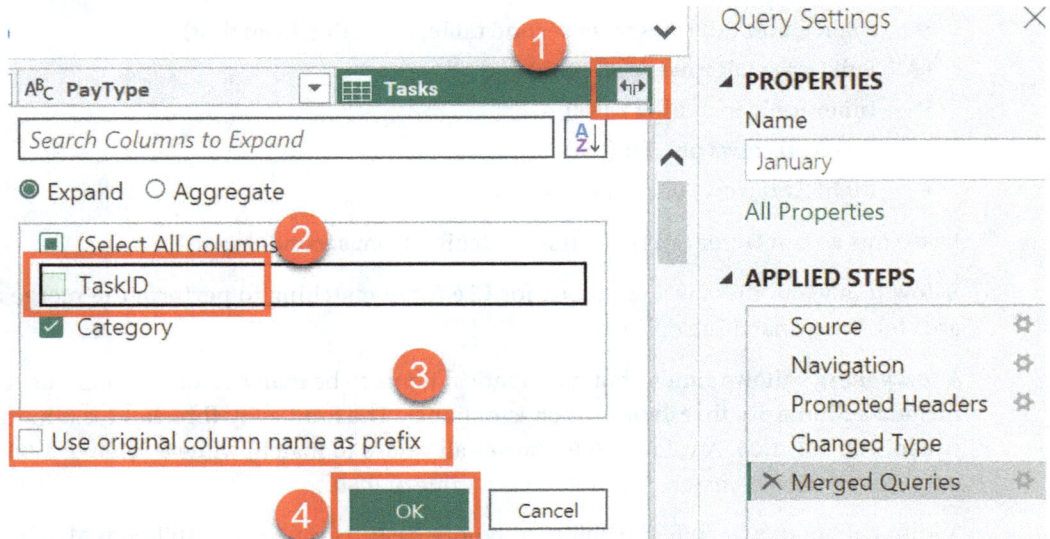

Figure 4.16 – Column expansion dialog

4. Click the **OK** button.

Note that the **Tasks** column changes to **Category** and that our task category values are listed in each row. Also, a step has been added to our query: **Expanded Tasks**.

With that, we have expanded the tables. Next, we will explore disabling queries from being loaded.

Disabling queries from being loaded

Now that we have merged our **Tasks** query with our **January** query, we don't need to load the **Tasks** query into a separate table in our semantic model. However, the **Tasks** query is still required to ingest the data. To disable loading the **Tasks** query, perform these steps:

1. Select the **Tasks** query in the **Queries** pane.
2. Right-click on the **Tasks** query and note that several options are presented.
3. Uncheck **Enable load**.

A warning dialog appears, informing us that this operation will not load data from this query into its own table and remove the table from our semantic model if it exists. This warning dialog is shown in the following screenshot:

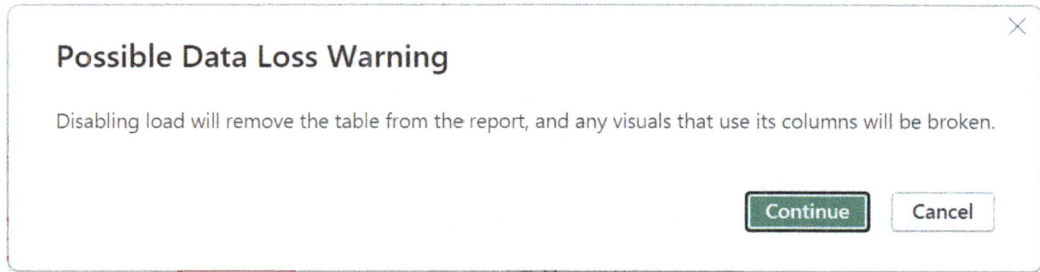

Figure 4.17 – Possible Data Loss Warning dialog

4.   Click the **Continue** button.

Back in **Power Query Editor**, note that the **Tasks** query name is now italicized. By disabling the loading of this query, our **January** query still loads the data using the **Merge queries** operation, but the **Tasks** query itself does not load into a separate table in our semantic model.

Duplicating queries

Now that we have modified our **January** query to merge in our **Tasks** information, we still need to bring in **February** and **March** data. We can do this easily by duplicating our **January** query and then changing the source. To duplicate the **January** query, do the following:

1.   In **Power Query Editor**, select the **January** query in the **Queries** pane.
2.   Right-click the **January** query and choose **Duplicate**. A new query called **January (2)** is created.
3.   Repeat this procedure to create a **January (3)** query.
4.   Click on the **January (2)** query in the **Queries** pane. Note that the **Applied Steps** section is identical to our original **January** query, including the **Merged Queries** and **Expanded Tasks** steps.

Now that we have duplicates of our **January** query, we want to change the data sources for our **January (2)** and **January (3)** queries to load data for February and March instead, respectively.

Changing sources

To change the sources for our queries, perform the following steps:

1.   Click on the **January (2)** query.
2.   In the **APPLIED STEPS** area of the **Query Settings** pane, click the gear icon next to the **Navigation** step.
3.   In the **Navigation** dialog, click **February**.
4.   Click the **OK** button.

Note that two additional steps have been added to our query, just below the **Navigation** step: **Promoted Headers1** and **Changed Type1**. If we click on the **Expanded Tasks** step in our query, we see that an error message is displayed. To fix this, perform the following steps:

1. Use the X icon to delete the **Promoted Headers1** and **Changed Type1** steps of our query.

2. In the **Delete Step** dialog that is displayed, choose the **Delete** button each time. After deleting these steps, all the warnings and errors will be removed.

3. Finally, under the **PROPERTIES** section of the **Query Settings** pane, change the **Name** property of the query from **January (2)** to **February**.

The preceding method is one way of changing the source for a query. But there is another way to change the source: by editing the underlying M code. To use this method, perform the following steps:

1. Click on the **January (3)** query in the **Queries** pane.

2. Click the **Navigation** step.

3. This time, edit the formula bar and replace the word **January** with the word **March** so that the formula for this step appears as follows:

```
= Source{[Item="March",Kind="Sheet"]}[Data]
```

4. Press the *Enter* key to complete the formula. This time, no additional steps are added to our query.

5. Rename the query to **March** using the **Name** setting in the **PROPERTIES** area of the **Query Settings** pane.

With that, we have finished changing the sources for our copied queries. Next, we will append the three queries to a single data table.

Appending queries

We now have three separate tables for hours data reported by employees, one each for **January**, **February**, and **March**. However, what we need is for all of this data to reside in a single table. We can accomplish this by using an **Append Queries** step, as follows:

1. In **Power Query Editor**, start by clicking on the **Home** tab of the Ribbon.

2. In the **Combine** section at the far right of the Ribbon, choose the **Append Queries** dropdown and choose **Append Queries as New**. This displays the **Append** dialog, as shown in the following screenshot:

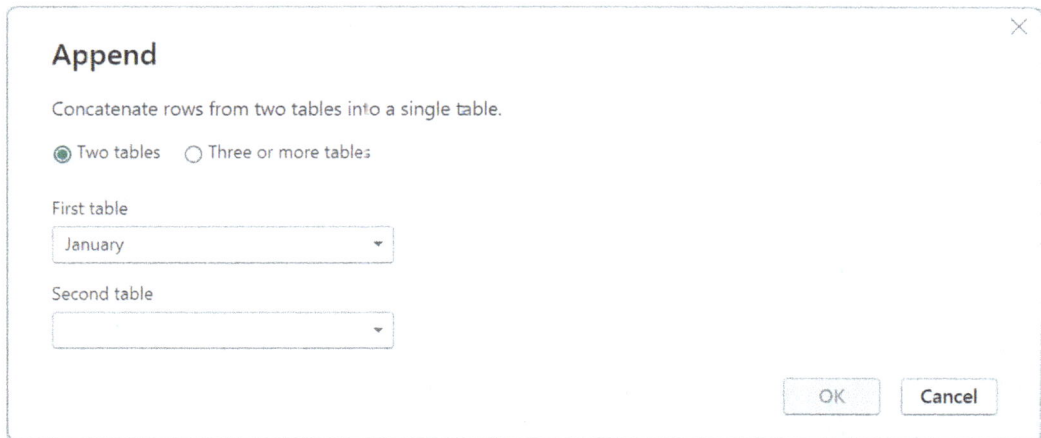

Figure 4.18 – Append dialog

3. In the **Append** dialog, select the radio button for **Three or more tables**.

4. Use the **Add >>** button to add the **January, February,** and **March** queries to **Tables to append**, as shown in the following screenshot. The order does not matter:

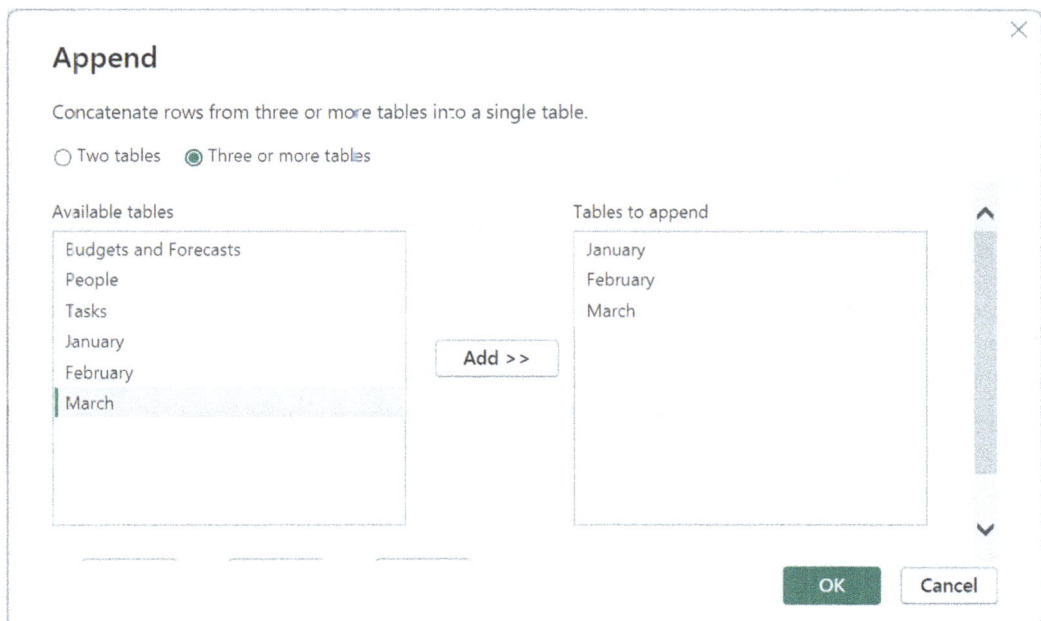

Figure 4.19 – Appending three or more tables

5. When finished, click the **OK** button.

This procedure creates a query called **Append1**. Note that the **Append1** query consists of a single step called **Source**. The formula that's displayed in the **Formula bar** for this step is as follows:

```
= Table.Combine({January, February, March})
```

Again, the order of the queries does not matter. We can now put some finishing touches on this query by performing a few additional steps, as follows:

1.   Select the **Append1** query in the **Queries** pane.

2.   Right-click the query and choose **Rename**. Rename this query **Hours**.

      The **Hours** query now contains all of the information from the **January**, **February**, and **March** queries. This means that we can disable loads on each of these queries. To do this, perform the following steps:

3.   In the **Queries** pane, right-click on each of the **January**, **February**, and **March** queries and uncheck **Enable load**.

4.   A warning dialog may appear when you uncheck **Enable load**. If so, simply click the **Continue** button. The warning dialog appears if the query has already been loaded into the semantic model versus if the query has never been loaded into the semantic model, the warning dialog does not appear.

We have used multiple pages in a single Excel workbook for the **Hours** query. In a production scenario, this would likely involve multiple Excel workbooks, one for each month. In this case, if you have many files in the same format, consider using a **Combine Binaries (Folder)** query: `https://docs.microsoft.com/en-us/power-bi/desktop-combine-binaries`.

Now that we have transformed our data, in the next section, we will verify the data and then load it into Power BI Desktop.

Verifying and loading data

Now that we are finished connecting to and transforming the data, there should be three active queries and four intermediate queries listed in the **Queries** pane.

The active queries include **Budgets and Forecasts**, **People**, and **Hours**. These should not be italicized. These are the active queries that will create tables in the semantic model. There are also four intermediate queries for **Tasks**, **January**, **February**, and **March** that are italicized. These queries will not create tables in the semantic model but are used by the active queries during data load.

The **Queries** pane should look as follows:

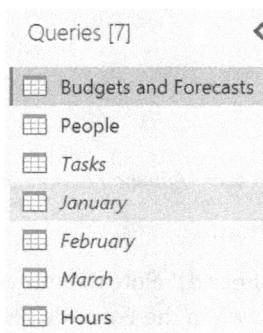

Figure 4.20 – Queries pane

We can view how our sources and queries are related to one another by viewing the query dependencies. We can do this by performing the following steps:

1. In **Power Query Editor**, click on the **View** tab of the Ribbon.

2. Click the **Query Dependencies** button in the **Dependencies** area of the Ribbon. This displays the **Query Dependencies** window, as shown in the following screenshot:

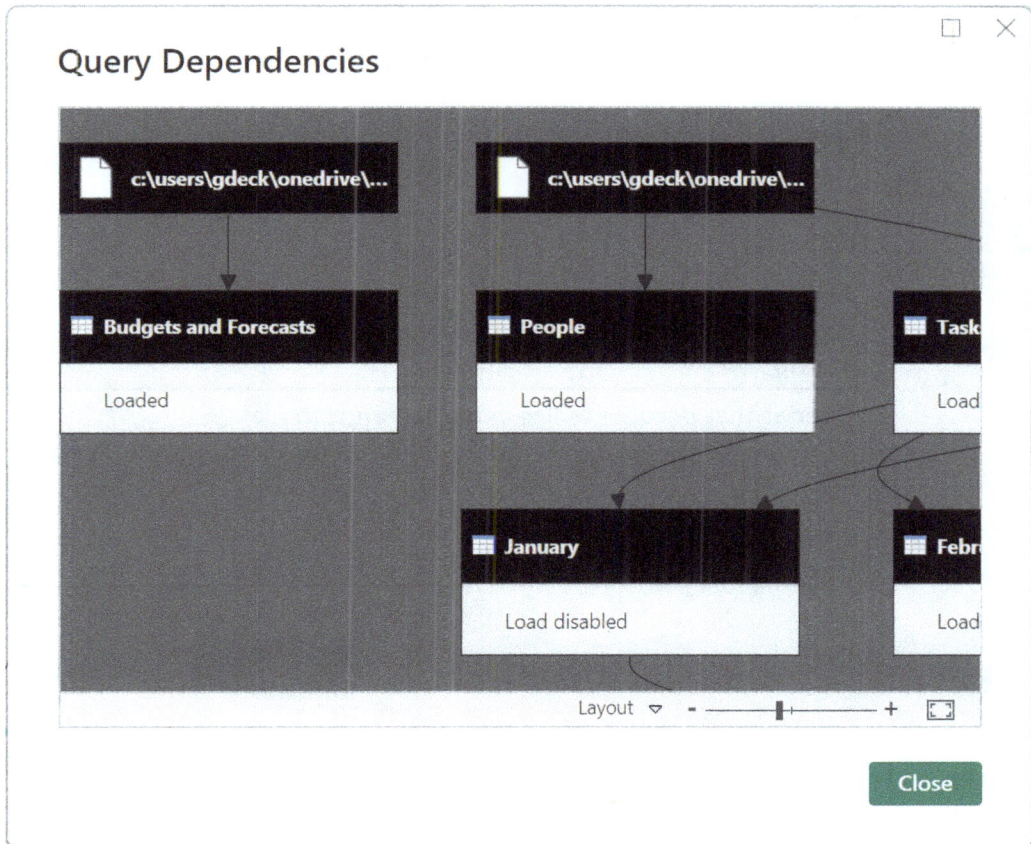

Figure 4.21 – Query Dependencies window

3. Click on the **Tasks** query to highlight the sources and other queries related to the **Tasks** query.

4. When you have finished exploring, click the **Close** button.

The **Query Dependencies** window is useful for understanding how queries are related to one another and how queries are organized.

Organizing queries

Now, let's organize our queries by grouping queries together. In this case, we will create groups for our active and intermediate queries. To do this, perform the following steps:

1. In **Power Query Editor**, in the **Queries** pane, right-click the **Hours** query and select **Move To Group** and then **New Group…**. The **New Group** dialog is displayed, as shown in the following screenshot:

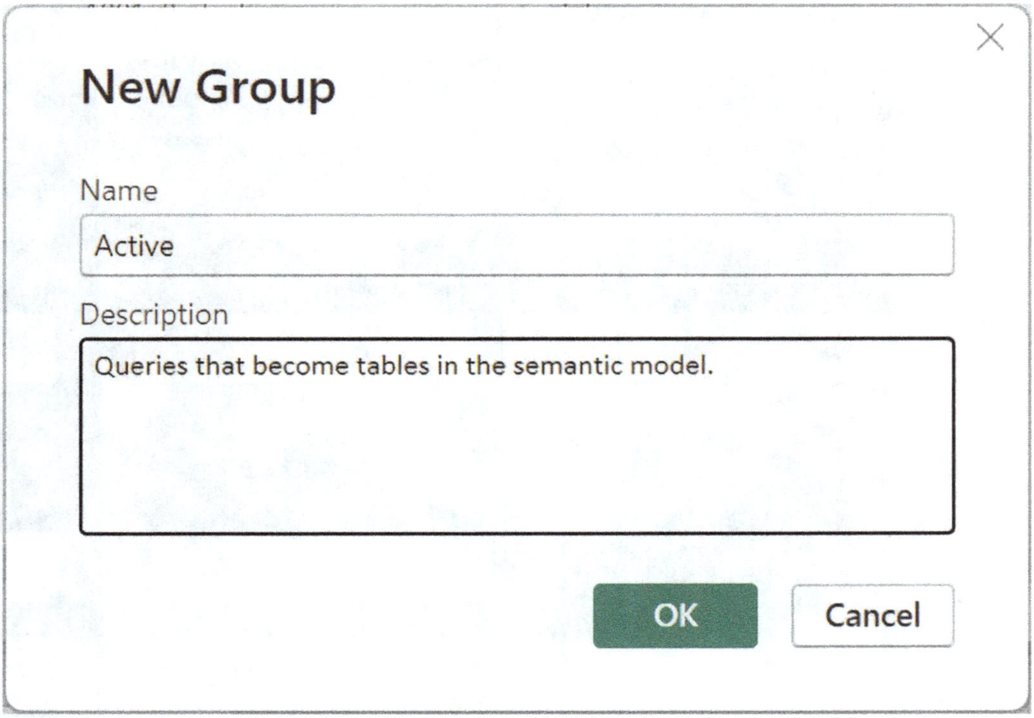

New Group

Name

```
Active
```

Description

```
Queries that become tables in the semantic model.
```

OK   Cancel

Figure 4.22 – New Group dialog

2. For **Name**, enter `Active` and, in the **Description** box, enter `Queries that become tables in the semantic model`.
3. Click the **OK** button. Note that two folders are created: an **Active** folder and an **Other Queries** folder.
4. Select the **Budgets and Forecasts** query and right-click it.
5. Choose **Move To Group** and then **Active**.
6. Repeat this process for the **People** query.

We now have our queries organized into **Active** queries and **Other Queries**. Organizing queries into groups is not required but beneficial, especially as more queries are added to your models.

Checking column quality, distribution, and profiles

As a final check before loading our data, **Power Query Editor** includes powerful tools that allow us to understand the quality of our data. These tools can be found on the **View** tab of the Ribbon, in the **Data Preview** section.

To use these features, perform the following steps:

1. Click on the **Hours** query in the **Active** group in the **Queries** pane.
2. Click the **View** tab of the Ribbon and check the box next to **Column quality** in the **Data Preview** section:

Figure 4.23 – Column quality for the EmployeeID column

As shown in the preceding screenshot, note that under the column headers, information is displayed regarding the quality of the data in each column. This information includes what percentages of row values are **Valid**, **Error**, or **Empty**. Errors can be caused by transformation steps in the query, especially when you're attempting to transform the data type of a column. For example, when changing a column to a **Date** data type, inserting a value of 12/32/2021 into a row creates an error because that value cannot be converted into a date.

3. In the **View** tab of the Ribbon, click the checkbox next to **Column distribution**. This same area now displays additional information regarding the distinct and unique values that were found in the rows of each column. This information is based on the first 1,000 rows returned by the query, therefore, there may be errors in the rest of the data that are not reported here:

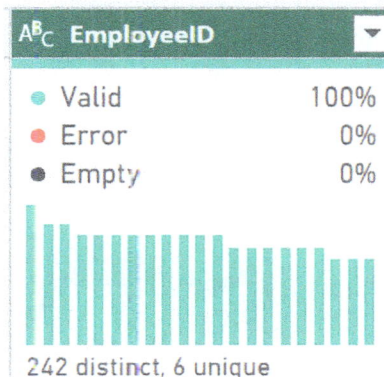

Figure 4.24 – Column distribution for the EmployeeID column

Note that the exact statistics found here may vary, depending on the order in which you appended your queries.

4. Finally, in the **View** tab of the Ribbon, click the checkbox next to **Column profile**. Note that two additional areas are displayed; that is, **Column statistics** and **Value distribution**:

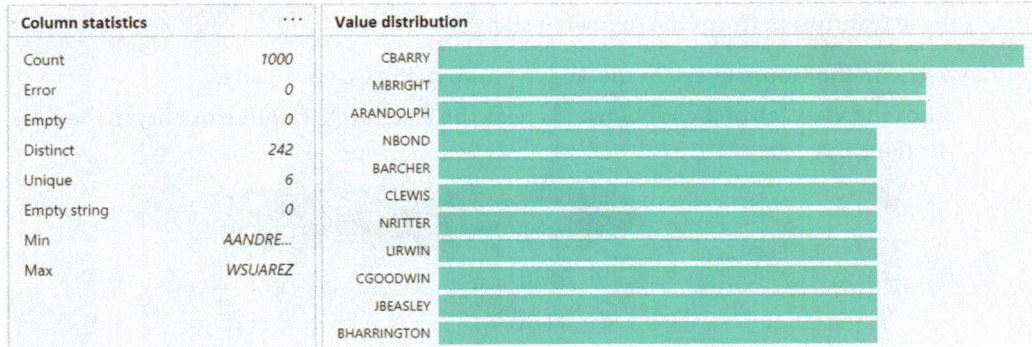

Column statistics	···
Count	1000
Error	0
Empty	0
Distinct	242
Unique	6
Empty string	0
Min	AANDRE...
Max	WSUAREZ

Figure 4.25 – Column profiling

Again, the exact statistics that are displayed will vary, depending on the order in which you appended your queries.

This completes the transformation process for our data. Our final step is to load the data into the semantic model.

Loading the data

Now that we have organized our queries and verified the data's quality, it is time to load the data from the queries into Power BI:

1. In **Power Query Editor**, click the **Home** tab of the Ribbon.
2. On the far left of the Ribbon, click the **Close & Apply** button.

    Clicking this button closes the **Power Query Editor** window and loads the data from the queries into Power BI Desktop. When this is complete, we will have four tables listed in the **Data** pane called **Budgets and Forecasts**, **Calendar**, **Hours**, and **People**, as shown here:

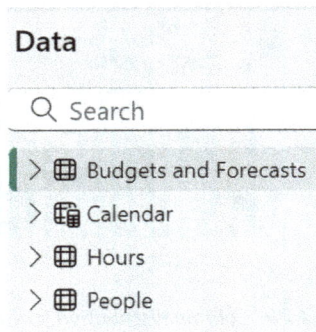

Figure 4.26 – Loaded tables

Now is a good time to save your work by clicking the **Save** icon in the Header or by choosing **File** and then **Save** in the Ribbon.

Summary

In this chapter, we explored Power Query Editor, the powerful sub-application that's used to ingest and shape data through the creation of queries. Queries are a series of recorded steps for connecting to and transforming data. We connected to multiple data files and learned how to clean up and transform the data to support further analysis. Next, we learned about more advanced operations such as how to merge, copy, and append queries. Finally, we explored some built-in data quality and profiling tools that summarize, visualize, and provide statistical information about the data we are ingesting.

In the next chapter, we will build a semantic model by connecting the tables created by these queries to one another via relationships. We will also build the necessary calculations that will complete our model.

Questions

As an activity, try to answer the following questions on your own:

- How many different connectors are available for ingesting data in Power BI?
- What is the powerful sub-application included with Power BI that's used for ingesting and shaping data?
- What is the name of the language that's used behind the scenes when creating queries?
- Turning columns into rows is called what?
- What icons are displayed in the headers of columns for text, whole number, decimal, and date columns?
- Joining two queries together based on columns is called what?
- What are the six different kinds of join operations that can be performed when joining queries?
- Adding one query to another query is called what?

Further reading

For more information on what was covered in this chapter, take a look at the following resources:

- *Data sources in Power BI Desktop*: `https://learn.microsoft.com/en-us/power-bi/connect-data/desktop-data-sources`
- *Excel*: `https://learn.microsoft.com/en-us/power-query/connectors/excel`
- *Query overview in Power BI Desktop*: `https://learn.microsoft.com/en-us/power-bi/transform-model/desktop-query-overview`
- *Perform common query tasks in Power BI Desktop*: `https://learn.microsoft.com/en-us/power-bi/transform-model/desktop-common-query-tasks`

Unlock this book's exclusive benefits now

Scan this QR code or go to packtpub.com/
unlock, then search for this book by name.

Note: Keep your purchase invoice ready before
you start.

5

Creating Semantic Models and Calculations

Even though we have loaded in some data, having raw data loaded into separate tables is not enough to enable analysis and visualization. In order to facilitate analysis and visualization, we must create a semantic model by building relationships between the individual tables, as well as calculations that can aid us in our analysis.

Building a semantic model with relationships between tables and required calculations allows us to create insightful reports for a business or organization. In this chapter, we will learn how to create a semantic model, create **Data Analysis Expressions (DAX)** calculated columns and measures, and understand the techniques for troubleshooting DAX calculations.

The following topics are covered in this chapter:

- Creating a semantic model
- Creating calculations
- Checking and troubleshooting calculations

Technical requirements

The following are needed in order to successfully complete the instructions provided in this chapter:

- An internet connection
- Microsoft Power BI Desktop
- Chapter 5 Start.pbix downloaded from GitHub at https://github.com/PacktPublishing/Learn-Microsoft-Power-BI_3E

Creating a semantic model

The concept of a **semantic model, data model,** or **dataset** is fundamental to Power BI. In short, a semantic model is defined by the tables that are created from Power Query queries, the metadata (data about data) regarding the columns within the tables, and finally, the relationships that are defined between tables. Relationships are needed to connect individual tables to one another. In Power BI, the semantic model is stored within an Analysis Services tabular cube. It is the creation of this semantic model that enables self-service analytics and reporting.

In *Chapter 4, Connecting to and Transforming Data,* we connected to various sources of data (three different Excel files) that in turn created seven different queries, which ultimately resulted in four queries that loaded data tables into our semantic model. We can now stitch those individual tables, along with our previously created data table, into a cohesive semantic model that is used for further analysis.

> If you are continuing from *Chapter 4,* continue to use the same Power BI Desktop file after completing that chapter. Otherwise, download and load Chapter 5 Start.pbix as specified in the *Technical requirements* section of this chapter.

Touring the Model view

So far, we have explored the overall architecture of Power BI Desktop and Power Query Editor. We will now explore the **Model** view within Power BI Desktop. To switch to the **Model** view, click the third icon from the top in the **Views** bar of Power BI Desktop.

The **Model** view is shown in the following screenshot:

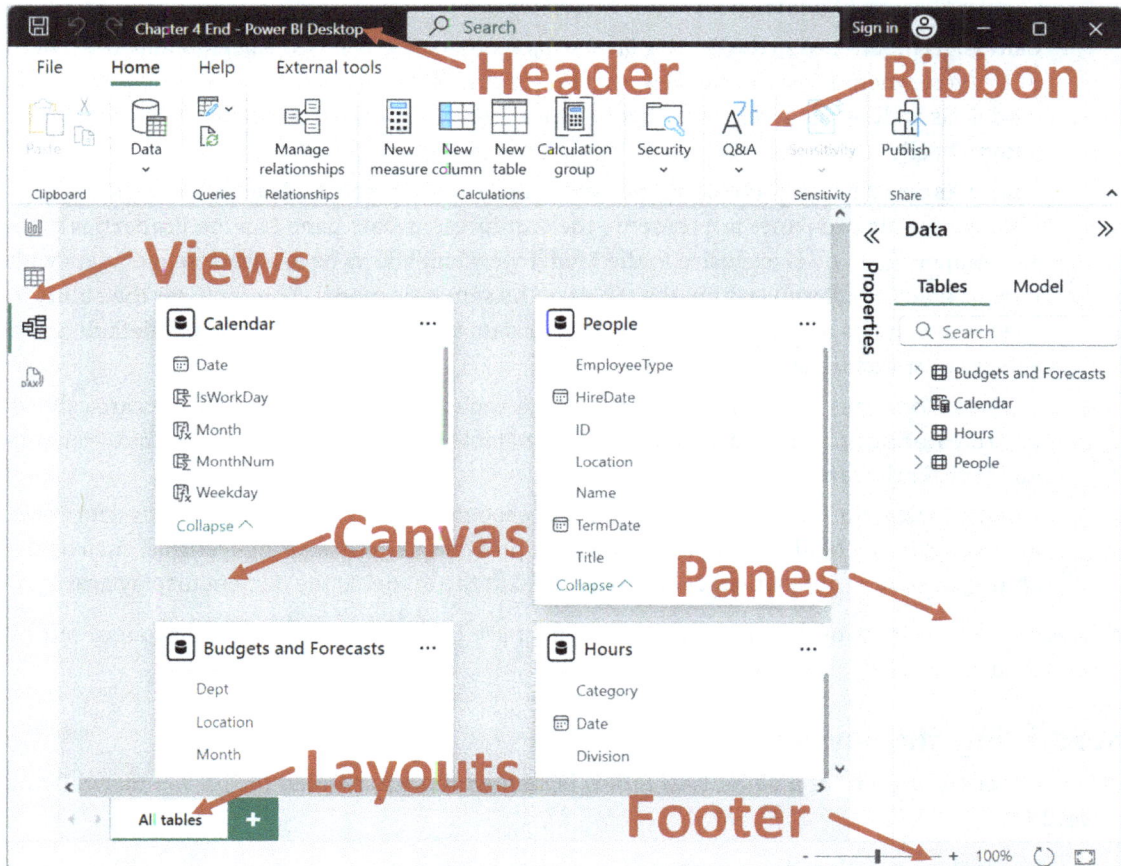

Figure 5.1 – Model view

The **Model** view provides an interface for building our semantic model. It does this by creating relationships between tables, as well as defining metadata for tables and columns. We can even create multiple layouts for our semantic model. The **Model** view interface is similar to other Desktop views, as shown in *Figure 5.1*:

- **Header:** As shown in *Figure 5.1*, the Header area is identical to what was described in the *Touring the Desktop* section of *Chapter 3*, *Up and Running with Power BI Desktop*.

- **Ribbon:** The **Ribbon** is nearly identical to what we described in the *Touring the Desktop* section of *Chapter 3*, *Up and Running with Power BI Desktop*, with the notable exception that only three tabs are available—that is, **File**, **Home**, and **Help**. If third-party extensions are installed, the **External tools** tab is also present.

- **Views:** The **Views** area is identical to what was described in the *Touring the desktop* section of *Chapter 3, Up and Running with Power BI Desktop*.

- **Canvas:** As mentioned in the *Touring the desktop* section of *Chapter 3, Up and Running with Power BI Desktop*, when in the **Model** view, this area displays layouts of tables within the semantic model, as well as their relationships to one another. A default **All tables** layout is created automatically.

- **Panes:** As described in the *Touring the desktop* section of *Chapter 3, Up and Running with Power BI Desktop*, only two panes are present—the omnipresent **Data** pane and the **Properties** pane. The **Properties** pane is exclusive to the **Model** view and allows us to associate metadata with various fields or columns within the tables of the semantic model. This includes the ability to specify synonyms and descriptions, as well as data types, data categories, and default aggregations or summarizations.

- **Layouts:** The **Pages** area from the **Report** view is replaced by **Layouts**. The **Layouts** area allows us to create multiple layouts or views of the data tables within the model, as well as to rename and reorder the layouts.

- **Footer:** As described in the *Touring the desktop* section of *Chapter 3, Up and Running with Power BI Desktop*, in the **Model** view, the **Footer** area provides various viewing controls, such as the ability to zoom in and out, reset the layout, and fit the model to the current display area.

This completes our tour of the **Model** view. Let's next see how we can change the layout of our semantic model.

Modifying the layout

In the **Model** view, we have a default **All tables** layout, which was created for us automatically by Power BI.

To modify this layout, follow these steps:

1. Minimize the **Data** and **Properties** panes by clicking on the arrow icon in the pane headers (>).

2. Click on the tables and drag them closer together. Use the **Fit to screen** icon at the far right of the **Footer** to zoom in on the table layout. You should now be able to clearly see the table names and columns in the tables.

3. Move the **Calendar** and **People** tables next to one another in the top center of the **Canvas** by clicking on and then dragging and dropping. Place the **Budgets and Forecasts** and **Hours** tables underneath these two tables. Use the **Fit to screen** icon in the footer to zoom in on the tables. Note that we cannot see all of the columns in the **Hours** table or the **Calendar** table. A right-hand scroll bar is present on both tables.

4. Use the sizing handle in the bottom-right corner of the table to adjust the size so that we can see all of the columns in the table. When finished, your **Canvas** should look similar to this:

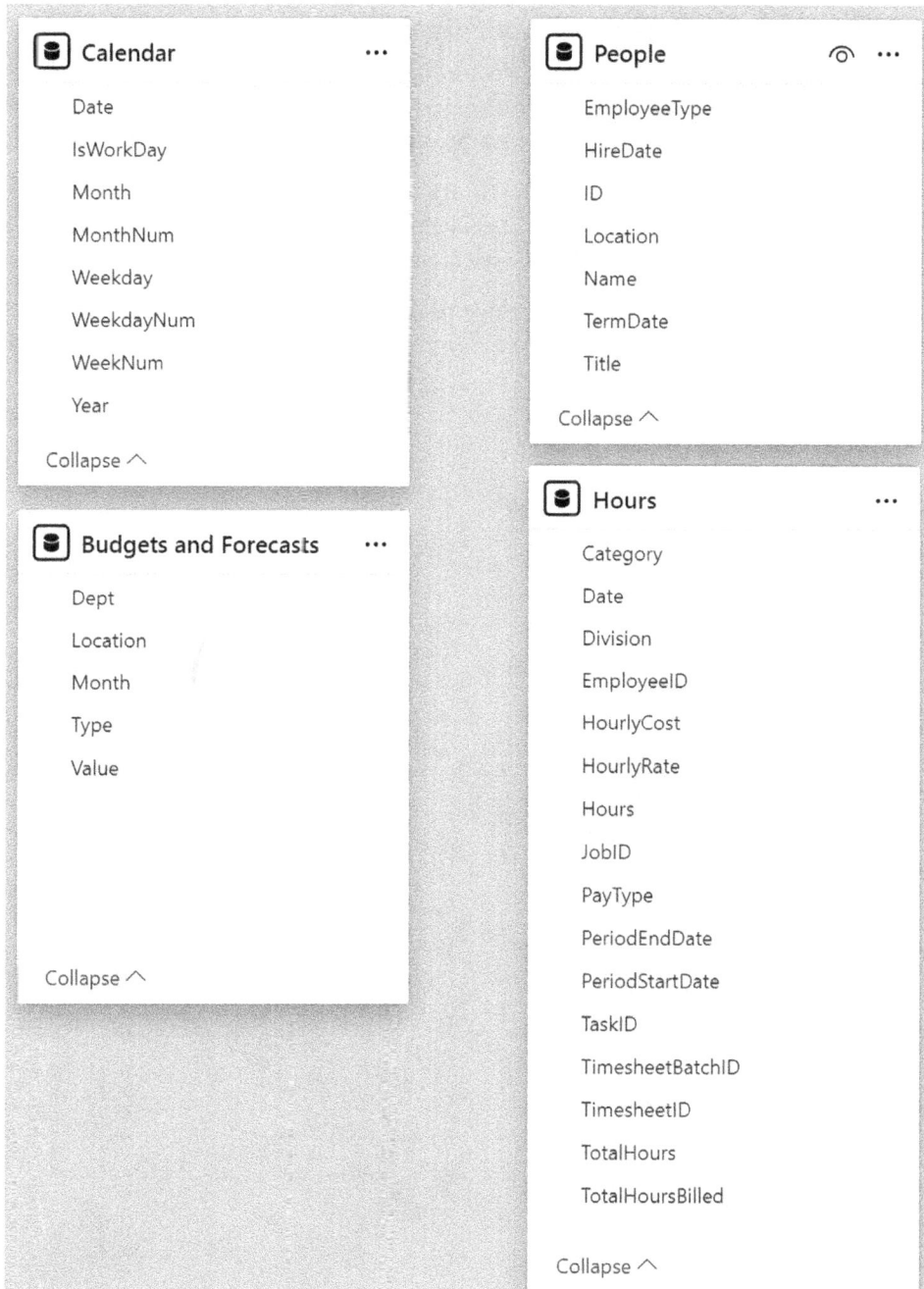

Figure 5.2 – Data tables in the model

Now that we have modified the layout such that we can easily see all tables on the screen, let's continue building our semantic model by defining relationships between the individual tables.

Creating and understanding relationships

Now that we can clearly see our tables and columns, we can create relationships between our tables. Creating relationships between tables allows calculations and aggregations to work across tables so that multiple columns can be used from separate, related tables.

For example, once the **People** table and the **Hours** table are related to one another, we can use the **ID** column from the **People** table and the `TotalHoursBilled` column from the **Hours** table. By doing this, `TotalHoursBilled` aggregates correctly for each user **Identifier** (**ID**) in the **People** table.

To create this relationship between the **People** table and the **Hours** table, click on the **ID** column in the **People** table and drag and drop it onto the `EmployeeID` column in the **Hours** table. The **New Relationship** dialog is displayed, as follows:

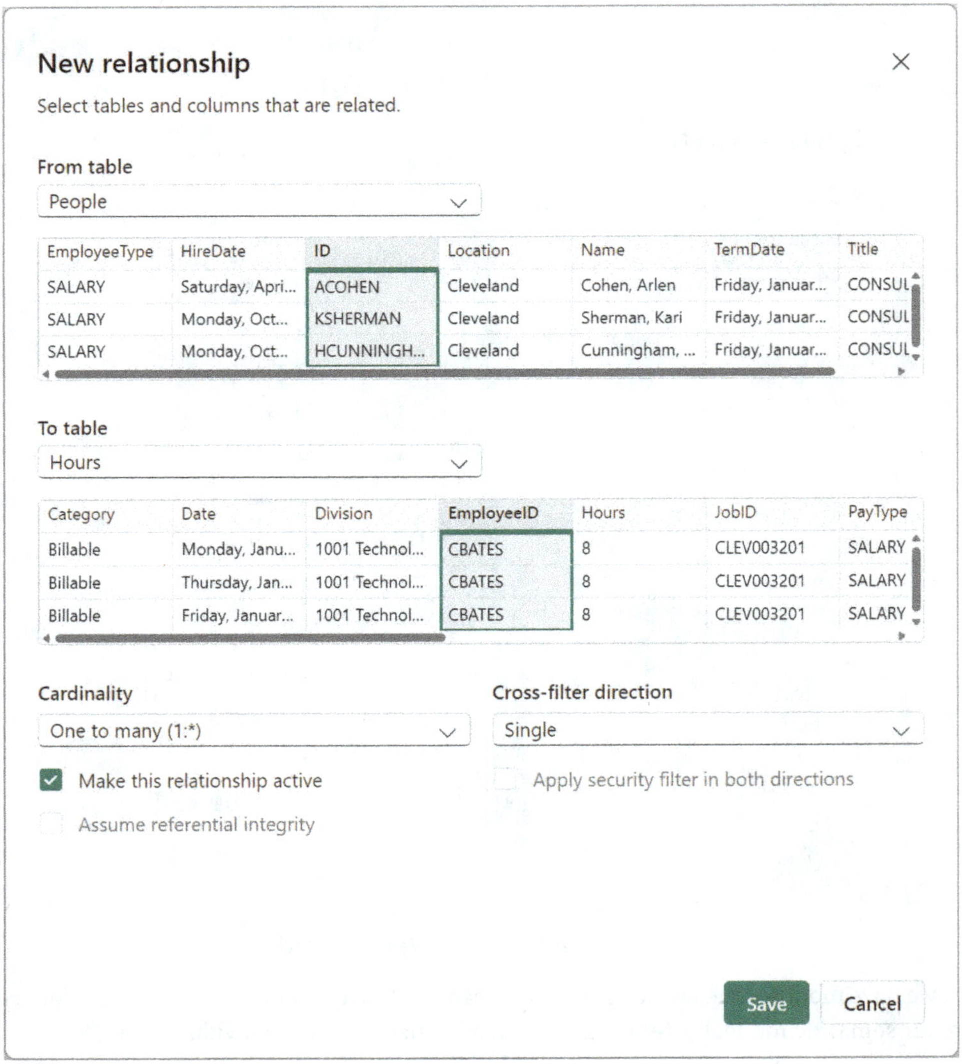

Figure 5.3 – New relationship dialog

Click the **Save** button and note that a line appears on the canvas that connects the **People** table to the **Hours** table. This creates a relationship between the ID column in the **People** table and the EmployeeID column in the **Hours** table.

You can check the columns that are involved in a relationship by hovering your mouse over the relationship line. The line changes slightly and the columns involved in the relationship become shaded.

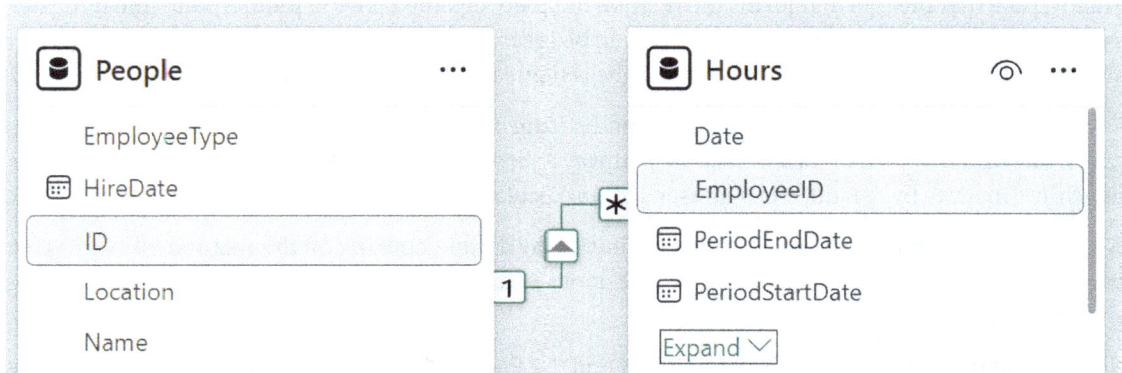

Figure 5.4 – Relationship between two tables

If you notice that ID and EmployeeID are not columns associated with the relationship, hover over the relationship line, right-click it, and choose **Delete**. Then, try again.

Note that the line has 1 next to the **People** table and * next to the **Hours** table. This means that this relationship is **one-to-many** or **many-to-one**.

In other words, there are unique row values in the **People** table that match multiple rows in the **Hours** table. This makes sense since each employee submits an **Hours** report for every day. The designation of 1 (unique) or * (many) defines the cardinality of the relationship between the tables.

There are actually four different cardinalities for relationships in Power BI, as outlined here:

- **One-to-one:** This means that there are unique values in each table.
- **Many-to-one:** This means that there are unique values in one table that match multiple rows in another table.
- **One-to-many:** This means that there are unique values in one table that match multiple rows in another table.
- **Many-to-many:** This means that neither table has unique values for rows. It is generally good practice to avoid these types of relationships because of their complexity and the amount of processing and resources required.

The designation of many-to-one versus one-to-many is simply a matter of which table is defined first within a relationship. In other words, the relationship between our **People** table and **Hours** table could be either many-to-one or one-to-many, depending on which table we defined first in our relationship.

Note that there is also an arrow icon in the middle of the line that points from **People** to **Hours**. This indicates that the **People** table filters the **Hours** table, but not vice versa. This is known as the cross-filter direction. Cross-filter directions can be either **Single** or **Both**, meaning that the filtering occurs only one way or bidirectionally. In simple semantic models, you generally don't have to worry about cross-filter direction, but it can become very important if the complexity of the semantic model increases.

Finally, note that the line that forms the relationship between the tables is solid. A solid line indicates an active relationship. Inactive relationships can be created between tables, and these are represented as a dashed line. In Power BI, there can only be a single active path between tables.

As models become more complex, multiple paths from one table to another can be created. In those cases, one or more of the relationships or pathways become inactive. However, even though the relationship is inactive by default, it can be used within calculations that specify using specific relationships.

We can view and modify the relationship definition by double-clicking on the relationship line. This brings up the **Edit relationship** dialog, which looks nearly identical to the **New relationship** dialog shown in *Figure 5.3*.

Note that since the **Hours** table is defined first and the **People** table is defined second, the **Cardinality** value of our relationship is **Many to one (*:1)**. Also, note that the relationship is active and that the **Cross filter direction** value is **Single**.

In many-to-one and one-to-many relationships, a **Cross filter direction** value of **Single** means that the one side of the relationship filters the many side. Finally, note that the EmployeeID column in the **Hours** table and the ID column in the **People** table are highlighted in gray. This shows us the columns that form a relationship between the two tables. Close the **Edit relationship** dialog by clicking the **Cancel** button.

Now, let's create another relationship, this time between our **Calendar** table and the **Hours** table. To do this, we can use the **Manage relationships** functionality, as follows:

1. Click on the **Home** tab of the ribbon. Then, in the **Relationships** section, choose the **Manage relationships** button. The **Manage relationships** dialog is displayed, as shown in the following screenshot:

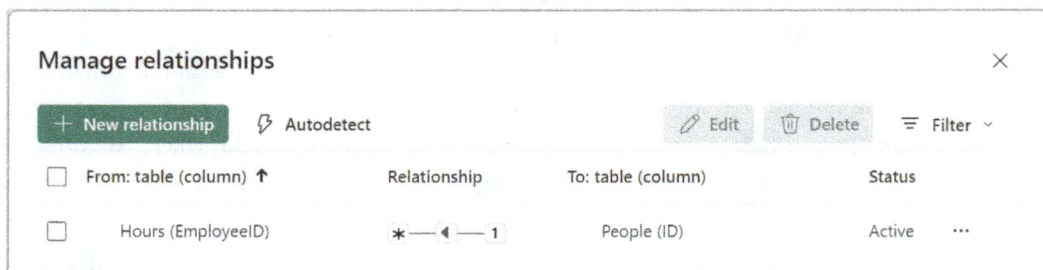

Manage relationships				×
+ New relationship ⌇ Autodetect		⌀ Edit 🗑 Delete ☰ Filter ⌄		
☐ From: table (column) ↑	Relationship	To: table (column)	Status	
☐ Hours (EmployeeID)	*—◀—1	People (ID)	Active	⋯

Figure 5.5 – Manage relationships dialog

Here, we can see our existing **Active** relationship between the **Hours** table and the **People** table, including the columns involved in the relationship in parentheses. From this dialog, we can **Edit** or **Delete** the relationship or have Power BI attempt to **Autodetect** relationships between tables. Power BI can sometimes autodetect relationships between tables based on the column names and row values.

2. Select the **+ New relationship** button. This displays the **New relationship** dialog, as shown in the following screenshot:

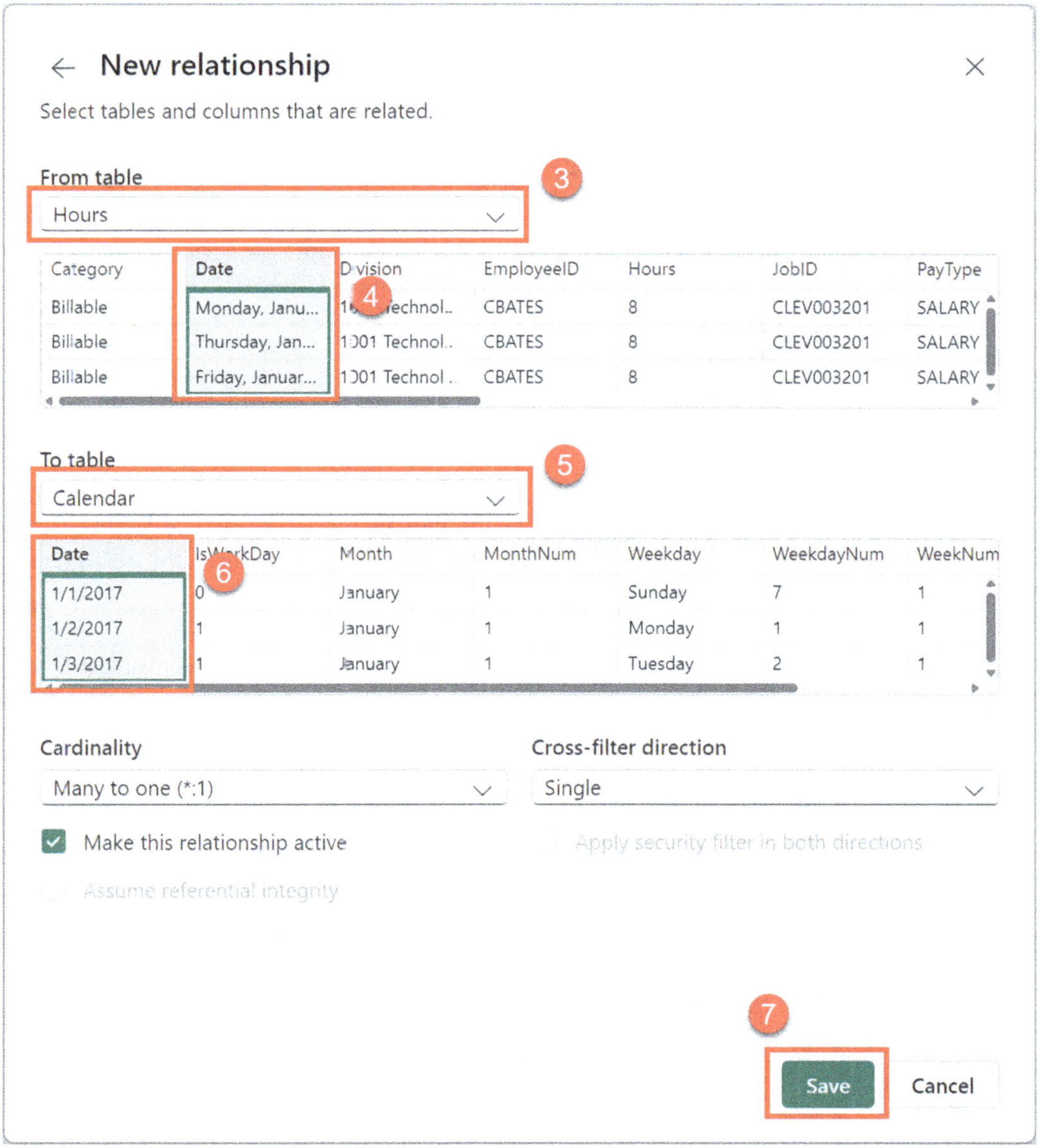

Figure 5.6 – Create relationship dialog

3. In the first drop-down menu, choose the **Hours** table. A preview of the table will be displayed.

4. Click the **Date** column.

5. Choose **Calendar** in the second drop-down menu. A preview of this table is displayed.

6. Choose the **Date** column from this table. Power BI detects the appropriate **Cardinality** and **Cross filter direction** values. Since there are no other relationships between these tables, Power BI checks the **Make this relationship active** checkbox.

7. Click the **Save** button to create this relationship. Note that this new relationship now appears in the **Manage relationships** dialog.

8. Click the **Close** button to close the **Manage relationships** dialog. In the canvas, there will now be a relationship line linking the **Calendar** table to the **Hours** table.

Congratulations—you have successfully linked the three separate tables to create a semantic model! For now, we won't link the **Budgets and Forecasts** table within our semantic model. This is a good time to save your work.

Now that our semantic model is created, let's explore our semantic model a little closer by creating some visuals.

Exploring the semantic model

Before we move on, let's do some exploration of our data in order to understand our data, our semantic model, and how this data can ultimately be viewed by end users. To do this, follow these steps:

1. Start by clicking on the **Report** view in the **Views** bar.

2. At the bottom of the report canvas, click the plus (+) icon next to **Page 1**. This creates a new blank page, **Page 2**. Double-click **Page 2** and rename it **Utilization**, and then press the *Enter* key. This changes the name of the page to **Utilization**.

3. Expand the **People** table in the **Data** pane by clicking the small arrow to the left of the **People** table. Check the box next to the **Name** field. This creates a **Table** visualization on our report canvas with the names of employees. Use the sizing handles for this visualization to resize the table to take up the entire page.

4. Expand the **Hours** table. Make sure that the table visual is selected and then check the box next to the **Hours** field. The number of hours reported by each employee is shown next to their name. This occurs because of the relationship between our **People** table and our **Hours** table. Because these tables are joined by a relationship based on the ID of each employee, we can use fields from both tables in visualizations. Due to this, the rows in the **Hours** tables are automatically filtered based on this relationship.

    Note that when the **Table** visualization is selected, the **Hours** and **People** tables have small checkmarks next to them. This indicates that the visualization contains fields from these tables.

5. We know that the **Category** field of the hours is important, regardless of whether the hours are billable or not. With the table selected, click on the **Matrix** visualization in the **Visualizations** pane. This icon is to the immediate right of the highlighted **Table** visualization. Note that the **Build visual** pane changes from just displaying a **Values** field well to now containing field wells for **Rows, Columns**, and **Values**. Our **Name** field is now under **Rows**, while our **Hours** field is under **Values** and shows up as **Sum of Hours**.

6. From the **Hours** table, click on **Category** and drag and drop this field into the **Columns** field well. We can now see a breakdown of the hours for each employee by category.

It is now obvious that we can calculate a simple version of our utilization metric by taking the number of **Billable** hours for each employee and dividing them by the **Total** number of hours for each employee. Save your work before continuing.

Let's now add to our semantic model by creating some calculations.

Creating calculations

We now have a workable semantic model that contains all of the raw data we will need to report on utilization. Recall that, in the section *Explaining the example scenario* from *Chapter 2, Planning Projects with Power BI*, with the rollout of unlimited **Paid Time Off** (PTO), it is imperative that employee utilization be tracked closely.

Utilization in this context is a calculation that involves the ratio of billable time versus the total time (billable and non-billable). From experience, the organization knows that, in order to remain profitable, the target utilization must be 80%. Therefore, our goal is to create this utilization calculation.

Calculated columns

Calculated columns are additional columns that are created in semantic model tables through the use of the **DAX** formula language. Calculated columns are computed for each row in a table at the time of the calculated column's creation, as well as during the refresh process. Hence, the data refresh process executes the queries defined in **Power Query Editor**. These queries create corresponding tables and/ or refresh the data in the semantic model. Then, Power BI recalculates any DAX calculated columns for each row in the table.

This means that calculated columns are always up to date, based on the latest data that's loaded into the semantic model. This also means that updates to the calculations only occur as part of the data refresh process. In other words, user interactivity, such as interacting with slicers or the application of filters, does not change the calculation of a calculated column for a row.

Understanding the context for calculated columns

Follow these steps to create a calculated column:

1. Click on the **Table** view in the **Views** bar.

2. Click on the **Hours** table in the **Data** pane. From the ribbon, choose the **Table tools** tab and then **New column** in the **Calculations** section. The formula bar is populated by **Column =**, and a new field called **Column** appears in the **Data** pane. Click the formula bar, enter the following formula, and press the *Enter* key:

```
Column = SUM( [Hours] )
```

A quick look at the results shows us that something is clearly not correct. The same number appears for every row in the table! We can see that this is the case by clicking on the drop-down arrow in the header for **Column**. Note that only a single value appears in the filter area—that is, **177997.15**, as shown in the following screenshot:

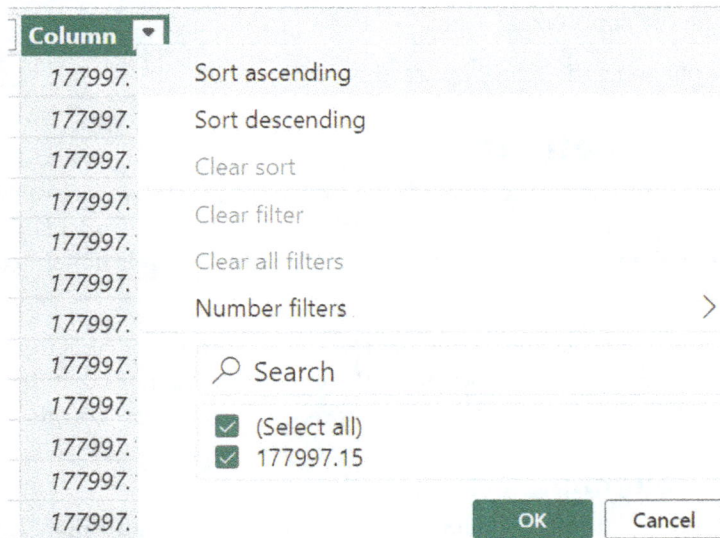

Figure 5.7 – Column filtering dialog

To understand what is going on here, it is important to understand the concept of evaluation context. Evaluation context is the context in which a DAX formula evaluates a calculation.

There are two types of evaluation contexts in DAX: row and filter contexts. Calculated columns, by default, evaluate within what is called row context. Row context means that when a DAX calculation evaluates, it only considers the current row, and nothing else.

However, certain functions, such as SUM, override this default context. In this case, the SUM function is overriding the row context of the calculated column and imposing a filter context of the entire table. Hence, the output for each of the rows is the sum of all of the hours in the entire table. All of the standard aggregation functions—that is, SUM, AVERAGE, MAXIMUM, MINIMUM, COUNT, and so on—exhibit this behavior in calculated columns.

In order to see row context in action, create another new calculated column and enter the following formula:

```
Column 2 = [Hours] / [TotalHours]
```

In this calculation, the TotalHours column contains the total number of hours that were reported during the entire reporting period specified by the PeriodStartDate and PeriodEndDate columns. Because no functions have been used that change the evaluation context from row to filter, only the current row is considered during the evaluation of the formula.

Hence, this formula simply divides the Hours column in each row by the TotalHours column in each row. Now, if we click on the drop-down arrow for **Column 2**, we will see that there are many different values.

Creating calculated columns for utilization

For the purposes of calculating utilization, we want the total hours billed by an employee divided by the total hours reported by an employee.

In order to get the first part of this—that is, the total hours billed—we need to create a third calculated column using the following formula:

```
Column 3 =
    VAR __Employee = [EmployeeID]
    VAR __Table =
        FILTER(
            ALL('Hours'),
            [Category] = "Billable" && [EmployeeID] = __Employee
        )
    VAR __Result = SUMX( __Table, [Hours] )
RETURN
    __Result
```

Use *Shift* + *Enter* and the *Tab* keys to create the correct formatting. *Shift* + *Enter* inserts a new line cr break, while *Tab* indents text that's entered.

Note the use of VAR and RETURN in this formula. VAR and RETURN are paired functions in DAX, which means that once VAR is used, there must be a RETURN statement as well. VAR allows the creation of temporary values or variables within a DAX formula. These variables can be referenced within the rest of the DAX formula. It is a good idea to prefix variable names with a single or double underscore in order to ensure that you do not run afoul of DAX reserved words.

The first variable, __Employee simply returns the value of the EmployeeID column for the current row using row context. The next variable, __Table uses filter context to filter the Hours table to just the rows that have a **Category** of **Billable** and an EmployeeID that equals the __Employee variable.

The FILTER function takes two parameters. The first parameter is the Hours table and the second is the filter clause. The ALL function returns an entire table stripped of all of its rows and filters. Although technically not required in this context, the ALL function ensures that we are operating against all of the rows in the table. The second parameter is the applied filter. This filter actually contains two parts joined by logical AND criteria, &&.

In DAX, && is a logical AND operator, while || is a logical OR operator. Hence, the first part ensures that the table that's returned by the FILTER function only contains rows that have a **Category** value of **Billable**. The second part ensures that the table that's returned by the FILTER function also only contains rows for the employee in the current row.

The final variable, __Result uses the SUMX function. The SUMX function takes two parameters: a table and a numeric column. These parameters are separated by a comma (,). The SUMX function iterates over the specified table and sums the specified column. Hence, in the preceding formula, the first parameter is the __Table variable, while the second parameter is simply the Hours column.

Therefore, the **Column 3** formula can be read in the following way:

1. Save the current row's EmployeeID value into a variable called __Employee.
2. Take the entire table (ALL) and filter this table down so that it only has rows where the **Category** column has a value of **Billable** and rows where the EmployeeID column matches the current row value for EmployeeID.
3. Sum the Hours column for this filtered table and store it in the variable __Result.
4. Use a RETURN statement to return the value of the __Result variable. Each row for an employee should return the exact same numeric value, which is the total hours that were reported by that employee that were **Billable** hours.

For the second part—that is, the total number of hours reported by an employee—we simply need to create another new column with a slight modification to remove the filter for only billable hours. This column can be written with the following formula:

```
Column 4 =
    VAR __Employee = [EmployeeID]
    VAR __Table =
        FILTER(
            ALL('Hours'),
            [EmployeeID] = __Employee
        )
    VAR __Result = SUMX( __Table, [Hours] )
RETURN
    __Result
```

Finally, to create our utilization calculation, create a new calculated column that utilizes row context, as follows:

```
Column 5 = DIVIDE( [Column 3], [Column 4], 0 )
```

While the preceding formula could have been written as Column 5 = [Column 3] / [Column 4], it is a good idea to use the DIVIDE function instead of the divide (/) operator. The DIVIDE function takes a third parameter, which allows for the return of an alternate number or blank value instead of an error in the event of an attempt to divide by zero.

We can now select **Column 5** by clicking on its header and change its formatting to be a percentage. To change the column to a percentage, we need to go to the **Formatting** section of the **Column tools** tab in the ribbon. From here, select the % icon.

Now that we have the desired calculation for utilization in **Column 5**, we can clean up some of our previously created columns. To perform this cleanup, execute the following steps:

1. Right-click the header for **Column** and choose **Delete**.
2. Confirm the deletion of this column in the **Delete column** dialog box by clicking **Yes**.
3. Repeat this procedure for **Column 2**.
4. Double-click the `TotalHours` column and rename this column `TotalHoursInPeriod`.
5. Rename **Column 3** `TotalBillableHours`, **Column 4** `TotalHours`, and **Column 5** `% Utilization`.

We are now ready to use these new calculated columns in visualizations. To use these columns in visuals, do the following:

1. Click on the **Report** view in the **Views** bar.
2. Shrink the existing matrix visualization horizontally to create space on the report canvas.
3. Click on an empty portion of the report canvas to deselect the existing matrix visual. Click **Name** from the **People** table to create a new table visualization in the blank area of the report canvas.
4. With this new table selected, click on **TotalBillableHours**, **TotalHours**, and **% Utilization** from the **Hours** table to add these to this second table visualization.

Note that the values that are returned in this second table are really large! This is because the default aggregation for numeric fields is **Sum**. Since all of the rows for each employee contain our desired number, summing these values doesn't make sense. To correct this, do the following:

1. In the **Values** field well of the **Visualizations** pane, select the drop-down arrow next to **Sum of TotalBillableHours** and choose **Average** instead of **Sum** as the aggregation.
2. Repeat this procedure for **Sum of TotalHours** and **Sum of % Utilization**.

Continuing with the scenario we introduced in *Chapter 2, Planning Projects with Power BI*, Pam is initially happy with the utilization calculation that she has created and decides to share her progress with her colleague, Mike, who is also in the finance department. Mike is impressed by the work so far, but as they start to talk through the utilization calculation, they start to identify some potential problems.

First, the utilization calculation is only taking into account the hours reported, not the potential billable hours. For example, if a user only reports 30 total hours within a particular week when there are really 40 potential billable hours for that week, then the current utilization calculation will be incorrect. Furthermore, managers will likely want to view utilization by particular weeks, months, or a range of dates.

The current utilization calculation is essentially static and based on all of the data within the **Hours** table. Since calculated columns are only calculated at the time of their creation and during data refresh, it is not possible to have the calculations be dynamically based on user interaction with the report.

Clearly, calculated columns are not the way to go. Pam needs to rethink how the utilization calculation occurs within Power BI.

Using calculated columns to resolve data granularity issues

While calculated columns may not be a fit for Pam's utilization calculation, calculated columns are useful in other ways. Recall that we did not create a relationship for the **Budgets and Forecasts** table. The main issue here is that the **Budgets and Forecasts** table has a data **granularity** of month while our **Hours** and **Calendar** tables have a data granularity of day. However, we can resolve this data granularity issue through the use of calculated columns as well as a calculated table.

To resolve the data granularity issue, start by creating the following calculated column in the **Budgets and Forecasts** table:

```
MonthYear = [Month] & "2019"
```

Here, we use DAX's & concatenation operator to concatenate each row's Month column value with the text value 2019 since the **Budgets and Forecasts** data is for the year **2019**. Similarly, we can create a calculated column in the **Calendar** table using the following formula:

```
MonthYear = LEFT([Month], 3) & [Year]
```

Here, we used the LEFT function to get the first three letters of the Month column since the **Calendar** table uses the full name of the month versus an abbreviation, as with the **Budgets and Forecasts** table. In addition, we can simply concatenate this with the **Year** column for each row.

We can now use the MonthYear columns in the **Budgets and Forecasts** table and the **Calendar** table to create a relationship between the tables. However, if we do that, we receive a warning when creating the relationship:

This relationship has cardinality Many-Many. This should only be used if it is expected that neither column (MonthYear and MonthYear) contains unique values, and that the significantly different behavior of Many-many relationships is understood.

Since the **Budgets and Forecasts** table contains a budget for each city for each month, there are multiple rows with duplicate MonthYear values. The same is true for the **Calendar** table. Relationships with **Many-Many** cardinality are allowed in Power BI since the July 2018 release of Power BI Desktop. They can be more complex than other relationship cardinalities, but with caution are acceptable to use.

Click **Save** to create the relationship. Note that the relationship has a **Cardinality** value of **Many-to-many** (*:*) and a filter direction of **Both**.

Now is a good time to save your work before continuing with an exploration of Measures.

Measures

As noted previously, Pam needs to rethink her utilization calculation because calculated columns are static once data is loaded or refreshed. Luckily, there are DAX calculations that are dynamically calculated based on user interaction. These calculations are called **measures**.

Measures can be either implicit or explicit. Implicit measures are created automatically by Power BI whenever a numeric field is used within a visualization and are sometimes created for text fields as well, within certain visualizations in certain circumstances. These implicit measures include the standard aggregations—such as sum, average, maximum, minimum, distinct count, count, standard deviation, variance, and median for numeric fields, and first, last, distinct count, and count for text fields.

We observed implicit measures when we created our table visualizations in the previous section, *Calculated columns*. When we placed the TotalBillableHours, TotalHours, and % Utilization columns in our table, the values were calculated via an implicit Sum measure that we changed to Average.

However, measures can also be explicitly defined by a user to have very specific, and potentially quite complex, calculations. As with calculated columns, writing explicit measures involves DAX code. However, unlike calculated columns, measures are dynamic in their calculation so that measures are calculated just in time, every time there is an interaction with the end user. Measures are not recalculated during data refresh but rather every time a user views or interacts with a report. This makes measures truly dynamic, and hence they are perfect for a scenario where end users may change the evaluation context on the fly.

Understanding the context for measurements

To demonstrate how measures are different compared to calculated columns, execute the following steps:

1. In the **Report** view, create a new page by right-clicking the **Utilization** page tab and selecting **Duplicate**. A new page called **Duplicate of Utilization** is created.

2. Remove the matrix visualization on the left by selecting the matrix and then clicking the *Delete* or *Del* key. This deletes the matrix visual from the canvas. Use the sizing handles to expand the remaining table visualization so that the table visual takes up the entire page.

3. Right-click the **Hours** table in the **Data** pane and choose **New measure**. The formula bar is activated. In the formula bar, enter the following formula:

```
Measure =
    VAR __Table =
        FILTER(
            'Hours',
            'Hours'[Category] = "Billable"
        )
    VAR __Result = SUMX( __Table, [Hours] )
RETURN
    __Result
```

Note that the formula for our Measure is extremely similar to the formula for our TotalBillableHours column from the *Creating calculated columns for utilization* section. The main difference is that we removed the EmployeeId filter clause.

While not strictly required in all circumstances, since measures can exist in any table, it is a good practice to refer to any column within a measure using both the table name and column name. If no table name is specified for a column, the measure assumes the current table, and this can cause problems when moving measures between tables when duplicate column names exist in multiple tables.

It is important to understand that, unlike calculated columns, measures have no implicit row context, only filter context. This means that when measures refer to a column in a table, multiple rows are being referenced. Since there are multiple rows involved when referencing columns in a measure, we must use an explicit aggregation function such as SUM, AVERAGE, MAX, MIN, and so on. This also means that while measures can be used within a calculated column formula, the row context for that calculated column simply becomes the initial filter context for the measure calculation.

We can now use this measure in our visualization by performing the following steps:

1. Place this **Measure** into the table visualization on the **Duplicate of Utilization** page and note that the results displayed are exactly the same numbers that we have for the average of our calculated column, Average of TotalBillableHours.
2. Shrink this table visualization horizontally.
3. Click on a blank area on the canvas and then select the **Slicer** visualization from the **Visualizations** pane.
4. Place **Month** from our **Calendar** table into the field well for our slicer.
5. Select **March** from within the slicer.

By doing this, we can see how calculated columns and measures are different. Observe that the value for the average of TotalBillableHours did not change, but the value for **Measure** is now much lower. If we select **February** or **January** in our slicer, again, the calculated column values do not change, while the values for **Measure** do.

To understand what is happening, it is important to recognize that, while the slicer filters the rows in the **Hours** table for both the calculated column and the measure, since the calculated column has the same value for every row per employee, the average of those values never changes.

With the measure, the summation calculation specified in the formula is performed within the combined context of the visualizations and the DAX formula to create a truly dynamic evaluation context.

This evaluation context actually comes from three different sources, as follows:

• The first source is the table visualization itself. Because we have the **Name** value of the employee in our table, this creates a filter context where **Measure** only considers rows within the **Hours** table that are related to the **Name** value of the employee from the **People** table for each row in the table visualization.

• The second source is the **Slicer** visualization. By selecting a particular **Month** value in the slicer, because of the relationship between the **Calendar** table and the **Hours** table, this adds extra filter context where the measure also only considers rows within the **Hours** table that are related to the **Month** value that's selected from our **Calendar** table in the slicer.

- Finally, our explicit definition of the measure adds a final filter context where the measure only considers rows in the **Hours** table that have a **Category** value of **Billable**.

Creating measures for utilization

Because measures can exist in any table, it is often considered good practice to place measures in their own table for ease of reference and use.

To create such a table, follow these steps:

1. Select the **Home** tab in the ribbon. Then, in the **Data** section, choose **Get data** and then **Blank query**. This opens **Power Query Editor**.
2. Rename **Query1** to **Calculations** in the **Query Settings** pane by editing the **Name** property.
3. Right-click the **Calculations** query in the **Queries** pane and uncheck **Include in report refresh**, as there is no reason to refresh a blank query.
4. From the ribbon, choose **Close & Apply**. Note that a new table, **Calculations**, appears below the **Budgets and Forecasts** table in the **Data** pane.
5. Back in **Power BI Desktop**, in either the **Report** or the **Table** view, select **Measure** in the **Hours** table by clicking on the name **Measure** (not the checkbox).
6. From the **Measure tools** tab of the ribbon, locate the **Home table** field in the **Structure** section of the ribbon. Then, from the drop-down menu, choose **Calculations**. **Measure** disappears from the **Hours** table and now appears in the **Calculations** table, along with a column called **Calculations**.
7. Right-click the **Calculations** column (not the table) and choose **Hide**. Note that the icon for the **Calculations** table changes and the **Calculations** table now appears at the top of the **Data** pane.
8. Right-click **Measure** in the **Calculations** table and **Rename** this measure **Total Billable Hours**.

Because measures can exist in any table, the name of a measure should not be the same as the name of any table, column, or any other measure within a semantic model.

There are many different schemes for helping to ensure uniqueness. A common practice is to prefix the names of measures with something such as an underscore (_), m, or #, in order to help guarantee uniqueness and denote that this is a measure. Some users utilize multiple measure prefixes, such as # to denote numeric measures, $ to denote measures formatted as currency, % for percentages, and @ for text. Prefixing measure names with special characters also has the benefit of keeping these measures at the top of tables. However, there are other schools of thought that specify that measure names should be intuitive to the end user, and this is the approach we use here.

The **Total Billable Hours** measure contains the calculation that we need for the numerator in our utilization calculation. Now, we need to create a measure for the denominator of our utilization calculation—that is, the total potential billable hours available within a period. We know that we cannot simply use the total hours reported, though, and that we must calculate the number of potential billable hours for any period of time in a different way.

To do this, we must have an independent way of calculating the number of hours and thus utilization within any arbitrary period of days. Follow these steps to do so:

1. While in the **Report** or **Table** view, right-click the **Calendar** table in the **Data** pane and choose **New column**. In the formula bar, enter the following formula:

    ```
    WorkHours = IF( [IsWorkDay], 8, 0 )
    ```

    Recall that we previously created a calculated column called `IsWorkDay` that returned 1 for Monday, Tuesday, Wednesday, Thursday, and Friday and 0 for Saturday and Sunday. Hence, this calculated column uses row context to return either 8 or 0 for each row in the **Calendar** table.

2. Right-click the **Calculations** table, choose **New measure**, and enter the following formula in the formula bar:

    ```
    Total Hours = SUM( 'Calendar'[WorkHours] )
    ```

    As mentioned in the *Understanding the context for measures* section, any reference to a column within a measure formula must be done within the explicit context of an aggregating function. In this case, we use the SUM function since we want the total potential number of billable hours within a period of days.

3. Right-click the **Calculations** table again, select **New measure**, and enter the following formula in the formula bar:

    ```
    % Utilization =
        DIVIDE(
            [Total Billable Hours],
            [Total Hours],
            0
        )
    ```

    Note that, when referencing other measures within a measure formula, we don't need to use any kind of aggregation function because measures, by definition, must include an aggregation.

4. While in the **Report** view, uncheck any selected values in the **Month** slicer.

5. Select the % **Utilization** measure in the **Data** pane (not the checkmark box).

6. From the **Measure tools** tab in the ribbon, select the % button from the **Formatting** section to format the % **Utilization** measure as a percentage.

7. Select the table visualization and add the **Total Hours** and % **Utilization** measures to the table. Observe that the table visualization exhibits some strange behavior. Many additional rows are displayed in the table; **Total Hours** for every row is very large and the same for each row—that is, 6,256. Considering that there are generally only about 2,080 working hours in a year, something is definitely wrong.

The issue here comes back to the filter context for our **Total Hours** measure. Our measure formula only takes into account the WorkHours column in our **Calendar** table. However, because the relationship between our **Calendar** table and our **Hours** table is unidirectional from **Calendar** to **Hours**, the **Calendar** table is not being filtered based on the employee. Hence, all of the rows within the **Calendar** table are being included in the calculation for **Total Hours**, and hence, we are returning a result even when the employee is a past employee who has not reported hours within our **Hours** table. In addition, even for employees who do have reported hours within the **Hours** table, all of the rows within the **Calendar** table are being included, versus just those dates that are being included in our **Hours** table for each employee.

Luckily, there is a simple fix for this. Follow these steps:

1. While in the **Report** view, select the **Modeling** tab of the ribbon and then choose **Manage Relationships** in the **Relationships** section.
2. Select the **Hours (Date)** to **Calendar (Date)** relationship by clicking the checkbox.
3. Click the **Edit** button.
4. Locate the **Cross-filter direction** option in the **Edit relationship** dialog and change this from **Single** to **Both**.
5. Finally, click the **Save** button and then the **Close** button.

The table visualization refreshes and any past employees disappear from the visualization. The **Total Hours** measure is now much closer to the values found in the Average of TotalHours column, although there are differences, and those differences are expected. Finally, % **Utilization** also generally looks correct, with most values being 104% or lower.

By changing the **Cross filter direction** setting to **Both** in our relationship, we added context to the calculation of our **Total Hours** measure so that, within the context of our table visual, the **Calendar** table becomes filtered based on the rows in the **Hours** table for each employee.

Looking more closely at our table visualization, we can see that the **Total** line for the table has a massive number for utilization: **2389.55%**. Obviously, this is not correct—well, yes and no. The calculation is correct, but not what is expected or desired. Note that the **Total** value for **Total Billable Hours** is **149,490.15**, and that the **Total** value for **Total Hours** is **6256**. Dividing these two numbers does indeed return **2389.55%**.

However, what we would expect is that the number for **Total Billable Hours** and **Total Hours** would simply be the sum of all of the numbers in our table. Unfortunately, the **Total** lines in the table and matrix visualizations do not work that way. The problem, again, is the filter context. The **Total** line in any table or matrix visualization is always evaluated in the context of ALL, and this results in what is commonly called the **measure totals problem**.

In the case of the **Total Hours** measure, the ALL context simply returns the sum of the WorkHours column from all of the rows from our **Calendar** table, resulting in **6256**. However, we actually need this number to be the sum of all of the available work hours, iterating over the available work hours of every employee.

This problem does not exist in the other core visuals within Power BI, and despite repeated and concerted attempts by the community to provide a toggle or other easy means to change total behavior in table and matrix visuals, Microsoft has thus far refused to address the issue in any meaningful way.

Luckily, there is a standard technique for solving the measure totals problem, although it does add some complexity to our DAX code. To implement this technique, follow these steps:

1. Rename the **Total Hours** measure to **Total Hours by Employee**.

2. Create a new **Total Hours** measure using the following formula:

    ```
    Total Hours =
        VAR __Table =
            SUMMARIZE(
                'People', 'People'[Name],
                "__Hours", [Total Hours by Employee]
            )
        VAR __Result = SUMX( __Table, [__Hours] )
    RETURN
        __Result
    ```

3. Since we renamed our original **Total Hours** measure to **Total Hours by Employee**, Power BI also modified the **% Utilization** measure to reflect this name change. Therefore, edit the **% Utilization** measure to again be the original formula, as follows:

    ```
    % Utilization =
        DIVIDE(
            [Total Billable Hours],
            [Total Hours],
            0
        )
    ```

4. Add the new **Total Hours** measure to the table visualization.

The formula creates a calculated table variable (__Table) within the DAX formula using SUMMARIZE, which emulates exactly how our information is displayed within our table visual. The SUMMARIZE function takes the name of a table, which in this case is **People**, the name of one or more columns within that table, which in this case is People[Name], and then allows for the creation of additional columns, in this case, __Hours, with some kind of aggregation being performed, which in this case is simply a reference to our **Total Hours by Employee** measure.

You can think of the SUMMARIZE function as a way to group rows within a table and apply aggregations to those groups of rows. This calculated table is then used as input to the SUMX function. By using this, we simply sum the hours in our __Hours column.

It is considered good practice to prefix things such as calculated tables, column names, and variables created within DAX formulas with something such as an underscore, a double underscore, or other identifying character or characters. This assists with readability and can reduce confusion when referring to objects within DAX formulas.

The net effect of this calculation is that for individual employee rows, the SUMMARIZE function returns a single row, the current row of the table visual. However, for the **Total** row, the SUMMARIZE function returns all of the rows of the table visual with their summarized **Total Hours by Employee** measure.

We can now observe that our **Total** line in our table visualization now appears to be correct, with a value for **Total Hours** of **178344** and a total value for **% Utilization** of **83.82%**. It should be noted that the **Total Billable Hours** measure does not exhibit the measure totals problem, while **Total Hours by Employee** does.

Hence, you may be curious about what determines whether a measure will exhibit this problem or not. Unfortunately, there is no straightforward answer to this question. The basic issue is that the measures in the **Total** rows get evaluated in the context of all the rows in the current context. In other words, the measure is being aggregated for all of the rows in the current context for the total lines, not for each row individually in the current context, and then being aggregated. Regardless, it is safe to assume that any measure could potentially exhibit the measure totals problem, and so you should always be diligent in checking the **Total** line when dealing with measures in table and matrix visualizations.

Looking more closely at our table visualization, we can observe that % **Utilization** is blank for some employees. The easiest way to see this is to click twice on the % **Utilization** column header in the table visualization in order to sort the table in an ascending fashion. This can also be done by selecting the table visualization and then clicking on the ellipses (...) in the upper-right or lower-right of the table visualization and choosing **Sort ascending**.

Blank values for % **Utilization** occur for employees who have no billable hours. We don't want % **Utilization** to be blank, but rather to display **0.00%** in such cases. Again, there is an easy fix for this. In the **Data** pane, select the % **Utilization** measure in the **Calculations** table by clicking anywhere on the measure name except the checkbox. The formula bar is displayed and lists the formula for the measure.

Edit this formula to the following:

```
% Utilization =
    VAR __Utilization =
        DIVIDE(
            [Total Billable Hours],
            [Total Hours],
            0
        )
    VAR __Result = __Utilization + 0
RETURN
    __Result
```

This edit to our % **Utilization** measure solves the issue of having blanks shown for % Utilization for employee rows. Unfortunately, this has also reintroduced the issue of having past employees show up in our table visualization.

One final tweak to our % Utilization measure fixes this, as illustrated in the following code snippet:

```
% Utilization =
    VAR __Utilization =
        DIVIDE(
            [Total Billable Hours],
            [Total Hours],
            0
        )
    VAR __Days = COUNTROWS( 'Hours' )
    VAR __Result =
        IF(
            ISBLANK( __Days ),
            BLANK(),
            __Utilization + 0
        )
RETURN
    __Result
```

Our % Utilization measure now adds an additional variable, __Days. The calculation for the __Days variable simply calculates the number of rows in the **Hours** table. Hence, for employees with no rows in the **Hours** table, the value for __Days is nothing (BLANK). The RETURN statement, therefore, checks whether __Days is blank (ISBLANK), and if so, returns nothing (BLANK). Otherwise, the __Utilization variable is returned, plus 0.

Now that we have our calculations, we need to check our calculations and troubleshoot any issues we find.

Using visual calculations

Visual calculations are a recent feature introduced into Power BI Desktop that attempts to make certain types of calculations easier for end users. To see how visual calculations work, perform the following steps:

1. Save your work.
2. Go to **File | Options and settings | Options**.
3. Click on **Preview features**.
4. Scroll down, click the box next to **Visual calculations,** and then click the **OK** button.
5. Restarting Power BI Desktop is required to activate preview features. Close Power BI Desktop and then reopen Power BI Desktop with your file.
6. On the **Duplicate of Utilization** page, select the table visual and then, in the ribbon of the **Home** tab, in the **Calculations** section, choose **New visual calculation**.
7. In the formula bar, create the following formula:

```
Calculation = EXPANDALL( SUM( [Total Hours by Employee] ), ROWS )
```

You can see in the preview for the table visual that the **Total** row for **Calculation** displays the correct value of **177,665.00** instead of the incorrect value for **Total Hours by Employee of 472**.

Thus, in theory, instead of adding additional DAX to the **Total Hours** measure that corrected the **Total** row, we could instead have used the original version and then added a similar visual calculation to arrive at the correct value. However, at that point, all subsequent calculations involving the **Total Hours** measure would instead need to be additional visual calculations based upon the visual calculation for **Total Hours**.

In addition, there are other drawbacks to visual calculations. One, the original columns that visual calculations are based on must remain in the visual. You can hide these columns, but they must be present in the visual in order for visual calculations to work. In addition, visual calculations are not reusable between visualizations, as is the case with measures, and instead must be recreated. Finally, visual calculations are still in preview and thus cannot be recommended for production reports. Even if visual calculations become generally available, there is much debate within the Power BI community regarding the efficacy of visual calculations, governance, maintainability, and other concerns.

Use the **Back to report** button in the upper-left corner to return to the **Report** view before proceeding to the next section, where we will do some checking and troubleshooting.

Checking and troubleshooting calculations

Now that we have our calculations seemingly correct, it is important to take a closer look so that we can discover any anomalies or instances that might throw off the calculations.

Boundary cases

A common method of performing checks is to look at boundary cases, or the maximums and minimums of our calculations. To do this, follow these steps:

1. Start by clicking on the % **Utilization** column header in our table visualization. This sorts the table in descending fashion, where our highest % **Utilization** number is at the top of the list. We can see what some anomalies of very high utilization might be, such as % **Utilization** at the top, which is **175.00%** for **Cole, Camille**.

2. To check this number, click on the **Table** view in the **Views** bar.

3. Click on the **Hours** table in the **Data** pane.

4. Find the EmployeeID field in the **Hours** table and click on the drop-down arrow in the column header.

5. Uncheck the **(Select all)** checkbox to unselect all of the values, and then scroll down and check the box next to **CCOLE**. You could also search for the value.

6. Click the **OK** button. We can see that 4 hours were billed on a **Sunday** and another 10 hours on a **Friday**. Therefore, this calculation is correct since there are only 8 potential billable hours between the two days, since Sundays are considered non-working days.

7. We can check the next highest case, which is for **Perkins, Caitlen,** by using the same process and deselecting **CCOLE** and selecting **CPERKINS.** Again, we can see multiple billable hours on Saturdays and Sundays. Hence, it appears that the maximums for our **% Utilization** calculation are actually correct.

8. Clicking back on the **Report** view, notice that while we have filtered the table in the **Table** view, we can still see all of the data in the **Report** view. This is because filtering data in the **Table** view does not impact the **Report** view in any way. The filtering and sorting capabilities that are provided in the **Table** view are solely for the report author to use when verifying the data.

9. Now, click the header for **% Utilization** in the **Table** visualization again. The data is now sorted in ascending order, with the lowest values for **% Utilization** shown at the top.

10. There are numerous instances of **0.00%** values for cases where **Total Billable Hours** is blank. However, there is one case for **Irwin, Rachelle** that shows **0.00%** for **% Utilization** but **Total Billable Hours** as **6.00**. We can filter for **RIRWIN** in the **Table** view of the **Hours** table by using the **Search** box just above the list of values that can be filtered.

11. We can see that the 6 hours were billed on a **Sunday.** Hence, our calculation is technically correct, and it is a good thing that we used the `DIVIDE` function with its ability to return a value in the case of a divide-by-zero!

12. Back in the **Report** view and continuing down the list of rows in the table visualization, the next potential anomaly is **Beasley, Joni,** who has only **2 Total Billable Hours** entries but **368 Total Hours** entries and thus a **0.54%** utilization. Again, by checking the **Table** view for **JBEASLEY,** we can see in the footer that there are **71** rows of reported hours, but that all of these rows except one are to a **Category** value other than **Billable.** A similar circumstance exists for **BMACDONALD** and **SHESTER.**

With these checks now complete, we can reasonably conclude that, overall, our calculation is returning valid results.

Slicing

Another common technique that's used for troubleshooting calculations is slicing. To use this technique, you need to create multiple slicers to slice the data based on different criteria and then check the results and boundary cases for the sliced data. To employ this technique, follow these steps:

1. In the **Report** view, click **March** on the **Month** slicer. Here, we can see the curious case of **Wagner, Letitia.** This employee has an **Average of TotalBillableHours** entry of **224,** but a **% Utilization** entry of **0.00%.**

2. Check the data in the **Table** view by filtering the **Hours** table for **LWAGNER** and then right-clicking and sorting the **Date** column by **Sort descending.** We can see that **LWAGNER** had no billable hours in **March** but did have billable hours in **February** and **January,** hence explaining what we are seeing.

3. With **March** still selected, sort **% Utilization** by descending and observe **Cox, Rex** at the top of the list with **151.17%** for **% Utilization.** Checking the data for **RCOX,** we can see that this individual was regularly billing more than 8 hours per day in March and even billed on a Saturday, hence explaining the high utilization.

4. Back on the **Report** view, resize the **Month** slicer if necessary to free up space on the canvas.

5. Click on a blank area of the canvas, select the **Slicer** visualization, and this time, place the EmployeeType column from the **People** table into the slicer. This displays a slicer that includes **ADMINISTRATION, ASSOCIATE, CONSULTANT, HOURLY, SALARY**, and **SUB-CONTRACTOR**.

Continuing with the scenario we introduced in *Chapter 2*, *Planning Projects with Power BI*, Pam immediately notices a problem. **ADMINISTRATION, ASSOCIATE**, and **CONSULTANT** should not appear in the list. **ADMINISTRATION** is a designation for internal employees such as herself who never bill, while **ASSOCIATE** and **CONSULTANT** are old designations for employees that have not been used in years. Pam doesn't want these employees to be considered on any of the pages of the report. To fix this, follow these steps:

1. In the **Report** view, expand the **Filters** pane.

2. Drag EmployeeType from the **People** table to the **Filters on all pages** area of the report. An EmployeeType filter will be created.

3. In this filter, select only **HOURLY, SALARY**, and **SUB-CONTRACTOR**.

4. Now, select **HOURLY** in the slicer. Again, Pam notices an immediate issue. Some of the values for % **Utilization** displayed are not 100.00%. Because **HOURLY** and **SUB-CONTRACTOR** employees are paid hourly, their % **Utilization** values should always be 100.00% unless they have not billed any hours. This is because **HOURLY** and **SUB-CONTRACTOR** employees are only paid for the time they work. This can be fixed by tweaking our **Total Hours** measure, as follows:

```
Total Hours =
    VAR __Table =
        SUMMARIZE(
            'People', 'People'[Name],
            "__Hours", [Total Hours by Employee]
        )
    VAR __Result =
        SWITCH( MAX( 'People'[EmployeeType] ),
            "HOURLY", [Total Billable Hours],
            "SUB-CONTRACTOR", [Total Billable Hours],
            "SALARY", SUMX( __Table, [__Hours] )
        )
RETURN
    __Result
```

Here, we have used the SWITCH function to modify the calculation of the __Result variable. The first parameter in a basic SWITCH function is an expression that returns a value. The SWITCH statement can then have as many conditions and return value pairs as necessary before ending in a return value that is essentially none of the aforementioned.

To see how this works, take a look at the first parameter, `MAX( 'People'[EmployeeType] )`. This returns the `EmployeeType` value of the current row of the visualization. Remember that, within measures, we must use an aggregation function when referring to columns. Hence, we could have also used `MIN` instead of `MAX` since our expectation is that each employee is listed individually on a row of our visualization. The next line checks to see whether the value that's returned by this expression is **HOURLY** and, if so, simply returns the measure for **Total Billable Hours**.

The next line checks whether the value that's returned is **SUB-CONTRACTOR** and, if so, also returns **Total Billable Hours**. The next line under that checks to see whether the value that's returned is **SALARY**; if so, our original code is used. Finally, the last condition is the default condition if no other conditions are met. In our case, we did not specify a default condition, and thus the implicit default condition returns nothing (**BLANK**) in the event that none of the other conditions are met.

Now, when we select either **HOURLY** or **SUB-CONTRACTOR** in our `EmployeeType` slicer and sort our table visualization in either direction according to **% Utilization**, we can see that all of the rows are **100.00%** except for a few **HOURLY** employees that display **0.00%**. These **HOURLY** employees are essentially unutilized, which is useful information to know. In addition, we can see that our **Total** line is also **100.00%** for both **HOURLY** and **SUB-CONTRACTOR** employees, which is as expected.

Grouping

As a final check, Pam wants to make sure that the **% Utilization** values roll up by **Division**. To do this, follow these steps:

1. Clear all slicer selections.

2. Select a blank area of the canvas and then, from the **Hours** table, select **Division**. This creates a new table with the different divisions listed, such as **1001 Technology**, **2001 Accounting**, and so on.

3. With this new table visual selected, add **% Utilization** to the **Columns** field well.

   Again, it is easy to see that there is some kind of issue. **% Utilization** for each **Division** is either **100.00%** or **0.00%**, and the **Total** value is **100.00%**. Worse, now that we are looking more closely, when we don't have any `EmployeeType` column selected in our slicer, the total in our original employee table visualization is also **100.00%**, which is also not correct. Clearly, we have introduced the measure totals problem into our **% Utilization** measure as a result of the change we made to the **Total Hours** measure.

4. A change to our **% Utilization** measure is required, as follows:

```
% Utilization =
    VAR __Utilization =
        DIVIDE(
            [Total Billable Hours], [Total Hours], 0 )
    VAR __Days = COUNTROWS( 'Hours' )
    VAR __Result =
        SWITCH( TRUE(),
```

```
                    ISINSCOPE( 'People'[Name] ) && ISBLANK( __Days ),
                    BLANK(),
                    ISINSCOPE( 'People'[Name]), __Utilization + 0,
                    //otherwise
                        VAR __Table =
                            SUMMARIZE(
                                'People',
                                'People'[Name],
                                "__billedHours", [Total Billable Hours],
                                "__totalHours", [Total Hours]
                            )
                        VAR __billedHours = SUMX( __Table, [__billedHours] )
                        VAR __hours = SUMX( __Table, [__totalHours] )
                    RETURN
                        DIVIDE( __billedHours, __hours )
                )
    RETURN
        __Result
```

In the preceding formula for **% Utilization**, we have taken the last iteration of our **% Utilization** measure and added the measure totals problem logic to return the correct aggregated value whenever our visualization does not display data based on individual employee rows.

In this case, we have added a SWITCH statement to our __Result variable. This is a special version of the SWITCH statement that uses the TRUE function as the first argument or parameter. When using this version of the SWITCH statement, we can construct logical TRUE/FALSE statements as the conditions that are evaluated instead of individual values, as is the case in the current **Total Hours** measure.

The first two condition/value pairs use the ISINSCOPE function for 'People'[Name]. ISINSCOPE is a fairly recent function and was specifically designed to aid in measure calculations for instances of matrix hierarchies, as well as the measure totals problem. The ISINSCOPE function returns TRUE when the specified column is the current level in a hierarchy of levels. Hence, 'People'[Name] is not in scope for **Total** lines within table and matrix visuals, but is in scope for the individual rows of our table visualization that list **% Utilization** by employee.

The first condition checks if 'People'[Name] is in scope, as well as checking if the __Days variable is blank. If both of these conditions are TRUE, then BLANK is returned. The next condition only checks if 'People'[Name] is in scope and, if so, returns our standard **% Utilization** calculation using the __Utilization variable plus 0.

The rest of the SWITCH statement covers the case when 'People'[Name] is not in scope. This uses the "otherwise" clause of the SWITCH statement, which has no condition and is simply the result returned when no other condition has been met. In this case, we are in a **Total** line or some other aggregation/grouping, such as **Division**.

When this is the case, we first create a table using SUMMARIZE and assign this to a variable called __Table. This table contains a summary of our table by employee **Name** and calculates the values of **Total Billable Hours** and **Total Hours** for each row in this table, assigning these values to columns named __billedHours and __totalHours, respectively. We then use SUMX to calculate the sum of both the __billedHours and __totalHours columns within __Table and assign the result to the __billedHours and __hours variables. Finally, we return the value from dividing __billedHours by __hours.

5. With this change made to our **% Utilization** measure, and by looking at both table visualizations, we can see that the **Total** lines now agree with one another and that we have correct **% Utilization** results by Division as well as by employee Name!

As demonstrated in the final calculation for **% Utilization**, VAR/RETURN pairs can be nested infinitely—well, as close to infinitely as you will likely ever need.

Make sure to save your work before proceeding to the next chapter.

Summary

In this chapter, we took a tour of the **Model** view of Power BI and learned how to build a semantic model by creating relationships between separate tables. In doing so, we learned about the different types of relationships, as well as the concept of cross-filter direction. Next, we explored the semantic model we created to understand how we can use fields from different tables in the same visualization to gain insights into our data. Then, we created calculations to fulfill our goal of reporting on utilization as well as building relationships between tables. First, we created utilization calculations using calculated columns and began to understand the limitations of calculated columns and when they should and should not be used. Then, we created utilization calculations using measures in order to enable truly dynamic calculations that respond to user interaction.

Finally, we troubleshot our measure calculations by using a variety of techniques, such as boundary condition checking, slicing, and grouping. Now that we have built the semantic model and required calculations, we are ready to start analyzing our data in order to understand how the data is organized.

In the next chapter, we will explore the many powerful features within Power BI that allow us to break down, analyze, and unlock insights about our data.

Questions

As an activity, try to answer the following questions on your own:

*   What are the seven major areas of the **Model** view in Power BI?
*   What are the four different types of relationship cardinalities that Power BI supports?
*   What is cross-filter direction, and what are the two types of cross-filter direction supported by Power BI?
*   What are the two ways to create relationships in Power BI?
*   What are calculated columns?
*   When are calculated columns calculated?

- What are measures?
- When are measures calculated?
- What is the measure totals problem?
- What are visual calculations?
- What are three ways of troubleshooting calculations?

Further reading

To learn more about the topics that were covered in this chapter, please take a look at the following references:

- *Create and manage relationships in Power BI Desktop*: https://learn.microsoft.com/en-us/power-bi/transform-model/desktop-create-and-manage-relationships
- *Work with Table View*: https://learn.microsoft.com/en-us/power-bi/connect-data/desktop-data-view
- *Create calculated columns in Power BI Desktop*: https://learn.microsoft.com/en-us/power-bi/transform-model/desktop-calculated-columns
- *Create measures for data analysis in Power BI Desktop*: https://learn.microsoft.com/en-us/power-bi/transform-model/desktop-measures
- *Apply many-to-many relationships in Power BI Desktop*: https://learn.microsoft.com/en-us/power-bi/transform-model/desktop-many-to-many-relationships

Join our community on Discord

Join our community's Discord space for discussions with the authors and other readers: https://discord.gg/hvqvgyGH

6

Unlocking Insights

Now that we have built and verified our semantic model, we can explore the many powerful features within Power BI that allow us to break down, analyze, and unlock insights about our data. These features allow the report author to create compelling stories about the data within the semantic model, guiding report viewers to the most important insights and information.

Unlocking insights is all about creating reports that allow business users to easily navigate a report seamlessly while providing visualizations that make logical sense to the viewer. This often means that raw data needs to be massaged into groups and hierarchies. In addition, it is important to reduce clutter and only provide data that is relevant to the viewer. Navigational aids allow viewers to seamlessly navigate complex reports intuitively, providing a superior user experience. Finally, advanced analysis techniques are useful for providing a deeper understanding of the data in a visually appealing way that adds to the overall utility of visualizations and reports.

In this chapter, we cover the following topics:

- Segmenting data
- Using report navigation features
- Advanced analysis techniques

Technical requirements

You will need the following to follow the instructions in this chapter:

- An internet connection.
- Microsoft Power BI Desktop.
- Download Chapter 6 Start.pbix from GitHub at https://github.com/PacktPublishing/Learn-Microsoft-Power-BI_3E

Segmenting data

Power BI provides several mechanisms for **segmenting data**. These include the ability to use **groups**, **hierarchies**, and **Row-Level Security (RLS)**. Segmenting data allows you to partition or group individual rows of data into logical units that make sense to an organization. This helps ensure that business rules are enforced or that metrics can be shown in a manner that is more easily digestible by business users, versus looking at individual rows of data.

In this section, we will learn how to create groups that provide business-relevant segmentation of data, as well as logical hierarchies that classify information based on business structures. Finally, we will explore how to automatically filter data so that only the data that's relevant to the viewer is displayed.

Creating groups

The easiest way to see grouping in Power BI is to use visualizations to summarize data. We can do this by following these steps:

1. If you are continuing from the last chapter, continue using the same Power BI Desktop file. Otherwise, download `Chapter 6 Start.pbix` from the GitHub repository. Save this file as `LearnPowerBI.pbix`.

2. Create a new page, *Page 2*, in Power BI Desktop on the **Report** view.

3. While on this page, expand the **Calendar** table in the **Data** pane and select the checkbox for the **Month** column to create a **Table** visualization.

4. Next, add the **Hours** column from the **Hours** table to this visualization.

5. Now, change the visual from a **Table** visual to a **Clustered Column Chart** visual using the **Visualizations** pane.

After following these steps, we should have an ad hoc grouping of the hours based on the month in which those hours were reported.

However, there is another way to use groups within Power BI. Instead of using ad hoc grouping, we can define groupings of information as part of the semantic model itself and then use those defined groups within visualizations.

Refer to the following steps to see how this is done:

1. Expand the **People** table in the **Data** pane. Right-click the **EmployeeType** column and choose **New group**. The **Groups** dialog opens. Here, we can define names for our groups, as well as defining the groups themselves. Leave the name of the group as **EmployeeType (groups)**.

2. In the **Ungrouped values** area, select **HOURLY, SALARY,** and **SUB- CONTRACTOR,** by clicking on **HOURLY** and then holding down the *Ctrl* key while clicking on **SALARY** and **SUB-CON-TRACTOR**. Now, click the **Group** button. A new group is created in the **Groups and members** section. Rename this group **Billable** by double-clicking the heading **HOURLY & SALARY & SUB-CONTRACTOR**.

3. Check the **Include Other group** checkbox and then click the **OK** button.

The **Groups** dialog is shown in the following screenshot:

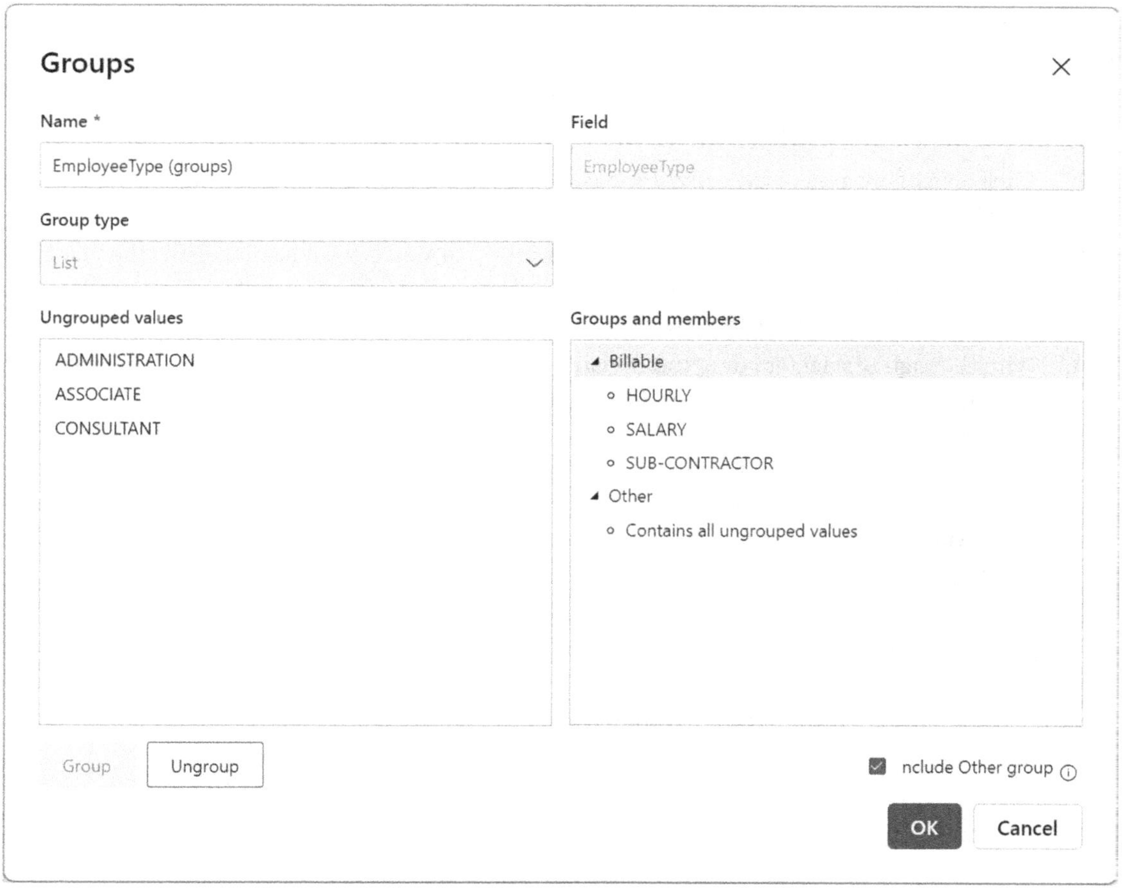

Figure 6.1 – Groups dialog

Note that, within the **People** table, an entry called **EmployeeType (groups)** appears underneath our **EmployeeType** column. This entry's icon is of a square segmented into four quadrants.

We can use this new collection of groups in visuals by removing the **EmployeeType** filter from all the pages.

1. Expand the **Filters** pane, find the **EmployeeType** filter under **Filters on all pages,** hover over this filter with the mouse, and click the small **x** to remove the filter.

2. Now, click on a blank area of the canvas and click on the checkbox next to **EmployeeType (groups)**. A **Table** visualization is created that contains two rows: **Billable** and **Other**. Add the **Hours** column from the **Hours** table to this visualization.

Defining groups within the semantic model is a convenient way to save time by creating reusable groupings of information that can be used within multiple visualizations.

Creating hierarchies

Hierarchies are a powerful feature of Power BI that allow data to be summarized, but also allow report viewers to drill down into the data to obtain additional details. Similar to groups, we can create ad hoc hierarchies, as well as defining hierarchies within our semantic model. The easiest way to see an ad hoc hierarchy is to use a **Matrix** visualization, as follows:

1. Click on a blank area of the canvas and click the checkbox next to the **Location** column in the **People** table.

2. Switch the visualization from a **Table** visualization to a **Matrix** visualization using the **Visualizations** pane. Some visuals work well with hierarchies, while others do not. **Table** visualizations are not particularly suited for use with hierarchies, while **Matrix** visualizations are.

3. With the matrix selected, drag the **Division** column from the **Hours** table into the **Rows** field well in the **Visualizations** pane. Make sure that the **Division** column appears underneath the **Location** column in the **Rows** field well. Note that several arrow icons appear above/below our **Matrix** visualization. In addition, small + icons appear to the left of each row in the matrix. Refer to the following screenshot. If you do not see the + icons, you can turn them on using the **Format** sub-pane of the **Visualizations** pane by expanding the **Row headers** card and then toggling the **+/- icons** to **On**.

4. Drag the **Hours** column from the **Hours** table into the **Values** field well of the **Matrix** visualization. Use the forked arrow icon (see the following screenshot) associated with the **Matrix** visualization to select **Expand all down one level in the hierarchy**. We can now see the reported hours broken down by **Location** and **Division** in our matrix:

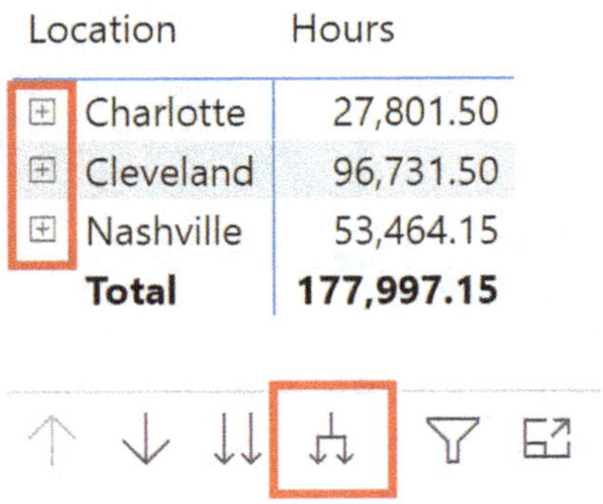

Location	Hours
⊞ Charlotte	27,801.50
⊞ Cleveland	96,731.50
⊞ Nashville	53,464.15
Total	**177,997.15**

↑ ↓ ↓↓ ⌄ ▽ ⤢

Figure 6.2 – Matrix visualization with an ad hoc hierarchy

We can also define hierarchies as part of our semantic model. However, unlike the previous case, where we created an ad hoc hierarchy from columns in separate tables, hierarchies that are created as part of the semantic model must have all of the columns in the hierarchy come from the same table.

Follow these steps to create a hierarchy within the semantic model:

1. Expand the **Hours** table in the **Data** pane.

2. Right-click the **Division** column and choose **Create hierarchy**. A Division Hierarchy element will be created within the **Hours** table and appear just below our **Division** column. Note that **Division** is the first element within our new hierarchy. This can be seen by clicking the > symbol to the left of **Division Hierarchy** in the **Data** pane, as shown in the following screenshot:

Figure 6.3 – Model hierarchy

3. Right-click the **JobID** column, choose **Add to hierarchy**, and then choose **Division Hierarchy**. **JobID** is added to **Division Hierarchy**, below **Division**.

Follow these steps to see our new hierarchy in action:

1. Click on the blank area of the canvas and then click the checkbox next to **Division Hierarchy** in the **Hours** table.
2. Switch the created visual from a **Table** visualization to a **Matrix** visualization using the **Visualizations** pane.
3. Add the **Hours** column from the **Hours** table to the **Values** field well.
4. Use the forked arrow icon for this new **Matrix** visualization to select **Expand all down one level in the hierarchy**. We can now see our hours broken down by **Division** and **JobID**.

Defining hierarchies within the semantic model is a convenient way to save time since these reusable hierarchies of information can be created once and then used within multiple visualizations.

Exploring hierarchies

So far, we have used the forked arrow icon to select **Expand all down one level in the hierarchy**. Now, let's take a look at the functionality of the other arrow icons:

1. In the latest **Matrix** visualization that we created using **Division Hierarchy**, use the up-arrow icon to select **Drill Up** within our hierarchy. This collapses our hierarchy to the **Division** level.
2. Switch the visualization to **Clustered column chart** using the **Visualizations** pane.
3. Click on the single down arrow icon to turn on **Drill down**. Note that the down arrow icon is now surrounded by a circle, as shown in the following screenshot:

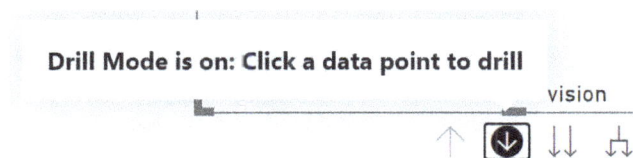

Figure 6.4 – Drill Mode is on

4. Click on the **3001 Management** column to drill down into the hierarchy for just the **3001 Management** data. We are now at the **JobID** level of the hierarchy, just within the **3001 Management** leaf of our hierarchy.

5. Click on the down arrow icon again to turn off **Drill down,** and then click on the up-arrow icon to drill back up to the top level of the hierarchy.

6. This time, click on the double-down arrow icon. This icon drills down into the second level of the hierarchy across all of the top-level leaves of our hierarchy.

7. Use the up-arrow icon to drill back up to the top level of the hierarchy.

The same four arrow icons for expanding/collapsing and drilling down and up through a hierarchy, which appear above or below a visualization that contains a hierarchy, are also available in the **Drill actions** section of the **Data/Drill** tab of the ribbon. In the **Data/Drill** tab of the ribbon, the forked arrow icon corresponds to **Expand next level**, while the double-arrow icon corresponds to **Switch to next level.**

Understanding Row Level Security

Row Level Security (RLS) is used to restrict data access for users viewing reports. Roles are created within Power BI Desktop by using DAX expressions to define filters. These filters restrict the data that's available to that role at the row level of the data. Users are added to roles from within the Power BI service. However, Power BI Desktop provides the ability to test role definitions by allowing the report author to view reports as a particular role or a particular user.

Creating roles

Let's try to understand RLS by continuing with the example scenario we introduced in *Chapter 2, Planning Projects with Power BI*. Pam knows that when she creates and publishes the final report, various job functions within the organization can look at the report. Two of these job functions are branch managers and division managers. Pam wants to ensure that each of these managers only sees the information that pertains to their area of management, without having to create separate reports for each job function and each user within those jobs. Pam can do this by creating roles for each using RLS.

Follow these steps to create the branch manager roles:

1. Click on the **Modeling** tab of the ribbon and then choose **Manage roles** from the **Security** section of the ribbon. The **Manage security roles** dialog is shown in the following screenshot:

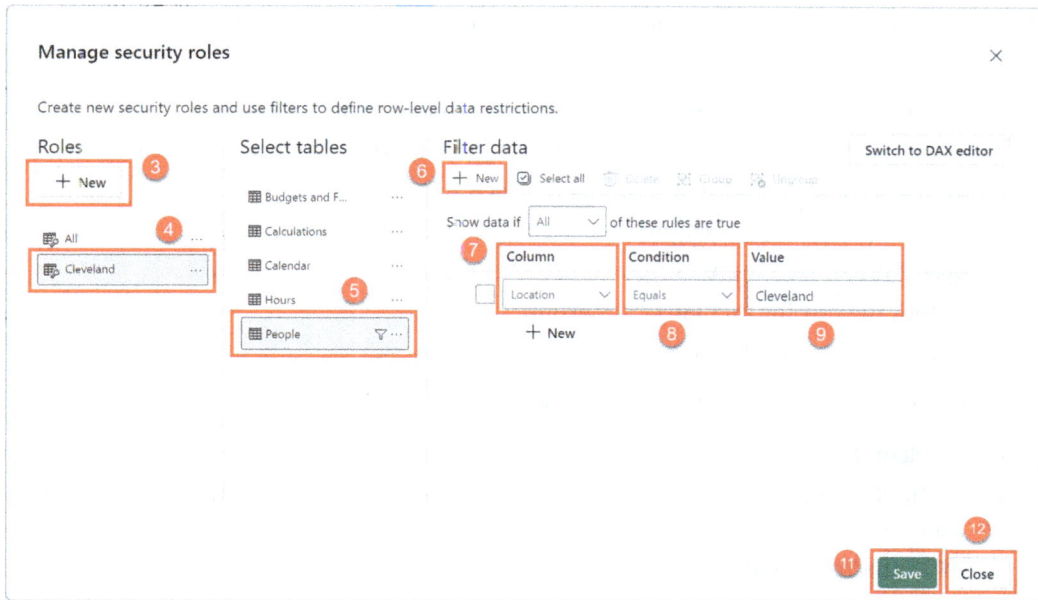

Figure 6.5 – Manage security roles dialog

2. In the **Manage security roles** dialog, under **Roles**, click the + New button to create a role. Name this role **All** by double-clicking the **Untitled** role. Since this role should see everything, we do not define any table filters.

3. Click the **+ New** button again as depicted in *figure 6.5*.

4. Rename this role `Cleveland`.

5. With the **Cleveland** role selected, select the **People** table in the **Select tables** section.

6. In the **Filter data** section, click the **+ New** button.

7. In the **Filter data** section, for the **Column** dropdown, choose the **Location** column.

8. Leave **Condition** as **Equals**.

9. For **Value**, type **Cleveland**.

10. Repeat *Steps 3* through *9* to create roles called **Nashville** and **Charlotte**. In *Step 9*, make **Value** **Nashville** and **Charlotte**, respectively. These four roles cover the branch managers within the organization, as well as those individuals who need to see all locations.

11. Click the **Save** button to save these roles.

12. Finally, click the **Close** button to exit the **Manage security roles** dialog.

Before we create any additional roles, let's define some additional groups within our semantic model, as follows:

1. While on the **Report** view, expand the **Hours** table in the **Data** pane.
2. Right-click the **Division** column (not **Division Hierarchy**) and choose **New group**.
3. Add **1001 Technology** to a group called **Technology**.
4. Similarly, add **2001 Accounting** to a group called **Accounting**.
5. Add **3001 Management** to a group called **Management**.
6. Check the box for **Include Other group**.
7. Finally, click the **OK** button.

Now, let's create roles for our division managers by performing these steps:

1. Click on **Manage roles** from the **Modeling** tab of the ribbon.
2. In the **Manage security roles** dialog, under **Roles**, click the **+ New** button and call this new role Technology.
3. With the **Technology** role selected, click the **Hours** table in the **Select tables** area.
4. In the **Filter data** area, click the **+ New** button. For **Column**, choose [**Division (groups)**].
5. Leave **Condition** as **Equals** and set **Value** to **Technology**.
6. Repeat steps 2 through 5 to create roles for the **Accounting**, **Management**, and **Other Services** roles with a **Value** filter of **Accounting**, **Management**, and **Other**, respectively.
7. When finished, click the **Save** button and then the **Close** button.

We have created all the roles we need in our model. Save your work before proceeding to test these roles.

Testing roles

It is important to test the roles so that we can be certain that the DAX filters defining the roles operate properly. To see our new roles in action, do the following:

1. First, click on a blank area of the canvas and select **Clustered column chart** using the **Location** column in the **People** table for **X-axis** and the **Hours** column from the **Hours** table for **Y-axis**.
2. Select the **Modeling** tab of the ribbon.
3. Click on **View as** in the **Security** section of the ribbon.
4. Select the checkbox for **Accounting**.

5. Click the **OK** button, as shown in the following screenshot:

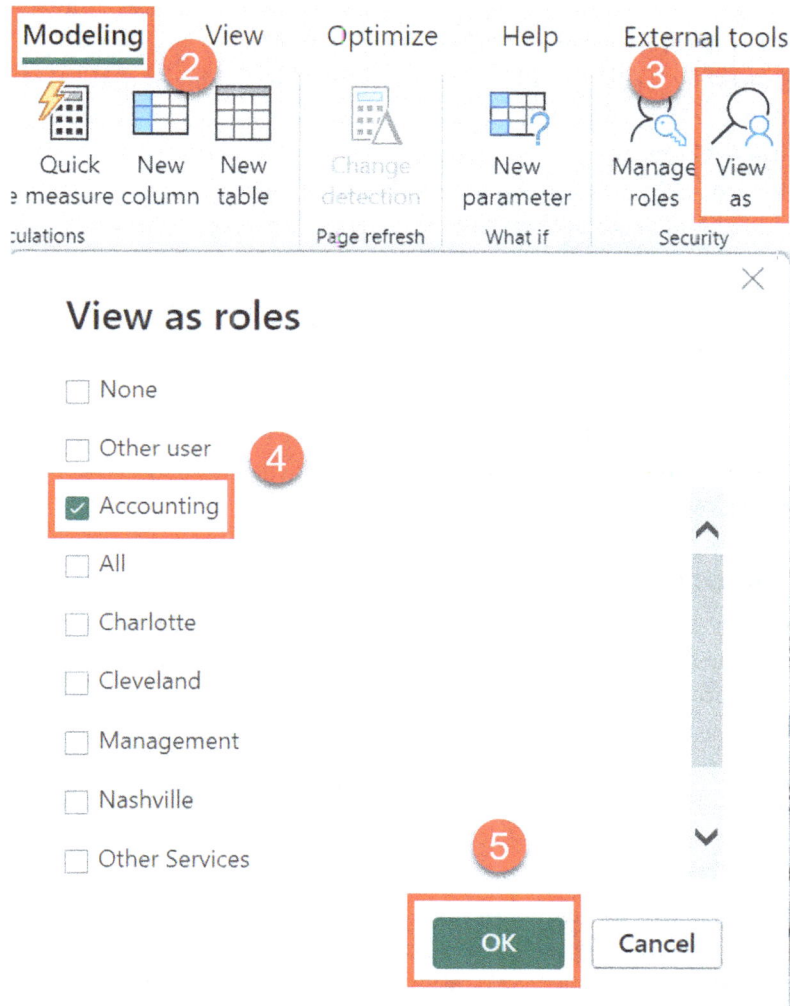

Figure 6.6 – View as roles

Note that the clustered column chart that displays **Hours** using **Division Hierarchy** now only displays **2001 Accounting**, and that our clustered column chart that displays **Sum of Hours by Location** displays all three locations; that is, **Cleveland, Charlotte**, and **Nashville**. Note the yellow information bar at the top of the canvas that reads **Now viewing as: Accounting**. You are now viewing the report using the RLS rules associated with the **Accounting** role.

6. Click the **View as** button in the ribbon again, uncheck **Accounting**, and then view the report as **Management**, then **Technology**, and finally by **Other Services**. Note that, when viewing as **Other Services**, we see all of our ungrouped divisions.

7. Next, test the **All** group by clicking on **View as**, unchecking any other roles and checking **All**, and then clicking on the **OK** button. Note that we now see all locations and divisions. When we click the **Stop viewing** button in the information bar, nothing changes.

8. Finally, test each of the location roles in turn and verify that the correct location – and only the correct location – is displayed in the clustered column chart that summarizes **Sum of Hours by Location**.

9. When finished, click the **Stop viewing** button in the information bar.

RLS is a powerful mechanism for segmenting data that allows a single semantic model to service multiple different roles within an organization while keeping that data secure.

Now that we have covered various methods of segmenting data, we will next look at how to use report navigation features, which help provide a superior user experience by allowing viewers to seamlessly navigate complex reports intuitively.

Using report navigation features

In addition to powerful capabilities related to segmenting data for analysis, Power BI also provides mechanisms for navigating between report pages. This can also be used as an aid for analysis. To this end, we will explore the drill through functionality, which allows report viewers to easily gain deeper insights from summary data, as well as buttons and bookmarks, which allow viewers to quickly navigate between pages or instantly focus on particular sets of data. Finally, we will explore the Q&A functionality, which empowers report viewers to answer questions about the data contained in reports.

Drill through

So far, we have seen how we can break down our data using groups, hierarchies, and RLS. Power BI provides another powerful method of breaking down and analyzing data called **drill through**. Drill through is a method that's used for segmenting data as well as navigating a report. Drill through allows us to connect pages of reports. A report page can be created that focuses on a particular data entity, such as a division, location, or employee. Users can then right-click on a data element on one page and drill through to a different page while maintaining the original filter context from the first page.

Using drill through

Let's learn how to use drill through by performing the following steps:

1. Start by creating a new page called **Page 3**. Rename this page to Details by triple-clicking on the page's name and then typing Details.

2. Now, click on the **Utilization** page and select the **Matrix** visualization on the left-hand side of the page. This is the matrix that has **Name** in **Rows**, **Category** in **Columns**, and **Sum of Hours** in **Values**. Use *Ctrl + C* to copy this visualization. Click back on the **Details** page and use *Ctrl + V* to paste this visualization onto the canvas.

3.   Now, click on **Page 2** and copy and paste the **Sum of Hours by Division** and **Sum of Hours by Location** visualizations onto the **Details** page. Adjust the locations and sizes of these visualizations as necessary. Make sure to shrink the matrix and other visualizations to leave some blank space at the top of the page.

4.   Click on a blank area of the page's canvas. Now, expand the **People** table and select the checkbox for the **Location** column in the **Data** pane.

5.   Change this visualization to a **Card** visualization and move this visualization to the top right-hand corner of the page. Adjust the size as necessary. Note that this **Card** visualization displays **First Location**, which is **Charlotte** alphabetically.

6.   Click on a blank area of the canvas. Then, in the **Visualizations** pane, drag and drop the **Location** column from the **People** table into the **Add drill through fields here** area of the **Drill through** section of the **Visualizations** pane. Note that the **Drill through** section is at the bottom of the **Visualizations** page:

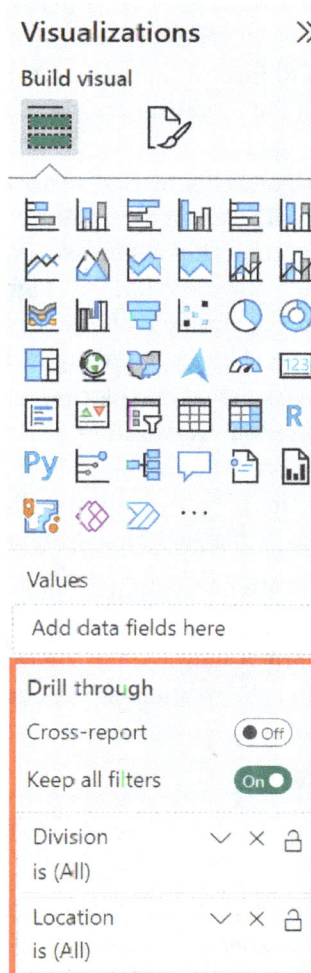

Figure 6.7 – Drill through filters

7. Also, drag and drop the **Division** column from the **Hours** table as a drill through field. Note that, in the top left-hand corner of the page, a left-pointing arrow icon will appear, surrounded by a circle, as shown in the following screenshot. This is added automatically to any report page that includes drill through fields:

Figure 6.8 – Back button

8. Click back onto **Page 2**. In the **Sum of Hours by Location** visualization, right-click the column for **Nashville**, choose **Drill through**, and then **Details**. Note that you are transported to the **Details** page and that only **Nashville** appears in the **Sum of Hours by Location** visualization. In addition, **Nashville** appears in our **Card** visualization as well. All the visualizations on this page are now being filtered to only show data that's linked to the **Nashville** location. You can verify this by hovering over each visual in turn, and then hovering over the funnel icon above or below the visualization to inspect the active filters on each visualization. Also, note that in the **Drill through** area of the **Visualizations** pane, **Division** is set to (**All**), while **Location** is set to **Nashville**.

9. Now, hold down the *Ctrl* key and click on the left arrow icon in the top-left corner of the page. This is a back button. You will be taken back to **Page 2**. Note that holding down the *Ctrl* key is only required during report authoring. When users view the report, they can simply click the back button without holding down the *Ctrl* key. Right-click on the **Cleveland** column in the **Sum of Hours by Location** visualization, choose **Drill through**, and then **Details**. This time, only **Cleveland** information will be displayed on the **Details** page.

10. Use the back button to go back to **Page 2**. This time, right-click the **3001 Management** column in the **Sum of Hours by Division** visualization, choose **Drill through**, and then **Details**. You are transported to the **Details** page once more. Note that only the **3001 Management** column is displayed in the **Sum of Hours by Division** visualization. This time, all of the information on the page is being filtered by the **3001 Management** division.

Note that the **Sum of Hours by Location** visualization only displays **Nashville** and **Cleveland**. This is because the employees who belong to the **3001 Management** division only work in **Nashville** and **Cleveland**. Why, then, does the **Card** visualization at the top of the page still say **Charlotte**? This is because the cross filter direction of the relationship in our model between the **People** and **Hours** tables is **Single**, from **People** to **Hours**.

To fix this, we need to do the following:

1. Click on the **Modeling** tab of the ribbon and choose **Manage relationships** from the **Relationships** section of the ribbon.

2. In the **Manage relationships** dialog, click anywhere on the **From Hours (EmployeeID) To People (ID)** relationship checkbox.

3. Now, click the **Edit** button.

4. Change **Cross filter direction** to **Both** and then click the **Save** button.

5. Click the **Close** button to close the **Manage relationships** dialog.

After making a brief update to the visualizations, our **Card** visualization now says **Cleveland**, since Cleveland is now the first location.

The **Data/Drill** tab of the ribbon contains a **Drill through** button in the **Data actions** section. This tab is activated whenever a visualization contains a hierarchy or can use drill through. Clicking on this button activates the drill through feature so that clicking on a visualization element displays the **Drill through** menu.

This completes our exploration of drill through. Save your work before starting to explore buttons.

Buttons

Our use of drill through has exposed another navigational aid within Power BI: **buttons**. When we added drill through filters to a page, Power BI automatically created a back button. However, other types of buttons can be used with Power BI. Let's go over them now.

Types of buttons

To explore the various buttons within Power BI, do the following:

1. Create a new page and rename this page **Buttons**.

2. Now, click on the **Insert** tab of the ribbon. In the **Elements** section of the ribbon, click on the **Buttons** icon. There are nine types of buttons in Power BI, as shown in the following screenshot:

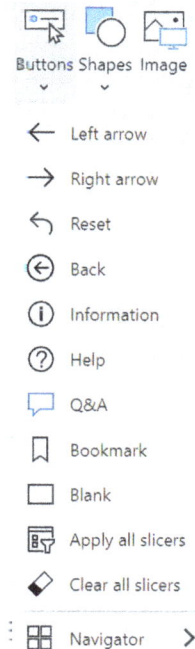

Figure 6.9 – Types of buttons

3. Create one of each button type.

4. Power BI automatically places buttons in the top left-hand corner of the screen. Move the buttons to a different area of the canvas so that no two buttons overlap.

5. Click on each of these buttons in turn. Notice that the **Visualizations** pane changes to include formatting options for each button and is now titled **Format button.**

Different buttons have different default formatting options that are either turned on or off by default. For example, the **Blank** button has the **Style | Border** formatting option turned on by default, while the other buttons do not. Most of the options in the **Format button** pane are simply options that allow you to change the look and feel of these buttons.

One of these formatting options is the **Style | Icon** option. All of the buttons have this option turned on except the **Apply all slicer** button, page navigator, and bookmark navigator buttons. If you expand the **Icon** sub-card, there is an **Icon type** setting. By clicking on the drop-down arrow for the **Icon type** setting, a list of icons is presented that mirror the same buttons that can be created (except for page and bookmark navigator buttons), plus an option for **Custom.**

In reality, each of the various button types in Power BI, other than the page and bookmark navigator buttons, isn't a button type at all, but rather default settings for a single type of element – a button! As you have likely caught on, the page and bookmark navigator buttons are special buttons, so let's cover these special buttons before looking at the buttons in general.

Page and bookmark navigator buttons

The **Page navigator** and **Bookmark navigator** buttons are special buttons known as **Navigator** buttons. **Navigator** buttons are specifically designed for report navigation purposes.

The **Page navigator** button actually displays a series of buttons, one for each page in the report. As one might expect, holding down the *Ctrl* key and then clicking on a button in the **Page navigator** changes the report to the corresponding page. Again, note that when users are viewing the report, there is no need to hold down the *Ctrl* key.

Selecting the page navigator button (without holding down the *Ctrl* key) changes the **Visualizations** pane to the **Format navigator** pane. The **Format navigator** pane includes a format card named **Pages.** Expanding the **Pages** format card and then the **Options** and **Show** sub-cards allows granular control over what types of pages and which specific pages to display in the page navigator. There is also a **Grid layout** format card that provides some control over the overall layout of the navigator, such as its orientation (either **Grid, Horizontal,** or **Vertical**) and the **Padding** (spacing) between buttons.

The **Bookmark navigator** button is essentially the same concept as the **Page navigator** button, but instead of displaying the pages of the report, this navigator displays the bookmarks in the report. Since we have not created any bookmarks, this navigator is empty. Bookmarks are explored after we finish exploring buttons.

Let's now continue our exploration of standard buttons in Power BI Desktop.

Button actions

The real magic of buttons rests with their ability to perform actions. The action of a button is controlled by the **Action** format card. With the **Blank** button selected, toggle on the **Action** format card and then expand the **Action** format card of the **Format button** pane. Under **Action sub-card**, click the down arrow next to the **Type** field and note the different types of action types, as shown in the following screenshot:

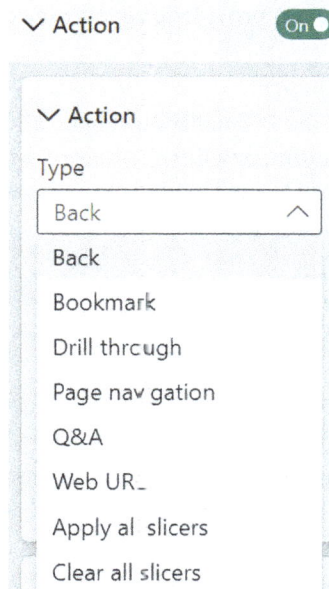

Figure 6.10 – Button action types

We have already seen how the **Back** action works and how it is useful when we are using features such as drill through. To see how we can use a web URL, do the following:

1. Select **Web URL** for **Type**.
2. A **Web URL** field is displayed. Type https://www.powerbi.com into the **Web URL** field.
3. Now, hold down the *Ctrl* key and click the **Blank** button. A web browser or a new browser tab will open, and you will be transported to the powerbi.com website!

Regarding the other action types, the **Drill through** action type acts exactly like choosing the **Drill through** button in the **Data/Drill** tab of the ribbon. The **Page navigation** action changes the page of the report. **Apply all slicers** and **Clear all slicers** do exactly what they indicate, either applying the selections from all slicers on the page or clearing the selections in all slicers on the page. We'll explore two other possible actions, **Bookmarks** and **Q&A**, in the upcoming sections, since these are powerful features of Power BI that may be used with or without the use of buttons.

Note that when using a type of **Drill through**, **Page navigation**, or **Web URL** for **Action**, an **fx** icon appears to the right of the **Destination** or **Web URL** setting. Clicking this icon allows the **Destination** or **Web URL** setting to be specified by a column in the semantic model or even a DAX measure.

The same actions that are available for buttons are also available for inserted images and shapes. Images and shapes can be inserted into a report page using the **Insert** tab of the ribbon in the **Elements** section. This means that you can use any image or shape just like a button!

Let's next explore visual cues that we can provide to report viewers regarding buttons.

Button states

The **Shape** and **Style** format cards in the **Format button** pane allow you to control the shape, display text, include an outline around the button, or a filled-in color for the button, etc. Each of these format settings includes a **State** setting that can be set to either **Default state**, **On hover**, **On press**, or **Disabled**. Each of these states can be set independently.

To configure these states, do the following:

1. Click on the **Blank** button and, under the **Button** tab, expand the **Style** format card and toggle the **Text** sub-card to **On**.
2. Expand the **Text** sub-card. Ensure that **State** in the **Apply settings to** sub card is set to **Default** state, and then in the **Text** sub-card, type the word `Default` in the **Text** field.
3. Now, change **State** in the **Applied settings to** sub-card to **On hover** and then, in the **Text** sub-card, type the word `Hover` in the **Text** field.
4. Finally, change **State** in the **Applied settings to** sub-card to **On pressed** and then, in the **Text** sub-card, type the word **Pressed!** in the **Text** field.

Note that the **Blank** button now contains text that says **Default**.

Hover your mouse over the button and note that the button text now says **Hover**, as shown in the following screenshot:

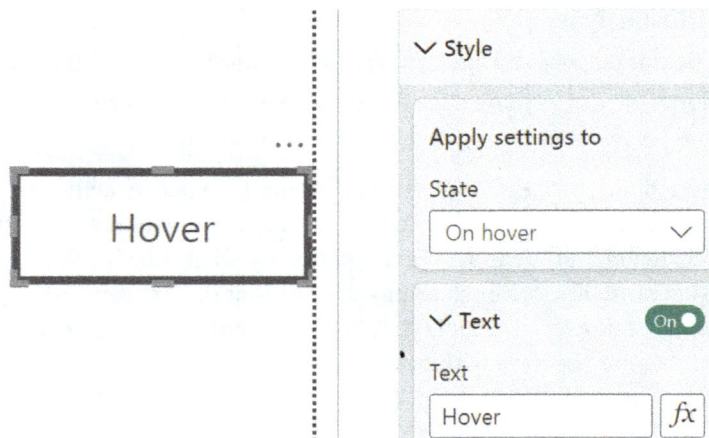

Figure 6.11 – Button states

Click on the button and note that the button's text changes to **Pressed!**.

Button states allow report authors to provide visual cues regarding the outcome of pressing a button. Let's now move on to exploring bookmarks.

Bookmarks

Bookmarks allow you to capture the state of a report page and save this state to be referred to later. When creating a bookmark, the following elements are saved as part of the bookmark's definition by default:

- The current page, along with all of the visuals on the page
- All filters, including the states of slicers and selections within visuals (such as cross-highlight filters)
- The sort order of visuals
- The drill to locations of visuals
- The visibility of visuals and shapes
- The **Focus and Spotlight** settings of visuals and shapes

There are many uses for bookmarks. Bookmarks are often used as an aid to report viewers so that users can reset the report page to a default state, removing all the filters and slicer selections they have chosen. Bookmarks are also created and grouped as a collection in order to create a step-by-step presentation to tell a story of interesting findings or insights. Finally, bookmarks are also used to provide alternative page navigation. This only begins to cover the uses for bookmarks within Power BI. Let us learn more about bookmarks in the following sections.

Creating and using bookmarks

To see how bookmarks work, follow these steps:

1. Click on the **Details** page while in the **Report** view.
2. In the **Visualizations** pane, look at the **Drill through** area and ensure that there are no active drill through filters. If there are, hover over the filter and remove it by clicking on the eraser icon (**Clear filter**), as highlighted in the following screenshot:

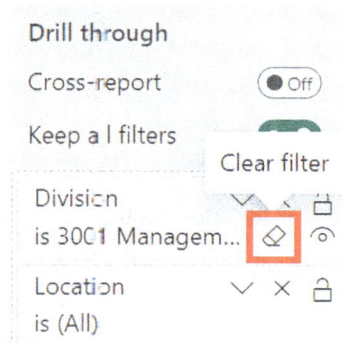

Figure 6.12 – The eraser icon, highlighted by a circle

🔍 **Quick tip:** Need to see a high-resolution version of this image? Open this book in the next-gen Packt Reader or view it in the PDF/ePub copy.

🔒 **The next-gen Packt Reader** is included for free with the purchase of this book. Scan the QR code OR go to `packtpub.com/unlock`, then use the search bar to find this book by name. Double-check the edition shown to make sure you get the right one.

When all of the drill through filters have been removed, you should see **Charlotte** at the top of the page in the **Card** visual. You should also see all of the divisions and all of the locations in the **Sum of Hours by Division** and **Sum of Hours by Location** visuals, respectively.

3. Now that the page is in its proper state, collapse the **Filters** pane and the **Visualizations** pane.

4. In the ribbon, select the **View** tab and, in the **Show panes** section of the ribbon, select **Bookmarks**. The **Bookmarks** pane appears between the collapsed **Filters** and **Visualizations** panes, as shown in the following screenshot:

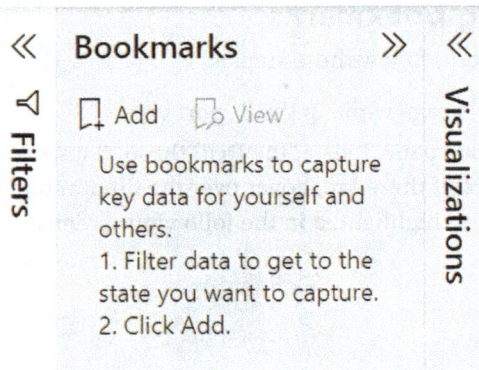

Figure 6.13 – Bookmarks pane

5. In the **Bookmarks** pane, click **Add**. **Bookmark 1** appears.

6. Rename this bookmark by double-clicking its name, typing `Default Details`, and then pressing the *Enter* key.

To use this new bookmark, follow these steps:

1. First, click on **Page 2** while in the **Report** view.

2. Right-click on **3001 Management** in the **Sum of Hours by Division** visual, choose **Drill through**, and then **Details**. Here, we can see **Cleveland** at the top in our **Card** visual and only **3001 Management** in our **Sum of Hours by Division** visual. Also, only **Cleveland** and **Nashville** appear in our **Sum of Hours by Location** visual.

3. Now, click on the **Default Details** bookmark in the **Bookmarks** pane. The page automatically resets to its state when the bookmark was defined, removing the **Drill through** filters!

4. Now, click back onto **Page 2**.

5. Click the **Default Details** bookmark again. You are transported to the **Details** page automatically!

As you can see, bookmarks can be used while on a page, as well as being used as navigational aids between pages.

Advanced bookmarks

Let's explore some more advanced options for bookmarks by following these steps:

1. Make sure that you are on the **Details** page with the **Bookmarks** pane visible.

2. In the **Bookmarks** pane, click the ellipsis (...) next to the **Default Details** bookmark and uncheck **Current page**.

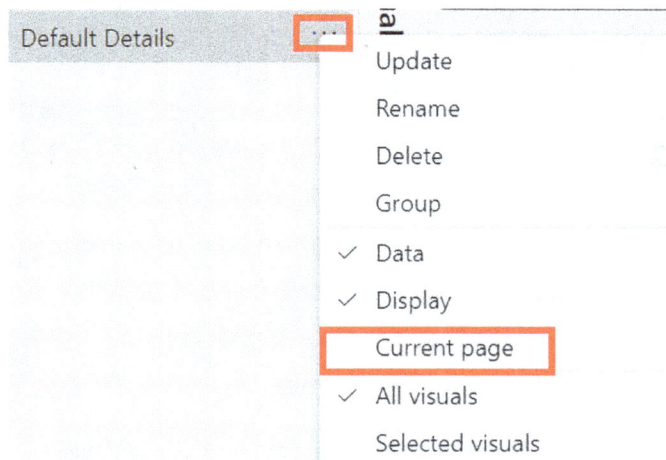

Figure 6.14 – Bookmarks options

3. Now, switch to **Page 2** and use drill through in the **Sum of Hours by Division** visualization to the **Details** page from **3001 Management**.

4. Click back onto **Page 2** and select the **Default Details** bookmark from the **Bookmarks** pane. You are no longer transported to the **Details** page. However, if you click on the **Details** page, you will see that the page has been reset to remove the **Drill through** filters.

5. Click on the ellipsis (...) for our **Default Details** bookmark in the **Bookmarks** pane and recheck **Current page**.

6. Now, click on the ellipsis (**...**) for the **Sum of Hours by Location** visualization and choose **Spotlight**. Note that the other visualizations fade into the background.

7. Add a new bookmark using the **Add** button in the **Bookmarks** pane and call this bookmark **Details Spotlight**.

8. Click on the ellipsis (**...**) for the **Details Spotlight** bookmark and uncheck **Data**.

9. Switch to **Page 2** and **Drill through** to **Details** for **3001 Management** in our **Sum of Hours by Division** visualization once more.

10. Note that the spotlight for the **Sum of Hours by Location** visual is gone.

11. Click on the **Details Spotlight** bookmark. Note that the data stays the same; the **Drill through** filters haven't been removed, but the spotlight returns for our **Sum of Hours by Location** visualization.

As you can see, the report author has a measure of control over what states a bookmark preserves. Let's create some additional bookmarks, this time using the **Selection** pane:

1. First, reset the **Details** page by clicking on the **Default Details** bookmark.

2. To activate the **Selection** pane, click on the **View** tab in the ribbon. Then, in the **Show panes** section, choose **Selection**. The **Selection** pane appears to the left of the **Bookmarks** pane, as shown in the following screenshot:

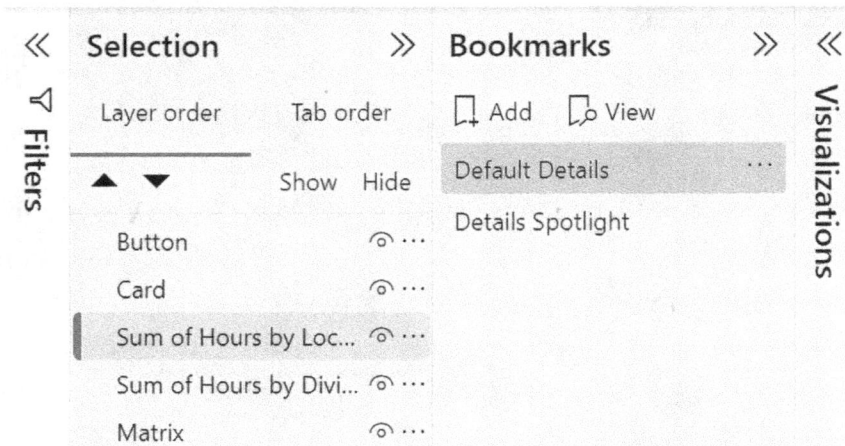

Figure 6.15 – Selection and Bookmarks panes

The **Selection** pane lists all of the visualizations and shapes on our report page:

- **Button** refers to the back button.
- **Card** refers to our **Card** visualization at the top right of our page.
- **Sum of Hours by Location** and **Sum of Hours by Division** refer to the respective visuals with the same titles.
- **Matrix** refers to our **Matrix** visualization.

To understand how to use the **Selection** pane, do the following:

1. In the **Selection** pane, under the word **Hide**, note the eyeball icons. These are a small circle with an arc over the top.

2. Click on the eyeball icon for **Sum of Hours by Location**. Note that the **Sum of Hours by Location** visualization disappears from the page and that there is now a slash through its eyeball icon in the **Selection** pane.

3. Hide the **Sum of Hours by Division** visual as well.

4. Now, use **Add** in the **Bookmarks** pane to add a bookmark called **Default One**.

5. Click on the **Default One** bookmark and drag and drop it above **Details Spotlight**, but below **Default Details**.

6. Click on the eyeball icon next to **Sum of Hours by Division** to show this visual on the page once more.

7. Add another bookmark called **Default Two** and drag and drop this visual underneath **Default One**.

8. Now, show the **Sum of Hours by Location** visual by selecting the eyeball icon in the **Selections** pane.

9. Create another bookmark called **Default Three** and drag and drop this bookmark below **Default Two**. Your bookmarks should now be ordered as follows:

   - Default Details
   - Default One
   - Default Two
   - Default Three
   - Details Spotlight

10. In the **Bookmarks** pane, select **View**. Note that, at the bottom of the page, a gray bar appears that replaces the page tabs. The left-hand side of the gray bar reads **Bookmark 1 of 5**, in the middle shows **Default Details**, and on the right are three icons.

11. Use the right-pointing **Next** icon to switch to the next bookmark in the list, that is, **Default One**.

12. Repeat this procedure to page through all of the bookmarks that we've created.

13. Click on the **X** icon in the bookmarks bar or **Exit** in the **Bookmarks** pane to exit this slideshow of bookmarks.

14. Reset the **Details** page by clicking on the **Default Details** bookmark.

15. Close the **Selection** and **Bookmarks** panes by unselecting them in the **View** tab of the ribbon.

You now have a good understanding of how to use bookmarks in conjunction with the **Selection** pane to structure a conversation about a report. Let's now move on to Q&A.

Questions and answers (Q&A)

Q&A is a powerful tool that has been built into the Power BI service since its inception. More recently, Q&A was added to Desktop as well. Q&A allows the user to use natural language to ask questions about the data contained within the semantic model. The answers received are in the form of visualizations.

Best practices for Q&A

There are several best practices to follow to use Q&A effectively:

- First, it is important to start with a good semantic model that has all of the proper relationships between tables.
- Second, naming tables and columns becomes critical when using Q&A. This is because Q&A uses the words that were typed into the question and tries to match the words with the names of tables and columns within the semantic model.
- Third, the columns and measures within the semantic model must be set to the correct **Data type**. This allows Q&A to return the correct results. For example, if a date column is set to text in the semantic model, Q&A can return unexpected results when using that date column.
- Fourth, it is important to configure the **Summarization** and **Data category** properties of the columns correctly. For example, we set the **Year** column in our **Calendar** table to have a default summarization of **Don't summarize**. This is because **Year** is a numeric column, but we do not wish to ever aggregate **Year**. Data categorization is also important, as this aids Q&A in choosing the correct visual to return as an answer.

We have followed all of these best practices except for the last one: data categorization. Data categorization is mainly used with geographic columns to denote the type of location element represented by data within the column. Using data categorization to tag these columns provides Power BI with hints regarding the type of information within the column and how it should be displayed. For example, categorizing a column as **Address**, **City**, **State or Province**, **Country**, or **Postal code** provides Power BI with the necessary hints to display this information on a **Map** visualization. To understand how to use data categorization, follow these steps:

1. While in the **Report** view, expand the **People** table in the **Data** pane.
2. Select the **Location** column by clicking anywhere on the name of the column (not the checkbox).
3. Now, click on the **Column tools** tab of the ribbon and in the **Properties** section, find the drop-down field next to **Data category**.
4. Currently, **Uncategorized** is selected. Change this to **City**.

   Note that a globe icon is now displayed next to the **Location** column in the **Data** pane, denoting that this column represents information that is geocoded (can be displayed on a map). This can be seen in the following screenshot:

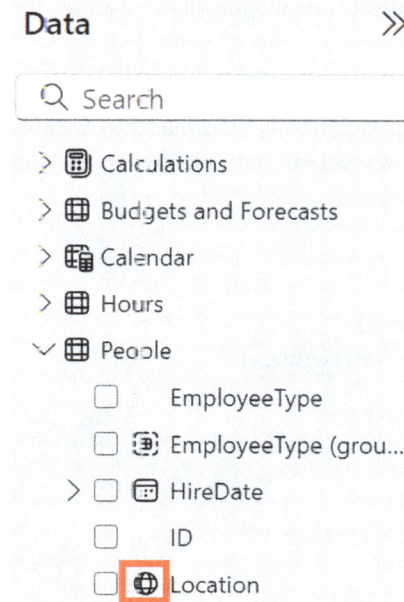

Figure 6.16 – Geocoding the data category icon

Now that we have learned about some of the best practices for Q&A, let's start using Q&A in our report!

Using a Q&A button

Let's understand how to use a Q&A button:

1. Switch to the **Buttons** page and click back on the **Blank** button we created earlier, expand the **Action** format card in the **Format button** pane, and change its **Type** to **Q&A**.

2. Hold down the *Ctrl* key and click the button. After a brief wait, the **Q&A** dialog is displayed, similar to the following:

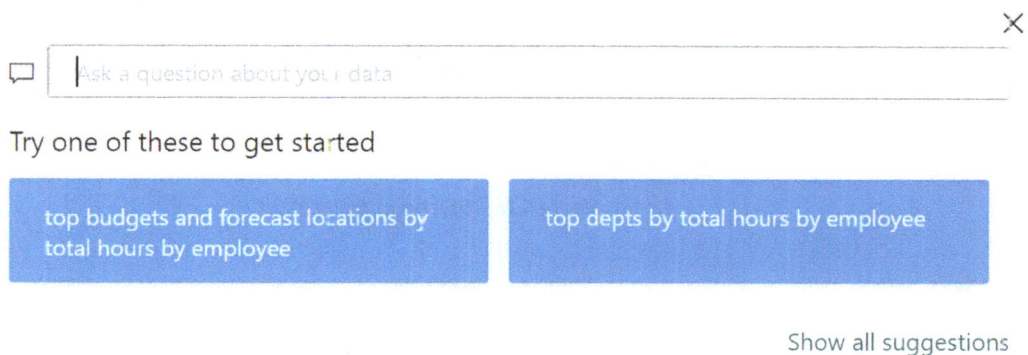

Figure 6.17 – Q&A dialog

Several example questions are displayed, as well as an entry area that says **Ask a question about your data.**

3. Click inside the **Ask a question about your data** box, type hours by location, and then press the *Enter* key. In the area formally occupied by example questions, a map will be displayed, showing bubbles over Cleveland, OH; Nashville, TN; and Charlotte, NC, as shown in the following screenshot:

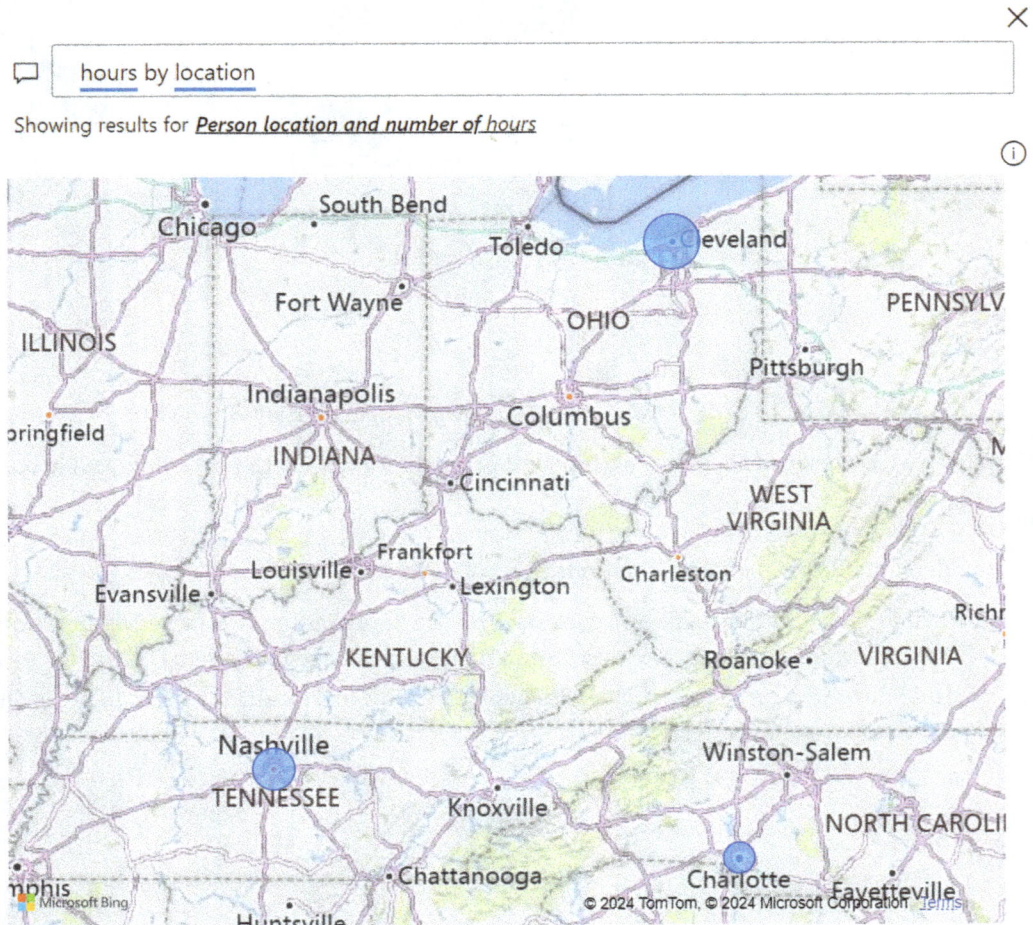

Figure 6.18 – Q&A hours by location

The size of the bubbles on the map denotes the total relative number of hours worked by employees in each location. Note that you can hover your mouse over the bubbles and receive a tooltip stating the **Location** and **Count of Hours** properties. **Count of Hours** is probably not what was intended. This means that the number is the count of the rows within the **Hours** table that are related to each location instead of the sum of hours for each location. Further confirmation that this is using **Count of Hours** can be found at the top of the map, where it says **Showing results for Person location and number of hours**. The exact phase may vary.

To fix this, note that hours and location are underlined where you entered the text **hours by location**. The underlined words indicate that Power BI has found a table or column name in the model.

4. Inside the text box where you entered the question, click on the underlined word **hours**. Note that there are multiple possible suggestions Q&A provides for semantic model entities that could refer to the word hours. Under **You could also try**, click **Show more** and review the options.

5. None of these look quite correct, so revise the question to **sum of Hours[Hours] by location**. Here, we are explicitly telling Q&A that we are referring to the **Hours** column in the **Hours** table. Now, click on **location** and note that there is an additional suggestion: **budgets and forecast location**. This is because we have a **Location** column in both the **People** table and the **Budgets and Forecasts** table. Because we have set the data categorization for the **Location** column in our **People** table to **City**, we can remove this ambiguity.

6. Click at the end of the question to place the cursor after **location**. Remove **location** and replace it with the word **city** so that our question now reads **sum of Hours[Hours] by city**. Note that the same visualization is displayed, but that the ambiguity has been removed.

7. Click the **X** in the top-right corner of the **Q&A** dialog to close the dialog.

The Q&A dialog can be a useful addition to reports as it lets report viewers answer ad hoc questions about the data.

Using Q&A in report authoring

Q&A can also be used for report authoring. To use Q&A in this manner, follow these steps:

1. Click on a blank area of the canvas on our **Buttons** page.

2. Select the **Insert** tab of the ribbon and, from the **AI visuals** section, choose **Q&A**. A blank visualization will appear on the page, along with a similar dialog to what we received previously, stating **Ask a question about your data**.

3. Type the same question as before; that is, **sum of Hours[Hours] by city**. Note that the same **Map** visualization is displayed and that we have the same underlined words in our question, as shown in the following screenshot:

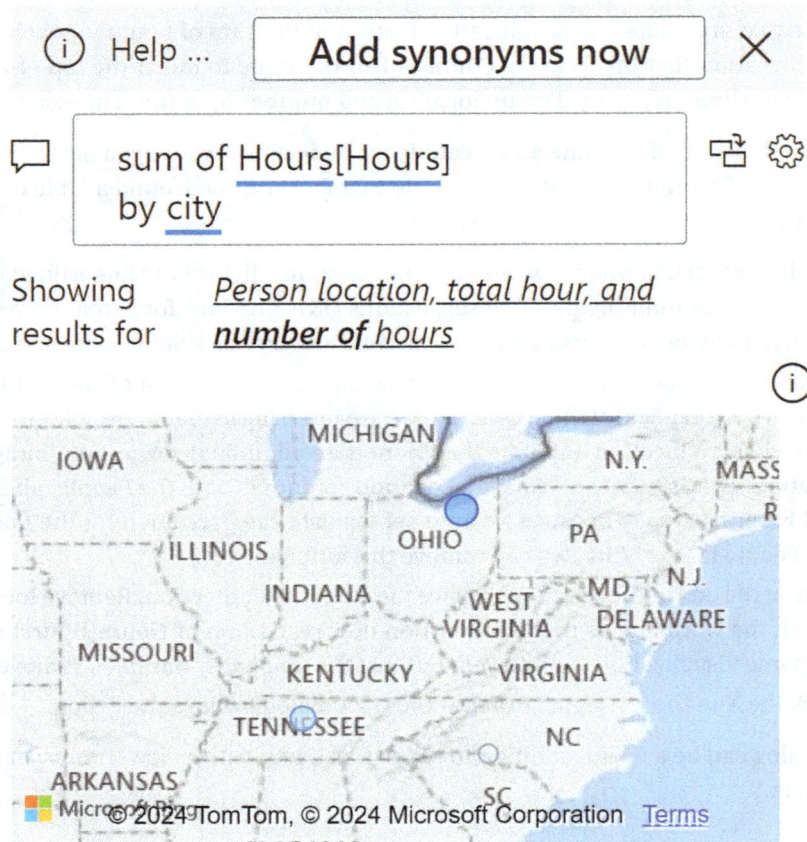

Figure 6.19 – Using Q&A to create visualizations

Just to the right of the question entry area are two icons. The right-most icon is a gear icon, which allows for advanced configuration of Q&A. When hovering over the other icon, a tip is displayed that reads **Turn this Q&A result into a standard visual**. Click this icon. The Q&A dialog goes away, and a standard **Map** visual is displayed with a title of **Sum of Hours and Count of Hours by Location**.

We now have a standard **Map** visualization that we can resize and move. The Q&A dialog is simply used as a means of creating the visualization. The Q&A feature can also be activated by simply double-clicking on a blank area of the canvas. To create a visual this way, do the following:

1. Double-click on a blank area of the canvas.
2. This time, ask the question **sum of Hours[H] by city as bar chart**. Note that Q&A follows the direction to create the visualization as a bar chart instead of a map visual.
3. Add this visual to the report, as we did previously.

We now have a second visualization that we've created via Q&A.

Synonyms

Power BI includes another useful feature that can significantly improve the Q&A experience. This feature is called **synonyms**. With synonyms, the report author can add additional names for tables, columns, and measures that Q&A will then recognize as referring to those semantic model entities.

For example, continuing with our example from *Chapter 2, Planning Projects with Power BI*, Pam knows that the three cities the company operates in are internally referred to as branches. If we double-click on a blank area of the canvas and type **sum of Hours[H] by branch**, Q&A recognizes the word *branch*, but only in the context of people's names; that is, Rocco Branch, Ellen Branch, and Gabriela Branch. To fix this, do the following:

1. Click the gear icon to the right of the question entry box. The **Q&A setup** dialog is displayed, as shown in the following screenshot:

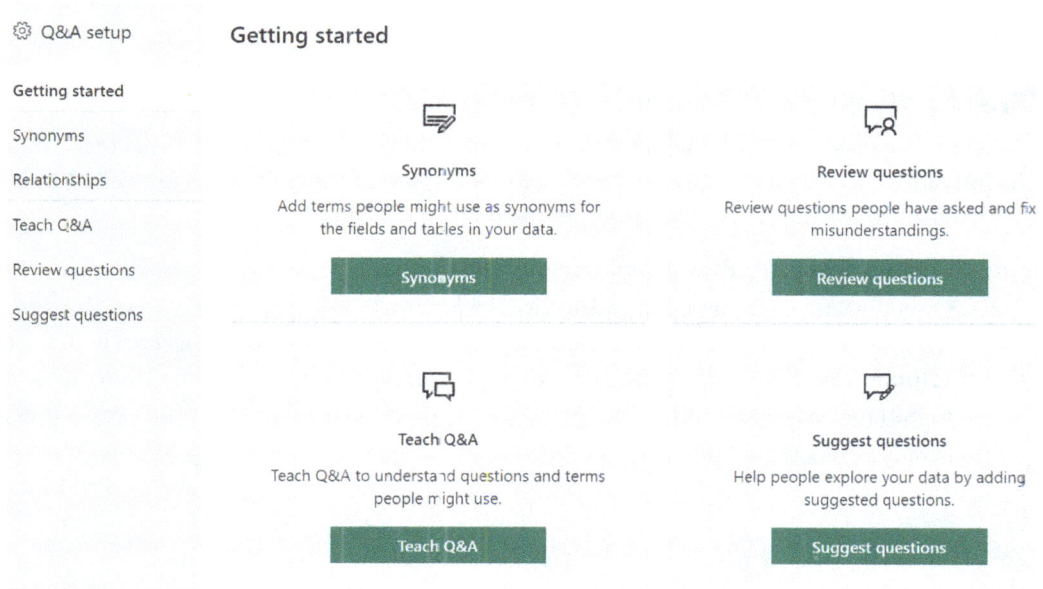

Figure 6.20 – Q&A setup

2. On the left-hand side of the dialog, click **Synonyms**.
3. Expand the **People** table and scroll down to the **Location** column.
4. Click the **Add +** button, type the word branch, and then press the *Enter* key.
5. Click the **X** icon at the top right to close the dialog.

The Q&A visual updates. Retype your question and Q&A now recognizes *branch* in the context of locations. Note that the **Q&A Setup** dialog can be accessed from the **Modeling** tab of the ribbon while you're in the **Report** view. In addition, synonyms can also be added using the **Properties** pane of the **Model** view.

Now that you understand the basics of report navigation features, we'll next explore some advanced analysis techniques that can aid business users in gaining a deeper understanding of data in a visually appealing way. Such analysis adds to the overall utility of visualizations and reports. Save your work before continuing.

Advanced analysis techniques

So far, we have seen how we can segment our data using groups and hierarchies, as well as how to use navigational features such as drill through, buttons, bookmarks, and Q&A to uncover and highlight insights into our data. But Power BI still has more to offer! There are also visual features that allow us to highlight information that is of particular interest or enable the analysis of our data in unique ways.

In this section, we cover a variety of features that enable business users to immediately gain additional detail and insights, including analysis and summarization, Top-N filtering, advanced visualizations, what-if parameters, conditional formatting, quick measures, and report page tooltips. Using these techniques as appropriate can greatly aid in understanding the raw data and unlock meaningful insights that are important to a business.

The Analyze and Summarize features

Power BI provides powerful machine learning and artificial intelligence features that can aid in exploring and analyzing data within a semantic model. Two of these features are called **Analyze** and **Summarize**. To see how these features operate, do the following:

1. Create a new page, **Page 3**, and rename it Analysis.
2. Copy the **Sum of Hours by Location** visual from the **Details** page to the **Analysis** page. Alternatively, recreate the visual on the **Analysis** page using a **Clustered column chart** with the **Location** column from the **People** table as **X-axis** and the **Hours** column from the **Hours** table as **Y-axis**.
3. Right-click anywhere in the visual, choose **Analyze**, and then click **Find where this distribution is different**.

4. A dialog is displayed titled **Here are the filters that cause the distribution of Sum of Hours by Location to change the most,** as shown in the following screenshot:

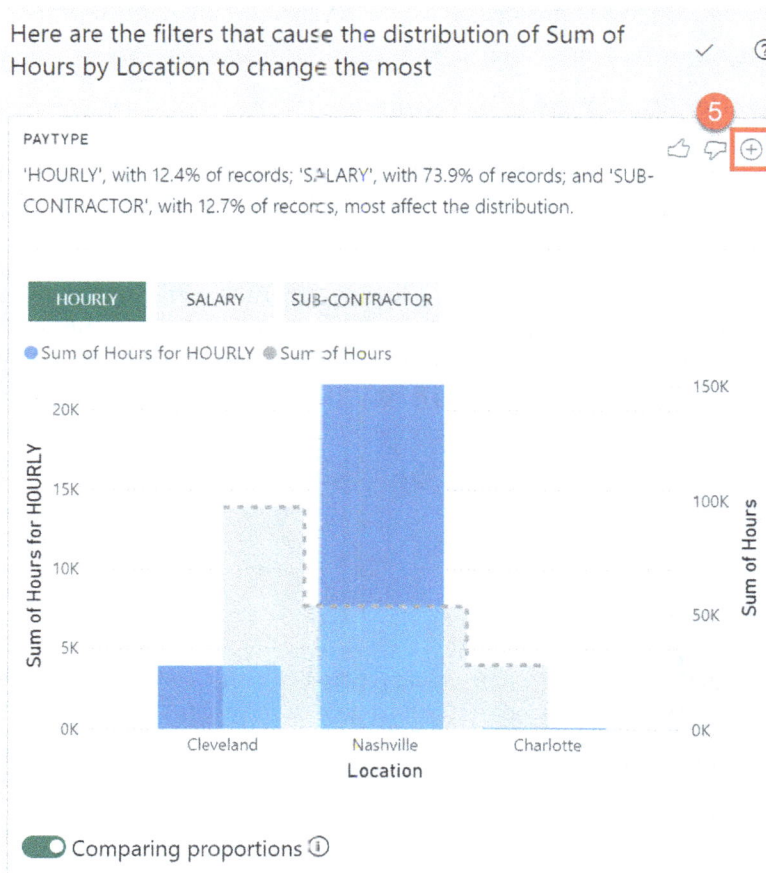

Here are the filters that cause the distribution of Sum of Hours by Location to change the most

PAYTYPE

'HOURLY', with 12.4% of records; 'SALARY', with 73.9% of records; and 'SUB-CONTRACTOR', with 12.7% of records, most affect the distribution.

Figure 6.21 – The Analyze feature

The **Analyze** feature analyzes the semantic model using automated machine learning algorithms to determine the factors that impact the distribution of data in the visual the most. In the preceding screenshot, we can see that the **Nashville** location has a high proportion of employees with a pay type of **HOURLY** compared to **Cleveland** and **Charlotte**. Note the gray, dotted outline of the original **Sum of Hours by Location** visual is included in this new visual.

5. Use the + icon at the top right of the insight card to add the visual to the current page (see *Figure 6.21*).

6. In the **Analyze results** window, scroll down until you find the **DIVISION (GROUPS)** insight card. Initially, **Management** is chosen and shows **Nashville** with a high proportion of **Hours for Management**.

7. Click the **Accounting** button to show that Cleveland has a high proportion of **Hours for Accounting**.

8. Click the + icon to add this insight card as a visualization on the current page.

9. Click anywhere not inside the dialog to close the dialog.

In **Sum of Hours for HOURLY** and **Sum of Hours by Location**, you can hover over the gray, dotted line to view the sum of hours by location. The vertical-colored bars include just the hours for a pay type of **HOURLY**. The y axis on the left represents the hours for the colored bars, while the y axis on the right is for the gray, dotted line. We can easily see from this visualization that while **Cleveland** has the most hours reported in total, the **Nashville** location has many more hours submitted by **HOURLY** employees.

By expanding the **Visualizations** pane and selecting the visual, note that the visual is a standard **Line and clustered column chart** with the **Location** column from the **People** table as **X-axis**, **Sum of Hours for HOURLY** as **Column y-axis**, and the **Sum of Hours** column from the **Hours** table as **Line y-axis**. While not added to the semantic model as a measure, **Sum of Hours for HOURLY** is an implicit DAX calculation equivalent to the following formula:

```
Sum of Hours for HOURLY = CALCULATE(
    SUM( 'Hours'[Hours] ),
    'Hours'[PayType] = "HOURLY"
)
```

💡 **Quick tip:** Enhance your coding experience with the **AI Code Explainer** and **Quick Copy** features. Open this book in the next-gen Packt Reader. Click the **Copy** button

(1) to quickly copy code into your coding environment, or click the **Explain** button

(2) to get the AI assistant to explain a block of code to you.

```
                                                      Copy      Explain
function calculate(a, b) {                              1          2
  return {sum: a + b};
};
```

🔒 **The next-gen Packt Reader** is included for free with the purchase of this book. Scan the QR code OR visit packtpub.com/unlock, then use the search bar to find this book by name. Double-check the edition shown to make sure you get the right one.

The **Analyze** feature can be a powerful tool for quickly finding insights about what factors have a big impact on a visualization. Another power tool is the **Summarize** or **Smart narrative** feature. To see how this feature operates, perform the following steps:

1. On the **Analysis** page, right-click the **Sum of Hours by Location** visualization and choose **Summarize**.

2. When prompted, choose the **Custom** button. We will explore **Copilot** later in this book.

3. A text box appears with a narrative describing the information in natural language. This includes insights around the total number of hours for each location, as well as percentages, such as **Cleveland accounted for 54.34% of Hours**.

Note that the **Summarize** functionality makes use of the **Narrative** visual.

As you can see, the **Analyze** and **Summarize** features can help you unlock insights about your data, as well as aiding in report authoring.

Top-N filtering

Continuing with the example scenario we introduced in *Chapter 2*, *Planning Projects with Power BI*, Pam is learning a lot about how to segment her data and use navigational features to highlight insights. However, Pam wants to do more to visually show important information such as the most utilized or least utilized employees. To this end, perform the following steps:

1. Create a new page called Page 3.

2. Create a table visualization along the right-hand side of the page using the **Name** column from the **People** table and the **% Utilization** measure from the **Calculations** table (not the **% Utilization** column from the **Hours** table). This list is very long, and Pam knows that managers are most likely only interested in the top and bottom performers. While the list can be sorted by clicking on the **% Utilization** column in the table, Pam wants to make it easier for managers to focus on the most important information.

3. Expand the **Filters** pane and then expand the **Name** filter by using the small down arrow icon in the header of the filter. **Filter type** is currently set to **Basic filtering**.

4. Use the drop-down menu to change **Filter type** to **Top N**.

5. The **Show items** field appears and is set to **Top**. In the box next to this, type 10.

6. Next, drag and drop the **% Utilization** measure from the **Calculations** table in the **Data** pane into the **Add data fields here** area underneath the **By value** label.

7. Now, click **Apply filter**. The visual only displays the top 10 employees based on their **% Utilization**.

8. In the **Visualizations** pane, click on the **Format** sub-pane (middle icon).

9. Expand the **Totals** format card and toggle **Values** to **Off**.

10. In the **Format visual** pane on the **General** tab, toggle **Title** to **On**.

11. Expand the **Title** section and, in the **Text** field, type **Top Performers**.

12. With the visualization selected, press *Ctrl + C* to copy the visualization.

13. Press *Ctrl + V* to paste the visualization and drag this new visualization underneath the first visualization.

14. Select this new visualization and, in the **Filters** pane, expand the **Name** filter and change **Show items** to **Bottom**.

15. Click **Apply filter**. Note that more than 10 names are displayed. This is because the bottom performers are all tied at 0%.

16. Use the **Format** pane to edit **Title text** to **Worst Performers**.

Proper use of Top-N filtering allows report viewers to quickly focus on the most important information within visualizations.

Gauges and KPIs

Continuing with the example scenario we introduced in *Chapter 2, Planning Projects with Power BI*, Pam also knows that the overall utilization compared to a target percentage of 80% is important. A good way to display a metric concerning a goal is to use a **gauge** visualization. To add a gauge visualization to the page, do the following:

1. Click on a blank area of the canvas and add a **Gauge** visualization to the page.

2. Add the **% Utilization** measure from the **Calculations** table in the **Value** field well.

3. The gauge visualization displays **84.79%** on a gauge, ranging from **0.00%** to **100.00%**.

4. Pam does not feel that the decimals are important, so select **% Utilization** from the **Data** pane. Then, on the **Measure Tools** tab of the ribbon, in the **Formatting** section, reduce the decimals that are displayed from 2 to 0. Now, the gauge visual displays **85%** on a gauge ranging from **0%** to **100%**.

5. Right-click the **Calculations** table and choose **New measure**.

6. Create a measure with the `% Target Utilization = 0.8` formula.

7. Select the **% Target Utilization** measure. Then, in the **Measure tools** tab of the ribbon, click the **%** icon in the **Formatting** section and set the number of decimal places to 0.

8. Select the gauge visual and add the **% Target Utilization** measure to the **Target value** field well. A line representing the target value is added to the gauge visualization, providing a convenient visual cue regarding whether the utilization is above or below the target:

% Utilization and % Target Utilization

Figure 6.22 – Gauge visualization

Pam likes this new visual but also wants to investigate the **Key Performance Indicator (KPI)** visual.

To experiment with the KPI visual, do the following:

1. Click on a blank area of the canvas and add a **KPI** visual to the page.
2. Drag and drop the **% Utilization** measure from the **Calculations** table into the **Value** field well.
3. Drag and drop the **% Target Utilization** measure into the **Target** field well.
4. Finally, drag and drop **Year** from the **Calendar** table into the **Trend axis** field well.

The KPI visual turns green and reports that the displayed **% Utilization** is +5.99% above the goal of **80%**.

What-if parameters

Continuing with the example scenario we introduced in *Chapter 2, Planning Projects with Power BI*, Pam is pleased with her new visuals but is concerned that the **% Target Utilization** measure is a static number. Managers may wish to increase or decrease their target utilization in the future. Pam wants to provide a way for managers to easily adjust their target utilization goals. To this end, we can create a **What-if parameter.**

To create a what-if parameter, do the following:

1. Click on the **Modeling** tab of the ribbon and, in the **What if** section, choose **New Parameter**. The **What-if parameter** dialog is displayed, as shown in the following screenshot:

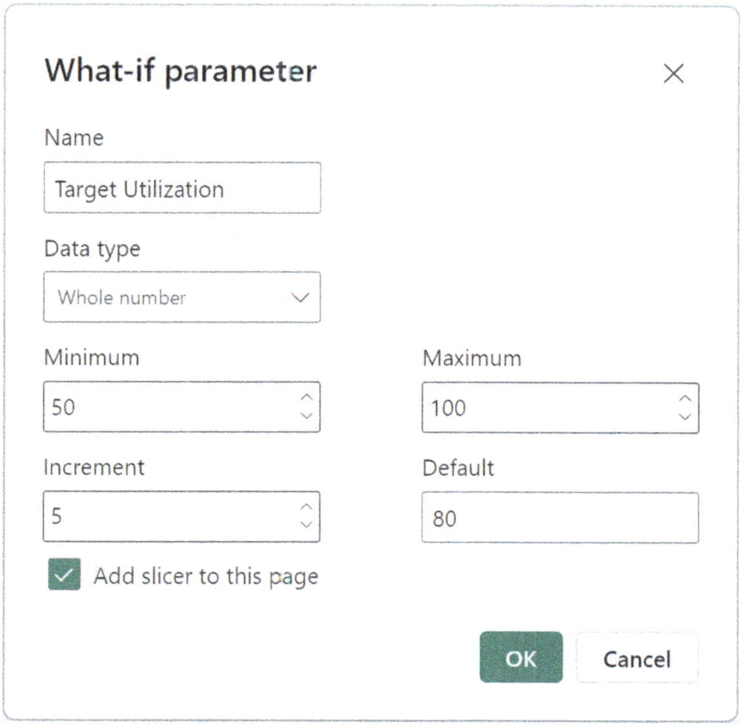

Figure 6.23 – What-if parameter dialog

2. As shown in the preceding screenshot, set **Name** to `Target Utilization`, **Data type** to **Whole number**, **Minimum** to 50, **Maximum** to 100, **Increment** to 5, and **Default** to 80.

3. Leave **Add slicer to this page** checked and then click the **OK** button. A single-value slicer is added to the page. This slicer includes a slider to adjust the value of the slicer.

4. Adjust the slider so that it reads **80**. Note that, in the **Data** pane, a new table was added called **Target Utilization**.

5. Expanding this table shows that two entities are listed: a column called **Target Utilization** and a measure called **Target Utilization Value**.

6. Click on the **Data** view and then select the **Target Utilization** table in the **Fields** pane. Row values exist for **50** through **100** in increments of **5**.

7. Observe that this table is defined by the following DAX formula:

```
Target Utilization = GENERATESERIES(50, 100, 5)
```

GENERATESERIES is a DAX function that takes three parameters: a minimum value, a maximum value, and an increment. GENERATESERIES returns a table of all of the values between the minimum and the maximum in the specified increment.

8. While in the **Data** view, expand the **Target Utilization** table and select the **Target Utilization Value** measure. Observe that the DAX formula for this measure is as follows:

```
Target Utilization Value = SELECTEDVALUE(
    'Target Utilization'[Target Utilization], 80
)
```

SELECTEDVALUE is a special DAX function that returns the currently selected value in a column specified as the first parameter. The second parameter specifies the value to return if no value is selected or if a single selection cannot be determined.

9. Since our utilization is expressed as a decimal, modify this formula in the formula bar to read as follows:

```
Target Utilization Value =DIVIDE(SELECTEDVALUE(
    'Target Utilization'[Target Utilization], 80),
    100,
    0.8
)
```

10. While the **Target Utilization Value** measure is selected, select the **Measure tools** tab of the ribbon, and click the % icon in the **Formatting** section. Also, set the number of decimal places to 0 if necessary.

11. Switch back to the **Report** view and, on **Page 3**, replace **Target value** for the gauge with the **Target Utilization Value** measure. Similarly, on the KPI visual, replace the % **Target Utilization** measure in the **Target** field well with the new **Target Utilization Value** measure.

12. Now, slide the **Target Utilization** slider to **90**. Note that we are now short of our goal on our gauge visualization and that our KPI visualization has turned red!

What-if parameters provide an easy and convenient mechanism for report viewers to interact with reports to set goals, control DAX calculations, and filter information on report pages.

Conditional formatting

In addition to the visual cues provided by the gauge and KPI visualizations, Power BI also supports visual cues in the form of **conditional formatting**. Conditional formatting can be used with tables and matrices to provide background colors, font colors, data bars, and icons for cells within the visualization. To see how this works, do the following:

1. Select the **Top Performers** visualization.

2. In the **Columns** field well, in the **Build visuals** tab of the **Visualizations** pane, right-click **% Utilization**, choose **Conditional formatting**, and then **Background color**. The conditional formatting dialog will be displayed.

3. Check the box for **Add a middle color** and then click the **OK** button, as shown in the following screenshot:

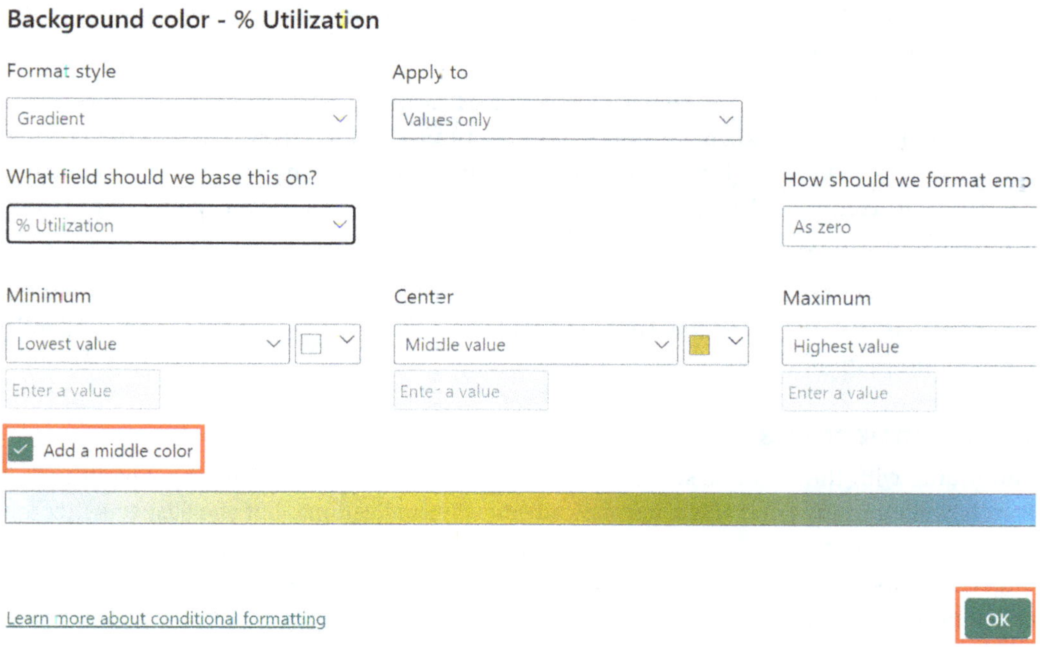

Figure 6.24 – Conditional formatting dialog

4. The **Top Performers** visualization's **% Utilization** column is now color-coded based on the highest and lowest values that appear in the column.

Continuing with the example scenario we introduced in *Chapter 2, Planning Projects with Power BI*, Pam can see how conditional formatting can be useful to create heat maps or otherwise highlight important information, but what she wants is for the **% Utilization** column to be green if the value is greater than or equal to the **Target Utilization Value** measure and red if the value is less than the **Target Utilization Value** measure.

To achieve this, do the following:

1. Create a new measure in the **Calculations** table with the following formula:

```
Goal Status Color = IF(
    [% Utilization] >= [Target Utilization Value],
    "#00FF00", "#FF0000"
)
```

2. Click back on the **Top Performers** visual and right-click % **Utilization** in the **Visualizations** pane. Then, choose **Conditional formatting** and then **Background color**.

3. In **Format style**, choose **Field value** from the drop-down menu instead of **Gradient**.

4. In the **What field should we base this on?** dropdown, choose the new **Goal Status Color** measure in the **Calculations** table.

5. Now, click the **OK** button. All of the cells for % **Utilization** in the **Top Performers** visual are now green.

6. Repeat this same conditional formatting for the **Worst Performers** visualization. All of these cells are now red.

Note that the #00FF00 and #FF0000 used in the Goal Status Color measure are hexadecimal color codes. The first two characters after the hash tag represent the amount of red, the next two green, and the latter two blue. Each character can be a number or text ranging from 0-9, as well as A-F. A is essentially 10 decimal and F represents 16 decimal. Thus, a value of 00 represents none of the specified color, while a value of FF represents all of the specified color.

Conditional formatting has many uses when it comes to highlighting information in information-dense visualizations, such as tables and matrices, and can aid report reviewers in visually identifying important information.

Quick measures

Continuing with the example scenario we introduced in *Chapter 2, Planning Projects with Power BI*, Pam is feeling pretty good about her new advanced visualizations, but she suspects that the managers might want to see a running total of all the hours accumulated during the year. However, Pam is uncertain about how to create a running total using DAX. Luckily, Power BI provides a feature called **Quick measures** that can help with much of the DAX heavy lifting. To see how quick measures can be used to create DAX formulas, do the following:

1. While in the **Report** view, in the **Data** pane, expand the **Hours** table, right-click the **Hours** column, and choose **New quick measure**. The **Quick measure** pane is displayed, as shown in the following screenshot:

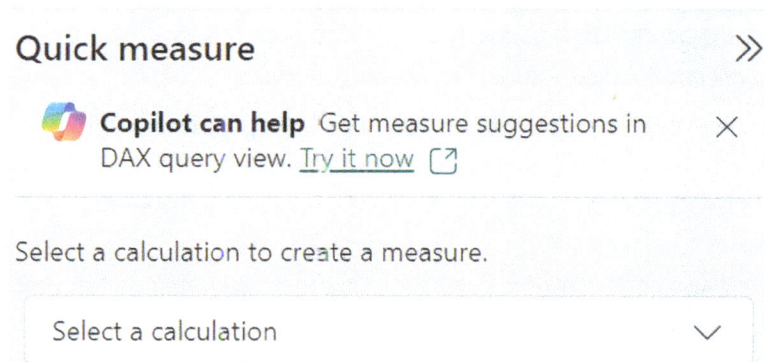

Figure 6.25 – Quick measure pane

2. Under **Select a calculation**, use the drop-down menu and note the various types of quick measures that can be created.

3. Under the **Totals** heading, find and select **Running total**.

4. Drag and drop the **Month** column from the **Calendar** table into the **Field** area where the **Add data** text is displayed.

5. Leave **Base value** as **Sum of Hours** and **Direction** as **Ascending** and click the **Add** button at the bottom of the **Quick measure** pane.

6. A new measure is created in the **Hours** table called **Hours running total in Month**.

7. Since Pam wishes to keep all of her measures together in her **Calculations** table, ensure that the **Hours running total in Month** measure is selected in the **Data** pane, and then select the **Measure tools** tab of the ribbon. In the **Properties** section, change **Home table** from **Hours** to **Calculations**. The **Hours running total in Month** measure now appears under the **Calculations** table.

8. In the **Report** view on **Page 3**, create a new visualization by clicking on a blank area of the canvas. Then, select the checkbox for the **Hours running total by Month** measure in the **Calculations** table and the **Month** column from the **Calendar** table.

9. Switch this visualization from **Clustered column chart** to **Line chart**. Note that, for months after March, the line remains horizontal since we do not have reported hours for months after March.

Quick measures provide us with an easy way to create dozens of common DAX calculations and can be particularly helpful when just beginning to use DAX.

Report tooltip pages

Continuing with the example scenario we introduced in *Chapter 2, Planning Projects with Power BI*, Pam has heard about another advanced visualization technique that she wants to try to make it easy for managers to gain insight into their utilization numbers. This feature is called **report tooltip pages**. Let's see what those are about.

Creating a report tooltip page

To create a report tooltip page, follow these steps:

1. Start by creating a new page and renaming this page **Tooltip1**.
2. While on this page, click the **Format** sub-pane within the **Visualizations** pane.
3. Expand **Page information** and toggle **Allow use as tooltip** from **Off** to **On**. Note that the canvas size changes automatically.
4. Click on **Page 3** and copy and paste the gauge visualization onto the **Tooltip1** page.
5. Adjust the size and position so that the gauge visualization takes up the top right quadrant of the page. Use the **Format** sub-pane of the **Visualizations** pane to toggle **Title** to **Off**. This is under the **General** sub-tab.
6. Copy and paste the **Top Performers** visualization from **Page 3** onto the **Tooltip1** page and adjust the size and position so that it takes up the left-hand side of the page.
7. For the **Top Performers** visualization, on the **Visual** tab of the **Format visual** sub-pane of the **Visualizations** pane, expand **Style presets** and set **Style** to **Condensed**. In addition, expand the **Column headers** and **Values** sections and set **Text size** to **8 pt**.
8. Create a new visualization positioned underneath the gauge visualization. Make this a **Table** visualization consisting of the **Weekday** column from the **Calendar** table and the **% Utilization** measure from the **Calculations** table.
9. Use the **Format** sub-pane of the **Visualizations** pane to modify this table visualization. Expand the **Style presets** section and set the section to **Condensed**. Also, expand the **Totals** section and toggle **Values** to **Off**. Finally, expand the **Column headers** and **Values** sections and set **Text size** to **8 pt**.
10. Make size adjustments to visuals as necessary.

When finished, your **Tooltip1** page should look similar to the following:

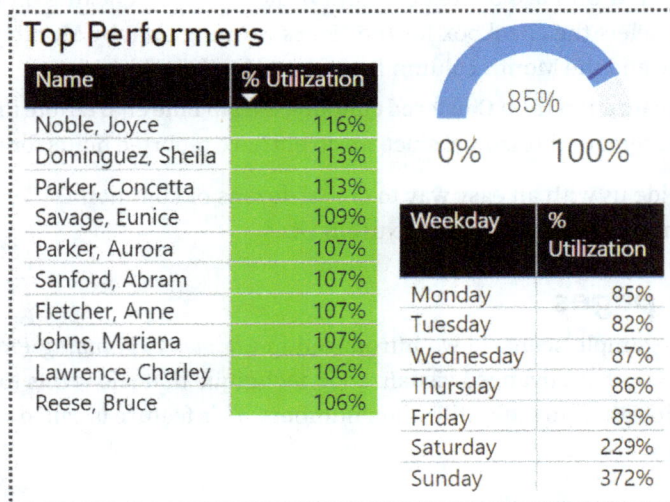

Figure 6.26 – Report tooltip page

Now that we have created our report tooltip page, let's explore how to use this page in a report.

Using a report tooltip page

To use our new report tooltip page, follow these steps:

1. Click back onto the **Page 3** page.

2. Create a new **Table** visualization using the **Division** column from the **Hours** table and the **% Utilization** measure from the **Calculations** table.

3. Select this new table visualization. Then, on the **General** tab of the **Format visuals** sub-pane of the **Visualizations** pane, scroll down and toggle **Tooltips** to **On**.

4. Expand the **Tooltips** format card and ensure that, on the **Options** sub-card, the **Type** is set to **Report page**. Also, change the **Page** setting from **Auto** to **Tooltip1**.

5. Now, use your mouse cursor to mouse over the divisions listed in the **Division** column of the table visualization.

Note that the **Tooltip1** page is displayed as a popup and filters the information for that particular division!

Key influencers

Pam has heard about one last advanced visualization feature of Power BI that she would like to try. This feature adds machine learning functionality to Power BI and is called the **key influencers** visual. To see this new visual in action, follow these steps:

1. Create a new page called Page 4.

2. Find the **Key influencers** visual in the **Visualizations** pane and add this visual to the page. You can also find the **Key influencers** visual by using the **Insert** tab of the ribbon.

3. Resize this visual so that it takes up the entire page.

4. Drag the **Hours** column from the **Hours** table into the **Analyze** field for this visual.

5. Add the following fields to the **Explain by** field:

    - Hours > Division (groups)
    - Hours > PayType
    - People > EmployeeType
    - People > Location

The **Key influencers** visual should now look similar to the following:

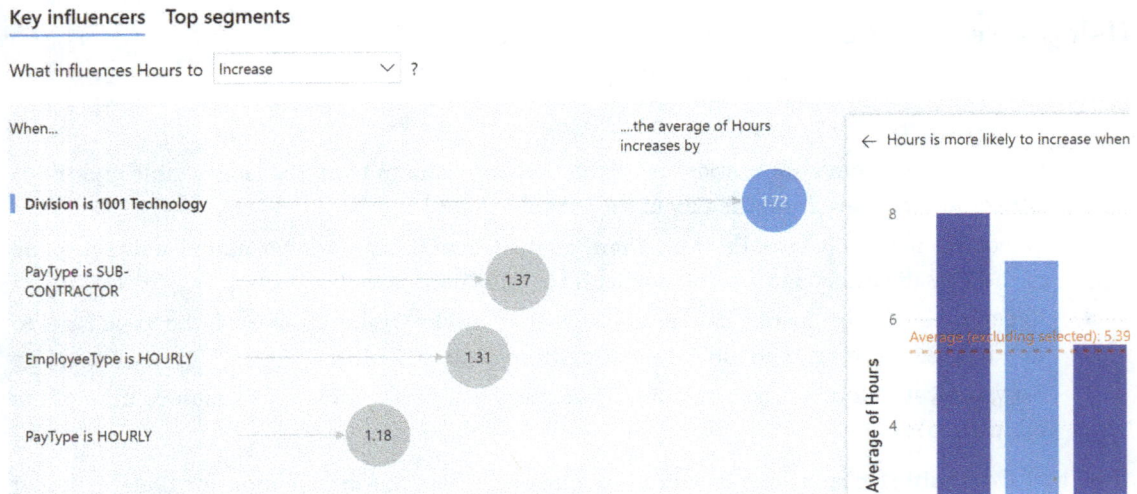

Figure 6.27 – Key influencers visual

The **Key influencers** visual packs a tremendous amount of analysis and insight into a small package. On the **Key influencers** tab, you can see the factors that are most likely to increase or decrease the chosen metric, which in this case is **Hours**. Clicking on the bubbles in the left-hand pane displays the associated visuals in the right-hand pane. The **Top segments** tab identifies clusters of values for when the chosen metric is more likely to be **High** or **Low**. The user can click on these bubbles to gain additional insights into these segments.

Summary

In this chapter, we built upon the semantic model and calculations we created in the previous chapter and learned how to take advantage of the powerful features within Power BI. These features include the ability to segment our data into groups and hierarchies. In addition, we learned how to expand, collapse, and drill up and down through hierarchies, as well as how to use RLS. Next, we learned how additional Power BI features such as drill through, buttons, bookmarks, and Q&A can be used to provide navigational pathways within reports that viewers can use to unlock self-service business intelligence insights.

Finally, we explored advanced analysis techniques such as Analyze, Summarize, Top-N filtering, gauge visualizations, KPI visualizations, what-if parameters, conditional formatting, quick measures, report tooltip pages, and the advanced key influencers visualization. These advanced analysis and visualization techniques allow the report author to build truly engaging and insightful reports that provide tremendous value to an organization.

Now that we have learned about all of the necessary techniques, in the next chapter, we will put what we have learned into use by building a final report.

Questions

As an activity, try to answer the following questions on your own:

- What are the two different methods of segmenting data in Power BI?
- What are the four operations for working with hierarchies?
- What feature would a report author use to ensure that people within different roles only see the information that's relevant to their particular role?
- How is drill through different from drilling up and down through hierarchies?
- What are the six actions buttons can perform?
- Why is data categorization important for Q&A?
- What are synonyms and where can they be added within Power BI Desktop?
- What is a bookmark and what information can it save as part of its definition?
- What advanced visualization feature allows you to create a measure that can be adjusted by a report viewer?
- What are the three settings that must be adjusted when creating a report tooltip page, and how is a report tooltip page activated for use?

Further reading

For more information about the topics that were covered in this chapter, take a look at the following resources:

- Using grouping and binning in Power BI Desktop: https://learn.microsoft.com/en-us/power-bi/create-reports/desktop-grouping-and-binning
- Row-level security (RLS) with Power BI: https://learn.microsoft.com/en-us/fabric/security/service-admin-row-level-security
- Set up drillthrough in Power BI reports: https://learn.microsoft.com/en-us/power-bi/create-reports/desktop-drillthrough
- Create buttons in Power BI reports: https://learn.microsoft.com/en-us/power-bi/create-reports/desktop-buttons?tabs=powerbi-desktop
- Specify data categories in Power BI Desktop: https://learn.microsoft.com/en-us/power-bi/transform-model/desktop-data-categorization
- Best practices to optimize Q&A in Power BI: https://learn.microsoft.com/en-us/power-bi/natural-language/q-and-a-best-practices
- Create report bookmarks in Power BI to share insights and build stories: https://learn.microsoft.com/en-us/power-bi/create-reports/desktop-bookmarks?tabs=powerbi-desktop
- Create and use parameters to visualize variables in Power BI Desktop: https://learn.microsoft.com/en-us/power-bi/transform-model/desktop-what-if
- Create tooltips based on report pages: https://learn.microsoft.com/en-us/power-bi/create-reports/desktop-tooltips?tabs=powerbi-desktop

Unlock this book's exclusive benefits now

Scan this QR code or go to packtpub.com/ unlock, then search for this book by name.

Note: Keep your purchase invoice ready before you start.

7

Creating the Final Report

We have spent the last few chapters importing, scrubbing, and shaping data, and then carefully crafting it into a semantic model. In addition, we have learned about the many powerful features of Power BI that can help us unlock insights into our data.

All of this hard work is about to pay off. In this chapter, we will put all of these tools and techniques together into a final report that we can share with the organization! This chapter provides detailed steps regarding how to create a polished report. This report will not only provide ease of use and valuable insights to the viewer but can also be easily updated and maintained over time.

In this chapter, we will cover the following topics:

- Preparing the final report
- Creating the final report pages
- Finishing up

Technical requirements

You will need to meet the following requirements to follow the instructions in this chapter:

- An internet connection.
- Microsoft Power BI Desktop.
- Download Chapter 7 Start.zip from GitHub at: https://github.com/PacktPublishing/ Learn-Microsoft-Power-BI_3E and uncompress the pbix file.

Preparing the final report

Before we start creating the final version of our report, it is important to take a moment to get things in order with regard to creating the report. A little bit of preparation can save a lot of time, headaches, and avoid rework. So, we'll start preparing for the final report in the following subsection.

Planning the final report

Continuing with the example scenario introduced in *Chapter 2, Planning Projects with Power BI*, Pam takes a moment to contemplate the various groups of individuals within the company that the final utilization report must serve.

The main groups include the following:

- C-level executives
- Division managers
- Branch managers

Each group is interested in utilization but in slightly different ways. The C-level executives simply want a quick summary of the utilization numbers, whether it is meeting the desired goals, how utilization is trending, and so on. Division managers, on the other hand, need to drill a little bit deeper and understand how utilization looks on individual projects as well as who the top and bottom individual contributors are on those projects. Branch managers are interested in the same sort of information as division managers, but only within their individual branches/locations.

Pam decides that her final report should include six pages:

- **Executive Summary:** A page summarizing the information at a high level, including relevant trends.
- **Division Management:** A summary page focused on division managers.
- **Branch Management:** A summary page focused on branch managers.
- **Hours Detail:** A page that includes a detailed hours breakdown.
- **Employee Details:** A page focused on breaking down the utilization of particular employees.
- **Introduction:** An introduction to the report and how to use it.

Now that we have the overall plan for the report, it is time to clean up some of our prior work.

Cleaning up

Before Pam begins working on the final report, she wants to clean up some of the pages within her current working draft. To do this, follow these steps:

1. If not continuing from the last chapter, download **Chapter 7 Start.pbix** from the GitHub repository and save the file as **LearnPowerBI.pbix**.
2. Delete all of the pages in the report that have been created thus far except for **Page 4**. This can be done by hovering over a page tab and clicking the small x icon or by right-clicking a page tab and selecting **Delete Page**.
3. While on **Page 4**, delete the **Key influencers** visualization and any other visualizations.

With that, you're all done cleaning up! Now, let's tackle applying a theme to our report.

Using a theme

Pam wants all of the pages of her report to be consistent and use corporate branding guidelines. To this end, she has created a theme file for use with Power BI Desktop. This theme file contains all of the approved corporate branding colors and standards, as well as larger default font size settings. This theme can save Pam a lot of time and effort when it comes to formatting the final report, and the viewers will appreciate the corporate branding as opposed to the default colors in Power BI Desktop, which, frankly, Pam is not very fond of.

The theme file is simply a text file that is named LearnPowerBI.json. This is a **JavaScript Object Notation (JSON)** file. Its content is as follows:

```json
{
    "name": "LearnPowerBI",
    "dataColors":[
      "#EC670F",
      "#3C3C3B",
      "#E5EAEE",
      "#5C85E6",
      "#29BCC0",
      "#7EAE40",
      "#20B2E7",
      "#D3DCE0",
    ],
    "background":"#EC670F",
    "foreground": "#FFFFFF",
    "tableAccent": "#29BCC0",
    "visualStyles": {
      "*": {
        "*": {
          "*": [
            {
              "fontSize":14,
              "fontFamily":"Segoe UI"
            }
          ],
          "general":[{"responsive":true}]
        }
      },
      "tableEx": {
        "*": {
```

```
    "columnHeaders":[
      {
        "autoSizeColumnWidth":true,
        "fontFamily":"Segoe (Bold)",
        "fontSize":14
      }
    ]
  }
 }
}
}
```

This theme file can be downloaded from GitHub here: https://github.com/PacktPublishing/Learn-Microsoft-Power-BI_3E.

There are many online Power BI theme generators, such as those from bibb (https://powerbithemegenerator.bibb.pro/), POINT (https://themegenerator.point-gmbh.com/en/Home), and powerbi.tips (https://themes.powerbi.tips/themes/wireframes). In addition, the Microsoft community site has a Themes Gallery where you can view and download theme files (https://community.fabric.microsoft.com/t5/Themes-Gallery/bd-p/ThemesGallery).

Of these, bibb's is perhaps the easiest to use, with the ability to upload an image such as a corporate logo to automatically generate a theme or generate a theme using a simple, descriptive phrase such as "a dark and stormy sea."

To use this theme, perform the following steps:

1. In Power BI Desktop, while in the **Report** view, click on the **View** tab.
2. In the **Themes** section, click the drop-down arrow.

3. Choose **Browse for themes,** as shown in the following screenshot:

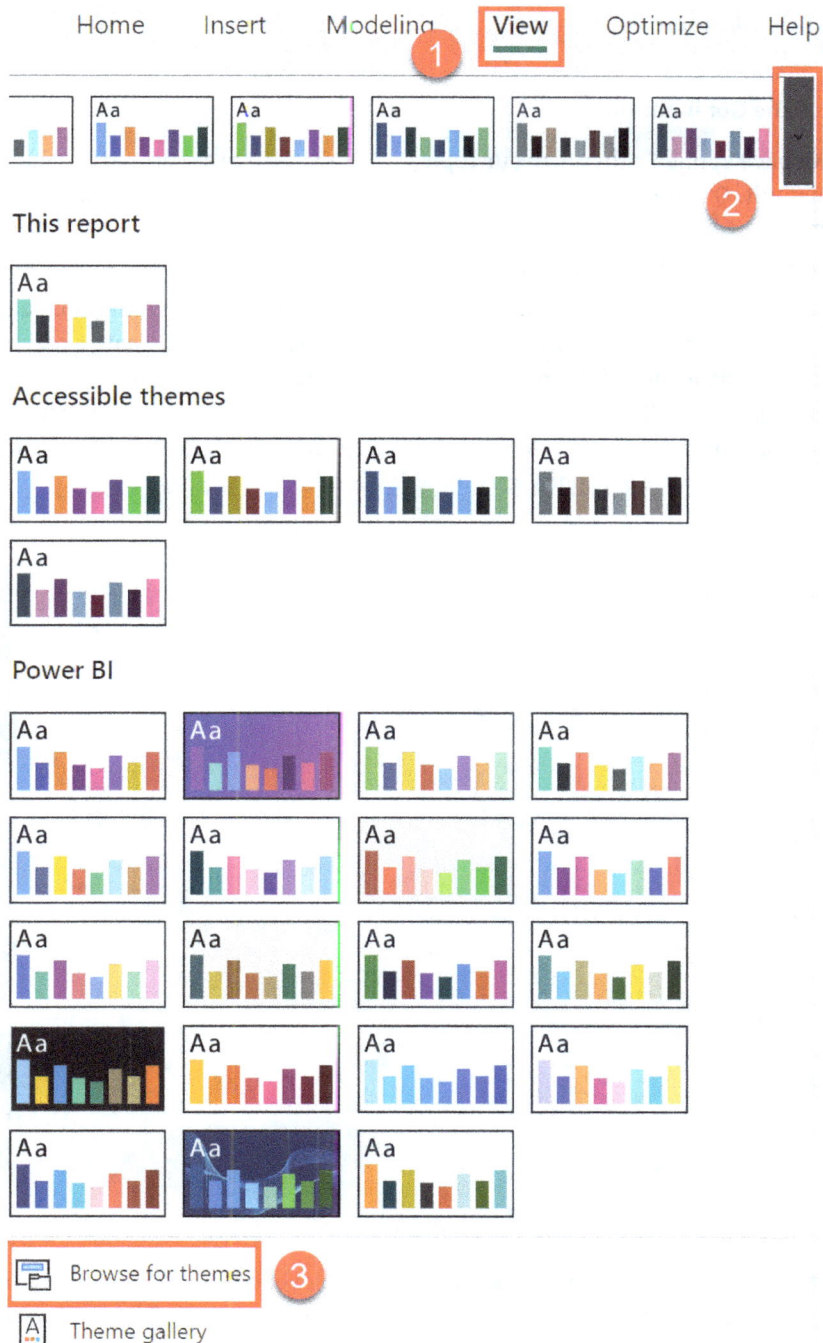

Figure 7.1 – Browse for themes in Power BI Desktop

4.   Navigate to the LearnPowerBI.json file, select it, and click the **Open** button.

An **Import theme** dialog appears, stating whether the theme file was imported successfully or not.

5.   Click the **Got it** button.

Now that we have applied a theme to our report, we only need to set properties that do not follow the theme by default. Our next step is to create a template for the final pages of the report.

Creating a page template

Pam decides that she wants all of her pages to have the same basic layout, look, and feel. Therefore, she decides that, as her next step in creating her final report, she will create a page template that can be used as the basis for all of the pages in her report. This will take some initial work to complete, but it will save a tremendous amount of time later on as pages are added to the report. Think of the value of a template page this way: instead of setting up the layout and format for each page of a report individually, we do these operations only once instead.

The **Template** page should look as follows when we are done:

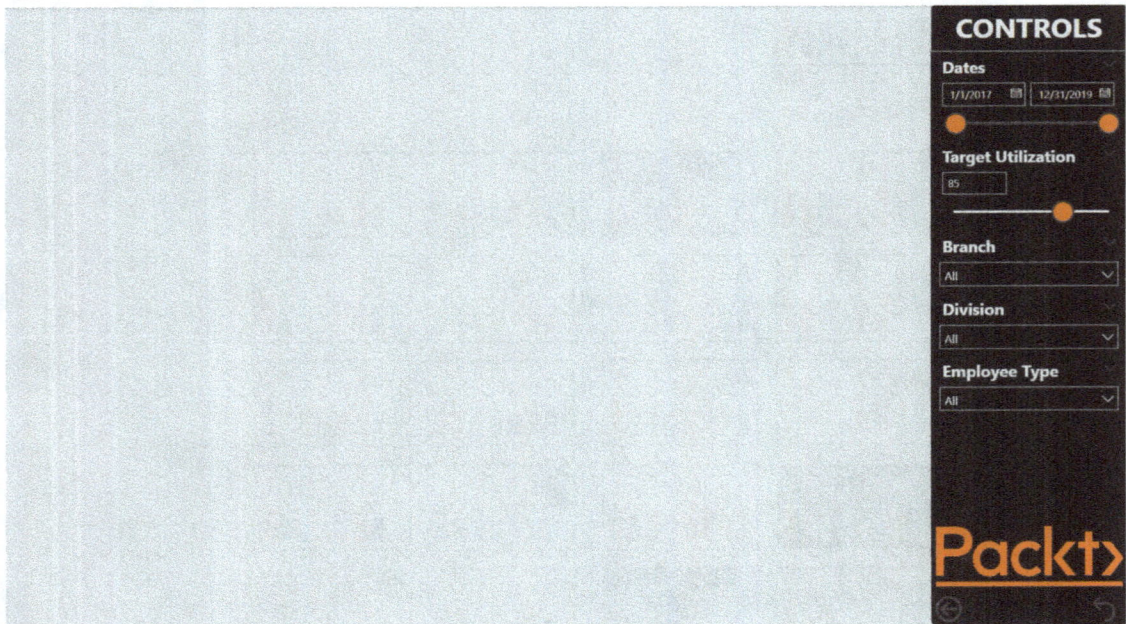

Figure 7.2 – Completed Template page

If you want to skip creating this template, download the LearnPowerBI_TemplateOnly.zip file from https://github.com/PacktPublishing/Learn-Microsoft-Power-BI_3E. Otherwise, complete the following steps to create the page template:

1.   Rename **Page 4** to Template.

2. Next, set the background color for the page by using the **Format** sub-pane of the **Visualizations** pane, expanding **Canvas background** and format card, and clicking the drop-down arrow under the **Color** setting.

3. Select the last color in the top row under **Theme colors**. The tooltip for this color is **#D3DCE0, Theme color 8**.

4. Set **Transparency** to 0%.

To aid her in laying out the visuals on her pages, Pam then decides to activate positioning and layout tools by clicking on the ribbon's **View** tab. In the **Page options** section, she checks the boxes next to **Gridlines** and **Snap to grid**.

Pam has decided that the right-hand side of each page will be reserved for slicers that the end users can use to create various views of the visualizations on the page focused on their desired information. To mark this area off as separate, Pam decides to create a rectangle to mark where she will place the slicers.

To do this, follow these steps:

1. Select the **Insert** tab of the ribbon and, in the **Elements** section, select **Shapes** and then **Rounded Rectangle**. Note that white dots appear on the canvas, marking the gridlines.

2. Position the rectangle in the top right of the page canvas.

3. Next, adjust the size of the rectangle so that it takes up the entire height of the page and the first two vertical grid lines from the right-hand side of the page. For the default **16:9** canvas setting, this should correspond to a **Height** of 720 and a **Width** of 224. You can check this by selecting the rectangle and in the **Format shape** pane, switch to the **General** tab and expand the **Properties** format card.

4. With the rectangle selected, on the **Shape** tab of the **Format shape** pane, expand the **Style** format card, expand the **Fill** sub-card, and change **Color** to the fourth color in the top row from the left, **#3C3C3B, Theme color 2**.

5. Expand the **Border** sub-card and change **Color** to this same color.

6. Finally, expand the **Shape** format card and adjust **Round corners** to 3%. Note, you can achieve the same effect by using a standard rectangle and adjusting the rounded corners to **10 px**.

Pam decides that she should title this area. To do so, follow these steps:

1. From the **Insert** tab of the ribbon, choose **Text box** from the **Elements** section.

2. Place this visual at the top of the rectangle and resize it so that the text box is the entire width of the rectangle and consumes seven grid dots of vertical height. Note that since **Snap to grid** is turned on, each "snap" when resizing is one grid dot. This corresponds to a **Height** of **56** and a **Width** of **224**.

3. Type CONTROLS into the text box.

4. Double-click the word **CONTROLS** and change its font to **Segoe (Bold)**.

5. Increase the font size to **24** and **Center** the text.

6. Change the font color to the fifth color from the left in the top row, **#E5EAEE, Theme color 3**.

7. In the **Format text box** pane, expand the **Effects** format card and toggle **Background** to **Off**.

The final position of the text box can be checked in the **Properties** section of the **Format text box** pane using the **Size** and **Position** cards:

- **Horizontal Position:** 1056
- **Vertical Position:** 0
- **Width:** 224
- **Height:** 56

Your page should look similar to the following:

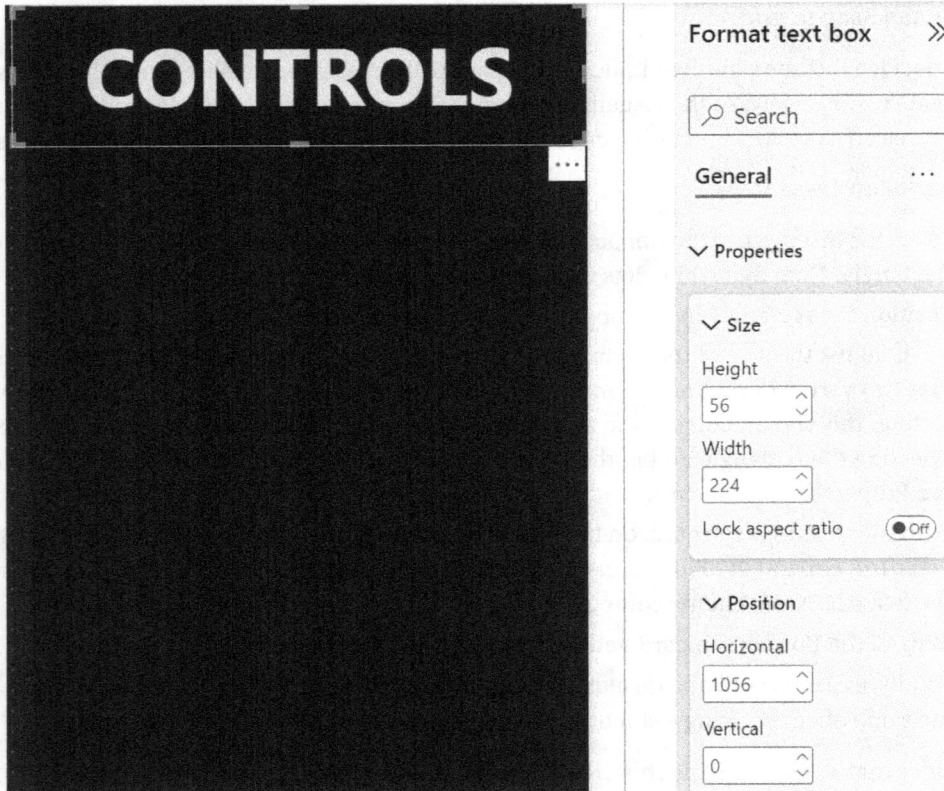

Figure 7.3 – CONTROLS text box position

Next, Pam wants to show a relative date slicer at the top of this rectangle. Follow these steps to add the slicer:

1. Click on a blank area of the canvas, expand the **Calendar** table in the **Data** pane, and select **Date**.
2. In the **Visualizations** pane, click the drop-down arrow for **Date** in the **Columns** field well and switch this to **Date** instead of **Date Hierarchy**.

3. Switch this new visualization to a slicer using the **Visualizations** pane.

4. Shrink this visual to where the bottom of the visual is at the bottom of the circular sliders, and then move this slicer so that it is centered directly underneath the **CONTROLS** text box. Red guidelines appear to aid in positioning.

5. Adjust the horizontal size as necessary so that it fits within the rectangle.

6. On the **General** tab of the **Format** sub-pane of the **Visualizations** pane, expand the **Effects** format card and toggle **Background** to **Off**.

7. On the **Visual** tab, expand the **Values** section and change **Font color** to the fifth color from the left in the top row, **#E5EAEE, Theme color 3**.

8. Expand the **Slicer header** section and change **Font color** to **#E5EAEE, Theme color 3**, **Title text** to **Dates**, **Text size** to **14**, and **Font family** to **Segoe UI (Bold)**.

9. Finally, adjust the vertical size of this slicer until the word **Dates** increases to its proper size.

The slicer should have the following sizes and coordinates, which you can check in the **Properties** sections of the **General** tab of the **Format** sub-pane using the **Size** and **Position** cards:

- **Horizontal Position:** 1056
- **Vertical Position:** 56
- **Width:** 224
- **Height:** 152

Your visuals should look similar to the following:

Figure 7.4 – CONTROLS text box and Dates slicer

Next, Pam wants to use the **Target Utilization** slicer she created earlier. To add this slicer to the page, perform the following steps:

1. Click on a blank area of the canvas, expand the **Target Utilization** table, and click the checkbox next to the **Target Utilization** column.

2. Resize this slicer and position it underneath the **Dates** slicer. It is okay if the visuals overlap.

3. On the **General** tab of the **Format** sub-pane of the **Visualizations** pane, expand the **Effects** format card and toggle **Background** to **Off**.

4. On the **Visual** tab, expand the **Values** format card and change the **Font color** property of **#E5EAEE, Theme color 3**.

5. Format **Slicer header** to have a **Font color** of **#E5EAEE**, **Theme color 3**, a **Text size** of **14**, and a **Font family** of **Segoe UI (Bold)**.

6. Finally, adjust the vertical size of this slicer until the words **Target Utilization** increase to their proper size and the yellow warning disappears from the **Slicer header** area.

The slicer should have the following sizes and coordinates, which you can check using the **Properties** section on the **General** tab of the **Format** sub-pane using the **Size** and **Position** cards:

*   **Horizontal Position:** 1056
*   **Vertical Position:** 160
*   **Width:** 224
*   **Height:** 152

The visuals on your page should look similar to the following:

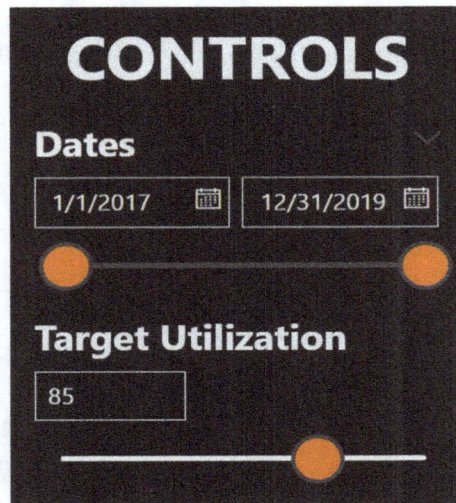

Figure 7.5 – Target Utilization slicer added

Pam also wants a slicer for branches. To create this, do the following:

1. Click on a blank area of the canvas and then expand the **People** table in the **Data** pane and choose the **Location** column.

2. Switch this visual to a slicer as well.

3. Shrink this slicer vertically and reposition this slicer underneath the **Target Utilization** slicer. It is okay if the visuals overlap.

4. Adjust the horizontal size as necessary so that it fits within the rectangle.

5. On the **General** tab of the **Format** sub-pane of the **Visualizations** pane, expand the **Effects** format card and toggle **Background** to **Off**.

6. On the **Visual** tab of the **Format** sub-pane of the **Visualizations** pane, expand the **Slicer settings** format card and then the **Selection** sub-card, and toggle **Show "Select All" option** to **On**. Set **Style** to **Dropdown**.

7. Expand the **Slicer header** format card and change **Title text** to **Branch**, **Font color** to **#E5EAEE**, **Theme color 3**, **Font size** to **14**, and **Font family** to **Segoe UI Bold**.

8. Expand the **Values** section and change **Font color** to **#E5EAEE**, **Theme color 3**, and **Font size** to **12**. Expand the **Background** sub-card and change **Color** to **#3C3C3B**, **Theme color 2**.

This slicer should have the following settings in the **Properties** section of the **General** tab for the **Size** and **Position** cards:

- **Horizontal Position:** 1056
- **Vertical Position:** 264
- **Width:** 224
- **Height:** 72

The visuals on your page should look similar to the following:

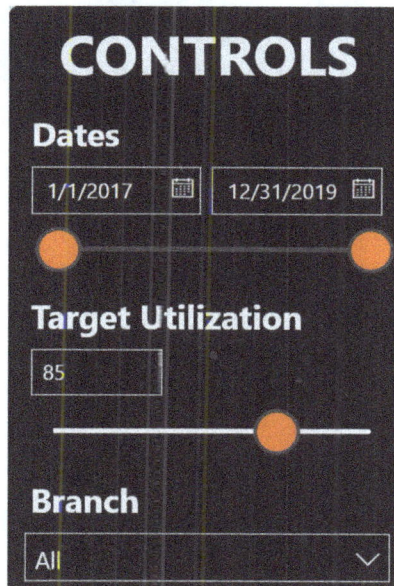

Figure 7.6 – Branch slicer added

To create a **Division** slicer, perform the following steps:

1. Select the **Branch** slicer and use *Ctrl + C* and *Ctrl + V* to copy and paste the slicer, respectively.

2. Reposition this slicer directly underneath the original **Branch** slicer.

3. Replace the slicer's **Field** with the **Division** column (not **Division (groups)** or **Division Hierarchy**) from the **Hours** table.

4. In the **Format** sub-pane of the **Visualizations** pane, expand the **Slicer header** section and change **Title text** to **Division**.

This slicer should have the following settings in the **Properties** section of the **General** tab for the **Size** and **Position** cards:

- **Horizontal Position:** 1056
- **Vertical Position:** 336
- **Width:** 224
- **Height:** 72

The **Division** slicer should be positioned directly underneath the **Branch** slicer, as shown in the following screenshot:

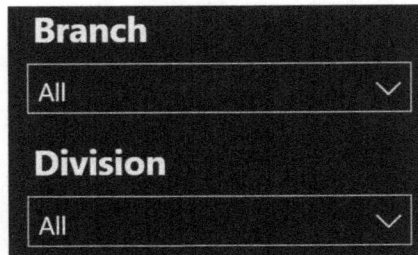

Figure 7.7 – The Division slicer underneath the Branch slicer

To create a slicer based on the type of employee, follow these steps:

1. Select the **Division** slicer and use *Ctrl + C* and *Ctrl + V* to copy and paste the slicer, respectively.
2. Position this slicer directly underneath the original **Division** slicer.
3. Replace this slicer's **Field** with the **EmployeeType** column (not **Employee Type (groups)**) from the **People** table.
4. In the **Format** sub-pane of the **Visualizations** pane, expand the **Slicer header** section and change **Title text** to **Employee Type.**

This slicer should have the following settings in the **Properties** section of the **General** tab for the **Size** and **Position** cards:

- **Horizontal Position:** 1056
- **Vertical Position:** 408
- **Width:** 224
- **Height:** 72

The **Employee Type** slicer should be positioned directly underneath the **Division** slicer, as shown in the following screenshot:

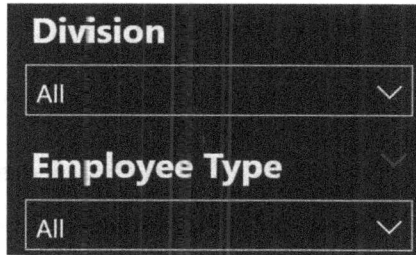

Figure 7.8 – The Employee Type slicer beneath the Division slicer

These are the common slicers that Pam envisions on each page. Pam also plans on creating a bookmark for each page that will reset all of the slicers and filters on the page. To plan for this, follow these steps:

1. Click on a blank area of the canvas. Then, on the **Insert** tab of the ribbon, choose **Buttons** and then **Reset**.
2. Shrink this button horizontally until just before the icon gets smaller and reposition this button in the lower right-hand corner of the page.
3. With the button selected, on the **General** tab of the **Format button** pane, expand the **Effects** section and ensure **Background** is toggled to **Off**.
4. Also, on the **Button** tab of the **Format button** pane, expand the **Style** section and toggle **Text** to **On**.
5. Expand the **Text** section and change the top dropdown from **Default** to **On hover**.
6. Enter **RESET** for **Text**.
7. Change **Font color** to **#E5EAEE, Theme color 3**, **Font family** to Segoe UI (Bold), and **Horizontal alignment** to **Center**.

Pam also plans on using drill through on some pages. To prepare for this, do the following:

1. Copy and paste the reset button and reposition it at the bottom left of the rectangle.
2. In the **Format button** pane, expand the **Style** format card on the **Button** tab and then expand the **Icon** sub-card and change **Shape** from **Reset** to **Back**.
3. Expand the **Text** card, change the state to **On hover**, and replace the word **RESET** with **BACK**.
4. Toggle the **Action** format card to **On** and ensure that **Type** is set to **Back**.

Finally, Pam wants to brand all of the report pages with the corporate logo. To add the logo, follow these steps:

1. Click on a blank area of the canvas, click the **Insert** tab of the ribbon, and select **Image** from the **Elements** section.
2. Select **Packtlogo.png**. This file can be downloaded from GitHub at `https://github.com/PacktPublishing/Learn-Microsoft-Power-BI_3E`.
3. Shrink this image as necessary and place the image just above the buttons.

The corporate logo and buttons are shown in the following screenshot:

Figure 7.9 – Corporate logo and buttons

The completed **Template** page should now look like what was shown in *Figure 7.2*.

All of these visuals are intended to remain exactly as they are and act like a group. To ensure that you do not accidentally move individual visuals around later, press the *Ctrl-A* keys to select all of the visuals. In the **Format** tab in the **Arrange** area of the ribbon, select **Group** and then **Group**. This groups the visuals together such that they act as a single unit while editing.

Now is a good time to save your work before looking at syncing slicers.

Using Sync slicers

Pam wants the slicers in the **CONTROLS** area to stay in sync across the pages of the report. This means that when a slicer is changed or adjusted on one page, all of the other pages of the report should reflect this change. To use the sync slicers feature, do the following:

1. Start on the **Template** page.
2. Click on the **View** tab of the ribbon. In the **Show panes** section, choose **Sync slicers**. The **Sync slicers** pane appears between the **Filters** pane and the **Visualizations** pane.
3. Select the **Dates** slicer. Note that, at the top, all of the page names in the report are listed – in this case, just **Template**. The visible (eyeball) icon indicates whether or not the slicer is present on the page. There is also a sync icon to the left of the visible icon that allows you to check which pages the slicer keeps in sync.
4. Expand the **Advanced options** section.
5. In the field, type *Dates* and then note that the checkboxes next to **Sync field changes to other slicers** and **Sync filter changes to other slicers** are checked automatically, as shown in the following screenshot. These options mean that any slicers with the same group name will be kept in sync, regardless of the pages they are on:

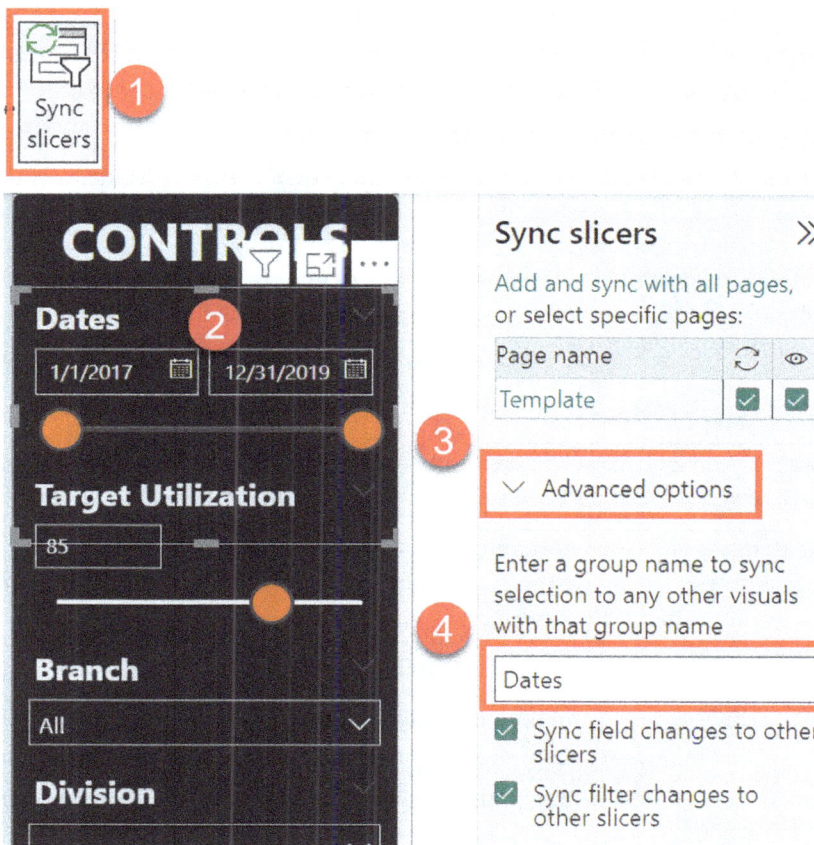

Figure 7.10 – Sync slicers pane

6. Click on the **Target Utilization** slicer and add a group name of *Target Utilization*.

7. Click on the **Branch** slicer and add a group name of *Branches*.

8. Click on the **Division** slicer and add a group name of *Divisions*.

9. Click on the **Employee Type** slicer and add a group name of *Employee Types*.

Pam is now done with the **Sync slicers** pane, so unselect the **Sync slicers** icon on the **View** tab of the ribbon.

Adjusting the calendar

Pam only wants dates that are contained within the report to be displayed in the **Dates** slicer. When Pam created the **Calendar** table, she used the CALENDAR function and used 1/1/2017 and 12/31/2019 as the beginning and end dates for the CALENDAR function's parameters, respectively. This means that the **Dates** slicer displays all these dates. This will not do for the final report.

To fix this, click on the **Calendar** table and edit the DAX formula definition so that it's now as follows:

```
Calendar = CALENDAR( MIN( 'Hours'[Date] ), MAX( 'Hours'[Date] ) )
```

This formula replaces the hardcoded date values with the minimum and maximum date values in the **Hours** table. The **Dates** slicer now only has available dates of 1/1/2019 to 3/22/2019. Pam knows that when she adds data to the report, this table will recalculate during the refresh, so the report's **Dates** slicer will always only have the dates that are available within the semantic model.

The CALENDARAUTO function can also help ensure that all of the calendar dates within the model are part of the calendar table. CALENDARAUTO is similar to CALENDAR in that it creates a table of dates, but CALENDARAUTO analyzes the semantic model and creates the calendar table between the minimum and maximum dates within the entire model. To control exactly what dates appear more accurately in your calendar/date table, it is recommended to use the CALENDAR function, as described here, instead of CALENDARAUTO.

Adding report filters

As a final preparation step, Pam wants to add overall report filters. **Report-level filters** filter all of the pages of the report, which will save time compared to placing these same filters on each page.

Pam knows that, for this report, management only cares about billable resources and not about back-office resources such as administrators, human resources, sales, and so on. Pam already created a group that groups billable resources.

To implement this report filter, perform the following steps:

1. Expand the **Data** pane and then the **People** table.
2. Right-click **EmployeeType (groups)**, choose **Add to filters**, and then choose **Report-level filters**.
3. Expand the **Filters** pane and in the **Filters on all pages** section, find **EmployeeType (groups)**.
4. Ensure that **Filter type** is set to **Basic filtering** and then check **Billable**.

The **Employee Type** slicer now only lists HOURLY, SALARY, and SUB-CONTRACTOR.

Similarly, Pam only wants to focus this report on the three main lines of consulting services the company provides, that is, technology, accounting, and management consulting.

To add this filter, do the following:

1. Expand the **Hours** table in the **Data** pane and add **Division (groups)** (not the **Division** column or **Division Hierarchy**) to the **Filters on all pages** area of the **Filters** pane.
2. Using **Basic filtering**, select **Technology**, **Accounting**, and **Management**.

The **Division** slicer now only shows the values for these three groups.

We are now done preparing for the creation of our final report pages. So, let's get to it!

Creating the final report pages

Pam is finally done with the preparation. However, all of this preparation is about to pay off by making the rest of the final report pages far easier and faster.

In the following subsections, we'll create each of the six pages of the final report.

Creating the Executive Summary page

The first page is the **Executive Summary** page. This page should display a quick snapshot of the most important information to the business executives. To create the **Executive Summary** page, follow these steps:

1. Right-click the **Template** page and choose **Duplicate Page**.
2. Rename **Duplicate of Template** to Executive Summary.

Because this page is a duplicate of the **Template** page, all of the slicers on this page have the same group names that were defined for the slicers on the **Template** page. This means that the slicers on this page will be kept in sync with the slicers on the **Template** page; any other pages that are created will be done by duplicating the **Template** page.

Pam wants this page to be a high-level summary of information that the executives can glance at and immediately understand the state of utilization across months, divisions, and branches. She wants big, bold, colorful visuals that convey a lot of information quickly. She remembers the **Key Performance Indicator (KPI)** visualization she created earlier and liked its color and ability to display a lot of information in a small amount of space. To add a KPI visualization, follow these steps:

1. On the **Executive Summary** page, click on a blank area of the canvas. Then, from the **Visualizations** pane, select the KPI visualization.
2. Place this visualization at the top left of the page and adjust its size so that it takes up half the page vertically and half of the light-gray area horizontally.
3. Place the **Month** column from the **Calendar** table in the **Trend Axis** field well, the **% Utilization** measure from the **Calculations** table in the **Value** field well, and the **Target Utilization Value** measure from the **Target Utilization** table in the **Target** field well.
4. Using the **General** tab of the **Format visuals** sub-pane of the **Visualizations** pane, expand the **Effects** format card and toggle **Background** to **Off**.
5. While still on the **General** tab, expand the **Title** format card and change **Title text** to **Current % Utilization vs. Target.**
6. Change **Text color** to **#3C3C3B**, **Theme color 2**, **Alignment** to **Center**, **Text size** to **24**, and **Font** to **Segoe UI (Bold)**.
7. Switch to the **Visual** tab, expand the **Callout value** section, and adjust the **Font** size to the maximum of **60**.
8. Expand the **Target label** section and change **Font color** to **#3C3C3B**, **Theme color 2**, **Text size** to **24**, and **Font** to **Segoe UI (Bold)**.

The next visual is a summary of **% Utilization by Division**. To create this visual, follow these steps:

1. Copy and paste the KPI visual and move the copied visual directly underneath the original KPI visual.
2. Change this visualization to a **Clustered** bar chart.
3. Replace the **Month** column in the **Y-axis** field well with the **Division** column from the **Hours** table.

4. Remove **Target Utilization Value** from the **X-axis** field well.

5. Using the **General** tab of the **Format visual** sub-pane of the **Visualizations** pane, expand the **Title** section and edit **Title Text** to **% Utilization by Division**.

6. On the **Visuals** tab, toggle **Title** for both **Y axis** and **X axis** to **Off** and change the **Color** values of both to **#3C3C3B, Theme color 2**.

7. Toggle **Data labels** to **On**, expand the format card, expand the **Value** sub-card, and change **Color** to **#3C3C3B, Theme color 2**.

8. Finally, click on the **Analytics** sub-pane in the **Visualizations** pane. The icon looks like a magnifying glass.

9. Expand **Average line** and click **+ Add line**.

Pam also wants a summary of **% Utilization by Branch**. To create this visual, perform the following steps:

1. Copy and paste the **% Utilization by Division** visual and reposition the copy next to the original.

2. Add the **Location** column from the **People** table to **Y-axis** and remove **Division**.

3. Change the visualization's **Title** to **% Utilization by Branch** and change the visual to be a **Clustered column chart**.

Finally, Pam wants to show the total utilization. To do this, follow these steps:

1. Copy and paste the KPI visual and reposition this new visual to the right of the original KPI visual.

2. Change the visual to a **Card** visualization and ensure that the **% Utilization** measure from the **Calculations** table is in **Fields** for this visualization.

3. Use the **Format** sub-pane of the **Visualizations** pane to toggle **Category label** to **Off**.

4. On the **General** tab, toggle **Title** to **On** and enter **Total % Utilization** as Title Text.

5. On the **Visual** tab, expand the **Callout value** section and set **Font size** to **Segoe UI Bold** and **60**, and **Color** to **#EC670F, Theme color 1**.

The final **Executive Summary** page should now look as follows:

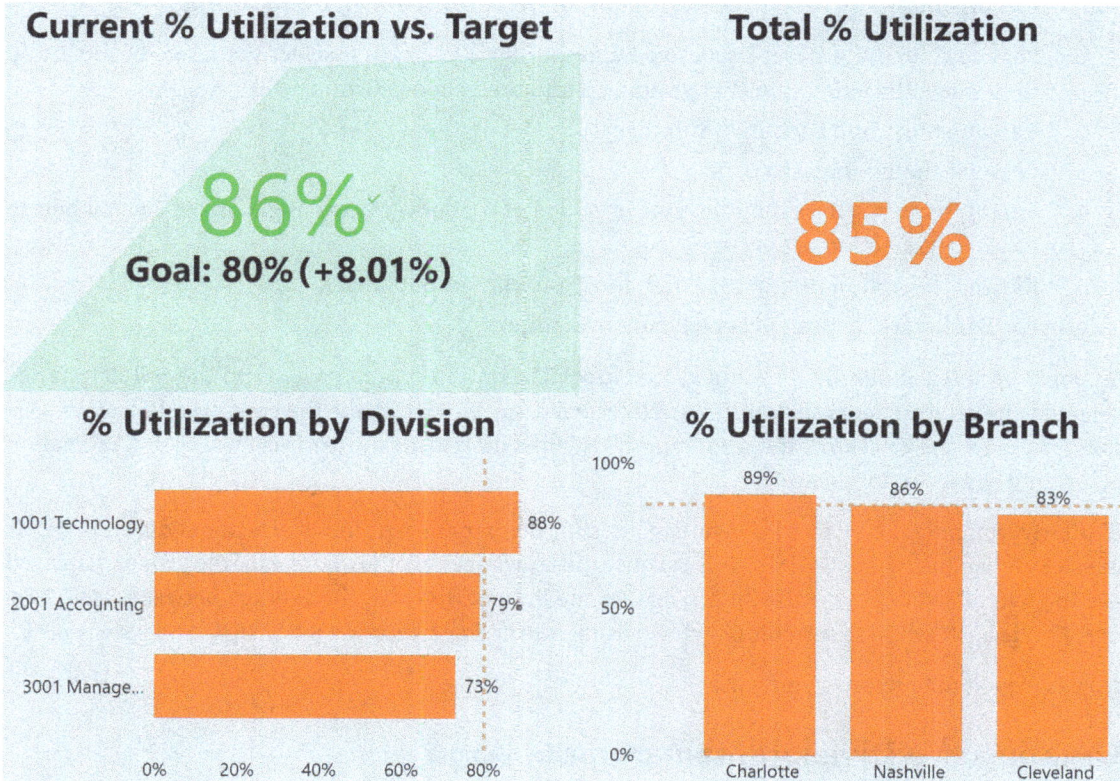

Figure 7.11 – The Executive Summary report page

Pam is satisfied with the **Executive Summary** page. In the KPI visualization, executives can now see the latest month's utilization, along with its trend in previous months and a comparison with the target utilization. They can also see the overall utilization by division and by branch. Finally, they can see the overall total utilization for all selected dates, branches, divisions, and employee types.

Before moving on, Pam needs to finish up a few details for the **Executive Summary** page. To finish off the **Executive Summary** page, do the following:

1. First, because she does not plan on this page being a drill-through page, select and delete the **Back** button at the bottom left of the dark gray rectangle.

2. Next, create a bookmark for this page by selecting the **View** tab of the ribbon. Then, in the **Show panes** section, select **Bookmarks**.

3. Set the **Target Utilization** slicer to **80**.

4. In the **Bookmarks** pane, choose **Add** and rename this bookmark to **Reset Executive Summary**.

5. The previously created bookmarks are no longer needed, so for each one, hover over the bookmark name, choose the ellipsis (**...**) next to the bookmark name, and choose **Delete**.

Pam is planning to create more bookmarks and wants to keep her bookmarks organized. To keep the bookmarks organized, we need to create groups for them. To do so, follow these steps:

1. For the remaining **Reset Executive Summary** bookmark, first select the name of the group, then select the ellipsis for that group (**...**), and then choose **Group**.
2. Rename the group **Executive Summary**.
3. Collapse the **Bookmarks** pane.
4. Finally, select the **Reset** button in the lower left of the dark gray rectangle. In the **Format button** pane, toggle **Action** to **On**.
5. Expand the **Action** format card and, for **Type**, choose **Bookmark**.
6. For **Bookmark**, choose **Reset Executive Summary**.

A couple of notes about the different values for % **Utilization** on the page. With the full date range selected and all the slicers set to **All**, the KPI visual displays **86%**, while the card visual displays **85%**. This is because the KPI shows the latest month's % **Utilization** while the card visual shows % **Utilization** calculated across all three months.

Similarly, you may notice that the **Average** lines for the bar and column charts are at different levels, one at **80%** and the other at **86%**. This is because these averages are the averages of the groups displayed, not the overall average % **Utilization**. Thus, in the bar chart visual, the average between **88%**, **79%**, and **73%** is **80%**, while in the column chart visual, the average between **89%**, **86%**, and **83%** is **86%**.

Now is a good time to save your work.

Creating the Division Management page

The next page in the report is the **Division Management** page. Division managers within the organization will use this page to display relevant information so that they can keep their division utilized.

To create this page, perform the following steps:

1. Right-click the **Executive Summary** page and choose **Duplicate Page**.
2. Rename **Duplicate of Executive Summary** to Division Management.
3. Pam plans on this page being available for drill-through. So, first, copy and paste the **Back** button from the **Template** page onto the **Division Management** page and reposition it as necessary.
4. Click on a blank area of the canvas, such as just to the right of the **Controls** group of visuals, and expand the **Visualizations** and **Data** panes.
5. Drag and drop the **Division** column from the **Hours** table into the **Add drill-through fields here** area. Since this page already contains a **Back** button, Power BI does not add one automatically to the page.

Pam knows that it is also important for the division managers to track utilization by the type of employee. To add this visual, perform the following steps:

1. Select the % **Utilization by Division** visual and replace **Division** in the **Y-axis** field well with the **EmployeeType** column from the **People** table.

2. On the **General** tab of the **Format visual** sub-pane of the **Visualizations** pane, expand the **Title** section, and set **Title Text** to **% Utilization by Employee Type**.

Pam knows that the division managers will want more detail than at the **Executive Summary** level. This means tracking hours and utilization by individual job codes. To create this visual, do the following:

1. Select the KPI visual and change this visual to a **Table** visual.
2. Replace **Month** in the **Columns** field well with the **JobID** column from the **Hours** table.
3. Replace **Target Utilization Value** in the **Columns** field well with the **Hours** column from the **Hours** table. Double-click **Sum of Hours** in the **Columns** field well and rename it to **Hours**.
4. In the **Columns** field well, ensure that the columns from top to bottom are **JobID**, **Hours**, and then % **Utilization**. If not, simply click on the columns in the **Columns** field well and drag and drop them as required.
5. On the **Visual** tab of the **Format visual** sub-pane of the **Visualizations** pane, expand the **Values** format card and then the **Values** sub-card, and change **Text color** and **Alternate text color** to **#E5EAEE, Theme color 3**.
6. Still on the **Visual** tab, expand the **Column headers** format card and the **Text** sub-card, and change **Text color** to **#E5EAEE, Theme color 3**, **Font** to **Segoe UI (Bold)**, and **Header alignment** to **Center**.
7. Still on the **Visual** tab, expand the **Totals** format card and change **Background color** to **#3C3C3B, Theme color 2** and **Text color** to **#E5EAEE, Theme color 3**.
8. Switch back to the **Build visual** sub-pane, right-click % **Utilization**, and choose **Conditional formatting** and then **Data bars**.
9. In the **Data bars** dialog, change the **Positive bar** color to **#3C3C3B, Theme color 2** and click the **OK** button.
10. Click on the % **Utilization** column in the **Table** visual to sort by descending order.
11. Click on the % **Utilization** column one more time to sort by ascending order.

Pam also believes that the division managers will want to see the total hours that were spent on different tasks. To create this visual, follow these steps:

1. Select the **Total % Utilization** card visual and shrink this visual vertically to about half its original size.
2. Copy and paste the **Total % Utilization** visual and reposition the visual directly underneath the original.
3. Change this to a **Clustered column chart** visual.
4. Replace % **Utilization** in the **Y-axis** field well with the **Hours** column from the **Hours** table.
5. Put the **Category** column from the **Hours** table into the **X-axis** field well.
6. On the **General** tab of the **Format visual** sub-pane of the **Visualizations** pane, expand the **Title** section, and set **Title** to **Hours by Category**.
7. On the **Visual** tab, change **Color** for **Values** for **X axis** and **Y axis** to **#3C3C3B, Theme color 2** and toggle both axis **Title** settings to **Off**.

Pam realizes that if users drill through to this page, they will not have any visual cues as to which division has been drilled into. Pam decides to create a dynamic title measure and visual. To create these items, follow these steps:

1. Right-click on **Calculations** and choose **New measure**. Use the following formula:

```
Divisions Title =
    VAR __AllCount = 3
    VAR __CurrentCount = COUNTROWS( SUMMARIZE( 'Hours',[Division] ) )
    VAR __Result =
        SWITCH(
            TRUE(),
            HASONEVALUE( 'Hours'[Division] ),
            MAX( 'Hours'[Division] ),
            __AllCount = __CurrentCount,
            "All Divisions",
            "Multiple Divisions"
        )
RETURN
    __Result
```

This measure uses a special form of the SWITCH DAX statement, where TRUE() is specified as the first parameter instead of a column or measure. This allows you to specify multiple complex logical statements that return either true or false. The first statement that returns true returns the corresponding calculation. The first check is whether there is a single unique value for the **Division** column. If so, then that value is returned. Next, if the counts for all divisions (__AllCount) equal the current count of divisions (__CurrentCount), then **All Divisions** is returned. Otherwise, **Multiple Divisions** is returned.

2. Shrink the **Table** visual vertically from the top to make room in the top-left corner of the page.
3. Click on this blank area of the canvas and then click on the **Card** visualization in the **Visualizations** pane.
4. Reposition and resize this visualization to take up the blank space.
5. Add the **Division Title** measure from the **Calculations** table to the **Fields** area for the visual.
6. Use the **Format** sub-pane of the **Visualizations** pane to toggle **Category label** on the **Visual** tab to **Off**, and also toggle **Background** under the **Effects** section of the **General** tab to **Off**.
7. On the **Visuals** tab, expand the **Callout value** section and change **Color** to #7EAE40, **Theme color 6**, and **Font** to **Segoe UI (Bold)** size **24**.

Picking a green color from the theme instead of the same title color as the other visuals provides a visual indication that this text is different than the titles for the other visualizations.

The completed **Division Management** page should look as follows:

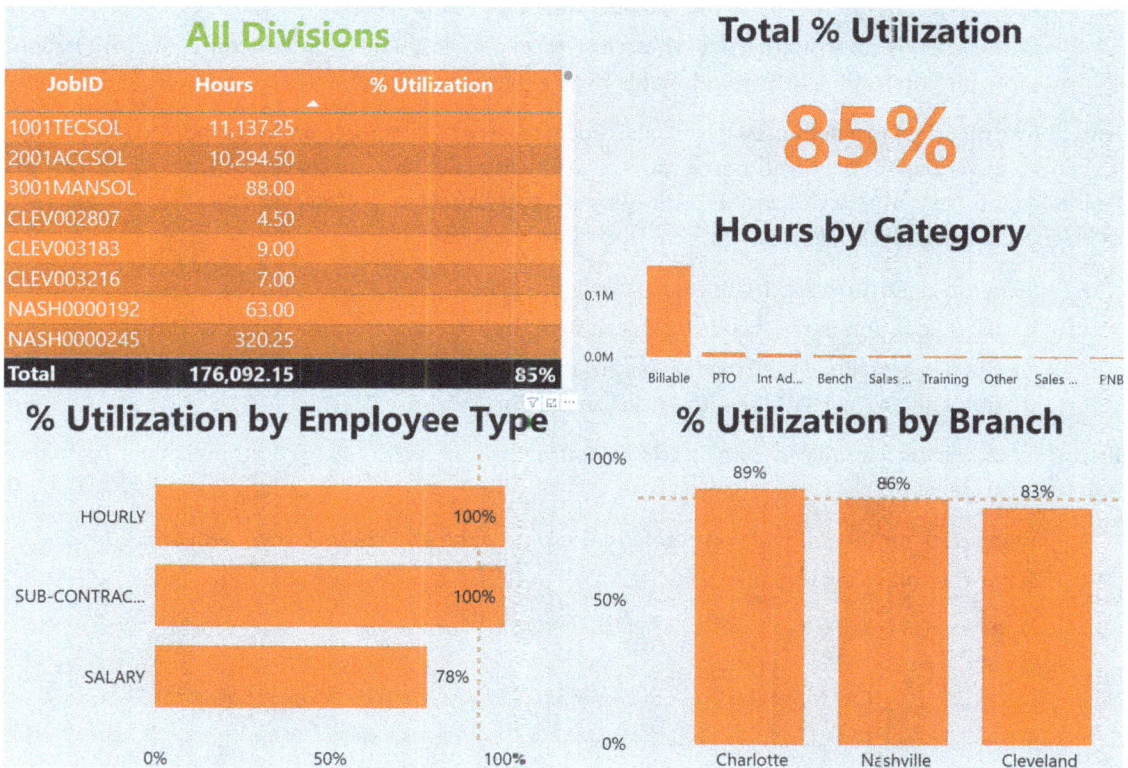

Figure 7.12 – The Division Management page

Pam is satisfied with the **Division Management** page. To finish this page, do the following:

1. In the **Bookmarks** pane, choose **Add** and rename this bookmark **Reset Division Management**.
2. Select the ellipsis (**…**) for this bookmark and choose **Group**.
3. Rename the group **Division Management**.
4. Collapse the **Bookmarks** pane.
5. Select the **Reset** button in the lower left of the dark gray rectangle.
6. In the **Format button** pane, expand the **Action** section and for **Bookmark**, choose **Reset Division Management**.

The **Division Management** page is now complete. Save your work before continuing.

Creating the Branch Management page

Pam also wants a page more focused on branch managers. Much of the information that's displayed, as well as the layout, is similar to the **Division Management** page. To create this page, follow these steps:

1. Right-click the **Division Management** page and choose **Duplicate Page**.
2. Rename the **Duplicate of Division Management** page to Branch Management.

3. Pam plans on this page being available for drill through. Therefore, click on a blank area of the canvas and then expand the **Visualizations** and **Data** panes.

4. Remove **Division** from the **Drill though** section and drag and drop **Location** from the **People** table into the **Add drill-through fields here** area.

Pam knows that the branch managers will also be interested in how their branch is performing across divisions, as well as their overall percentage of utilization. So, she can leave the **Total % Utilization, Hours by Category**, and **% Utilization by Employee Type** visuals as is. However, the other visuals need to be changed slightly. To do this, perform the following steps:

1. Select the **% Utilization by Branch** visual.

2. Replace **Location** in the **X-axis** field well with the **Division** column from the **Hours** table.

3. On the **General** tab of the **Format visual** sub-pane of the **Visualizations** pane, expand the **Title** section and change **Title text** to **% Utilization by Division**.

Pam wants to create a similar dynamic title measure for branches as she did for divisions. To do this, follow these steps:

1. Right-click on the **Calculations** table in the **Data** pane and choose **New measure**.

2. Enter the following formula:

```
Branch Title =
    VAR __AllCount = 3
    VAR __CurrentCount = COUNTROWS( SUMMARIZE( 'People',[Location] ) )
    VAR __Result =
        SWITCH(
            TRUE(),
            HASONEVALUE( 'People'[Location] ),
            MAX( 'People'[Location]),
            __AllCount = __CurrentCount, "All Branches",
            "Multiple Branches"
        )
RETURN
    __Result
```

3. Select the card visual in the top-left corner and replace **Divisions Title** in the **Fields** field well with **Branch Title**.

Pam also needs to change the **Table** visualization. To do so, follow these steps:

1. Select the **Table** visual.
2. In the **Values** field well, replace **JobID** with the **Name** column from the **People** table.
3. In the **Values** field well, right-click **% Utilization**, choose **Remove conditional formatting**, and then **All**.
4. Shrink the **% Utilization** column in this visual so that it is just wide enough that the **% Utilization** text does not wrap.

Pam wants to create a colored indicator for the **Table** visualization denoting whether or not each employee is meeting **Target Utilization**. Pam previously created a **Goal Status Color** measure. The **Goal Status Color** measure returns the hex color code for green (#00FF00) if the target goal is met or exceeded, and returns red (#FF0000) if not. This measure can be used to create a graphical indicator. To do this, follow these steps:

1. Drag the **Goal Status Color** measure from the **Calculations** table into the **Columns** field well.
2. Double-click the **Goal Status Color** in the **Columns** field well in the **Build visual** sub-pane of the **Visualizations** pane and change its name to **Status**.
3. Click the drop-down arrow for **Status** in the **Columns** field well and choose **Conditional formatting** and then **Icons**.
4. In the **Icons** dialog, under **Rules**, change the first rule's **Text** to be #FF0000.
5. Delete the second rule using the X icon on the right.
6. Edit the last **Text** to be #00FF00.
7. Under **Icon Layout**, change the dropdown from **Left of data** to **Icon only**.
8. Click the **OK** button to close the dialog.

Pam is happy with the icons but does not like #00FF00 appearing in the **Status** column's **Total** row. To fix this, do the following:

1. On the **Visual** tab of the **Format visual** sub-pane of the **Visualizations** pane, expand the **Specific column** section.
2. In the **Apply settings to** card, change the **Series** dropdown to **Status**.
3. In the **Values** card, set **Text color** to #3C3C3B, **Theme color 2**.
4. Change **Alignment** to **Center**.
5. Toggle **Apply to total** to **On**.

The completed **Branch Management** page should look as follows:

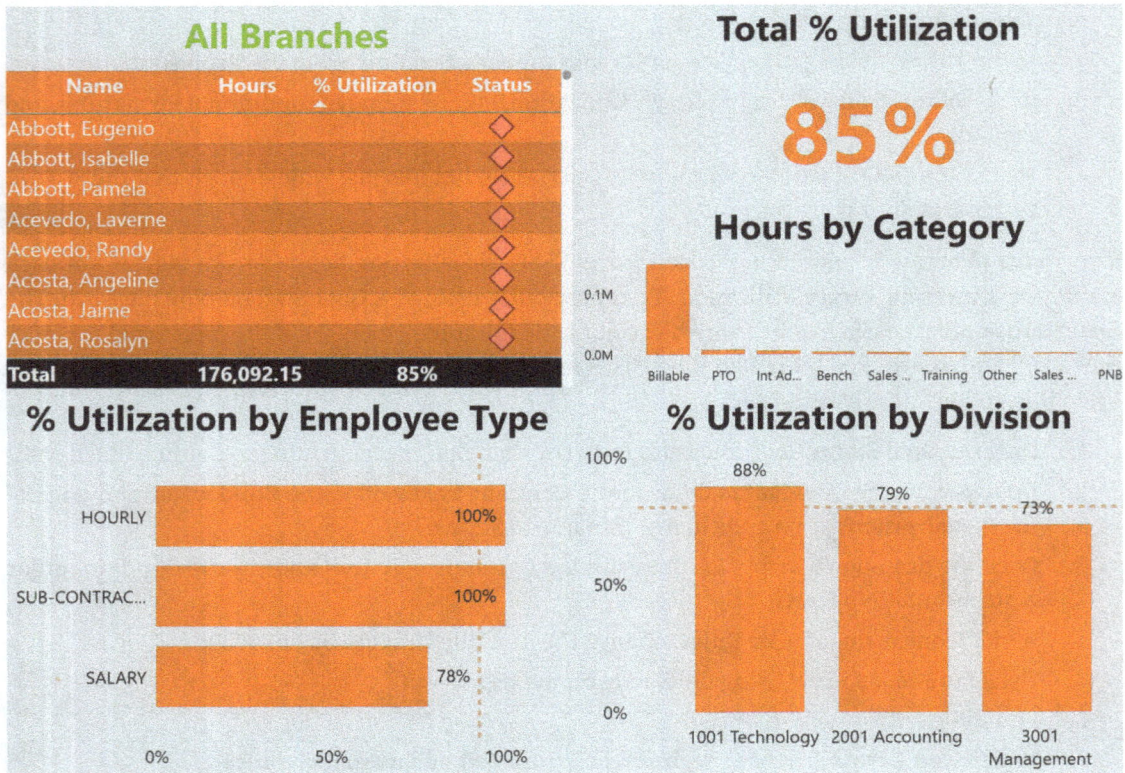

Figure 7.13 – The Branch Management page

Pam is satisfied with the **Branch Management** page. To finish off this page, do the following:

1. In the **Bookmarks** pane, choose **Add** and rename this bookmark **Reset Branch Management**.

2. Select the ellipsis (**...**) for this bookmark and choose **Group**.

3. Rename the group **Branch Management**.

4. Collapse the **Bookmarks** pane.

5. Select the **Reset** button in the lower left of the dark gray rectangle.

6. In the **Format button** pane, expand the **Action** section, and for **Bookmark**, choose **Reset Branch Management**.

The **Branch Management** page is now complete. Save your work before continuing.

Creating the Hours Detail page

Pam now has three pages that summarize information for managers at a high level. But she knows that there may be times when these managers will want more details about employees and how their time is being spent at work. Therefore, she decides to create a page dedicated to showing the breakdown of hours by employee. To start creating this page, follow these steps:

1. Right-click the **Branch Management** page and choose **Duplicate Page**.

2. Rename **Duplicate of Branch Management** to **Hours Detail**.

3. Pam plans on this page being available for drill through. Therefore, click on a blank area of the canvas and expand the **Visualizations** and **Data** panes.

4. Drag and drop the **Division** column from the **Hours** table below the **Location** column in the **Drill through** area of the **Visualizations** pane. Also add the **EmployeeType** column from the **People** table as a **Drill through** filter.

5. Delete all of the visuals on the page except the **Controls** group, **All Branches** card visual, and table visual.

6. Change the table visual to a **Matrix** visualization and expand this visual so that it takes up the entire canvas except the **CONTROLS** area and **All Branches** visual.

7. Remove **% Utilization** and **Status** from the **Values** field well.

8. Place the **Category** column from the **Hours** table in the **Columns** field well.

9. Since there is a lot of information to fit onto one page, use the **Format** sub-pane of the **Visualizations** pane to reduce **Text size** to 12 for the Values, Column headers, Row headers, Column subtotals, Row subtotals, and Column grand total and Row grand total format cards.

10. On the **Build visual** tab, in the **Rows** field well, rename **Name** to **Employee**.

Pam notices a problem, however: the order of the categories is alphabetical, so they're not in the same order that the managers are used to seeing in other reports. To fix this, do the following:

1. Start by clicking on the **Modeling** tab of the ribbon and selecting **New Table**.

2. Enter the following formula for the table:

```
tmpTable = DISTINCT('Hours'[Category])
```

3. This creates a table of all of the distinct values in the **Category** column of the **Hours** table, ensuring that all of the categories are present and that all of the spellings are the same.

4. Switch to the **Table** view, right-click this table in the **Data** pane, and choose **Copy Table**.

5. From the **Home** tab in the **Data** section, click on **Enter data**. **Enter data** queries provide a convenient mechanism so that you can hand-enter short lists of data.

6. Press *Ctrl* + *V*. The rows of the table are pasted into the first column, and the first row of the table, **Category**, is promoted to a column header!

7. Rename the table **Categories** using the **Name** field.

8. Click on the + column to add a column and rename this column **Order**.

9. Provide the orders shown in the following screenshot. When you're done, click the **Load** button:

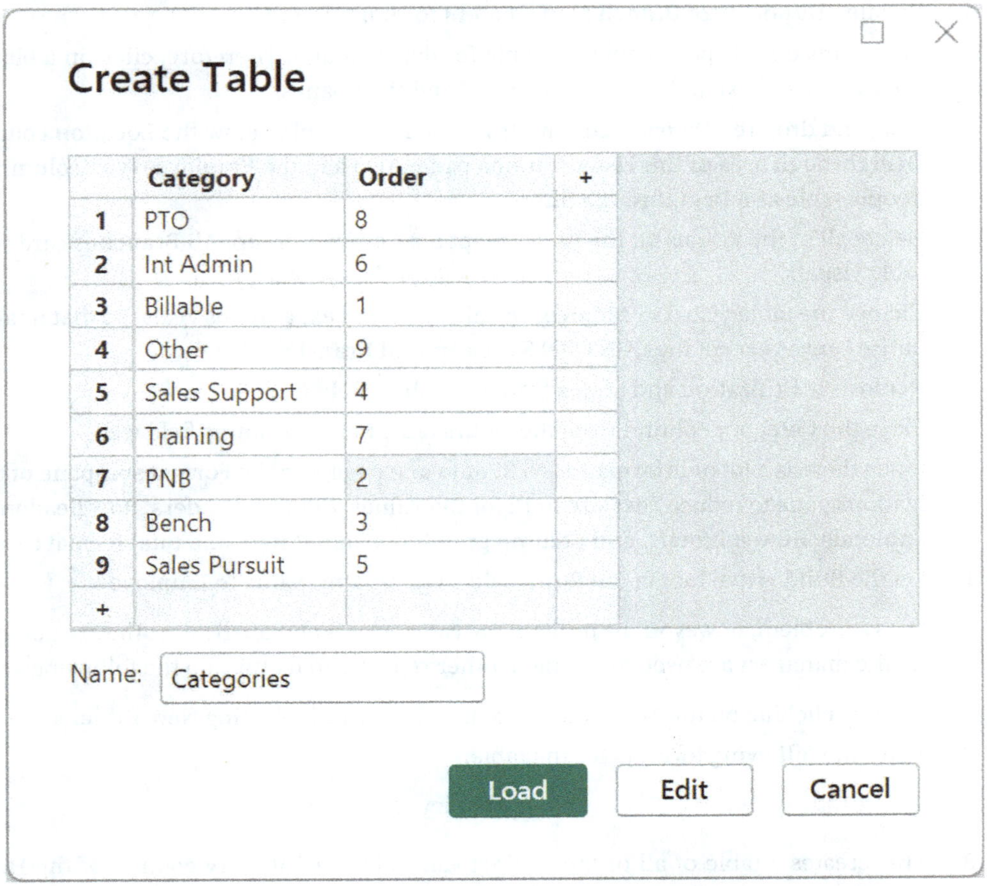

Create Table

	Category	Order	+
1	PTO	8	
2	Int Admin	6	
3	Billable	1	
4	Other	9	
5	Sales Support	4	
6	Training	7	
7	PNB	2	
8	Bench	3	
9	Sales Pursuit	5	
+			

Name: Categories

Load   Edit   Cancel

Figure 7.14 – Create Table using an Enter data query

10. A new table, **Categories**, is added to the semantic model.

> **Important note**
>
> **Enter data** queries support a limited amount of information. If you run into a limitation, you can always copy the table in Power BI and then paste it into Excel. Once you've done this, you can add the required information in Excel, save it, and then import this Excel file into Power BI.

11. Switch to the **Model** view and confirm that Power BI has added a relationship between the new **Categories** table and **Hours**. If not, add the relationship between the **Category** columns in both tables.

12. In the **Data** pane, right-click **tmpTable**, choose **Delete from model**, and, when prompted, choose **Yes** to delete the table.

13. Switch back to the **Report** view.
14. Expand the **Data** pane and select the **Order** column in the **Categories** table (not the checkbox).
15. Click on the **Column tools** tab and ensure that the **Order** column has a **Data type** of **Whole number**. If not, set **Data type** to **Whole number**.
16. Click on the **Category** column in the **Categories** table (not the checkbox).
17. From the **Column tools** tab, click on **Sort by column** and choose **Order**.
18. Add the **Category** column from the **Categories** table to the **Columns** field well for the matrix and remove the original **Category** column. The column headings are now sorted in numerical order based on the **Order** column.

Pam likes this visualization but also wants to see **% Utilization** as a total. To do this, follow these steps:

1. Add **% Utilization** from the **Calculations** table to the **Values** area of the matrix visualization.
2. In the **Values** area, rename **% Utilization** to **%**.
3. Unfortunately, this adds a second level under each **Category**, with each **Category** now containing two sub-columns for **Hours** and **%**.
4. To fix this, switch to the **Visual** tab of the **Format visual** sub-pane of the **Visualizations** pane, expand the **Values** section, and toggle **Text wrap** to **Off**. Repeat this for **Column headers** as well.
5. Now, in the matrix visualization, use the top **Category** column header row and carefully shrink the columns for each category except the **Total** column, until **%** is no longer displayed.
6. On the **Visual** tab of the **Format visual** sub-pane of the **Visualizations** pane, expand the **Column headers** section and then the **Options** card and toggle **Auto-size column width** to **Off**.
7. Finally, click on the **%** column to sort this column in descending order.

Since this page supports drillthrough, Pam wants to use her dynamic title visuals. To use these visuals, follow these steps:

1. Reposition the **Branch Title** card visual to the middle of the gray area of the page horizontally.
2. Copy the **Division Title** card visual from the **Division Management** page and paste it onto the **Hours Detail** page.
3. Arrange these cards across the top of the page and adjust their horizontal size to be a third of the width of the matrix visual.

Since the users can also drill through on **EmployeeType**, Pam needs an additional dynamic title measure. To do this, follow these steps:

1. Right-click on the **Calculations** table in the **Data** pane and choose **New measure**.
2. Enter the following formula:

```
Type Title =
    VAR __AllCount = 3
    VAR __CurrentCount = COUNTROWS( SUMMARIZE(
        'People',[EmployeeType]))
    VAR __Result =
```

```
                   SWITCH(
                       TRUE(),
                       HASONEVALUE( 'People'[EmployeeType] ),
                       MAX( 'People'[EmployeeType] ),
                       __AllCount = __CurrentCount, "All Types",
                       "Multiple Types"
                   )
               RETURN
                   __Result
```

3. Copy the **Branch Title** card visual and paste a copy onto the page.

4. Arrange this card visual across the top and replace its **Fields** property with the **Type Title** measure.

    The final report page should now look as follows:

	All Divisions				**All Branches**					**All Types**		
Category	**Billable**	**PNB**	**Bench**	**Sales S...**	**Sales P...**	**Int Ad...**	**Training**	**PTO**	**Other**	**Total**	
Employee	**Hours**	**Hours**	**Hours**	**Hours**	**Hours**	**Hours**	**Hours**	**Hours**	**Hours**	**Hours**	**%**
Noble, Joyce	148.00							8.00		156.00	116%
Dominguez, Sheila	524.50						2.50	16.00		543.00	113%
Parker, Concetta	9.00									9.00	113%
Savage, Eunice	515.00							8.00		523.00	109%
Parker, Aurora	507.00					12.50				519.50	107%
Sanford, Abram	503.50							8.00		511.50	107%
Fletcher, Anne	409.25								12.00	421.25	107%
Johns, Mariana	468.75							27.00		495.75	107%
Lawrence, Charley	502.50					25.50		8.00	3.50	539.50	106%
Reese, Bruce	450.00									450.00	106%
Goodwin, Carey	348.00									348.00	106%
Westerman, Scott	100.00									100.00	104%
Rogers, Cortez	474.00									474.00	104%
Erickson, Darius	490.00							8.00		498.00	104%
Hull, Luisa	264.00									264.00	103%
Ingram, Lavonne	484.00						14.00	8.00		506.00	103%
Bond, Deidre	481.00	2.50		2.50		35.00	0.50	8.00	5.00	534.50	102%
Carter, Carolina	480.25					1.00	11.00	16.00	9.50	517.75	102%
Schmitt, Leonor	479.50							16.00		495.50	102%
Gill, Isabella	437.50									437.50	101%
Mendez, Neville	421.00							8.00	4.00	433.00	101%
Underwood, Ronda	473.50					3.00		8.00		484.50	100%
Stewart, Estelle	473.00							8.00		481.00	100%
Adkins, Rita	464.00									464.00	100%
Allen, Susana	72.00									72.00	100%
Total	**148,282.40**	**952.50**	**3,731.75**	**3,315.00**	**1,281.25**	**5,940.25**	**2,636.75**	**7,493.75**	**2,458.50**	**176,092.15**	**85%**

Figure 7.15 – The Hours Detail page

Pam is satisfied with the **Hours Detail** page. To finish the page, perform the following steps:

1. In the **Bookmarks** pane, choose **Add** and rename this bookmark **Reset Hours Detail**.

2. Select the ellipsis (**...**) for this bookmark and choose **Group**.

3. Rename the group **Hours Detail**.

4. Collapse the **Bookmarks** pane.

5. Select the **Reset** button in the lower left of the dark gray rectangle.

6. In the **Format button** pane, toggle **Action** to **On**.

7. Expand the **Action** section and for **Type**, choose **Bookmark**.

8. For **Bookmark**, choose **Reset Hours Detail**.

The **Hours Detail** page is now complete. Save your work before continuing.

Creating the Employee Details page

In addition to the **Hours Detail** page, Pam wants another page focused on displaying detailed information for one or more employees.

To create this page, do the following:

1. Right-click the **Division Management** page and choose **Duplicate Page**.

2. Rename the **Duplicate of Division Management** page to **Employee Details**.

3. Pam plans on this page being available for drill through. Therefore, click on a blank area of the canvas and then expand the **Visualizations** and **Data** panes.

4. Remove **Division** from the **Drill through** section and drag and drop the **Name** column from the **People** table into the **Add drill-through fields here** area.

5. Select the **Hours by Category** visual.

6. In the **Build visual** sub-pane of the **Visualizations** pane in the **Y-axis** field well, right-click **Sum of Hours** and choose **Show value as** and then **Percent of grand total**.

7. Click on the **Visual** tab of the **Format visual** sub-pane and toggle **Data labels** to **On**.

8. Expand the **Data labels** section, expand the **Value** card, and change **Color** to **#3C3C3B, Theme color 2**.

9. On the **General** tab, expand the **Title** section and change **Text** to **% Hours by Category**.

10. Delete the **% Utilization by Employee Type** and **% Utilization by Branch** visualizations.

11. Click on a blank area of the canvas. Now, select the **Date** column from the **Calendar** table and then add the **% Utilization** measure from the **Calculations** table to this visual.

12. In the **Columns** field for this visual, right-click **Date** and change this from **Date Hierarchy** to **Date**.

13. Now, change this visual to a **Line chart**. Expand the visual horizontally and vertically to consume the entire bottom of the light-gray area of the report page.

14. On the **General** tab of the **Format visual** sub-pane of the **Visualizations** pane, expand the **Effects** section and toggle **Background** to **Off**.

15. Expand the **Title** section and change **Text** to **% Utilization and Forecast**.

16. In the **Title** section, change **Text color** to **#3C3C3B, Theme color 2**, **Alignment** to **Center**, and **Font** to **Segoe UI (Bold)** and **24**.

17. On the **Visual** tab, change the **Color** values for **X axis** and **Y axis** to **#3C3C3B, Theme color 2** and toggle both axis **Title** settings to **Off**.

18. Finally, switch to the **Analytics** sub-pane and toggle **Forecast** to **On**.

Since this page also uses drill through, Pam wants to create a dynamic employee title measure. To create and use this measure, perform the following steps:

1. Right-click on the **Calculations** table in the **Data** pane and choose **New measure**.

2. Enter the following formula:

```
Employee Title =
    IF(
        HASONEVALUE('People'[Name]),
        MAX('People'[Name]),
        "Multiple Employees"
    )
```

3. Select the card visual at the top left and replace the **Fields** property with **Employee Title**.

    The final report page should now look as follows:

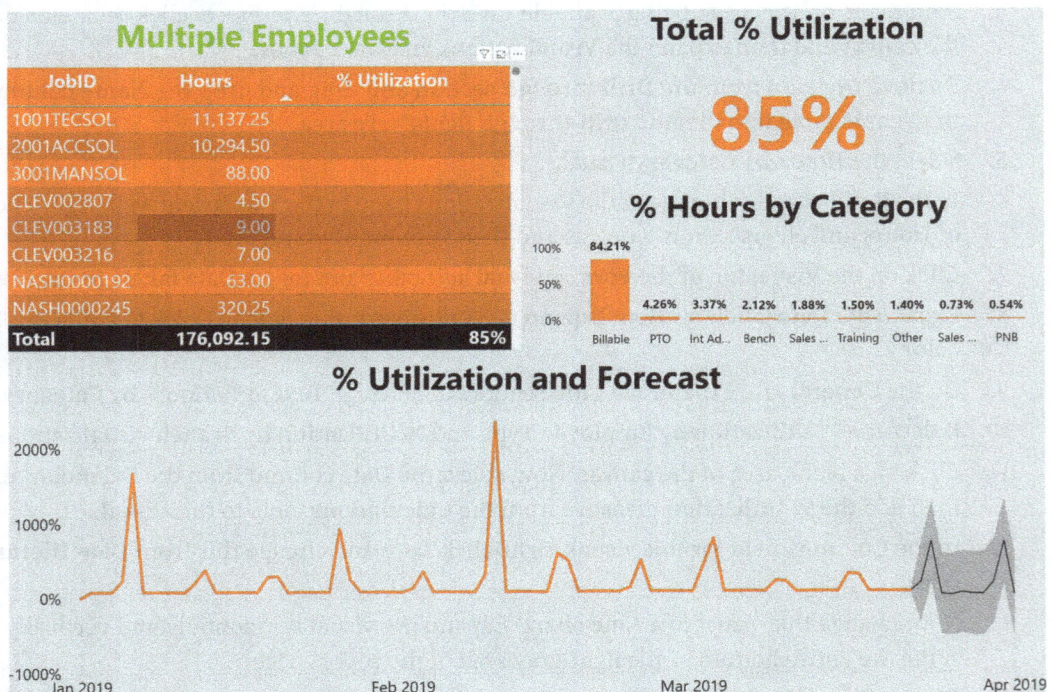

Figure 7.16 – The Employee Details page

Pam is satisfied with the **Employee Details** page. To finish this page, do the following:

1. In the **Bookmarks** pane, choose **Add** and rename this bookmark **Reset Employee Details**.

2. Select the ellipsis (**…**) for this bookmark and choose **Group**.

3. Rename the group **Employee Details**.

4. Collapse the **Bookmarks** pane.

5. Select the **Reset** button in the lower left of the dark gray rectangle.

6. In the **Format button** pane, expand the **Action** section and, for **Bookmark**, choose **Reset Employee Details**.

The **Employee Details** page is now complete. Save your work before continuing.

Creating the Introduction page

Pam knows that a good report includes an introduction on how to use it. To create an **Introduction** page, do the following:

1. Right-click the **Template** page and choose **Duplicate Page**.

2. Rename the **Duplicate of Template** page to **Introduction**.

3. Click on the **Introduction** page's tab and drag this page between the **Template** page and the **Executive Summary** page.

4. Click on the **Insert** tab of the ribbon and choose **Text box** from the **Elements** section.

5. On the **General** tab of the **Format text box** pane, expand the **Effects** section and toggle **Background** to **Off**.

6. Resize this text box so that it's the full size of the light gray area.

7. Enter text into the text box explaining the report, such as what is displayed in *Figure 7.17*.

The **Introduction** page should look similar to the following:

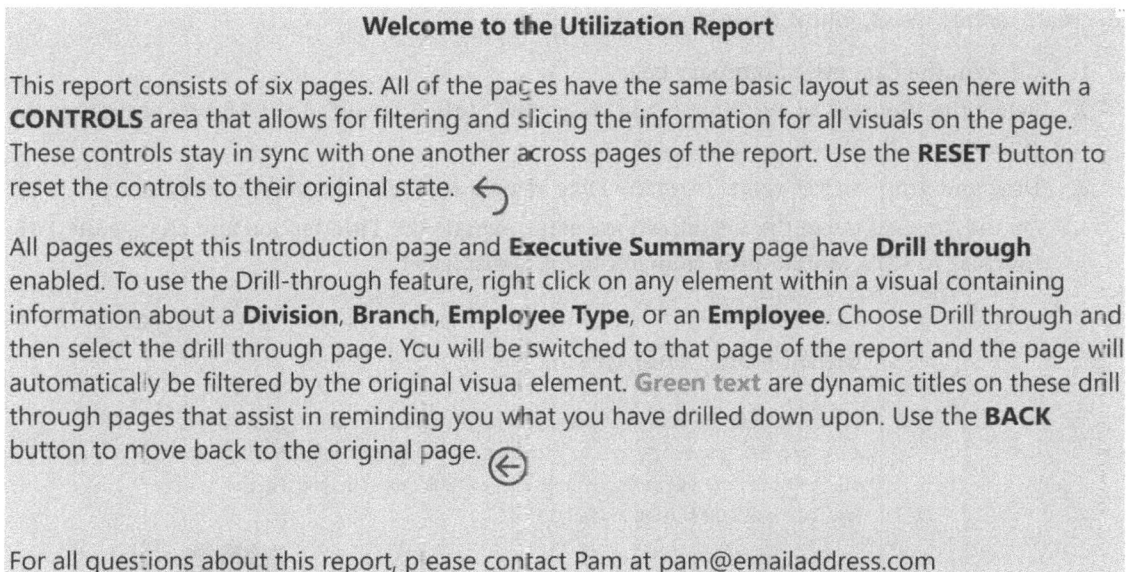

Welcome to the Utilization Report

This report consists of six pages. All of the pages have the same basic layout as seen here with a **CONTROLS** area that allows for filtering and slicing the information for all visuals on the page. These controls stay in sync with one another across pages of the report. Use the **RESET** button to reset the controls to their original state. ↰

All pages except this Introduction page and **Executive Summary** page have **Drill through** enabled. To use the Drill-through feature, right click on any element within a visual containing information about a **Division**, **Branch**, **Employee Type**, or an **Employee**. Choose Drill through and then select the drill through page. You will be switched to that page of the report and the page will automatically be filtered by the original visual element. Green text are dynamic titles on these drill through pages that assist in reminding you what you have drilled down upon. Use the **BACK** button to move back to the original page. ⟵

For all questions about this report, please contact Pam at pam@emailaddress.com

Figure 7.17 – The Introduction page

A good introduction page includes some or all of the following information:

- Contact information
- Data sources
- Pages included
- Explanation of special features such as slicers, buttons, drill through, dynamic titles, etc.

We are now done creating the pages of our report. Now, it is time to perform some finishing touches.

Finishing up

Even though Pam has finished building her report, she still needs to test the report and clean up some loose ends.

In the following subsections, we will perform some final testing and cleanup on the report to ensure that everything works correctly and that the report is ready for business users to consume. However, prior to that, Pam wishes to create some mobile views for the report.

Creating mobile views

The Power BI ecosystem includes mobile apps that allow users to access reports from their phone or tablet. Pam knows that executives and managers will sometimes want to access the report from their phones while they are traveling.

To create mobile views, follow these steps:

1. Click on the **Executive Summary** page.
2. Select the **View** tab in the ribbon and then click **Mobile layout** in the **Mobile** section of the ribbon.
3. Drag and drop the KPI visual from the **Page visuals** area onto the mobile layout.
4. On the **General** tab in the **Visualizations** pane, expand the **Title** section and change the **Title** font size to **12**. A **Mobile-only changes** dialog is displayed.

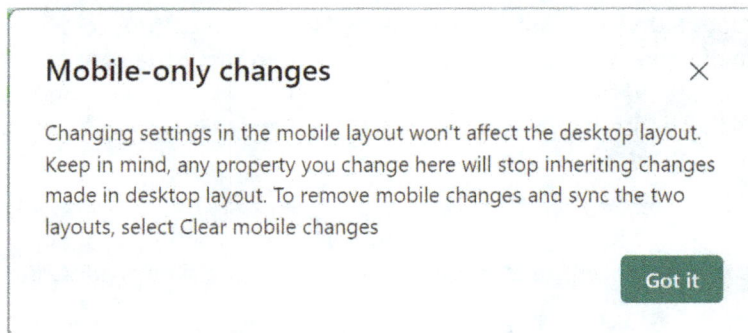

Mobile-only changes   ✕

Changing settings in the mobile layout won't affect the desktop layout. Keep in mind, any property you change here will stop inheriting changes made in desktop layout. To remove mobile changes and sync the two layouts, select Clear mobile changes

Got it

Figure 7.18 – Mobile-only changes dialog

5. Continue adding visuals and modifying settings until you achieve an acceptable mobile view, such as the following:

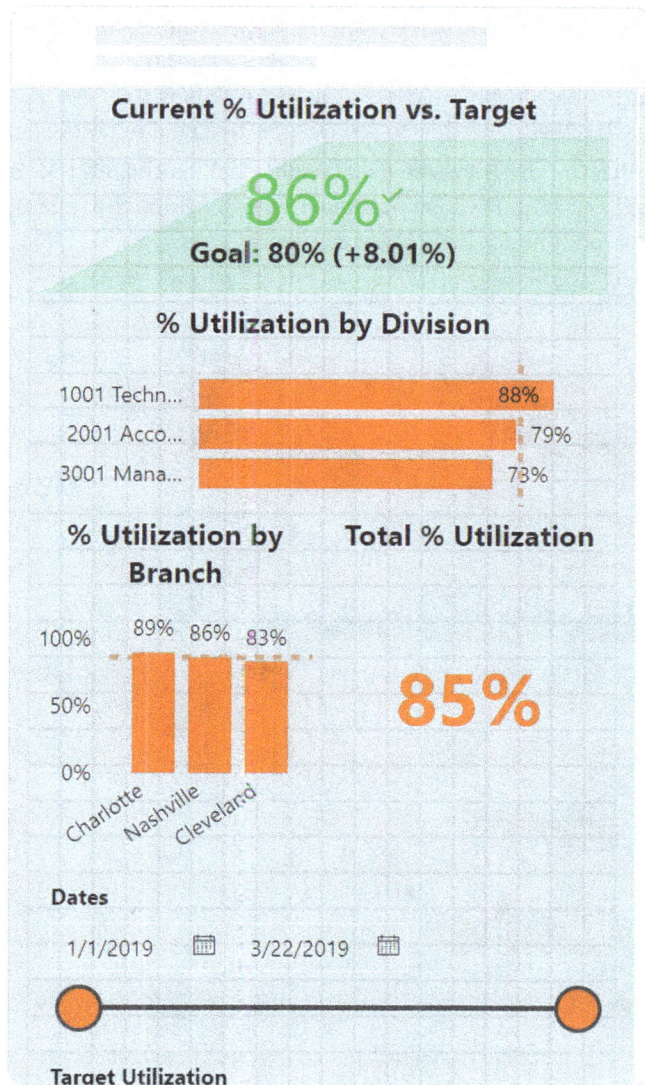

Figure 7.19 – Mobile view

Note that the mobile view is scrollable, so you can continue to add visuals infinitely.

6. Repeat this process for the **Division Management** and **Branch Management** pages.

Save your work before continuing.

Testing

Pam decides to work through an example scenario to see how the report performs. To perform this test, do the following:

1. Start on the **Executive Summary** page. Here, we can see that the overall utilization is good and above our goal. All of the branches are above our target utilization. However, one division, in particular, is noticeably below the average. This is the **3001 Management** division. Let's investigate this division further to see what is driving down utilization.

2. In the **% Utilization by Division** visual, right-click on the **3001 Management** bar and choose **Drill through** and then **Division Management**. Checking the green dynamic title text, we can see that it correctly states **3001 Management**.

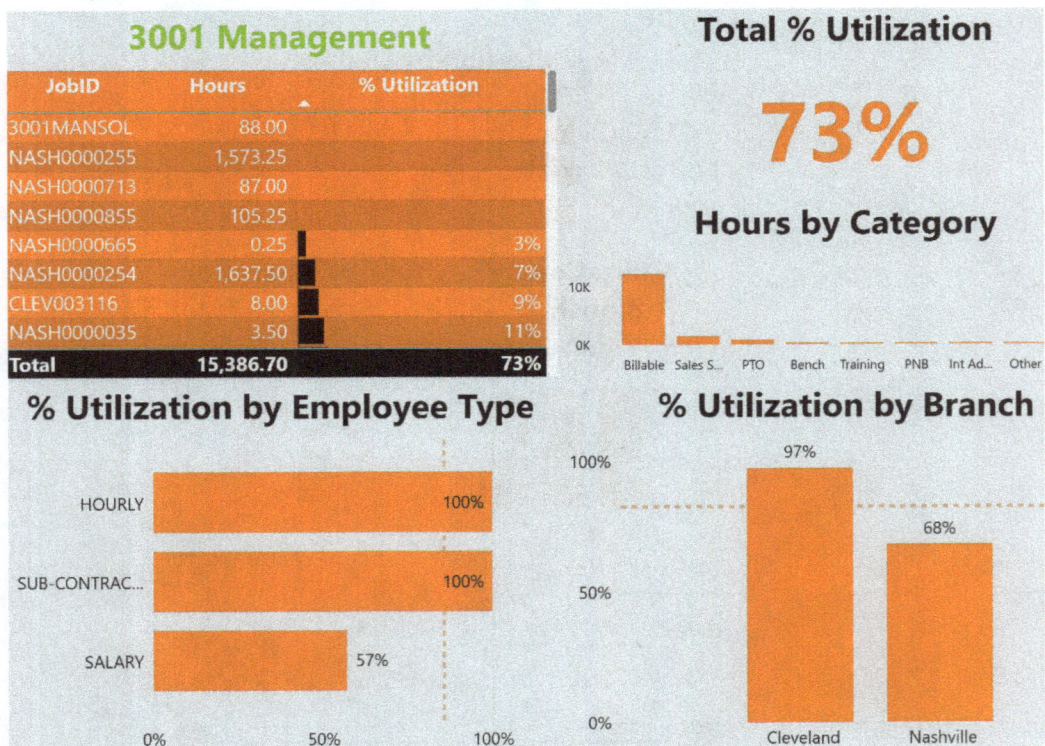

Figure 7.20 – 3001 Management utilization

3. We can see that our utilization for salaried employees is quite low and that utilization is particularly suffering in Nashville.

4. To investigate this further, right-click on the **Nashville** column in the **% Utilization by Branch** visual and choose **Drill through** and then **Hours Detail**. When checking our green dynamic title text, we are looking at resources for only **3001 Management** and **Nashville**.

5. Click on the % column header to sort by ascending order. Have a look at the following screen-shot:

3001 Management				Nashville						All Types	
Category Employee	Billable Hours	PNB Hours	Bench Hours	Sales S... Hours	Sales P... Hours	Int Ad... Hours	Training Hours	PTO Hours	Other Hours	Total Hours	%
Irwin, Rachelle	6.00									6.00	0%
Schaefer, Gustavo	14.50		176.00	272.00				8.00	4.00	474.50	3%
Beltran, Elvira	22.00	45.00		38.00				232.00		387.00	5%
Huerta, Lavern	30.00		36.00				65.00	23.00		154.00	12%
Harrington, Bradly	79.75	5.50		308.75				36.00		430.00	17%
Watts, Cassie	42.00									42.00	17%
Rivers, Gwen	60.00									60.00	18%

Figure 7.21 – 3001 Management Nashville utilization

6. It looks like the least utilized person, **Irwin, Rachelle**, was just recently hired. Her utilization is low, but so are her total hours.

7. On the next line down, however, is **Schaefer, Gustavo**. This individual only has **3%** utilization but has logged almost **500** hours.

8. We want to check out how **Schaefer, Gustavo** is spending his time. Right-click on the row containing **Schaefer, Gustavo** and choose **Drill through** and then **Employee Details**.

9. In the **% Hours by Category** visual, we can see that this individual is mostly spending their time doing sales support.

10. We want to check out the next person on the list. Click the **Back** button (hold down the *Ctrl* key while clicking).

11. Our **Hours Detail** page is just like how we left it.

12. Right-click the row containing **Beltran, Elvira** and choose **Drill through** and then **Employee Details**.

13. We can quickly see that this person has been taking a lot of PTO! Clicking on the first **JobID** code, we can see that over **72%** of the **320** hours that were logged to this code are for **PTO**. This individual is already on the unlimited PTO plan!

14. Finally, Pam tests the **Reset** button. On the **Employee Details** page, hold down the *Ctrl* key and then press the **Reset** button.

15. Also reset the **Hours Detail** and **Division Management** pages.

Pam is satisfied that there is an intuitive flow to the report and that the report is in working order.

Cleaning up

Pam needs to do a little cleanup on the report before she can publish and share her hard work. To clean things up, do the following:

1. Hide the **Template** page by right-clicking the page tab and choosing **Hide**. An eyeball icon with a slash through it appears next to the page's name. As the report author, you can see this page, but the viewers of the report will not.

2. Pam can also hide unused tables within the report. Click on the **Table** view.

3. Right-click the **Budgets and Forecasts** table and choose **Hide in report view**.

4. Hide the **Target Utilization** table as well.

5. Pam can also hide columns and measures. For example, the % **Target Utilization** measure in the **Calculations** table is no longer used.

6. Expand the **Calculations** table, right-click % **Target Utilization**, and choose **Hide in report view**.

> **Important note**
>
> Hiding pages, tables, columns, and measures that are not intended to be used by report viewers or by self-service business intelligence users can greatly aid these users by not overwhelming and confusing them with unnecessary data elements that should not be used in reporting and are rather simply semantic modeling artifacts

7. Finally, Pam clicks back to the **Report** view. On the **View** tab of the ribbon, she unchecks **Gridlines** and **Snap to grid**, and then checks **Lock objects**.

Now that Pam is done authoring the report, the positioning aids are no longer required, and locking the positions of the objects on the pages prevents visuals from accidentally being moved or resized.

Summary

In this chapter, we learned about the importance of proper planning when creating a final report. Planning a report by thinking about how users will use and interact with the report makes the report creation process go more smoothly and helps ensure that users find the report intuitive and easy to use. Thinking ahead about using sync slicers and report filters can save time and effort. Using a theme ensures that colors are consistent throughout the report and can also save time by reducing the amount of formatting that's required for visuals. Creating a page template can also save time and effort when creating multiple report pages.

While creating the various pages of the utilization report, we learned valuable lessons about how to overcome the limitations of certain visuals by using DAX, as well as how to use DAX to create dynamic titles that are helpful when working with the drill through feature and how to add visual cues by using icons. Finally, we learned how we can clean up certain report and semantic model elements by hiding them from report viewers, making the report cleaner and more user-friendly.

Now that we have created the final report, the next step is to publish and share our report with others. In the next chapter, we introduce the Power BI service and demonstrate how to publish and share the report.

Questions

As an activity, try to answer the following questions on your own:

- What Power BI feature allows the report author to preset elements such as colors and font sizes?
- What are the three preparation steps that are taken before creating the final report pages?
- What feature keeps the settings for slicers consistent across pages?
- What type of visual can display the current value of a metric and the trend of that metric and track that metric against a goal?
- What two features of Power BI are used to allow report viewers to reset the slicers on a page?
- What DAX function can be used to determine whether a column has a single value?
- What Power BI feature allows ad hoc information to be entered into the semantic model?
- What two analytics features were used on the report pages?
- What report and data elements can be hidden from report viewers?

Further reading

To learn more about the topics that were covered in this chapter, please take a look at the following references:

- *Using Report Themes in Power BI Desktop*: https://learn.microsoft.com/en-us/power-bi/create-reports/desktop-report-themes
- *Using gridlines and snap-to-grid in Power BI Desktop reports*: https://learn.microsoft.com/en-us/power-bi/create-reports/desktop-gridlines-snap-to-grid?tabs=powerbi-desktop
- *Add text boxes, shapes, and smart narrative visuals to Power BI reports*: https://learn.microsoft.com/en-us/power-bi/create-reports/power-bi-reports-add-text-and-shapes?tabs=powerbi-desktop
- *Apply conditional formatting in tables and matrices*: https://learn.microsoft.com/en-us/power-bi/create-reports/desktop-conditional-table-formatting
- *Sort one column by another column in Power BI*: https://learn.microsoft.com/en-us/power-bi/create-reports/desktop-sort-by-column?tabs=powerbi-desktop
- *Create report bookmarks in Power BI to share insights and build stories*: https://learn.microsoft.com/en-us/power-bi/create-reports/desktop-bookmarks?tabs=powerbi-desktop
- *Using the Analytics pane in Power BI Desktop*: https://learn.microsoft.com/en-us/power-bi/transform-model/desktop-analytics-pane
- *Tips and tricks for creating reports in Power BI Desktop*: https://learn.microsoft.com/en-us/power-bi/create-reports/desktop-tips-and-tricks-for-creating-reports
- *Getting started formatting report visualizations*: https://learn.microsoft.com/en-us/power-bi/visuals/service-getting-started-with-color-formatting-and-axis-properties
- *Slicers in Power BI*: https://learn.microsoft.com/en-us/power-bi/visuals/power-bi-visualization-slicers?tabs=powerbi-desktop

Join our community on Discord

Join our community's Discord space for discussions with the authors and other readers: `https://discord.gg/hvqvgyGH`

Part 3

The Service

Now that you have created reports in Power BI Desktop, in this part of the book you will publish your work to the Power BI service, understand how to share and collaborate with others, and enable automatic refreshing of your report.

This part of the book includes the following chapters:

- *Chapter 8, Publishing and Sharing*
- *Chapter 9, Using Reports in the Power BI Service*
- *Chapter 10, Understanding Dashboards, Apps, Metrics, and Security*
- *Chapter 11, Refreshing Content*

8

Publishing and Sharing

A tremendous amount of work has gone into the report that we've created so far, from importing the data to creating the semantic model and calculations to designing and formatting report pages. The report is looking good, but the value of the report is minimal if only the report author has access to it. To maximize the value of the report, the report must be shared with other members of the organization. This chapter introduces the Power BI service, demonstrating how to publish your finalized report to the service and how to share your report with others.

After reading this chapter, you will have a basic understanding of the overall layout and features of the Power BI service as well as how to publish and share reports created in Power BI Desktop.

In this chapter, we will cover the following topics:

- Creating an account
- Introducing the service
- Publishing and sharing

Technical requirements

You will need the following requirements to complete this chapter:

- An internet connection
- Microsoft Power BI Desktop
- A Microsoft 365 account and Microsoft Fabric trial
- If you have skipped any of the previous chapters, you can download `LearnPowerBI.pbix` from GitHub at `https://github.com/PacktPublishing/Learn-Microsoft-Power-BI_3E`

Creating an account

Publishing and sharing work is typically done through the Power BI service. As we covered in *Chapter 1, Introduction to Business Intelligence and Power BI*, the Power BI service is a cloud-based **Software as a Service (SaaS)** online platform used for report creation, report editing, and data ingest, as well as for sharing, collaborating, and viewing reports.

However, in order to use the Power BI service, you need to have a Microsoft 365 account. Once you have a Microsoft 365 account, you can sign up for a free Power BI trial.

Microsoft 365

If you already have a Microsoft 365 account, then you are all set. You can use that account's email address to sign up for a free trial of Power BI or have your IT department or Microsoft 365 administrator assign you a free or Pro Power BI license. If you do not have a Microsoft 365 account, then you will need to sign up for a free Microsoft 365 trial. You can sign up for a free trial here: `https://www.microsoft.com/en-us/microsoft-365/try`. Under the **Explore Microsoft 365 for free** heading, click on **Start your free trial**. The free trial is for one month, which should give you plenty of time to read the rest of this chapter!

Microsoft Fabric trial

Once you have a Microsoft 365 account, you will also need a Microsoft Fabric trial license, Power BI Pro license, or Power BI **Premium Per User (PPU)** license. Your IT administrator or Microsoft 365 administrator can assign you a Pro or PPU license for Power BI. Otherwise, follow these steps to register for a trial of Microsoft Fabric and Power BI:

1. In a web browser, enter `https://powerbi.com` into the browser bar and press the *Enter* key.
2. Enter your Microsoft 365 email address and follow the prompts from there.

After signing up and activating your Microsoft Fabric/Power BI trial, you are ready to log in to the service.

Introducing the service

The **Power BI service**, or simply the **service**, is a web-based SaaS product that is complementary to Power BI Desktop. The service provides a means by which Power BI users can create new semantic models and reports as well as publish, share, and collaborate on semantic models and reports that are created in Power BI Desktop. The service is built around storing reports, dashboards, workbooks, semantic models, dataflows, and other content.

Let's take a brief look at the service and the major capabilities it provides.

Touring the service

Once logged in to the service, the Power BI service interface is somewhat reminiscent of the Power BI Desktop interface, although somewhat simpler.

The Power BI service's user interface is comprised of three main areas, as shown in the following screenshot:

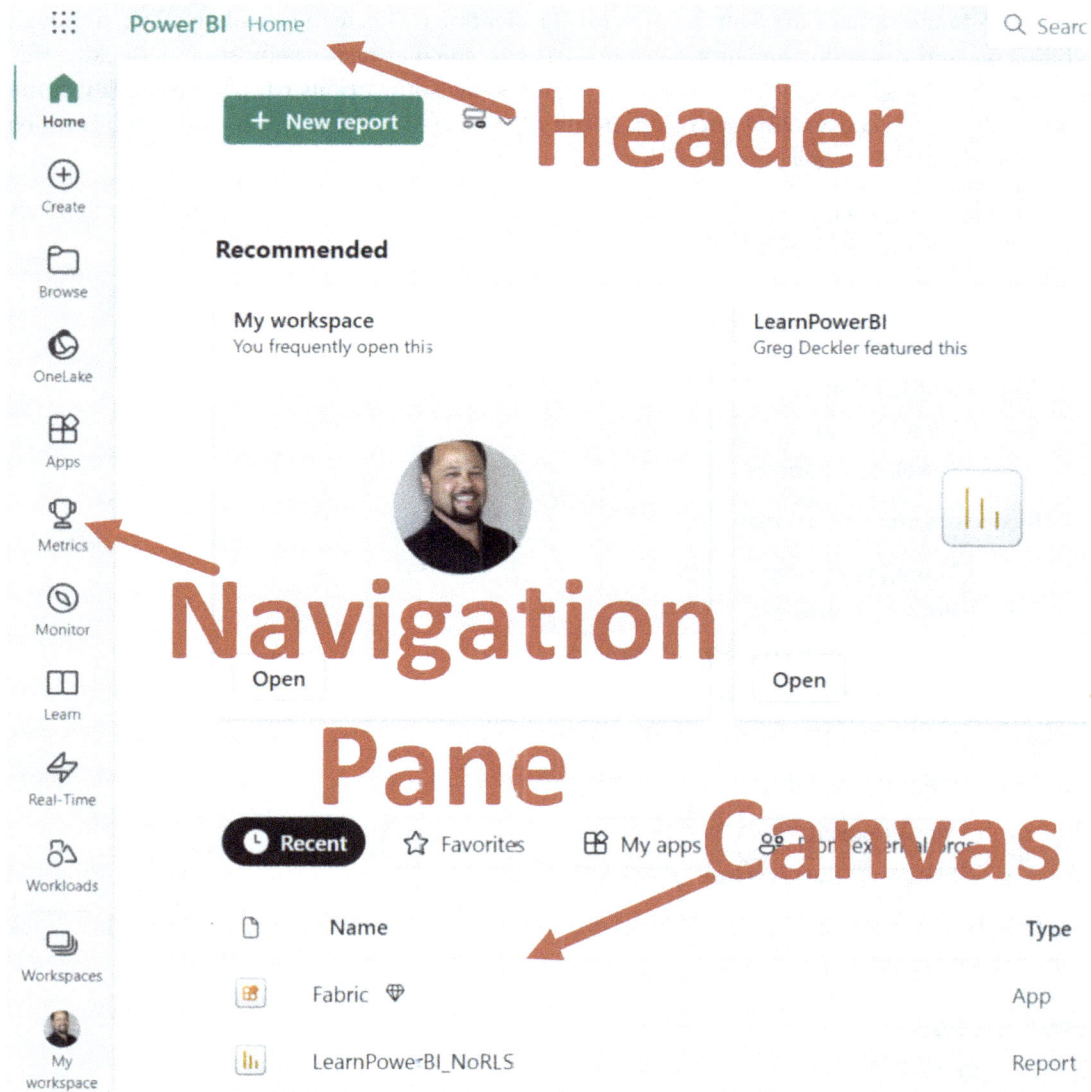

Figure 8.1 – A tour of the service

We will now investigate these three areas more closely. Please refer to *Figure 8.1* throughout the upcoming sections regarding the header, navigation pane, and canvas.

Header

The header area contains a number of useful items. On the far left is a waffle icon, which, when clicked, provides links to other Microsoft 365 applications. On the right-hand side of the Power BI text is a breadcrumb widget that helps you keep track of where you are within the Power BI service. At the top-center of the screen, there is a Search bar and some icons.

The first icon to the right of the **Search** bar is for **Notifications**. This icon looks like a bell, although depending on your resolution and browser zoom settings, you may just see ellipses (...). Clicking this bell icon or the ellipses and then **Notifications** presents the **Notifications** pane as an overlay of the right-hand side of the canvas. Any important notices can be viewed here. This includes notifications from Microsoft, as well as any data alerts that you might configure.

The next icon to the right of the **Notifications** icon is a gear. The gear icon provides links for **Settings** in a drop-down menu. The menu options are as follows:

- Preferences:

  - **General**
  - **Notifications**
  - **Item settings**
  - **Developer settings**

- Resources and extensions:

  - **Manage personal storage**
  - **Power BI settings**
  - **Manage connections and gateways**
  - **Manage embed codes**
  - **Azure Analysis Services migrations**

- Governance and insights:

  - **Admin portal**
  - **Microsoft Purview hub (preview)**

Your **Settings** options may be slightly different depending on your permissions. Let's take a brief look at each of these options:

Preferences

Under this option, we have the following sub-options:

- **General** – Allows you to set **Language** and **Privacy** options for Q&A and close your account
- **Notifications** – Allows you to manage subscriptions and alerts and control whether you receive notifications in email and Microsoft Teams
- **Item settings** – Allows you to activate or deactivate ArcGIS for Power BI
- **Developer settings** – Controls whether to use developer mode when creating custom Power BI visuals

Resources and extensions

Under this option, we have the following sub-options:

- Selecting **Manage personal storage** presents information in the canvas regarding your storage. At the top of this page is a graphic that allows you to see how much personal storage you have consumed. Power BI Pro users get 10 GB of personal storage. This page also lists the semantic models owned by the current user and lists how much space each of the semantic models consumes, along with the associated reports, dashboards, and other information. This page is a convenient location for removing unused semantic models and related artifacts.

- The **Power BI settings** option provides a central location to manage settings for **Dashboards**, **Semantic models**, **Workbooks**, **Reports**, and **Dataflows**.

- The **Manage connections and gateways** link allows you to view and edit gateway connections as well as on-premises and virtual network data gateways within the organization. We cover gateways in *Chapter 11, Refreshing Content*.

- **Manage embed codes** provides a page that you can use to manage your own embed codes. Embed codes are how Power BI content is shared externally to the Power BI service. This area differs from the Admin portal's embed code management as the Admin portal allows all embed codes within the organization to be managed, while this area only lists the currently logged-in user's embed codes.

- The **Azure Analysis Services migrations** link provides the ability to migrate the Azure Analysis Services semantic model to Fabric.

Governance and insights

Under this option, we have the following sub-options:

- Depending on whether or not you are an administrator, you may or may not have access to all or part of the **Admin portal**. The **Admin portal** provides an interface where you can see usage metrics, manage users, view audit logs, adjust tenant and capacity settings, manage embed codes and organizational visuals, as well as manage dataflow settings and workspaces, etc.

- The **Microsoft Purview hub** link is a preview feature that allows you to explore, secure, and govern data within Microsoft Fabric.

The third icon to the right of the **Search** bar, a down arrow, provides **Download** links so that you can download various components of Power BI, including the following:

- **Power BI Desktop**
- **Data Gateway**
- **Paginated Report Builder**
- **Power BI for Mobile**
- **Analyze in Excel updates**
- **Power BI for PowerPoint**
- **OneLake File Explorer**

The fourth icon to the right of the **Search** bar, a question mark, provides **Help & Support** links that are helpful if you want to learn and get support for Power BI. The fifth icon provides **Feedback** links. The sixth icon provides information on your account, tenant, license type, and Fabric trial.

Regardless of where you are in the service, the header area remains a constant fixture, providing immediate access to the icons and links covered in this section.

Navigation pane

The navigation pane contains a number of useful navigational links. We will briefly cover each of these links here:

- The **Home** link takes you to a page that serves as an overall entry point to the Power BI service. This page lists reports that have been favorited and are frequently accessed, as well as recent reports and workspaces. In addition, reports that have been shared with you will appear here, as well as recommended apps and useful links that you can use to explore learning opportunities.

- The **Create** option allows you to enter data manually or choose a published semantic model and then begin creating a report with the chosen data. In addition, if using a Fabric trial, you can create Microsoft Fabric items such as a Lakehouse, Notebook, Warehouse, etc. Microsoft Fabric is covered in greater detail later in this book.

- The **Browse** link lists workspaces, semantic models, dashboards, reports, and other content items that you have recently used or favorited, or that have been shared with you.

- The **OneLake data hub** option lists semantic models as well as Fabric items such as Lakehouses and Warehouses.

- The **Apps** option lists apps that you have installed. **Apps** are collections of dashboards and reports that can be easily shared and deployed to large numbers of specific business users or an entire organization in order to empower people throughout the business to make data-driven decisions. Apps are covered in *Chapter 10, Understanding Dashboards, Apps, Metrics, and Security*.

- The **Metrics** link allows for the creation of Scorecards. Scorecards are covered in *Chapter 10, Understanding Dashboards, Apps, Metrics, and Security*.

- The **Monitor** option provides success and failure information for the refresh of semantic models and dataflows.

- The **Learn** link provides access to sample reports and training materials.

- The **Real-Time hub** link provides access to the **Real-Time hub**, which is for streaming data.

- The **Workloads** link provides access to all Power BI and Fabric workloads such as:

    - **Data Factory**
    - **Industry Solutions**
    - **Real-Time Intelligence**
    - **Data Engineering**
    - **Data Science**
    - **Data Warehouse**
    - **Databases**
    - **Power BI**

- **Workspaces** is a fly-out menu that lists any workspaces that have been created by, or shared with, the currently logged-in user. Workspaces are a way of organizing your dashboards, reports, workbooks, semantic models, dataflows, and other content. Workspaces also serve as shared environments for a group of users, and a workspace is the technology underlying apps in Power BI. Every user starts with one workspace, **My workspace**. Users can create as many other workspaces as desired and each of these workspaces can also contain multiple dashboards, reports, workbooks, semantic models, and dataflows. Creating workspaces other than the default **My workspace** workspace is a Power BI Pro license feature. Selecting a workspace displays the workspace below the **Workspaces** icon in the navigation pane.
- The ellipses (...) provide access to additional navigation pane items such as **Deployment pipelines**.

At the bottom of the navigation pane is the **Experiences** icon. Currently, this displays the Power BI logo and the words **Power BI**. If using a Microsoft Fabric trial, clicking this icon provides access to Fabric. The navigation pane is useful for quickly switching between major content areas in the Power BI service.

Canvas

Similar to the canvas area in Desktop, the particular content and use of the canvas area in the service depend on exactly where you are in the service and what you are doing. Suffice it to say that this is the main area where you view and interact with reports and other content within the service.

Publishing and sharing

Continuing with the example scenario we introduced in *Chapter 2, Planning Projects with Power BI*, Pam is excited to share the new utilization report with the rest of the organization. She decides that using the Power BI service is the best and most secure way to do this, especially since she wants to leverage **Row-Level Security** (RLS) in order to keep people focused on the information that is most important to their role. Pam's organization does not have a Microsoft Fabric capacity so this means that everyone viewing the report will need a Power BI Pro license.

In order to publish and share a report, we first need to create a workspace to store the report, so let's do that next.

Creating a workspace

Pam decides to create a workspace specifically for the reports that she will publish to the service. She expects to publish many more reports other than just her new utilization report, so she decides to create a new workspace for these reports instead of cluttering up her default **My workspace** workspace.

We follow these steps to get started:

1. Click on **Workspaces** and then, at the bottom of the fly-out menu, click **+ New workspace**.
    The **Create a workspace** dialog is displayed on the right-hand side of the screen, as shown in
    Figure 8.2:

Create a workspace

Name *

    Learn Power BI

✔ This name is available

Description

    Describe this workspace

Domain ⓘ

    Assign to a domain (optional)

Learn more about workspace settings [↗]

Workspace image

↑ Upload

↩ Reset

Advanced ⌄

Figure 8.2 – Create a workspace dialog

2. Enter a name for the workspace, such as Learn Power BI, and then click the **Apply** button. The new workspace is created, and you are transported to the workspace's home page, as shown in *Figure 8.3*:

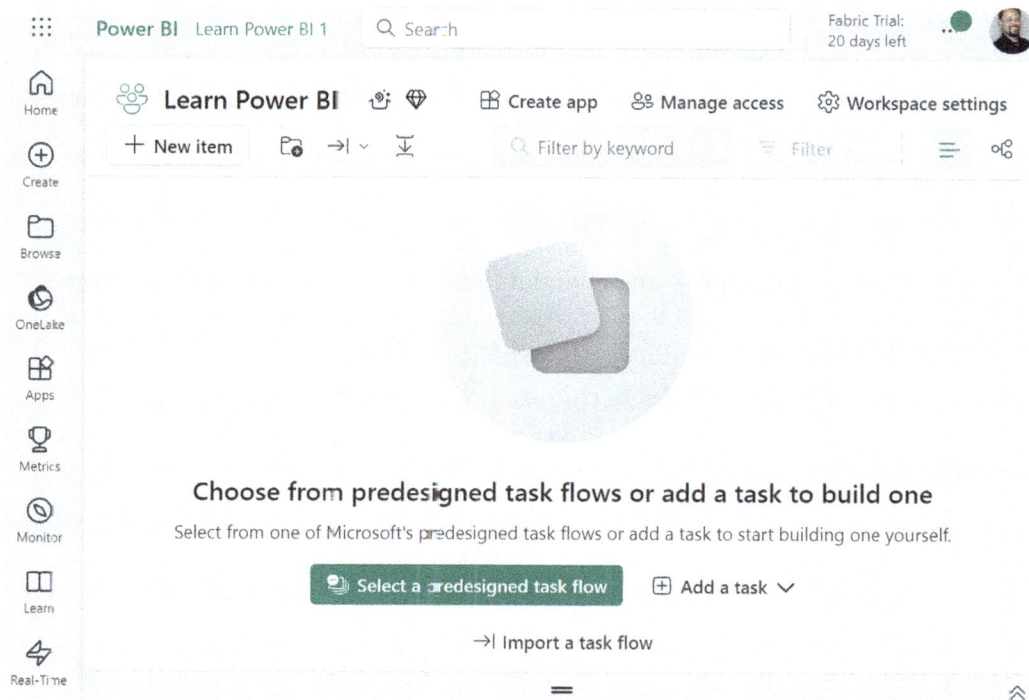

Figure 8.3 – Workspace home page (Get data page)

You may be curious about the optional **Domain** setting. Domains are Microsoft's way of implementing a data mesh, a decentralized data architecture for organizing data by business units such as sales, operations, marketing, etc. In Power BI, domains are both a logical grouping of content as well as a security container.

Now that we have created a workspace, we can publish our report.

Publishing

Let's publish our report to the service. To publish the report, we must switch back to Power BI Desktop. Follow these steps to publish the report:

1. Open Power BI Desktop.
2. Open the most recent saved copy of your saved report by selecting the **File** tab on the ribbon and then **Open report**.

3. Click the **Browse reports** button, navigate to the most recent copy of your report, and then click the **Open** button. Remember, you can download `LearnPowerBI.pbix` from GitHub at `https://github.com/PacktPublishing/Learn-Microsoft-Power-BI_3E`.

Before proceeding and publishing the report, navigate to each page of the report and reset the filters by holding down the *Ctrl* key and then pressing the **Reset** button in the lower-right corner of each page. Finally, before proceeding, choose the page you wish to be displayed initially to users; in this case, this will be the **Introduction** page. Publishing the report to the service publishes the report with any and all current filters and slicer selections. In addition, the currently selected page at the time of publishing becomes the default page for the published report.

4. If not already signed in, click on the **File** tab of the ribbon again and choose **Sign in**. The **Sign in** option appears at the bottom of the **File** menu. Sign in to the Power BI service using an existing work account or the account created in the *Getting an account* section of this chapter.

5. On the **Home** tab of the ribbon, click **Publish** in the **Share** area.

6. Save your work if prompted by clicking the **Save** button.

7. The **Publish to Power BI** dialog is displayed. This dialog displays all the workspaces under the **Select a destination** heading, as shown in *Figure 8.4*:

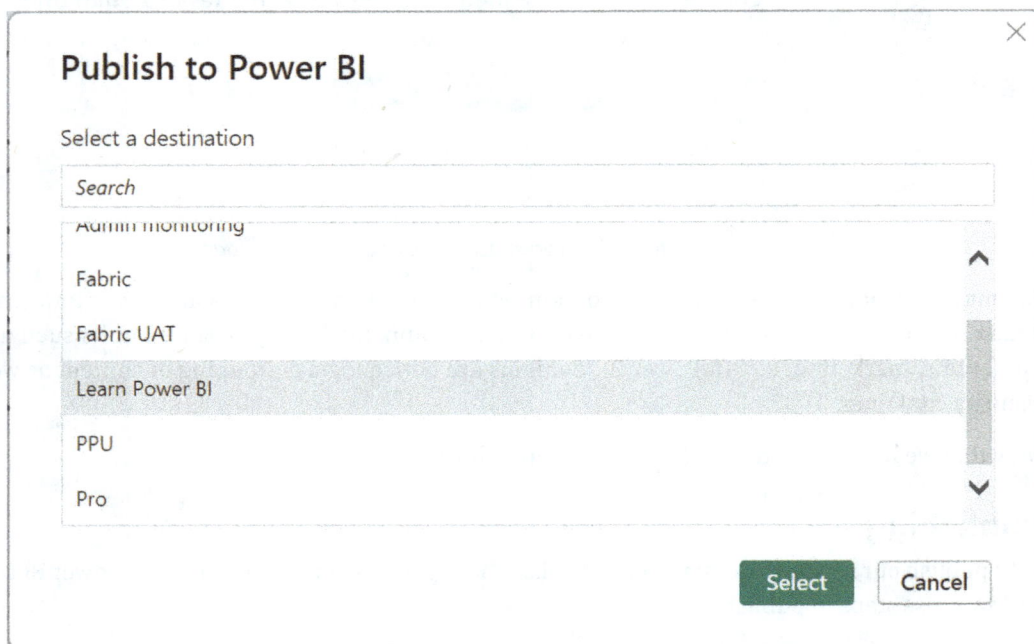

Publish to Power BI

Select a destination

Search
Admin monitoring
Fabric
Fabric UAT
Learn Power BI
PPU
Pro

Select   Cancel

Figure 8.4 – Publish to Power BI dialog

8. Select the workspace you created previously in the *Creating a workspace* section of this chapter and then click the **Select** button.

9. The **Publishing to Power BI** dialog is displayed:

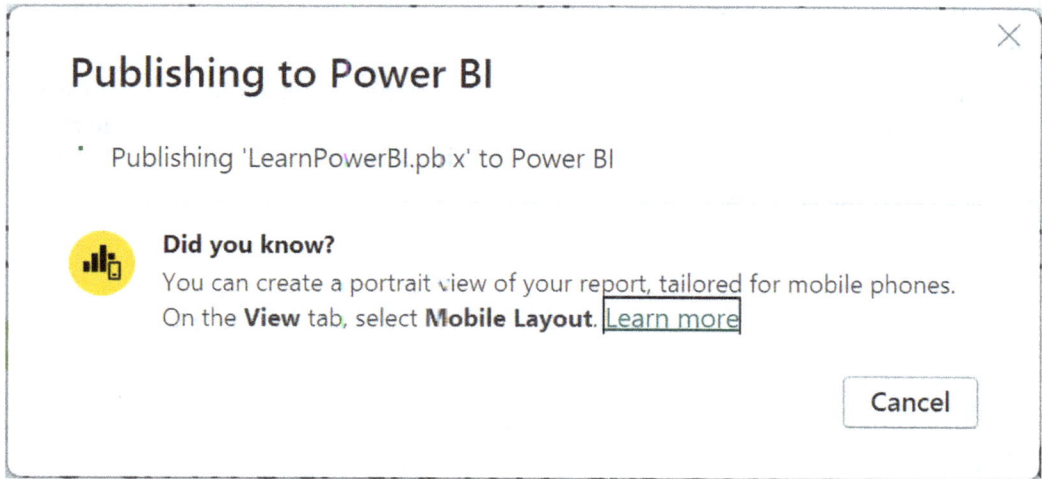

Figure 8.5 – Publishing to Power BI dialog in progress

10. Once publishing is complete, this dialog changes to indicate success or failure:

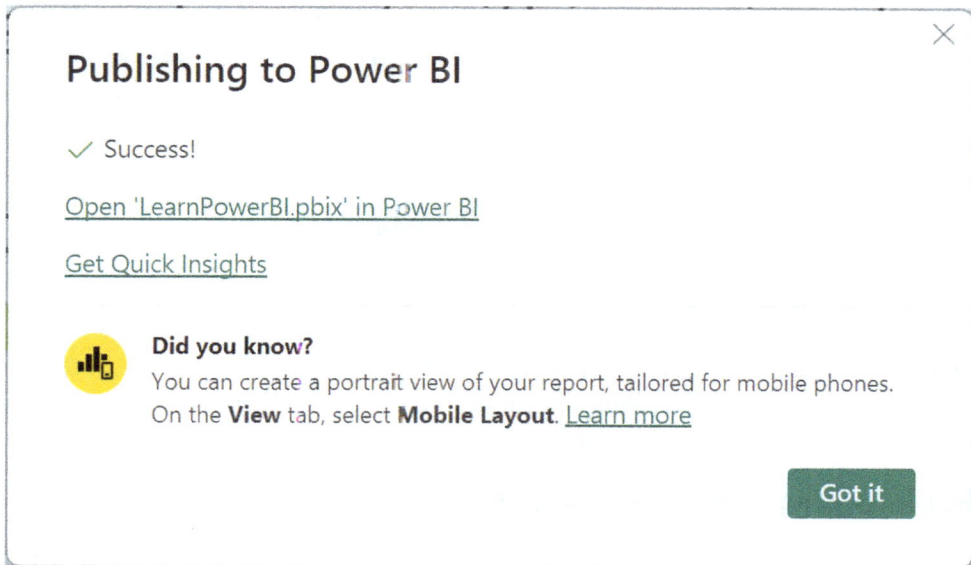

Figure 8.6 – Publishing to Power BI dialog; publishing complete

11. Upon getting a **Success!** message, click the **Open 'LearnPowerBI.pbix' in Power BI** link beneath the **Success!** message, as shown in *Figure 8.6*. Clicking this link opens a browser window or tab that opens the report in the Power BI service. You may be prompted to log in to the service.

The published report in the service should now look and operate exactly like it does within Power BI Desktop, including all the slicers, filters, buttons, bookmarks, and other features. In some cases, there may be slight discrepancies in the display of certain visual elements, but these are rare.

Note that the **Filters** pane is displayed by default but, in the default reading view of the report, the **Visualizations** and **Fields** panes are not displayed in the service. Also note that instead of page tabs at the bottom of the report, a collapsible **Pages** pane is displayed to the left of the report. Finally, note that an icon for the report is included in the navigation pane:

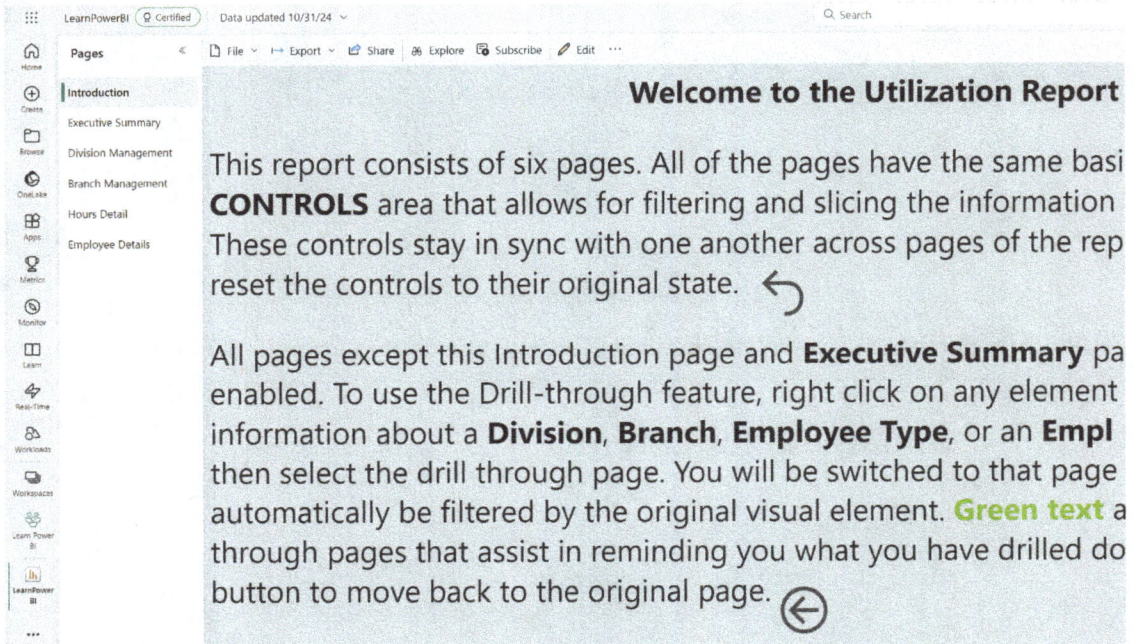

Figure 8.7 – Published report in the service

Click on each page of the report to confirm that each page looks correct. You can also work through the *Testing* subsection of the *Finishing up* section of *Chapter 7, Creating the Final Report*, but this time, using the published report in the service.

What happens when you publish?

When a report is published from Power BI Desktop to the service, multiple objects are created in the Power BI service. To understand this behavior, click on the **Learn Power BI** workspace in the navigation pane. If the Learn Power BI workspace is not visible, click on **Workspaces** in the navigation pane and then select the Learn Power BI workspace.

Your screen should now resemble *Figure 8.8*:

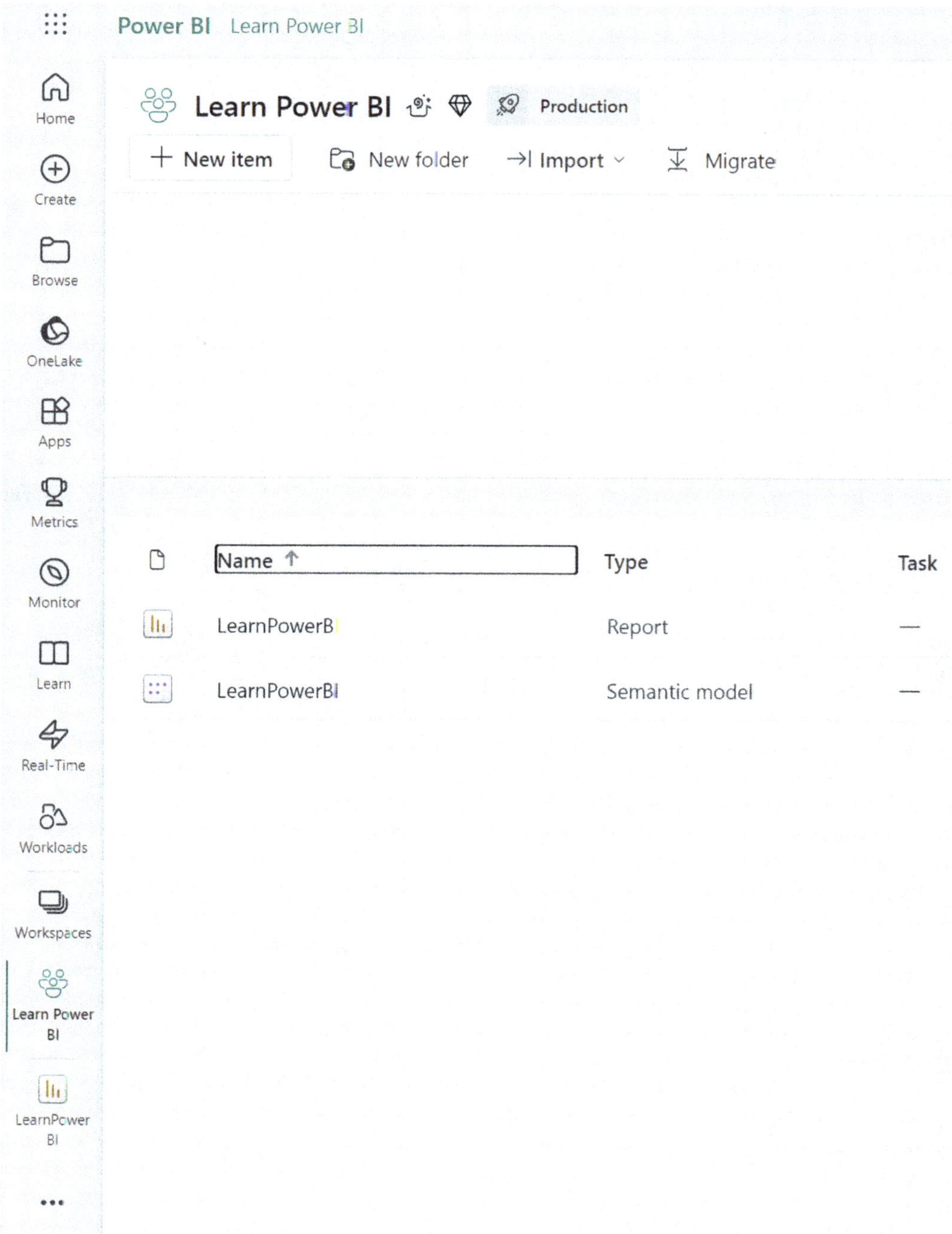

Figure 8.8 – Workspace subsections

As seen in *Figure 8.8*, the filename of the Power BI Desktop file published to the workspace appears as both a **Report** and **Semantic model** type. During publishing, Power BI takes the underlying semantic model in the report and publishes this as a semantic model. The report pages are published as a separate report object and this report object is linked to the published semantic model. Publishing these as separate, but linked, objects allows the semantic model to be reused for the creation of additional, independent reports from within the service. We will discuss this in the next chapter, *Chapter 9, Using Reports in the Power BI Service.*

Sharing

Now that the report has been published, the next step is to share your work with other users within the organization.

Sharing is a paid feature that requires a Power BI Pro or PPU license. This means that all of the users who can view a shared report must have a Power BI Pro license to view it. Power BI PPU works similarly. If the user publishing the report publishes the report to a PPU workspace, then all users must have a PPU license to view it.

However, some Microsoft Fabric capacities work differently. With Microsoft Fabric capacities, reports that are published to an F64+ workspace only require the report publisher to have a Power BI Pro license. Individuals with whom a report is shared only need a Fabric free license to view reports that are published to an F64+ workspace.

Make sure that you are viewing the report in the service. Note that a visual element analogous to the ribbon in Power BI Desktop exists in the service when viewing a report. This ribbon provides access to common features and operations within the service that are specific to reports.

To share the report with others, perform the following steps:

1. Ensure that you are viewing the report in the service.
2. In the report ribbon, click the **Share** link, as shown in *Figure 8.9*:

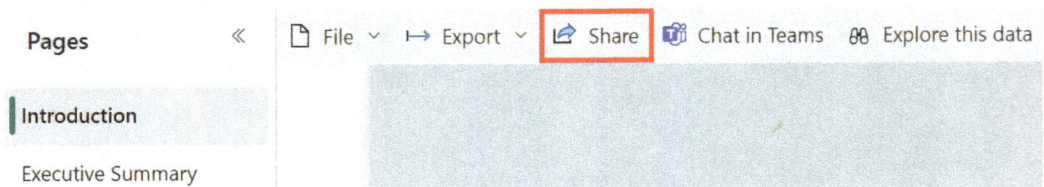

Figure 8.9 – The ribbon and Share link in the service

The **Send link** dialog is displayed, as shown in *Figure 8.10*:

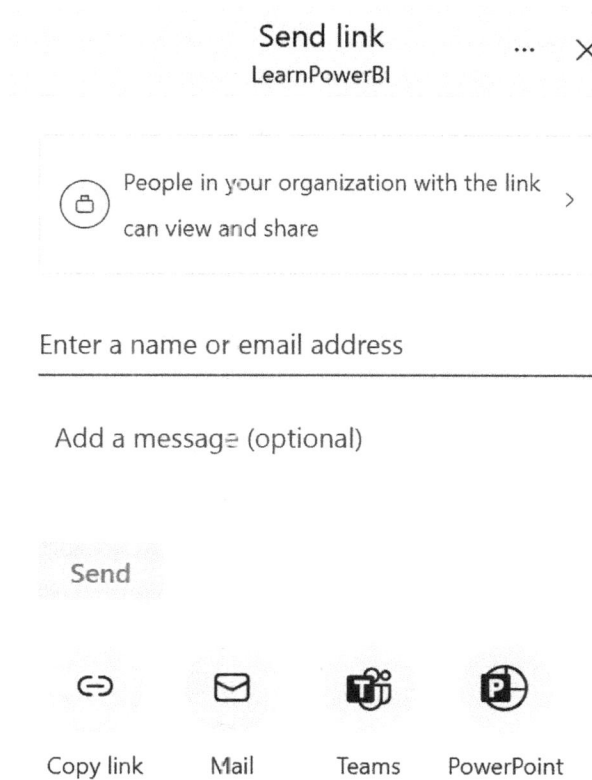

Send link ... ✕

LearnPowerBI

People in your organization with the link can view and share >

Enter a name or email address

Add a message (optional)

Send

Copy link   Mail   Teams   PowerPoint

Figure 8.10 – The Send link dialog in the service

3. First, determine what type of sharing link you wish to create. The default option is **People in your organization with the link can view and share,** as shown in *Figure 8.10*. To change this, click the box that contains the text **People in your organization with the link can view and share,** and the dialog changes to *Figure 8.11*:

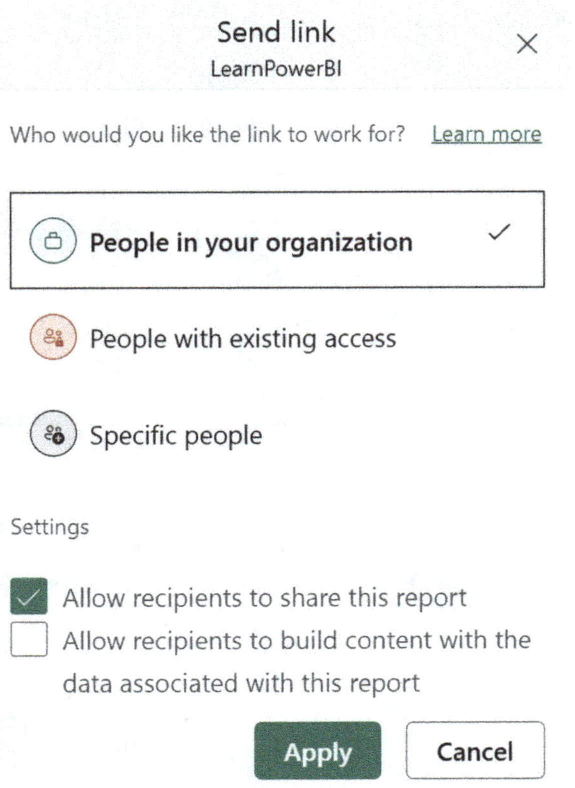

Figure 8.11 – Send link dialog options

4. Select **Specific people** and ensure that both **Allow recipients to share this report** and **Allow recipients to build content with the data associated with this report** are unchecked.

5. Click the **Apply** button.

6. You are now back to the **Send link** dialog shown in *Figure 8.10*. However, instead of the text **People in your organization with the link can view and share,** you now see **Specific people can view.**

7. Where the dialog says **Enter a name or email address**, enter the email address or name of a user with whom you wish to share the report.

    These email addresses can be internal to the Power BI/Microsoft 365 tenant or external email addresses, such as @gmail.com and @outlook.com addresses. These can also be email addresses of groups within Microsoft Entra ID. If the email addresses are external, a warning message is displayed, noting that the report is being shared with users external to the organization. Note that if you're sharing with email addresses external to the tenant, those users will need to have a Microsoft 365/Entra AD login, as well as a Power BI Pro license, in order to view the report.

8. Optionally, use the **Add a message (optional)** field to include a personalized message alongside the notification users receive when sharing the report.

9. When ready, click the **Send** button or choose one of the four icons: **Copy link**, **Mail**, **Teams**, or **PowerPoint**.

10. **Copy link** copies the link to the clipboard. **Mail** brings up a dialog to choose a messaging app and creates a message in that app with the link in the body of the message. **Teams** launches a **Share to Microsoft Teams** dialog, allowing you to share the link with a person, group, or channel in Teams. **PowerPoint** displays an **Embed live data in PowerPoint** dialog allowing you to copy a report page link.

Once a report has been shared with a user, that report will now appear when they select the **Shared with me** link after selecting the **Browse** link in the navigation pane. Note that sharing individual reports and other content is generally inefficient and you should instead be leveraging workspace permissions or, in particular, apps, which we will cover in *Chapter 10, Understanding Dashboards, Apps, Metrics, and Security*.

Summary

In this chapter, we introduced the Power BI service. First, we introduced multiple ways to get a Power BI account that we can use with the service. We then took a tour of the major interface elements within the service. Next, we learned how to publish a report that's been developed in the Desktop version to the service. This included learning how to create workspaces and understanding exactly what occurs when a Desktop file is published to the service. Once published, we then learned how to share a report with other individuals and groups, both within an organization and outside it.

In the next chapter, we will explore everything that can be done with reports in the service, including viewing, exporting, embedding, editing, and creating them!

Questions

As an activity, try to answer the following questions on your own:

- What are the two ways of getting a Power BI account?
- What are the three main interface elements of the Power BI service?
- What is a workspace and why would you use one?
- Do you publish reports from the Desktop version or the service?
- What two objects are created/updated in the Power BI service when a report is published?
- True or false? Reports can only be shared with internal users of an organization.
- True or false? Reports can only be shared with single users.
- What options are available when sharing reports?

Further reading

- *Tutorial: Get started creating in the Power BI service*: https://learn.microsoft.com/en-us/power-bi/fundamentals/service-get-started

- *Publish semantic models and reports from Power BI Desktop*: https://learn.microsoft.com/en-us/power-bi/create-reports/desktop-upload-desktop-files

- *Ways to collaborate and share in Power BI*: https://learn.microsoft.com/en-us/power-bi/collaborate-share/service-how-to-collaborate-distribute-dashboards-reports

- *Workspaces in Power BI*: https://learn.microsoft.com/en-us/power-bi/collaborate-share/service-new-workspaces

Unlock this book's exclusive benefits now

Scan this QR code or go to packtpub.com/unlock, then search for this book by name.

Note: Keep your purchase invoice ready before you start.

9

Using Reports in the Power BI Service

Now that we have published a report in the **Power BI service** and understood the basics of how to operate within the service, there are many other features of the service that are important to understand. The service has its own extensive feature set, such as sharing and commenting, that adds significant capabilities to Power BI in addition to just using the Desktop version alone. Understanding these features and capabilities allows us to maximize the value of Power BI for any organization. Chief among these is how to use reports within the service. This chapter explores the different features available when using reports in the service, including how to collaborate on reports, receive regular updates, use bookmarks, and so on.

To understand the full capabilities of reports within the Power BI service, the following topics are covered in this chapter:

* Viewing and using reports
* Editing and creating reports

Technical requirements

You will need the following requirements to successfully complete this chapter:

* An internet connection.
* A **Microsoft 365** account or Fabric trial account.
* If you have skipped any of the previous chapters, you can download LearnPowerBI.zip from GitHub at https://github.com/PacktPublishing/Learn-Microsoft-Power-BI_3E/tree/main/Chapter8.

Viewing and using reports

The reporting interface within Power BI provides numerous useful functions when viewing reports. Some of these functions are similar to features within Power BI Desktop, while others are unique to the service. Different options are available depending on certain tenant settings and whether you own a report or have read permissions for a report. The features and functionality described here encompass all of the options present as if you owned the report.

The first difference between Power BI Desktop and the Power BI service that most users will notice when viewing a report is that there is a **Pages** pane located to the left of the report versus the **Page** tabs at the bottom of the report in the Desktop version. All pages in the report except for hidden pages are listed in the **Pages** pane. This **Pages** pane can be collapsed or expanded using the << and >> icons, respectively.

The functions for reports within the service are accessed by using the slim ribbon bar that appears above the report, as shown in the following screenshot:

Figure 9.1 – Report ribbon in the service

Additional items in the report ribbon include the following:

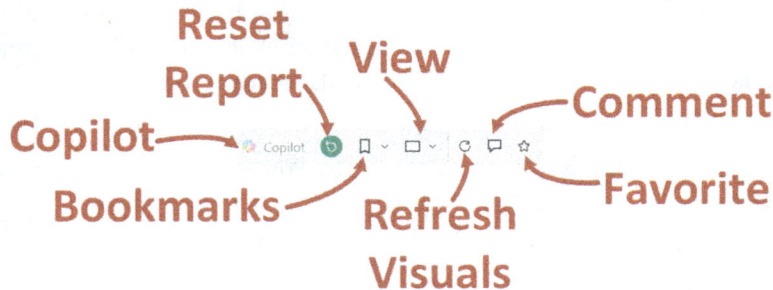

Figure 9.2 – Additional report ribbon options in the service

Let's explore the various options and functionality present within this ribbon bar.

File menu

The **File** menu provides a variety of important options and features for managing and working with reports while in the service, as illustrated in the following screenshot:

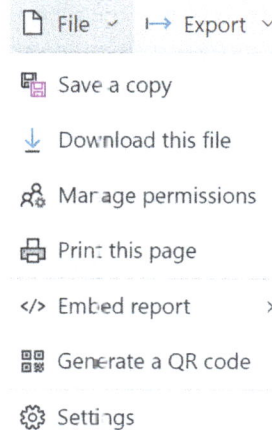

Figure 9.3 – File menu in the service

Let's explore all of the options shown in *Figure 9.3*.

Save a copy

Clicking **Save a copy** brings up a **Save your report** dialog that allows you to enter a new name for your report as well as to pick a workspace. Once you click the **Save** button, your report is saved under a new name within the selected workspace. Note that you can also create a **New folder** within this dialog as well.

Download this file

The **Download this file** menu option creates a **Power BI Desktop (PBIX)** file that is then downloaded from the service. This PBIX file can either contain a copy of the data within the associated semantic model or a live connection to the semantic model in the service.

Manage permissions

Clicking **Manage permissions** allows you to manage the sharing of **Links** created, users with **Direct Access** to the report, as well as **Pending** access requests, **Shared views**, and users with **Access via related items**:

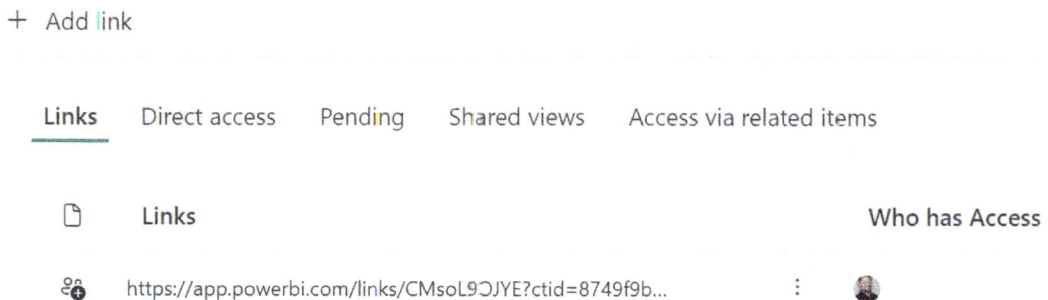

Figure 9.4 – Manage permissions dialog in the service

The **Links** tab displays any sharing links created for the report and allows you to add new links via an **Add link** button. Clicking the **Add link** button brings up the same dialog as clicking the **Share** button in the report ribbon. Links can be edited and removed.

The **Direct access** tab displays all users that currently have direct access to the report and allows you to add new users via an **Add user** button. When adding a user, as shown in the following screenshot, the user is added with **Read** permissions to the report and can also be granted reshare and build rights as well. These rights allow the user to reshare the report with others or build new reports based on the underlying semantic model, respectively. Users can also be removed or have their permission settings changed on this tab:

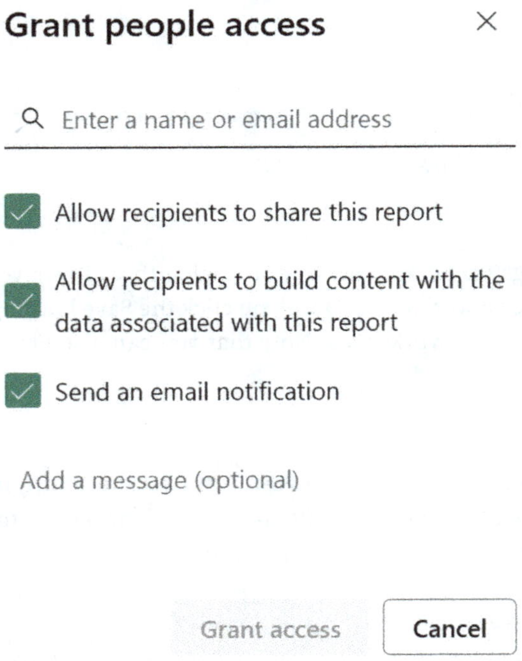

Grant people access   ✕

Q Enter a name or email address
_____

✓ Allow recipients to share this report

✓ Allow recipients to build content with the
    data associated with this report

✓ Send an email notification

Add a message (optional)

Grant access   Cancel

Figure 9.5 – Add user dialog in the service

The **Pending** tab allows you to accept or reject pending requests to view the report. When attempting to view a report in the service that you do not have access to view, you are provided the option of requesting access to the report. Those requests appear on the **Pending** tab.

When sharing a report, if you have made changes to the filters, slicers, or selected visual elements, there is an **Include my changes** option. Selecting this option creates a temporary shared view for the report. The **Shared views** tab lists these temporary views.

If access to the report is granted via a related content item (such as a dashboard), those users are listed on the **Access via related items** tab.

Print this page

Perhaps surprisingly, printing is a function that's only available in the Power BI service and not Power BI Desktop, although Power BI Desktop does include the ability to export to PDF. Clicking the **Print this page** link brings up a **Print** dialog that allows you to print a report using local or network printers. The **Print** dialog is shown in the following screenshot:

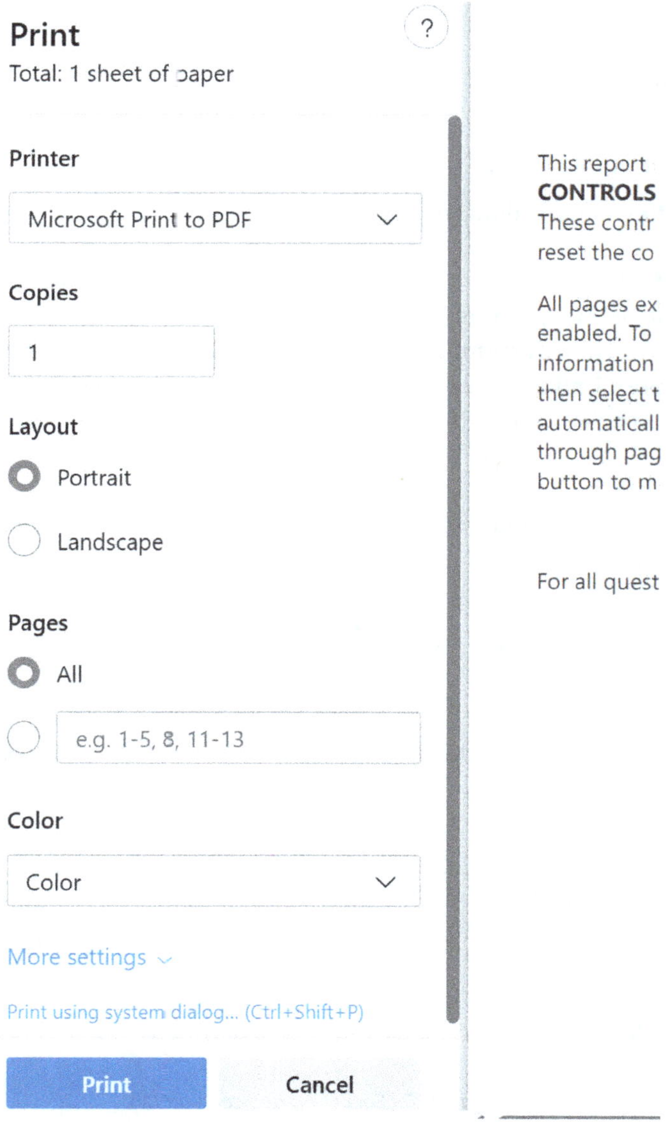

Figure 9.6 – Print dialog

Make sure to switch the **Layout** setting to **Landscape** to maximize your report's size and ensure that visuals are not cut off of the page.

Embed report

Embedding allows reports to be inserted into websites so that just the report canvas area is displayed. Embedding reports can be done in four different ways, as outlined here:

- SharePoint Online
- Website or portal
- Publish to web (public)
- Developer Playground

Let's explore the different embedding options.

SharePoint Online

Clicking **SharePoint Online** generates a secure embed code that's specifically designed for use in SharePoint Online. As with other embed codes, this embed code enforces authentication and all security within the report. Unlike other embed codes, SharePoint embed codes do not support the filter query string parameter. See *Using URL parameters with embed codes* in this section.

Website or portal

Clicking the **Website or portal** option brings up the **Secure embed code** dialog, as shown in the following screenshot:

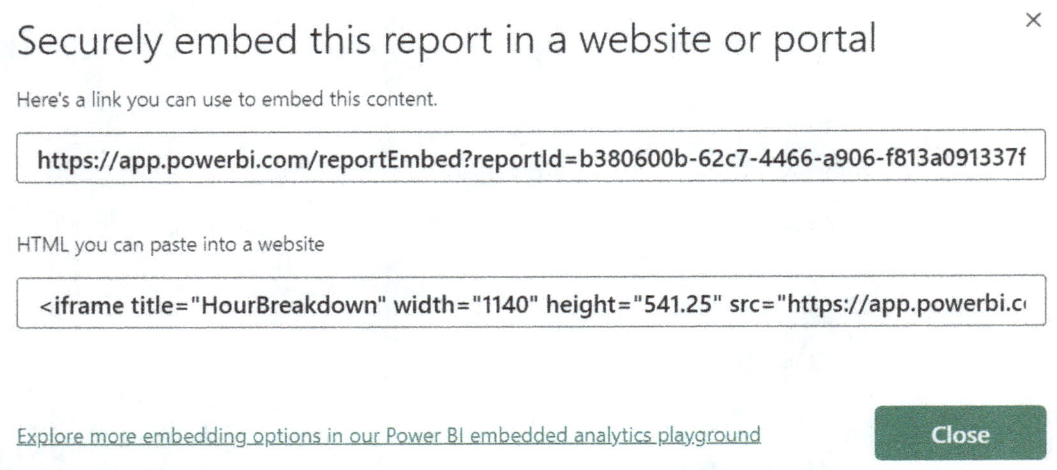

Securely embed this report in a website or portal   ×

Here's a link you can use to embed this content.

https://app.powerbi.com/reportEmbed?reportId=b380600b-62c7-4466-a906-f813a091337f

HTML you can paste into a website

<iframe title="HourBreakdown" width="1140" height="541.25" src="https://app.powerbi.c

Explore more embedding options in our Power BI embedded analytics playground   Close

Figure 9.7 – Secure embed code dialog

This secure embed code is designed to be used within external websites. Secure embed codes require authentication to the Power BI service in order to display reports. All report security, such as **Row-Level Security (RLS)**, is enforced within the embedded report.

Creating a secure embed code does not grant permissions to a report. Permissions to the report must be set separately by using the **Share** function or in the **Manage permissions** interface. This means that viewers of the report that use the embed code must have a Power BI Pro or **Premium Per User (PPU)** license, or the report must be published to a Microsoft Fabric F64+ capacity.

There are two types of embed codes: a **raw embed code** (the top link in the preceding screenshot) and a **HyperText Markup Language (HTML) embed code** (the bottom link in the preceding screenshot). The raw embed code is simply a secure link to the report. This link can be used within any website or portal that provides the ability to embed by using such a link. Alternatively, this link can be used as a direct link to the report. For example, the top link presented in the dialog can be pasted directly into a browser's **Uniform Resource Locator (URL)** bar.

The HTML embed code is an **Inline Frame (IFRAME) HTML snippet**. IFRAMEs are HTML tags that are used to include content from other websites within a web page. Thus, to use the HTML embed code, the snippet of HTML must be pasted within the HTML code of a web page. When using the HTML embed code snippet, you may need to adjust the width and height parameters of the snippet in order to properly display the report within your website.

Publish to web (public)

The **Publish to web** option works identically to the **Website and portal** option, with one important difference: security is not enforced. This means that anyone with the embed code or HTML snippet can view the report free of any security. As such, the **Publish to web** option is not available on reports that include RLS. In addition, there are numerous other restrictions when using **Publish to web** embed codes regarding the type of visuals and features supported. Some of the restrictions include the following:

- Cannot use R or Python visuals
- Cannot use ArcGIS Maps visuals
- Cannot use Q&A visuals
- Cannot use live connections
- Cannot use shared or certified semantic models

If a report uses RLS or any of these features, the **Publish to web** option does not appear as an option.

When clicking the **Publish to web** option, you are initially presented with a screen informing you of the terms of use, stating that you can only use the code on a public website. Click the **Continue** button to proceed. You are then informed on a second screen that anyone who has the embed code can view the report. Click the **Publish** button to proceed.

Clicking **Publish** displays an **Embed code** dialog that includes a preview of the report:

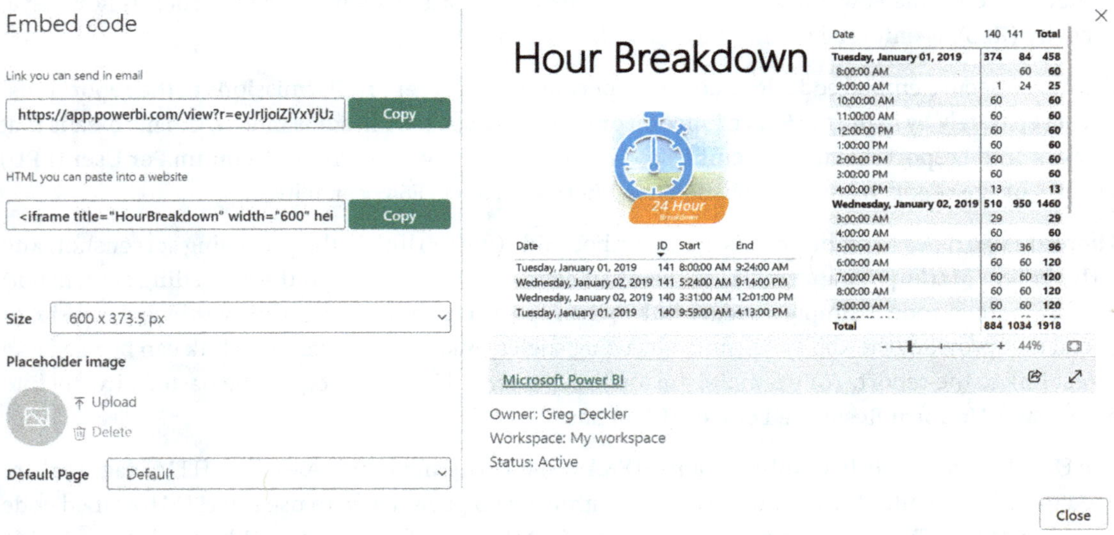

Figure 9.8 – Embed dialog for Publish to web

Obviously, you should not use **Publish to web** when sharing secure or sensitive information. **Publish to web** is only intended to be used when sharing work that could potentially be seen by anyone in the world. Because security is not enforced, anyone who has the embed code can turn around and resend or share that embed code with additional people, and those individuals could also see the report.

This feature is used heavily for community content such as on the Power BI Community website (`https://community.fabric.microsoft.com/t5/Power-BI-forums/ct-p/powerbi`). The Data Stories Gallery (`https://community.fabric.microsoft.com/t5/Data-Stories-Gallery/bd-p/DataStoriesGallery`) and Quick Measures Gallery (`https://community.fabric.microsoft.com/t5/Quick-Measures-Gallery/bd-p/QuickMeasuresGallery`) are good examples of proper use of the **Publish to web** feature.

As mentioned, once a **Publish to web** embed code is created, anyone with the code can access the report, free of any security, including authentication. These embed codes can be managed so that you can retrieve the embed codes or delete them. To manage embed codes, do the following:

1. To access the **Manage embed codes** interface, click the gear icon in the header area of the Power BI service. You may instead see ellipses (**…**) instead of a gear icon. If so, click the ellipses and then **Settings**.

2. Choose **Manage embed codes**, as shown in the following screenshot:

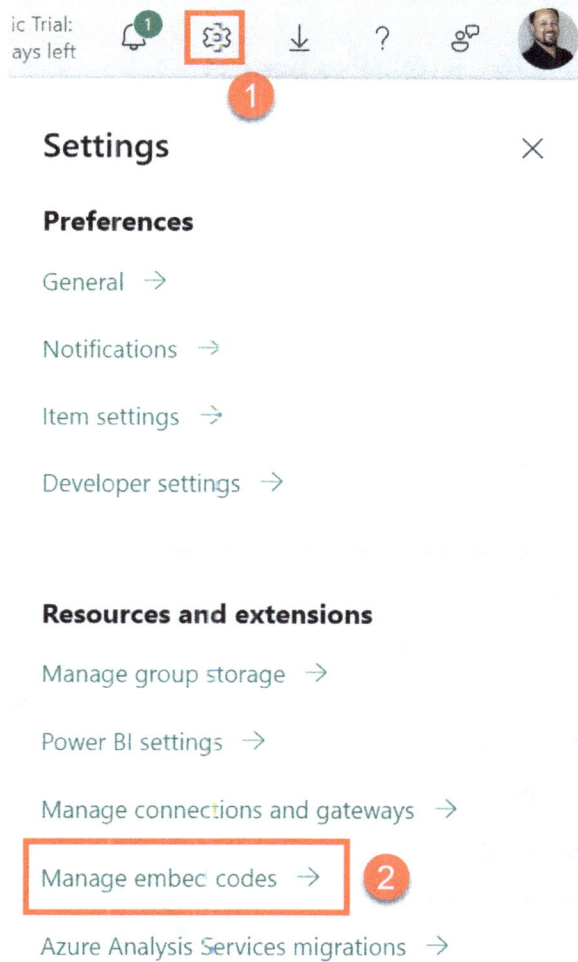

Figure 9.9 – Accessing Manage embed codes

3. Choosing this option brings up the **Manage embed codes** interface, which lists embed codes created in the current workspace, as illustrated in the following screenshot:

Greg Deckler Pro license

Associated Report ↑	Status	Date Created		
BrowserContents	Active	10/31/2024, 11:50:09 AM	</>	🗑
Fabric Lore	Active	2/16/2024, 5:12:28 PM	</>	🗑
HourBreakdown	Active	4/9/2024, 1:30:11 PM	</>	🗑
IncreasedDecreasedStayedTheSame	Active	4/9/2024, 2:52:21 PM	</>	🗑
LongestStreak	Active	7/20/2024, 11:37:23 AM	</>	🗑
MapsPublishToWeb	Active	3/26/2024, 11:11:05 AM	</>	🗑

Figure 9.10 – Manage embed codes page

4. From this interface, as shown in *Figure 9.10*, **Publish to web** embed codes can be retrieved (</>) as well as deleted (trash can icon).

The last option is **Developer Playground**.

Developer Playground

Developer Playground is a special interface where JavaScript or TypeScript developers can experiment with embedding reports, visuals, and other elements. **Power BI embedded** allows all or part of a report to be embedded in a custom website or other application.

Now that we have covered the different types of embed codes, let's next take a look at how you can use URL parameters with the different types of embed codes to create links that show specific information.

Using URL parameters with embed codes

Both **Web and portal** and **Publish to web** embed codes include the ability to use special URL parameters in order to control the display of the embedded report. These parameters are included in the query string portion of the URL.

The query string portion of a URL is the portion of the URL that is after the question mark (?). For example, note the bold ? character in the following code snippet:

```
https://app.powerbi.com/reportEmbed?reportId=0982-4e14-bbf7-ddb60a89ab43&autoAu
th=true&ctid=373a-43d2-827b-003f4c7ba1e5
```

> 💡 **Quick tip:** Enhance your coding experience with the **AI Code Explainer** and **Quick Copy** features. Open this book in the next-gen Packt Reader. Click the **Copy** button
>
> (1) to quickly copy code into your coding environment, or click the **Explain** button
>
> (2) to get the AI assistant to explain a block of code to you.

```
                                            Copy        Explain
function calculate(a, b) {
  return {sum: a + b};                       1            2
};
```

> 🔒 **The next-gen Packt Reader** is included for free with the purchase of this book. Scan the QR code OR visit packtpub.com/unlock, then use the search bar to find this book by name. Double-check the edition shown to make sure you get the right one.

Multiple query string parameters can be used by separating the parameters with an ampersand (&) sign. For example, the preceding URL includes three separate query string parameters, as follows:

* `reportId`
* `autoAuth`
* `ctid`

There is an additional parameter, the `filter` parameter. The `filter` parameter can also be used to filter the initial display of the report. The **filter** parameter has the following format:

```
filter=Table/Field eq 'Value'
```

To add a particular filter to the embed code that initially only displays the `1001 Technology` division, the URL can be edited like so:

```
https://app.powerbi.com/reportEmbed?reportId=0982-4e14-bbf7-ddb60a89ab43&aut
oAuth=true&ctid=373a-43d2-827b-003f4c7ba1e5 &filter=Hours/Division eq '1001
Technology'
```

The `Table` and `Field` portions of the parameter are *case-sensitive* to the names in the semantic model, while the `Value` portion is not. You can also use ne (not equal) and in operators such as:

```
&filter=People/Location in ('Cleveland', 'Charlotte')
```

Generate a QR code

The **Generate a QR code** option creates a **Quick Response (QR)** code that links to the report in the service, as shown in the following screenshot. This code can be downloaded and shared with others:

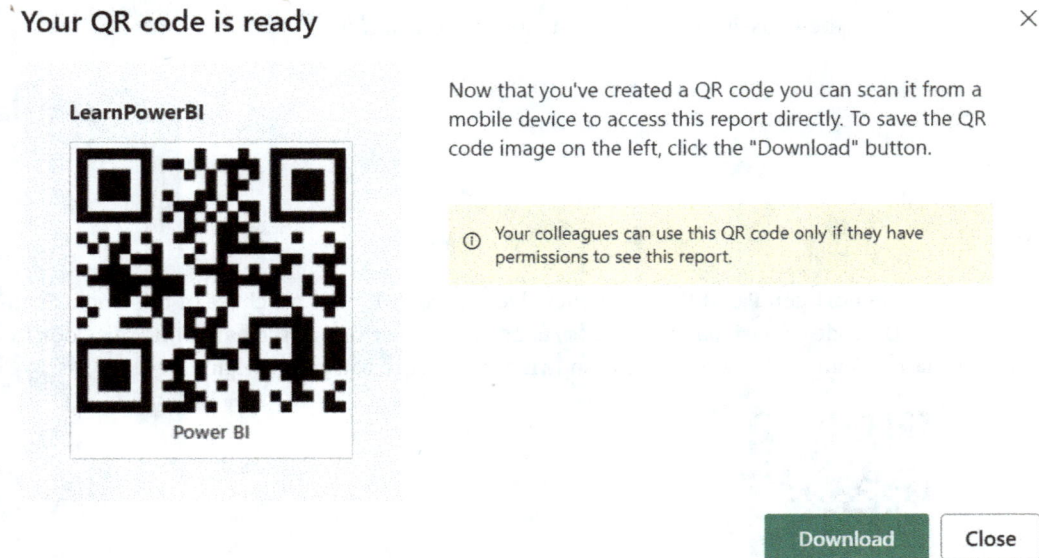

Figure 9.11 – Generate a QR code dialog

Next, let's look at **Settings**!

Settings

Choosing **Settings** from the **File** menu opens a pane on the right-hand side of the screen that lists many different settings that can be enabled, disabled, or changed for the report. These settings mainly control the experience of others viewing the report and include the following:

- **Report name:** The name of the report.
- **Description:** A description of the report.
- **Contact:** Who to contact regarding the report.
- **Snapshot:** An image snapshot of the report.
- **Endorsement:** Endorsing a report helps other organizational users find your report and trust that its content is reliable. **Endorsement** can be set to **None**, **Promoted**, or **Certified**. The **Certified** option may be grayed out, depending upon your Power BI administrator settings. You can also check the box for **Feature on Home** to display the report in the **Features** section of the Power BI home screen.
- **Persistent filters:** Enables or disables the ability of other users to save filters on the report.
- **Pages pane:** Controls whether the report pages are displayed in the **Pages** pane or as tabs along the bottom of the report, as in the Desktop version.

- **Visual options:** Visual options include the ability to enable or disable the header for visuals when in reading view, whether to use the modern visual header with updated styling options, and whether the default interaction between visuals is cross-highlighting or cross-filtering.

- **Export data:** This setting controls the kind of data users are allowed to export from the report and whether this can be done at all. The options include **Summarized data and data with current layout, Summarized data, data with current layout and underlying data,** and **None.** The **Summarized data and data with current layout** option essentially allows users to export the data presented in a visual. The data export is the information presented by the visual. Thus, if the three markets, Charlotte, Nashville, and Cleveland had 89%, 86%, and 83% utilization, then this would be the information exported. Conversely, **Summarized data, data with current layout and underlying data** would allow users to export the individual data records that were summarized to arrive at the data displayed in the visual.

- **Filtering experience:** These settings allow you to enable or disable the ability of users to change filter types as well as to enable or disable search functionality for the **Filters** pane. Filter types refer to such things as manual filters, auto filters, include/exclude filters, drill-down filters, and so on. See the *Further reading* section of this chapter for more information on filter types.

- **Cross-report drill through:** Enables or disables the ability of visuals in the report to use other reports as drill-through targets.

- **Comments:** You can either enable or disable comments for the report.

- **Personalize visuals:** Toggles on or off the ability of users to personalize visuals.

- **Modern visual tooltips:** Enables or disables modern visual tooltips. See the following screenshot for a representation of this:

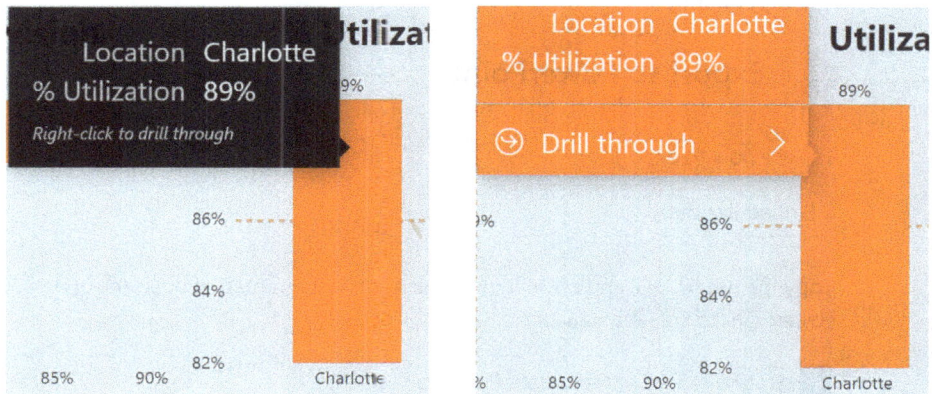

Figure 9.12 – Traditional tooltips (on the left) versus modern tooltips (on the right)

- **Tooltips auto-scale (preview):** Controls whether tooltips automatically scale based on canvas size.

- **Insights (preview):** Enables notifications if key insights are available for a report.

- **Default summarizations:** If enabled, aggregated fields always show the default summarization type.

After changing a setting, you must click the **Save** button and then refresh the report page in the browser. We are now finished with exploring the **File** menu and will now continue to explore the rest of the menu options in the ribbon.

Export menu

The **Export** menu provides three different options, as follows:

- Analyze in Excel
- PowerPoint
- PDF

Analyze in Excel

Choosing this option results in an Excel file being created on OneDrive that contains a live link to the Power BI semantic model for the report. A button is provided to open the file in Excel Online. To utilize the file, you need to enable external data connections when prompted in Excel. Once enabled, you may use the semantic model's tables and columns to create **PivotTables** and **PivotCharts** within the Excel file.

PowerPoint

The **PowerPoint** option is used to export or embed all of the pages of a report to a PowerPoint file. Use the following steps to export a report or portions of a report to PowerPoint:

1. Click on the **PowerPoint** option to display the **Export to PowerPoint** dialog, as shown in the following screenshot:

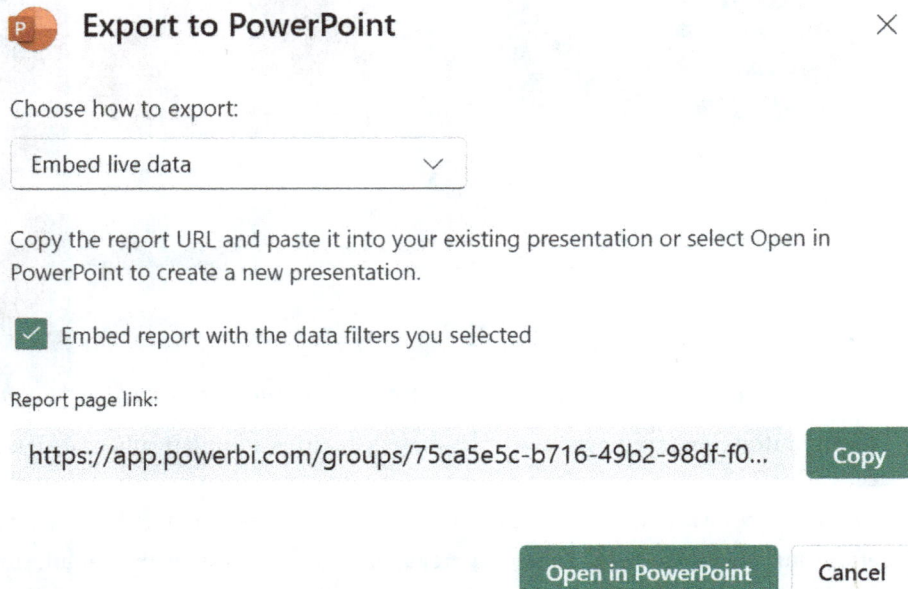

Figure 9.13 – PowerPoint Export dialog in the service

2. As shown, you have the ability to copy a **Report page link** using the **Copy** button or create a new PowerPoint using the **Open in PowerPoint** button. If copying the link, you can use the **Insert** tab of the ribbon in PowerPoint, choose **Power BI**, and then paste the embed link into the **Paste a URL from Power BI here** field.

3. Change the dropdown for **Choose how to export** to **Export as image**. Exporting as an image allows the presentation to be used while offline.

4. Use the **Export with** radio buttons to export the report with either the current values (filters and slicers) within the report or the default values for the report.

5. To not include hidden report tabs, check the **Exclude hidden report tabs** checkbox.

6. You can export all of the pages of the report, or to only export the current page, click the **Only export current page** checkbox.

7. Click the **Export** button to create a PowerPoint file. This may take some time. The file automatically downloads to your Downloads folder once created.

Let's look at the next option, **PDF**!

PDF

The PDF option is used to export all of the pages of the report to a **Portable Document Format (PDF)** file. Clicking on the **PDF** option displays the same **Export** dialog options as when using the **Export as an image** option for exporting as **PowerPoint**.

Share

Clicking the **Share** button in the ribbon opens the **Send link** dialog, as shown in the following screenshot:

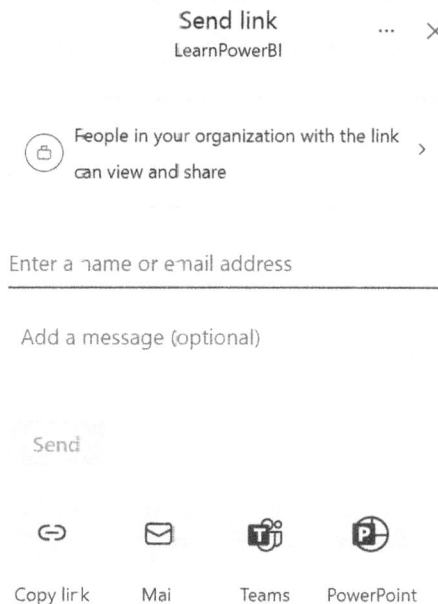

Send link   ···   ✕
LearnPowerBI

People in your organization with the link   >
can view and share

Enter a name or email address

Add a message (optional)

Send

⊖   ▢   📱   📑
Copy link   Mail   Teams   PowerPoint

Figure 9.14 – Send link dialog in the service

The dialog defaults to generating a link that everyone within your organization can use to view and reshare a report. You can add the names of individuals to send this link to and then click the **Send** button. Alternatively, you can use the four icons at the bottom to simply copy the link to your clipboard, open a messaging program with the link contained in the body of the email, post the link to a particular person, group, or channel in Microsoft Teams, or create a PowerPoint live embed link.

You can edit the permissions for the link created by clicking on **People in your organization with the link can view and share** in order to display the second page of the **Send link** dialog, as shown in the following screenshot:

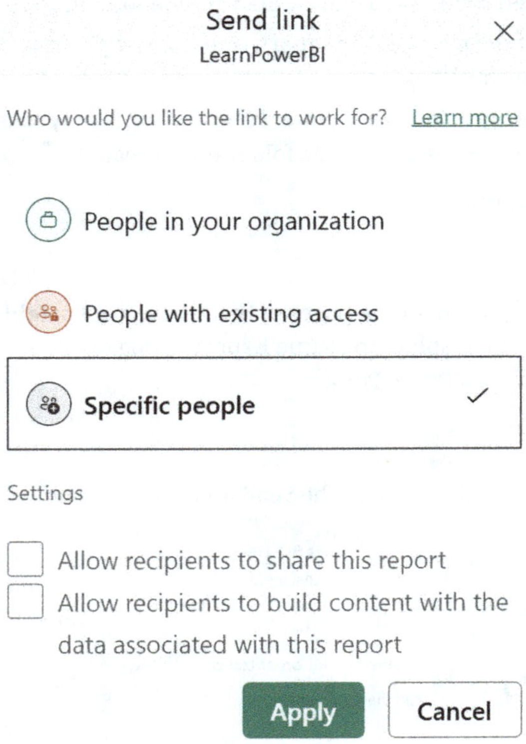

Figure 9.15 – Secondary Send link dialog in the service

As shown in *Figure 9.15*, you can control who the link functions for as well as permissions. For example, in *Figure 9.15*, the permissions have been changed such that the link is intended to only work for specific people, and when using that link, the user can't reshare the report or build new reports based on the underlying data. When you have configured the settings, click the **Apply** button to return to the original **Send link** dialog displayed in *Figure 9.14* with the updated settings.

The **Send link** dialog shown in *Figure 9.14* also provides access to a **Manage permissions** function via the ellipsis (**...**) in the header, as shown in the following screenshot:

Figure 9.16 – Manage permissions function

Choosing **Manage permissions** opens the **Manage permissions** pane on the right side of the screen. This pane displays links that have already been created, as well as those users with direct access to the report, as shown in the following screenshot:

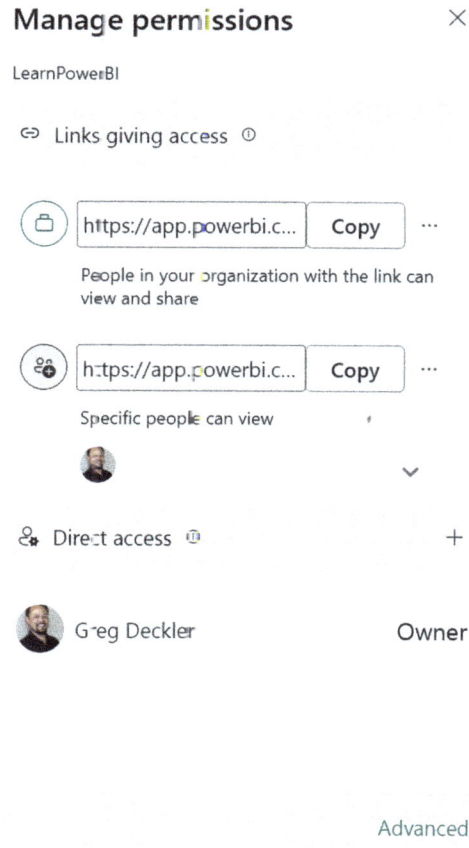

Figure 9.17 – Manage permissions dialog in the service

Users with direct access to the report can be added using the + icon in the **Direct access** header. Clicking the + icon brings up the same interface as shown in *Figure 9.5* and functions identically. Links can be copied using the **Copy** button next to the link. In addition, clicking the ellipsis (...) to the immediate right of the **Copy** button allows the link's permissions to be edited and deleted. The **Advanced** link functions identically to choosing **File | Manage permissions** from the report ribbon.

Teams

Clicking the **Teams** button as shown in *Figure 9.14* opens the **Share to Microsoft Teams** dialog, as shown in the following screenshot:

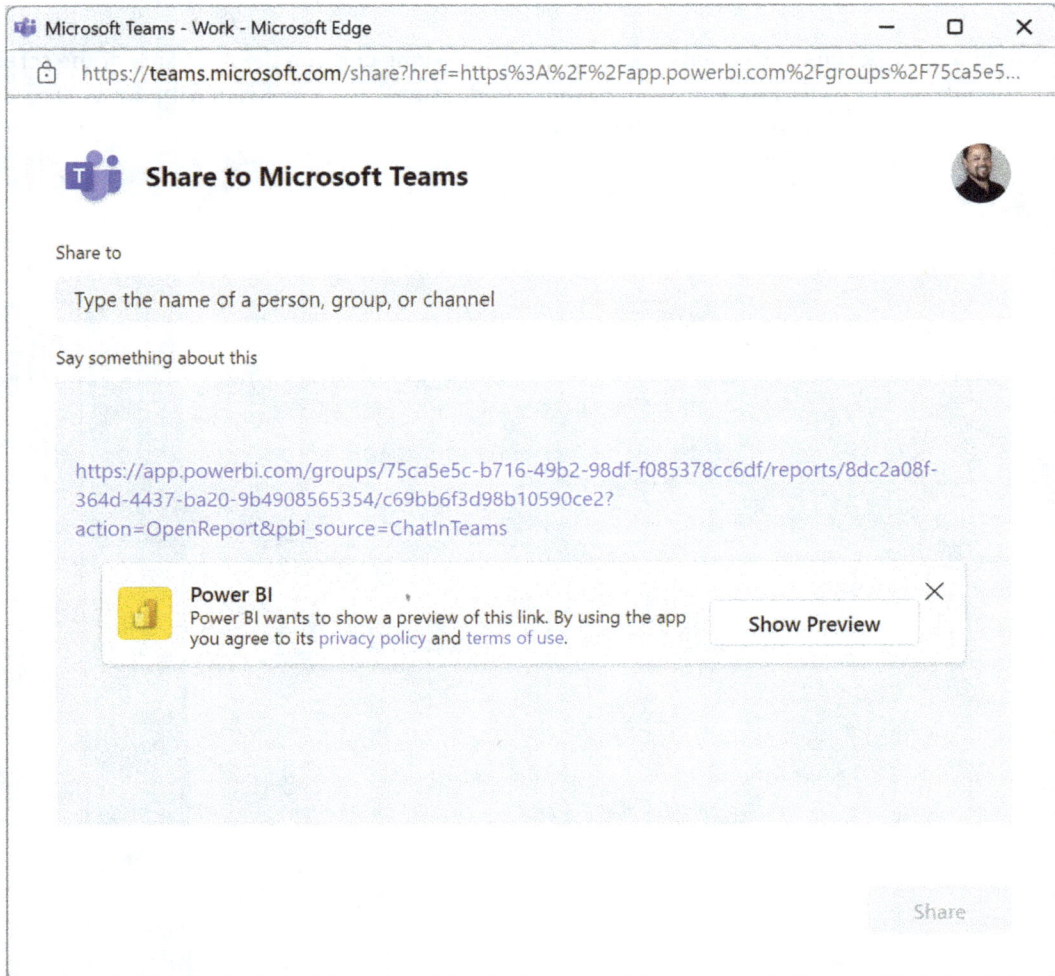

Figure 9.18 – Share to Microsoft Teams dialog in the service

The **Share to Microsoft Teams** dialog allows you to choose a person, team, or channel in **Microsoft Teams** to share a link with.

Explore

The **Explore** option is a preview feature that opens an interface that provides a limited authoring experience as shown:

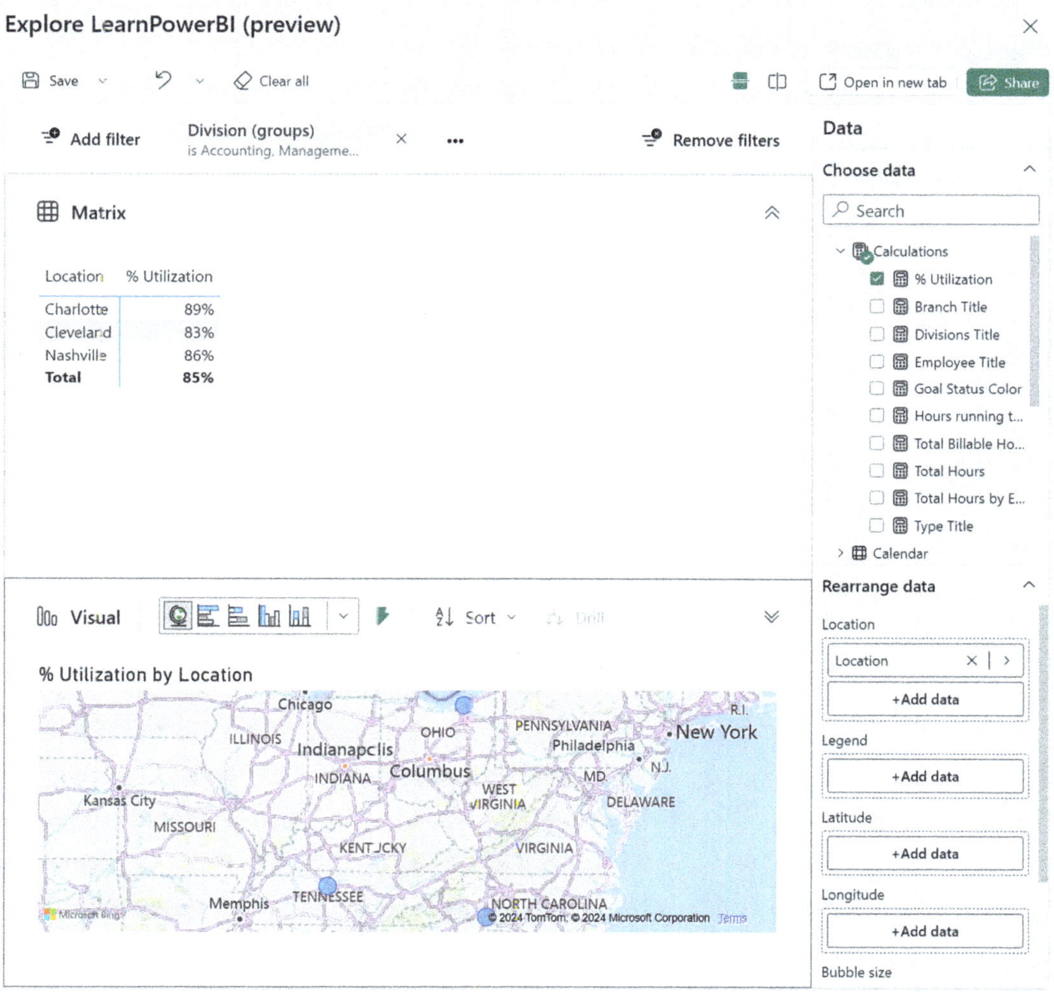

Figure 9.19 – Explore this data interface

The experience is somewhat similar to working in Power BI Desktop as the tables, columns, and measures are presented in the **Data** pane on the right-hand side. You can select these items in order to create a matrix and associated visual. Unlike Power BI Desktop, the **Filters** pane is replaced with a **filter** header. The **Save** button of the ribbon allows you to save the content as either an exploration or as a report.

Subscribe to report

The Power BI service provides the ability for you to subscribe to reports. This means that you will receive an email with an image of a particular page of a report with a link to open the report in a browser or mobile application. The frequency of these emails is set at the time of subscribing to the report.

To create a subscription to a report, do the following:

1. First, click on the report page to which you wish to subscribe.
2. Next, click the **Subscribe** button in the ribbon. This opens the **Subscriptions** pane, as shown in the following screenshot:

Subscriptions   ✕

Keep track of your data by subscribing to this report.

Manage all ⌄

No subscriptions yet

Stay up-to-date on this report and set up
a recurring email for yourself or others.

Create a subscription

Figure 9.20 – Subscriptions pane

3. If there are existing subscriptions, the subscriptions are listed in the pane. Additional subscriptions can be added by clicking the **Create a subscription** button.
4. Clicking the **Create a subscription** button presents two options, creating a **Standard** subscription or a **Dynamic per recipient** subscription. Select creating a **Standard** subscription.

5. The **Subscriptions** pane changes to display the following:

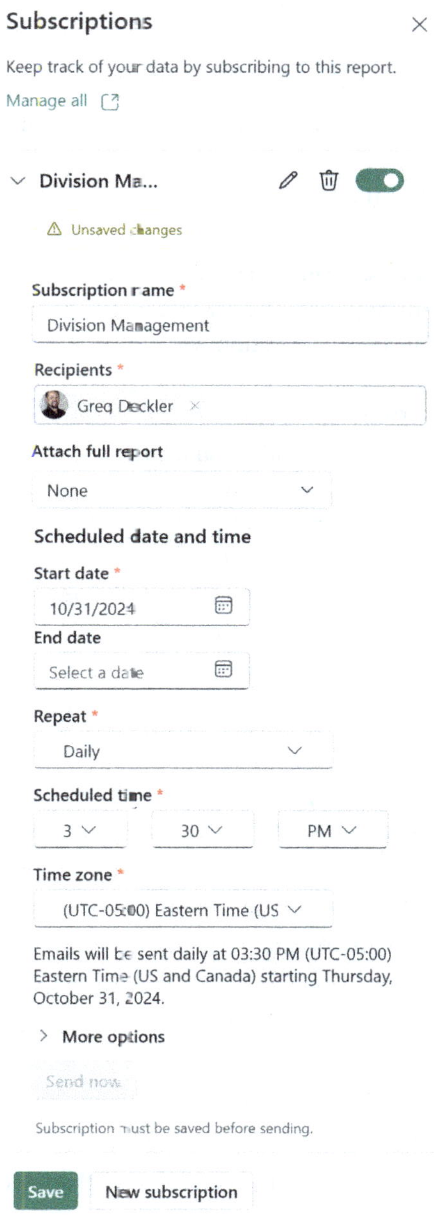

Subscriptions

Keep track of your data by subscribing to this report.

Manage all

⌄ **Division Ma...**

⚠ Unsaved changes

Subscription name *

Division Management

Recipients *

👤 Greg Deckler ×

Attach full report

None ⌄

Scheduled date and time

Start date *

10/31/2024

End date

Select a date

Repeat *

Daily ⌄

Scheduled time *

3 ⌄ | 30 ⌄ | PM ⌄

Time zone *

(UTC-05:00) Eastern Time (US ⌄

Emails will be sent daily at 03:30 PM (UTC-05:00) Eastern Time (US and Canada) starting Thursday, October 31, 2024.

> **More options**

Send now

Subscription must be saved before sending.

Save | New subscription

Figure 9.21 – Creating a Standard subscription

When adding a subscription, the service sets a number of default settings. If these settings are acceptable, simply click on the **Save** button at the bottom of the pane. Otherwise, adjust these settings as necessary, as follows:

- **Subscription name:** The name of the subscription.
- **Recipients:** This field allows you to subscribe yourself and other users to the report by entering email addresses or names of users.
- **Attach full report:** This allows you to attach the entire report as either a PDF or PowerPoint attachment.
- **Start date** and **End date: Start date** is the date upon which a subscription becomes active. This defaults to the current day. Use **End date** to automatically end a subscription. Leaving **End date** blank means that the subscription will continue indefinitely.
- **Repeat:** The repeat frequency can either be **Hourly**, **Daily**, **Weekly**, **Monthly**, or **After data refresh (once daily)**. **Daily** subscriptions are sent every day of the week at the prescribed **Scheduled Time**. **Weekly** subscriptions allow the user to choose the days of the week on which they receive subscription emails. **Monthly** subscriptions allow the user to choose the days of the month on which they receive subscription emails. **After data refresh** only sends a subscription email immediately after a report's data is refreshed, but no more than once per day.
- **Scheduled time:** This is the time at which subscription emails are sent. Subscription emails will be sent within 15 minutes of this time. This field is not displayed when the **Repeat** setting has been set to **After data refresh**.
- **Time zone:** Sets the time zone for the **Scheduled time** setting.
- **More options:**
    - **Email Subject:** The **Subject** field of the email message received from the service. If no subject is provided, the default subject for the email is used in the form of **Subscription for Report Name (Page Name)**, where **Report Name** is the name of the report and **Page Name** is the name of the page of the report to which you are subscribing.
    - **Message:** This is an optional message that can be included in the email.
    - **Report page:** This is the name of the report page to which the user is subscribing.
    - **Permission to view the report in Power BI:** Enables the recipient to view the report in the Power BI service.
    - **Link to report in Power BI:** Includes a link to the Power BI report in the email.
    - **Report page preview:** Includes a preview image of the report page in the email.
    - **Activator:** Provides a link to the **Fabric Activator** documentation. Data Activator is a Microsoft Fabric feature.
    - **My changes:** Checking this box includes any changes to filters, drill through, slicer choices, spotlights, etc.

Managing subscriptions

Your subscriptions for a particular report can be managed within the **Subscriptions** pane. This includes adjusting subscription settings, turning subscriptions on and off, running a subscription immediately, or deleting a subscription. At the top of the **Subscriptions** pane is a **Manage all** link. This link takes you to a page that lists all the subscriptions you have created.

Set alert

Set alert opens a **Set alert** pane on the right-hand side of the page. **Set alert** is a **Data Activator** feature that allows you to set alerts based on the visuals on report pages. **Data Activator** evaluates these alerts each time the semantic model for the report is refreshed. In the following example, an alert is set based on the **Total % Utilization** card dropping below **80%**:

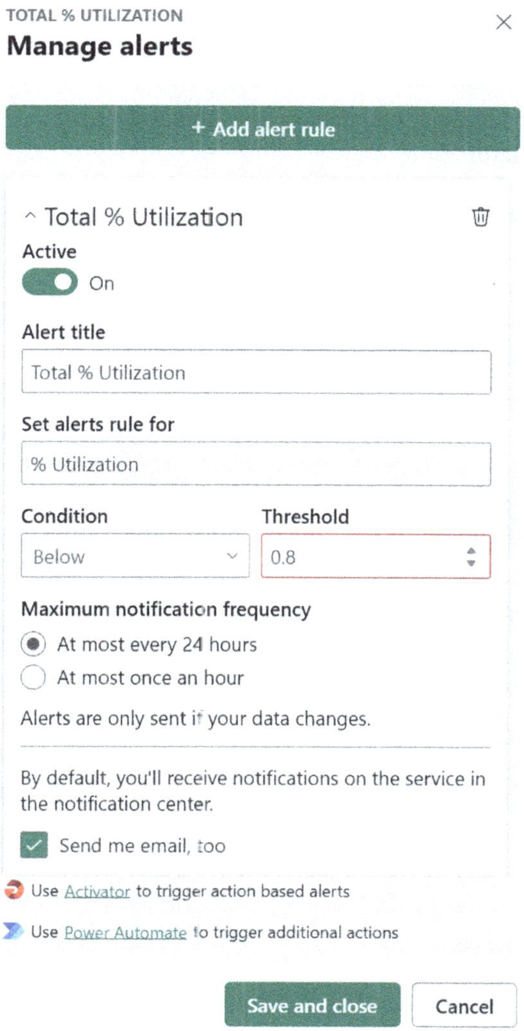

TOTAL % UTILIZATION

Manage alerts

+ Add alert rule

∧ Total % Utilization

Active

On

Alert title

Total % Utilization

Set alerts rule for

% Utilization

Condition

Below

Threshold

0.8

Maximum notification frequency

⦿ At most every 24 hours

◯ At most once an hour

Alerts are only sent if your data changes.

By default, you'll receive notifications on the service in the notification center.

✓ Send me email, too

⟳ Use Activator to trigger action based alerts

➤ Use Power Automate to trigger additional actions

Save and close   Cancel

Figure 9.22 – Set alert pane

Clicking the **Create** button creates the alert in **Data Activator**.

Edit

Microsoft has put tremendous effort into providing the ability to edit reports within the Power BI service. More information about editing reports is included in the *Editing and creating reports* section later in this chapter.

Ellipsis (...)

The ellipsis in the report ribbon provides additional functions, including the following:

- **Get insights:** Insights are available for PPU and F64+ capacities. Clicking Get insights opens a collapsable pane on the right-hand side. These insights include anomalies, trends, and KPI analysis and are presented as a series of cards.
- **See related content:** Displays related dashboards and semantic models related to the report in a pane on the right-hand side of the screen.
- **Open workspace lineage:** Opens a page that displays related dashboards and semantic models as well as the relationships between those content items graphically, as illustrated in the following screenshot:

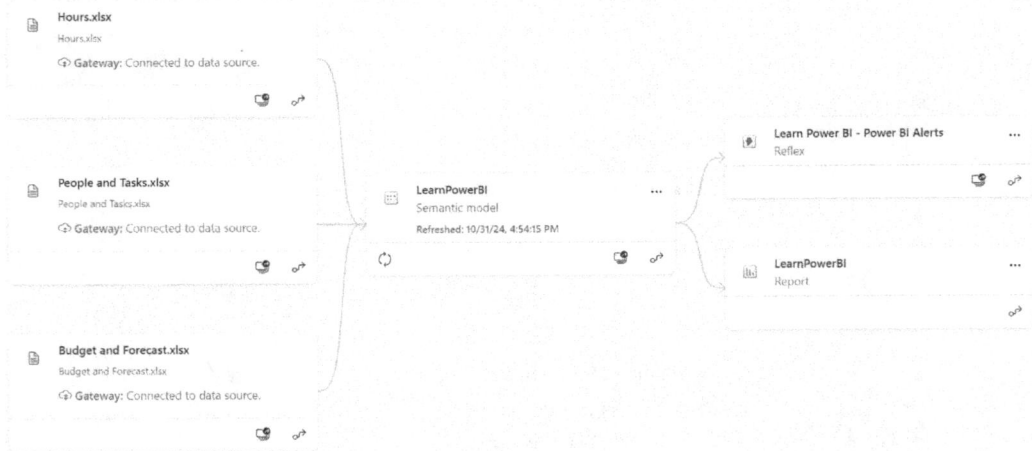

Figure 9.23 – Lineage view in the service

- **Open usage metrics:** This opens a report that displays how many users are accessing the report, including the total views of the report, total viewers, views by user, views per day, and unique viewers per day.
- **Pin to a dashboard:** Pins the entire report page to a dashboard of your choosing.

- **View semantic model:** Opens an interface for exploring the semantic model, as shown in the following screenshot:

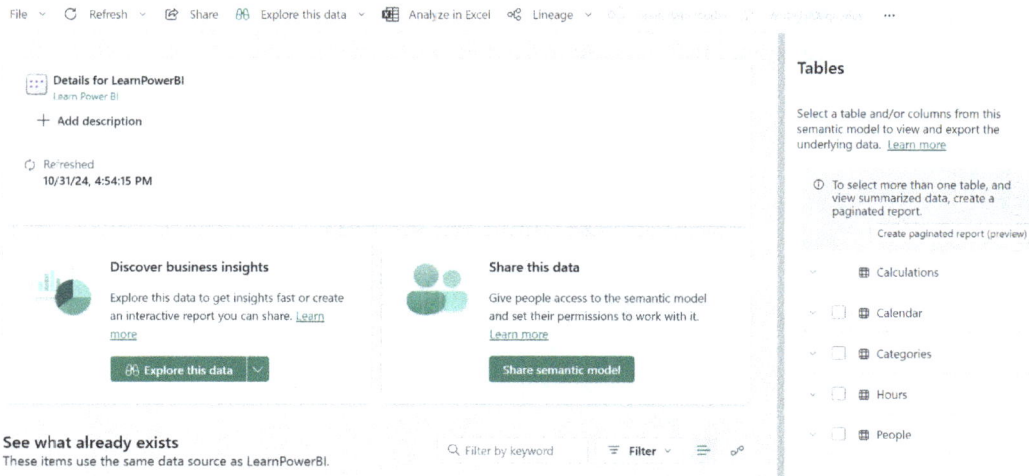

Figure 9.24 – View semantic model interface

Let's continue looking at additional features available in the ribbon.

Reset

The **Reset** button returns a report to its original state at the time of publishing, clearing all persistent filters and personal bookmark filters. If you are having trouble seeing information in a report, your first step should be to click **Reset** to restore a report to its original, published state.

Note that this icon only appears if something is changed compared to how the report was originally published.

Bookmark

The Power BI service provides expanded functionality for bookmarks. In addition to bookmarks that are created by the report author in Power BI Desktop, users in the Power BI service can create their own personal bookmarks. In fact, the service includes three types of bookmarks, as follows:

- Report bookmarks
- Personal bookmarks
- Persistent filters

Report bookmarks

Similar to Power BI Desktop, the Power BI service includes a **Bookmarks** pane that can be displayed to the right of the **Filters** pane. This pane is activated by clicking the **Bookmarks** icon in the ribbon and then **Show more bookmarks**, as seen in the following screenshot:

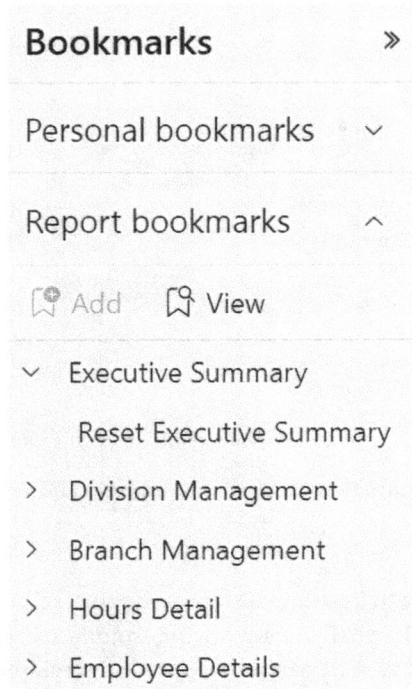

Figure 9.25 – The Bookmarks pane in the ribbon

As shown in *Figure 9.25*, the **Bookmarks** pane displays any bookmarks that were created by the author of a report under the **Report bookmarks** heading. These bookmarks operate just like they do in the Desktop version.

Personal bookmarks

Personal bookmarks are bookmarks created by report viewers and not the report author. Personal bookmarks can be created by doing the following:

1. To add a personal bookmark, either expand the **Personal bookmarks** section of the **Bookmarks** pane and choose **Add** or click on the **Bookmarks** icon in the ribbon and then choose **Add a personal bookmark**. The following screenshot shows a bookmark being added from the ribbon:

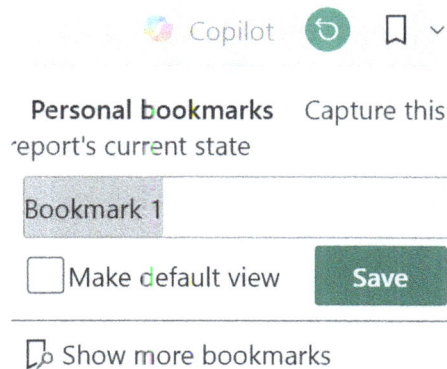

Figure 9.26 – Adding a personal bookmark

🔍 **Quick tip:** Need to see a high-resolution version of this image? Open this book in the next-gen Packt Reader or view it in the PDF/ePub copy.

🔒 **The next-gen Packt Reader** is included for free with the purchase of this book. Scan the QR code OR go to packtpub.com/unlock, then use the search bar to find this book by name. Double-check the edition shown to make sure you get the right one.

Both methods provide identical options for naming your bookmark.

2. Once you have entered a name, click the **Save** button to save the personal bookmark.

3. In addition, if you want your personal bookmark to be the default view when you view the report, check the **Make default view** checkbox prior to saving your bookmark.

4. Once saved, personal bookmarks appear in the **Personal bookmarks** section of the **Bookmarks** pane, as well as when clicking on **Bookmarks** in the ribbon.

Manually adding bookmarks in Power BI Desktop and the Power BI service is not the only way to create bookmarks. The Power BI service also supports the automatic creation of bookmarks. Let's look at these next.

Persistent filters

Persistent filters use the underlying technology of bookmarks to automatically save a report's state. This means that you can interact with a report, and your adjusted settings are automatically saved for the next time you return to view a report. The following settings are available:

- Filter settings
- Slicer selections
- Sorting selections
- Drill through location

To use persistent filters, you do not need to do anything. The current state of a report is automatically saved each time you adjust any of the preceding settings. To clear any adjusted settings and return to the original report's state, simply click the **Reset** button in the ribbon.

Marking a personal bookmark as **Make default view** overrides the persistent filter's functionality for that report.

View

Listed under the **View** menu in the ribbon are various options for controlling the size of the report in relation to the browser window, including the following:

- **Full screen:** Enters full screen mode; click the *Esc* key to exit this mode
- **Fit to page:** Fits the report into the overall page's width and height
- **Fit to width:** Fits the report into the width of the page but not the height
- **Actual size:** Displays the report at its actual size, regardless of the width or height of the browser window

The **View** menu in the ribbon also contains options for viewing the report using high-contrast colors, including the following:

- **None:** Displays the report with the original colors
- **High contrast #1:** Displays the report on a black background with neon yellow font and accents
- **High contrast #2:** Displays the report on a black background with neon green font and accents
- **High contrast black:** Displays the report on a black background with white font and accents
- **High contrast white:** Displays the report on a white background with black font and accents

Finally, the **View** menu also includes the preview feature **Show visuals as tables**. Selecting this option displays any non-table visuals such as bar charts, column charts, and line charts as tables instead of the original visuals. Certain visuals, such as matrixes and card visuals are not affected by this setting.

Refresh visuals

This refreshes the report visuals based on the semantic model. *It is important to understand that this does not refresh the data within the semantic model from the source data.*

Comment

Individuals with any kind of permission for the report can comment on reports as well as individual visuals. To comment on a report or to see all report and visual comments, follow these steps:

1. Click the **Comment** button in the ribbon. Clicking this button in the ribbon displays the **Comments** pane on the right-hand side of the page, as shown in the following screenshot:

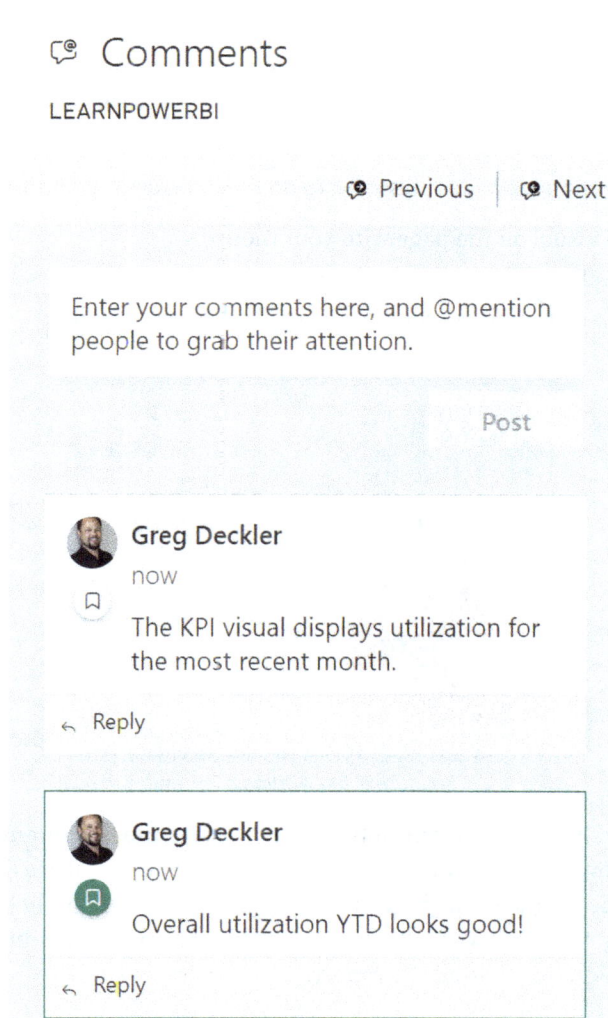

Figure 9.27 – Comments pane in the service

There can be many pages of comments. Use the **Previous** and **Next** buttons to navigate between multiple pages of comments.

2. To post a new comment, click your mouse inside the area just below the **Previous** and **Next** buttons, type a comment, and then click the **Post** button. The comment will appear directly underneath the **Post** button as comments are always displayed from newest to oldest.

Comments can be replied to by clicking on the **Reply** link in the lower-left corner of the comment. Replies are threaded within the original comment block. Comments and replies can also be deleted by hovering over the comment or reply and clicking the small trashcan icon that appears in the upper-right corner of the comment.

Use the @ symbol in a comment, immediately followed by someone's name or email address. This flags the comment for the attention of a particular user, sending that user an email message from the Power BI service.

You can also comment on individual visuals. To do this, perform the following steps:

1. Hover over a visual on the page with your mouse.
2. Click on the ellipsis (**...**) menu in the visual's header that appears above or below the visual.
3. Choose **Add a comment**, as shown in the following screenshot:

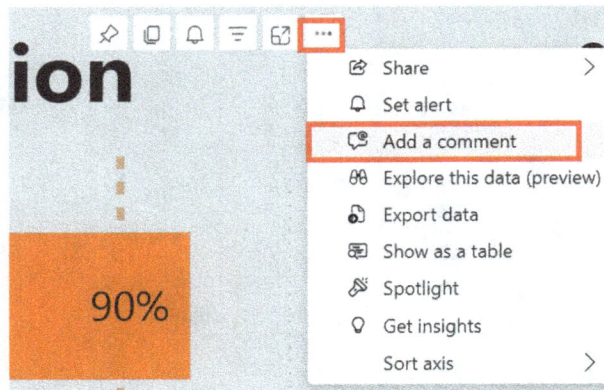

Figure 9.28 – Adding a comment to a visual

Selecting the **Add a comment** option also displays the **Comments** pane if it is not already displayed; however, only comments for that individual visual are displayed in the **Comments** pane. In addition, the visual is given a spotlight effect to highlight the visual on which you are commenting. When viewing all comments, clicking on a comment for a particular visual also highlights that visual within the report.

4. To close the **Comments** pane, either click the **Close** button at the bottom of the pane or click on the **Comments** icon in the ribbon.

Comments are a great way to collaborate and communicate about a report.

Add to Favorites

The **Add to Favorites** (star) icon adds a report to **Browse | Favorites** in the **Navigation** pane. When viewing a report marked as a favorite, the icon will be filled in.

This completes this section on viewing and using reports in the service. However, you can also edit reports and even create new reports in the service, so let's explore that next.

Editing and creating reports

In addition to adding features and capabilities to reports that are published from Power BI Desktop, the Power BI service also includes an interface for editing reports and even building entirely new reports on top of existing semantic models. Being able to edit and create reports is dependent upon a user's permissions on the report and semantic model. These permissions are covered in detail in *Chapter 10, Understanding Dashboards, Apps, Metrics, and Security.*

Editing reports

To edit a report, follow these steps:

1. While viewing a report, click the **Edit** link in the ribbon.
2. The report canvas changes to **Edit** mode. This changes the ribbon so that it provides editing options. It also activates the **Visualizations** and **Data** panes, as shown in the following screenshot:

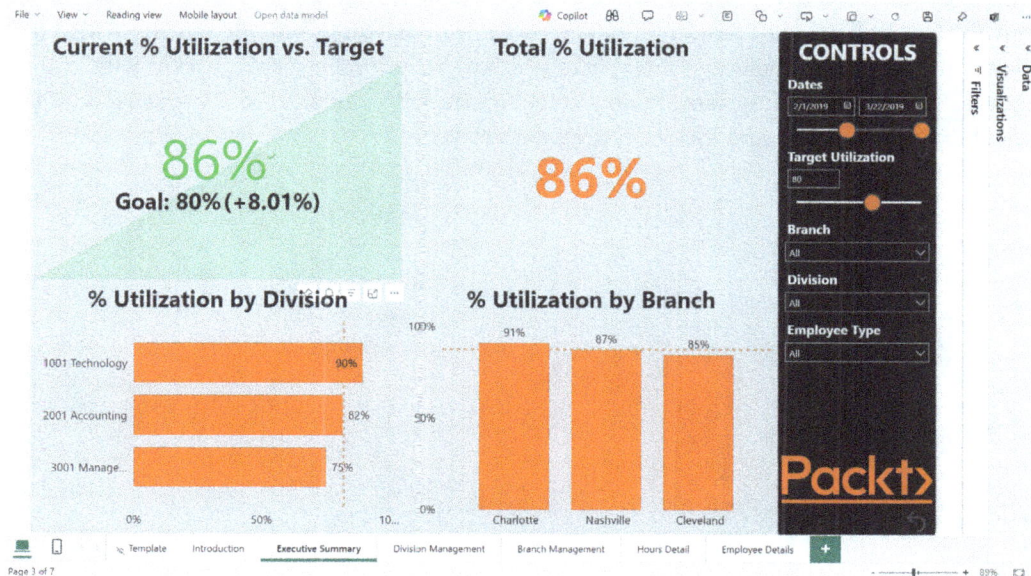

Figure 9.29 – Editing a report in the service

When in edit mode, the ribbon and layout change to be more similar to Power BI Desktop, with the pages as page tabs at the bottom of the report, and options for inserting shapes and textboxes and editing visual interactions.

In general, the editing experience mirrors the editing experience in the Desktop version. However, not all of the editing features of the Desktop version are included in the Power BI service. Most noticeably, there is no access to the underlying data, semantic model, or relationships, hence there is no way to create new columns or measures. To exit edit mode, click **Reading view** in the ribbon.

It is critical to remember that if you make edits to a report in the service and then later republish the original Desktop file, you will lose all of your changes. Hence, it is highly recommended that once you edit a report in the service, you use the **Download this file** option in the **File** menu and replace your original PBIX file.

Creating a mobile layout

While in edit mode, the **Mobile layout** option allows you to create a version of the report that's been optimized for mobile devices. This is the same interface as the Desktop version when we're using the **Mobile layout** option in the **View** tab of the ribbon. Once in the **Mobile layout** view, you can page through the report to create a mobile version of each page. To switch back, click the **Web Layout** link in the ribbon.

Creating a report

Power BI also allows the creation of new reports from existing semantic models. This brings up an identical interface to the one that appears when we're editing a report, except with a blank report canvas. To access this interface, simply select a semantic model from a workspace. In the ribbon, select **Explore this data** and then **Create a blank report**:

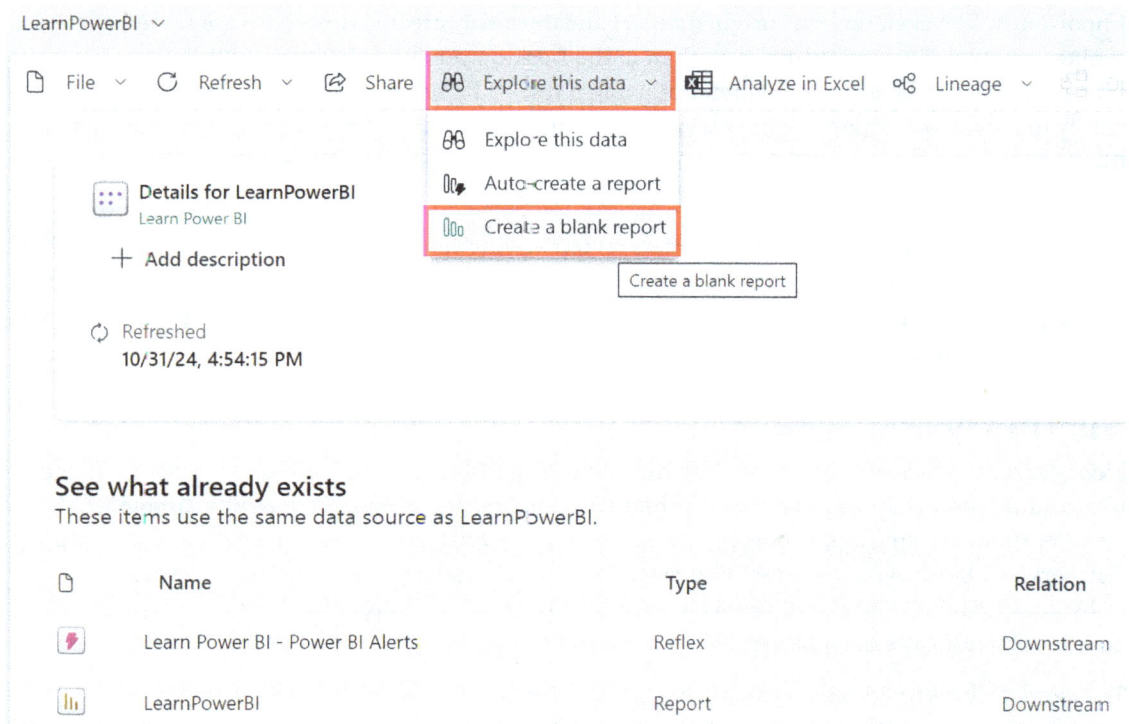

Figure 9.30 – Creating a new report in the service

Using this interface to create a new report is strikingly similar to creating a report in the Desktop version. However, you cannot create new measures or columns; otherwise, the experience is nearly identical.

Creating a new report is analogous to creating a new PBIX file in the Desktop version, meaning that the report pages created are not associated with the report pages that were originally published to the Power BI service. This means that, once you create a new report in the service, if you use the **Download this file** option on the original report, the new report pages that were created will not be included.

Importantly, however, both the original report and the newly created report use the same underlying semantic model. This is very different than in the Desktop version, where each PBIX file contains its own semantic model and data (when not using a **live** or **DirectQuery** connection). This makes the ability to create new reports in the service a powerful feature as a semantic model can be created in the Desktop version and published to the Power BI service. Then, the Power BI service can be used to create multiple reports from the same underlying semantic model.

Consider using the Desktop version to create an underlying semantic model with only a single, blank report page and publishing to the Power BI service, then use the service to create actual reports. This separates publishing the semantic model from the reports, allowing each to be worked on and updated independently.

Summary

This chapter has been all about using reports in the Power BI service. The service extends the functionality around reports far beyond what is provided in the Desktop version. It does this through enabling collaboration, printing and exporting, embedding, and even the editing and creation of new reports. The service allows report authors and viewers to collaborate by commenting on entire reports or individual visuals. In addition, report users can subscribe to reports in order to receive automated emails containing the current contents of reports.

The service also provides the critical ability to print reports, which is missing from the Desktop version, in addition to allowing reports to be exported in various formats, such as PowerPoint and PDF. The service also allows reports to be securely embedded in other websites and SharePoint Online. Finally, the service allows you to edit reports directly within the service or even create new reports from existing semantic models.

In the next chapter, we move beyond reports and explore other objects that can be created within the Power BI service, such as dashboards, scorecards, and apps. In addition, there is a comprehensive coverage of security for reports, semantic models, dashboards, and other content.

Questions

As an activity, try to answer the following questions on your own:

- How do you tag another user in a comment?
- What are the key differences between report bookmarks, personal bookmarks, and persistent filters?
- Which formats can users export Power BI reports to?
- What are three different ways in which reports can be embedded in other websites?
- True or false: Using the **Publish to web** feature maintains the security of a report.
- Once **Publish to web** is used, how do you remove an embed link?
- What is the most important thing to remember about editing reports in the Power BI service?

Further reading

To learn more about the topics that were covered in this chapter, please take a look at the following references:

- *Embed a report in a secure portal or website*: https://learn.microsoft.com/en-us/power-bi/collaborate-share/service-embed-secure
- *Filter a report using query string parameters in the URL*: https://learn.microsoft.com/en-us/power-bi/collaborate-share/service-url-filters
- *Embed a report web part in SharePoint Online*: https://learn.microsoft.com/en-us/power-bi/collaborate-share/service-embed-report-spo
- *Publish to the web from Power BI*: https://learn.microsoft.com/en-us/power-bi/collaborate-share/service-publish-to-web
- *Announcing Persistent Filters in the Power BI Service*: https://powerbi.microsoft.com/en-us/blog/announcing-persistent-filters-in-the-service/
- *Create report bookmarks in Power BI to share insights and build stories*: https://learn.microsoft.com/en-us/power-bi/create-reports/desktop-bookmarks?tabs=powerbidesktop
- *Email subscriptions for reports and dashboards in the Power BI Service*: https://learn.microsoft.com/en-us/power-bi/collaborate-share/end-user-subscribe?tabs=creator
- *Types of filters in Power BI reports*: https://learn.microsoft.com/en-us/power-bi/create-reports/power-bi-report-filter-types

Join our community on Discord

Join our community's Discord space for discussions with the authors and other readers: https://discord.gg/hvqvgyGH

10

Understanding Dashboards, Apps, Metrics, and Security

While reports are what you will primarily interact with the most in the service, there are other aspects of the service that are quite powerful and can add tremendous value. It is important to understand the capabilities of objects such as dashboards and apps to determine the best method of sharing and collaborating on your work. In addition, scorecards and metrics can help you keep track of important business KPIs. The goal of this chapter is to familiarize you with all of the other objects within the service and understand how these different objects interrelate with one another in terms of security.

The following topics will be covered in this chapter:

- Understanding dashboards
- Creating and using apps
- Working with metrics
- Understanding security and permissions

Technical requirements

You will need the following to successfully complete this chapter:

- An internet connection.
- A Microsoft 365 account or Fabric trial.
- If you have skipped any of the previous chapters, you can download and publish `LearnPowerBI.zip` from GitHub at `https://github.com/PacktPublishing/Learn-Microsoft-Power-BI_3E/tree/main/Chapter8`.

Understanding dashboards

Dashboards are single-page canvases that contain visualizations called **tiles**. These tiles are visualizations pinned from reports, other dashboards, **Question and Answer (Q&A)** displays, or other sources such as quick insights. Single visuals or entire report pages can be pinned.

At first, you may be confused regarding the purpose of dashboards versus reports since both are essentially a collection of visualizations. The most important difference is that reports can only contain visuals based upon a single semantic model, versus Power BI dashboards which can contain visuals from many different reports and thus many different semantic models within the same workspace. In addition, dashboards have exclusive features, such as setting alerts, setting a featured dashboard, and control over navigation.

Because dashboards can contain information from one or more reports and one or more semantic models, dashboards allow end users to create a single, customized view of all of the information within an organization that is most important to them.

Creating a dashboard

To create a simple dashboard, perform the following steps:

1. Make sure that you are viewing the **LearnPowerBI** report in the service. Then, click on the **Executive Summary** report page.

2. Hover your mouse over any of the visualizations on the page and note that several icons appear in the upper-right or lower-right corner of the visualization. The first icon on the left is the **Pin visual** icon, as shown in the following screenshot:

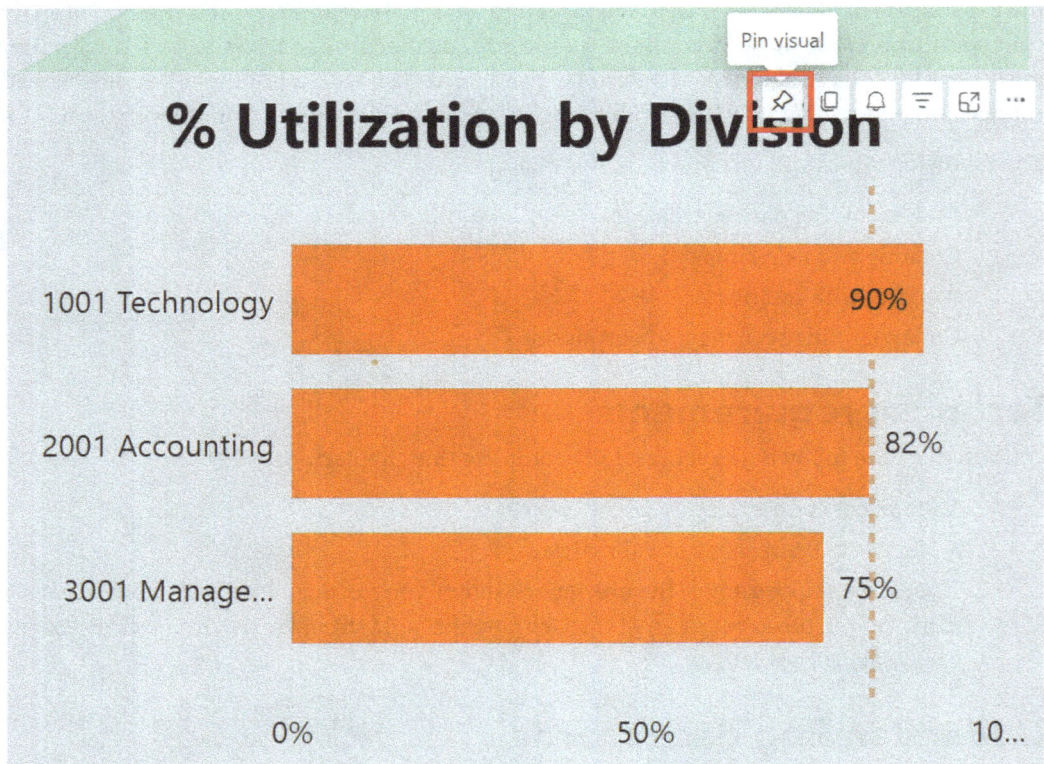

Figure 10.1 – Pin visual icon

3. Click the **Pin visual** icon and the **Pin to dashboard** dialog is displayed, as shown in the following screenshot:

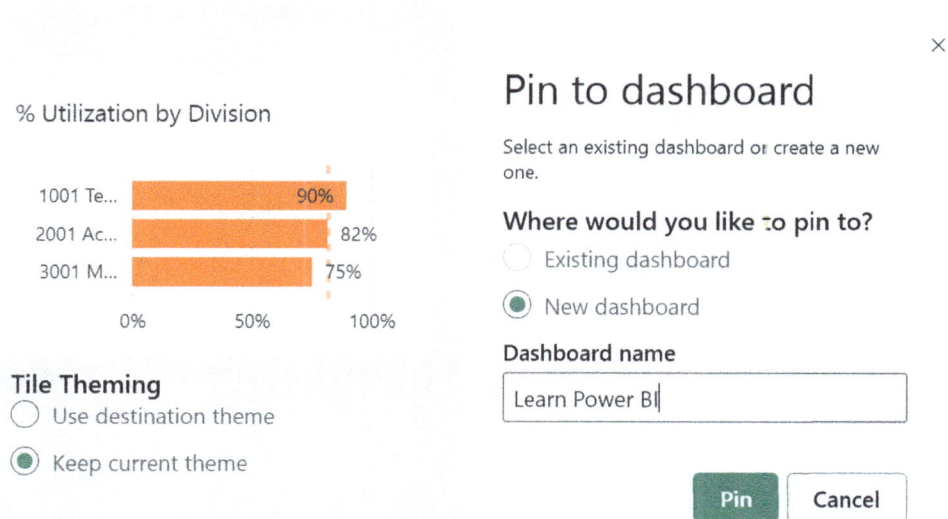

Figure 10.2 – Pin to dashboard dialog

4. Enter Learn Power BI in the **Dashboard name** field and then click the **Pin** button.

5. When viewing the workspace, **Learn Power BI** now appears as a dashboard content item. Clicking on this dashboard displays the pinned visualization as a tile on the dashboard.

It is important to remember that when pinning a report visual, the report visual is pinned with all current filters active on that visual such as filters from the **Filters** pane, slicers, and cross-highlighting/cross-filtering from other visuals. These filters persist on the dashboard tile even after the underlying semantic model is refreshed or if the filters on the report are changed.

Now that we have created a simple dashboard, we can explore how to work with dashboards in the service.

Working with dashboards

Working with dashboards in the service is in some ways very similar to working with reports. In this section, we explore the various options and features of dashboards in the service.

Once a dashboard is created, the new dashboard appears in the content area when viewing a workspace:

🗋	Name		Type
⊙	Learn Power BI		Dashboard
⚡	Learn Power BI - Power BI Alerts		Reflex
ılı	LearnPowerBI		Report
⠿	LearnPowerBI		Semantic model

Figure 10.3 – Dashboard interface in the service

Viewing dashboards in the service presents a ribbon with various functions, including the following:

- **File**
- **Share**
- **Chat in Teams**
- **Comment**
- **Subscribe to dashboard**
- **Edit**
- **Ellipsis (...)**

The **Share**, **Chat in Teams**, **Comment**, and **Subscribe to dashboard** options essentially work the same for dashboards as reports, thus we will not explore these options in depth here.

Let's take a look at the rest of the ribbon features.

The File menu

The **File** menu contains the following options:

- **Save a copy**
- **Manage permissions**
- **Print this page**
- **Settings**

Save a copy, **Manage permissions**, and **Print this page** work similarly to the equivalent options under the **File** menu for reports. The **Settings** menu is also similar to the **Settings** menu option for reports, except for the **Q&A** option.

The Q&A toggle

Q&A in the service works similarly to **Q&A** functionality in the desktop, allowing dashboard users to ask questions about the underlying data and receive answers in the form of visuals. For dashboards with **Q&A** enabled, you can access and use **Q&A** by following these steps:

1. Ensure that the **Q&A** toggle is on in the **Settings** menu for the dashboard.

2. Click the **Ask a question about your data** text that appears at the upper left of the dashboard canvas. Clicking on this brings up the Q&A interface within the service, as shown in the following screenshot:

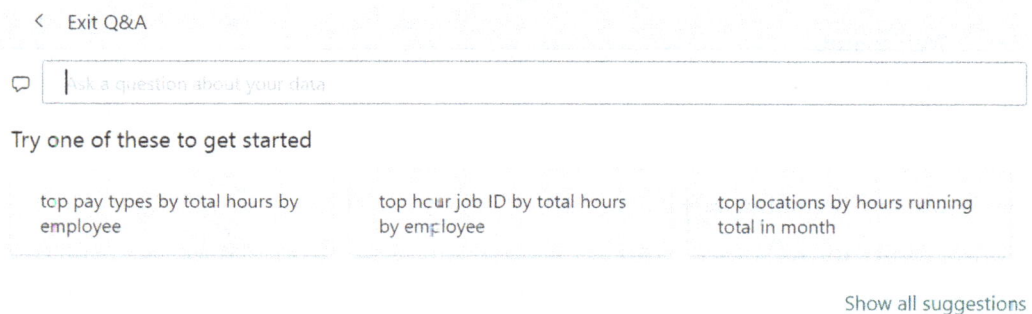

< Exit Q&A

Ask a question about your data

Try one of these to get started

| top pay types by total hours by employee | top hour job ID by total hours by employee | top locations by hours running total in month |

Show all suggestions

Figure 10.4 – Q&A interface in the service

3. Suggested questions are presented to aid the dashboard user in forming acceptable questions. Your suggested questions may be different than those in *Figure 10.4*.

4. Enter your own question, such as sum of hours by location where category is PTO, in the **Ask a question about your data** field.

5. Once you find a visual that you like, click **Pin visual** in the ribbon area:

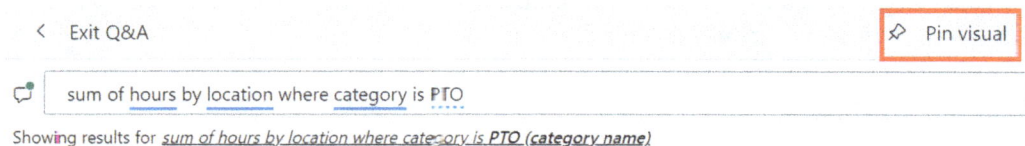

< Exit Q&A   ⚲ Pin visual

sum of hours by location where category is PTO

Showing results for *sum of hours by location where category is PTO (category name)*

Figure 10.5 – Pin Q&A visual

6. Click the **Pin** button to pin the tile to your current, existing dashboard.

7. Once you're back on the Q&A interface, click **Exit Q&A** in the ribbon to return to your dashboard and see your new tile.

Now that we have explored the **File** menu, let's move on to the **Edit** menu.

Edit

The **Edit** menu contains the following three options:

- **Add a tile**
- **Dashboard theme**
- **Mobile layout**

Let's explore these options further.

Add a tile

While tiles can be added from a variety of sources, certain types of tiles can be added directly to the dashboard. These types of tiles are listed here:

*   **Web content**
*   **Image**
*   **Text box**
*   **Video**
*   **Custom Streaming Data**

Choosing **Add a tile** brings up the **Add a tile** pane. This pane walks you through creating the desired type of tile. Note that **Web content** and **Video** may be disabled due to a default tenant setting. For images and videos, these simply require a **Uniform Resource Locator** (**URL**) link to the desired content. For videos, these must be YouTube or Vimeo URLs. Uploading your own images and videos isn't supported. Textboxes simply require you to enter the text that you want displayed, along with any desired formatting. Web content tiles take an embed code, which is generally in the form of an **Inline Frame (IFRAME)**.

> **Note**
>
> There is also an option for **Custom Streaming Data**. However, Microsoft has announced the deprecation of that functionality.

Dashboard theme

Choosing the **Dashboard theme** option brings up the **Dashboard theme** pane, as shown in the following screenshot:

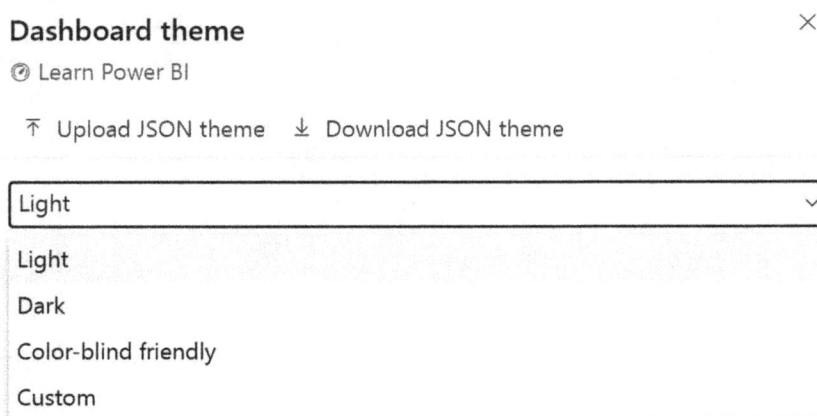

Dashboard theme   ✕

⊙ Learn Power BI

⤒ Upload JSON theme   ⤓ Download JSON theme

Light   ⌄
Light
Dark
Color-blind friendly
Custom

Figure 10.6 – Dashboard theme pane in the service

The drop-down field provides various pre-built themes, including the following:

- **Light**
- **Dark**
- **Color-blind friendly**
- **Custom**

The **Custom** option allows you to create a custom theme by selecting colors, tile opacity, and whether to use a background image. This theme can be downloaded by clicking on **Download JSON theme**. Downloading a **JavaScript Object Notation (JSON)** theme allows you to edit the JSON file in a text editor. This provides additional levels of control over the theme.

For example, the following theme file can be created:

```
{
    "name":"LearnPowerBI",
    "foreground":"#FFFFFF",
    "background":"#EC670F",
    "dataColors": [
        "#EC670F","#3C3C3B","#E5EAEE","#EC85E6","#29BCC0",
        "#7EAE40","#20B2E7","#D3DCE0","#FF6B0F"
    ],
    "tableAccent":"#20B2E7",
    "tiles": {
        "background":"#3C3C3B",
        "color":"#E5EAEE",
        "opacity":1.00
    },
    "visualStyles": {
        "*": {
            "*": {
                "*": [
                    {
                        "color": {
                            "solid": {
                                "color":"#E5EAEE"
                            }
                        }
                    },
                    {
                        "labelColor": {
                            "solid": {
                                "color":"#E5EAEE"
```

```
                }
              }
            }
          ]
        }
      }
    },
    "backgroundImage":null
}
```

You can download this theme file, `LearnPowerBIDashboardTheme.json`, from the following link: `https://github.com/PacktPublishing/Learn-Microsoft-Power-BI-3E/tree/main/Chapter10`. Once this file has been created or downloaded, follow these steps to implement the theme:

1. Use **Upload JSON theme** to upload the theme file.
2. Browse for the file and select **Open**.
3. Click the **Save** button in the dialog to activate this theme.

Your dashboard should now have a color scheme similar to the theme used to create your final report.

Mobile layout

As with reports, dashboards can have a custom mobile layout. Choosing this option presents an **Edit mobile layout** interface similar to the mobile layout when editing reports, allowing you to build a custom view for phones and mobile devices. Tiles can be pinned and unpinned from this interface, as well as resized and moved around the canvas. This phone view is automatically saved once created. To exit the **Edit mobile layout** interface, choose **Web layout** in the ribbon. To delete the custom mobile layout, while in **Edit mobile layout**, choose **Delete mobile layout** in the ribbon.

Ellipsis menu

The ellipsis (...) menu provides a number of useful options for dashboards, including the following:

*   **See related content**
*   **Open workspace lineage**
*   **Open usage metrics**

All of these options work identically to the same options for reports.

Working with tiles

The size and position of tiles can be adjusted on the dashboard canvas. Tiles provide additional functionality, such as the creation of alerts and overall navigation.

Sizing and position

To reposition a tile, simply click anywhere on the tile and drag the tile to a new location on the canvas. Note that for some tiles, such as map visual tiles, you cannot click on the map area of the visual when repositioning and must click on the header of the tile.

To change the size of a tile, hover over the bottom-right corner of the tile with your mouse and then use the sizing handle that appears. Tiles can be resized to preset tile dimensions. As you resize a tile, these various possible tile dimensions are shown as a shadow on the canvas.

Tile options

Options for tiles can be accessed by hovering over a tile and then clicking on the ellipsis (...) in the upper-right corner of the tile. This options menu provides a number of actions, including the following:

- **Add a comment**
- **Chat in Teams**
- **Copy visual as image**
- **Go to report**
- **Go to Q&A**
- **Open in focus mode**
- **Manage alerts**
- **Export to .csv**
- **Edit details**
- **View Insights**
- **Pin tile**
- **Delete tile**

Not all options are available for all types of dashboard tiles. For example, only tiles created via Q&A will list the **Go to Q&A** option.

Most of these options work similarly to information we have already covered for reports and dashboards or need no real explanation. For example, **Copy visual as an image** does exactly that, simply copies the tile as an image to your copy-and-paste clipboard. However, **Manage alerts** and **Edit details** deserve further explanation.

Manage alerts

Only simple numeric tiles such as card tiles and **Key Performance Indicator** (**KPI**) tiles have the **Manage alerts** option. Choosing the **Manage alerts** option displays the **Manage alerts** dialog, as shown in the following screenshot:

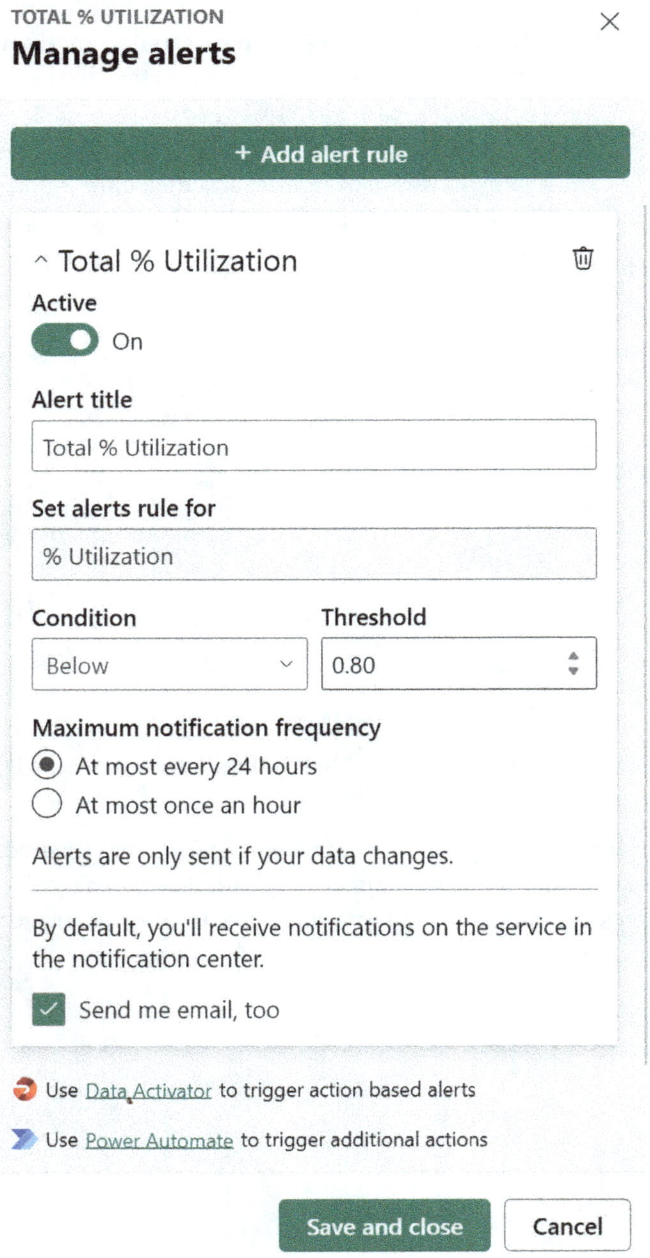

TOTAL % UTILIZATION   ✕

Manage alerts

+ Add alert rule

⌃ Total % Utilization   🗑

Active

🟢 On

Alert title

Total % Utilization

Set alerts rule for

% Utilization

Condition   **Threshold**

Below   ⌄   0.80   ⬍

Maximum notification frequency

◉ At most every 24 hours

◯ At most once an hour

Alerts are only sent if your data changes.

By default, you'll receive notifications on the service in the notification center.

☑ Send me email, too

🔴 Use Data Activator to trigger action based alerts

▶ Use Power Automate to trigger additional actions

Save and close   Cancel

Figure 10.7 – Manage alerts dialog

Use the + **Add alert rule** button to add a new alert. Alert rules automatically notify you whenever the metric represented by a tile meets a certain condition, such as falling below a certain value.

Edit details

Choosing the **Edit details** option displays the **Tile details** dialog, as shown in the following screenshot:

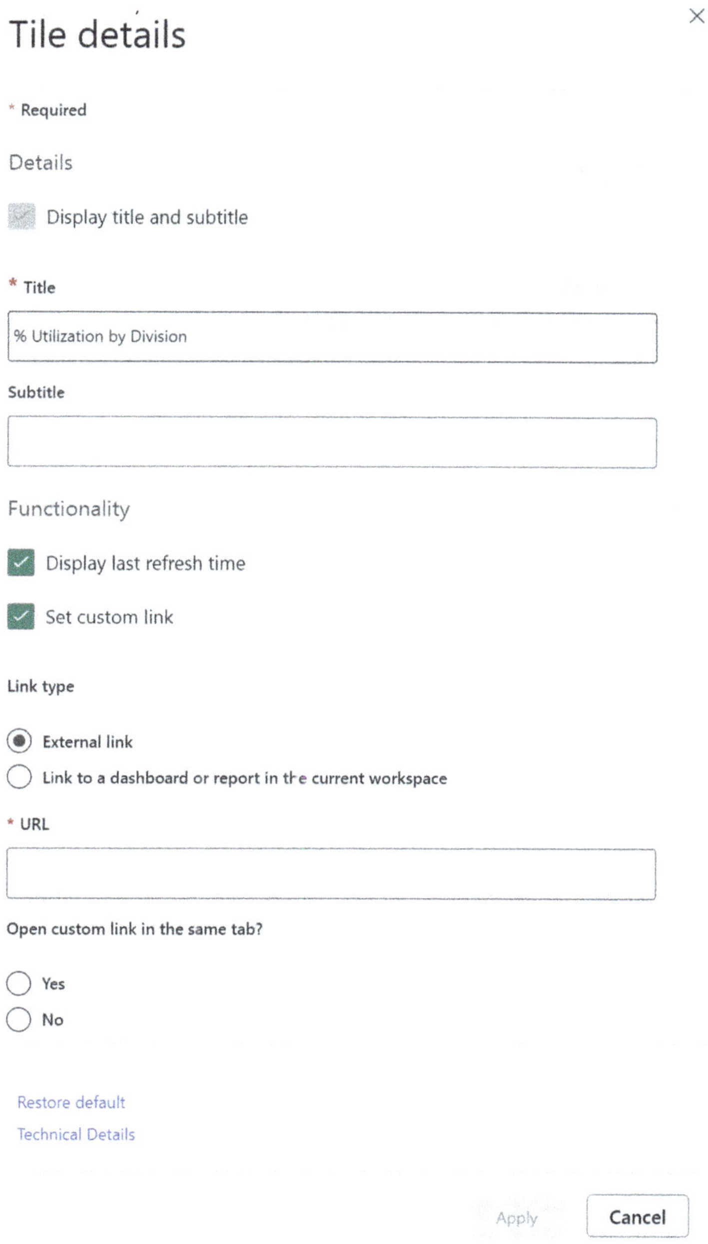

Tile details   ✕

* Required

Details

☑ Display title and subtitle

* Title

| % Utilization by Division |

Subtitle

| |

Functionality

☑ Display last refresh time

☑ Set custom link

Link type

◉ External link
○ Link to a dashboard or report in the current workspace

* URL

| |

Open custom link in the same tab?

○ Yes
○ No

Restore default

Technical Details

Apply   **Cancel**

Figure 10.8 – Tile details dialog

A useful setting for dashboard tiles is the **Display last refresh time** setting. Checking this box displays the last time the underlying semantic model was refreshed.

In addition, the **Set custom link** option allows you to configure a custom link for the tile. When clicking on a tile in a dashboard, the default behavior is to transport the user to the underlying report page from where the tile was originally pinned or, in the case of Q&A tiles, transport the user to the Q&A dialog. The **Set custom link** option overrides this default behavior and allows you to control the destination when clicking a tile.

Now that we have looked at dashboards, let's next take a look at apps.

Creating and using apps

Apps are a method of bundling multiple dashboards and reports into a single object that is then published and shared within the organization. Hence, instead of sharing individual dashboards and reports or granting permissions to an entire workspace, apps allow the author to choose exactly what content to bundle and share, providing an effective means of organizing shared content and controlling access.

Creating an app

Before we create an actual app, let's add some content to our workspace so that we can understand how workspace objects are included and excluded from our app. We will create an additional dashboard and report within our workspace by simply duplicating our existing dashboard and report.

To create a copy of the existing dashboard, follow these steps:

1. Navigate to the existing dashboard.
2. From the **File** menu, click **Save a copy**.
3. Leave the dashboard name, **Learn Power BI (copy)**, as is and click the **Duplicate** button.
4. From the **Edit** menu, choose **Dashboard theme**, change the theme to **Dark**, and click the **Save** button.

Now that we have a copy of the dashboard and can distinguish between the two versions, we can create a copy of the existing report. Follow these steps:

1. Navigate to the existing report.
2. From the **File** menu in the ribbon, choose **Save a copy**.
3. For the name of the report, enter *Copy of report* and click the **Save** button.
4. Click **Edit** in the ribbon to edit the report.
5. Click on one of the visuals to select it and then press the *Del* key on your keyboard to delete the visual.
6. Click on the **File** menu in the ribbon and choose **Save**.
7. Exit editing by clicking **Reading view** in the ribbon.

Now that we have additional content, we can create an app by following these steps:

1. Click on the workspace name under **Workspaces** in the **Navigation** pane to display the workspace interface, which defaults to listing all of the content within the workspace, as shown in the following screenshot:

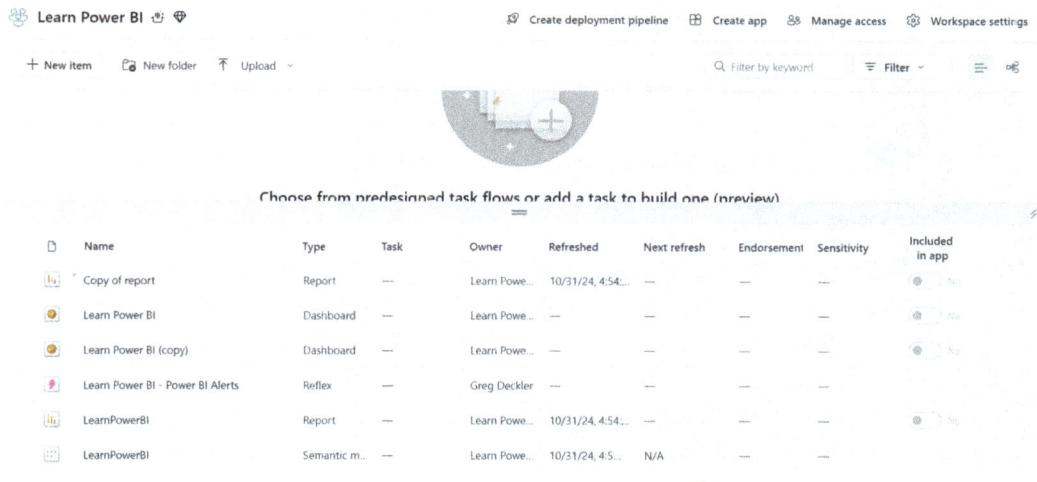

Figure 10.9 – Workspace interface

2.   Click the **Create app** button to display the app's publishing interface, as shown in the following screenshot:

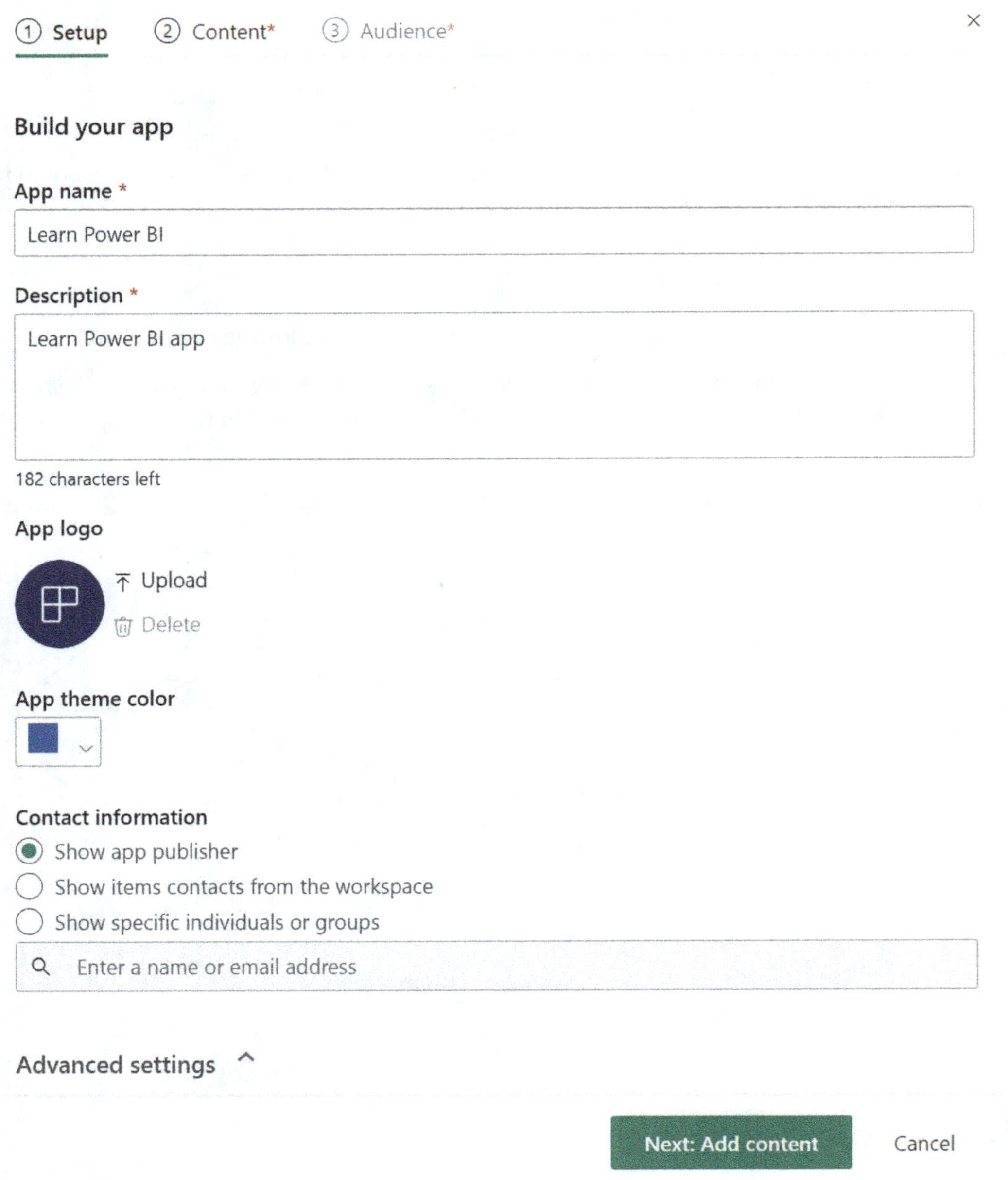

① **Setup**   ② Content*   ③ Audience*   ✕

Build your app

App name *

| Learn Power BI |

Description *

| Learn Power BI app |

182 characters left

App logo

⤴ Upload
🗑 Delete

App theme color

| ⬛ ∨ |

Contact information

◉ Show app publisher
◯ Show items contacts from the workspace
◯ Show specific individuals or groups

    🔍   Enter a name or email address

Advanced settings ⌃

                                                        Next: Add content   Cancel

Figure 10.10 – App publishing interface: the Setup tab

3. The app publishing interface consists of three tabs: **Setup**, **Content**, and **Audience**. The **Setup** tab is displayed initially. You must fill in the **App name** and **Description** fields and can optionally change the default **App logo** option provided by uploading an image, change **App theme color**, or edit **Contact information**. **Advanced settings** allow you to know about how the app's navigation pane works, permissions to hidden content, global app settings, and setting a support website URL.

4. Click on **Next: Add content | Add content** button and select the following items:

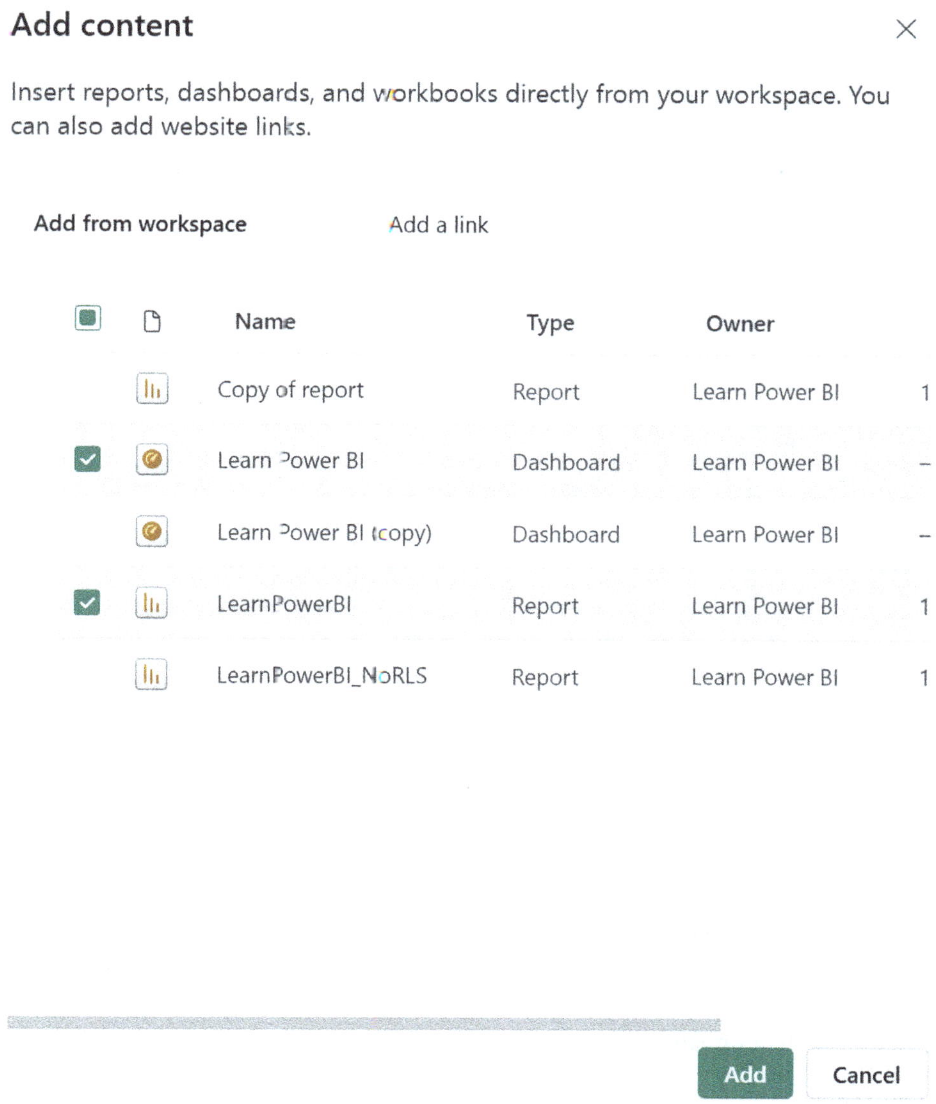

Add content   ✕

Insert reports, dashboards, and workbooks directly from your workspace. You can also add website links.

Add from workspace   Add a link

☑	☐	Name	Type	Owner	
	📊	Copy of report	Report	Learn Power BI	1
✓	◉	Learn Power BI	Dashboard	Learn Power BI	–
	◉	Learn Power BI (copy)	Dashboard	Learn Power BI	–
✓	📊	LearnPowerBI	Report	Learn Power BI	1
	📊	LearnPowerBI_NoRLS	Report	Learn Power BI	1

Add   Cancel

Figure 10.11 – Adding content to an app

5. Click the **Add** button to add the content.

6. Click the **Next: Add audience** button.

7. Click on the **Audience** tab. This tab is shown in the following screenshot:

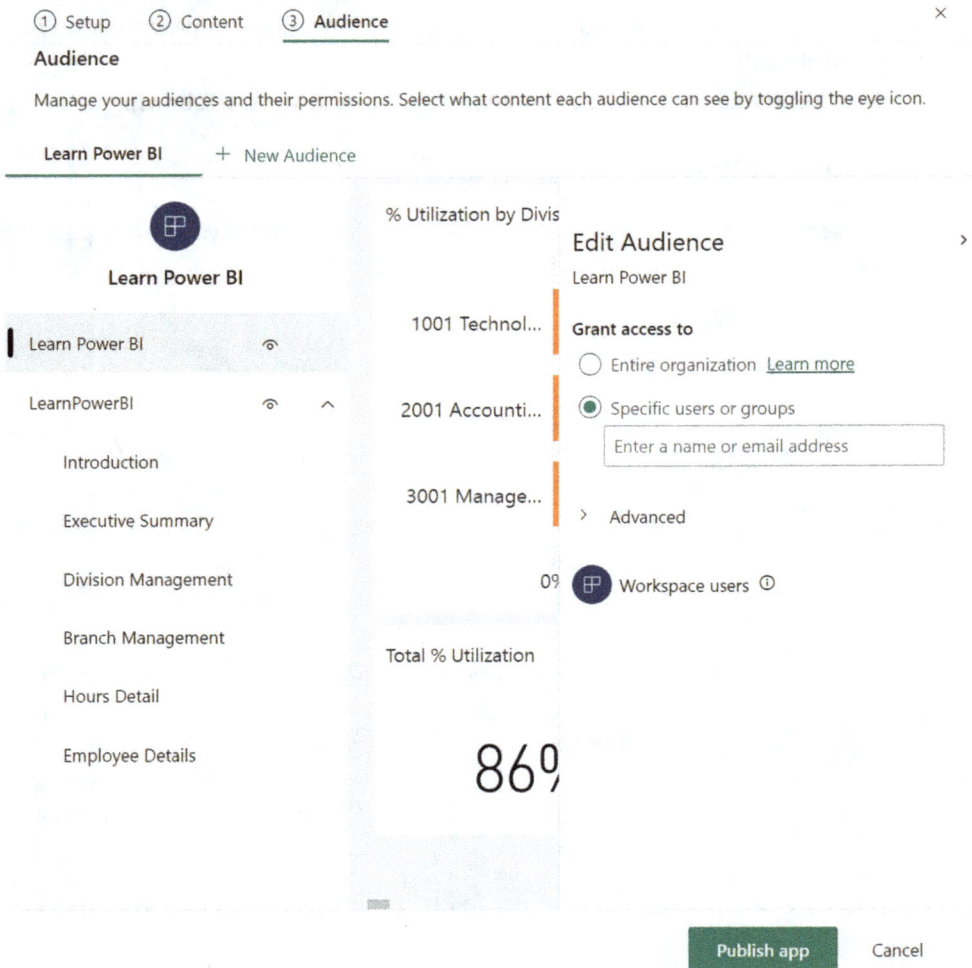

Figure 10.12 – App publishing interface: the Permissions tab

8. Click on the radio button next to **Entire organization** to share the app with the whole organization. The **Audience** tab also allows sharing with groups, distribution lists, internal users, and external users, although your organization may disable sharing with external users.

9. Click on the **Publish app** button to publish the app.

10. The app publishing dialog is displayed, as shown in the following screenshot:

Learn Power BI   ✕

When you publish an app that has large distribution, it might take a little while to process. Typically, the content will be available within 5-10 minutes, but it can take up to one day.

> **Publish**   Cancel

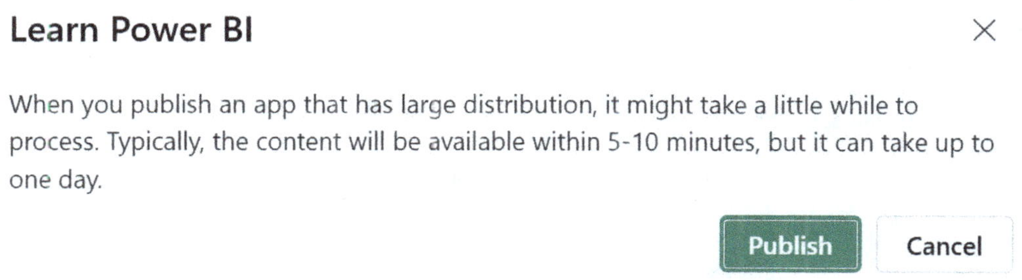

Figure 10.13 – App publishing dialog

11. Click the **Publish** button.

When successfully published, the **Successfully published** dialog is displayed, as shown in the following screenshot. You can either copy the link to the app and email the link to users or direct authorized users to get the app by using the **Apps** link in the **Navigation** pane:

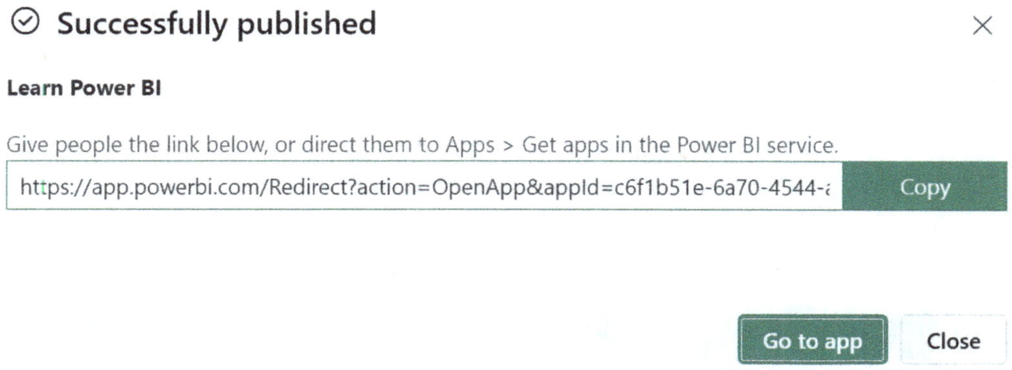

⊘ Successfully published   ✕

Learn Power BI

Give people the link below, or direct them to Apps > Get apps in the Power BI service.

> https://app.powerbi.com/Redirect?action=OpenApp&appId=c6f1b51e-6a70-4544-a   Copy

> **Go to app**   Close

Figure 10.14 – Successfully published dialog

12. Finally, click on the **Close** button.

Now that we have created and published an app, let's explore how to deploy and use the app.

Getting and using apps

Once an app has been published, the app can be accessed directly through the link that's provided when publishing the app. Alternatively, you can follow these steps:

1. Click on **Apps** in the **Navigation** pane. The **Apps** dialog is displayed on the canvas, listing any existing apps you have installed.

2. Click the **Get apps** button that appears in the upper-right corner of the canvas. The **Power BI apps** dialog is displayed, as shown in the following screenshot:

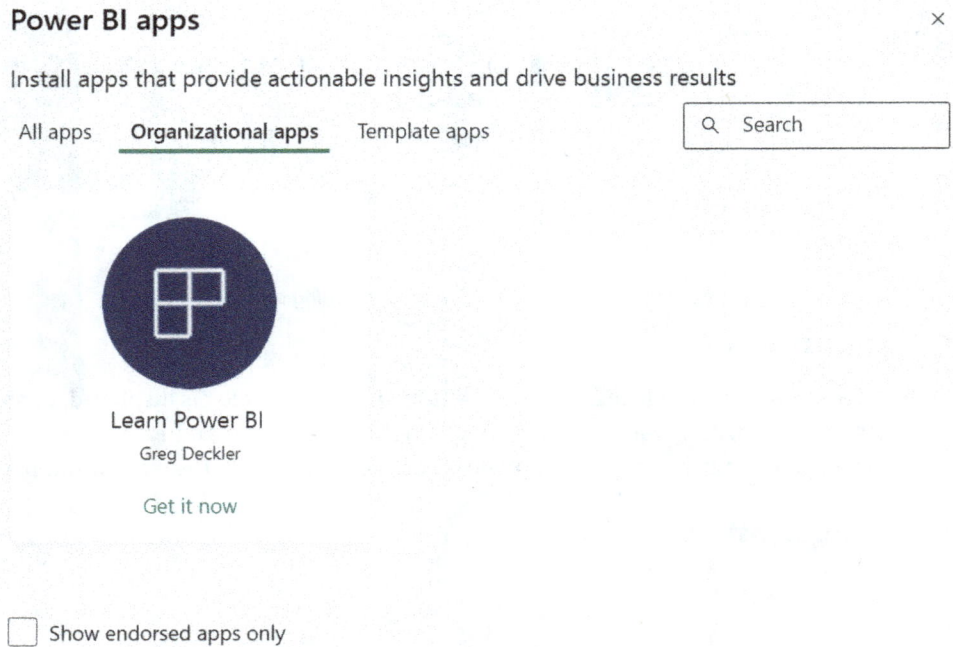

Figure 10.15 – Power BI apps dialog

3. Ensure that the **Organizational apps** tab is selected and click the **Get it now** link for the desired app. The app is displayed in the browser, as shown in the following screenshot:

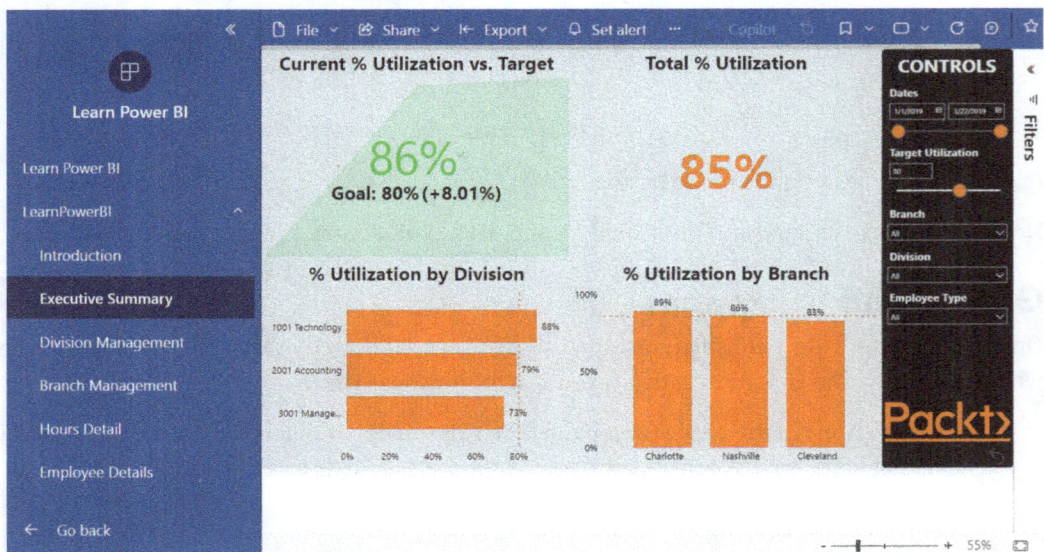

Figure 10.16 – The app

This app functions like an independent application with much of the functionality of the Power BI service, including **Comments**, **Subscribe**, **Bookmarks**, and other functionalities.

We are now done exploring apps in the service. To get back to the service, and exit the app, click the **Go back** link in the bottom-left corner of the app. Note that the **Learn Power BI** app now appears in your list of apps.

Let's move on to looking at goals and scorecards.

Working with metrics

Metrics consist of scorecards that allow users to track key goals against business objectives. Goals provide the ability for teams to measure their progress toward achieving business objectives, with the ability to share updates and analyze detailed data when necessary. Goals are organized into scorecards, which can incorporate content from multiple workspaces in order to provide a single window into the health of an organization.

Creating scorecards and goals

To create a new scorecard, do the following:

1. Click **Metrics** in the **Navigation** pane.
2. Click the **New scorecard** button. This displays the **Create scorecard** dialog, as shown in the following screenshot:

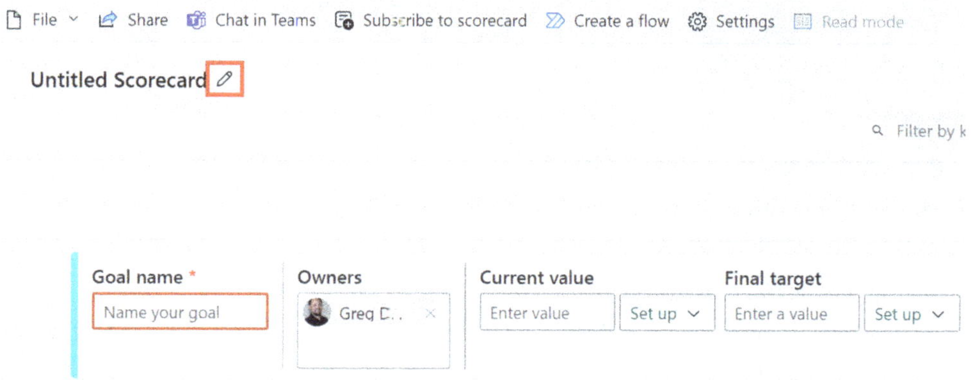

Figure 10.17 – Create scorecard dialog

3. Provide a name for your scorecard by clicking the pencil icon that appears when hovering over **Untitled Scorecard**.

4. Create a manual goal, like the one configured in the following screenshot:

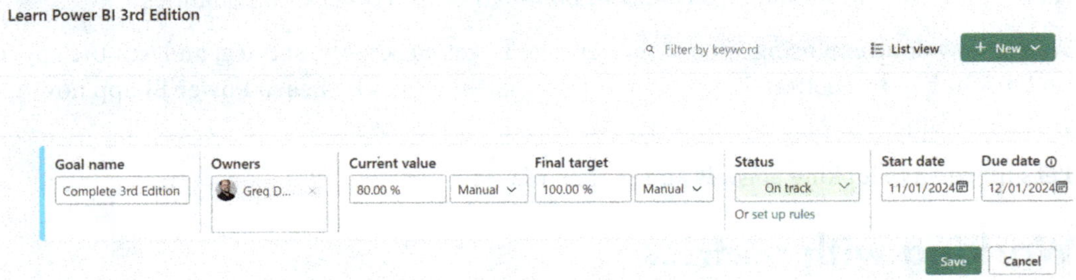

Figure 10.18 – Creating a goal

5. Click the **Save** button. A scorecard is presented, as shown in the following screenshot:

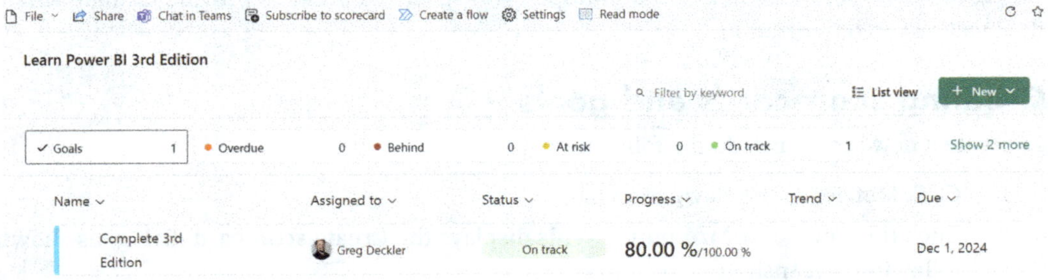

Figure 10.19 – A completed scorecard

While this is a simple example, you can see how goals and scorecards can provide an easy way to track progress against a variety of different goals. Let's now explore how to use scorecards and goals.

Using scorecards and goals

Let's explore some things that we can do with scorecards and goals. First, let's update our goal's progress. To do this, perform the following steps:

1. Hover over the goal and click the **Notes** icon.

2. Click on the **New check-in** button to create a new check-in for the goal, as shown in the following screenshot:

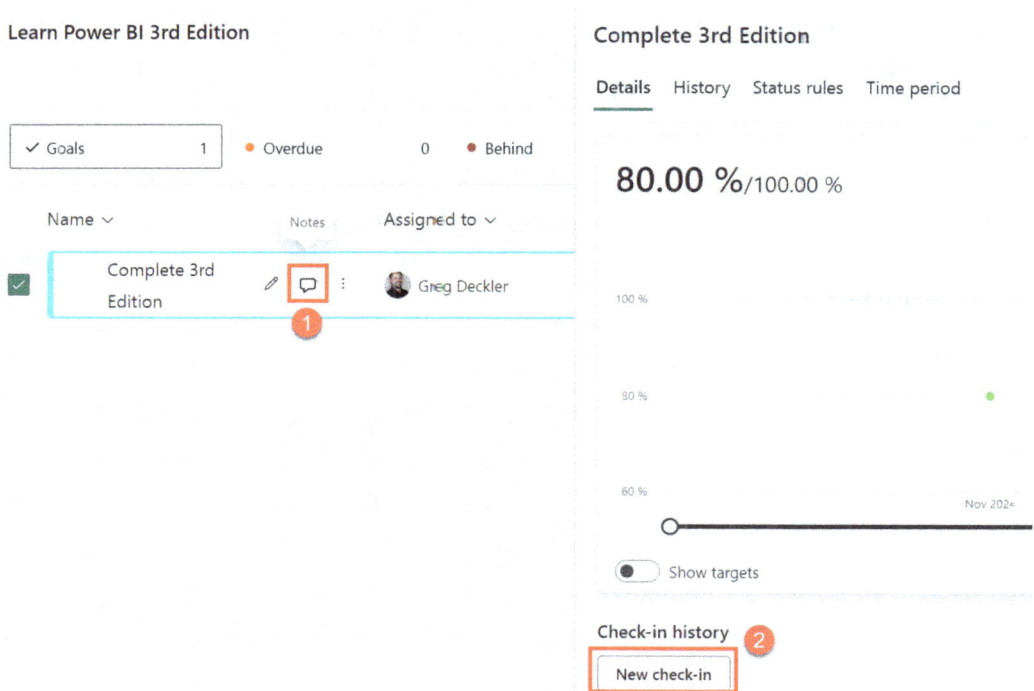

Figure 10.20 – New check-in

3. Enter a new check-in and click the **Save** button.

Creating check-ins allows the progress toward the goal to be updated and tracked over time. Next, let's add a data-driven goal. To do this, follow these steps:

1. On the scorecard, click **Edit** in the ribbon if not already in **Edit** mode.
2. Click the **New** button and then the **New goal** button.
3. Provide a name for your goal in the **Goal name** field.
4. In the **Current value** area, click the **Set up** dropdown and then choose **Connect to data...**.

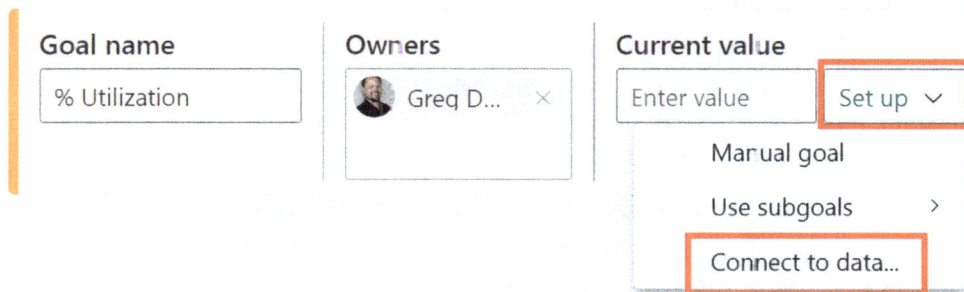

Figure 10.21 – Creating a data-driven goal

5.   Select the LearnPowerBI report from the list of reports and then click the **Next** button.

6.   Navigate to the **Executive Summary** page of the report, click the % **Utilization vs. Target by Month** KPI visual, and then click the **Connect** button.

7.   Back on the scorecard edit screen, enter a **Target** value of *.8* and then click the **Save** button.

8.   Hover over the new goal and click the **Notes** icon.

9.   Click the **Status rules** tab and then click the **New rule** button.

10. Configure the **Status rules** settings, as shown in the following screenshot, and then click the **Save** button:

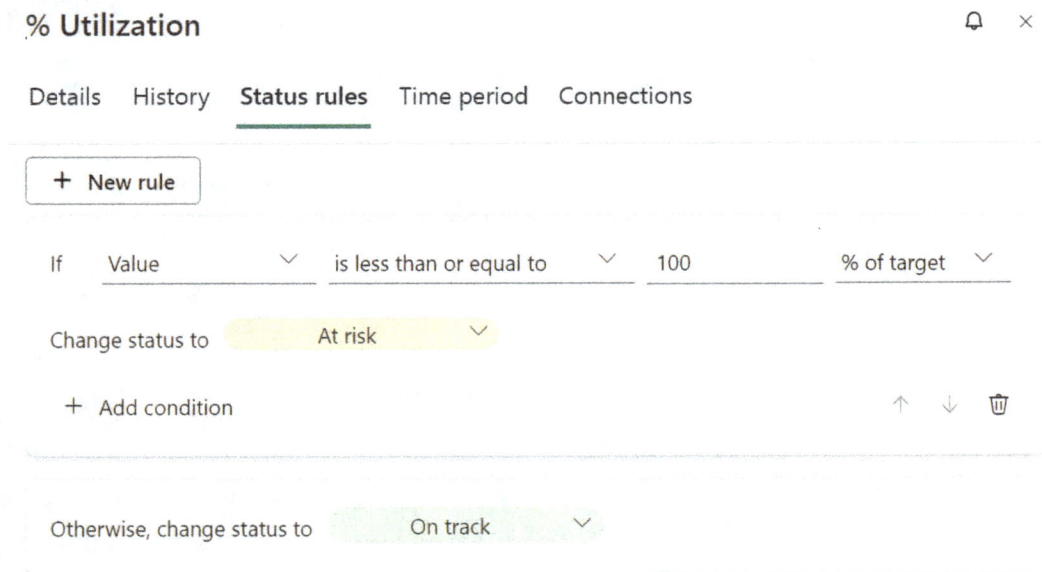

% Utilization   🔔   ✕

Details   History   **Status rules**   Time period   Connections

+ New rule

If   Value   ⌄   is less than or equal to   ⌄   100   % of target   ⌄

Change status to   At risk   ⌄

+ Add condition   ↑   ↓   🗑

Otherwise, change status to   On track   ⌄

Figure 10.22 – Creating a data-driven goal

Now, instead of having to update the status manually via check-ins, the status of the goal is updated automatically every time the semantic model refreshes. Let's now take a look at security and permissions.

Understanding security and permissions

There are several levels of security and permissions within the Power BI service. It is important to understand these various permission levels to ensure that users can only access the appropriate reports, dashboards, apps, and data.

The main levels of permissions within Power BI are listed as follows:

*   Workspace permissions
*   App permissions
*   Object permissions (dashboards, reports, scorecards, and semantic models)
*   **Row-Level Security (RLS)**

Let us understand each of these in the following sections.

Workspace permissions

Workspaces serve as logical containers in which you store dashboards, reports, scorecards, workbooks, semantic models, and dataflows. So far, we have only worked with a single report and semantic model. But workspaces can contain dozens or even hundreds of different dashboards, reports, scorecards, workbooks, semantic models, and dataflows. Assigning security at a workspace level provides access to all the objects within the workspace. This means that workspace access should only be assigned to individuals or groups of individuals who should see everything that is published or could be published to the workspace.

To assign workspace permissions, perform the following steps:

1. In the **Navigation** pane, click **Workspaces** and then the name of the workspace, which, in this case, is **Learn Power BI**. This changes the canvas to display the workspace interface.
2. Click the **Manage access** link in the ribbon of the workspace interface. The **Manage access** dialog is displayed, as shown in the following screenshot:

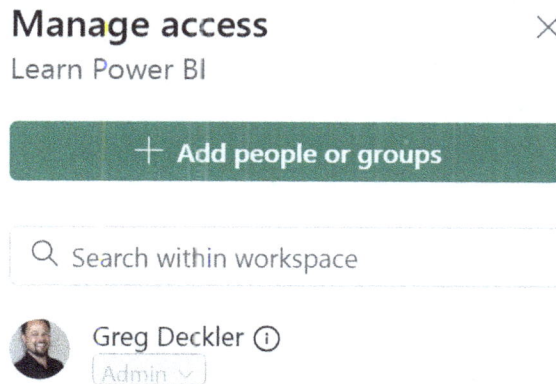

Figure 10.23 – Manage access dialog in the service

3. Similar to sharing a report, clicking the + **Add people or groups** button allows you to enter names or email addresses in the **Enter name or email** field. **Entra** (Azure Active Directory) groups can be assigned as well as individuals.

There are four different security roles for workspaces. These roles are listed as follows:

* **Viewer**
* **Contributor**
* **Member**
* **Admin**

The **Viewer** role provides the following permission:

* View items within the workspace.

The **Contributor** role includes the **Viewer** role permission, plus the following permissions:

- Publish reports to the workspace and delete content.
- Create, edit, and delete content in the workspace.

The **Member** role includes all of the **Contributor** and **Viewer** role permissions, plus the following permissions:

- Allow others to reshare items.
- Share an item or share an app.
- Publish and update an app.
- Add members or others with lower permissions.

The **Admin** role includes all of the **Member**, **Contributor**, and **Viewer** role permissions, plus the following permissions:

- Add/remove people, including other admins.
- Update and delete the workspace.

By default, the creator of a workspace is assigned the **Admin** role.

Because groups can be assigned permissions to a workspace, individuals may be assigned to multiple roles for a workspace. If a user is assigned multiple roles, that individual receives the highest level of access that's provided by the roles they are assigned.

App permissions

App permissions relate to the users that are allowed to get and view a published app. We have already seen how to set app permissions when publishing an app.

To update an app's permissions, do the following:

1. Navigate to the workspace in the **Navigation** pane.
2. Click on **Update app** in the ribbon. The **Update app** option replaces the **Publish app** option in the ribbon once an app has been published.
3. Simply adjust the **Audience** tab and republish the app.

Consider that the same app can be shared with different audiences with different navigation items either hidden or not hidden.

Let's continue our exploration of permissions by next looking at object permissions.

Object permissions

Object permissions refer to permissions that are assigned to individual objects within the Power BI service, such as dashboards, reports, and semantic models. Unlike workspace permissions, which assign access to all the objects within a workspace, object permissions only assign permissions to an individual object. However, there is a hierarchy to these object permissions so assigning permissions at one level of this hierarchy will, by default, assign certain permissions to related objects lower in the hierarchy.

To understand how object permissions work, consider that the hierarchy for dashboards, reports, and semantic models is as follows:

- Dashboards
- Reports
- Semantic models

This is a logical hierarchy, as dashboards are built from reports and reports rely upon semantic models. This means that when a report is shared, permissions are assigned for the report and are also assigned to the related semantic model for that report. However, no permissions are assigned to any dashboards. The hierarchical flow of permissions is required since dashboards, reports, and semantic models are all separate yet related objects that are dependent on objects lower in the hierarchy.

For example, assigning a user permission to view a report would be useless without that user also being able to have permission to read the underlying semantic model for that report. Similarly, assigning permissions when sharing a dashboard assigns the corresponding permissions for any related reports and semantic models. Scorecards currently sit completely outside of this hierarchy.

Four permissions can be assigned to objects outside of workspace permission settings. These permissions are listed as follows:

- Read
- Build
- Reshare
- Write

Remember that objects can be shared either via the creation of shared links or via direct access. However, the same permissions apply in both cases. While sharing and permissions can be accessed from a variety of locations within the Power BI service, the most consistent method that works for all objects is outlined as follows:

1. Navigate to the object via the **Navigation** pane.
2. In the ribbon, click the **Share** option. This allows you to generate a sharing link.
3. To view existing permissions, click the ellipsis (...) in the header of the sharing dialog and choose **Manage permissions**.
4. In the bottom right-hand corner, click the **Advanced** link.
5. The **Links** tab lists generated share links, while the **Direct access** tab lists individuals and groups with direct access to the object.

Individuals and groups with workspace access are listed under the **Direct access** tab with the corresponding **Permissions** description, as follows:

- **Workspace Admin**
- **Workspace Member**
- **Workspace Contributor**
- **Workspace Viewer**

Sharing an object grants read access to the object. **Reshare** permissions can be added for all objects, allowing the user or group members to share the object with others. **Build** permissions can only be added for semantic model objects, and this allows users or group members to build new reports and content from the semantic model.

RLS

In addition to workspace-level permissions, which assign permissions to everything within a workspace, and object-level permissions, which assign permissions to one or more objects, individual rows of data within a semantic model can be secured as well. This is the purpose of RLS, which was first introduced in *Chapter 6, Unlocking Insights*. In that chapter, roles were created in the Power BI Desktop application. These roles had **Data Analysis Expressions (DAX)** calculations that limited the rows of data that users within those roles could see.

When a Power BI Desktop file is published to the Power BI service, any roles that were created within Power BI Desktop are published to the service as part of the semantic model for the report. Once published, these roles are available within the service. To assign users to these roles, follow these steps:

1. To access these roles within the service, navigate to a workspace.

2. Hover over the semantic model, click the ellipses (**...**), and then click **Security**, as shown in the following screenshot:

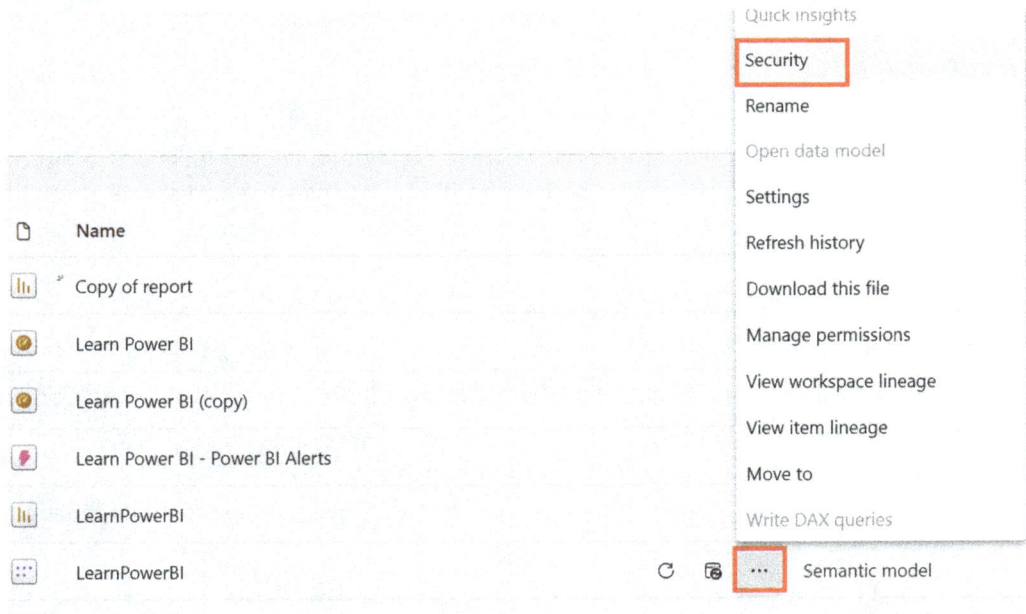

Figure 10.24 – Accessing the RLS interface in the service

3. Clicking on the **Security** link brings up the **Row-Level Security** interface, as shown in the following screenshot:

Row-Level Security

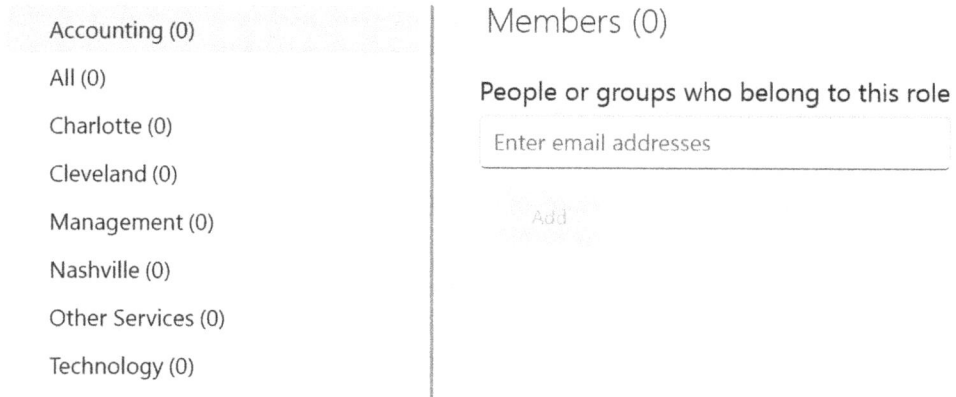

Accounting (0)	**Members (0)**
All (0)	
Charlotte (0)	**People or groups who belong to this role**
Cleveland (0)	Enter email addresses
Management (0)	
Nashville (0)	Add
Other Services (0)	
Technology (0)	

Figure 10.25 – RLS interface in the service

4. Adding users to roles is as simple as clicking on a role, entering a user's name or email address, and then clicking the **Add** button.

Note that RLS does not affect any other security permissions at a workspace or object level; RLS simply limits the rows of data within a semantic model that a user can read. Finally, it is vital to remember that users assigned **Admin**, **Member**, or **Contributor** permissions on the workspace are immune to (not affected by) RLS. The **Viewer** role, however, is affected by RLS.

Summary

This chapter introduced three important types of objects in the Power BI service: dashboards, apps, and scorecards.

Dashboards are a powerful feature that allows end users to bring together all of the most important information from multiple reports, semantic models, other dashboards, Q&A, and other sources into a single-page canvas consisting of tiles. These tiles can be adjusted on the canvas and allow for the creation of data alerts to immediately inform users when key metric thresholds are met.

Apps, on the other hand, allow multiple dashboards and reports to be bundled together as an independent application and published to users. These apps provide similar features and functionality to the full Power BI service.

Scorecards allow users to track and share goals. These goals can be dynamically driven by data and rules to automatically track progress.

In addition to understanding dashboards, apps, and scorecards, we also took an in-depth look at security within the Power BI service. Power BI provides multiple levels of interrelated security settings for workspaces, apps, scorecards, dashboards, reports, semantic models, and even individual rows of semantic models.

In the next chapter, we focus on how to keep semantic models that have been published to the service refreshed.

Questions

As an activity, try to answer the following questions on your own:

- What is a dashboard and what purpose does it serve?
- Which types of tiles can be added to dashboards?
- Which tiles allow for the creation of a data alert?
- What is an app and why would you use one?
- What are the two publishing methods that can be used with apps?
- Once an app has been published, how can the app be modified?
- What are the three main security/permission levels within the Power BI service?
- What are the four roles that are available for workspaces?
- What is the hierarchy of objects within the Power BI service?
- What are the four permissions that are available for objects?

Further reading

To learn more about the topics that were covered in this chapter, please take a look at the following references:

- *Introduction to dashboards for Power BI designers*: https://learn.microsoft.com/en-us/power-bi/create-reports/service-dashboards
- *Intro to dashboard tiles for Power BI designers*: https://learn.microsoft.com/en-us/power-bi/create-reports/service-dashboard-tiles
- *Add images, text, video, and more to your dashboard*: https://learn.microsoft.com/en-us/power-bi/create-reports/service-dashboard-add-widget
- *Publish an app in Power BI*: https://learn.microsoft.com/en-us/power-bi/collaborate-share/service-create-distribute-apps
- *Get started with metrics in Power BI*: https://learn.microsoft.com/en-us/power-bi/create-reports/service-goals-introduction
- *Give users access to workspaces in Power BI*: https://learn.microsoft.com/en-us/power-bi/collaborate-share/service-give-access-new-workspaces
- *Semantic model permissions*: https://learn.microsoft.com/en-us/power-bi/connect-data/service-datasets-permissions

Unlock this book's exclusive benefits now

Scan this QR code or go to packtpub.com/ unlock, then search for this book by name.

Note: Keep your purchase invoice ready before you start.

11

Refreshing Content

So far, we have spent quite a bit of time in the Power BI service working with reports, dashboards, apps, and security. Throughout this book, we have learned how to create semantic models and reports and then publish and share our work using the Power BI service. However, it is the nature of data to change over time. New data gets added or existing rows are deleted or changed. Hence, once our work is in the Power BI service, how do we keep our work up to date with new data without having to manually refresh the data on the desktop and republish it? Luckily, the Power BI service contains even more functionality that allows us to keep our data refreshed.

In this chapter, we will cover how to install and configure data gateways, which can keep our data up to date. Then, we will learn how to configure our semantic models to use these gateways.

The following topics will be covered in this chapter:

- Installing and using data gateways
- Refreshing semantic models

Technical requirements

You will need the following to complete this chapter:

- An internet connection.
- A Microsoft 365 account or a Power BI trial.
- If you have skipped any of the previous chapters, you can download LearnPowerBI.zip from GitHub at https://github.com/PacktPublishing/Learn-Microsoft-Power-BI_3E/tree/main/Chapter8.

Installing and using data gateways

As mentioned in the introduction, it is the nature of data to change over time. The Power BI service includes functionality to keep our data refreshed. However, when the data exists on-premises and not in the service, we require a bridge between the Power BI service in Microsoft's cloud and the on-premises environment. This bridge is handled by the on-premises data gateway.

The **on-premises data gateway**, or simply **data gateway**, is software that's installed on an on-premises computer that provides a secure connection between local, on-premises data and a variety of services that reside in Microsoft's cloud, including the Power BI service. Once installed, the Power BI service can use this gateway to refresh semantic models that have been published to the Power BI service, as shown in the following diagram:

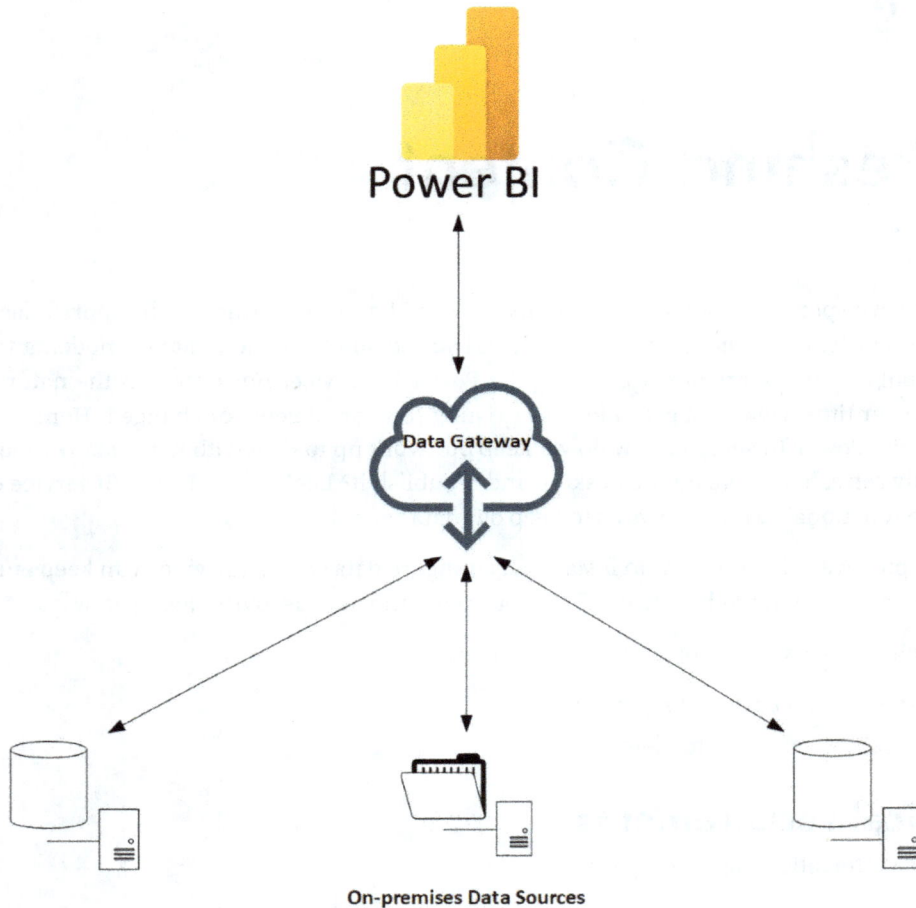

Figure 11.1 – Data gateway

There are two ways the gateway can operate, as follows:

*   Standard
*   Personal

The reason to install a gateway in one mode versus the other comes down to the scenario in which you plan to use the gateway. You want to use the standard mode if the following applies:

*   You want other users within the organization to use a single, centralized gateway.
*   You need **DirectQuery**, as well as import mode semantic models.

- You wish to use the gateway for Power Apps, Azure Logic Apps, Power Automate, Azure Analysis Services, and dataflows, as well as for Power BI.
- You can run the installation as an administrator.
- The computer that you are installing the gateway on is not a domain controller.

Many end users often start by installing the gateway in personal mode because they are often not administrators of their local computer. In this scenario, they can only use import mode and only use the gateway with Power BI. For these users, it is advisable to get the **Information Technology** (IT) department involved to install the gateway in standard mode if additional functionality is required.

Downloading and installing a data gateway

To install a data gateway in either mode, follow these steps:

1. Log in to the Power BI service.
2. In the header area, click the down arrow icon or the ellipsis. Choose **Data Gateway**. This is a link that takes you to Microsoft's data gateway home page, https://powerbi.microsoft.com/gateway/, which should look similar to the following:

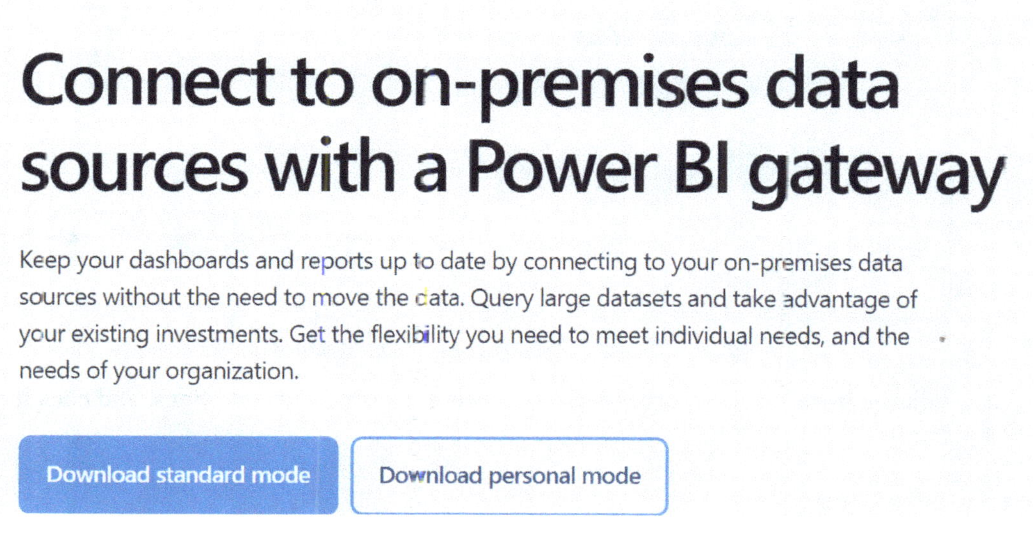

Connect to on-premises data sources with a Power BI gateway

Keep your dashboards and reports up to date by connecting to your on-premises data sources without the need to move the data. Query large datasets and take advantage of your existing investments. Get the flexibility you need to meet individual needs, and the needs of your organization.

Download standard mode   Download personal mode

Figure 11.2 – Power BI gateway page

3. Click either the **Download standard mode** or **Download personal mode** button. The file that's downloaded is GatewayInstall.exe for standard mode and On-premises data gateway (personal mode).exe for personal mode.
4. Save the file to your Downloads directory or another location on your local computer. Once the file has finished downloading, open the folder on your computer where you downloaded the file.

Next, we install the gateway in personal mode.

Personal mode installation

To install the gateway in personal mode, follow these steps:

1. Right-click the On-premises data gateway (personal mode).exe file and choose **Open**. The installation splash screen is displayed, as shown in the following screenshot:

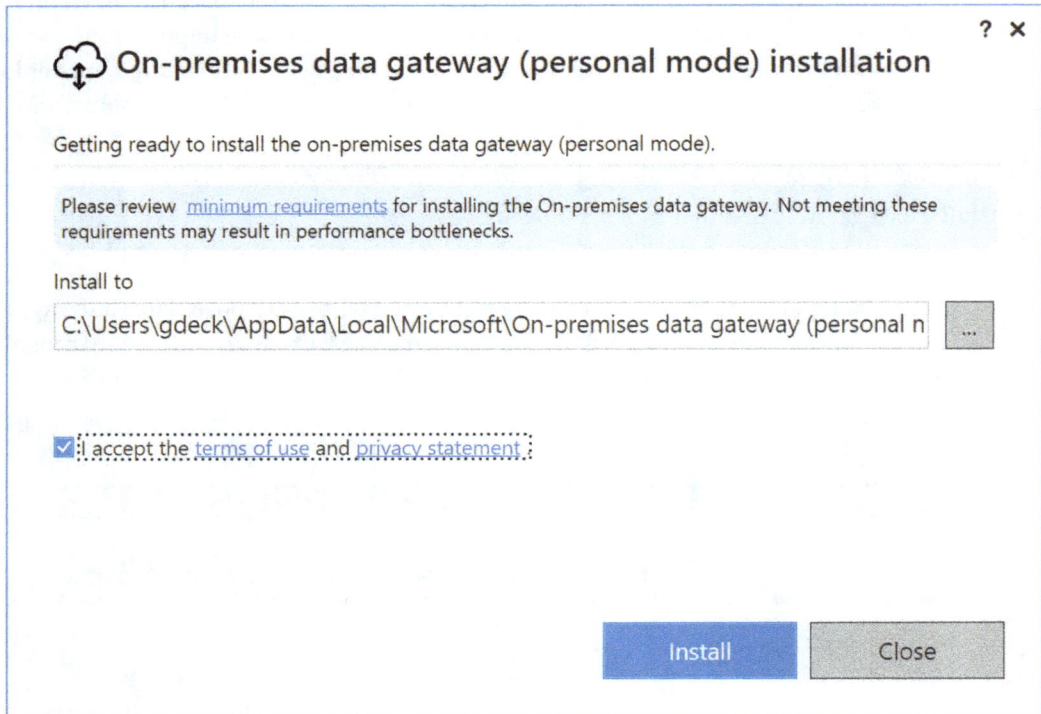

☁ On-premises data gateway (personal mode) installation   ? ✕

Getting ready to install the on-premises data gateway (personal mode).

Please review minimum requirements for installing the On-premises data gateway. Not meeting these
requirements may result in performance bottlenecks.

Install to

C:\Users\gdeck\AppData\Local\Microsoft\On-premises data gateway (personal n   ...

☑ I accept the terms of use and privacy statement.

[Install]   [Close]

Figure 11.3 – Data gateway installer splash screen (personal mode)

2. Edit the **Install to** directory if desired, accept the terms and conditions, and click the **Install** button.

3. It may take a few minutes for the installation to complete. After the installation completes, enter the email address that you use to log into the Power BI service and click the **Sign in** button:

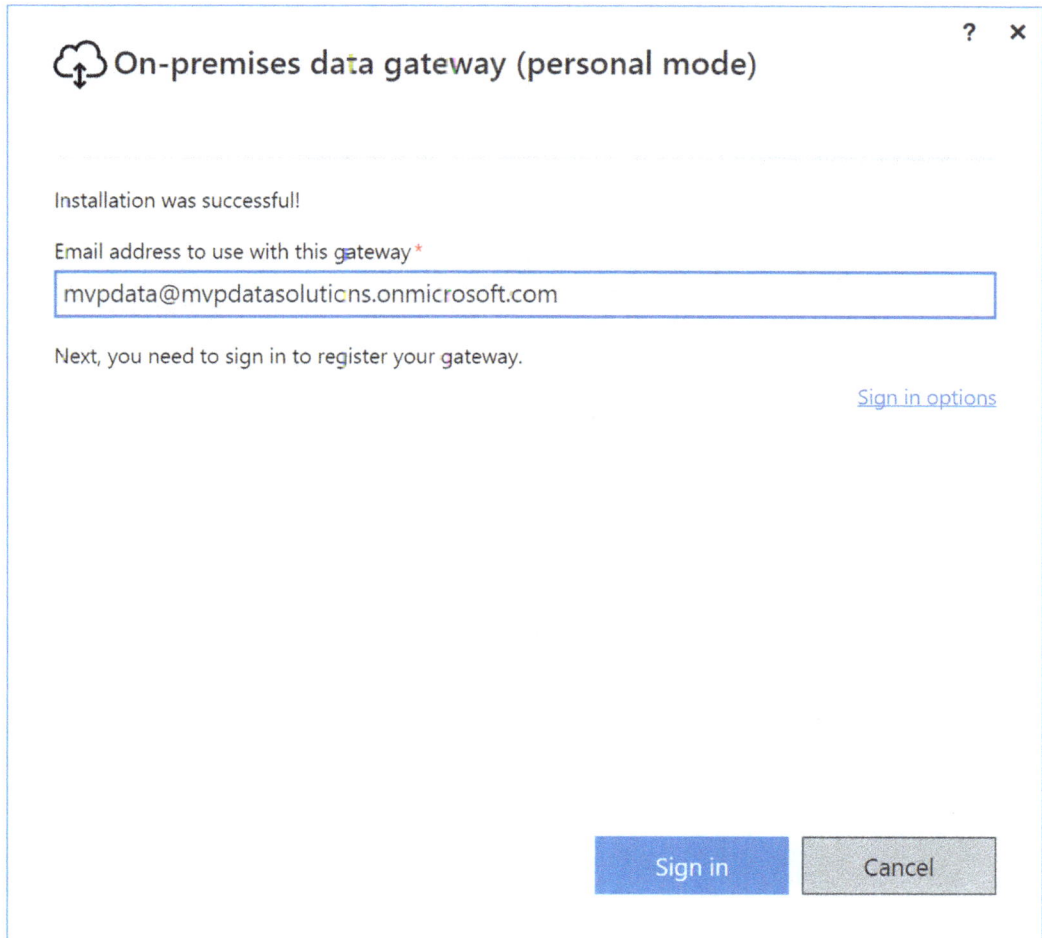

Figure 11.4 – Data gateway email address (personal mode)

4. Sign in to the Power BI service to register the gateway.

5. Once you've successfully signed in, the gateway is installed and ready to use:

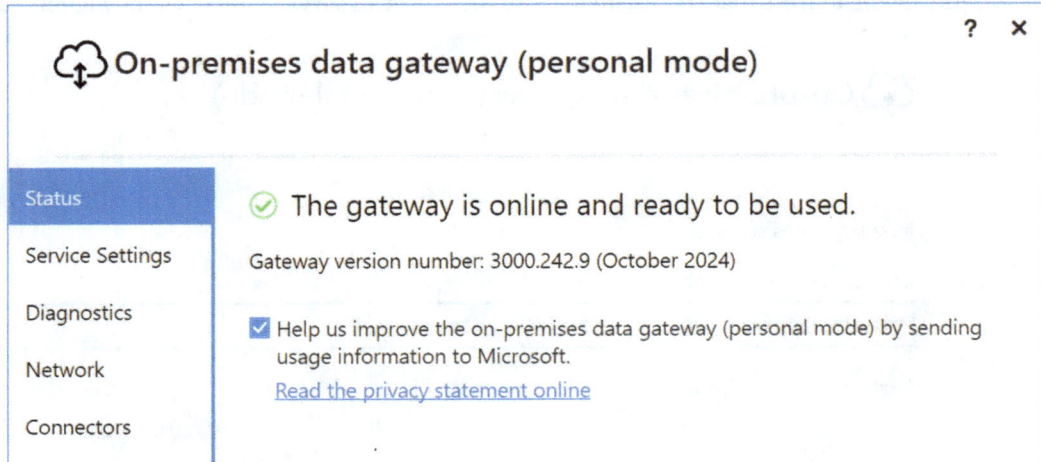

Figure 11.5 – Data gateway administration screen (personal mode)

Now, let's look at how to install the gateway in standard mode.

Standard mode installation

To install the gateway in standard mode, follow these steps:

1. Right-click the `GatewayInstall.exe` file and choose **Run as administrator**. The installation splash screen is displayed:

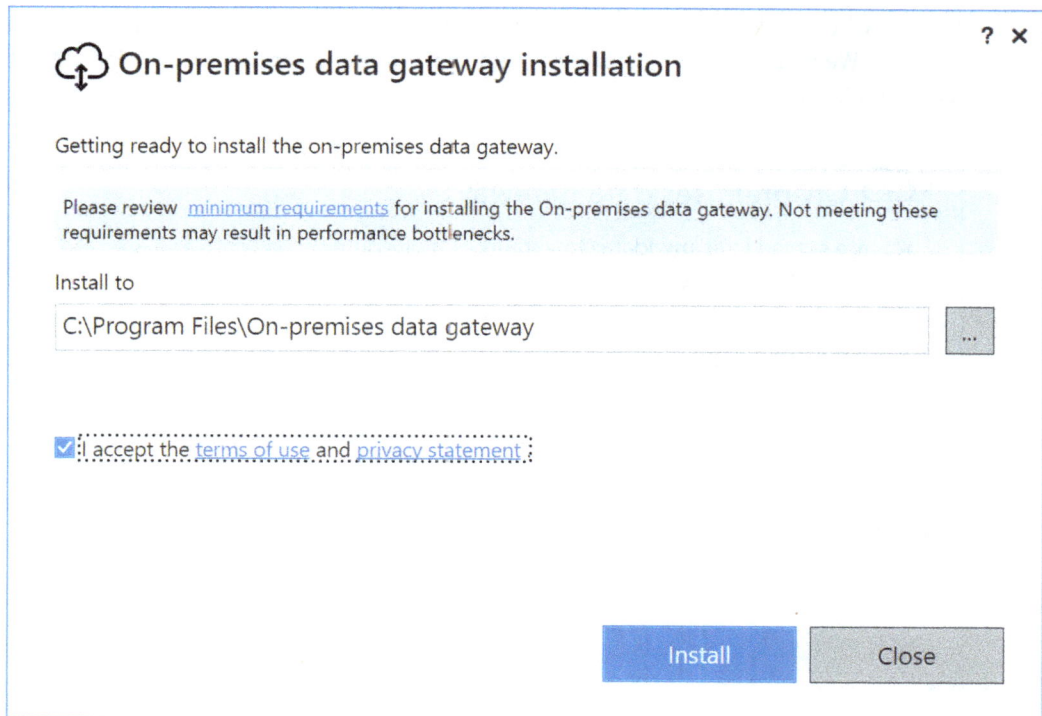

Figure 11.6 – Data gateway installer splash screen (standard mode)

2. Edit the **Install to** directory if desired, accept the terms and conditions, and click the **Install** button.

3. It may take a few minutes for the installation to complete. After the installation completes, enter the email address that you use to log into the Power BI service and click the **Sign in** button. This screen is similar to *Figure 11.4*.

4. Sign in to the Power BI service.

5. Choose whether you wish to register a new gateway or migrate/restore/takeover an existing gateway. We will choose **Register a new gateway on this computer** and click the **Next** button, as shown in the following screenshot:

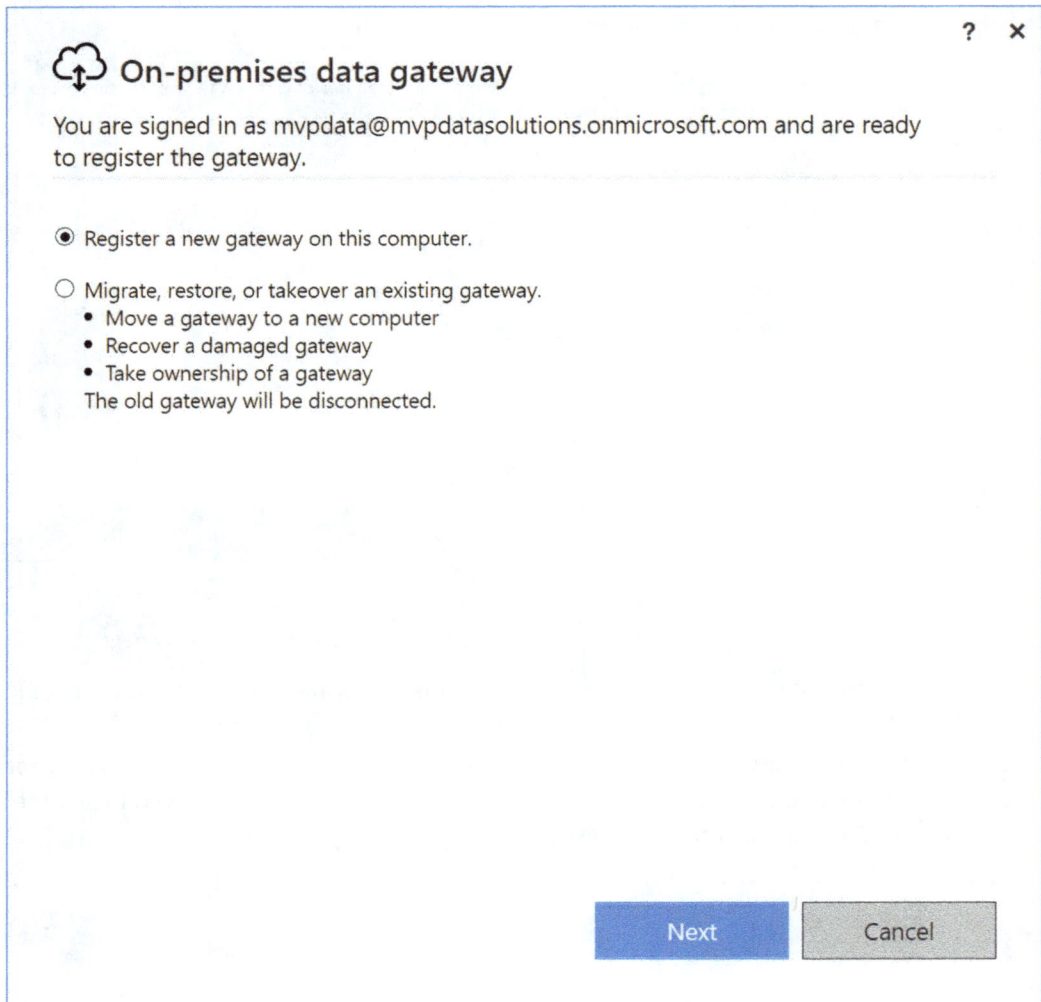

> ? ✕
>
> ## ☁ On-premises data gateway
>
> You are signed in as mvpdata@mvpdatasolutions.onmicrosoft.com and are ready to register the gateway.
>
> ⦿ Register a new gateway on this computer.
>
> ○ Migrate, restore, or takeover an existing gateway.
> * Move a gateway to a new computer
> * Recover a damaged gateway
> * Take ownership of a gateway
> The old gateway will be disconnected.
>
> [Next]   [Cancel]

Figure 11.7 – Register gateway (standard mode)

6. Enter a name for the gateway, provide a recovery key, and click the **Configure** button.

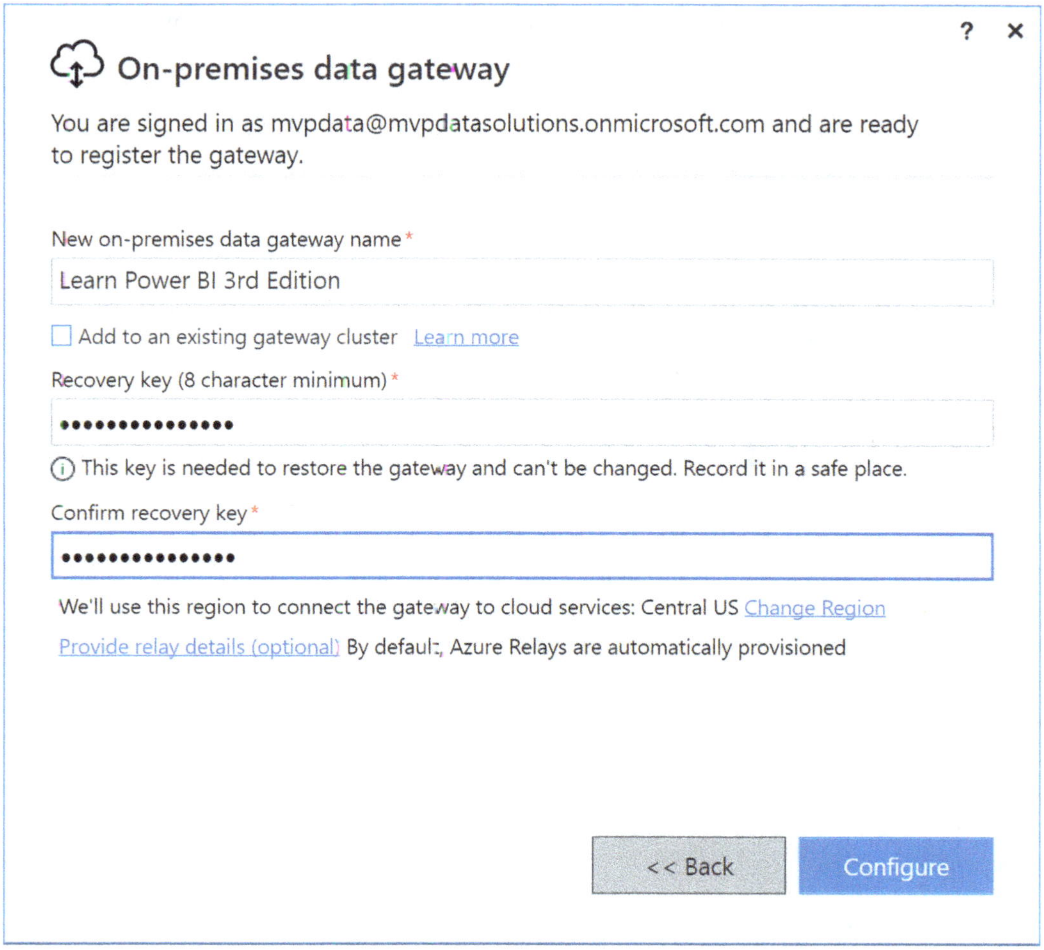

Figure 11.8 – Gateway name and recovery key (standard mode)

The recovery key is needed if you need to restore the gateway or wish to add additional gateways to the gateway cluster, so make sure that you record this recovery key in a safe place. You have the option to add a gateway to an existing cluster. Only do this if you have already installed a gateway and wish to enable redundancy. In addition, at the bottom of the screen, you have the option to change the region that your gateway operates in. Only do this if you understand what you are doing. The gateway's region is based on the Power BI tenant that's tied to your login. If you install the gateway for another region, it will not operate correctly with that tenant's region.

7. The data gateway should now be installed and ready to use, as shown in the following screen-shot:

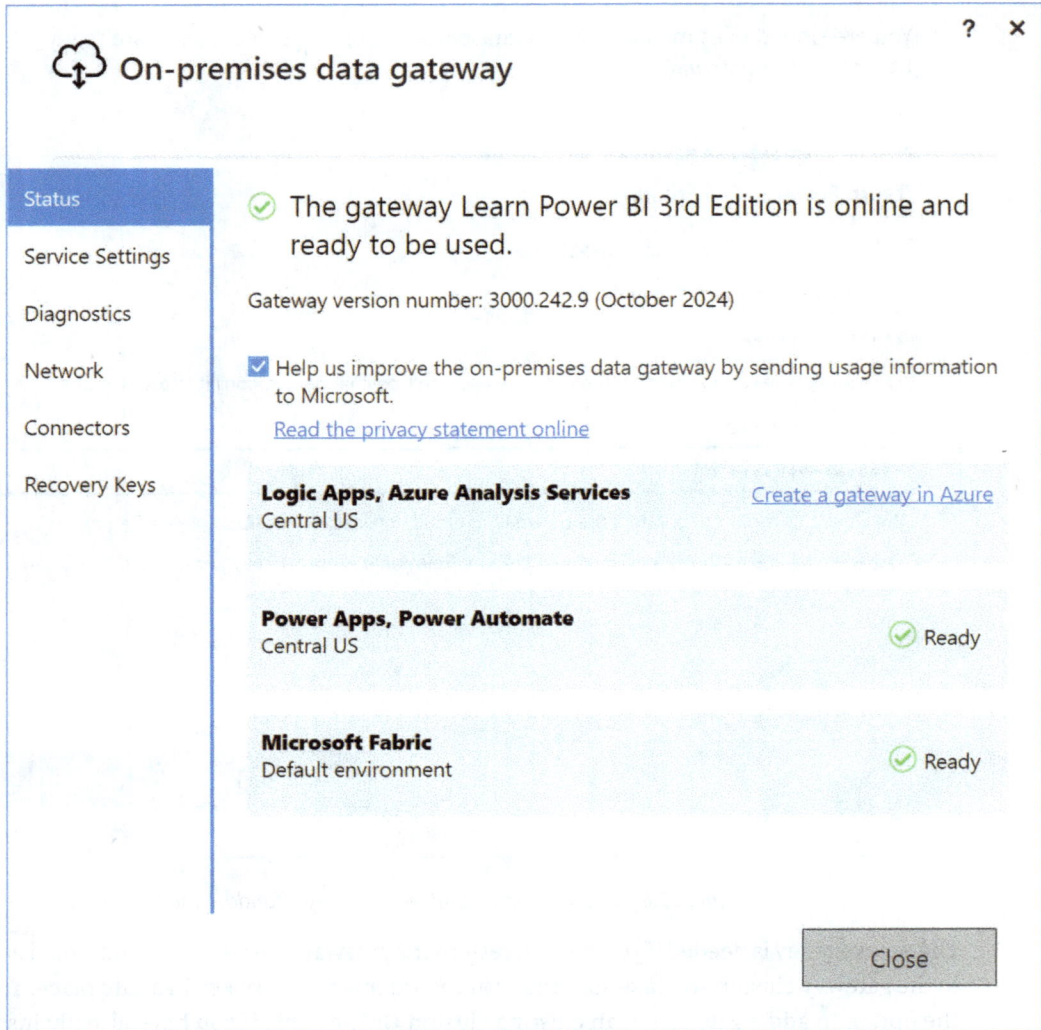

Figure 11.9 – Data gateway administration screen (standard mode)

Now that the gateway is installed, we can move on to how to operate and use it.

Running a data gateway

The data gateway runs as either an application or a service on the computer that the installation was run on, depending on which mode – either personal or standard – was used for the installation.

Personal mode

When installed in personal mode, the gateway runs as a background process called **Microsoft.PowerBI.DataMovement.PersonalGateway**. This background process continues to run even if you close the gateway administration screen that appears at the end of the installation. This administration screen is the **PersonalGatewayConfigurator** application. The **PersonalGatewayConfigurator** application is enabled to start automatically by default. To prevent the gateway from starting automatically after rebooting, follow these steps:

1. Use the Windows Start menu to launch **Task Manager.** The Power BI gateway background process can be found on the **Processes** tab, as shown here:

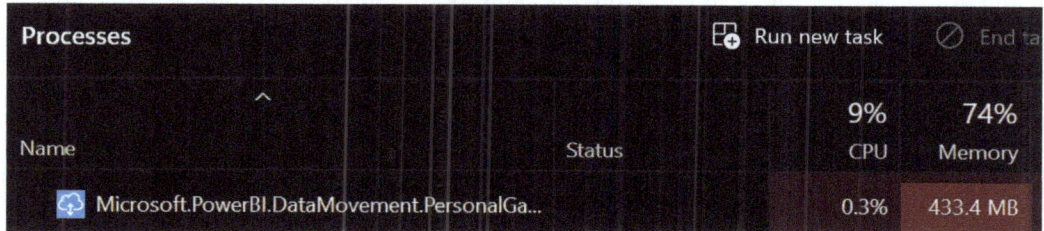

Figure 11.10 – Task Manager

2. If desired, you can select **Microsoft.PowerBI.DataMovement.PersonalGateway** and click the **End task** button to stop the gateway.

3. In the **Task Manager** window, switch to the **Startup apps** tab, as shown in the following screenshot, to view your startup tasks:

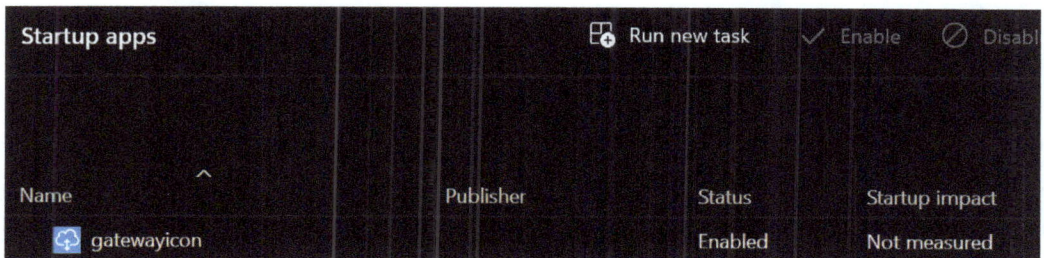

Figure 11.11 – Task Manager – the Startup tab

4. If you do not want the personal gateway to start automatically, right-click **PersonalGateway-Configurator** and choose **Disable.**

Now that we have explored running the data gateway in personal mode, let's look at standard mode.

Standard mode

When installed in standard mode, the gateway runs as a Windows service, which is why you need to run the installation as an administrator. This service's name is **PBIEgwService** with a **Description** of **On-premises data gateway service**, and the background process is called **Microsoft.PowerBI.EnterpriseGateway**.

Once installed, this service is set to automatically start when the computer is rebooted. This Windows service continues to run even if you close the gateway administration screen that appears at the end of the installation. This administration screen is the **EnterpriseGatewayConfigurator** application. If you close the administration application, you can bring the administration screen back up by finding and running **On-premises data gateway** in the Windows Start menu.

Now that you have a data gateway installed, it is time to configure the data gateway, so let's do that next.

Configuring a data gateway

The data gateway has some additional configuration settings that are worth understanding. These configuration settings are available from the gateway administration application that appears at the end of the installation. We already saw the **Status** page of the application at the end of the *Downloading and installing a data gateway* section. The additional pages are as follows:

- Service Settings
- Diagnostics
- Network
- Connectors
- Recovery Keys

Let's look at these pages in detail.

Service Settings

The **Power BI Service Settings** page is shown in the following screenshot:

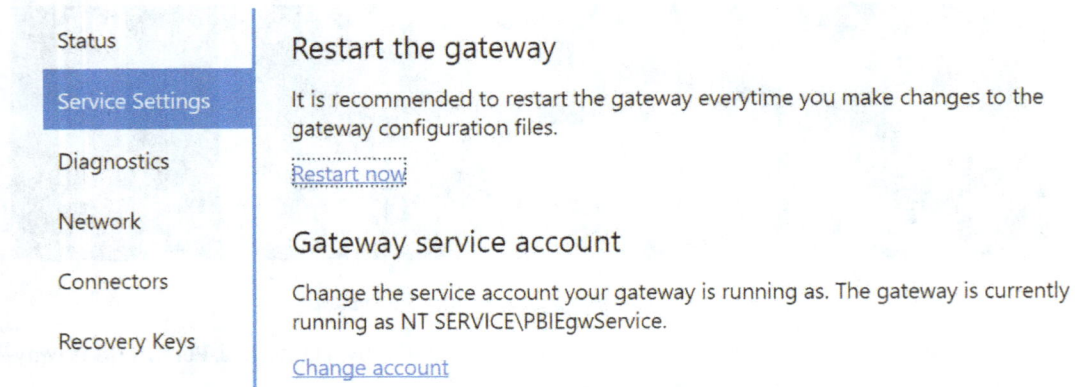

Status

Service Settings

Diagnostics

Network

Connectors

Recovery Keys

Restart the gateway

It is recommended to restart the gateway everytime you make changes to the gateway configuration files.

Restart now

Gateway service account

Change the service account your gateway is running as. The gateway is currently running as NT SERVICE\PBIEgwService.

Change account

Figure 11.12 – Service Settings page

Both the personal mode and standard mode configurators allow you to restart the gateway by clicking the **Restart now** link. It is advisable to restart the gateway any time a configuration setting is changed. Standard mode also allows you to change the account that's used to run the Windows service. You can do so by clicking the **Change account** link if you are already signed in. By default, the Power BI service runs as the internal account known as NT SERVICE\PBIEgwService. This can be changed if you wish to run the Power BI service as an Active Directory domain account.

Diagnostics

The **Diagnostics** page, as shown in the following screenshot, is the same for both modes of the gateway. If you are having an issue with your gateway, then this is a good place to start troubleshooting. This page allows you to enable detailed logging by moving the **Additional logging** slider to the right. These logs can be used for troubleshooting purposes, but should not be enabled unless you are experiencing issues with the gateway. This is because enabling added logging can cause performance issues. These logs can be exported to a single .zip file by selecting the **Export logs** link under the **Gateway logs** heading. New gateway installations include support for **Even Tracing for Windows (ETW)** logging as well.

You can also ensure that the communication pathways are open between the gateway and the Power BI service by selecting the **Start new test** link under the **Network ports test** heading. This is useful if you wish to see whether there might be something such as a firewall blocking communication:

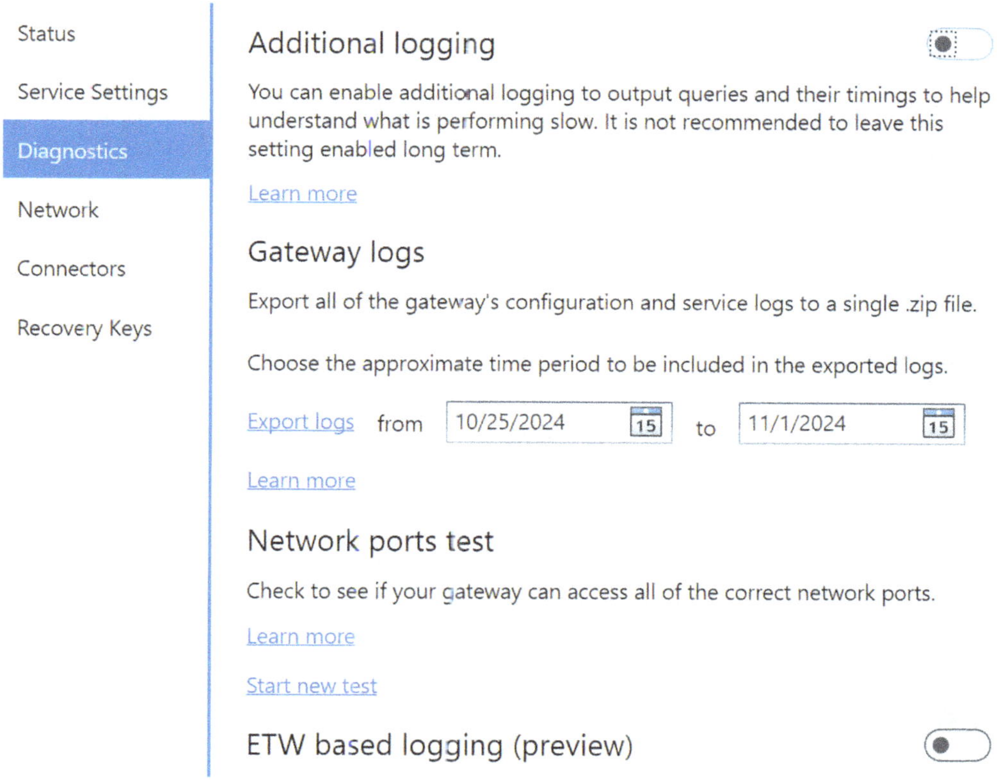

Status	**Additional logging**
Service Settings	
Diagnostics	You can enable additional logging to output queries and their timings to help understand what is performing slow. It is not recommended to leave this setting enabled long term.
Network	
Connectors	Learn more
Recovery Keys	**Gateway logs**

Export all of the gateway's configuration and service logs to a single .zip file.

Choose the approximate time period to be included in the exported logs.

Export logs   from   10/25/2024   to   11/1/2024

Learn more

Network ports test

Check to see if your gateway can access all of the correct network ports.

Learn more

Start new test

ETW based logging (preview)

Figure 11.13 – Diagnostics page

Now, let's look at the **Network** page.

Network

The **Network** page, as shown in the following screenshot, is the same for both modes of the gateway. Here, you can see the status of the network connectivity between the gateway and the Power BI service.

In addition, you can turn HTTPS mode on or off to force the gateway to use either **HyperText Transfer Protocol Secure (HTTPS)** or **Transmission Control Protocol (TCP)** as the network communication protocol. In either mode, network traffic is encrypted. It is recommended that you leave HTTPS mode with its default settings. If HTTPS mode is off, the gateway will still automatically switch to using HTTPS mode if it is unable to communicate via direct TCP. This setting always reflects the current network communication protocol being used by the gateway:

Figure 11.14 – Network page

Now, let's look at the **Connectors** page.

Connectors

The **Connectors** page, as shown in the following screenshot, is nearly identical for both modes of the gateway. Power BI is an extremely extensible platform, and this is also true of the data gateway. The **Connectors** page specifies the file location where custom data connectors are installed. Custom data connectors allow developers to create data connectors to applications, services, and data sources that aren't currently supported:

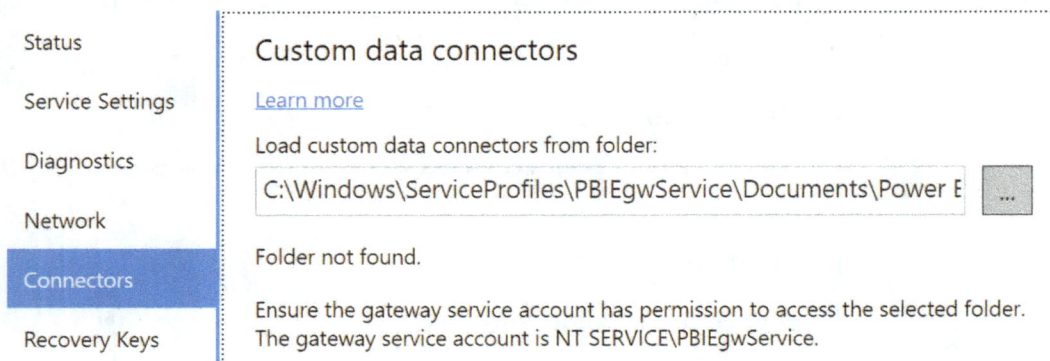

Figure 11.15 – Connectors page

Recovery Keys

The **Recovery Keys** page only appears when you sign in to the data gateway. This page simply allows you to set new recovery keys. You will need the current recovery key to set a new recovery key, so make certain to keep your recovery keys safe!

Now that we have investigated the additional configuration settings for the data gateway, let's look at managing gateways in the Power BI service.

Managing a data gateway

Once the gateways have been installed and configured, standard mode gateways can be managed via the Power BI service. To manage a standard mode gateway, do the following:

1. Log in to the Power BI service.
2. Click the gear icon at the top right and choose **Manage connections and gateways**, as shown in the following screenshot. Depending on your screen resolution and level of zoom, you may need to click on the ellipses (...) to the right of the **Search** box, then **Settings**, and then **Manage connections and gateways**:

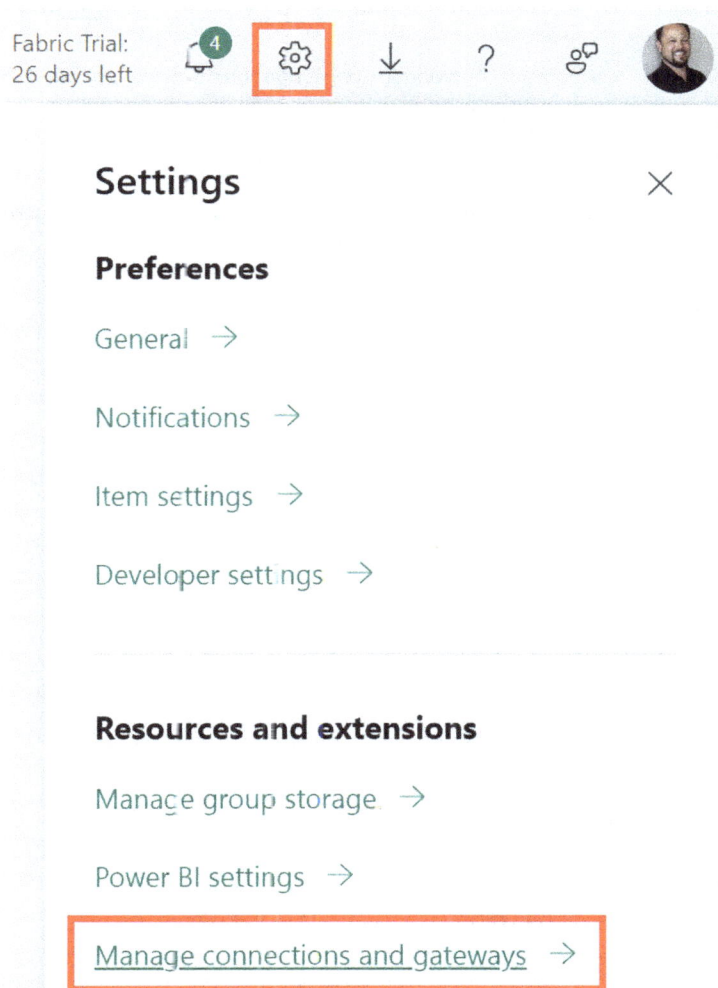

Figure 11.16 – Accessing the Manage connections and gateways link

After selecting the **Manage connections and gateways** link from the gear icon in the Power BI service, the **Manage Connections and Gateways** page is displayed, as shown in the following screenshot:

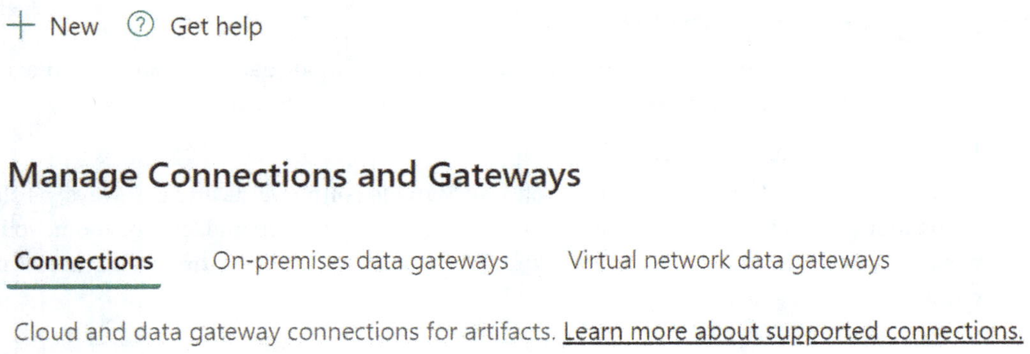

$+$ New   ⑦ Get help

Manage Connections and Gateways

<u>Connections</u>   On-premises data gateways   Virtual network data gateways

Cloud and data gateway connections for artifacts. <u>Learn more about supported connections.</u>

Figure 11.17 – Manage Connections and Gateways page

The **Connections** tab lists all of the data source connections contained in the semantic models in the service. New connections can be created using the **+ New** button.

The **On-premises data gateways** tab lists all installed gateways owned by the user. Selecting a gateway activates several options, including the ability to configure **Settings**:

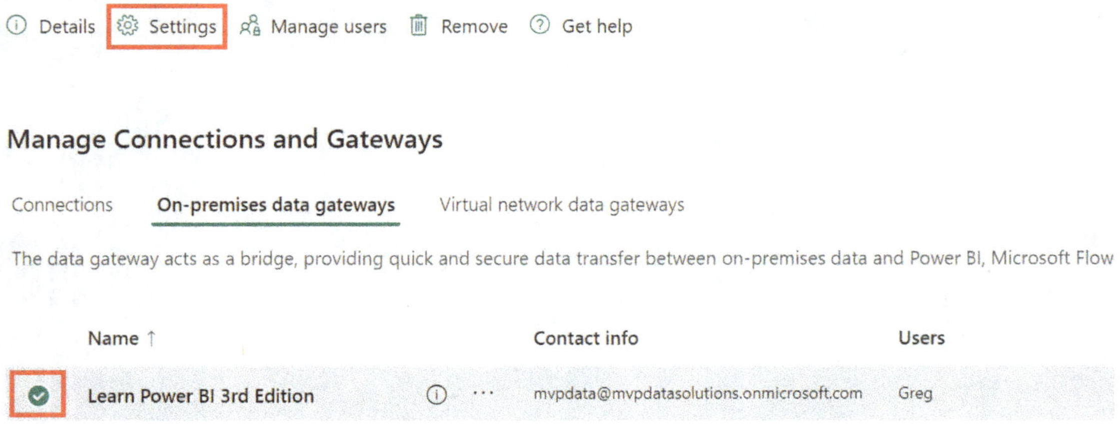

ⓘ Details   ⚙ Settings   ♟ Manage users   🗑 Remove   ⑦ Get help

Manage Connections and Gateways

Connections   **On-premises data gateways**   Virtual network data gateways

The data gateway acts as a bridge, providing quick and secure data transfer between on-premises data and Power BI, Microsoft Flow

Name ↑			Contact info	Users
✅ **Learn Power BI 3rd Edition**	ⓘ	⋯	mvpdata@mvpdatasolutions.onmicrosoft.com	Greg

Figure 11.18 – Managing on-premises data gateways

Selecting **Settings** displays the **Settings** pane on the right-hand side of the page:

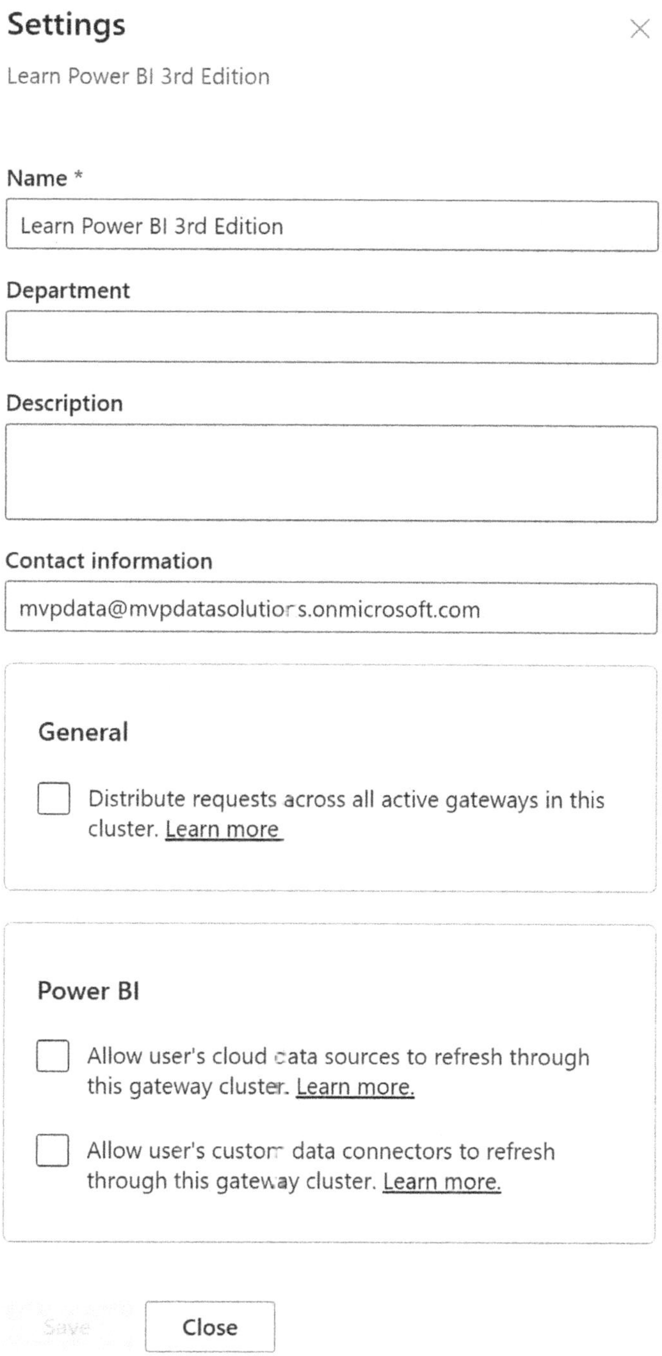

Settings   ✕

Learn Power BI 3rd Edition

Name *

Learn Power BI 3rd Edition

Department

Description

Contact information

mvpdata@mvpdatasolutiors.onmicrosoft.com

General

☐ Distribute requests across all active gateways in this cluster. Learn more

Power BI

☐ Allow user's cloud data sources to refresh through this gateway cluster. Learn more.

☐ Allow user's custom data connectors to refresh through this gateway cluster. Learn more.

Save   Close

Figure 11.19 – Gateway settings

The first four settings listed are primarily informational. These include **Name, Department, Description**, and **Contact information**. However, it is important to understand the three checkboxes after these four informational fields, which are as follows:

- The first checkbox is **Distribute requests across all active gateways in this cluster**. Installing a gateway creates a single gateway cluster. If additional gateways are installed within that single cluster, the load balancing across gateways within the cluster is random by default. Checking this box forces refresh requests to be distributed evenly across all of the gateways in the cluster. Only enable this checkbox if you're using multiple gateways in a single cluster and you wish for the load balancing to not be random.

- The next checkbox is **Allow user's cloud data sources to refresh through this gateway cluster**. This setting is used when you wish to have a single query that merges or appends both cloud and on-premises data sources. It is a good idea to enable this setting since, if this setting is not enabled, any queries that merge with both cloud and on-premises data sources within a single query will fail to refresh.

- The third checkbox is **Allow user's custom data connectors to refresh through this gateway cluster**. This setting allows custom data connectors to be refreshed through this gateway. Note that the custom data connector must be installed in the gateway's custom data connector's folder, as specified on the **Connectors** page of the gateway configuration application. You should only enable this checkbox if you're using custom data connectors.

Next to the **Settings** button is the **Manage users** button. This allows you to designate other administrators or connection creators for the gateway besides yourself. Simply enter the email address of someone within your Power BI tenant:

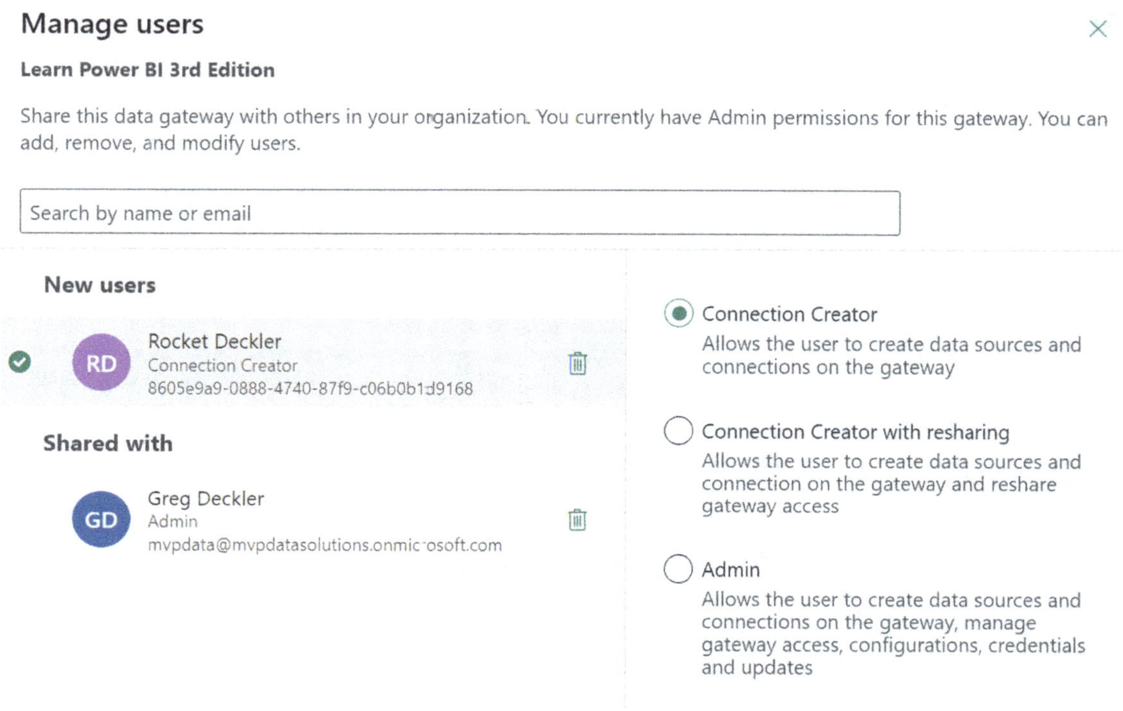

Manage users   ✕

Learn Power BI 3rd Edition

Share this data gateway with others in your organization. You currently have Admin permissions for this gateway. You can add, remove, and modify users.

Search by name or email

New users

⊘ **RD** Rocket Deckler
Connection Creator
8605e9a9-0888-4740-87f9-c06b0b1d9168   🗑

Shared with

GD Greg Deckler
Admin
mvpdata@mvpdatasolutions.onmicrosoft.com   🗑

◉ Connection Creator
Allows the user to create data sources and
connections on the gateway

◯ Connection Creator with resharing
Allows the user to create data sources and
connection on the gateway and reshare
gateway access

◯ Admin
Allows the user to create data sources and
connections on the gateway, manage
gateway access, configurations, credentials
and updates

Figure 11.20 – Manage gateway users

Gateway administrators and users can also be removed by selecting the trash can icon next to their names.

Next to the **Manage users** button is the **Remove** button. Even if you uninstall a gateway from a computer or turn off the computer that a gateway is installed on, the gateway cluster remains registered in the Power BI service. Therefore, to remove the gateway from the service, you must select the gateway and click **Remove**.

Let's now take a look at adding connections to a gateway in the service.

Adding connections

Unlike personal gateways, which automatically map themselves to available semantic model connections, standard mode gateways must have their connections created and then mapped to data sources. To create a connection, do the following:

1. On the **Connections** tab, choose **+ New**. The **New connection** pane is displayed:

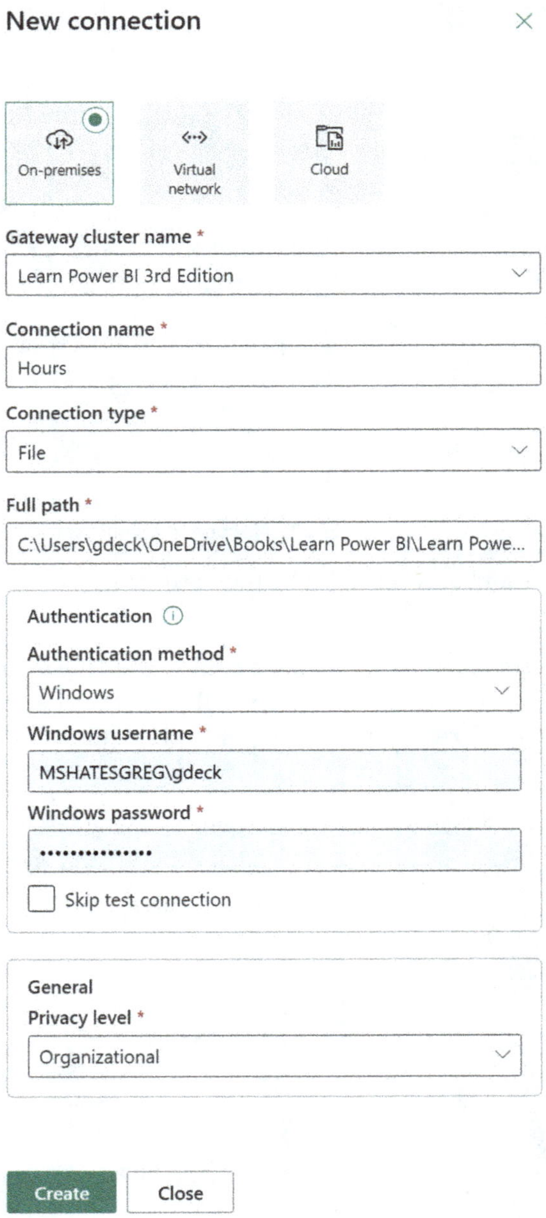

Figure 11.21 – Manually adding a data source

This page varies, depending on the **Connection type** parameter that's selected. However, in general, this page allows the gateway administrator to manually define a data source that can be refreshed using the gateway. Once a connection is created, selecting the connection on the **Connections** tab allows you to manage users. This controls who is allowed to use the connection on the gateway:

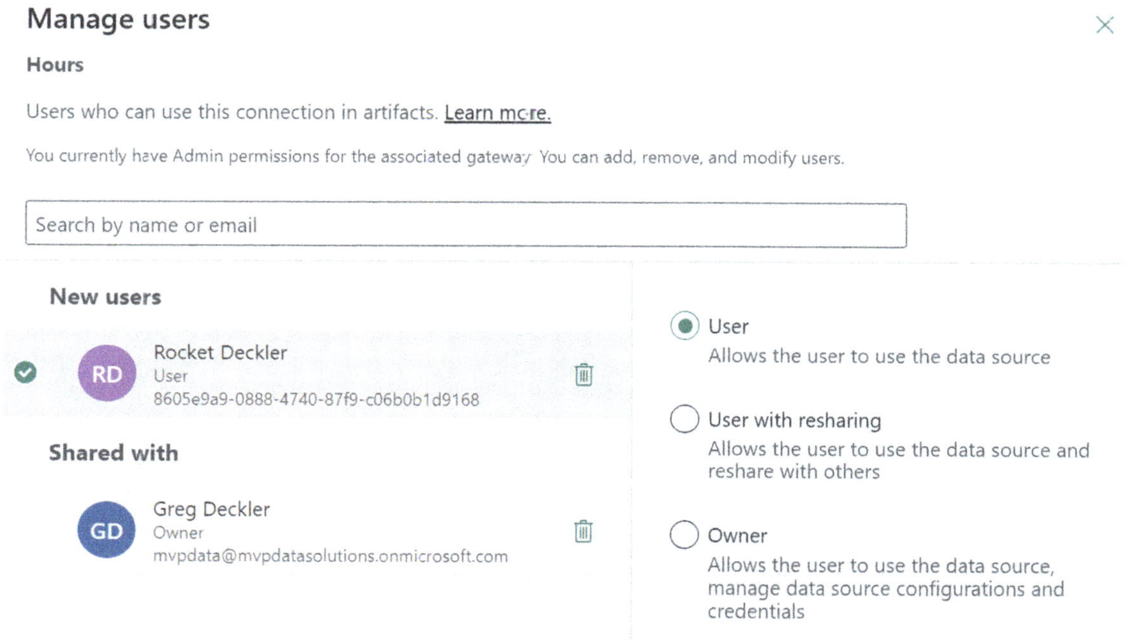

Figure 11.22 – Manage connection users

Now that you understand the management of gateways and connections, let's move on to how to refresh semantic models.

Refreshing semantic models

Now that a gateway is installed and configured, it is time to enable our semantic model so that it can automatically refresh. This means that if we add to or replace the data in our file or database, the Power BI service can automatically refresh that data within the published semantic model so that the associated dashboards and reports are kept up to date.

Scheduling a refresh

To schedule a refresh for a semantic model, do the following:

1. Log in to the Power BI service. Navigate to your workspace.

2. For the desired semantic model, hover over your semantic model, click the ellipsis (...), and choose **Settings**:

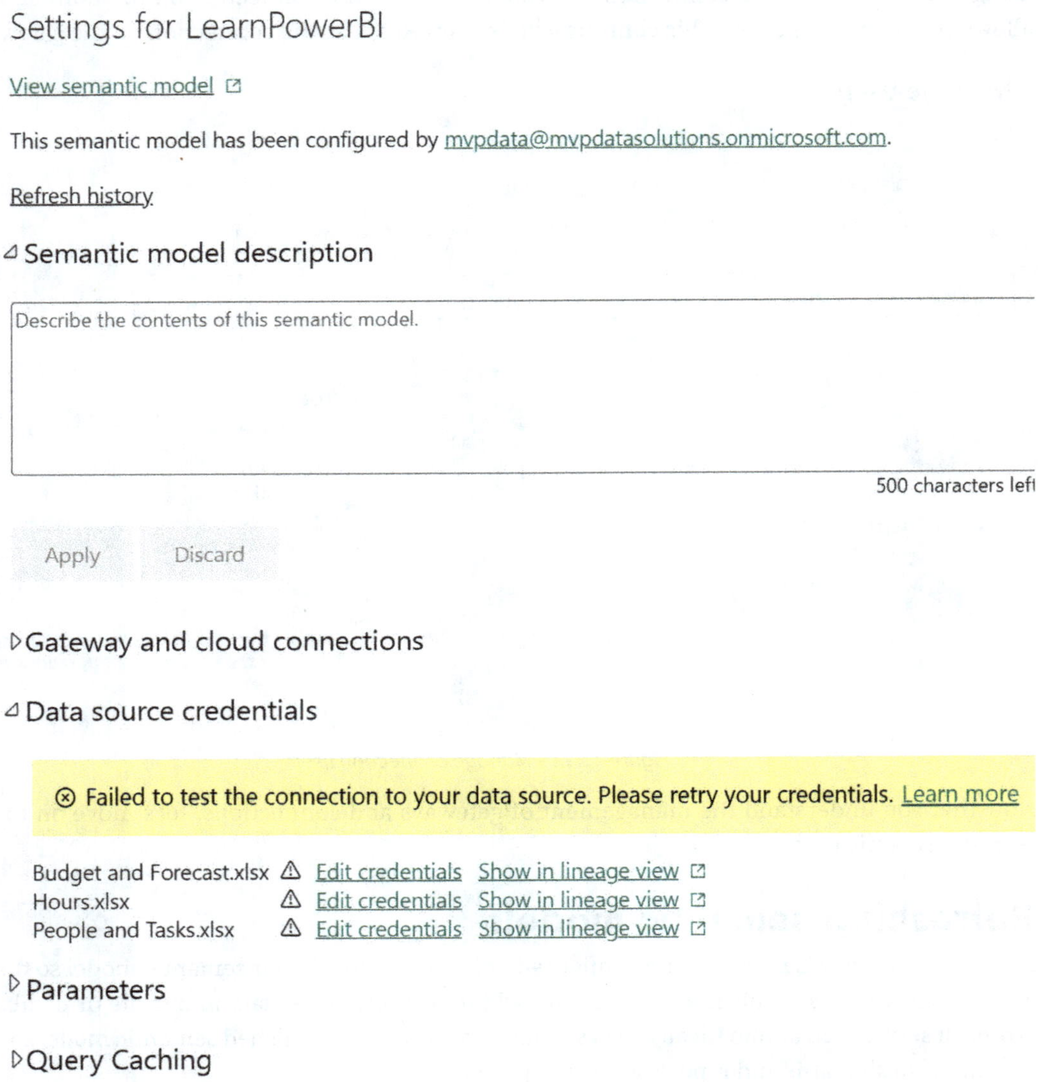

Settings for LearnPowerBI

View semantic model ⟐

This semantic model has been configured by mvpdata@mvpdatasolutions.onmicrosoft.com.

Refresh history

◁ Semantic model description

Describe the contents of this semantic model.

500 characters left

Apply   Discard

▷ Gateway and cloud connections

◁ Data source credentials

⊗ Failed to test the connection to your data source. Please retry your credentials. Learn more

Budget and Forecast.xlsx ⚠ Edit credentials Show in lineage view ⟐
Hours.xlsx   ⚠ Edit credentials Show in lineage view ⟐
People and Tasks.xlsx   ⚠ Edit credentials Show in lineage view ⟐

▷ Parameters

▷ Query Caching

Figure 11.23 – The semantic model's settings page

3. Expand the **Gateway and cloud connections** section, as shown here:

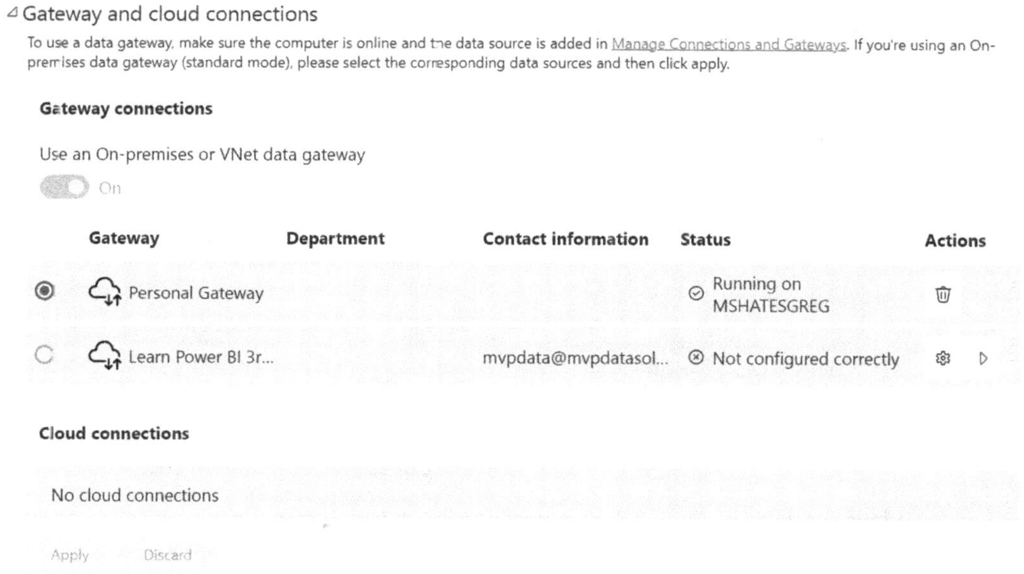

◿ Gateway and cloud connections

To use a data gateway, make sure the computer is online and the data source is added in Manage Connections and Gateways. If you're using an On-premises data gateway (standard mode), please select the corresponding data sources and then click apply.

Gateway connections

Use an On-premises or VNet data gateway

⬤ On

	Gateway	Department	Contact information	Status		Actions
⦿	☁ Personal Gateway			⊘ Running on MSHATESGREG		🗑
○	☁ Learn Power BI 3r...		mvpdata@mvpdatasol...	⊗ Not configured correctly		⚙ ▷

Cloud connections

No cloud connections

Apply   Discard

Figure 11.24 – Gateway and cloud connections section

Note that any installed personal gateways, as well as any standard mode gateways that you have access to, appear under this section. As shown in the preceding screenshot, the personal mode gateway displays a checkbox under **Status** indicating that it is properly configured to refresh the semantic model.

However, the standard mode gateway status is **Not configured correctly**. This is because the data sources that are used by the semantic model haven't been added to the gateway. This is an important distinction between the different modes of the gateway. Gateways that are installed in personal mode do not require data sources to be added to the gateway and managed, but gateways that are installed in standard mode require additional steps to be used. If you're using **Personal Gateway**, skip to *Step 11*; otherwise, continue with *Step 4*.

4. **Standard mode only:** To add the data sources to our standard mode data gateway, click the right arrow icon beneath **Actions**. This displays a **Data sources included in this semantic model** list, as shown in the following screenshot:

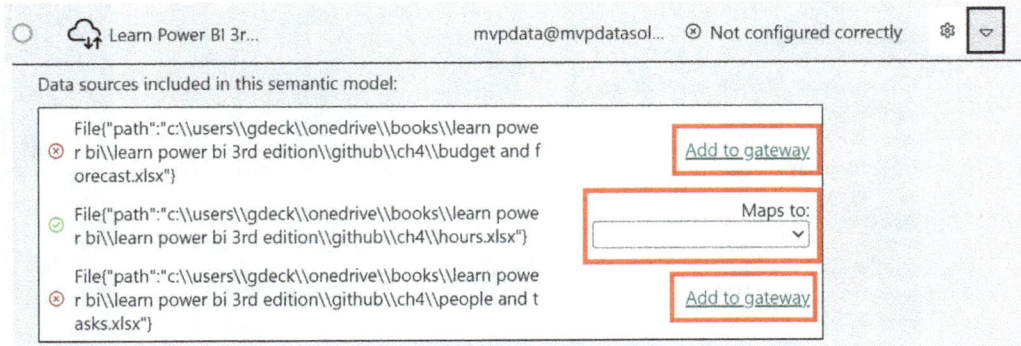

Figure 11.25 – Data sources included in this semantic model

5. **Standard mode only:** To add data sources to the data gateway, simply click the **Add to gateway** link next to the data source. This transports you to the **New connection** page for the gateway, as shown in *Figure 11.21*:

    Again, this page will vary, depending on the type of data source, but by default, **Connection type** and some other information will already be filled in on the page. Complete any other required information; in this case, provide a descriptive name, as well as your **Authentication** settings. When you're finished, click the **Create** button.

6. **Standard mode only:** After clicking the **Create** button, if the data source has been set up and tested successfully, you will be transported back to the semantic model's settings page. Expand the **Gateway connections** section and click the right arrow icon in the **Actions** area for the standard mode gateway, as shown in the following screenshot:

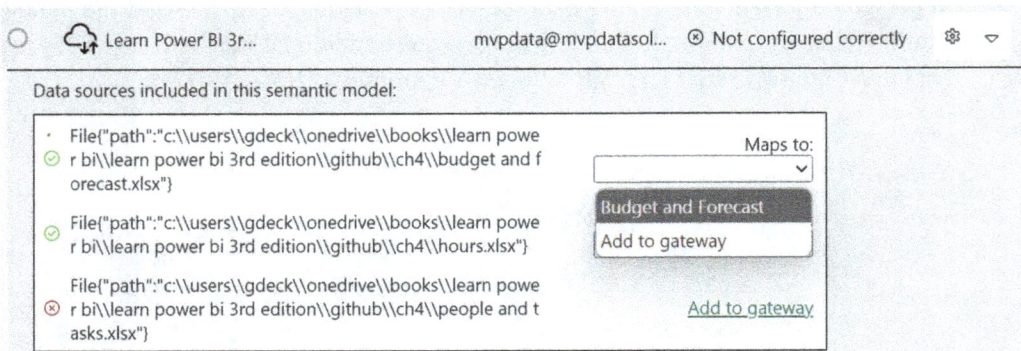

Figure 11.26 – Mapping a data source

7. **Standard mode only:** This time, you should have a green checkmark instead of a red **x** next to your first data source. In addition, instead of an **Add to gateway** link, there should be a **Maps to** drop-down box. Click this drop-down box and note that the name of your newly created gateway data source definition appears, which, in this case, is **Budget and Forecast**. This is why it is important to provide good, descriptive names when defining data sources for a gateway!

8. **Standard mode only:** Repeat *Step 5* and *Step 7* for the two additional data sources. When you are finished, your standard mode gateway should show green text and a status of **Running on**. In addition, your data sources should display green checkmarks and have **Maps to** drop-down boxes, as shown in the following screenshot:

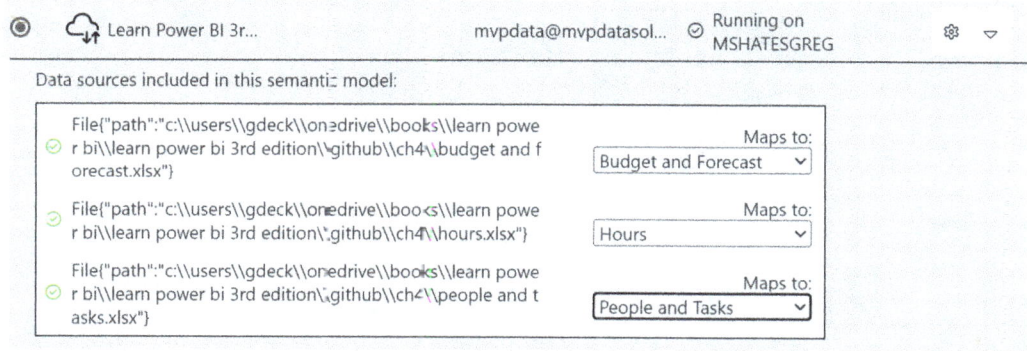

Figure 11.27 – Successfully added and mapped data sources

9. **Standard mode only:** Map each of the data sources to their corresponding gateway data source definitions using the **Maps to** drop-down menu and click the **Apply** button. Note that, in the **Data source credentials** section, the yellow warning banner goes away, and that you are no longer required to enter your credentials. This is because the credentials have been defined as part of the gateway connection definitions. Skip to *Step 12*.

10. **Personal mode only:** If you're using a gateway in personal mode, you must enter the authentication credentials that will be used to access the data in the **Data source credentials** section. Any data source that has a warning icon next to the **Edit credentials** link must have credentials entered for it. To do this, click the **Edit credentials** link next to a data source and sign in. Repeat this for each data source. Note that the warning icon disappears once the data source has been correctly configured. Once all of the data sources have been correctly configured, the yellow warning banner will disappear:

Figure 11.28 – Correctly configured credentials for a personal mode gateway

11. Now that the appropriate gateway and credentials have been configured, it is time to configure the refresh schedule. Expand the **Refresh** section, as shown here:

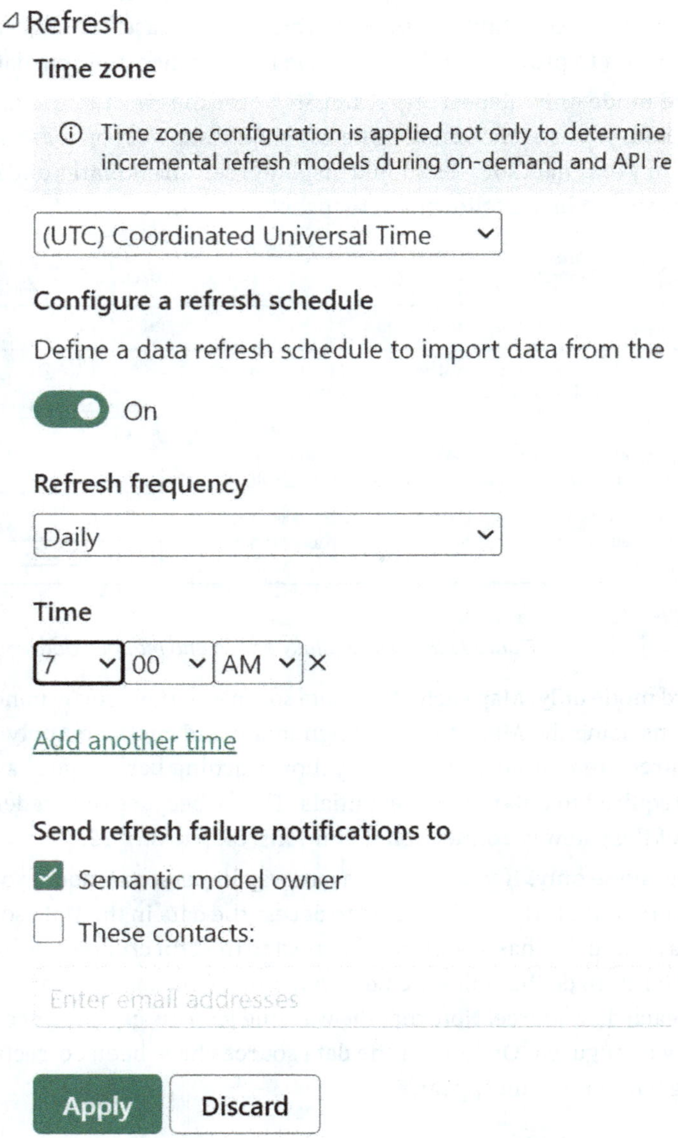

◁ Refresh

Time zone

    ⓘ Time zone configuration is applied not only to determine
       incremental refresh models during on-demand and API re

| (UTC) Coordinated Universal Time ⌄ |

Configure a refresh schedule

Define a data refresh schedule to import data from the

🟢◯ On

Refresh frequency

| Daily ⌄ |

Time

| 7 ⌄ | 00 ⌄ | AM ⌄ | ✕

Add another time

Send refresh failure notifications to

☑ Semantic model owner

☐ These contacts:

| Enter email addresses |

Apply **Discard**

Figure 11.29 – Scheduled refresh

12. Toggle **Configure a refresh schedule** to **On**. You can set **Refresh frequency** to either **Daily** or **Weekly**, as well as setting **Time zone**. Click **Add another time** under the **Time** area.

13. Use the drop-down boxes to set the desired time for the refresh. If you're using a **Weekly** refresh schedule, you can also select the days of the week when refreshes occur. Multiple times can be added to keep a semantic model refreshed by clicking the **Add another time** link. Up to eight scheduled refreshes can be configured per day with Power BI Pro and up to 48 refreshes per day with Premium Per User and Fabric SKUs (formally, Power BI Premium).

14. Once you've finished adding the specified refresh times, you can add an email address that notifications will be sent to if there is a problem with the data refresh. Then, you can click the **Apply** button.

With that, you have finished learning about the basics of how to keep your data refreshed!

Summary

This chapter was all about how to configure Power BI to keep semantic models that are published to the Power BI service up to date automatically. We learned how to download, install, and configure the on-premises data gateway in both standard (enterprise) and personal modes. We also learned how to manage gateways within the Power BI service, as well as to configure data sources for use in gateways. Finally, we learned how to schedule the semantic models for automatic refresh by the Power BI service.

You have now learned all of the basic skills that you will need when working with Power BI, which has opened the door to an entirely new and exciting world. In the next chapter, we dive deeper into the world of deploying, governing, and adopting Power BI.

Questions

As an activity, try to answer the following questions on your own:

- What is the purpose of the on-premises data gateway?
- In what two modes can the data gateway be installed?
- What must you do to ensure that the data gateway starts after rebooting the computer that the gateway is installed on?
- What feature allows for redundancy and load balancing when you're refreshing data?
- What two methods can be used to add a data source to a data gateway?
- How many times can a semantic model be refreshed per day?

Further reading

You can check out the following links for additional information regarding this chapter's topics:

- *What is an on-premises data gateway?*: https://learn.microsoft.com/en-us/power-bi/connect-data/service-gateway-onprem
- *Installing an on-premises data gateway*: https://learn.microsoft.com/en-us/data-integration/gateway/service-gateway-install
- *On-premises data gateway in-depth*: https://learn.microsoft.com/en-us/power-bi/connect-data/service-gateway-onprem-indepth

- *On-premises data gateway architecture*: `https://learn.microsoft.com/en-us/data-integration/gateway/service-gateway-onprem-indepth`

- *Use a personal gateway in Power BI*: `https://learn.microsoft.com/en-us/power-bi/connect-data/service-gateway-personal-mode`

- *Troubleshooting gateways – Power BI*: `https://learn.microsoft.com/en-us/power-bi/connect-data/service-gateway-onprem-tshoot`

- *Getting started with data connectors*: `https://github.com/Microsoft/DataConnectors`

- *Data refresh in Power BI*: `https://learn.microsoft.com/en-us/power-bi/connect-data/refresh-data`

- *Configuring scheduled refresh*: `https://learn.microsoft.com/en-us/power-bi/connect-data/refresh-scheduled-refresh`

Join our community on Discord

Join our community's Discord space for discussions with the authors and other readers: `https://discord.gg/hvqvgyGH`.

Part 4

The Future

You are now well on your way to a rewarding career in business intelligence or enhancing your current job with your new Power BI knowledge. This part covers what comes next, including how Power BI is deployed, governed, and adopted within an organization, how Microsoft Fabric and Copilot can be used to enhance your solution, and some job and career advice.

This part of the book includes the following chapters:

- *Chapter 12, Deploying, Governing, and Adopting Power BI*
- *Chapter 13, Working with Microsoft Fabric and Copilot*
- *Chapter 14, Putting Your Knowledge to Use*

12

Deploying, Governing, and Adopting Power BI

Now that you have learned the fundamentals of working with Power BI and have seen Power BI's powerful analytics and visualization features firsthand, it is time to turn our attention to the broader topics of deployment, governance, and the adoption of Power BI within an organization. This chapter is designed to help you understand the organizational issues and requirements of Power BI within an enterprise.

Understanding the bigger picture when it comes to Power BI will help you better understand and navigate the journey of Power BI use and adoption within your organization. To this end, we cover the various deployment and usage scenarios used by most organizations. In addition, we cover the important organizational topics of governance and administration, providing detailed information on the configuration of Power BI tenant settings, as well as a phased deployment process for the development and creation of Power BI content. Finally, we cover the topic of adoption and propose adoption strategies that can assist in diffusing the disruptive technology of self-service analytics and business intelligence throughout an organization.

The following topics are covered in this chapter:

- Understanding usage models
- Governing and administering Power BI
- Adopting Power BI

Technical requirements

You will need the following to successfully complete this chapter:

- An internet connection.
- A Microsoft 365 account or Power BI trial.
- If you have skipped any of the previous chapters, you can download the LearnPowerBI.zip file from GitHub at https://github.com/PacktPublishing/Learn-Microsoft-Power-BI_3E/tree/main/Chapter8.

Understanding usage models

Power BI provides considerable flexibility regarding how organizations deploy and adopt the technology. There are nearly limitless ways to organize and use such things as workspaces, apps, and scorecards, as well as how organizations choose to share and distribute content. We call the overall architecture and plan for how organizations deploy and utilize Power BI **usage models**. Usage models encapsulate how an organization adopts and utilizes the various components of Power BI in order to provide governance and processes around the use of Power BI.

The following sections explore some of the more common usage models for Power BI. However, keep in mind that there are nearly unlimited usage models as organizations can combine aspects of different ones in different ways in order to facilitate the particular needs of their organization. The usage models covered here can be thought of as archetypes, or base usage scenarios, that demonstrate particular desired outcomes or traits.

Anarchy model

Many Power BI implementations start as near chaos or anarchy, the grassroots adoption of Power BI by end users. This model is depicted in *Figure 12.1*:

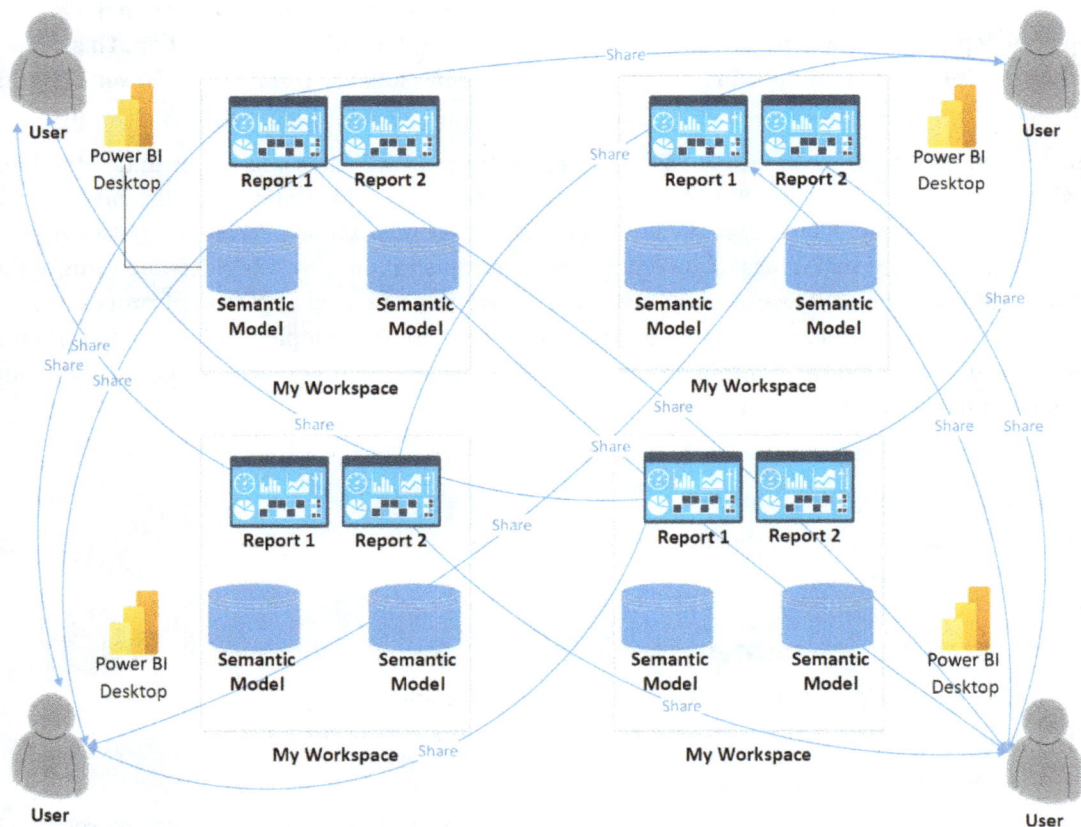

Figure 12.1 – Anarchy: no governing model for report development and sharing

If *Figure 12.1* looks messy, that is intentional. In the **anarchy model**, end users just start connecting to data sources, building semantic models, reports, and dashboards, and then sharing those reports with whomever. This is the epitome of grassroots, self-service business intelligence and mimics how many organizations use Excel. Under this model, there is little to no governance or control.

While the anarchy model empowers business users, there are definite drawbacks. For example, there is no real single source of truth. Different business users may calculate various business metrics differently. There can also be a tremendous amount of duplication of effort. Finally, without any *official* reporting, there is no guarantee that users are able to access and view the appropriate reports and dashboards.

It is important to understand that while the anarchy model should absolutely not be the end journey of an organization's Power BI usage model, the anarchy model is present with all deployments of Power BI. All Power BI users get their own workspace, **My workspace**, where they can create their own semantic models, reports, and dashboards. This is okay and is, in fact, a good thing. The anarchy model represents the citizen data analyst and citizen data scientist. It is a key component of building a data culture within an organization. And if anarchy is not occurring in Power BI, it is certainly occurring somewhere else, such as in Excel. By leveraging Power BI for anarchy, users are free to explore and harness data and share their insights with others.

Centralized model

At the opposite end of the spectrum from the anarchy model is the **centralized model.** In the centralized model, a single individual or group of individuals (often the IT department) controls the creation of all official semantic models, reporting, and distribution. The centralized model is shown in *Figure 12.2*:

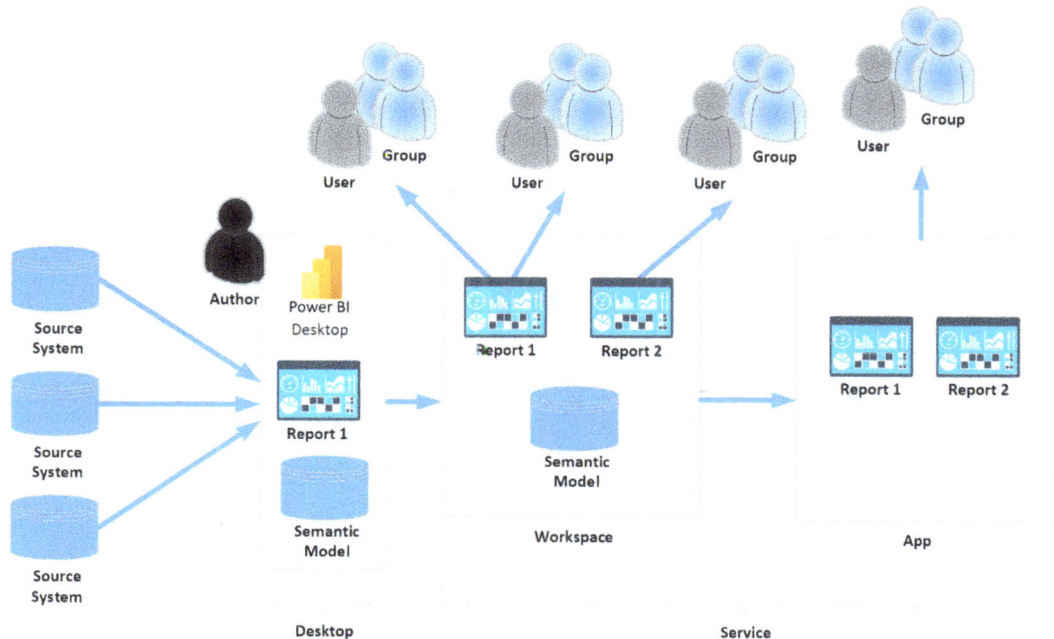

Figure 12.2 – Centralized: a central group controls report development and sharing

The main strengths of the centralized model are trust, governance, and efficiency. Because the semantic models and reports are created by a central team of business intelligence professionals, the organization can trust that the metrics presented are consistent and accurate. In addition, efficiency is achieved since business intelligence professionals are likely more skilled than the average business user, and as there is central control, it is unlikely that there is excessive duplication of effort.

The main weakness of the centralized model is difficulty scaling to large-sized organizations. The centralized model creates a funnel point for all official reporting, and it is common for this to be a constraint to the business. Business users desiring certain information or metrics are required to make requests to the centralized team. It is not uncommon for there to be more requests for reports than the centralized team can handle within a timeframe the organization desires, creating a backlog and leaving organizational users wanting more.

An additional weakness of the centralized model is one of requirement gathering. It is often necessary for a liaison to exist between the centralized IT team and the business users. IT people tend to know a lot about the technology side of the equation but are often not deeply knowledgeable about the actual business, the metrics important to the business, and exactly how the business users wish to view and interact with the data.

Federated model

To solve the scale issues inherent in the centralized model, organizations can adopt the **federated model** instead, as depicted in *Figure 12.3*:

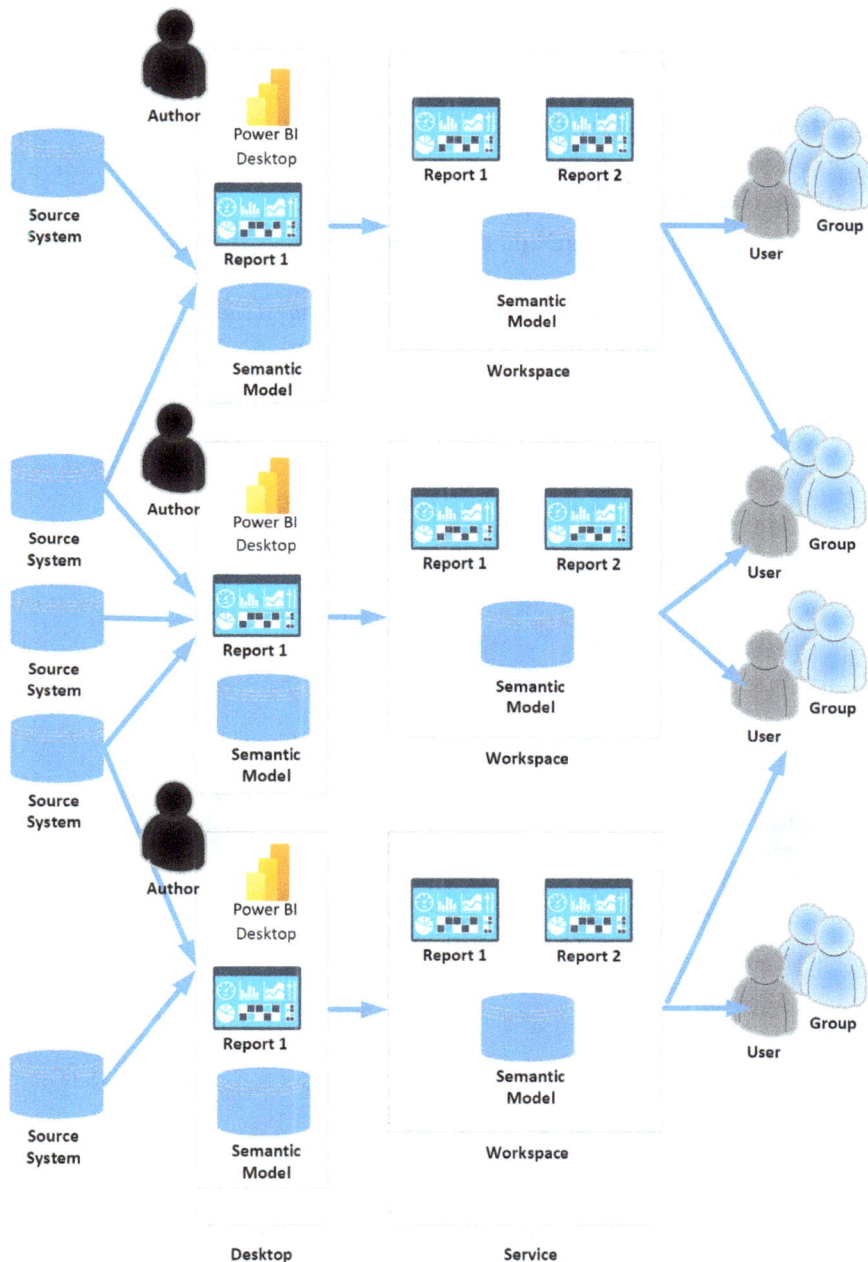

Figure 12.3 – Federated: report development and sharing is spread throughout the organization

Similar in concept to the centralized model, the federated model solves the scaling problem by creating multiple teams of semantic model and report authors, such as one per organizational unit or department. For example, the sales, finance, and supply chain departments would each have their own team of business intelligence professionals responsible for the creation of semantic models and reports for their respective departments.

While the federated model solves the scaling problem inherent in the centralized model, the federated model can lead to the duplication of effort and metrics being calculated differently and does not necessarily solve the need to translate requirements between the business and the federated teams of business intelligence professionals.

Golden semantic model

A popular method of asset development and deployment includes the concept of creating multiple reports from a single, central semantic model that effectively serves as a sort of datamart, sometimes called a **golden semantic model**. This model is depicted in *Figure 12.4*:

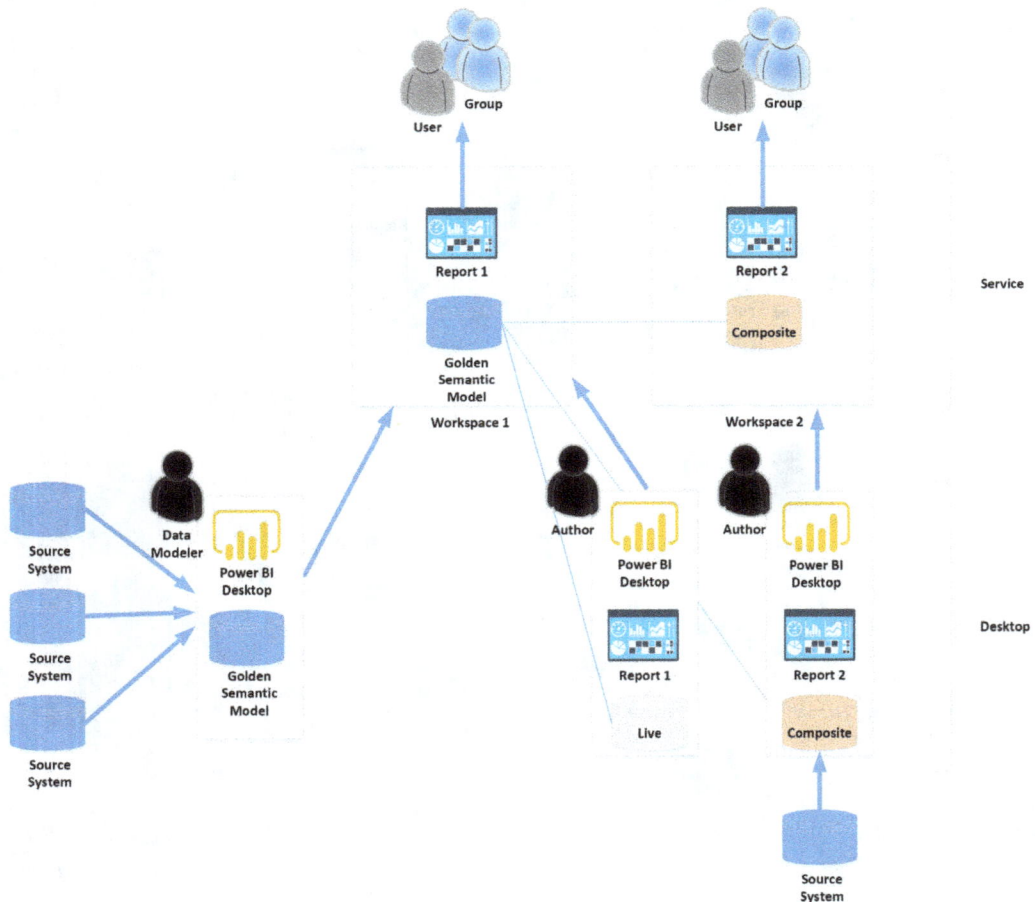

Figure 12.4 – Golden semantic: one group controls the semantic models, and another group controls report creation and sharing

A golden semantic model is derived from the term *gold standard*. A golden semantic model represents the single source of truth (or *gold standard*) of cleansed data and consistent business metrics. Under the golden semantic model paradigm, a central team of business intelligence professionals (usually IT) is solely responsible for the creation of semantic models and business metric calculations. These semantic models are often created and published without any official reporting.

The report creation is done by separate teams of content creators who connect live to the semantic model within their own PBIX files and develop reports. Content creators may use only the golden semantic model for their content or may create **composite models** that combine the golden semantic model with additional data.

The golden semantic model paradigm is popular because it facilitates the separation of duties between the IT team and the business. The IT team is concerned with data lineage, semantic model sprawl, and the accuracy and consistency of metrics and governs and controls the creation of semantic models, while the business users, who deeply understand their business domain and desire speedy analysis and reporting, control the creation of content. In this way, the golden semantic model paradigm provides the *best of both worlds* between the centralized and distributed model approaches.

Hybrid model

It is not uncommon for multiple usage models to be used simultaneously within the same organization in order to accommodate different needs within the organization. One such hybrid model is shown in *Figure 12.5*:

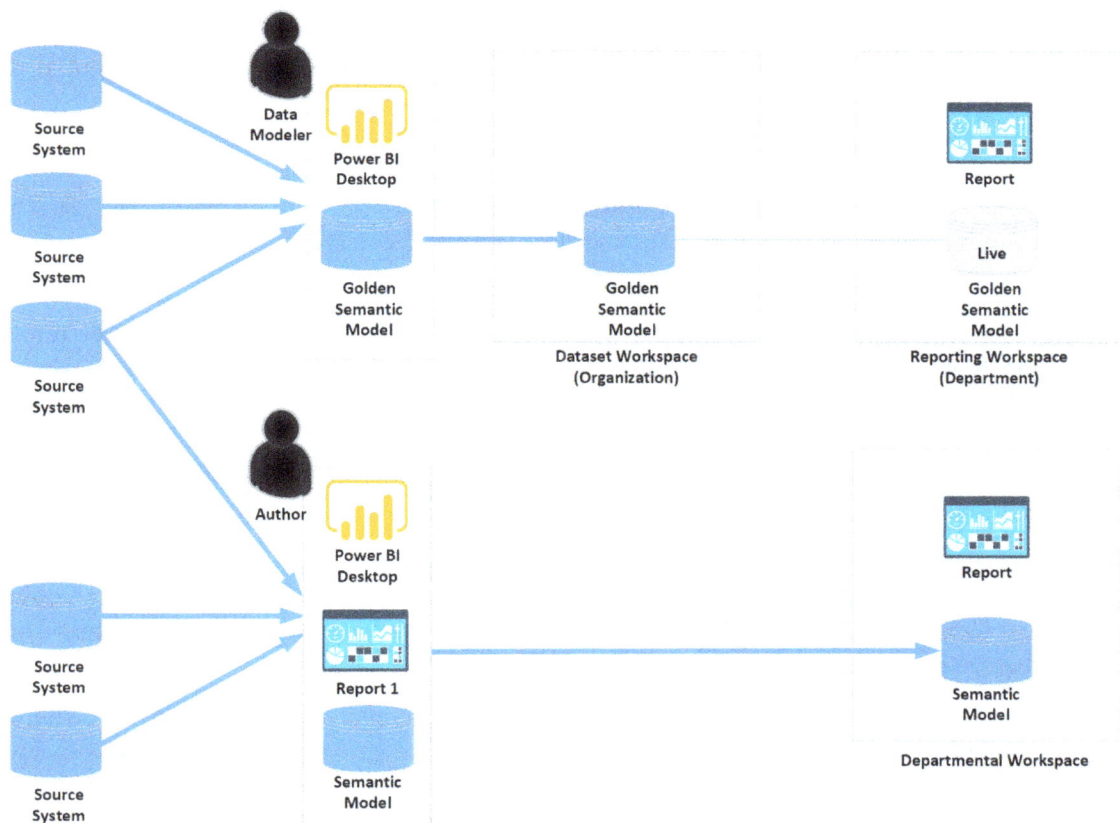

Figure 12.5 – Hybrid: a combination of multiple governance models

In the hybrid model depicted in *Figure 12.5*, the organization has chosen to combine the golden semantic model with the federated model. Golden semantic models are used for official organizational content created by the centralized team of IT business professionals. However, departmental workspaces are also created to allow the individual departments within the organization flexibility in creating content that is used internally within the department.

The examples covered here are simply examples of some of the more common usage models found within organizations that use Power BI and are certainly not the only ways in which organizations might deploy and leverage Power BI. However, keeping these base archetypes in mind can help you determine the correct usage model or combination of usage models that will meet the needs of your organization.

Now that we have learned about several different usage models for Power BI, let's next take a closer look at governing and administering Power BI.

Governing and administering Power BI

Governance of Power BI is a broad and potentially complex subject that can encompass the overall data governance within an organization as well as Power BI Desktop and the Power BI service. However, at its core, governance for Power BI is simply a set of established rules and policies regarding what people can do with organizational data.

The overall goals of governance in the context of Power BI are as follows:

- Empower business users to use data for making decisions.
- Comply with applicable government, industry, and contractual regulations.
- Establish rules that comply with organizational requirements.

The usage models in the *Understanding usage models* section within this chapter are one way of implementing governance. For example, controlling who is allowed to publish *official* semantic models is an example of governance. By centralizing the creation of semantic models and metrics, business users can be empowered because this ensures that those metrics or **key performance indicators** (**KPIs**) are consistent and accurate. In addition, those creating the semantic models can ensure that only appropriate data is exposed to the business, thereby avoiding regulatory compliance issues.

Many of these governance and administration settings are controlled in the **Admin portal**. To go to the **Admin portal**, select the gear icon in the upper-right corner of the Power BI service and choose **Admin portal** under **Governance and insights**. Alternatively, click the ellipsis (**...**) in the upper-right corner, then **Settings**, and then **Admin portal**.

The following sections explore additional important governance controls, such as classifying content, tenant settings, organizational visuals, deploying Power BI content, gateway governance, and Purview.

Classifying content

Power BI includes a number of different methods for classifying content within the Power BI service. Classifying content helps users discover relevant information more easily. Types of classification include:

- Domains
- Tags
- Endorsements
- Featured content

Let's briefly explore each of these types of classification methods.

Domains

Domains are Microsoft's attempt to support a federated data architecture or data mesh. Domains can be particularly useful if employing the federated usage model covered earlier in this chapter.

Domains are simply a logical container or tag, enabling workspaces to be organized based on domains and users to filter content by domain. To create a domain, perform the following steps:

1. Go to the **Admin portal**.
2. Select **Domains**.
3. Select **Create new domain**:

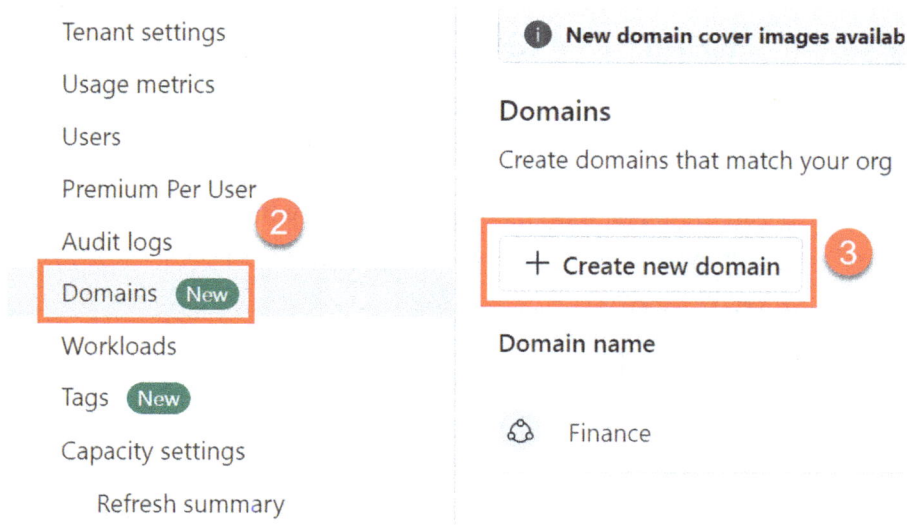

Figure 12.6 – Creating a domain

4. Enter a name for the new domain and, optionally, specify **Domain admins**. The user creating the domain is automatically assigned as a domain admin.

5.   Click the **Create** button:

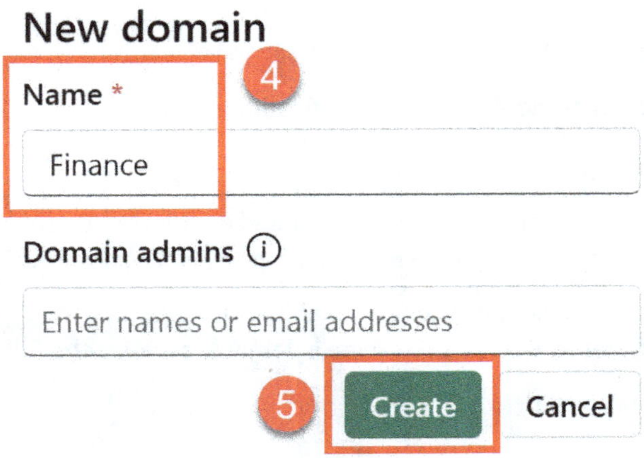

Figure 12.7 – New domain dialog

6.   On the **Domains** page, click the newly created domain name:

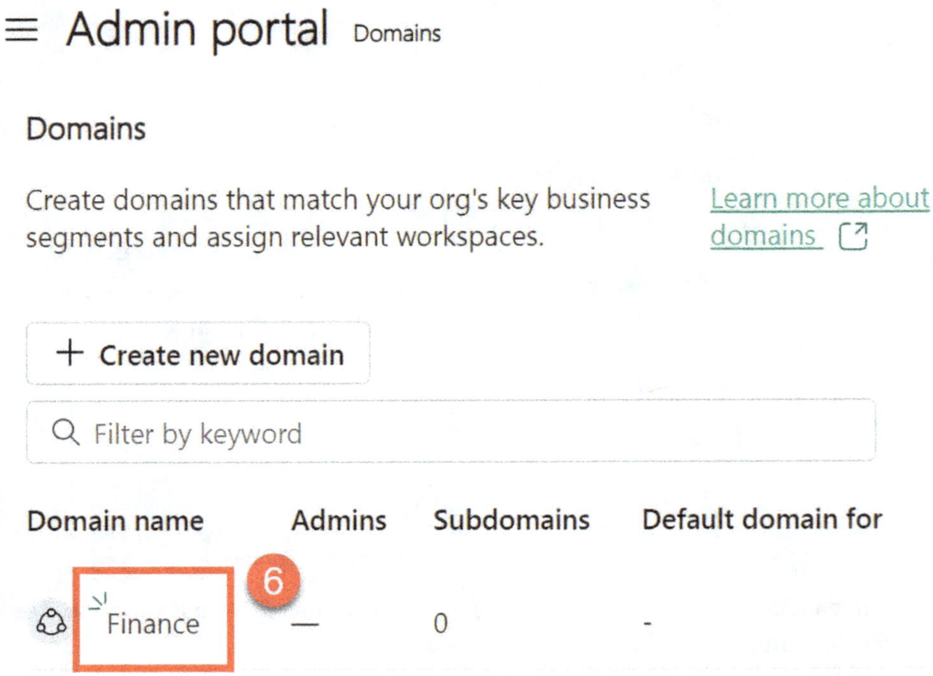

Figure 12.8 – Domains page

The page for the new domain enables you to assign workspaces to the domain, create one or more new subdomain(s), and configure **Domain settings**.

With the basics of domains understood, let's move on to tags.

Tags

Tags are simply additional labels or metadata that can be applied to content items such as reports, dashboards, semantic models, and other content items. Like domains, tags help increase or otherwise enhance the discoverability, organization, and data categorization of content.

To create a tag, follow these steps:

1. Go to the **Admin portal.**
2. Select **Tags (preview).**
3. Select **Create your first tags:**

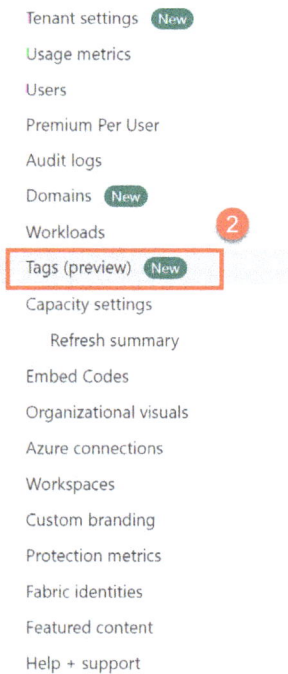

Figure 12.9 – Creating tags

4. In the **Name your tags** dialog, enter one or multiple tags separated by commas.

5. Click the **Create** button:

Figure 12.10 – Name your tags dialog

🔍 **Quick tip:** Need to see a high-resolution version of this image? Open this book in the next-gen Packt Reader or view it in the PDF/ePub copy.

🔒 **The next-gen Packt Reader** is included for free with the purchase of this book. Scan the QR code OR go to `packtpub.com/unlock`, then use the search bar to find this book by name. Double-check the edition shown to make sure you get the right one.

6. Navigate to **Settings** for a report, dashboard, semantic model, or other content item.

7. Use the **Apply tags to this item** area to assign tags.

8. Click the **Save** button:

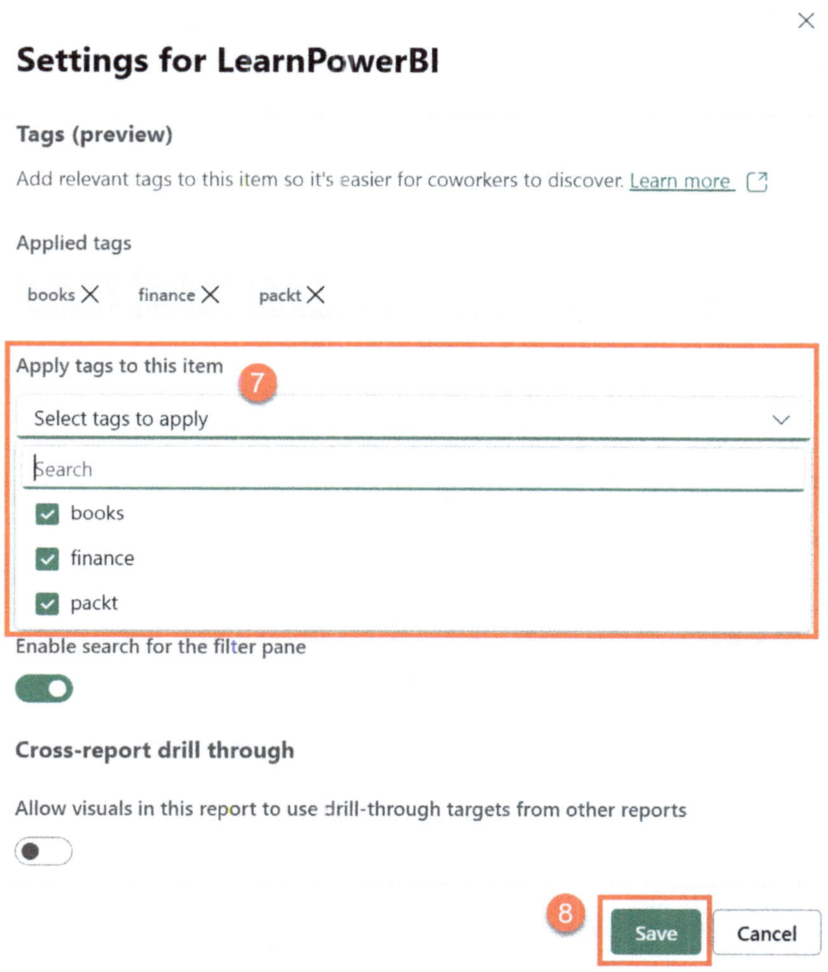

×

Settings for LearnPowerBI

Tags (preview)

Add relevant tags to this item so it's easier for coworkers to discover. Learn more ⬀

Applied tags

books ✕   finance ✕   packt ✕

Apply tags to this item ⑦

| Select tags to apply   ⌄ |

| Search |

☑ books

☑ finance

☑ packt

Enable search for the filter pane

⬤◯

Cross-report drill through

Allow visuals in this report to use drill-through targets from other reports

◯

⑧ **Save**   Cancel

Figure 12.11 – Apply tags to an item

The tags are now viewable next to the content item, as shown:

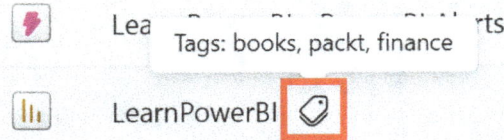

Figure 12.12 – Applied tags

In addition, in the **Filter** area for a workspace, the available filters include tags:

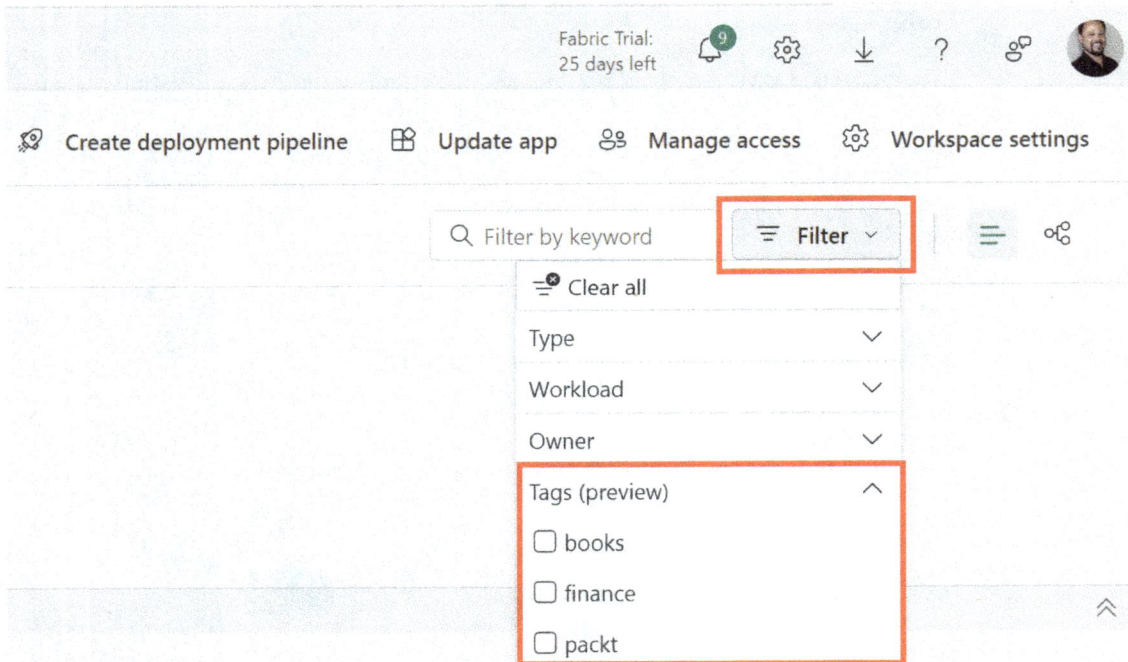

Figure 12.13 – Applied tags

Now that you understand tags, let's next look at endorsements and featured content.

Endorsements and featured content

Endorsements and featured content are related concepts in Power BI. Endorsements are another method of classifying content as either **Promoted** or **Certified**. In general, a promoted item simply highlights content that the user deems as valuable or worthwhile to others, while certified items indicate that the content is aligned with an organization's overall quality requirements, meaning that it is an authoritative and reliable source of information.

To endorse a content item, navigate to **Settings** for a report, app, semantic model, or dataflow. Use the **Endorsement** section to mark the content as either **Promoted** or **Certified.** Semantic models can also be marked as **Master data**.

You can optionally use the **Feature on Home** setting to display the content in the **Featured** section on the Power BI Home page:

Endorsement

Help coworkers find your quality content by endorsing this report. Learn more

○ None

  The report will appear in search results but isn't endorsed.

◉ Promoted

  When you're ready to distribute the report to your coworkers, promote it to let them know.

○ Certified

  Certify your report to show coworkers that it's been reviewed and meets your org's certification criteria. How do I get my report certified?

☑ Feature on Home

  Display this report in the Featured section on Power BI Home for people with access to it.

Figure 12.14 – Endorsement area in the Settings for a report

Now, when listed as content in the Power BI service, the endorsement is visible:

	Name	Type	Opened	Location	Endorsement	Sensitivity
📊	LearnPowerBI ⬦	Report	now	Learn Power...	⚲ Certified	—

Figure 12.15 – Viewing the endorsement area

🔍 **Quick tip:** Need to see a high-resolution version of this image? Open this book in the next-gen Packt Reader or view it in the PDF/ePub copy.

🔒 **The next-gen Packt Reader** is included for free with the purchase of this book. Scan the QR code OR go to packtpub.com/unlock, then use the search bar to find this book by name. Double-check the edition shown to make sure you get the right one.

As shown in the example, when endorsing content, it is also possible to feature that content on the Power BI Home page. This concludes our exploration of different methods of classifying content, so let's next look at tenant settings.

Tenant settings

As explained in *Chapter 1, Understanding Business Intelligence and Power BI*, a **tenant** is simply a logical slice of the Power BI service particular to a single organization. Each Power BI tenant must have at least one account that is deemed the **tenant administrator**. The tenant administrator or administrators control which features and functionality are enabled within the tenant. This section explains the various tenant settings within Power BI along with suggestions and recommendations for their enablement or disablement. For tenant administrators, it is important to understand these tenant settings and carefully consider the implications of each with regard to empowering business users and complying with regulatory and organizational requirements. For business users, it is also important to understand which available features may be disabled by tenant administrators so that requests can be made to enable those features should the need arise to make use of them.

Tenant settings are accessed in the Power BI service by clicking on the gear icon in the upper-right corner of the Power BI service, choosing **Admin portal**, and then **Tenant settings**. Alternatively, click on the ellipsis (…) in the upper-right corner, then **Settings**, **Admin portal**, and finally, **Tenant settings**.

Once enabled, many tenant settings allow the tenant administrator to choose whether the feature is enabled for the entire organization or for specific security groups (Entra groups). In addition, tenant administrators can also exclude specific security groups if desired.

The common dialog for setting tenant security is shown in *Figure 12.16*:

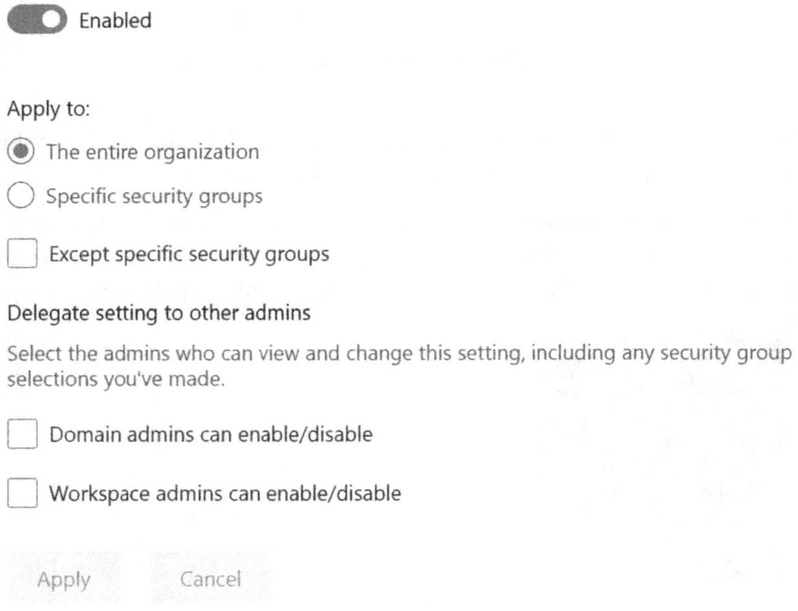

Enabled

Apply to:
- The entire organization
- Specific security groups

Except specific security groups

Delegate setting to other admins

Select the admins who can view and change this setting, including any security group selections you've made.

Domain admins can enable/disable

Workspace admins can enable/disable

Apply   Cancel

Figure 12.16 – Tenant security settings

In general, it is advisable to use the least privileges approach to tenant settings. That is, only enable the features required by the organization and only enable those features for the groups of business users that require the use of those features.

It is important to understand that tenant settings are constantly evolving, with new tenant settings added frequently.

Therefore, the following list highlights some of the more important and helpful tenant settings.

Microsoft Fabric

The Microsoft Fabric tenant settings control various aspects of Microsoft Fabric, the umbrella service of which Power BI is a part. In general, these tenant settings control who can and cannot create various Microsoft Fabric content items such as lakehouses, warehouses, real-time dashboards, AI skill item types, etc. Microsoft Fabric is covered in greater detail in *Chapter 13, Working with Microsoft Fabric and Copilot.*

Help and support settings

Help and support settings include options to control help and support links as well as notifications about service outages, the use of enhanced features on a trial basis, and custom messages when publishing content. Let's look at them briefly:

*   **Publish "Get Help" information:** This setting allows the administrator to change certain menu links in the service to point to internal help and support resources. Enabling this can be helpful for large organizations in order to point business users toward internal support organizations and content. Configuring this option would generally be done for the entire organization and provides the ability to replace certain links in the Power BI help menu (**?** **Help & Support**) with custom links.

    Table 12.1 shows the different settings that can be customized as well as which menu links are changed:

Setting	Changes
Training documentation	Adds a link for training documentation
Discussion Forum	Discussion forum
Licensing requests	Licensing requests
Help Desk	Help desk

Table 12.1 – Customizable help and support links

*   **Receive email notifications for service outages or incidents:** If enabled, the specified mail-enabled security groups receive email notifications if there is an outage or other issue with the Power BI tenant. It is recommended that this option be enabled for specific mail-enabled security groups such as IT support and the help desk or anyone responsible for the administration and governance of Power BI.

- **Users can try Microsoft Fabric paid features**: If enabled, users can sign up for a Microsoft Fabric trial for 60 days. In general, it is recommended that this option be disabled.

- **Show a custom message before publishing reports**: This feature is useful for organizations that wish to inform content creators of any organizational policies or procedures that should be followed when publishing content. When content creators publish a report, they'll see a custom message prior to publication. Enable this feature if your organization wishes to inform publishers of organizational policies, although you may wish to exempt certain groups such as IT.

Domain management settings

Domain management settings control whether or not tenant and domain admins are allowed to override workspace assignments. The assignment of workspaces to domains can be based upon the name of the domain but also based upon a workspace admin or by capacity. In other words, all workspaces with a particular admin or within a particular capacity can be mass-assigned to a domain. This setting allows tenant and domain admins to override these assignments.

Workspace settings

Workspace settings control who and what types of workspaces can be created as well as the use of semantic models between workspaces:

- **Create workspaces**: If enabled, users can create new workspaces within the Power BI service. It is recommended that this be enabled for only authorized security groups within the organization in order to avoid the proliferation of workspaces within the tenant.

- **Use semantic models across workspaces**: Users in the organization can use semantic models across workspaces if they have the required build permission. It is recommended that this be enabled for specific security groups within the organization and is generally a required setting for usage models such as golden semantic models.

- **Define workspace retention period**: There is a default retention period of 7 days in which to recover a deleted workspace. This setting allows this default retention period to be extended up to 90 days. Workspaces can be restored by using the **Workspaces** link within the **Admin portal**.

Information protection

Information protection settings control the application and use of sensitivity labels for Power BI content. Sensitivity labels are discussed in more detail in the *Purview* section of this chapter.

Export and sharing settings

Export and sharing settings control guest user access to the tenant, export formats for reports, the ability of users to certify and promote content, and additional sharing and collaboration functionality.

Only enable external sharing of content, guest users, and the ability of users to accept external sharing requests if necessary. In general, the export settings apply to both Power BI reports and paginated reports. In addition, the export settings apply to the interface for exporting in the service as well as the Power BI REST API. Enabling these settings can be beneficial to end users but some organizations may see exporting as a security risk and, therefore, would disable these settings.

Some of the more specific settings available are as follows:

- **Publish to web:** If enabled, users can publish public reports to the web. When reports are published to the web, those reports do not require authentication in order to view them; anyone with the link can view the report. It is highly advised that this setting be disabled as this can result in severe security and compliance issues for most organizations. If enabled, tenant administrators should regularly review generated embed codes via the **Embed Codes** page in the **Admin portal** in order to ensure that no confidential information has been published to the web.

- **Copy and paste visuals:** This enables or disables the ability for users to copy and paste dashboard tiles or report visuals as static images. There is no real security benefit in disabling this feature as users can still take screenshots or take pictures of tiles and visuals using their mobile device.

- **Export to ...:** This enables or disables the ability of users to export data from report visuals or paginated reports to an Excel file or comma-separated value (.csv) file. Note that the .csv setting also allows exporting from dashboard tiles.

- **Download reports:** This enables or disables the ability of users to download Power BI Desktop (.pbix) files or paginated report (.rdl) files.

- **Users can work with semantic models in Excel using a live connection:** This enables or disables the ability of users to connect live to Power BI semantic models. Disabling this feature effectively disables the Analyze in Excel functionality in the service, as the Excel files generated by Analyze in Excel use a live connection to the semantic model. Enabling this feature is a requirement for the golden semantic model usage model.

- **Export reports as ...:** This enables or disables the ability of users to export reports to PowerPoint, PDF, MHTML, Word, XML, or images.

- **Print dashboards and reports:** This enables or disables the ability of users to print dashboards, reports, and paginated reports. Enabling this setting allows content to be printed regardless of applied sensitivity labels (see the *Purview* section).

- **Certification** and **Endorse master data:** Enabling these features allows users to certify semantic models, dataflows, reports, and apps. **Endorse master data** only applies to semantic models. See the *Endorsements and featured content* section of this chapter for additional information.

- **Users can se tup email subscriptions:** This enables or disables the ability of users to create email subscriptions for reports, paginated reports, and dashboards.

- **Featured content:** This enables or disables the ability of users to promote dashboards, reports, and paginated reports to the **Featured** section of the Power BI **Home** page. This setting should only be enabled for trusted contributors. See the *Endorsements and featured content* section of this chapter for additional information.

- **Allow connections to featured tables:** This enables or disables the ability of users to access and perform calculations on data from featured tables. Featured tables are defined in the modeling view of Power BI Desktop. Featured tables can be viewed using the data types gallery of Excel. To view the data types gallery in Excel, use the **Data** tab of the ribbon and then expand the dropdown in the **Data Types** group.

- **Allow shareable links to grant access to everyone in your organization:** This enables or disables the ability of users to create links that enable anyone within the organization to view the content (assuming the correct license type). This link cannot be used by user accounts outside of the organization's tenant. Only enable this setting if necessary and only for specific groups.

- **Enable Microsoft Teams integration:** This enables or disables the ability for users to access features associated with integration for Microsoft Teams, including launching Teams experiences from the Power BI service such as chats, the Power BI app for Microsoft Teams, and receiving Power BI notifications in Teams. To completely enable or disable Teams integration, use the **Manage apps** section of the Teams administrator site to allow or block the Power BI app. If enabling this feature, it is recommended to also enable **Install Power BI app for Microsoft Teams automatically** as well.

- **Enable Power BI add-in for PowerPoint:** This enables or disables the ability of users to embed Power BI data in PowerPoint presentations.

- **Allow DirectQuery connections to Power BI semantic models:** This enables or disables the ability of users to make changes to existing semantic models or use DirectQuery to build composite data models.

Discovery settings

Discovery settings control whether or not users can discover content within the Power BI service to which they do not have permission. Enabling these settings can be viewed as a security risk and is thus generally not recommended.

App settings

App settings control the ability of users to create apps, push those apps to end users, and publish apps to the entire organization. It is recommended to restrict these permissions to trusted content creators only.

Integration settings

Integration settings control the integration and use of third-party systems within the Power BI service. These include **single sign-on (SSO)** integrations with Dremio, Snowflake, Redshift, and Google BigQuery, which should only be enabled if actually using those systems. In addition, the use of map visuals such as ArcGIS Maps, Azure Maps, and other default map visuals can be enabled or disabled.

Some specific integration settings include the following:

- **Allow XMLA endpoints and Analyze in Excel with on-premises semantic models:** If enabled, users can use the Analyze in Excel functionality to create Excel files that link to Power BI semantic models. In addition, this setting allows XMLA endpoint connections. XMLA endpoints are required for certain tools such as the ALM Toolkit. Enabling this setting can be beneficial to end users but some organizations may see this as a security risk and, therefore, would disable this setting. This setting should at least be enabled for administrative security groups.

- **Semantic Model Execute Queries REST API:** This enables or disables the use of the Power BI REST API to query semantic models using DAX.

- **Use global search for Power BI**: This enables or disables the **Search** bar present in the header of the Power BI service. Search functionality is provided by Azure Search's external search index. It is generally recommended to enable this setting.

- **Integration with SharePoint and Microsoft Lists**: This enables or disables the ability of users to launch Power BI from SharePoint lists and Microsoft Lists. Enabling this setting can be very beneficial to end users.

- **Microsoft Entra single sign-on for data gateway**: This enables or disables SSO for the on-premises data gateway. When enabled, user information such as the user's name and email address is sent to the SSO-supported data source for the purposes of authentication.

There are also a number of integration settings for OneDrive, SharePoint, Microsoft Lists, Power Platform, and OneLake. Review these settings carefully and only enable the integrations necessary for your organization.

Power BI visuals

Power BI visuals settings control the use of custom visuals within the Power BI service:

- **Allow visuals created using the Power BI SDK**: This enables or disables the ability of users to add, view, share, and interact with custom visuals in the Power BI service. It is recommended that this setting be disabled and that you use organizational visuals to control what custom visuals are allowed. This setting does not apply to organizational visuals. Organizational visuals can be managed within the **Organizational visuals** page of the Admin portal. See the *Organizational visuals* section of this chapter for more information.

- **Add and use certified visuals only (block uncertified)**: If enabled, users can only use certified visuals. It is recommended that this setting be disabled and that you use organizational visuals to control what custom visuals are allowed. This setting does not apply to organizational visuals. Organizational visuals can be managed within the **Organizational visuals** page of the Admin portal. See the *Organizational visuals* section of this chapter for more information.

Additional settings allow or disallow custom visuals to access the browser's local storage, access Microsoft Entra ID access tokens, and allow users to download data from custom visuals.

R and Python visual settings

R and Python visual settings control whether or not users are permitted to use R and Python visuals within the Power BI service:

- **Interact with and share R and Python visuals**: This enables or disables the ability of users to use visuals created with R and Python scripts. Only enable this setting if absolutely necessary as this setting can only be applied to the entire organization and R and Python scripts could pose a significant security risk.

Audit and usage settings

Audit and usage settings control the collection of audit logs and metrics as well as the ability of users to view and access these logs and metrics. For more information about audit and usage logs, see the *Further reading* section in this chapter:

- **Usage metrics for content creators**: This enables or disables the ability for users to see usage metrics for dashboards and reports to which they have permission. Enabling this setting is beneficial to end users and is generally recommended.

- **Per-user data in usage metrics for content creators**: This enables or disables the ability of content creators to view usage metrics that include the display names and email addresses of users accessing the content. There are several schools of thought on this topic. However, transparency tends to promote better security, and thus it is recommended that this be enabled for the entire organization.

- **Azure Log Analytics connections for workspace administrators**: This enables or disables the ability for administrators of workspaces to send their workspace logs to Azure Log Analytics. It is generally recommended to enable this setting.

- **Microsoft can store query text to aid in support investigations**: It is generally advisable to enable this setting, as disabling it can potentially impact the ability of Microsoft to provide support.

Dashboard settings

Dashboard settings control the type of content available in dashboards as well as whether data classification is available for dashboards:

- **Web content on dashboard tiles**: This enables or disables the ability of users to create web content tiles on dashboards. It is highly recommended that this setting be disabled as this may expose your tenant to malicious software.

Developer settings

Developer settings control the use of embedding as well as the use of Power BI APIs and resource keys. For more information about Power BI APIs, see the *Further reading* section in this chapter:

- **Embed content in apps**: This enables or disables the ability of users to embed dashboards and reports in web applications using the **Embed for your customers** method. Only enable this setting if necessary.

- **Service principals to use Fabric APIs**: This enables or disables the ability for assigned service principals to access web apps registered in **Microsoft Entra ID** without a signed-in user. If a security group is specified for this setting, that security group must include the service principal. This setting should be disabled unless this functionality is required.

- **Allow service principals to create and use profiles**: This enables or disables this functionality. Note that this setting does not impact API functionality.

- **Block ResourceKey Authentication**: If enabled, it blocks users from using a resource key for streaming semantic models. Only disable this setting if you require authentication via resource keys.

Admin API settings

Admin API settings control the use of Power BI admin APIs and the information contained within the responses from admin API requests. For more information about admin APIs, see the *Further reading* section in this chapter:

- **Service principals can access read-only admin APIs**: This enables or disables the ability of service principals assigned to registered Microsoft Entra ID to access Power BI admin APIs without having a signed-in user. The service principal must be included in an allowed security group. Enabling this setting provides the service principal read-only access to all the information available through the admin APIs. Only enable this setting if necessary.
- **Enhance admin APIs responses with detailed metadata**: If enabled, additional information is included in Power BI admin API requests by allowed users and service principals. If enabling the prior setting, then it is recommended to also enable this setting.
- **Enhance admin APIs responses with DAX and mashup expressions**: If enabled, additional information is included in Power BI admin API requests by allowed users and service principals regarding the metadata about queries and expressions comprising Power BI items. Only enable this setting if necessary.

Gen1 dataflow setting

This enables or disables the ability of users to create Gen1 dataflows. This setting can only be enabled for the entire organization. However, dataflows cannot be created in **My workspace** workspaces, so only administrators, members, and contributors to non-**My workspace** workspaces can create dataflows. It is recommended that you enable this setting and utilize dataflows to curate data connections. Additional information about dataflows can be found in *Chapter 13, Working with Microsoft Fabric and Copilot*.

Template app settings

Template app settings control whether users can publish or install template apps. For more information about template apps, see the *Further reading* section in this chapter.

Q&A settings

Q&A settings control whether or not semantic model owners are able to review questions asked by other users as well as whether synonyms can be shared between semantic models. If using Q&A within your organization, it is recommended that these features be enabled so that semantic model owners can improve their Q&A settings over time and content creators can view **Suggested terms** when defining synonyms for a semantic model.

Semantic model security

The semantic model security setting controls who is allowed to republish semantic models within Power BI. If enabled, it blocks anyone except the semantic model owner from publishing updates. This includes semantic model deployment updates from Power BI deployment pipelines. Enabling this setting may be viewed as a security feature by organizations but carefully consider the broader implications around usability and administration before enabling this feature.

Advanced networking

Advanced networking controls whether or not users can access the Power BI tenant via a private link and/or public internet. See the *Further reading* section of this chapter to learn more about these features.

Metric settings

Metrics settings control whether or not users are allowed to create and use goals and scorecards.

User experience experiments

This setting controls whether users experience variations in the Power BI service user interface based on Microsoft experiments. It is highly recommended to disable this feature as it can cause support issues and benefits no one other than Microsoft.

Share data with your Microsoft 365 services

This section controls the Power BI tenant's ability to interact with a Microsoft 365 tenant. If enabled, it permits the Power BI tenant to share information with a Microsoft 365 tenant. This allows certain features such as favorites and search results to function the same when using either the Power BI tenant or the Microsoft 365 tenant. Generally, it is recommended to enable this setting if both tenants are in the same geographic region. Sharing data with tenants in different geographic regions can be controlled separately.

Insight settings

Insight settings control the ability of users to receive automatic insights about their reports.

Datamart setting

This enables or disables the creation of datamarts. Datamarts are a special content type within Power BI that predates Microsoft Fabric. Generally, it is recommended to disable the use of datamarts.

Data model setting

This enables or disables the ability of users to edit data models within the service. You may wish to disable this setting in order to avoid the possibility that edits made in the service are later overwritten.

Scale-out settings

These settings only apply to semantic models that use the large semantic model storage format. There are generally no security concerns with enabling this feature.

OneLake settings

These settings control various features related to OneLake. OneLake is covered in more detail in *Chapter 13, Working with Microsoft Fabric and Copilot.*

Git integration

These settings control integration with Git. Git is a source control repository system owned by Microsoft.

Copilot and Azure OpenAI Service

These settings control various features related to Copilot and Azure OpenAI. Copilot is covered in more detail in *Chapter 13, Working with Microsoft Fabric and Copilot*.

Additional workloads

These settings control various features related to Fabric workloads. Workloads are developed using the Microsoft Fabric Workload Development Kit. More information about Fabric is covered in *Chapter 13, Working with Microsoft Fabric and Copilot*.

Now that we have covered the various Power BI tenant settings, let's next take a look at governing the deployment of Power BI content.

Organizational visuals

Organizational visuals allow administrators to control exactly which custom visuals users are allowed to use within their Power BI reports. In addition to the array of default visuals included with Power BI Desktop, additional visuals are available via **AppSource**. You can access these visuals from Power BI Desktop via the **Visualizations** pane:

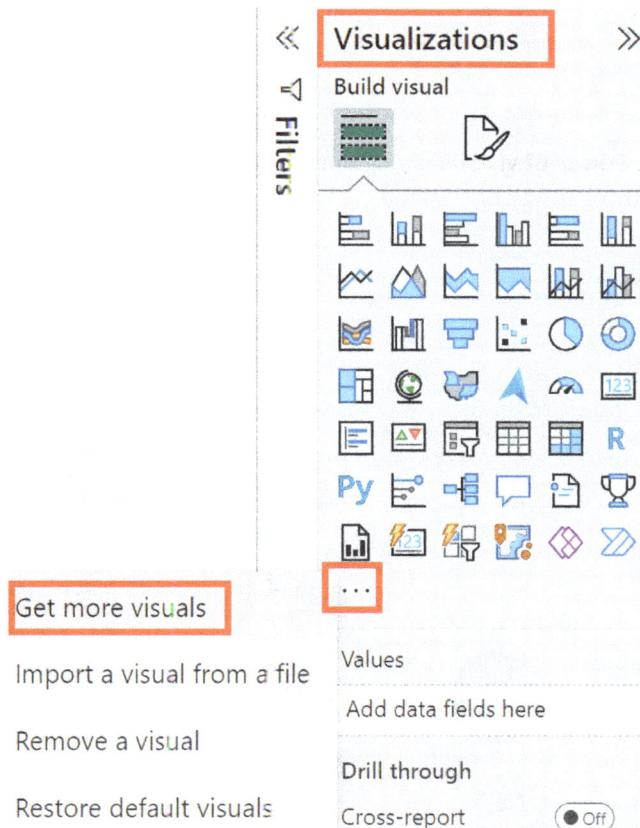

Figure 12.17 – Get custom visuals in Power BI Desktop

There are hundreds of custom visuals available from both Microsoft and various third parties. To govern and control the use of custom visuals, refer to the *Power BI visuals tenant settings* reference in the *Further reading* section and then perform the following steps:

1. Go to the **Admin portal**.
2. Select **Organizational visuals**.
3. On the **Organizational visuals** page, select **+ Add visual** and then **From AppSource**:

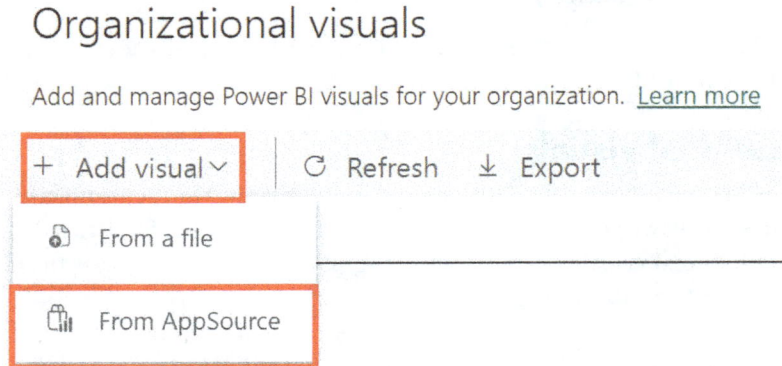

Figure 12.18 – Manage organizational visuals in the Power BI service

4. The **AppSource Power BI visuals** dialog opens. This is the same interface as displayed when getting visuals from Power BI Desktop.

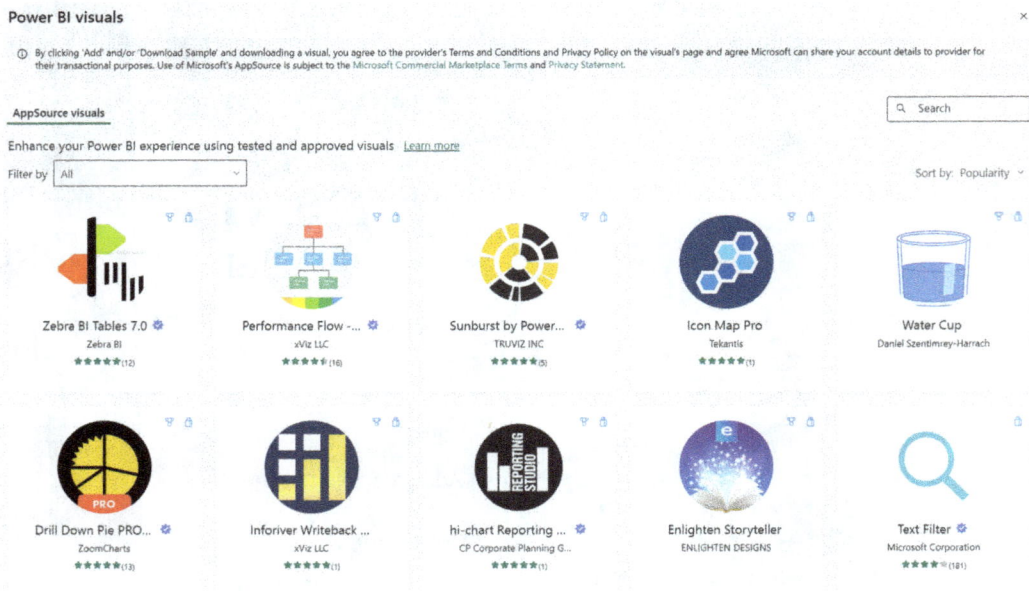

Figure 12.19 – AppSource Power BI visuals

5. Select a visual from **AppSource** and then click the **Add** button.

Once added to the **Organizational visuals** list, the visual can be selected and then the **Enable for Visualization Pane** option can be selected in the ribbon. This setting displays the custom visual in Power BI Desktop's **Visualizations** pane.

With an understanding of organizational visuals, let's next look at deploying Power BI content.

Deploying Power BI content

Another way in which governance is commonly enforced is through the use of a phased approach for the development and deployment of content. A common approach used in software testing and engineering is called **DTAP**, short for **Development, Testing, Acceptance,** and **Production.** The letters of the acronym denote the environments and steps used during the engineering and testing of software, and the particular steps and environments used can vary between three and five.

For example, the following steps might be followed as part of a software development DTAP process:

1. While the software is being developed, this development occurs in a development environment that only the software developers can access.
2. Once the software is deemed ready, the software is deployed to a test environment that closely mimics the target production environment.
3. If tests are completed successfully, the software is then deployed to an acceptance environment where end users can test that the software meets business requirements.
4. Once acceptance is achieved, the software is finally deployed to production.

Well-governed Power BI deployments should also follow a similar DTAP process for the creation of content. Power BI query parameters and the ability to publish content to multiple workspaces facilitate this process. While a DTAP process can be performed manually, Premium users can leverage **Power BI deployment pipelines** to facilitate and automate this process.

To create and use a Power BI deployment pipeline, follow these steps:

1. In the Power BI service, create a workspace and publish the `LearnPowerBI.pbix` report to this workspace.
2. Open the workspace in the Power BI service and choose **Create deployment pipeline** in the ribbon:

Figure 12.20 – Create deployment pipeline

3. Provide a pipeline name such as *Learn Power BI* and click the **Next** button.

4. Select the **Create and continue** button to accept the default pipeline stages, **Development**, **Test**, and **Production**. Alternatively, you can add, remove, and rename stages as desired.

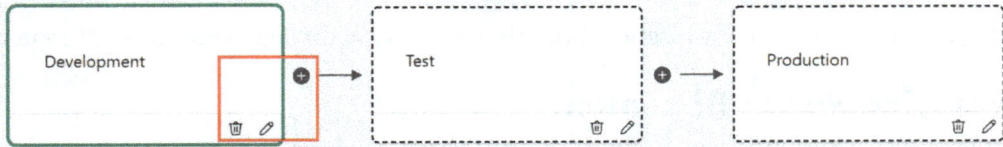

Figure 12.21 – Customize stages

5. Assign the deployment stage for the workspace as **Production** and click the **Assign** button:

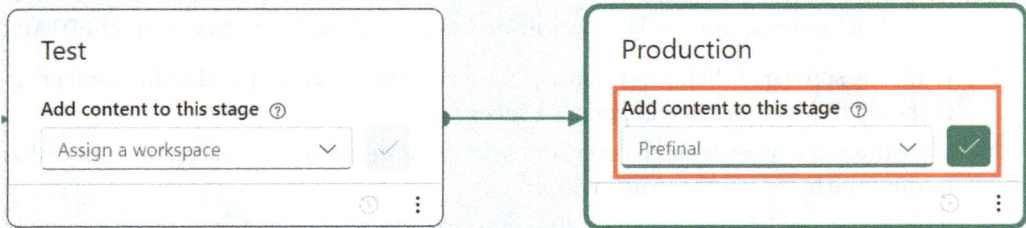

Figure 12.22 – Assign a workspace to the Production stage of the pipeline

6. If a warning is displayed regarding unsupported items, simply click the **Continue** button.

7. Click on the **Test** stage. Select both the semantic model and report and then click the **Deploy** button:

Figure 12.23 – Deploy content to the previous stage

8. Again, if a warning is displayed regarding unsupported items, simply click the **Continue** button.

9. In the **Deploy back to this stage** dialog, click the **Deploy** button.

10. A new workspace called **Learn Power BI [Test]** is created and the content is deployed to that workspace.

11. Once the copying of content is complete, repeat the procedure in *step 7* using the **Development** stage in order to create and deploy content to the **Development** stage. This creates a **Learn Power BI [Development]** workspace and deploys the content to that workspace:

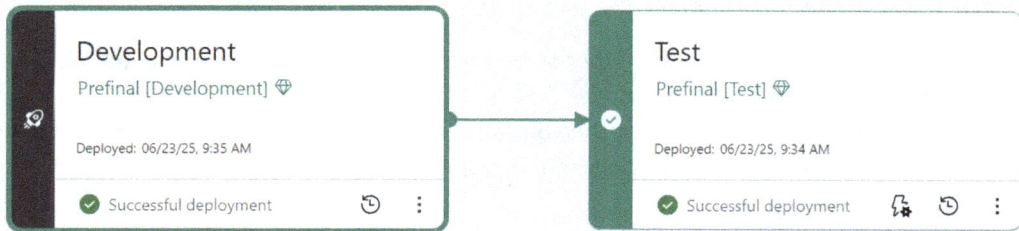

Figure 12.24 – Development and Test stages of a Power BI deployment pipeline

Once a deployment pipeline is deployed between stages, green checkboxes are present, indicating that the content in both stages is the same or in sync with one another. If new or updated content is subsequently deployed to the **Development** stage, this icon indicates that the content is not in sync:

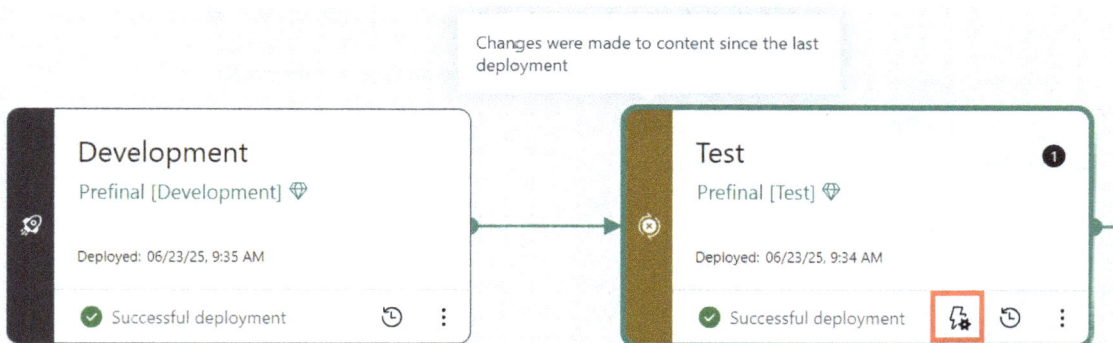

Figure 12.25 – Content is different between the Development and Test stages

To deploy the updated content from the **Development** stage to the **Test** stage, click the Test stage, select the modified content and click the **Deploy** button.

In addition to making deployment between workspaces easy, pipelines also allow you to define rules for the different pipeline stages. These rules allow you to repoint data sources, for example, from Development systems to Test and Production systems. The ability to define deployment rules is accessed by clicking the lightning bolt icon of the appropriate stage, as shown in *Figure 12.25*.

Let's next turn our attention to governing gateways in the Power BI service.

Gateway governance

While we already covered the basics of managing gateways and connections in *Chapter 11*, *Refreshing Content*, there is also the ability to govern who can install data gateways if you have the **Global Admin** or **Fabric Admin** role within **Entra**. To see how this is done, do the following:

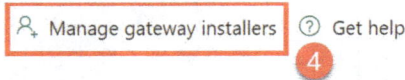

1. Select the gear icon in the upper-right corner of the Power BI service and choose **Manage connections and gateways** under **Resources and extensions**. Alternatively, click the ellipsis (**...**) in the upper-right corner, then **Settings**, and then **Manage connections and gateways**.

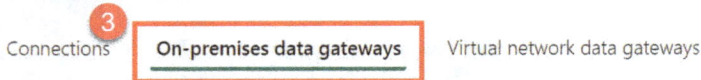

2. In the upper-right corner, toggle **Tenant administration** to **On**.

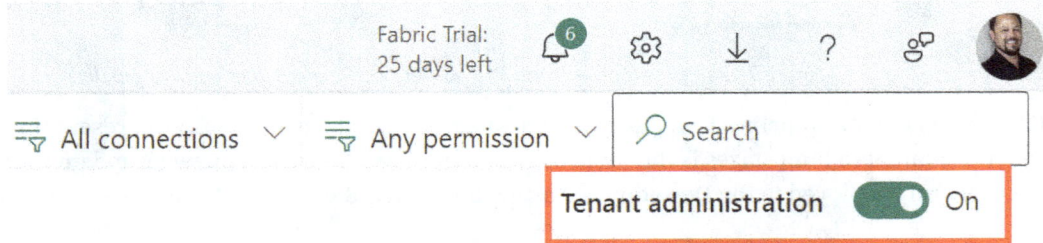

Figure 12.26 – Tenant administration for gateways and connections

3. Select the **On-premises data gateways** tab.

4. Select **Manage gateway installers**.

Figure 12.27 – Manage gateway installers

5. The **Manage gateway installers** pane opens on the right-hand side of the page. Toggle **Restrict users in your organization from installing gateways** to **On**.

6. Under **Users who can install gateways**, use the **Search by name or email** field and the **Add** button to add gateway installers.

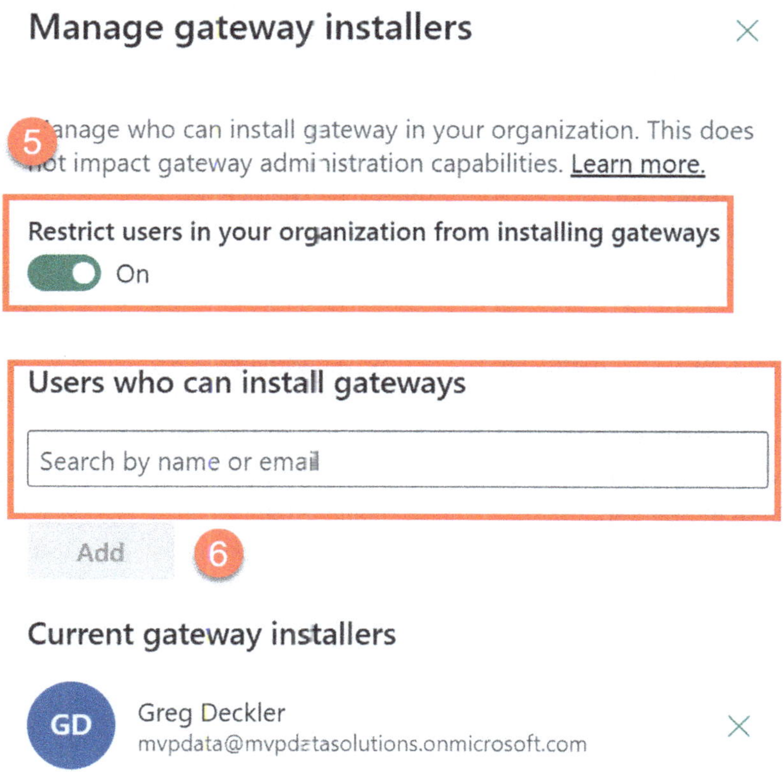

Manage gateway installers ✕

⑤ Manage who can install gateway in your organization. This does not impact gateway administration capabilities. <u>Learn more.</u>

Restrict users in your organization from installing gateways

🟢 On

Users who can install gateways

Search by name or email

Add   ⑥

Current gateway installers

GD Greg Deckler
mvpdata@mvpdatasolutions.onmicrosoft.com   ✕

Figure 12.28 – Manage gateway installers pane

Now that you know how to govern gateway installers, let's briefly explore Purview.

Purview

Microsoft Purview assists organizations in managing, protecting, and governing their data. In fact, Microsoft Purview is essentially an umbrella for a number of previous loosely related data security and compliance solutions, including:

- Data Loss Prevention
- Information Barriers
- Information Protection
- Insider Risk Management
- Privileged Access Management

Certain Microsoft Purview functionality is included in a Microsoft Fabric trial. However, to make full use of Purview requires separate licensing, such as Purview Information Protection for Office 365 licenses.

Of most relevance for Power BI, Purview Information Protection allows the application of sensitivity labels for Power BI content in both Power BI Desktop and the Power BI service. Sensitivity labels, such as Confidential, are visible within many different areas of Power BI and Fabric and can control what operations a user may perform on data exported from Power BI content with applied sensitivity labels.

Purview Data Loss Prevention policies can also be applied to Power BI content, allowing policy tips to be attached to items that have sensitive content and alerts to be triggered that can be reviewed in the Microsoft Purview compliance portal.

Basic Purview reporting is built into the Power BI service. To access this reporting, perform the following steps:

1. Select the gear icon in the upper-right corner of the Power BI service and choose **Microsoft Purview hub** under **Governance and insights**. Alternatively, click the ellipsis (**…**) in the upper-right corner, then **Settings**, and then **Microsoft Purview hub**.

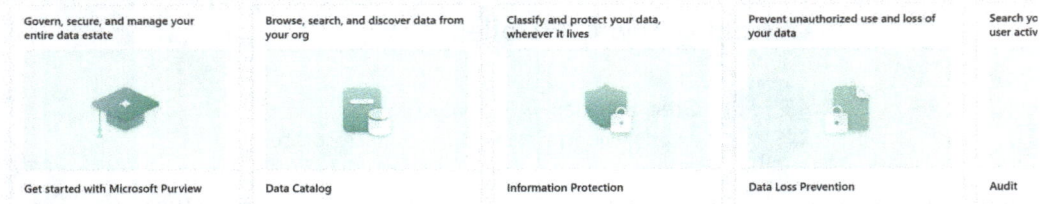

2. The Microsoft Purview hub page is displayed. Reporting can be found under the Microsoft Fabric data heading:

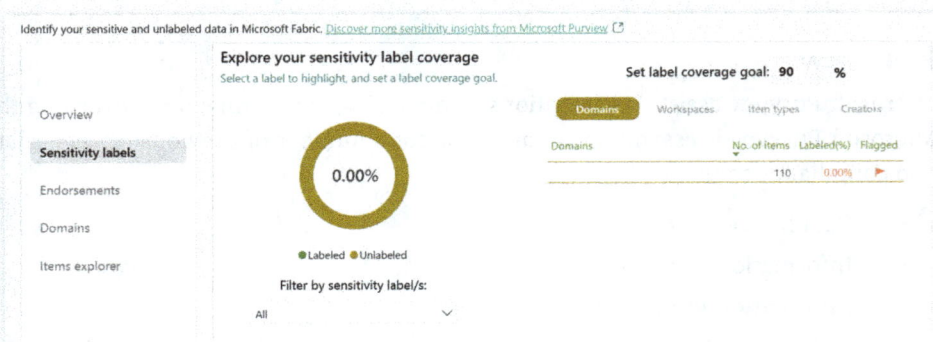

Figure 12.29 – Microsoft Purview hub

We have now covered many different settings and methods for governing Power BI. Let's next explore the important topic of promoting the adoption of Power BI throughout an organization.

Adopting Power BI

The subject of an organization adopting a disruptive technology such as Power BI is vast and complex and a complete treatment of this subject is beyond the scope of this book. However, this section introduces the topic and provides the essential strategies for adopting Power BI within an organization.

Adoption as covered here is the diffusion of a disruptive technology within an organization. It means that a technology progresses from being used infrequently by a small percentage of an organization to being used by the entire organization on a daily basis. Power BI, a self-service business intelligence technology, should be viewed as a disruptive technology that must be evangelized in order to promote its use throughout an organization.

The basic underpinnings of the diffusion of technology within a society is a well-researched subject within scientific literature, popularized in 1962 by Everett Rodgers' seminal work, *Diffusion of Innovation*. The diffusion of innovation theory is most often presented as a bell curve similar to *Figure 12.30*, where adopters are classified into five categories:

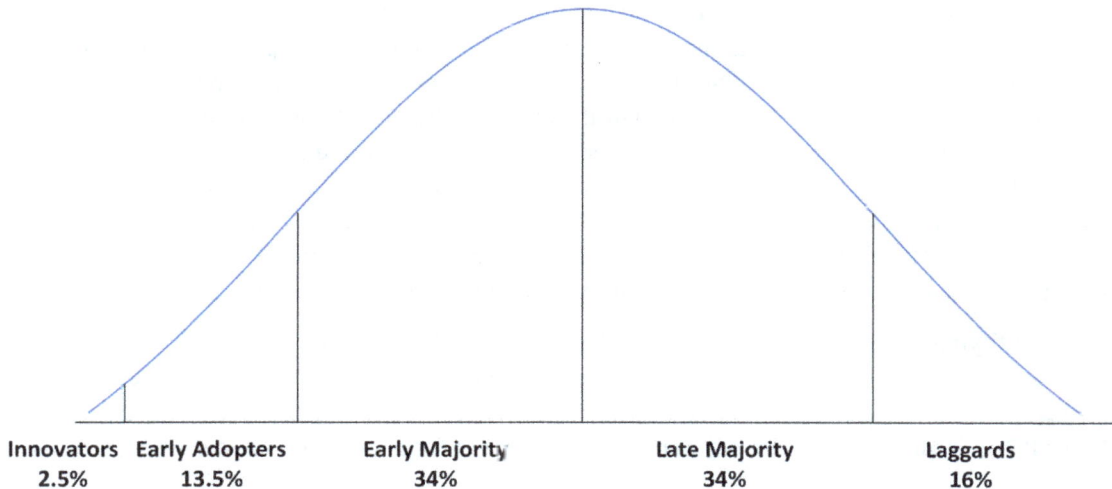

| Innovators | Early Adopters | Early Majority | Late Majority | Laggards |
| 2.5% | 13.5% | 34% | 34% | 16% |

Figure 12.30 – Diffusion of innovation bell curve

Geoffrey Moore later extended the diffusion of innovation work by Everett Rodgers and identified an *adoption chasm* between the early adopters and the early majority. While Rodgers' and Moore's work mainly dealt with disruptive technologies adopted by society as a whole, many of the same principles and challenges apply to disruptive technologies such as Power BI when considering adoption by an organization.

Adoption strategies

If you are the first or one of the first Power BI users within your organization, then you fall into the Innovators category of the diffusion of innovation bell curve. As an innovator, you are more prone to take risks and learn new technologies. As an innovator using Power BI, you understand the intrinsic business value that Power BI can bring to an organization regarding self-service business intelligence.

The data analytics and visualization capabilities of Power BI can help organizations make better business decisions and improve the efficiency and effectiveness of business processes, making the business more profitable. However, not everyone within an organization is willing to take risks, learn new technologies, or understand the potential business value of Power BI. Therefore, your first goal is to identify the potential early adopters of Power BI, but not all early adopters are created equal.

Early adopters should be considered based on their authority and influence within an organization. Early adopters who are executive leaders and/or whose opinions are respected by their peers should be sought out when targeting early adopters because their opinions carry weight within their peer group, and this influence or clout can further drive adoption by their peers. Early adopters who have little authority and are not influential within their peer groups are far less effective at driving adoption.

Once an appropriate group of early adopters has been identified, the next step is to identify a need or pain point that is compatible with a Power BI solution. This need or pain point could be many different things. For example, the need or pain point may take the form of the creation of manual processes for creating reports in Excel. A common theme is that raw data is imported into Excel, massaged, and then reported on. This process may take an hour or two every week. Power BI can help solve this problem by effectively eliminating this manual process. Another example is perhaps a regularly scheduled meeting that reviews different projects or initiatives within the organization. Often, these types of meetings require managers to review data from multiple systems in order to determine the health of each project or initiative. Power BI can help solve this problem by bringing together data from multiple source systems and reporting on that information in a visual way that makes the health of each project or initiative immediately clear. These are just two examples, but it should be clear that any task where Power BI can save people time and energy is a good candidate because eliminating monotonous, manual effort is generally a winning theme for most individuals and organizations.

After identifying a need or pain point, the next step is to create a quick **Proof-Of-Concept (POC)**. This POC does not have to be elaborate or even have real data behind it. Rather, the purpose of a POC is to convey the *what-if* scenario. What if the need or pain point of the early adopter could be solved by Power BI? A simple POC that visually demonstrates the antidote or cure for the early adopter's pain.

Assuming the POC is received favorably, the next step is to propose a business intelligence project that implements the concept demonstrated by the POC. Once this goal is reached, refer to *Chapter 2, Planning Projects with Power BI*, to plan and implement the solution.

Once you complete your first solution, there is no time to rest on your laurels. Evangelize the solution with peers and coworkers, but more importantly, repeat the process with the next pain point and/or early adopter. A single success is not likely to create the bandwagon effect necessary to hurdle the adoption chasm between early adopters and the early majority. Repeated successes, however, can create the necessary tension and envy within other parts of the organization that allow you to bridge and eventually cross the adoption chasm.

Summary

This chapter diverged from the step-by-step, hands-on learning of Power BI to encompass the larger topics of the overall deployment, usage, governance, administration, and adoption of Power BI within an organization. This chapter explored various strengths and weaknesses of different usage models representing the *big picture* of how Power BI is deployed and used within an organization. When Power BI is deployed and used by an organization, the topics of governance and administration naturally come to the fore, and thus this chapter also covered important governance and administrative topics such as tenant settings and the process of deploying Power BI content. Finally, Power BI used by a single individual is powerful, but when used by an entire organization, it can create a data culture that makes the entire organization more efficient and effective. Thus, we covered the topic of adoption and proposed adoption strategies that can assist in diffusing the disruptive technology of self-service analytics and business intelligence throughout an organization.

In the next chapter, we leave the big picture and organizational issues behind and explore the exciting new world of Microsoft Fabric and Copilot.

Questions

As an activity, try to answer the following questions on your own:

- What is a Power BI usage model?
- What usage model is used by many new Power BI deployments?
- What are the strengths and weaknesses of the centralized usage model?
- How do the federated and golden semantic model usage models address the weaknesses of the centralized usage model?
- What are the overall goals of governance in terms of Power BI?
- What are three ways to classify content in Power BI?
- What approach is recommended when it comes to configuring Power BI tenant settings?
- How are Power BI tenant settings accessed?
- How do organizational visuals assist in governance?
- A phased approach for the development and deployment of content is called what?
- What feature in Power BI Premium enables the phased development and deployment of content?
- What Entra roles allow the governance of gateway installers?
- What is Microsoft Purview?
- What is an important trait of early adopters?

Further reading

To learn more about the topics that were covered in this chapter, please take a look at the following references:

- *What is the admin portal?*: https://learn.microsoft.com/en-us/fabric/admin/admin-center
- *Fabric domains*: https://learn.microsoft.com/en-us/fabric/governance/domains
- *Tags in Microsoft Fabric*: https://learn.microsoft.com/en-us/fabric/governance/tags-overview
- *Endorse your content*: https://learn.microsoft.com/en-us/power-bi/collaborate-share/service-endorse-content
- *Manage Power BI visuals admin settings*: https://learn.microsoft.com/en-us/fabric/admin/organizational-visuals
- *About tenant settings*: https://learn.microsoft.com/en-us/fabric/admin/about-tenant-settings
- *Using the Power BI REST APIs*: https://learn.microsoft.com/en-us/rest/api/power-bi/
- *Configure Azure Log Analytics for Power BI*: https://learn.microsoft.com/en-us/power-bi/transform-model/log-analytics/desktop-log-analytics-configure
- *Private lines for secure access to Fabric*: https://learn.microsoft.com/en-us/fabric/security/security-private-links-overview
- *The deployment pipeline process*: https://learn.microsoft.com/en-us/fabric/cicd/deployment-pipelines/understand-the-deployment-process
- *Learn about Microsoft Purview*: https://learn.microsoft.com/en-us/purview/purview
- *Sensitivity Labels in Power BI*: https://learn.microsoft.com/en-us/power-bi/enterprise/service-security-sensitivity-label-overview
- *Microsoft Fabric adoption roadmap*: https://learn.microsoft.com/en-us/power-bi/guidance/fabric-adoption-roadmap

13

Working with Microsoft Fabric and Copilot

Pam's presentation of the final report was well received by her boss, Mike, as well as the rest of the C-level executives within the organization. They immediately want to put the report into production so that department and geographic managers can begin using the insights to better manage the organization.

At the same time, Mike and the other executives want to scale the report created by Pam to include years of historical information as well as future-proof the solution for many years to come. To this end, Paul, their IT architect, has been tasked with creating a revised solution that can scale.

After analyzing the situation, Paul decides to leverage Microsoft Fabric to scale Pam's solution and make the solution enterprise-ready. Microsoft Fabric is Microsoft's data analytics platform and a superset of Power BI. In addition to Power BI, Microsoft Fabric provides enterprise tools for ingesting and transforming data, real-time event handling, and data alerts. These services are provided through a series of workloads such as Data Factory, Data Warehouse, Data Engineering, Data Science, Real-Time Analytics, Activator, and Databases.

The following topics are covered in this chapter:

- Leveraging Data Factory
- Working with Data Warehouse
- Using Microsoft Fabric items
- Working with Copilot

Technical requirements

You will need the following to successfully complete this chapter:

- An internet connection.
- A Microsoft 365 account or Power BI trial.
- A Microsoft Fabric trial.

- For Copilot, you must have a *reserved* F64+ SKU.
- An operational data gateway.
- Source files for Chapter 13 from the GitHub repository at a: `https://github.com/PacktPublishing/Learn-Microsoft-Power-BI_3E`.

Leveraging Data Factory

When looking at Pam's solution, Paul quickly realizes that a single Excel file holding all the hours for every year and month on separate tabs is not going to scale. Instead, Paul decides to separate the hours for each month and year into separate files. These files will then be placed in a single directory to provide the source of the information for Microsoft Fabric.

In addition, instead of creating a Power BI Desktop file to store the queries that access this source data, Paul decides to use dataflows. Dataflows are reusable queries created in the service. These queries can then be used across multiple solutions both within Power BI Desktop as well as within the service.

To demonstrate how to use dataflows, do the following:

1. Download `January.xlsx`, `February.xlsx`, `March.xlsx`, and `People and Tasks.xlsx` from the *Chapter13* folder in the GitHub repository for this book.
2. Create a new folder and place all three files into the folder.
3. Log in to the Power BI service.
4. Create a new workspace and assign the workspace to your Fabric trial capacity. This is done by expanding the **Advanced** section in the **Create a workspace** pane and choosing the **License mode** as **Trial**. Then click the **Apply** button.

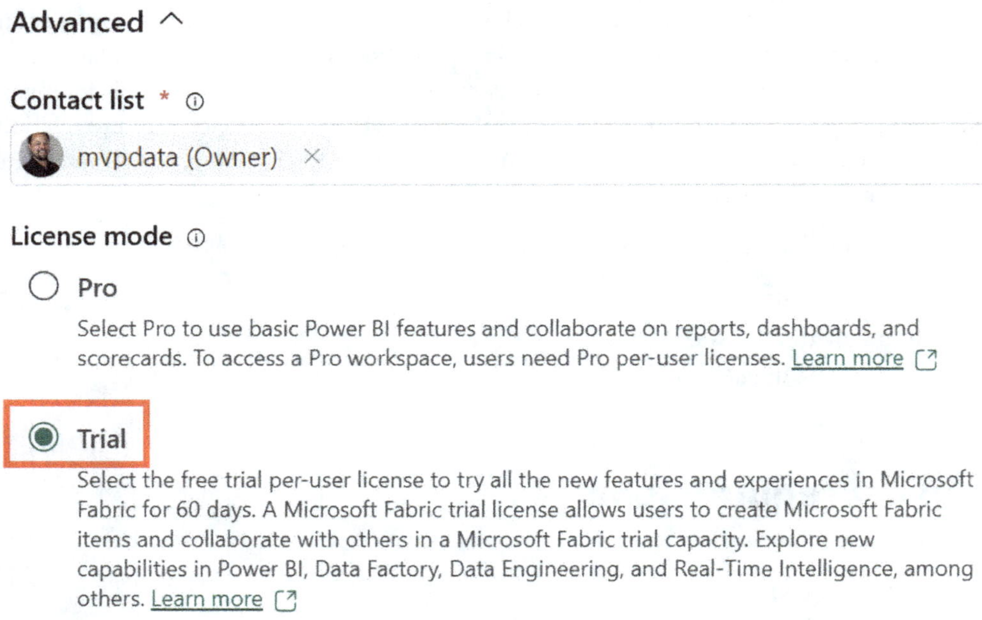

Advanced ^

Contact list * ⓘ

👤 mvpdata (Owner) ✕

License mode ⓘ

◯ Pro

   Select Pro to use basic Power BI features and collaborate on reports, dashboards, and scorecards. To access a Pro workspace, users need Pro per-user licenses. Learn more ↗

◉ Trial

   Select the free trial per-user license to try all the new features and experiences in Microsoft Fabric for 60 days. A Microsoft Fabric trial license allows users to create Microsoft Fabric items and collaborate with others in a Microsoft Fabric trial capacity. Explore new capabilities in Power BI, Data Factory, Data Engineering, and Real-Time Intelligence, among others. Learn more ↗

Figure 13.1 – Assigning a workspace to the Fabric trial capacity

5. While in the new workspace, click the **+ New item** button at the upper left of the page:

Figure 13.2 – New item

6. In the **New item** pane, choose **Dataflow Gen2**.

7. Click the **Create** button.

8. You are now presented with an interface that looks almost exactly like Power Query Editor. Choose **Get data** (first icon) and then **More...** from the **Home** tab of the ribbon.

9. In the **Choose data source** dialog, select **Folder**.

10. Enter the **Connection settings** information including the **Folder path, Connection name, Data gateway, Username,** and **Password,** and then click the **Next** button.

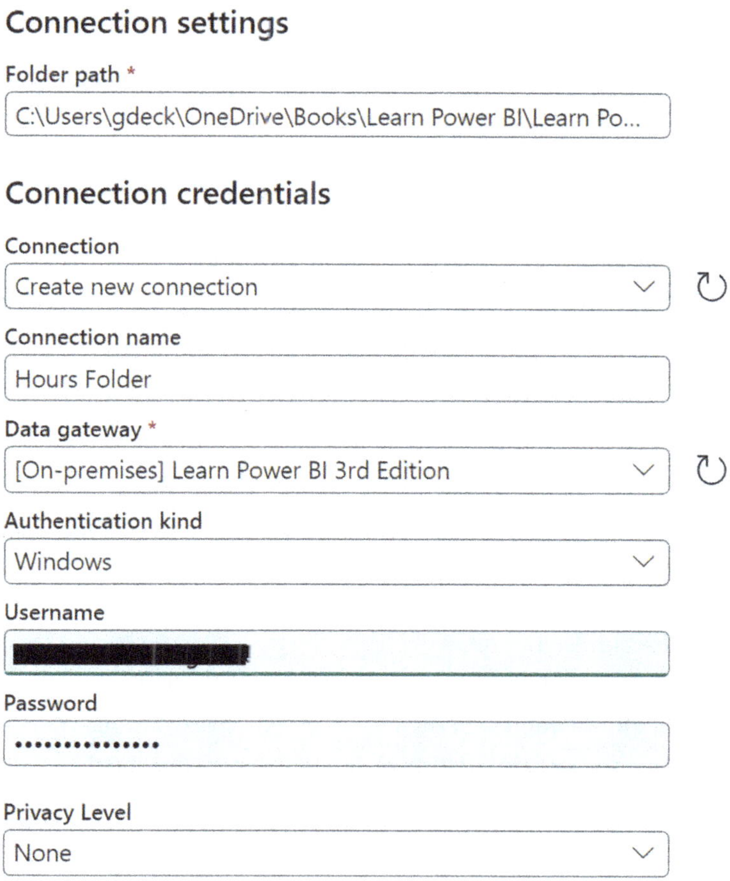

Figure 13.3 – Folder connection settings

11. On the **Preview** folder data dialog, click the **Combine** button.

12. In the **Combine files** dialog, keep **Example file** as **First file** and choose the **Hours** table, as shown here:

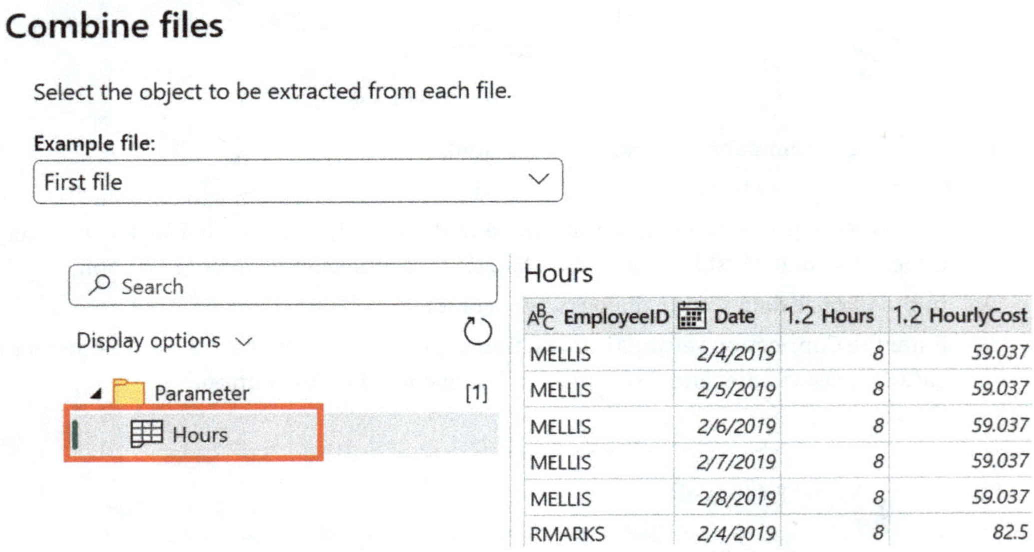

Combine files

Select the object to be extracted from each file.

Example file:

First file   ∨

🔍 Search		
Display options ∨		↻
▲ 📁 Parameter	[1]	
▦ Hours		

Hours

^{ABC} EmployeeID	📅 Date	1.2 Hours	1.2 HourlyCost
MELLIS	2/4/2019	8	59.037
MELLIS	2/5/2019	8	59.037
MELLIS	2/6/2019	8	59.037
MELLIS	2/7/2019	8	59.037
MELLIS	2/8/2019	8	59.037
RMARKS	2/4/2019	8	82.5

Figure 13.4 – Combine files dialog

13. Click on the **Create** button.

14. Additional transformations can now be applied to the data. However, in this case, simply rename the dataflow by clicking on **Dataflow 1** at the upper left and renaming the dataflow to **Hours**.

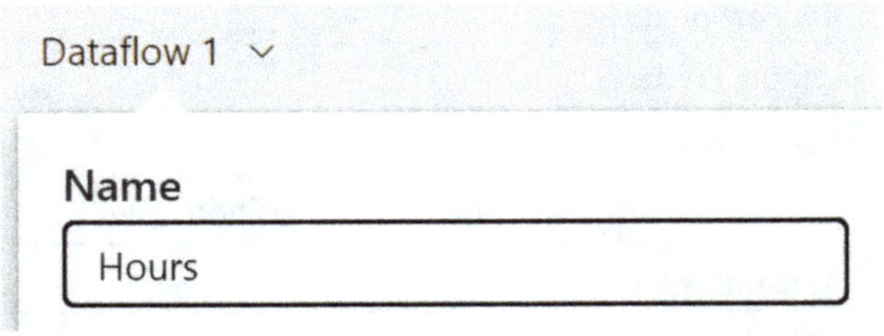

Dataflow 1 ∨

Name

Hours

Figure 13.5 – Renaming a dataflow

15. Now click the **Publish** button.

16. In the workspace, click the **New item** button and then choose **Dataflow Gen2**.

17. Name the dataflow **People** and then click on the **Create** button.

18. This time, choose **Get data** (first icon) and then **Excel workbook**.

19. On the **Connect to data source** page, this time, enter the full path to the People and Tasks. xlsx file. Use **People and Tasks** as the connection name.
20. Click the **Next** button.
21. On the **Choose data** dialog, choose the People table and then click the **Create** button.
22. Click the **Publish** button.

There are actually two different types of dataflows: Gen1 and Gen2. While both allow you to author dataflows, Gen1 dataflows offer the unique abilities to use Direct Query, incremental refresh, and AI insights support. Conversely, Gen2 dataflows have improved monitoring and refresh support, can integrate with data pipelines, and support high-scale compute.

In addition to dataflows, Data Factory also supports pipelines and Spark jobs for data ingestion and transformation. Pipelines provide a no-code, low-code environment like dataflows. However, pipelines support about 30 connectors and can only handle lightweight data transformation. Dataflows have more than 150 connectors and can support complex data transformation. Pipelines are generally used for process orchestration while dataflows are used for data transformation. Spark jobs require the ability to code in Scala, Python, Spark SQL, or R.

Now that Paul has two separate Dataflow Gen2 queries for Hours and People, it is time to create a data warehouse.

Working with Data Warehouse

Microsoft describes Fabric Data Warehouse as a next-generation solution consisting of a lake-centric warehouse with a SQL analytics endpoint and a Fabric data warehouse. This may sound extremely confusing considering that Fabric also supports the ability to create an object called a Lakehouse as well. In short, create a data warehouse when dealing with structured data, if you need multi-table transactions, or you want to develop using T-SQL. Create a Lakehouse when dealing with unstructured and structured data, if you need only single table transactions, or if you want to develop using Spark.

Since the data in this scenario is structured data, Paul chooses to build a data warehouse to store the data that will come from the dataflows created earlier in the *Leveraging Data Factory* section of this chapter. To create a data warehouse, do the following:

1. Navigate to the workspace in your Fabric trial.
2. Click the **New item** button in the ribbon and then choose **Warehouse** under the **Store data** heading in the **New item** pane.

3. In the New warehouse dialog box, type **Learn Power BI Warehouse** for the name and then click the **Create** button:

New warehouse

Name

Learn Power BI Warehouse

Create Cancel

Figure 13.6 – Creating a Fabric data warehouse

4. Once the warehouse is created, click back on the workspace in the left navigation pane.

5. Hover over the **Hours** dataflow, click the ellipsis (**...**), and then choose **Edit**.

Hours   Dataflow Gen2

Learn Power BI   Delete

Learn Power BI (copy)   Edit

Figure 13.7 – Editing a dataflow

6. Once the query loads, choose **Get data** (first icon) and then **Excel workbook** from the **Home** tab of the ribbon.

7. On the **Connect to data source** page, this time, enter the full path to the **People and Tasks.xlsx** file. Note that this reuses your **People and Tasks** connection created earlier.

8. Click the **Next** button.

9. On the **Choose data** dialog, choose the **Tasks** table and then click the **Create** button.

10. Once the table loads, click the **Use first row as headers** in the **Transform** area of the **Home** tab of the ribbon. Use the down-arrow chevron on the far right of the ribbon to expand the ribbon.

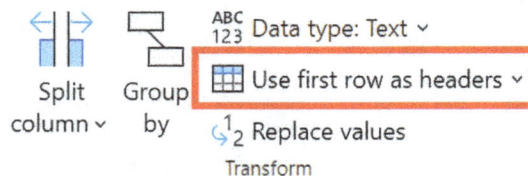

Split   Group   Data type: Text ∨
column ∨   by   Use first row as headers ∨
                       Replace values
                       Transform

Figure 13.8 – Use first row as headers

11. Click on the **Hours** query.

12. Choose **Merge queries** in the **Combine** section of the **Home** tab of the ribbon.

13. In the **Merge** dialog, select **Tasks** as **Right table for merge** and select the **TaskID** columns in both queries:

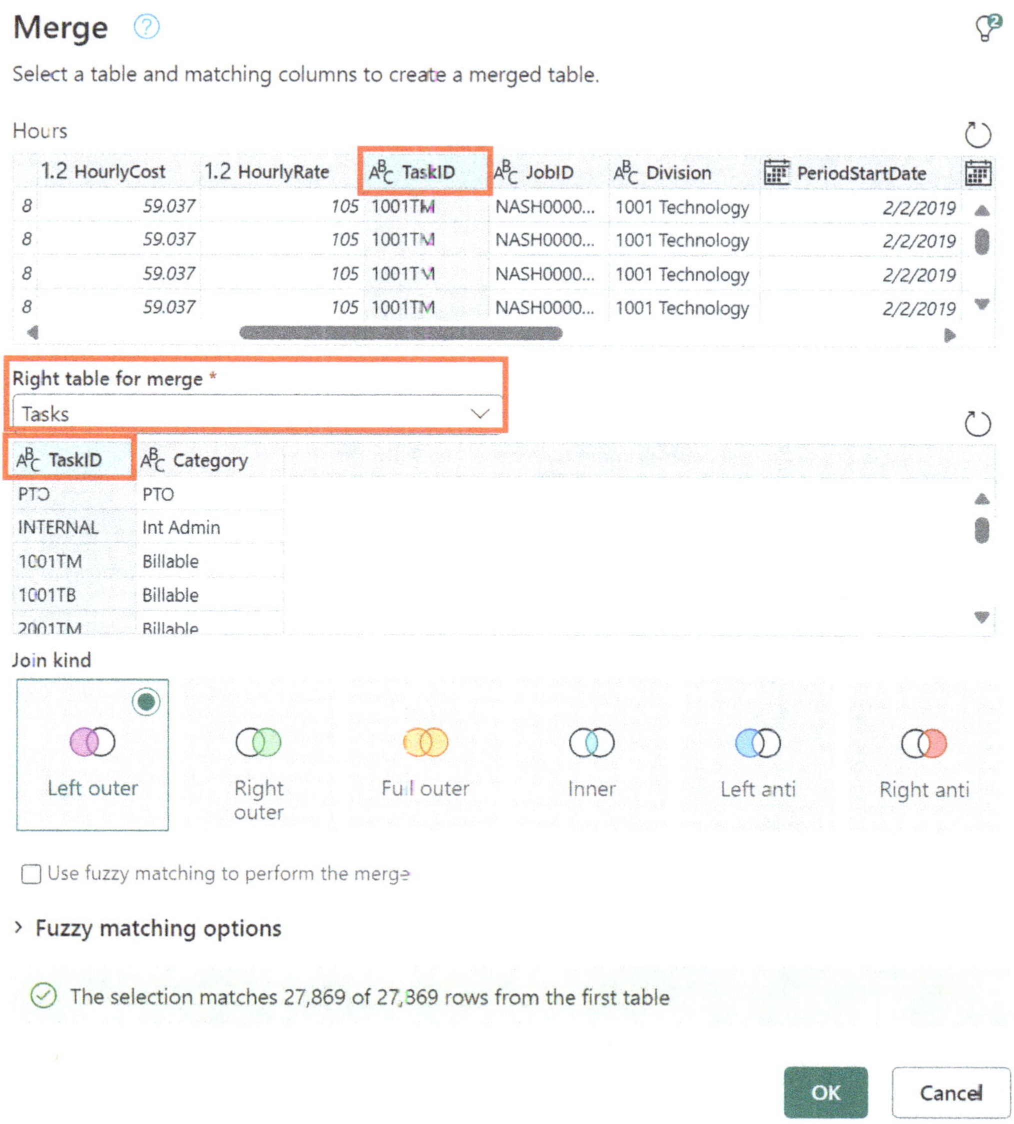

Merge ⑦

Select a table and matching columns to create a merged table.

Hours

1.2 HourlyCost	1.2 HourlyRate	A^B_C TaskID	A^B_C JobID	A^B_C Division	PeriodStartDate
8	59.037	105 1001TM	NASH0000...	1001 Technology	2/2/2019
8	59.037	105 1001TM	NASH0000...	1001 Technology	2/2/2019
8	59.037	105 1001TM	NASH0000...	1001 Technology	2/2/2019
8	59.037	105 1001TM	NASH0000...	1001 Technology	2/2/2019

Right table for merge *

Tasks

A^B_C TaskID	A^B_C Category
PTO	PTO
INTERNAL	Int Admin
1001TM	Billable
1001TB	Billable
2001TM	Billable

Join kind

Left outer	Right outer	Full outer	Inner	Left anti	Right anti

☐ Use fuzzy matching to perform the merge

> **Fuzzy matching options**

⊘ The selection matches 27,869 of 27,869 rows from the first table

OK   Cancel

Figure 13.9 – Merge queries dialog

14. Click the **OK** button. If you receive a message about privacy levels, simply ignore the privacy levels.

15. In the header of the **Tasks** column, click the diverging arrows icon, deselect **TaskID**, and then click the **OK** button:

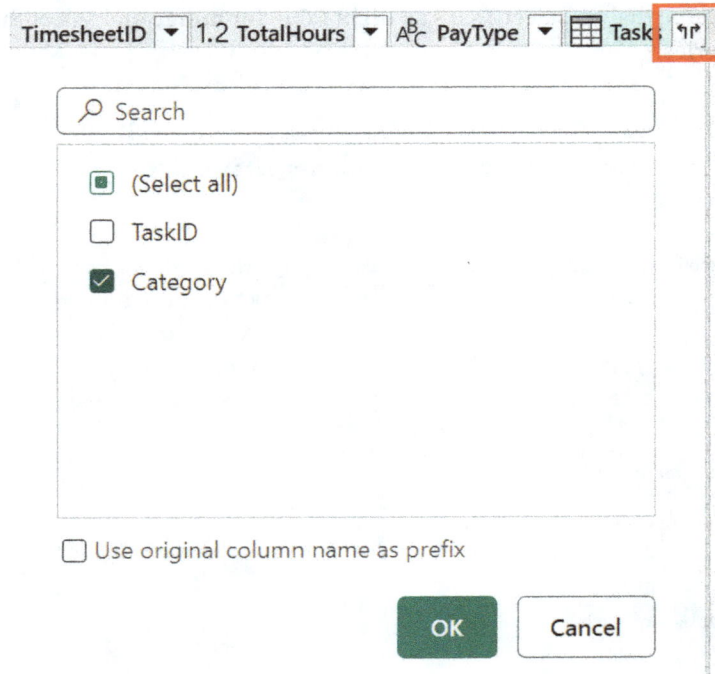

Figure 13.10 – Expanding the table

16. In the **Query** section of the **Home** tab of the ribbon, select **Add data destination** and then select **Warehouse**.

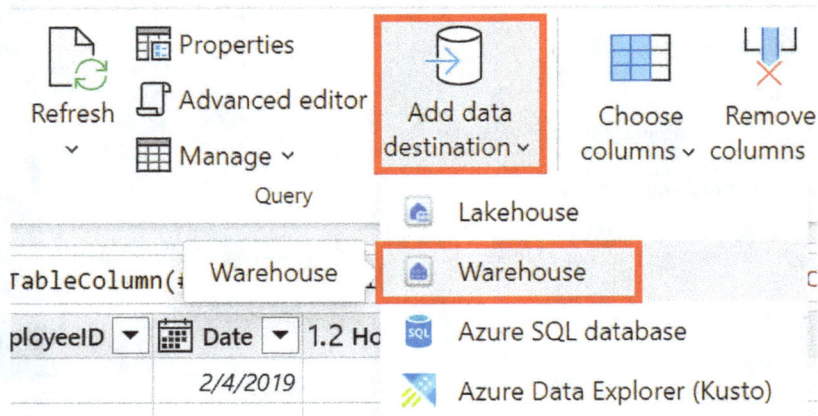

Figure 13.11 – Add data destination

17. On the **Connect to data destination** page, click the **Sign in** button and sign in if necessary.
18. Click the **Next** button.
19. On the **Choose destination target** dialog, select **Learn Power BI Warehouse** and leave **Table name** as **Hours** as shown in the following screenshot:.

Choose destination target

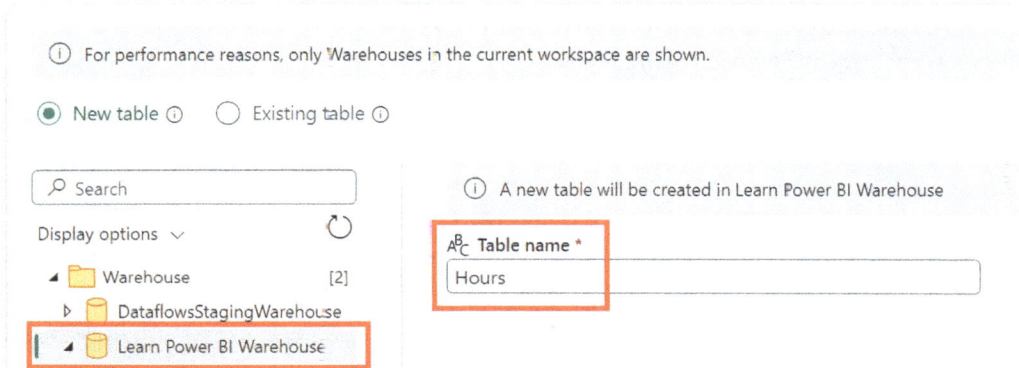

ⓘ For performance reasons, only Warehouses in the current workspace are shown.

⦿ New table ⓘ　　◯ Existing table ⓘ

🔍 Search

Display options ⌄　　↻

▲ 📁 Warehouse　　　　[2]
　▷ 🗄 DataflowsStagingWarehouse
│　▲ 🗄 Learn Power BI Warehouse

ⓘ A new table will be created in Learn Power BI Warehouse

ᴬᴮC Table name *

Hours

Figure 13.12 – Choose destination target

20. Click the **Next** button.
21. On the **Choose destination settings** dialog, choose the **Save settings** button.
22. Click the **Publish** button.
23. Back in the workspace, select **Learn Power BI Warehouse**:

🔷 Learn Power BI Warehouse 🗿　　　　　　　　　　　Warehouse

　└ ⠿ Learn Power BI Warehouse　　　　　　　　　Semantic model (default)

Figure 13.13 – Warehouse selection

24. In the **Explorer** panel, expand **Learn Power BI Warehouse**, expand **Schemas**, expand **dbo**, expand **Tables,** and click on the **Hours** table to view the first 1,000 rows. If the **Hours** table is not present, you will need to wait until the **Hours** dataflow completes its refresh.

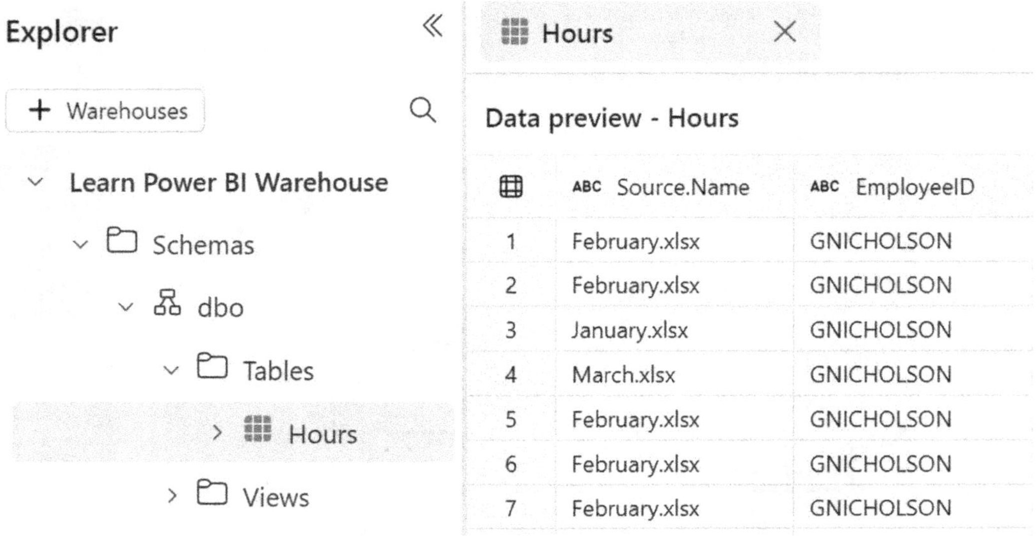

Explorer	≪		⊞ Hours	✕

Data preview - Hours

⊞	ABC Source.Name	ABC EmployeeID
1	February.xlsx	GNICHOLSON
2	February.xlsx	GNICHOLSON
3	January.xlsx	GNICHOLSON
4	March.xlsx	GNICHOLSON
5	February.xlsx	GNICHOLSON
6	February.xlsx	GNICHOLSON
7	February.xlsx	GNICHOLSON

Explorer panel:
- **+ Warehouses**
- ⌄ **Learn Power BI Warehouse**
  - ⌄ 🗁 Schemas
    - ⌄ ⛗ dbo
      - ⌄ 🗁 Tables
        - ＞ ⊞ Hours
      - ＞ 🗁 Views

Figure 13.14 – Explorer panel

25. Click on the workspace in the left navigation pane.
26. Edit the **People** query and add a data destination of **Learn Power BI Warehouse.** Use the same connection already created.
27. While in the workspace, click on **Learn Power BI Warehouse** to open the warehouse.
28. Confirm that the **People** table exists in the **Explorer** pane.
29. In the **Explorer** pane, click on **Model layouts.**

30. Create a relationship between the **EmployeeID** column in the **Hours** table and the **ID** column in the **People** table by dragging and dropping:

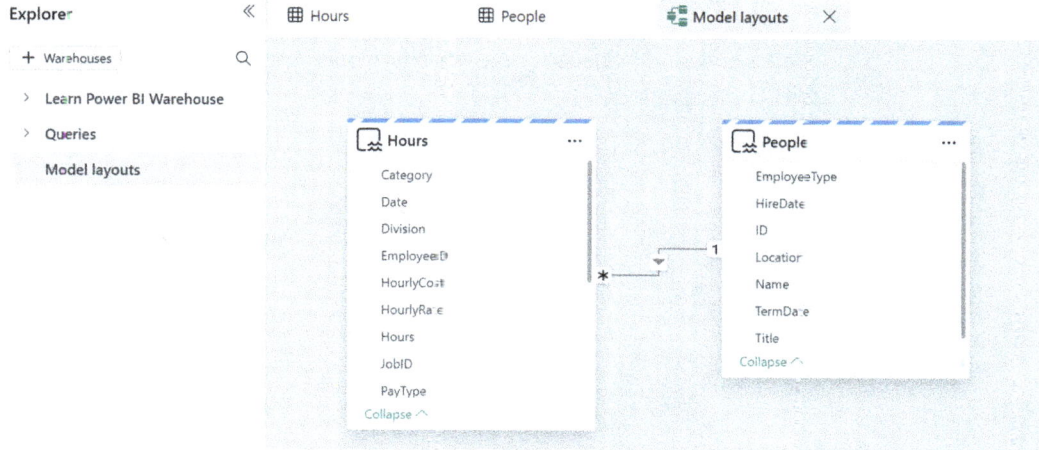

Figure 13.15 – Model layouts

31. Click the **Reporting** tab of the ribbon and then select **Manage default semantic model**.

Figure 13.16 – Manage default semantic model

32. In the **Manage default semantic model** dialog, check the **Select all** checkbox.

Manage default semantic model

Select or deselect objects for the semantic model. Only objects that can be shown. Learn more ⎘

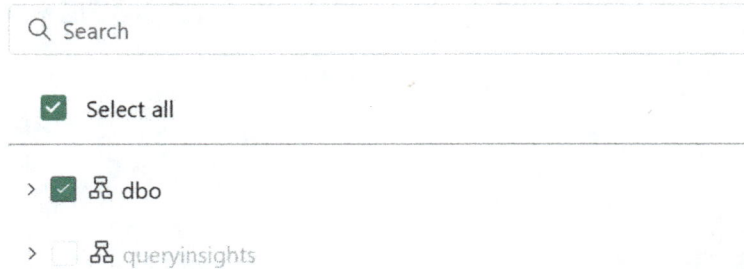

🔍 Search

✅ Select all

> ✅ 🗂 dbo

> ☐ 🗂 queryinsights

Figure 13.17 – Manage default semantic model dialog

33. Click the **Confirm** button.
34. On the **Reporting** tab of the ribbon, click **Automatically update semantic model**.

As you can see, you can create one or more semantic models based on the warehouse. You can also explore the data in the semantic model as well as create reports. To see how this is done, do the following:

1. Navigate back to the workspace in your Fabric trial.
2. Click on **Semantic model (default) Learn Power BI Warehouse**. Note, select the semantic model, not the warehouse.
3. In the ribbon, select **Explore this data** and then select **Explore this data**:

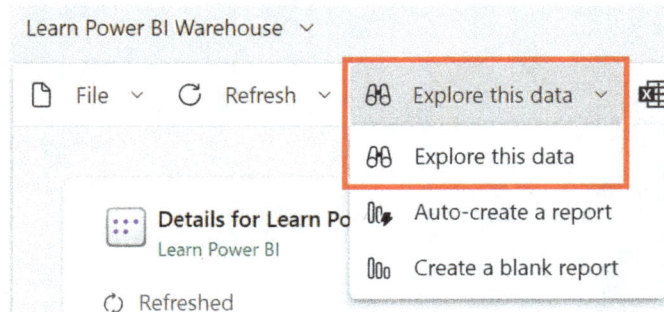

Learn Power BI Warehouse ⌄

📄 File ⌄   C Refresh ⌄   👓 Explore this data ⌄   📊

👓 Explore this data

▦ Details for Learn Po   📊 Auto-create a report
   Learn Power BI
                          📊 Create a blank report
C Refreshed

Figure 13.18 – Explore this data

4. In the **Explore Learn Power BI Warehouse** dialog, in the **Data** pane, select the **EmployeeType** column from the **People** table and the **TotalHours** column from the **Hours** table.
5. Both a **Matrix** and a **Visual** chart are created.

6. An alternate visual can be shown by clicking the **Visual** text and then selecting a different visual type:

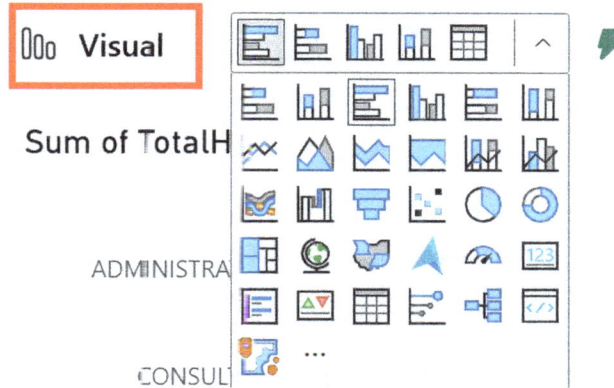

Figure 13.19 – Changing the visual type

7. You can also add filters by clicking the **Add filter** text above **Matrix**. In the dropdown, expand **All data**, expand **Hours**, and then choose the **Category** column.

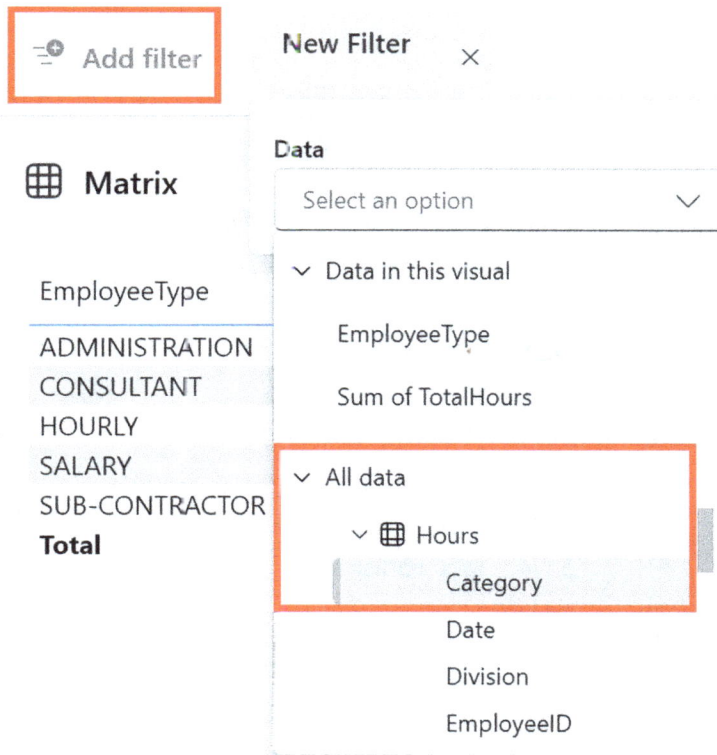

Figure 13.20 – Adding a filter

8. For the filter, choose **Billable** and then click the **Apply** button:

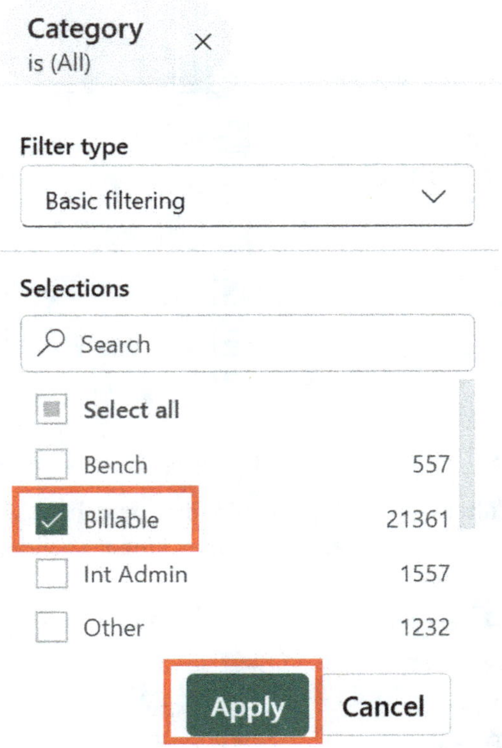

Figure 13.21 – Applying a filter

9. If desired, you can save this as an exploration or as a report using the **Save** button in the ribbon.

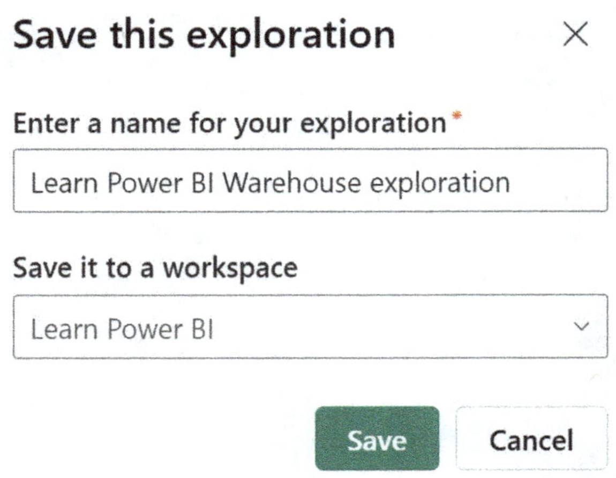

Figure 13.22 – Saving an exploration

10. Close out of the exploration dialog by clicking the **X** icon in the upper-right corner.

11. In the ribbon, select **Explore this data**, but this time, choose **Auto-create a report**.

12. Watch for a notification to appear in the upper-right corner, and when it does, select **View report now**:

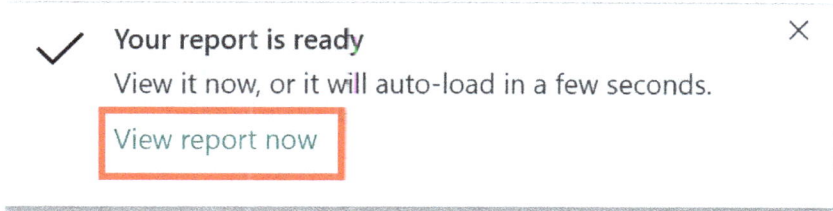

Figure 13.23 – Report is ready notification

13. The report will open as follows:

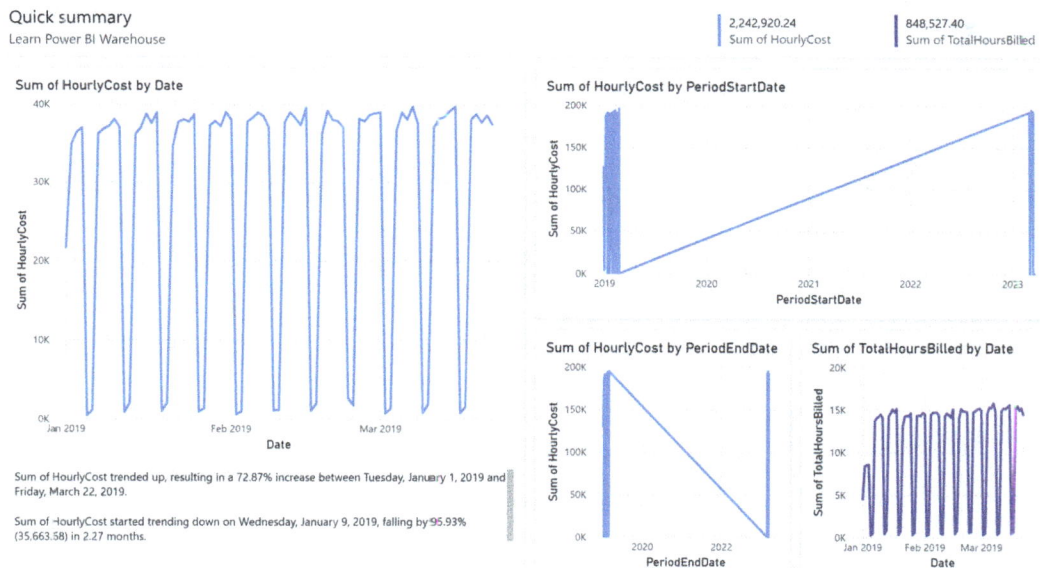

Figure 13.24 – Automatically created report

14. Click the **Save** button in the ribbon to save the report.

15. In the **Save your report** dialog, enter a name for your report and then click the **Save** button.

This completes our creation and exploration of data warehouses in Microsoft Fabric. Now that we have created these items in Fabric, we can use them in multiple ways.

Using Microsoft Fabric items

Once Microsoft Fabric content such as dataflows and warehouses are created, there are multiple ways to use these items within the Power BI/Fabric service as well as in Power BI Desktop. To demonstrate how to use these Fabric items in Power BI Desktop, do the following:

1. Open Power BI Desktop and create a blank report.
2. On the **Home** tab of the ribbon, select **Get data** and then choose **Dataflows**.
3. Sign in to your organizational account and then choose the **Connect** button.
4. In **Navigator**, expand **Dataflows**, expand your workspace (in this case, **Learn Power BI**), expand **Hours** and select the **Hours** table, and expand **People** and select the **People** table, as shown:

Navigator

Display Options ▼

▲ Dataflows [2]
  ▷ Environments
  ▲ Workspaces [2]
    ▷ Fabric
    ▲ Learn Power BI [3]
      ▲ Hours [2]
        ☑ Hours
        ☐ Tasks
      ▲ People [1]
        ☑ People

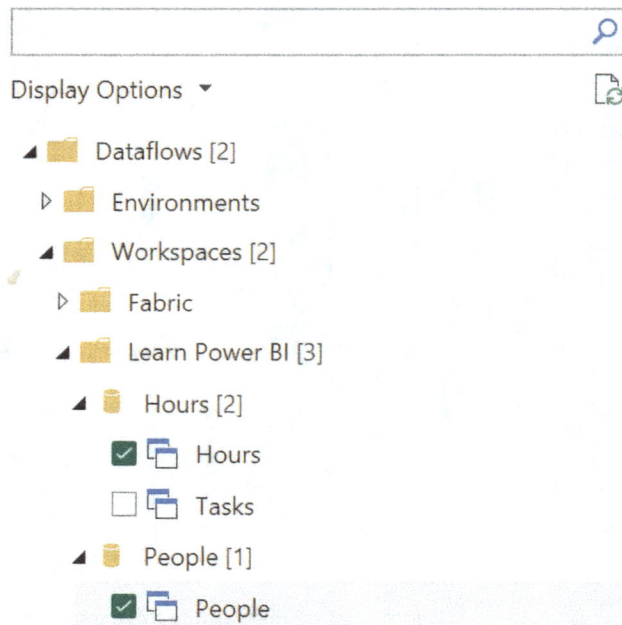

Figure 13.25 – Dataflows Navigator

5. Select the **Load** button when finished.
6. If prompted for credentials, choose Microsoft account, sign in with your organizational account, and then choose the **Connect** button.

7. When prompted for **Privacy levels**, check the box to ignore privacy levels.

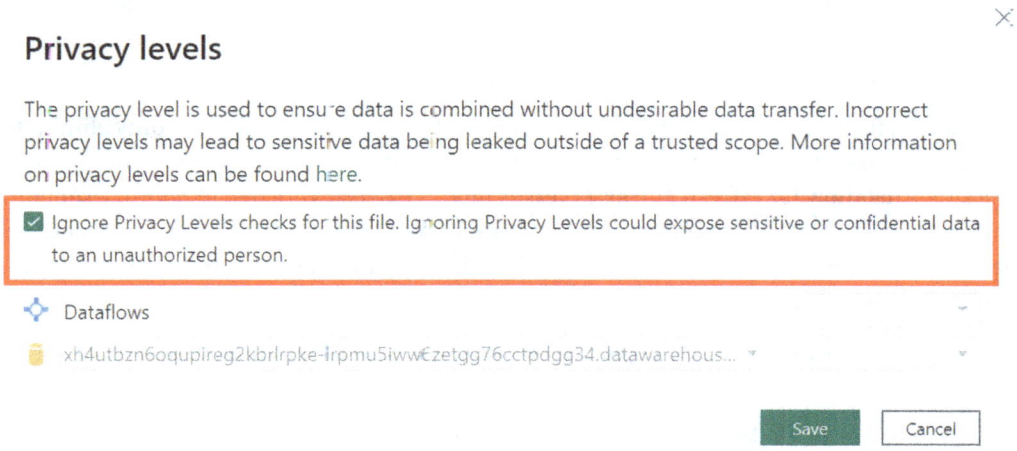

Privacy levels

The privacy level is used to ensure data is combined without undesirable data transfer. Incorrect privacy levels may lead to sensitive data being leaked outside of a trusted scope. More information on privacy levels can be found here.

☑ Ignore Privacy Levels checks for this file. Ignoring Privacy Levels could expose sensitive or confidential data to an unauthorized person.

◇ Dataflows

🗄 xh4utbzn6oqupireg2kbrlrpke-irpmu5iwwEzetgg76cctpdgg34.datawarehous... ▾

Save   Cancel

Figure 13.26 – Ignore privacy levels

8. Click the **Save** button.

9. In the **Set storage mode** dialog, leave the storage modes as **Import** and then click the **OK** button:

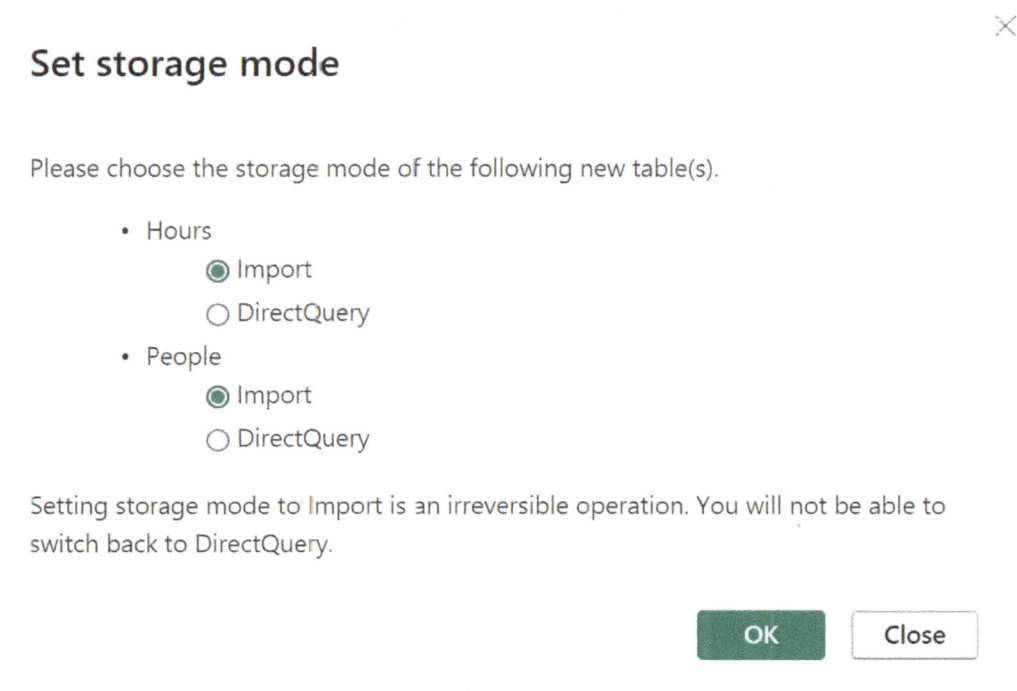

Set storage mode

Please choose the storage mode of the following new table(s).

- Hours
  - ◉ Import
  - ○ DirectQuery
- People
  - ◉ Import
  - ○ DirectQuery

Setting storage mode to Import is an irreversible operation. You will not be able to switch back to DirectQuery.

OK   Close

Figure 13.27 – Set storage mode dialog

10. The **Load** dialog appears, wait for it to complete.

The advantage of dataflows should now be clear. The next time Pam or anyone else wants to build a report based on the people in the organization and the hours worked, they simply need to connect to the appropriate dataflow. Since the data has already been transformed, less work is required on the part of the end user.

In addition, the same dataflows can be used across multiple reports. This not only eliminates duplication but can also improve the operation of the entire system since source systems are only accessed by a single dataflow for refresh purposes versus multiple queries created in multiple semantic models. This is because dataflows access the source systems and load the data into Azure Data Lake Storage Gen2 storage blobs. Other semantic models or objects that utilize these dataflows pull the data from the Azure storage blob versus the actual source systems themselves.

You can also use the warehouse object as well as its associated semantic model in Power BI Desktop. To demonstrate, do the following:

1. In Power BI Desktop, create a new blank report.
2. From the **Home** tab of the ribbon, choose **Get data** and then **Power BI semantic models**.
3. Choose the **Learn Power BI Warehouse** semantic model and then click the **Connect** button.
4. You are now connected live to the **Learn Power BI Warehouse** semantic model.
5. Create another blank report.
6. From the **Home** tab of the ribbon, choose **Get data** and then **More....**
7. In the **Get Data** dialog, choose **Microsoft Fabric**, **Warehouses**, and then **Connect:**

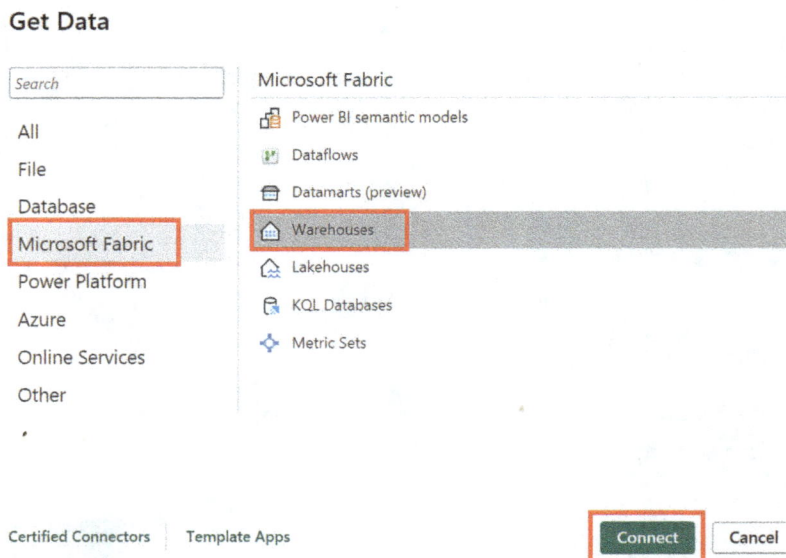

Figure 13.28 – Getting data from Microsoft Fabric warehouses

8.   Choose **Learn Power BI Warehouse** and then click the **Connect** button.

9.   You are now connected live to the **Learn Power BI Warehouse** semantic model.

Both of these methods create a **Live** connection to the **Learn Power BI Warehouse** semantic model. However, you can also connect to the SQL endpoint for the warehouse. To do this, perform the following steps:

1.   In the Power BI service, navigate to the workspace where you created your data warehouse.

2.   Select **Learn Power BI Warehouse** (the **Warehouse**, not the **Semantic model (default)**.

3.   On the **Home** tab, click the gear icon:

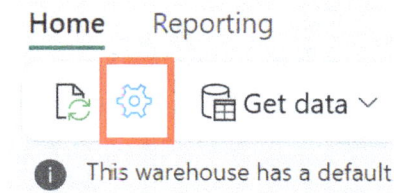

Figure 13.29 – Settings icon

🔍 **Quick tip:** Need to see a high-resolution version of this image? Open this book in the next-gen Packt Reader or view it in the PDF/ePub copy.

🔒 **The next-gen Packt Reader** is included for free with the purchase of this book. Scan the QR code OR go to packtpub.com/unlock, then use the search bar to find this book by name. Double-check the edition shown to make sure you get the right one.

4.   Under **SQL connection string,** click the copy icon to copy the connection string:

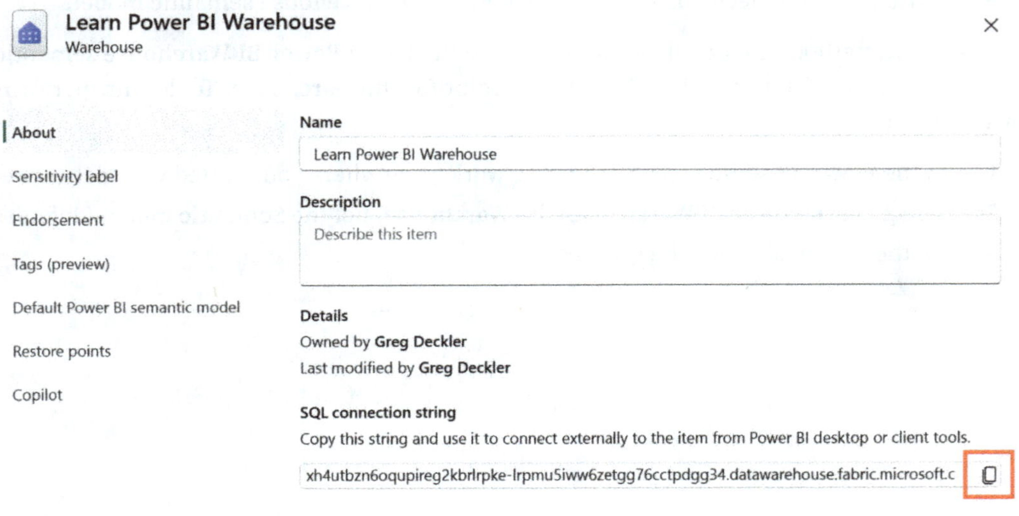

Learn Power BI Warehouse
Warehouse   ×

| About |
| Sensitivity label |
| Endorsement |
| Tags (preview) |
| Default Power BI semantic model |
| Restore points |
| Copilot |

Name

Learn Power BI Warehouse

Description

Describe this item

Details
Owned by **Greg Deckler**
Last modified by **Greg Deckler**

SQL connection string
Copy this string and use it to connect externally to the item from Power BI desktop or client tools.

xh4utbzn6oqupireg2kbrlrpke-lrpmu5iww6zetgg76cctpdgg34.datawarehouse.fabric.microsoft.c   []

Figure 13.30 – SQL connection string

5.   Create a new blank report in Power BI Desktop.

6.   On the **Home** tab of the ribbon, choose **Get data** and then **SQL Server.**

7.   For **Server,** paste in the connection string and then click the **OK** button.

8.   In **Navigator,** expand **Learn Power BI Warehouse** and note that you can select the **Hours** and **People** tables.

We are now done exploring how to use Microsoft Fabric items. Let's finally turn our attention to **Copilot,** Microsoft's generative artificial intelligence platform.

Working with Copilot

Copilot is Microsoft's generative AI feature designed to enable alternative ways to create reports and visuals, analyze and transform data, and generate insights.

Using Copilot in Microsoft Fabric and Power BI requires a reserved Fabric capacity of F64 or higher, although Microsoft has recently announced that Copilot will be available for all Fabric capacities. Copilot is not enabled for trial Fabric capacities and is not available in sovereign clouds (government clouds). Copilot must be enabled in **Tenant settings** within the Power BI/Fabric tenant. See *Chapter 12, Deploying, Governing, and Adopting Power BI.*

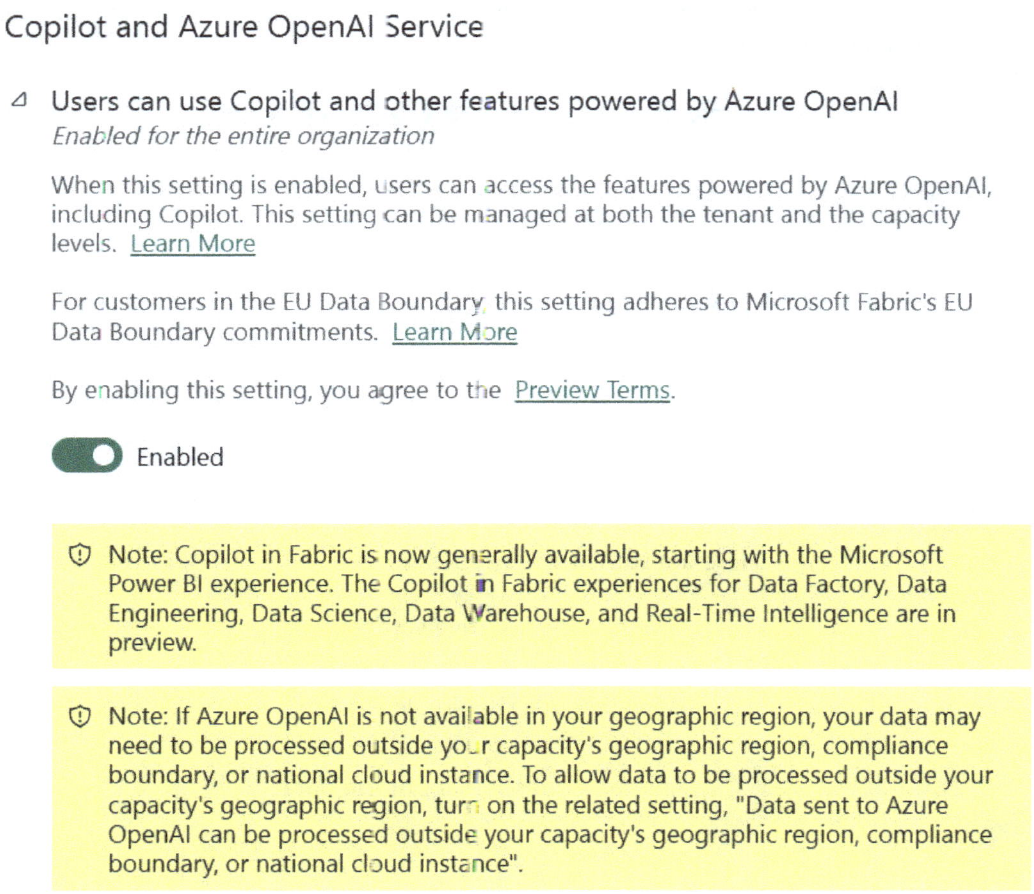

Copilot and Azure OpenAI Service

△ Users can use Copilot and other features powered by Azure OpenAI
Enabled for the entire organization

When this setting is enabled, users can access the features powered by Azure OpenAI, including Copilot. This setting can be managed at both the tenant and the capacity levels. Learn More

For customers in the EU Data Boundary, this setting adheres to Microsoft Fabric's EU Data Boundary commitments. Learn More

By enabling this setting, you agree to the Preview Terms.

◯ Enabled

> ⓘ Note: Copilot in Fabric is now generally available, starting with the Microsoft Power BI experience. The Copilot in Fabric experiences for Data Factory, Data Engineering, Data Science, Data Warehouse, and Real-Time Intelligence are in preview.

> ⓘ Note: If Azure OpenAI is not available in your geographic region, your data may need to be processed outside your capacity's geographic region, compliance boundary, or national cloud instance. To allow data to be processed outside your capacity's geographic region, turn on the related setting, "Data sent to Azure OpenAI can be processed outside your capacity's geographic region, compliance boundary, or national cloud instance".

Figure 13.31 – Copilot and Azure OpenAI Service tenant settings

Once Copilot is enabled, you must assign at least one workspace to an F64+ reserved capacity. Once enabled, Copilot appears in the ribbon of the service when viewing certain content such as reports, dataflows, and data warehouses.

For example, when viewing a report, a Copilot icon appears on the far right of the ribbon. Clicking the Copilot icon opens the Copilot pane, as shown here:

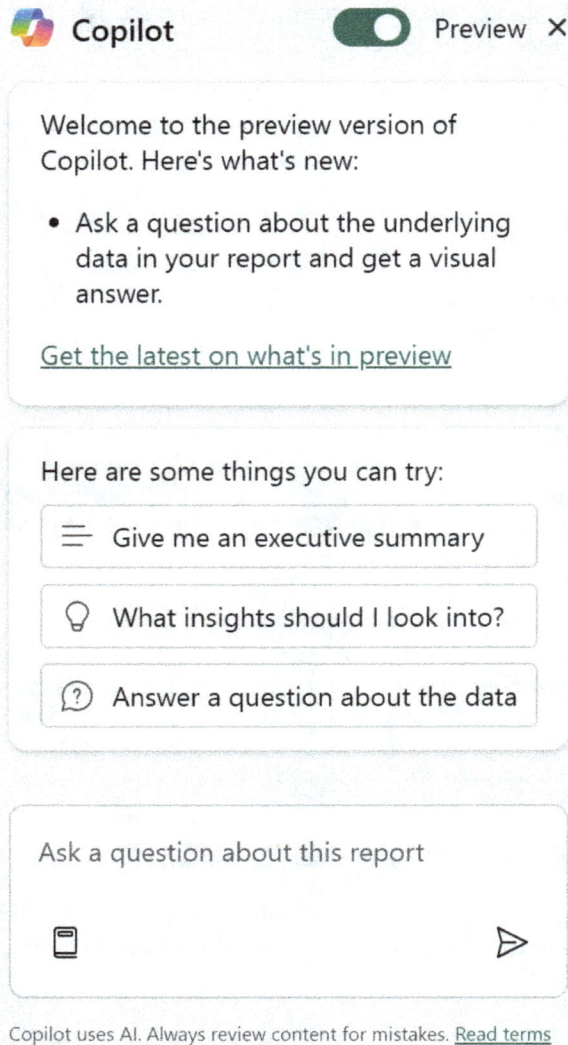

Figure 13.32 – Copilot pane

Asking a question about the data generates a text response within the Copilot pane. You can also use Copilot when editing a report. Doing so provides options such as **Suggest content for a new report page**. Selecting this option provides a response that includes a button for creating the suggested page:

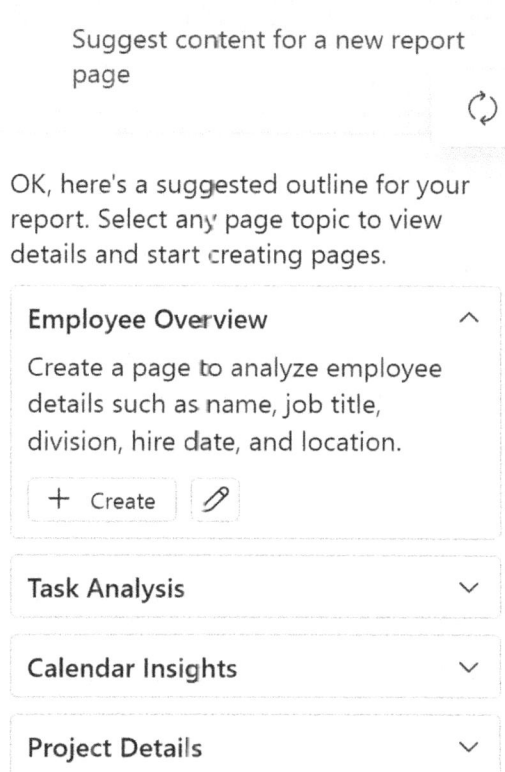

Suggest content for a new report
page

OK, here's a suggested outline for your report. Select any page topic to view details and start creating pages.

Employee Overview ∧

Create a page to analyze employee details such as name, job title, division, hire date, and location.

\+ Create ✎

Task Analysis ∨

Calendar Insights ∨

Project Details ∨

Figure 13.33 – Copilot pane for suggesting content for a new report page

Clicking the + **Create** button creates the page in the report.

Copilot can also be used with Data Factory and Data Warehouse workloads. In Data Factory, Copilot can be used with Dataflow Gen2 dataflows as well as data pipelines. With Dataflow Gen2 dataflows, the following actions are supported:

- Summarize an existing query.
- Create a new query.
- Create new transformation steps for an existing query.

With data pipelines, the following actions are supported:

- Summarize an existing pipeline.
- Create a new pipeline.
- Provide an explanation of error messages.

For Data Warehouse, Copilot supports the following actions:

- Create a SQL query using a natural language description.
- Help complete the code.
- Provide an explanation of how to fix an existing query via the **Fix** quick action in the SQL query editor.
- Provide a summary of a query via the Explain quick action in the SQL query editor.
- Receive intelligent observations and suggestions based on the schema and metadata of your warehouse.

Copilot is available for similar tasks in other Fabric workloads such as Data Engineering, Data Science, Real-Time Intelligence, and SQL Databases.

Copilot can also be used in Power BI Desktop. To see how this works, do the following:

1. Open the `Learn Power BI.pbix` file in Power BI Desktop.
2. While in **Report view**, on the **Home** tab of the ribbon, select the Copilot icon:

Figure 13.34 – Copilot icon in Power BI Desktop

3. If this is the first time using Copilot in Power BI Desktop, click the **Select a workspace** button.
4. In the **Copilot workspace** dialog, choose a workspace and press the **OK** button.
5. The Copilot pane now operates identically to when editing a report in the Power BI service.

With this, we have understood how Copilot works in Microsoft Fabric.

Summary

This chapter introduced Microsoft Fabric and Copilot. Microsoft Fabric provides enterprise capabilities with regard to data ingestion, data transformation, and data storage. Data Factory allows the creation of reusable queries via dataflows and data pipelines. These queries can then be used to ingest data into warehouses and lakehouses, as well as Power BI Desktop reports. Warehouses allow enterprises to create a data warehouse within the Fabric service. These warehouses can then feed semantic models and can also be queried as a SQL database.

Microsoft Copilot for Fabric brings generative AI features to both the Power BI/Fabric service as well as Power BI Desktop. Copilot can be used to aid in the creation of dataflows, data pipelines, and warehouses, as well as visualizations and reports.

In the next chapter, we will focus on you, the individual, and how you can leverage your knowledge of Power BI to advance your career.

Questions

As an activity, try to answer the following questions on your own:

- What are the seven Fabric workloads mentioned in this chapter?
- What are the three primary types of objects that can be created in Data Factory?
- What are the differences between Gen1 and Gen2 dataflows?
- When should you use a warehouse versus a lakehouse in Fabric?
- True or false? Copilot is available for all Fabric capacities, including trial capacities and capacities in sovereign clouds.

Further reading

To learn more about the topics that were covered in this chapter, please take a look at the following references:

- *What is Microsoft Fabric?*: https://learn.microsoft.com/en-us/fabric/get-started/microsoft-fabric-overview
- *What is Data Factory in Microsoft Fabric?*: https://learn.microsoft.com/en-us/fabric/data-factory/data-factory-overview
- *What is data warehousing in Microsoft Fabric?*: https://learn.microsoft.com/en-us/fabric/data-warehouse/data-warehousing
- *Overview of Copilot in Fabric*: https://learn.microsoft.com/en-us/fabric/get-started/copilot-fabric-overview

Join our community on Discord

Join our community's Discord space for discussions with the authors and other readers: https://discord.gg/hvqvgyGH

14

Putting Your Knowledge to Use

Now that you have a basic understanding of Power BI and **Business Intelligence (BI)** as a field, it is time to put that knowledge to use by finding a job or growing your career! This chapter focuses on the overall BI and data analytics market, citing industry reports on current value and expected growth. In addition, this chapter covers the various types of jobs and career paths you can find working within the BI and data analytics market. We also cover various search strategies for finding a job in BI as well as interviewing and compensation negotiation tips. Finally, we provide a wealth of resources to help you continue your journey of learning and discovery!

The following topics are covered in this chapter:

- Understanding the BI opportunity
- Growing your job and career
- Continuing your journey

Technical requirements

There are no technical requirements for this chapter.

Understanding the BI opportunity

The BI market is a vast and fragmented space with at least 20 different companies making Gartner's list for their *Magic Quadrant for Analytics and Business Intelligence Platforms*. Market reports generally place the total estimate of the global market for BI solutions and services at about 33 billion USD for 2024. The market is estimated to reach nearly double that amount (60 billion USD) by 2030.

That's a lot of numbers, but the important thing to realize is that the BI market is growing, as BI is important to all types of organizations, which are becoming increasingly reliant on it in order to make informed business decisions about how to operate more efficiently, effectively, and profitably.

The data analytics and BI space has seen explosive growth over the last few years, and everything indicates that this exponential growth will continue for years to come. Power BI is at the forefront of the market, as one of the fastest-growing, most capable, and most heavily used BI tools on the planet.

As of 2021–2024, Gartner's *Magic Quadrant for Analytics and Business Intelligence Platforms* placed Microsoft furthest to the right for completeness of vision and furthest up in the ability to execute for three years in a row.

However, the BI market is even bigger than just Power BI. There are many other tools and systems, such as Tableau, Qlik, and others, that comprise the software component of the BI market. In addition, the BI market consists of the services provided in conjunction with BI software. This services component is provided by a variety of different jobs and roles within organizations. The upcoming sections explore the types of jobs and roles that comprise the services aspect of the BI market.

Understanding the types of BI jobs and roles

The kinds of jobs available in the BI space are quite varied and diverse. While the exact roles, responsibilities, and requirements vary between organizations, here we cover the more common types of jobs and roles available in the BI sector, including typical responsibilities and requirements. This information is helpful in determining the type of job and career best suited to your particular skills and also helps you determine the skills you need to foster and learn in order to succeed in the growing BI market and get the job you truly desire.

BI analysts

A BI analyst, or simply analyst, is a diverse and popular job in the BI space. In many ways, business analysts are a jack-of-all-trades when it comes to the BI space. Part-requirements gathering, part-data analysis, part-data modeling, and part-report development, business analysts often form the bridge between the business side and the technical side of an organization.

Analysts collect the needs and requirements of the business or organization and then attempt to use data to answer questions posed by the business or fulfill the particular business need or requirement. What kinds of problems is the business trying to solve? What kinds of key performance indicators and other metrics are important for the business to track? Exactly what is important to any particular business or organization can be extremely diverse. For more detailed information on requirement gathering, refer to *Chapter 2, Planning Projects with Power BI*. Analysts are often involved early in the process to help plan and coordinate BI projects as well as throughout such projects to ensure that the voice of the business is being heard.

BI analysts often utilize data to project business and market trends in order to enable organizations to operate more efficiently, effectively, and profitably. Analysts collect the required data in numerous ways, such as using software like Power BI to mine corporate data sources as well as data from industry trends and competitors. Analysts evaluate the data, including looking at current conditions and past trends. Again, Power BI can be an important and effective tool in this process. Once analysts effectively analyze the data, they communicate their findings with business managers, often at the highest levels of the organization.

Typical responsibilities

Typical job responsibilities for a BI analyst include the following:

- Gather requirements from business stakeholders.
- Work with all levels of the organization to turn requirements into valuable insights and deliverables.
- Assist with the development of internal and external self-service reporting/dashboarding capabilities and products.
- Contribute to the development of advanced algorithms and metric definitions.
- Present solutions to a wide variety of audiences and senior leadership.
- Explore new tools and technologies and make recommendations for improvements and strategic direction for BI.
- Research business problems and create models that help analyze historical trends and options for solutions.
- Assist with data quality efforts, documentation, and socialization of terms and metrics.
- Enhance organizational data with external sources of information when needed.
- Improve data collection procedures to enhance information with relevant information.
- Assist in the evaluation of existing reporting channels, focusing on the strategic consolidation and enhancement of existing sources and models.

Typical requirements

Typical requirements for a BI analyst include the following:

- Bachelor's degree in statistics, economics, business, information science, or similar
- 2+ years of experience using SQL, MySQL, Oracle, DB2, or a similar database system
- 2+ years of experience with BI visualization tools, data blending, and advanced statistical model generation
- 2+ years of experience with Microsoft Office
- Experience with R, Python, or similar languages a plus
- Be a self-starter who is resourceful and creative in your solutioning
- Good, applied statistics skills, such as distributions, statistical testing, regression, and so on
- Have the vision, intellectual curiosity, and business acumen to generate new metrics and insights that assist in driving key decisions and outcomes
- Excellent written and verbal communication skills

Typical salaries

Average salaries for BI analysts vary by source as well as by years of experience and location, but in the United States, expect an average salary of approximately $85,900 per year, ranging between $55,000 and $150,000 or more.

BI developers

The role of the BI developer, or simply developer, can also be quite diverse and varied. In larger organizations, there are generally three distinct types of BI developers: report developers, data transformation developers for **Extract, Transform, Load** (ETL), and data modelers. Report developers are responsible for constructing the final reports viewed by the business. In Power BI, this is the combining of visualizations supported by the underlying data model. Data transformation developers are responsible for ingesting and cleansing data from various sources in order to support the development of a data model. Data modelers take the ingested and cleansed data and create the underlying data model that supports the development of reports.

These three specific types of developer roles can be combined in different ways within organizations. Small organizations just starting their BI journey often combine all three types of developers into a single role while also combining the developer role with the analyst role. In this book, you have learned all of the essential skills for performing the BI developer role using Power BI, including report development, data transformation development, and data modeling.

Typical responsibilities

Typical job responsibilities for BI developers include the following:

- Develop data transformation jobs to extract data from source systems
- Develop data models to support self-service reporting and dashboarding
- Develop internal and external self-service reporting/dashboarding capabilities and products
- Create custom database queries, stored procedures, and tables to enhance data insights and accessibility
- Leverage existing BI assets such as data warehouses to develop insightful reports, analyses, and dashboards, using a combination of Excel, SQL, Power BI, and other analytics tools
- Maintain and analyze data feeds to ensure the accuracy of data
- Integrate datasets from disparate sources, stored using various technologies to provide unified views and practical outcomes of the data
- Work cross-functionally within the organization to research, develop, and implement data solutions to business challenges

Typical requirements

Typical requirements for BI developers include the following:

- Bachelor's degree in statistics, mathematics, economics, finance, information science, or similar
- 3+ years of experience using SQL, MySQL, Oracle, DB2, or a similar database system
- 3+ years of experience with BI visualization tools, data blending, and advanced statistical model generation
- 3+ years of experience working with data transformation technologies, such as **SQL Server Integration Services (SSIS)**, Power Query, or Alteryx

- Proficiency in SQL, DAX, Power Query (M), or similar coding languages
- Experience with R, Python, or similar languages a plus

Typical salaries

Average salaries for BI developers vary by source, as well as by years of experience and exact location, but in the United States, expect an average salary of approximately $95,000 per year, ranging between $70,000 and $130,000.

BI administrators

BI administrators, or just administrators, are responsible for the overall management, governance, and security of BI systems within organizations and often assist with the deployment of BI assets, such as datasets, reports, and dashboards. Within organizations using Power BI, administrators are responsible for Power BI tenant settings, the creation of workspaces, the assignment of workspace owners, and the creation and management of deployment pipelines.

Within larger organizations, there are often multiple administrators who manage the various systems that comprise the entirety of an organization's BI infrastructure or systems. This might include administration of underlying source data systems, such as SQL and Oracle databases, or even data warehouses built on technologies such as Azure Synapse and Snowflake. Smaller organizations may combine this role with the business analyst or developer roles.

Typical responsibilities

Typical job responsibilities for BI administrators include the following:

- Maintain, set up, configure, and secure BI-related software
- Maintain and patch software and hardware for BI-related applications and systems
- Proactively monitor the health and performance of BI systems and infrastructure
- Document existing and future BI systems' architecture and technology portfolio
- Assist in developing strategy, standards, and best practices, and ensure compliance with applicable government and industry regulations and standards
- Enact governance controls to optimize the usage of BI systems
- Assist in the deployment of BI assets

Typical requirements

Typical requirements for BI administrators include the following:

- Bachelor's degree in information technology or a related field
- 5+ years of related experience
- Experience with SQL Server or other database and BI platforms
- Experience in building enterprise data warehouses
- Experience in maintaining and monitoring BI environments
- Experience in working with development teams and end users to resolve issues

Typical salaries

Average salaries for BI administrators vary by source, as well as by years of experience and exact location, but in the United States, expect an average salary of approximately $90,000 per year, ranging between $60,000 and $170,000.

BI project managers

BI project managers, or simply project managers, work with other professionals to establish plans for projects that define the requirements, schedule, and resources required for BI projects. Project managers monitor and report on the progress of BI projects, implement and manage necessary changes, and monitor risks. Project managers help ensure that BI solutions are implemented within an agreed-upon time frame and meet the specified requirements. In addition, project managers assist in ensuring that solutions are cost-effective and are completed within a specified budget. Project managers regularly communicate with business stakeholders and other business professionals throughout the duration of projects.

Typical responsibilities

Typical job responsibilities for project managers include the following:

- Assist in gathering requirements from business stakeholders
- Assist in documenting BI requirements, including complex business logic and key metrics
- Work with all levels of the organization to turn requirements into valuable insights and deliverables
- Create BI project plans and manage the project throughout the full development life cycle
- Track and report on key project tasks, including technical development items and key milestones within the business
- Identify key risks, issues, and dependencies that may impact the project
- Prepare mitigation strategies to alleviate and resolve risks and issues
- Collaborate with technical teams to design dashboard prototypes and refine them through iterative development
- Partner with internal QA teams to define key test cases and establish success criteria
- Conduct high-level reviews to assess data quality and evaluate dashboard performance
- Provide a demo of prototypes and deliverables to key business stakeholders and senior leadership
- Coordinate user acceptance testing and provide end user training

Typical requirements

Typical requirements for project managers include the following:

- 3+ years of relevant experience in technical project management and/or BI projects
- Experience with project management tools such as Microsoft Project, Jira, Confluence, or similar tools

- Knowledge of BI and analytics, with some experience in the specific technology being a huge plus
- **Project Management Institute (PMI)** certifications highly desirable
- Business analytics experience
- Work well in a highly collaborative, matrixed, and team-oriented environment
- Superior verbal, written, and interpersonal communication skills with both technical and non-technical audiences

Typical salaries

Average salaries for BI project managers vary by source, as well as by years of experience and exact location, but in the United States, expect an average salary of approximately $85,000–115,000 per year, ranging between $60,000 and $185,000.

Data warehouse architects

Within larger enterprises, a data warehouse is often at the center of BI systems. Raw data, metadata, and other data assets from source transactional business systems are ingested into a data warehouse, which, in turn, provides an organized and verified data structure that is then used by BI and reporting solutions. Data warehouses are often built on top of database systems, such as Microsoft SQL Server or Oracle databases, as well as in the cloud, using systems such as Azure Synapse and Snowflake.

Data warehouse architects, or simply architects, are responsible for designing data warehouse solutions and working with and implementing data warehousing technologies that support an organization's overall business objectives. Architects seek to understand the overall BI goals of an organization and then develop a specific architecture or plan that can achieve those goals.

Typical responsibilities

Typical job responsibilities for data warehouse architects include the following:

- Work with various business departments to help develop the organization's data warehouse
- They are responsible for the conception, design, development, and deployment of data architecture and data models
- Develop physical and logical data models
- Translate business needs into feasible and acceptable data-centric semantic layer designs
- Document and present relationships between business entities using Kimball, Inmon, and other modern frameworks
- Assist in prioritizing and balancing the technical and business needs of the conceptual and logical data warehouse
- Architect and document the normalized data warehouse models
- Architect and document the denormalized dimensional presentation layer of the data warehouse

- Improve existing models to ensure compliance with standard methodologies around **Master Data Management (MDM)** and data architectures across technology platforms
- Design, develop, document, and advocate the enterprise data warehouse and/or data lake architecture

Typical requirements

Typical requirements for data warehouse architects include the following:

- 5+ years of experience in data architecture design and development
- Experience designing data warehouses, including the structure of how data is stored and retrieved
- Proficient with Microsoft SQL Server or other database technologies, such as Oracle, DB2, Snowflake, Azure Synapse, Azure Data Lake, Azure Analysis Services, and so on
- Proficient with ETL tools, such as SSIS, Azure Data Factory, Alteryx, and so on
- Experience with data pipeline development, orchestration, monitoring, and ETL processing
- Understanding of multidimensional and tabular modeling and other warehousing modeling techniques
- Expertise in data query technologies, such as SQL, Power Query, and so on

Typical salaries

Average salaries for data warehouse architects vary by source, as well as by years of experience and exact location, but in the United States, expect an average salary of approximately $125,000–130,000 per year, ranging between $90,000 and $195,000.

BI managers

BI managers, or simply managers, oversee particular aspects of an organization's BI systems and teams. For example, an enterprise may have individual managers who are responsible for data warehousing, MDM, and reporting. Managers coordinate teams of BI analysts, project managers, and developers, and may also supervise additional support staff and serve as liaisons for external contractors and service providers. Managers are responsible for the overall efforts related to the design, implementation, and operation of their slice of the BI systems within an organization and take a lead role in driving and executing the overall BI strategy.

Typical responsibilities

Typical job responsibilities for BI managers include the following:

- Design and implement data strategies and systems.
- Lead, motivate, and manage technical teams of BI professionals.
- Assist in the collection, storage, management, governance, and quality of data within the enterprise.
- Assist in the implementation of data privacy policies and compliance with applicable government and industry regulations.

Typical requirements

Typical requirements for BI managers include the following:

- Bachelor's degree in mathematics, statistics, information technology, data science, or related field
- 5+ years of experience in senior BI roles
- Strong leadership, management, and project management experience
- Excellent multitasking skills, with the ability to complete milestones and work toward multiple deadlines simultaneously
- Superior verbal, written, and interpersonal communication skills with both technical and non-technical audiences
- Extensive knowledge of BI systems
- A breadth and depth of knowledge regarding relevant BI applications, data solutions, and tools

Typical salaries

Average salaries for BI administrators vary by source, as well as by years of experience and exact location, but in the United States, expect an average salary of approximately $120,000–125,000 per year, ranging between $80,000 and $210,000.

BI directors or CDOs

Within mid- to large-sized organizations, there is often a vice president or director assigned to lead the overall strategy for BI within the organization. This position typically reports directly to a C-level position within the organization, such as the Chief Information Officer (CIO), Chief Operations Officer (COO), or Chief Marketing Officer (CMO). Within very large enterprises, this position is sometimes elevated to a C-level position, the Chief Data Officer (CDO). The relatively recent advent of the CDO is an indication of just how increasingly critical BI is to the success of organizations.

BI directors, or simply directors, are in charge of the overall strategy for BI within an organization and lead the design and development of BI activities within that organization. Directors work to understand the overall goals and objectives of an organization and then create strategies around how BI can help the organization reach those goals and objectives. Directors strive to make the organization as a whole more efficient, effective, and profitable. Directors provide leadership to a variety of other BI professionals and conduct and supervise training activities. Directors often participate in meetings with the business side of an organization in order to recommend ideas and modifications for future BI solutions.

Typical responsibilities

Typical job responsibilities for BI directors or CDOs include the following:

- Thoroughly understand the overall business, including goals, objectives, and data strategy
- Design and implement data strategies and systems
- Lead, motivate, and manage large technical teams of BI professionals

- Oversee the collection, storage, management, governance, and quality of data within the enterprise
- Oversee the implementation of data privacy policies and compliance with applicable government and industry regulations
- Assist in improving the efficiency, effectiveness, and profitability of the organization through insights gleaned from data analysis
- Effectively communicate the importance, value, and status of organizational data to executive leadership

Typical requirements

Typical requirements for BI managers or CDOs include the following:

- Bachelor's degree in mathematics, statistics, information technology, data science, or related field, with a preference for a master's degree
- 5–10 years of experience in a senior-level data management role
- Strong leadership, management, and project management experience
- Excellent multitasking skills, with the ability to complete milestones and work toward multiple deadlines simultaneously
- Superior verbal, written, and interpersonal communication skills with both technical and non-technical audiences
- The ability to make decisions and communicate choices in clear, non-technical language
- The ability to compile analytics and BI information, organize that information, and clearly present it to leadership teams
- Extensive knowledge of BI systems
- A breadth and depth of knowledge regarding relevant BI applications, data solutions, and tools

Typical salaries

Average salaries for BI directors vary by source, as well as by years of experience and exact location, but in the United States, expect an average salary of approximately $145,000–155,000 per year, ranging between $110,000 and $220,000. For organizations that are large enough to have a CDO, salaries are even larger, with an average salary of $190,000–310,000, ranging between $110,000 and $500,000.

Now that you understand the opportunities available in BI, let's explore how you can grow your job and career in the BI space.

Growing your job and career

As covered in the *Understanding the BI opportunity* section, there are many exciting jobs and roles available in the BI market. In addition, the jobs and roles available form a potential career path, from starting as a BI analyst, developer, or project manager to becoming the CDO of an organization. However, there is even more diversity when it comes to a career in the BI space. Let's dig deeper into the different jobs and career paths available to BI professionals.

Understanding the employment and career opportunities

It is important to understand that organizations deliver BI solutions to the business in one of two ways:

- Leveraging internal employees who fulfill the jobs and roles as identified and explained in the *Understanding the BI opportunity* section
- Leveraging consulting firms that employ BI professionals

In terms of you, as someone new to the BI world, you need to understand that there are two very different career paths ahead of you: that of an internal employee within an organization and that of a BI consultant employed by a consulting services firm. Understanding the use of internal employees is rather straightforward. However, understanding the employment and career opportunities with consulting firms deserves further explanation. Let's take a closer look.

Consulting services

Consulting firms deliver BI services to other organizations in a business-to-business relationship by providing organizations with specialists in the following roles:

- BI analysts
- BI developers
- BI administrators
- BI project managers
- Data warehouse architects

Consulting firms do not typically fulfill the following types of roles:

- BI managers
- BI directors or CDOs

However, within consulting services firms, there are somewhat equivalent roles within BI teams. Larger consulting services firms have managers and directors who oversee the overall health and operation of the BI consulting services practice within the consulting services firm. Thus, there are equivalent career paths even within consulting services firms, and it is not uncommon for successful BI consultants to eventually become employed by organizations in leadership roles within BI teams.

Consulting firms that deliver BI services typically deliver those services in one of two ways:

- Staffing
- Project services

These two approaches to providing consulting services are very different from one another, and it is important to understand these differences and why organizations choose to employ one or the other.

Staffing

Staffing refers to when an organization contracts with a consulting firm to fulfill a specific role within the organization. The BI professional is contracted through a consulting firm for a fee per hour. Under a staffing contract, the BI professional serves at the direction of internal organizational employees to complete tasks on behalf of the organization.

The BI professional generally completes tasks and behaves as if they are part of the organization, but they are actually employed and paid by the consulting services organization. Staffing contracts typically only specify a required set of skills and not a specific scope of work or specific expected deliverables (things that should be completed). In addition, staffing contracts are typically set to be a service length of six months to a year and are often renewed multiple times.

There are a variety of reasons why organizations will employ a staffing strategy instead of hiring their own internal employees:

- The potentially high cost of hiring and turnover
- Reduction in the risk of making a bad hire
- Industry talent shortages
- Scale issues caused by rapid growth

In many circumstances, organizations choose to take a staffing approach in order to reduce the costs of fulfilling a position, reduce the risks associated with hiring internal employees, and address issues of scale caused by rapid growth or a shortage of talent within the market.

Project services

Consulting organizations also provide BI expertise and resources through project services. Project services are fundamentally different from staffing engagements, as projects completed under a project services approach generally have the following traits:

- The project has a defined scope of work and specific deliverables.
- The project may be as short as four to six weeks, although many projects may last months or years.
- The consulting resources comprise all, or a significant portion, of the BI team, and the work is mostly managed by the consulting services organization in coordination with the customer's internal management resources.

Under a project services approach, organizations create a request to achieve a specified outcome. Consulting services firms respond to this request with a proposal or statement of work that defines how they intend to approach the work, the required work tasks, risks and assumptions, and a timeline, duration, and cost to complete the project. Consulting services organizations may propose completing the identified scope of work on either a time and materials basis or a fixed-fee basis. Time and material proposals include an expected range of hours for each required role in the project, as well as an hourly cost for each of those resources. Fixed-fee proposals provide a single cost for completing the identified work.

Understanding the differences between consultants and employees

There are various pros and cons between being a consultant and an internal employee when it comes to choosing a BI career path. One of the biggest differences is in the breadth and depth of experience gained.

As an internal employee, you are likely to become an expert regarding the BI needs and goals of a particular organization and develop deep knowledge of how that organization operates. This, in turn, provides a way to gain industry expertise within the particular industry in which that organization operates, such as financial services, manufacturing, and so on. In addition, internal employees are more likely to fulfill a single job function or role within the BI space, such as a BI analyst or a BI report developer. This does not mean that internal employees may not switch job functions or roles during the course of their careers, but they may often spend years fulfilling their designated role before switching roles or advancing. Thus, the focus of internal employees tends to be on acquiring a depth of expertise in a particular BI job role, industry, and organization.

Conversely, BI consultants tend to acquire more breadth of knowledge since consultants generally work across many industries, organizations, and even job functions or roles during their careers. Since most consulting services firms work across different industries and with many different customers, consultants have the opportunity to witness and understand a diverse set of BI needs and goals. In addition, consultants often fulfill different BI jobs or roles, depending upon the needs of the customer. This means that a BI consultant may serve as an analyst on one project, a report developer on the next project, and a project manager on the project after that.

There is no right or wrong answer when it comes to choosing a career path within BI. Different individuals have different goals and may find one of the other career paths, consultant or internal employee, more suited to their individual temperament and desired outcomes.

Now that you understand the different employment avenues, let's cover some tips for finding and getting a job in BI.

Job search strategies

When it comes to finding your dream job within BI, it is important to have a plan and approach that helps you achieve your goals. To this end, there are a number of job search strategies that you can employ to help you succeed in the exciting world of BI, as follows:

- **Be selective:** Search for the right jobs and roles that interest you on job search sites such as inceed.com, monster.com, ziprecruiter.com, glassdoor.com, careerbuilder.com, and so on. Target specific organizations that you would like to work for. Perform research on the organizations you select in order to know and understand their business. Understanding exactly what you want to do and who you want to work for can help you feel confident about the position and company when speaking to the hiring manager. In addition, demonstrating knowledge of the interviewing organization and role helps your passion for the position come across during interviews, which increases your likelihood of being hired.

- **Get noticed:** Maintaining a strong digital presence can be key to landing your dream job. Employers often search for so-called *passive* candidates, qualified individuals who are not necessarily actively looking for a new job but may be interested if the right job comes along. This means making certain that your social media accounts such as X/Twitter and professional networking sites such as LinkedIn are updated with your latest skills and achievements and speak to the type of job that interests you.

Check through your social media and professional networking profiles and tailor these profiles with specific keywords that recruiters and hiring managers are likely to search for when trying to find job candidates with your skill set. To identify those keywords, search job search sites for open positions in your desired role and identify the keywords those companies are using. Also, make sure that your profile tagline or title speaks of your passion for BI. Finally, use your name for the URL if possible. Many sites, including LinkedIn and X/Twitter, allow you to choose a vanity URL for your profile. This helps recruiters and hiring managers find you on the internet.

Post messages or articles on social media and professional networking sites pertinent to BI topics. This helps recruiters and hiring managers understand that you are passionate about BI and keep up with the latest developments within the BI space. You may also want to consider starting your own personal blog or website focused on BI topics. This allows you to share your knowledge and demonstrate your expertise and can be done for free on sites such as wordpress. com. Finally, in the Power BI world, participate on the Power BI Community site, community. powerbi.com. Rising to the rank of Super User and/or **Microsoft Most Valuable Professional (MVP)** is certainly a feather in your cap that can impress potential employers.

- **Network:** Networking has always been the most effective job search strategy available and the way most people find jobs. Join a local Power BI user group or similar professional BI group. Most metropolitan areas have local Power BI user groups, which you can find on sites such as meetup.com or the Power BI Community site. Joining and attending user group meetings or attending professional meetups is a great way to learn new skills and find organizations with BI needs. The more people you connect with and communicate that you are open to opportunities, the more likely you are to learn about open positions of interest. In addition, joining and participating in user groups and professional networks signals to potential employers your passion and commitment to BI.

- **Get personal:** While creating a professional resume is important, it is also important that you personalize your resume to each job position and organization. Personalizing your résumé and/ or cover letter allows you to highlight the specific skills and expertise being sought. Recruiters and hiring managers are often inundated with résumés for open positions. Highlight your expertise in key skill areas by moving those skills and experiences to the top of the résumé and/or by putting keywords and phrases in bold; this will make your resume more likely to be chosen by recruiters and hiring managers for an interview. Follow up after an interview with a personal thank-you email or note. Individuals who send thank-you notes or emails get hired more than those who do not. You can also use the thank-you note as an opportunity to restate why you are the best candidate for the job and to clarify any interview answers you feel you might have answered vaguely or incorrectly.

By following these simple job search strategies, you maximize your chances of finding and landing your dream job.

Interviewing tips

Once you move to the next step in your job search and land the interview for your dream job in BI, it is important for you to ace the interview. Succeeding in an interview is all about proper preparation.

To this end, make sure you do the following prior to any interview:

- **Research:** While you may have researched the companies you wish to work for as part of your job search strategy, it is time to go a level deeper in your research for the particular organization with which you are interviewing. This means researching the benefits the organization provides as well as the organization's leadership. Try to learn as much as you can about the organization's operations and the industry in which the organization operates. Expand your research to include current events and recent news headlines on the internet and in business journals. Use this research strategically during the interview to connect your skills and experience to the job description and the overall goals and needs of the organization.

- **Practice:** Practice your answers to common interview questions. Recruit a friend or colleague to perform a mock interview. By practicing interview questions and practicing interviewing, you will gain confidence in your ability to answer questions coherently and effectively. You should have stock answers for common questions, such as whether you are willing to travel, explaining gaps in your résumé, your qualities as a leader, why you are interested in the position, and why you are looking to change roles/jobs. Finally, be prepared for and practice answering a technical question that you do not know the answer to. This includes the ability to confidently state that you do not know the answer to the question and a detailed explanation regarding how you would approach researching and finding the answer.

- **Preparation:** Make sure you are prepared for your interview. This means picking out clothes and shoes for your interview well ahead of time. Make sure you have an interview *kit* that includes extra copies of your résumé, a notepad, a pen, and possibly an umbrella (unpredictable weather!). Write down questions for the interviewer and have them ready during the interview. Almost all interviews include the interviewer asking the interviewee whether they have any questions. Not having questions ready can make you appear apathetic toward the position.

  If you have to drive to the interview, make sure you know the route and how much time is required for travel. Plan for extra time in the event of an accident or traffic jam. If possible, drive the route at least once prior to the interview, understand where to park, and how long and which route to take from the parking location to the interview location. Remember, being on time for an interview means being early.

  If you are interviewing virtually, ensure that you have any and all technology set up, configured, and tested prior to the interview. For example, ensure that your camera works, that you have a stable internet connection, and that you are comfortable with the technology being used.

- **Stay calm:** Stress is one of the most often cited reasons why interviews are not successful. Researching, practicing, and preparing for an interview helps build your confidence and reduce stress. During the interview, maintain eye contact with the interviewer and make sure to pay close attention to the interviewer's questions by actively listening to the entire question and only answering it once the interviewer has finished speaking. If you need to compose your thoughts, take a moment to pause and repeat the interviewer's question back to them to allow yourself time to think and mentally prepare a response. For example, you could say, *If I heard you correctly, what you are asking is...*

- **Build rapport:** Before the interview, write down the interviewer's name and use their name during the interview. If possible, research the interviewer online and note where they are located and any interests or hobbies they may have. Review any social media posts or other materials on the internet. Use this information during the interview to build rapport and connect on a personal level with your interviewer.

   An often overlooked aspect of building rapport during an interview is being honest. In particular, if you do not know the answer to a technical question, state that you do not currently know the answer and then proceed to explain how you would approach researching and discovering the answer. Be specific in terms of what materials and websites you might use to find the answer.

- **Follow-up:** Always follow up an interview with a thank-you note or email reiterating your interest in the position.

Following these interview tips will help make you fully prepared and confident going into, during, and after an interview. Confidence is key to interviewing, and being fully prepared through research, practicing, and preparation helps build the confidence necessary for you to ace any interview.

Negotiating benefits and compensation

After a successful interview, any offer of a job provides the opportunity for negotiation of terms that are the most beneficial to you. While the salary is an important component of this negotiation, it is not the only important aspect of a job. It is important to know, understand, and keep in mind that there are many things that are negotiable in addition to your salary. Other factors include the following:

- **Hiring bonus:** A hiring bonus is a one-time cash payment made on the first day of employment. If there is a gap between what the market is paying and what the employer is offering, you may be able to convince the employer that you deserve a hiring bonus, particularly if the job has been open for a long time and it is hard to find skilled candidates.

- **Vacation time:** Many organizations offer two or three weeks of vacation time. However, negotiating for an extra week of vacation is not uncommon and often granted, especially if you currently have more weeks of vacation with your current employer than are being offered.

- **Timing of your first review:** Most organizations conduct annual reviews for employees. Negotiating for an early first review, such as after six months, is a reasonable compromise, particularly if the starting salary is less than you desire. An early review provides you the opportunity to prove yourself worthy of additional compensation sooner rather than later.

- **Relocation costs:** If the job requires you to relocate, most organizations will grant requests to be compensated for the costs of relocation. Do your research so that you understand the full costs of relocating.

- **Flexible work schedule:** There are many times when a flexible work schedule is more desirable than a higher salary. This includes the ability to come in early/late and leave early/late, a work schedule of four 10-hour days, or the ability to telecommute. With the recent worldwide pandemic, organizations are more likely than ever to grant requests to work remotely.

- **Goals and achievement bonuses:** Many positions offer annual bonuses or bonuses based on certain achievements. For example, consulting organizations often have a *utilization* bonus that compensates consultants who work more hours than expected.

- **Stock options or units:** Organizations that are publicly traded often offer stock to their employees on a regular basis, either in place of or in addition to annual bonuses.

- **Retirement benefits:** Be certain to understand the pension or matching 401(k) contributions offered by the employer.

- **Health and wellness benefits:** Many organizations offer medical, dental, and vision plans for their employees. The differences in how much you pay for such benefits and the comprehensiveness of those benefits can vary widely between different organizations.

- **Insurance programs:** Many employers offer basic life, accidental death, and disability insurance for little or no cost to employees. Be certain to understand these benefits and how they might defer or eliminate costs you currently pay for such insurance.

- **Educational reimbursement and training programs:** Most organizations have an interest in employees who are well educated and keep up to date with the latest technologies and innovations. To this end, these organizations may reimburse obtaining advanced degrees or regularly pay for training and obtaining certifications. Certifications and technical training are particularly important for consulting firms, as employing a certain number of individuals with particular training and certifications may be required to maintain partnerships with firms such as Microsoft, Amazon, and Google.

- **Perks:** Make sure to understand any perks associated with the position, such as gym memberships, cellphone reimbursement, reimbursement for travel, or even for costs such as the internet service.

When evaluating and comparing any offer, keep in mind the full scope of benefits and compensation being offered and not just the salary. Certain organizations may pay less but make up for this by offering much better non-salary benefit packages. Negotiating favorable benefits can help make up for a lower salary and promote a better work-life balance. However, at some point, you are going to have to discuss and negotiate the salary being offered.

Negotiating the salary

Most people looking for jobs are not skilled negotiators. Conversely, employers tend to have recruiters and hiring managers skilled in negotiation. In order to close this gap in negotiation skills, do the following:

- **Research:** Use internet websites such as payscale.com, glassdoor.com, and other job search websites to determine average salaries for comparable positions within the local market and with comparably sized organizations. Be prepared with your research when negotiating your salary in order to provide justification for your requested salary.

- **Determine your range:** You need to settle on two numbers in order to be an effective negotiator of your salary. These two numbers are your ideal salary and the lowest salary you are willing to settle for. Negotiate to achieve your ideal salary and be prepared to end negotiations if the employer cannot meet your lowest salary figure. However, do not forget about the impact of employment benefits outside of your salary when considering whether to end negotiations.

- **Practice:** It can often be beneficial to enlist a friend or colleague to help you practice negotiating. Negotiating is a skill that is acquired, not something that is generally an innate ability. Thus, practicing negotiating helps you to be more confident and better at dealing with different types of negotiation styles.

- **Be patient:** Delay the discussion of salary for as long as possible. Make the employer fall in love with the idea of you being on their team before addressing the subject of salary. If you make an employer relish the idea of hiring you, they are more agreeable if your salary requirements are more than they were hoping. Wait for the employer to put a number on the table. If the employer asks you how much you require in salary, deflect the question by asking the employer how much is budgeted for the position or what they typically pay for similar positions.

- **Always counter:** You should resist the urge to accept the first number given by a recruiter or hiring manager. It is in the best interests of an organization to employ the most skilled individuals possible for the least amount of money. Therefore, it is almost certain that the initial offer is not their best offer. Be prepared to explain the reasons for your counter-offer and why you believe you deserve additional compensation. Speak honestly and plainly and be confident but not in a demanding way. Be respectful and convey that you appreciate the offer but that you were expecting more.

Negotiating benefits and compensation can be stressful and awkward for many people. By following these negotiation tips, you can be more confident and less stressed when negotiating with potential employers. Remember that everything is on the table when it comes to the negotiation of benefits and compensation and ensure that you maintain a clear focus on what you will and will not accept. Always be professional, respectful, and impartial when negotiating compensation and benefits, and do not be offended if the employer rejects your counter-offer. Finally, be prepared that potential employers may withdraw an offer of employment if they feel that your demands are excessive. You should also be prepared to walk away if the employer cannot meet your minimum compensation target.

Negotiating with consulting firms

Negotiating your salary or hourly rate with a consulting firm is a special case. The reason is that while the exact economics of many complex organizations are difficult (if not impossible) to determine, the economics of professional services firms are exceedingly simple and nearly universal. Therefore, by asking a few simple questions and/or making some basic assumptions, it is relatively easy to determine how much you should be paid by a consulting services firm.

First, you should determine whether the position is a staffing position or a project services position. If it is for a staffing position, then you have much less negotiating room, as staffing positions generally have clearly stated target rates and staffing work generally has a significantly lower gross margin than project services work. However, the specified target rates are generally provided as a range. That said, generally, the consulting services firm can only negotiate within the boundaries of the specified target rates for the position and only exceed that range in special circumstances.

Second, you should determine whether the position is an hourly position or a full-time (exempt) position. Obviously, this is important when considering vacation and other applicable benefits but is also important for understanding the overhead costs the consulting services firm is likely to incur by employing you. This has a direct impact on how much you can be paid by the consulting services firm. While overhead cost factors vary, a decent estimate is to assume a cost overhead factor of around 1.2 for hourly positions and 1.4 for salaried positions. The overhead cost factor is simply an easy method of accounting for the costs of benefits, insurance, and other compensation factors over and above an employee's salary and also covers a proportion of corporate overhead in the form of rent and the overhead cost of non-billable employees, such as managers, recruiters, and other staff.

Next, you need to ask the consulting services firm the following questions:

- What is the typical hourly rate that you charge customers for the types of services I provide?
- What is the expected target percentage utilization for billable employees?
- What is the firm's target gross margin percentage on consulting services?

If the consulting services firm refuses to answer the last two questions, good assumptions for an average consulting firm are a target utilization percentage of 85% and a target gross margin of around 40%.

Because consulting services organizations make money by mostly simply charging a particular rate for each hour of consulting services, with the above information regarding overhead cost factor, the hourly rate charged to customers, expected percent utilization, and target gross margin percentage, you can easily calculate the maximum amount that the consulting services organization is likely to pay you for a salaried position based on the following formulas:

$$Revenue = Hourly\ bill\ rate * 2080 * \%Utilization$$

$$Maximum\ Salary = \frac{Revenue - \%GM * Revenue}{Overhead\ cost\ factor}$$

Therefore, for a consultant billed out at $150 an hour with an overhead cost factor of 1.4 and an expected utilization of 85%, this means that the consulting firm expects to generate $265,200 of revenue for that consultant during a year (2,080 hours in a year). $150 x 2080 x 85% = $265,200. This means that to meet an expected 40% gross margin (%GM), the maximum salary is $113,657.14 or ($265,200 - 40% x $265,200) ÷ 1.4. Thus, in the circumstance where the consulting services firm is offering less than $113,657 for such a position, you should be confident in negotiating toward that amount.

For hourly employees, the calculation is a bit different. First, as an hourly employee, you are only paid for the hours you work. This means that utilization is effectively 100% for hourly employees. In addition, it is probable that instead of talking in terms of salary, the consulting services firm will talk in terms of the hourly rate you will be paid. Therefore, the calculation simply becomes as follows:

$$Maximum\ hourly\ rate = \frac{(Hourly\ bill\ rate - \%GM * Hourly\ bill\ rate)}{Overhead\ cost\ factor}$$

Thus, for an hourly position with a bill rate of $150/hour, a target gross margin percentage of 30%, and an overhead cost factor of 1.2, the maximum hourly rate is $87.50 or ($150 - 30% x $150) ÷ 1.2.

Keep in mind that for non-billable positions within consulting firms, the calculations regarding salary follow different economics.

You are now prepared to find and land your dream job in BI! However, the journey for data insights and BI is never-ending. In the next section, we will cover resources where you can continue your journey of discovery and exploration!

Continuing your journey

The goal of *Learn Power BI* is to introduce you to the exciting world of Power BI and BI. But this is not the end of the journey! There is certainly far more to learn about Power BI and BI than any single book can cover. In addition, there are constantly new developments in the world of BI and Power BI. Power BI Desktop is updated every month with dozens of new features and functionality. Therefore, it is important that you continue your journey of learning and discovery!

The following table provides resources where you can do just that:

Creator(s)	Name	Link
Brian Julius	Follow on LinkedIn	`https://www.linkedin.com/in/brianjuliusdc/`
Rick de Groot	BI Gorilla	`https://gorilla.bi/`
Melissa de Korte	Follow on LinkedIn	`https://www.linkedin.com/in/melissa-de-korte/`
Greg Deckler	Microsoft Hates Greg	`https://www.youtube.com/@microsofthatesgreg`
Rick de Groot	PowerQuery.How	`https://powerquery.how`
Greg Deckler	DAX For Humans	`https://www.youtube.com/@daxforhumans`
Chandeep Chabra	Goodly	`https://goodly.co.in/blog/`
Pragati Jain	Data Vibe	`https://datavibe.co.uk/`
Ruth Pozuelo	Curbal	`https://curbal.com/`
Chris Webb	Crossjoin	`https://blog.crossjoin.co.uk/`
Soheil Bakhshi	BI Insight	`https://biinsight.com/`
Gilbert Quevauvilliers	Fourmoo	`https://www.fourmoo.com/`
Warren Dean	DataTale	`https://datatale.com.au/`
Marco Russo and Alberto Ferrari	SQL BI	`https://www.sqlbi.com/`
Imke Feldman	The BIccountant	`https://www.thebiccountant.com/`
Parv Chana	PeryTUS	`https://perytus.com/`
Reid Havens	Havens Consulting	`https://www.havensconsulting.net/`
Matt Allington	Excelerator BI	`https://exceleratorbi.com.au/`
Phil Seamark	DAX Tips	`https://dax.tips/`
Daniil Maslyuk	XXL BI	`https://xxlbi.com/`
Reza Rad	RADACAD	`https://radacad.com/`
Seth Bauer and Mike Carlo	PowerBI.Tips	`https://powerbi.tips/`
David Eldersveld	DataVeld	`https://dataveld.com/`

Table 14.1 – Recommended Resources for Continuing Your Power BI and Business Intelligence Learning Journey

After this, we have a list of blogs that showcase Power BI features and tools, along with practical examples of how to use them:

Blogger(s)	Blog	URL
Michael Carlo and Seth Bauer	PowerBI.Tips	`http://powerbi.tips`
Chris Webb	Crossjoin	`https://blog.crossjoin.co.uk`
Rob Collie and others	P3 Adaptive	`https://powerpivotpro.com`
Alberto Ferrari Marco Russo	SQL BI	`http://www.sqlbi.com`
Kasper De Jonge	Kasper On BI	`https://www.kasperonbi.com`
Matt Allington	Excelerator BI	`http://exceleratorbi.com.au/blog`
Ruth Martinez	Curbal	`https://curbal.com/blog`
Reza Rad	RADACAD	`http://radacad.com/blog`
Imke Feldman	The BIccountant	`http://www.thebiccountant.com`
Brett Powell	Insight Quest	`https://insightsquest.com`
Gilbert Quevauvilliers	Fourmoo	`https://www.fourmoo.com/blog`
Tom Martens	Mincing Data	`https://www.minceddata.info/blog`
Nicky van Vroenhoven	Power BI, Power Platform, Data Platform	`https://www.nickyvv.com/`
Debbie Edwards	Debbie's Microsoft Power BI, SQL and Azure Blog	`http://bit.ly/3eQsb2G`
Zoe Douglas	DataZoe	`https://www.datazoepowerbi.com/blog`
Ibarrau	LaDataWeb (Spanish)	`https://blog.ladataweb.com.ar/`
David Eldersveld	DataVeld	`https://dataveld.com/`
Pragati Jain	Data Vibe	`https://datavibe.co.uk/`
Adam Saxton and Patrick Leblanc	Guy in a Cube	`http://bit.ly/2o21RqU`
Various	Power BI Community Blog	`http://bit.ly/3qIoDl9`
Various	Power BI Weekly	`https://powerbiweekly.info/`

Figure 14.1 – A list of blogs that detail Power BI features and tools with examples of how to use them

As you can see, there is a large, active community of Power BI professionals who contribute content on the internet regarding Power BI. Some of these professionals come from within Microsoft, others are BI consultants, and still others are professionals in various industries that happen to use Power BI as part of their profession. For example, Guy in a Cube, Kasper On BI, and DataVeld are all run by Microsoft employees, while the rest of the blogs listed are from non-Microsoft employees. In addition, some of the websites listed are not exclusive to Power BI and cover the wider world of BI, such as Microsoft SQL Server, Azure, and Office 365 tools and services.

Summary

This chapter has been all about the exciting opportunities and jobs available in the world of BI and Power BI. We highlighted the growing demand for BI professionals and covered in detail the various types of jobs and roles available, including detailed lists of typical responsibilities and requirements of such jobs and each job's typical salary. Next, we covered the different ways you might engage in a BI job, either as an internal employee or as a consultant, and the major differences between these types of employment. Then, we provided guidance on how to find a job within the BI market, including job search strategies, interviewing tips, and negotiating tips. Finally, we provided resources for you to continue your journey of learning and discovery since BI and Power BI are constantly morphing and changing.

This is the end of the third edition of *Learn Power BI*. It is my sincere hope that you have found this book useful and that it propels you forward in your job and career.

Questions

As an activity, try to answer the following questions on your own:

- Where is Power BI positioned in Gartner's *Magic Quadrant for Analytics and Business Intelligence Platforms*?
- What are seven different jobs or roles available within the BI market?
- What are the two different ways that you might engage in a job within the BI market?
- What are two ways in which consulting services firms engage in work?
- What are some of the differences between being an internal employee versus a consultant?
- What are four job search strategies you can use to help you find a job in BI?
- What are six interviewing tips that can help you ace your interview?
- When negotiating benefits and compensation, what other things can be negotiated besides salary?
- What are five salary negotiating tips?

Further reading

To learn more about the topics that were covered in this chapter, please take a look at the following references:

- *Power BI Fabric User Groups*: https://community.powerbi.com/t5/Power-BI-User-Groups/ct-p/pbi_usergroups
- *Payscale*: https://www.payscale.com
- *Glassdoor*: https://www.glassdoor.com
- *Monster*: https://www.monster.com
- *ZipRecruiter*: https://www.ziprecruiter.com
- *Indeed*: https://www.indeed.com
- *CareerBuilder*: https://www.careerbuilder.com
- *How to Negotiate Compensation*: https://www.wikihow.com/Negotiate-Compensation

Unlock this book's exclusive benefits now

Scan this QR code or go to packtpub.com/unlock, then search for this book by name.

Note: Keep your purchase invoice ready before you start.

‹packt›

packtpub.com

Subscribe to our online digital library for full access to over 7,000 books and videos, as well as industry leading tools to help you plan your personal development and advance your career. For more information, please visit our website.

Why subscribe?

- Spend less time learning and more time coding with practical eBooks and Videos from over 4,000 industry professionals
- Improve your learning with Skill Plans built especially for you
- Get a free eBook or video every month
- Fully searchable for easy access to vital information
- Copy and paste, print, and bookmark content

At www.packtpub.com, you can also read a collection of free technical articles, sign up for a range of free newsletters, and receive exclusive discounts and offers on Packt books and eBooks.

Other Books You May Enjoy

If you enjoyed this book, you may be interested in these other books by Packt:

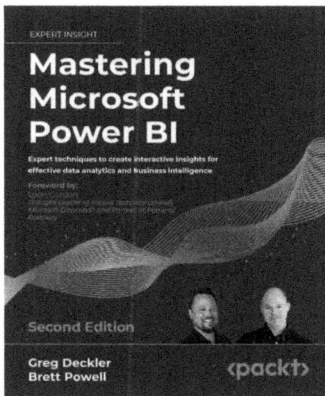

Mastering Microsoft Power BI – Second Edition

Greg Deckler, Brett Powell

ISBN: 978-1-80181-148-4

- Build efficient data retrieval and transformation processes with the Power Query M language and dataflows
- Design scalable, user-friendly DirectQuery, import, and composite data models
- Create basic and advanced DAX measures
- Add ArcGIS Maps to create interesting data stories
- Build pixel-perfect paginated reports
- Discover the capabilities of Power BI mobile applications
- Manage and monitor a Power BI environment as a Power BI administrator
- Scale up a Power BI solution for an enterprise via Power BI Premium capacity

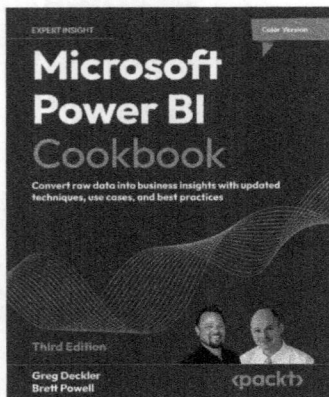

Microsoft Power BI Cookbook – Third Edition

Greg Deckler, Brett Powell

ISBN: 978-1-83546-427-4

- Analyze and integrate business data using Microsoft Data Fabric
- Create impactful visualizations and manage Hybrid tables
- Develop shared cloud connections and advanced scorecards
- Enhance report accuracy and dynamics using real-time data processing
- Implement efficient data governance and security measures within Power BI

Packt is searching for authors like you

If you're interested in becoming an author for Packt, please visit authors.packt.com and apply today. We have worked with thousands of developers and tech professionals, just like you, to help them share their insight with the global tech community. You can make a general application, apply for a specific hot topic that we are recruiting an author for, or submit your own idea.

Share your thoughts

Now you've finished *Learn Microsoft Power BI, Third Edition*, we'd love to hear your thoughts! Scan the QR code below to go straight to the Amazon review page for this book and share your feedback or leave a review on the site that you purchased it from.

https://packt.link/r/1836647417

Your review is important to us and the tech community and will help us make sure we're delivering excellent quality content.

Index

P

W

Y

www.ingramcontent.com/pod-product-compliance
Lightning Source LLC
Chambersburg PA
CBHW081224220326
41598CB00037B/6864